Computer Modern Typefaces

COMPUTERS & TYPESETTING / E

Computer Modern Typefaces

DONALD E. KNUTH *Stanford University*

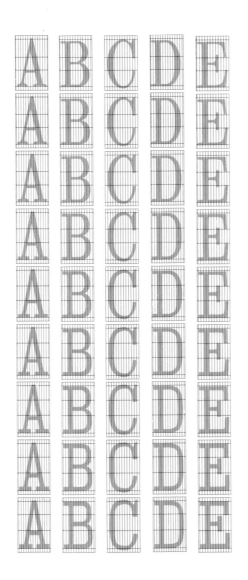

**ADDISON WESLEY
PUBLISHING COMPANY**

Reading, Massachusetts
Menlo Park, California
Don Mills, Ontario
Wokingham, England
Amsterdam · Mexico City
San Juan · Bogotá · Sydney
Santiago · Singapore · Tokyo

The quotations on pages 7 and 351 have been excerpted from the *Electra* file in the Dwiggins Collection of the Boston Public Library.

METAFONT is a trademark of Addison Wesley Publishing Company.

TEX is a trademark of the American Mathematical Society.

The programs for Computer Modern are in the public domain, and readers may freely generate and hand-tune their own fonts using the algorithms of this book. However, use of the names is restricted: Any fonts whose names `cmr10` or `cmbx12` or $\cdots$ are identical to the standard font names of this book should be fully compatible with the fonts defined here; i.e., fonts with the same names are supposed to have precisely the same character coding schemes and precisely the same font metric files.

Library of Congress Cataloging-in-Publication Data

```
Knuth, Donald Ervin, 1938-
    Computer Modern typefaces.

    (Computers & Typesetting ; E)
    Includes indexes.
    1. Type and type-founding--Data processing.
2. Printing--Specimens.  3. METAFONT (Computer system).
4. Computerized typesetting.  I. Title.  II. Series:
Knuth, Donald Ervin, 1938-      .  Computers &
typesetting ; E.
Z253.3.K568  1986        686.2'2544        86-1235
ISBN 0-201-13446-2
```

ISBN 0-201-13446-2
ABCDEFGHIJ–HA–89876

To Martin E. Frost:
Who nurtured the systems

Preface

G REEK AND ROMAN LETTERFORMS, together with punctuation marks, numerals, and a large collection of mathematical symbols, are the subject of this book. Indeed, all of the characters printed in this volume were produced by the "programs" found here. By changing the parameters of these programs, it is possible to generate an extensive array of fonts, known as the Computer Modern family of typefaces.

Since this book is somewhat unusual, I had better try to explain what it contains and why a person might want to read it. Most of the following pages are filled with somewhat cryptic code in the METAFONT language, accompanied by annotated diagrams that illustrate what the METAFONT system might draw when presented with the given code. A preparatory chapter introduces the parameters of Computer Modern; this material explains how it is possible to generate many different alphabets from the same general specifications. The book concludes in a more traditional way, with samples of text showing the Computer Modern typefaces in use.

What is the value of such a book? Well, in the first place, it's fun just to look at mechanically constructed letters, even if the details of their generation aren't entirely understood. Secondly, people can easily make customized, one-time-only variations of Computer Modern for their personal use by learning how to assign new values to the parameters. Thirdly, people can make new symbols, or variations on the standard symbols, by mimicking the programs found here and making comparatively simple changes. Carefully crafted new symbols can be effective in many types of publications. Finally, this book provides hundreds of examples of METAFONT in use. The METAFONT system of typeface design is quite different from its predecessors, and a large collection of examples helps to demonstrate the principles that are involved.

The programs that appear in this book were developed over a period of years, and they have lost much of their original simplicity because of this long history of refinements. For example, the '*stem_corr*' parameter, which specifies slight adjustments to stem widths at high resolutions, was not part of the original design; hence many of the original programs were substantially shorter. Additional complications have been introduced by special instructions that round the lines and curves to desirable raster positions. Although the resulting META-FONT statements are not as straightforward as textbook examples would be, I think it is valuable to show the actual "optimized" code that has evolved; so I haven't held back any tricks of the trade that have contributed to the quality of these fonts. These are the real programs, without the simplifications that were introduced for expository purposes in *The METRFONTbook*.

My colleague Charles Bigelow has kindly volunteered to write an introduction about "modern" fonts in general, so that the Computer Modern types can be understood in historical context. Although the so-called modern style of type is nearly 200 years old, I have always liked it because it was used in most of my favorite textbooks. Indeed, modern typefaces have been associated with technical publications of the highest quality for many generations. The Computer Modern designs are based to a considerable extent on the letterforms of "Monotype Modern 8A," which was used to typeset the first volumes of my books on *The Art of Computer Programming*.

The task of obtaining satisfactory typefaces with parametric variations has turned out to be much, much more difficult than I ever imagined when I began this work in 1977. But I've had the advantage of expert help; indeed, it has been my good fortune to make the acquaintance of several of the world's finest type designers, who have unselfishly given me a great deal of tutelage. At first I was blissfully unaware of the subtleties of the subject, because such things have rarely been described in print; when I completed the first "Computer Modern proto-type" in January 1980, I had been almost entirely self-taught, although I had spent much time in libraries looking for clues. Then in February of 1980, I had the great pleasure of demonstrating the first experimental METAFONT system to Hermann Zapf, who worked intensively with me for two weeks as we improved many of the character shapes. He taught me many things that I was able to use during the succeeding months. In 1981, I made several hundred specimen sheets of the fonts as they existed then, and I was privileged to receive detailed critiques of these specimens from Zapf in Germany as well as from Matthew Carter in England, and Charles Bigelow and Kris Holmes in America. Then Richard Southall came to Stanford during the month of April 1982, and we made extensive changes, especially to the sans-serif letters (for which he contributed a brand-new design). These changes spawned a completely new METAFONT language, which incorporated many ideas of Zapf, Bigelow, and Southall. Finally, the Computer Modern programs were rewritten again, in terms of the new METAFONT; the final draft, made during the spring of 1985, benefited greatly from detailed criticisms by Southall and Carter, as well as by N. N. Billawala, who also contributed a new design of the calligraphic letters. It is clear that I did not suffer from lack of expert assistance!

Another piece of luck came my way in 1984, when I learned that the original bronze patterns used to make the molds of Monotype 8A were in San Francisco. For years I had been working with indirect and imprecise information about the fonts that had stimulated this work. First I had worked from photographic blowups of letterpress original pages from *The Art of Computer Programming*; then Richard Southall had prepared enlargements from original proofs he had located in England. At last I found the actual 80-year-old patterns that had generated the metal type. The present owner of these patterns, Mr. Othmar Peters, kindly consented to let me borrow them while I was preparing the final draft of Computer Modern, and I learned much by measuring them with calipers. It never was my intention to make a slavish copy of any particular typeface, but the chance to work with these real artifacts made it possible to understand many of the intentions of the original designer.

If the Computer Modern typefaces have any merit, the credit should go to Zapf, Carter, Southall, Billawala, Bigelow, Holmes, and the anonymous original designer of Monotype 8A. I have tried to translate some of their wisdom into precise mathematical expressions. On the other hand, if these typefaces have deficiencies, the blame should be directed at me, because I did not always do what I was told.

I am dedicating this book to Martin E. Frost, who made it all possible by providing the WAITS and SAIL programming environments that have worked so efficiently for me during the past eight years. His yeoman service to Stanford has included countless rescue missions in the middle of the night, and he has introduced many system changes to accommodate the new equipment needed for our experiments.

The pleasant design of this book is due to Cleo Huggins, who found a nice way to fit illustrations and programs into the framework already established in *The METAFONTbook*.

I also want to reiterate my thanks to the many others acknowledged in previous volumes of this series—in particular, to my wife, Jill, and to my principal research sponsors, the National Science Foundation and the System Development Foundation.

Boston, Massachusetts
February 1986

— D. E. K.

Modern Typefaces

Typography is a conservative art: The style that is called "modern" in English typographic terminology is two hundred years old. The first types in the modern style were cut late in the 18th century, toward the close of the age of enlightenment and the beginning of the industrial revolution. The principal originators of the style were Giambattista Bodoni, a printer and punch-cutter of Parma, and Firmin Didot, a typefounder member of an illustrious Parisian printing family. These were contemporaries of Thomas Jefferson, and if today we regard Jefferson as a man modern in many respects, it may not be too far-fetched to call the types of his time "modern" as well.

An alternative term for modern is "neoclassical." This places the style in the context of the classical revival in 18th century European art, and it avoids confusion with the 20th century avant-garde styles that are also called modern. However, typography is not simply a subset of the arts; the evolution of type forms is also part of the broader history of literacy.

To distinguish typography from the pictorial and plastic arts and to emphasize its unique achievements, many typographers now prefer a nomenclature devised by the French typographic savant, Maximilien Vox. In the Vox classification, the modern style is called "Didone," a neologism coined from the names of Didot and Bodoni. In paying homage to the original designers, the term reminds us that typefaces are public artifacts created with a personal vision.

Whatever we choose to call it, the modern style has several characteristic features. Analytically, these are:

- high contrast between thick and thin letter elements;
- rectangular stems and serifs without brackets;
- abrupt graduation from thin, elongate hairlines to thick bowls;
- emphasis on bilateral symmetry with a vertical axis in "shading" (or "stress"—the orientation of thick and thin elements);
- rectangularization of curved bowls toward cartouche-like shapes;
- reduction of variation in the widths of capital and lower-case letters;
- repeatability of component letter parts;
- regulated, sculptural treatment of details such as terminals, based on engraving rather than on writing.

The mæstro Bodoni himself tells us, more intuitively, that the main features of the modern face are: regularity; neatness and polish; good taste; and grace.

A modern type produces a brilliant texture on the page. Refined hairlines and serifs contrast with dark stems and bowls in a glittery chiaroscuro. Assimilated shapes and widths emphasize the vertical regularity of the letterforms. The emergent text pattern connotes an elegant sophistication.

After its beginnings in Italy and France, the modern style was established in England in 1800 by the London typefounder Robert Thorne, and soon after in Germany by the Weimar founder Justus Erich Walbaum. Modern types were popular throughout the 19th century, and were among the earliest adopted for mechanical composition equipment. The English Monotype Corporation produced Moderns No. 1, 7, 13, and 14 in its early days, and its American cousin firm produced Modern No. 8A, among others. The Monotype Modern families came to be liberally provided with additional characters, including the sorts necessary for mathematical and technical composition, hence the designs have had an enduring presence in scientific publishing.

In the 19th century, modern engendered a variant called Clarendon, similar in structure but with much heavier serifs and hairlines. Century Schoolbook, a text book face, and Corona, a newspaper text face, are 20th century versions of the Clarendon style in popular use today.

But typographic taste changes, and there have been significant reactions against modern. The Arts & Crafts printers of the turn of the century thought it degenerate, preferring to revive Medieval and Renaissance styles. Also rejecting modern as decadent, the proponents of the "new typography" championed sansserif types in the 1920s and 30s.

Despite periodic reactions against it, the modern style has a stern beauty that continues to attract the attention of typographers even in our computer era. Revivals of the cuts of Bodoni, Didot, and Walbaum are available on most digital typesetting systems, and type designers have explored the idiom with fresh vision. Adrian Frutiger's Iridium is a lively evocation of the potentials of modern for photocomposition; Hermann Zapf's Marconi is an elegant modern designed for digital composition; and Donald Knuth's Computer Modern, the subject of this book, is a reinterpretation of Monotype Modern No. 8A.

In letterpress printing, modern fonts were technically troublesome because their delicate hairlines and serifs were particularly susceptible to damage; the broken letters produced a degraded text image. In digital typesetting with sufficient resolution, the delicate forms of modern can be rendered precisely. Computer typesetting and photolithographic printing are capable of reproducing modern typefaces with a clarity and sharpness unobtainable at the time of the original development of the style.

Because writing preserves the forms of expression as well as the contents, we can maintain continuity with the literate images of past eras. In a type style like modern we can find inspiration to create letterforms that are contemporary and yet whose texture alludes to another time, another place, in much the way that a floral scent suffuses a winter room with the memory of a summer garden.

San Francisco, California   — Charles A. Bigelow
January 1986

*The modern or new-fashioned faced printing type at present in use
was introduced by the French, about twenty years ago:
the old shaped letters being capable of some improvement,
it was judged expedient to re-model the alphabet
to render them more agreeable to the improved state of printing;
but unfortunately for the typographic art,
a transition was made from one extreme to its opposite:
thus instead of having letters somewhat too clumsy,
we now have them with hair lines so extremely thin
as to render it impossible for them to preserve their delicacy
beyond a few applications of the lye-brush, or the most careful distribution;
thus may types be said to be in a worn state ere they are well got to work.
The hair lines being now below the surface of the main strokes of the letters,
the Printer, in order to get an impression of all parts of the face,
is obliged to use a softer backing, and additional pressure.*

— RICHARD AUSTIN, *Specimen of Printing Types* (1819)

*As far back as 1732, Fleischman,
the letter-engraver for the Enschedé Foundry of Holland,
gave more roundness to the round letters of the lower-case,
but his teachings found no imitative pupil.
Bodoni of Italy was more successful.
He increased the roundness suggested by Fleischman,
lengthened the ascending and descending strokes,
extended serifs, put more white space between the lines,
and thereby gave improved readability to his types.*

— T. L. DE VINNE, *The Types of the De Vinne Press* (1907)

Bodoni's type displayed in a marked manner an attenuation of the thin lines,
with a reduction of the graduated portion of the curves to a minimum.
The letters are thereby weakened in construction
and turn a page into a maze of heavy lines
fretted here and there with grayness,
so that the eye is constantly readjusting its focus.
Morris says of it that it is the most illegible type ever cut,
with its preposterous thicks and thins;
he even speaks of "the sweltering hideousness of the Bodoni letter."
— F. W. GOUDY, *The Alphabet* (1918)

Likely enough it was Baskerville's 1773 edition of Ariosto's Orlando Furioso,
handsomely printed in Italian, which excited the admiration of Bodoni.
... Bodoni, however, cut several series of his own design;
he strengthened the thick lines and refined the thins,
thus producing that sharpness of contrast which,
exaggerated by the brilliance of his impression and the luxury of his paper,
seduced every European typographer from allegiance to
the more soundly built letters of obviously finer design
known to printers as the "old faces."
— STANLEY MORISON, *Four Centuries of Fine Printing* (1924)

The Didot modern face remained the standard letter in France,
and for the mass of books is still the normal design in use to-day.
Although some French printers have joined in the revival of old face,
the general typography has changed far less than in England.
A glance at any dozen recent novels printed in France
will show that the Didot tradition is by no means broken.
— A. F. JOHNSON, *Type Designs* (1934)

In pursuit of lively curves combined with a general "modern face" atmosphere,
we turned to one of the types that Bulmer used,
cut for him by William Martin around 1790—
and here seemed a good place to start again.
... The finishing strokes at the bottoms of letters,
cut straight across without "brackets,"
making sharp angles with the upright stems,
add "snap" to many of the old "modern face" designs—
and why not to Caledonia?
— W. A. DWIGGINS, *A New Printing Type, Caledonia* (1939)

Supplementary Bibliography

Readers who want to study more about typeface design with METAFONT may find a number of additional documents helpful. A complete bibliography of relevant literature would be extremely long; therefore this list has been limited to publications of the TEX project at Stanford University. Further information can be found in *TUGboat* (the journal of the TEX Users Group, published since 1980), and in the papers cited in the bibliographies of the papers cited here.

- "Mathematical Typography" by Donald E. Knuth, *Bulletin of the American Mathematical Society* (new series) **1** (March 1979), 337–372. [Reprinted as part 1 of *TEX and METAFONT: New Directions in Typesetting* (Providence, R.I.: American Mathematical Society, and Bedford, Mass.: Digital Press, 1979).] *Discusses the author's motivation for starting to work on METAFONT, and illustrates the results achieved during the first six months of experiments.*

- "The Computer Modern family of typefaces" by Donald E. Knuth, Stanford Computer Science Report 780 (Stanford, California, January 1980), 406 pp. *The first draft of what has developed into the present book and the present fonts. Includes complete programs written in the (now obsolete) METAFONT79 language, and discusses the early days of Computer Modern development.*

- *The METAFONTbook* by Donald E. Knuth (Reading, Mass.: Addison Wesley, 1986), xii+361 pp. [Also published as *Computers and Typesetting*, Volume C.] *The definitive user manual for METAFONT; a prerequisite for fully understanding the programs in the present book. Includes numerous examples, exercises, illustrations, lies, and jokes.*

- "The concept of a meta-font" by Donald E. Knuth, *Visible Language* **16** (1982), 3–27. [See also pp. 308–359 for sixteen reviews of this paper.] *Illustrates the notion of variable parameters in typeface design.*

- "Lessons learned from METAFONT" by Donald E. Knuth, *Visible Language* **19** (1985), 35–53. *Discusses the author's experiences with METAFONT79 and the early attempts at Computer Modern; illustrates several "meta-flops."*

- "The letter S" by Donald E. Knuth, *The Mathematical Intelligencer* **2** (1980), 114–122. *Illustrates Renaissance approaches to this difficult letter, and develops the geometric theory that underlies the S's of Computer Modern.*

- "My first experience with Indian Scripts" by Donald E. Knuth, *CALTIS-84*, a conference on calligraphy, lettering, typography of Indic scripts (New Delhi:

February 11–13, 1984), 49. *An example meta-character of the Devenagari alphabet, worked out hastily with the help of Matthew Carter.*

■ "An approach to type design and text composition in Indian scripts" by P. K. Ghosh, Stanford Computer Science report 965 (Stanford, California, April 1983), 148 pp. *Demonstrates that the methods developed for western languages and western alphabets work also for Devenagari and Tamil.*

■ "A Chinese meta-font" by Gu Guoan and J. D. Hobby, Stanford Computer Science report 974 (Stanford, California, July 1983), 22 pp.; reprinted in *TUGboat* **5**,2 (November 1984), 119–136. *Explains how to generate three different styles of Chinese characters satisfactorily by using only one program for each character; the different styles are obtained by defining nineteen general subroutines for basic strokes.*

■ "A course on METAFONT programming" by Donald E. Knuth, *TUGboat* **5**,2 (November 1984), 105–118. *Describes a series of 27 lectures by Charles A. Bigelow, Richard F. Southall, and the author about the history and frontiers of type design. These lectures were given while the implementation of METAFONT was being completed. Includes examples of numerous border designs as well as a "typeface" designed by the class participants.*

■ *The Euler Project at Stanford* by David R. Siegel (Stanford, California: Department of Computer Science, 1985), ii+31 pp. *Explains how METAFONT was adapted to copy a large set of drawings by Hermann Zapf for the Euler typeface commissioned by the American Mathematical Society.*

■ "Designing new typefaces with METAFONT" by Richard Southall, Stanford Computer Science report 1074 (Stanford, California, September 1985), 38 pp. *Presents a consistent terminology and a new typeface design created with METAFONT; evaluates the usefulness of symbolic programming languages as a tool for designers.*

■ "Meta-Marks: Preliminary studies for a Pandora's Box of shapes" by N. N. Billawala, Stanford Computer Science report (to appear). *Lavishly illustrated studies in parameter variation, leading to the design of a new typeface called Pandora.*

Contents

Grandjean, Baskerville, Bodoni and the Didots
had a mischievous influence on type-forms;
for the derivations *from types that their work made popular culminated in*
a kind of letter which was capable of greater vulgarity and degradation
than was ever the case with older fonts.

— D. B. UPDIKE, *Printing Types* (1927)

Introduction to the Parameters

Infinitely many alphabets can be generated by the programs in this book. All you have to do is assign values to 62 parameters and fire up the METAFONT system; then presto—out comes a new font of type.

The purpose of this introductory chapter is to explain the significance of each of the 62 parameters that define a Computer Modern typeface. The parameters divide naturally into several groups.

First come vertical measurements that define the heights and depths of most of the characters:

- *body_height* is the height of parentheses and other symbols like '/';
- *asc_height* is the height of lowercase letters with ascenders (b d f h k l);
- *cap_height* is the height of uppercase letters (A B C ⋯ Z);
- *fig_height* is the height of numerals (0 1 2 ⋯ 9);
- *x_height* is the height of lowercase letters without ascenders (a c e g m ⋯);
- *desc_depth* is the depth of lowercase letters with descenders (g j p q y);
- *comma_depth* is the depth of comma, semicolon, and 'Q';
- *math_axis* determines the middle of parentheses and certain other symbols (/ = + ⋯);
- *bar_height* determines many things, including the position of the bar line in 'e' and 'æ'.

Some characters have heights and depths determined indirectly from these quantities and other parameters; for example, the height of 'i' and 'j' is

$$\min\left(asc\_height, \tfrac{10}{7}\, x\_height + .5\max(dot\_size, cap\_curve)\right)$$

and the height of 't' is $\min(asc\_height, \tfrac{10}{7}\, x\_height)$. The diagrams of characters in this book have horizontal lines that show *body_height*, *asc_height*, *x_height*, *bar_height*, the baseline, *desc_depth*, and *body_depth*, where *body_depth* exceeds *desc_depth* by the same amount that *body_height* exceeds *asc_height*.

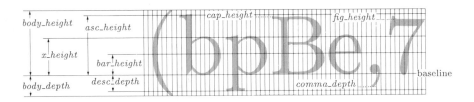

The *bar_height* parameter is somewhat delicate, because the author used it too frequently in his first designs of 1977; he never had the courage to abandon this early idea. If you increase *bar_height*, certain features of the lowercase letters will move upward in possibly unexpected ways; in fact, *bar_height* even influences characters like '4', 'G', and '&'! Therefore it is safest to keep *bar_height* between about 50% and 55% of *x_height*. The other height-and-depth parameters can be varied more freely.

Character shapes often "overshoot" the stated heights and depths. For example, an 'e' actually descends slightly below the baseline and ascends slightly above the *x_height*; this makes it visually compatible with letters like 'x' that do not overshoot. Two parameters are involved:

- *o* governs the overshoot of curved lines like the top and bottom of 'O';
- *apex_o* governs the overshoot at corners like the top of 'A' and the bottom of 'V'.

(The actual amount of overshoot varies from character to character. For example, letters like 'C', 'O', and 'S' overshoot their nominal height and depth by *o*, but 'e' and 'o' rise only .75*o* above *x_height* and descend only .5*o* below the baseline. The letters 'V' and 'W' dip below the baseline by *apex_o*, but 'v' and 'w' go down only half as much.) Small corrections like this are generally adjusted last, after the more significant measurements of a font have been established.

The widths of characters are determined primarily by a ubiquitous parameter that retains traces of its Monotype heritage:

- *u* is the basic unit of width.

There are essentially 18*u* to an em in the Computer Modern designs, and most characters have a prescribed width that is a multiple of *u*. For example, 'A' is 13*u* wide, and 'a' is 9*u*; the widths of the fundamental stem-letters 'l', 'n', and 'm' are respectively 5*u*, 10*u*, and 15*u*.

Characters aren't constrained to be an integer number of units wide, as they were in Monotype casting machines; but the old system provides a good reference point, and *u* is still a convenient unit to work with. The vertical lines in all character diagrams of this book are one unit apart. Increasing the value of *u* makes a font more extended; decreasing *u* makes it more condensed.

The proper fitting of letters is a subtle problem, hence character widths don't depend on *u* alone. Four additional parameters are available for finer adjustments:

- *serif_fit* is added to intercharacter spacing where lowercase serifs appear;
- *cap_serif_fit* is added to intercharacter spacing where uppercase serifs appear;
- *letter_fit* is added to the intercharacter spacing at the left and right of every character;
- *width_adj* is added to the widths of some letters (H M N) and subtracted from the widths of others (E F L O Q T).

(The *width_adj* attempts to reconcile competing notions about how wide certain letters ought to be; it is usually zero in a font with serifs, and between 0 and *u* in a font without serifs.) A sans-serif font usually has negative values for *serif_fit* and *cap_serif_fit*, to compensate for the fact that serifs are not present; on the other hand, the font cmr10 used in this sentence has *serif_fit* = 0, and its *cap_serif_fit* is slightly positive. A positive *letter_fit* puts more space between letters; this is often appropriate for small sizes of type. A negative *letter_fit* makes letters touch or nearly touch; this is sometimes appropriate in large title fonts.

The darkness or "weight" of a Computer Modern character is affected by quite a few parameters, of which the most important for lowercase letters are called *hair*, *vair*, *stem*, *curve*, and *flare*:

- *hair* is the horizontal breadth of thin "hairline" strokes;
- *vair* is the vertical breadth of thin "hairline" strokes;
- *stem* is the breadth of straight stem lines;
- *curve* is the breadth of curved stem lines;
- *flare* governs the diameter of bulbs or other terminal strokes.

A "monoline" font in which there is little or no contrast between thick and thin strokes often has *hair* = *stem* = *curve*, although *vair* is usually a bit smaller than this common value. The cmr10 font you are now reading has *hair* = $^9/_{36}$ pt, *vair* = $^8/_{36}$ pt, *stem* = $^{25}/_{36}$ pt = 1.25u, *curve* = $^{30}/_{36}$ pt = 1.5u, and *flare* = $^{33}/_{36}$ pt; here *curve* exceeds *stem*, to give the illusion of equal weight.

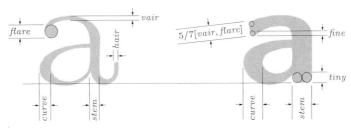

Computer Modern fonts with serifs have "bulbs" on letters like 'a', 'c', 'f', etc.; these bulbs are replaced in sans-serif fonts by slightly flared terminal strokes. The weight is controlled in both cases by the stated amount of *flare*, often in combination with *vair*.

Several other weight-oriented parameters are also necessary:

- *thin_join* controls thickness in critical parts of 'e', 'h', etc.;
- *bar* is the thickness of the crossbar in 'f' and 't';
- *slab* is the vertical thickness of serifs and arms;
- *dot_size* is the diameter of dots in 'i', ':', '!', etc.;
- *ess* is the stroke breadth in the middle of 's';
- *rule_thickness* is the breadth of strokes in mathematical symbols like '+', '/', and '='.

The *slab* value affects all serifs, and it is important also in sans-serif fonts because it governs the thickness of so-called arms in letters like 'E'. An independent *ess* parameter seems to be necessary even though it affects only one letter, because subtle combinations of *x_height*, *u*, *hair*, *vair*, and *curve* seem to influence the apparent thickness of this special stroke; the *ess* value should be fine-tuned after the rest of the font is in place.

Uppercase letters use the lowercase values of *vair*, *flare*, and *slab*, but they have their own parameters for other kinds of weights:

- *cap_hair* is the horizontal breadth of uppercase hairlines;
- *cap_stem* is the breadth of straight uppercase stem lines;
- *cap_curve* is the breadth of curved uppercase stem lines;
- *cap_ess* is the stroke breadth in the middle of 'S';
- *cap_bar* is the thickness of bar lines in 'E', 'F', 'G', 'H';
- *cap_band* is the thickness of horizontal strokes in 'A', 'B', 'D', 'P', 'R'.

There's not really a clear-cut distinction between *cap_bar* and *cap_band*, which are equal to each other in most of the standard Computer Modern fonts; the sans-serif case seems to work best if *slab* $\geq$ *cap_bar* $\geq$ *cap_band*.

If all stems are made exactly the same breadth, some of them will appear to be darker than others, because our eyes are influenced by other parts of the character shapes. Therefore small corrections are made:

- *stem_corr* controls small refinements to stems;
- *vair_corr* controls small refinements to hairlines.

For example, *stem_corr* is taken away from the stem inside the lobe of the 'P' (but the lower part of that stem is left untouched). The thickness at the top of 'O' is increased by *vair_corr*, and it is increased by $1.5vair\_corr$ at the bottom.

Three important parameters are available to control the "softness" of corners in the letter shapes:

- *crisp* is the diameter of serif corners;
- *tiny* is the diameter of rounded corners;
- *fine* is the diameter of sharply rounded corners.

For example, setting *crisp* $= 0$ gives perfectly square corners to serifs (as in cmr10); but if *crisp* $=$ *slab*, the serifs end in semicircles (as in cmtt10).

Serifs and "arms" can be varied in several ways by diddling with another set of parameters:

- *jut* is the amount by which lowercase serifs protrude;
- *cap_jut* is the amount by which uppercase serifs protrude;
- *serif_drop* is the amount by which certain serifs slope;
- *dish* is the amount erased at top or bottom of serifs;
- *bracket* is the vertical distance from serif to stem tangent;
- *beak* is the vertical protrusion of beak serifs at the ends of arms;
- *beak_jut* is the horizontal protrusion of beak serifs.

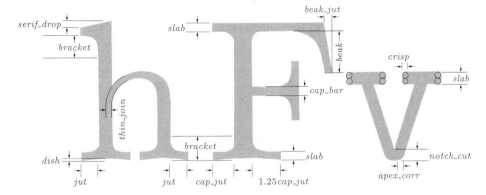

When diagonal strokes come together, the Computer Modern routines have two ways to keep the junction from filling in and looking too dark: The strokes are first spread apart by *apex_corr*; then the inner edge is opened, if necessary, until the height of the intersecting strokes is *notch_cut* or less.

- *apex_corr* is the extra external stroke width at diagonal junctions;
- *notch_cut* is the maximum vertical thickness at lowercase diagonal junctions;
- *cap_notch_cut* is the uppercase counterpart of *notch_cut*.

In cmr10 the *apex_corr* is zero, and *notch_cut* is 10 pt; this effectively disables such corrections, since they are unnecessary in a font with strong contrast between thick and thin strokes. However, cmtt10 has *apex_corr* = $^{10}/_{36}$ pt and *notch_cut* = $^{25}/_{36}$ pt.

The 48 parameters named so far have all been "ad hoc dimensions," which must be specified as physical units of measure in terms of inches, centimeters, or points, etc. The next several parameters are different; they are "pure numbers," i.e., dimensionless quantities.

- *slant* is the change in horizontal position per unit of vertical distance from the baseline, in italic or oblique fonts.

For example, the fonts cmr10 and cmsl10 are generated by exactly the same parameter values, except that cmr10 has *slant* = 0 while cmsl10 has *slant* = 1/6.

- *fudge* is a factor applied to the stem thicknesses of certain "heavy" characters.

For example, the stroke widths of 'w' are based on *fudge* × *hair* and *fudge* × *stem*, not simply on *hair* and *stem*. Font cmr10 has *fudge* = 1, so the fudge factor has no effect; but cmtt10 has *fudge* = 0.81.

- *math_spread* tells how "open" certain mathematical symbols are.

For example, cmr10 has *math_spread* = 0, cmr9 has *math_spread* = 1/5, ..., cmr5 has *math_spread* = 1; this makes more space between the bars of '=' signs and spreads out several other symbols in small sizes of type.

- *superness* is the parameter used in superelliptical bowls.

For example, the symbols '0', 'O', and 'O' have respective supernesses of 0.71, 0.77, and 0.84. (Chapter 14 of *The METAFONTbook* explains more about *superness*.)

- *superpull* is an amount by which superelliptical bowls are thinned.

The inside of the bowl is pulled toward the outside by this factor.

- *beak_darkness* governs the thickness of beaks.

The inside edge of a beak moves outward as *beak_darkness* increases. Font `cmr10` has *beak_darkness* = 11/30, while `cmtt10` has *beak_darkness* = 0.

- *ligs* controls the number of ligatures in the font.

If *ligs* = 0 you get only Spanish punctuation marks as ligatures; if *ligs* = 1 you get also double quotes and dashes; if *ligs* = 2 you get also the f-ligatures 'ff', 'fi', 'fl', 'ffi', and 'ffl'.

We have now covered 55 of the 62 parameters. The remaining seven all have true/false values; i.e., they're boolean, not numeric.

- *serifs* tells whether serifs and bulbs should be attached;
- *square_dots* tells whether dots should be square, not rounded.
- *hefty* tells whether weight-reducing strategies should be used.
- *monospace* tells whether the characters should all be forced to have the same width.
- *variant_g* tells whether 'g' should be used instead of 'g';
- *low_asterisk* tells whether '*' should be used instead of '*';
- *math_fitting* tells whether to produce special spacing for TeX math mode.

These parameters are fairly straightforward, except for '*hefty*'. When *hefty* is *true*, several characters are drawn in a special style that tends to avoid clusters of heavy strokes.

It's not easy to describe all the effects of each parameter. The index to this book should be consulted if you want to discover every place in which a certain parameter is used in the designs.

Many of the 62 parameters depend on each other in subtle ways, so you cannot expect to obtain a very good font if you simply select 62 values at random. The proper balance between *stem* and *curve* is particularly important. Several dozen combinations of values are given in this book as examples of possibilities that do seem to work; and thousands of variations that are reasonably near these "standard" values can be expected to produce satisfactory results. But if you try parameter settings that differ widely from those the author actually had time to examine while writing these programs, you will probably encounter cases in which individual shapes need to be adjusted.

The parameter values must, in fact, satisfy certain minimum conditions, or disaster will almost certainly ensue. The following relations are implicitly assumed to hold in all applications of the Computer Modern routines:

1) The *asc_height* must be larger than the *x_height*. Indeed, *asc_height* should be enough bigger that there is room for accents and for the distinctive features of letters like 'f', 'i', 'j', 't'.

2) The stem weights should satisfy

$$curve \geq stem; \qquad cap\_stem \geq stem; \qquad cap\_curve \geq curve.$$

3) The stem weights must not be less than the corner diameters. More precisely, each of the values

$$thin\_join, \; hair, \; vair, \; stem, \; curve, \; ess, \; flare, \; dot\_size, \; bar, \; slab,$$
$$cap\_hair, \; cap\_stem, \; cap\_curve, \; cap\_ess, \; cap\_bar, \; cap\_band$$

must be greater than or equal to each of the values

$$crisp, \; tiny, \; fine.$$

4) The "second-order refinement" values *stem_corr* and *vair_corr* should be very small. More precisely, *stem_corr* should not exceed

$$\tfrac{1}{5}cap\_hair, \qquad \tfrac{1}{6}stem, \qquad \tfrac{1}{4}fudge \times stem, \qquad \tfrac{1}{12}curve;$$

and *vair_corr* should not exceed $\tfrac{1}{4}slab$. If *hefty* is *true*, the stricter relation

$$stem\_corr \leq \tfrac{1}{16}fudge \times hair$$

should in fact be valid.

Trouble might also arise if the device-specific parameter called *blacker* is made negative. (The *blacker* value is not a parameter of Computer Modern, but it is a parameter of plain METAFONT, which is assumed to underlie the Computer Modern routines; see Chapter 11 of *The METAFONTbook*.) Since *blacker* is added to all stem weights behind the scenes, and since it is not added to the corner diameters, a relation like '*thin_join* $\geq$ *tiny*' might be violated when *blacker* < 0.

The programs will fail at extremely low resolutions, when there are fewer than 100 or so pixels per inch; some of the key points will be too close together, if there aren't enough pixels to go around. However, the standard fonts have all been tested successfully at a resolution of 101 per inch.

Electra Italic, really an oblique roman—
and the first to be available for machine composition in America—
is so readable a letter, that entire texts may readily be set in it.
— MERGENTHALER LINOTYPE COMPANY, *Electra* (1936)

A publisher called me up today and suggested that
a bold version of the original Electra Italic (oblique roman)
would make a wonderful letter in its own right,
and inquired if we had any intention of cutting it.
— C. H. GRIFFITH, *Letter to W. A. Dwiggins* (1941)

Organization of
the Files

The programs for Computer Modern consist of hundreds of little pieces that are grouped together in dozens of files. There are four main types of files:

- The *parameter files* define parameters for specific typefaces.
- The *driver files* control the font-generation process and define ligature and kerning conventions.
- The *program files* contain short programs for individual characters.
- The *base file* contains macros and declarations that are used by all the programs.

There also are *utility files* that facilitate the testing of new characters; these are described in Appendix E of *The METAFONTbook*.

When you want to generate a new font for a particular device (e.g., for the hypothetical *luxo* printer described in *The METAFONTbook*), you simply invoke METAFONT with a command line like

```
\mode=luxo; input cmr10
```

and stand back. The machine will begin by reading the parameter file cmr10.mf; then cmr10.mf will call in the base file cmbase.mf, followed by a driver file called roman.mf. The driver file, in turn, will input program files like romanu.mf, generating characters one by one; your terminal will look something like this:

```
(cmr10.mf (cmbase.mf) (roman.mf (romanu.mf
The letter A [65]
The letter B [66]
        ⋮
```

A verbose printout has appeared because *luxo* mode sets *tracingtitles* := 1, according to Chapter 11 of *The METAFONTbook*. If you're using a mode for which *tracingtitles* = 0, you won't see titles like 'The letter A'; in this case your screen will say

```
(cmr10.mf (cmbase.mf) (roman.mf (romanu.mf [65] [66] [67]
[68] [69] [70] [71] [72] [73] [74] [75] [76] [77] [78] [79]
[80] [81] [82] [83] [84] [85] [86] [87] [88] [89] [90])
(romanl.mf [97] [98] [99] [100] [101] [102] [103] [104]
[105] [106] [107] [108] [109] [110] [111] [112] [113] [114]
[115] [116] [117] [118] [119] [120] [121] [122]) (greeku.mf
```

```
[0] [1] [2] [3] [4] [5] [6] [7] [8] [9] [10]) (romand.mf
[48] [49] [50] [51] [52] [53] [54] [55] [56] [57])
(romanp.mf [36] [38] [63] [62]) (romspl.mf [16] [17] [25]
[26] [27] [28]) (romspu.mf [29] [30] [31]) (punct.mf [33]
[60] [35] [37] [39] [40] [41] [42] [43] [44] [46] [47] [58]
[59] [61] [64] [91] [93] [96]) (accent.mf [18] [19] [20]
[21] [22] [23] [24] [32] [94] [95] [125] [126] [127])
(romlig.mf [11] [12] [13] [14] [15]) (comlig.mf [34] [45]
[92] [123] [124])
```

at the end of the run. The driver file `roman.mf` has input 11 program files called `romanu.mf`, `romanl.mf`, `greeku.mf`, `romand.mf`, `romanp.mf`, `romspl.mf`, `romspu.mf`, `punct.mf`, `accent.mf`, `romlig.mf`, and `comlig.mf`.

Other driver files—such as `textit.mf`, which is used for text italic fonts like `cmti10`—will input different combinations of program files. For example, both `roman.mf` and `textit.mf` make use of `romanu.mf` for uppercase letters; but roman style lowercase letters come from `romanl.mf`, while the italic style comes from another program file called `itall.mf`.

In this book we shall examine the contents of all the files. First we'll look at parameter files (which are the easiest); then we'll consider the eight standard driver files (which are necessary but boring); and then we will get to the real meat of the matter, the 30 program files that describe approximately 500 characters. Parts of the base file `cmbase.mf` will be introduced together with the program files, since subroutines are most easily understood when they can be seen in use. Finally we'll wrap everything up by listing and discussing the remaining parts of `cmbase.mf`.

A comprehensive index at the back of this book makes it easy to find the uses of all the variables and the definitions of all the macros. There's also an index that takes you from character shape and/or font position to the relevant program page.

If you want to generate a new Computer Modern font with personalized parameters, you simply need to create a new parameter file analogous to the files found in this book. You might also want to go further and make your own driver file and/or program files, analogous to those presented here. Nothing in this book is "sacred," although you're not supposed to use the standard font names (`cmr10`, `cmtt10`, etc.) after you have made changes.

Parameter Files

There are altogether 75 standard parameter files in the Computer Modern family, hence there are 75 standard fonts. The "most standard" of all is `cmr10`, since the 10-point roman characters of Monotype Modern 8A served as the original starting point for all the Computer Modern designs.

Here is a transcript of the file `cmr10.mf`, which is typical of all the others. Notice that it defines the 62 parameters we discussed earlier, and it also does a little more: It prescribes a **font_identifier**, "CMR" (which characterizes a subfamily of Computer Modern that is useful in some schemes for font library maintenance); and it specifies a **font_size** of 10 points (so that, for example, TeX users can ask for 'cmr10 at 20pt' if they want two-fold magnification).

```
% Computer Modern Roman 10 point
if unknown cmbase: input cmbase fi                          % ensure that cmbase is present

font_identifier := "CMR"; font_size 10pt#;
```

$u^\# := {}^{20}\!/_{36}pt^\#;$ % unit width

$width\_adj^\# := 0pt^\#;$ % width adjustment for certain characters

$serif\_fit^\# := 0pt^\#;$ % extra sidebar near lowercase serifs

$cap\_serif\_fit^\# := {}^{5}\!/_{36}pt^\#;$ % extra sidebar near uppercase serifs

$letter\_fit^\# := 0pt^\#;$ % extra space added to all sidebars

$body\_height^\# := {}^{270}\!/_{36}pt^\#;$ % height of tallest characters

$asc\_height^\# := {}^{250}\!/_{36}pt^\#;$ % height of lowercase ascenders

$cap\_height^\# := {}^{246}\!/_{36}pt^\#;$ % height of caps

$fig\_height^\# := {}^{232}\!/_{36}pt^\#;$ % height of numerals

$x\_height^\# := {}^{155}\!/_{36}pt^\#;$ % height of lowercase without ascenders

$math\_axis^\# := {}^{90}\!/_{36}pt^\#;$ % axis of symmetry for math symbols

$bar\_height^\# := {}^{87}\!/_{36}pt^\#;$ % height of crossbar in lowercase 'e'

$comma\_depth^\# := {}^{70}\!/_{36}pt^\#;$ % depth of comma below baseline

$desc\_depth^\# := {}^{70}\!/_{36}pt^\#;$ % depth of lowercase descenders

$crisp^\# := 0pt^\#;$ % diameter of serif corners

$tiny^\# := {}^{8}\!/_{36}pt^\#;$ % diameter of rounded corners

$fine^\# := {}^{7}\!/_{36}pt^\#;$ % diameter of sharply rounded corners

$thin\_join^\# := {}^{7}\!/_{36}pt^\#;$ % width of extrafine details

$hair^\# := {}^{9}\!/_{36}pt^\#;$ % lowercase hairline breadth

$stem^\# := {}^{25}\!/_{36}pt^\#;$ % lowercase stem breadth

$curve^\# := {}^{30}\!/_{36}pt^\#;$ % lowercase curve breadth

$ess^\# := {}^{27}\!/_{36}pt^\#;$ % breadth in middle of lowercase 's'

$flare^\# := {}^{33}\!/_{36}pt^\#;$ % diameter of bulbs or breadth of terminals

$dot\_size^\# := {}^{38}\!/_{36}pt^\#;$ % diameter of dots

$cap\_hair^\# := {}^{11}\!/_{36}pt^\#;$ % uppercase hairline breadth

$cap\_stem^\# := {}^{32}\!/_{36}pt^\#;$ % uppercase stem breadth

$cap\_curve^\# := {}^{37}\!/_{36}pt^\#;$ % uppercase curve breadth

$cap\_ess^\# := {}^{35}\!/_{36}pt^\#;$ % breadth in middle of uppercase 's'

$rule\_thickness^\# := .4pt^\#;$ % thickness of lines in math symbols

$dish^\# := {}^{1}\!/_{36}pt^\#;$ % amount erased at top or bottom of serifs

$bracket^\# := {}^{20}\!/_{36}pt^\#;$ % vertical distance from serif base to tangent

$jut^\# := {}^{28}\!/_{36}pt^\#;$ % protrusion of lowercase serifs

$cap\_jut^\# := {}^{37}\!/_{36}pt^\#;$ % protrusion of uppercase serifs

$beak\_jut^\# := {}^{10}\!/_{36}pt^\#;$ % horizontal protrusion of beak serifs

$beak^\# := {}^{70}\!/_{36}pt^\#;$ % vertical protrusion of beak serifs

$vair^\# := {}^{8}\!/_{36}pt^\#;$ % vertical diameter of hairlines

$notch\_cut^\# := 10pt^\#;$ % maximum breadth above or below notches

$bar^\# := {}^{11}\!/_{36}pt^\#;$ % lowercase bar thickness

$slab^\# := {}^{11}\!/_{36}pt^\#;$ % serif and arm thickness

$cap\_bar^\# := {}^{11}\!/_{36}pt^\#;$ % uppercase bar thickness

$cap\_band^\# := {}^{11}\!/_{36}pt^\#;$ % uppercase thickness above/below lobes

$cap\_notch\_cut^\# := 10pt^\#;$ % max breadth above/below uppercase notches

$serif\_drop^\# := {}^{4}\!/_{36}pt^\#;$ % vertical drop of sloped serifs

$stem\_corr^\# := {}^{1}\!/_{36}pt^\#;$ % for small refinements of stem breadth

$vair\_corr^\# := {}^{1}\!/_{36}pt^\#;$ % for small refinements of hairline height

$apex\_corr^\# := 0pt^\#;$ % extra width at diagonal junctions

$o^\# := {}^{8}\!/_{36}pt^\#;$ % amount of overshoot for curves

$apex\_o^\# := {}^{8}\!/_{36}pt^\#;$ % amount of overshoot for diagonal junctions

$slant := 0;$ % tilt ratio $(\Delta x/\Delta y)$

$fudge := 1;$ % factor applied to weights of heavy characters

$math\_spread := 0;$ % extra openness of math symbols

$superness := 1/\mathrm{sqrt}\ 2;$ % parameter for superellipses

$superpull := {}^{1}\!/_{6};$ % extra openness inside bowls

$beak\_darkness := {}^{11}\!/_{30};$ % fraction of triangle inside beak serifs

$ligs := 2;$ % level of ligatures to be included

$square\_dots := \textbf{false};$ % should dots be square?

$hefty := \textbf{false};$ % should we try hard not to be overweight?

$serifs := \textbf{true};$ % should serifs and bulbs be attached?

$monospace := \textbf{false};$ % should all characters have the same width?

$variant\_g := \textbf{false};$ % should an italic-style 'g' be used?

$low\_asterisk := \textbf{false};$ % should the asterisk be centered at the axis?

$math\_fitting := \textbf{false};$ % should math-mode spacing be used?

generate roman   % switch to the driver file

All of the dimension-oriented parameters have been given in terms of "sharped" units (involving $pt^\#$), according to the conventions of plain METAFONT. The **font_setup** routine in cmbase will convert device-independent values such as $u^\#$ and $hair^\#$ into pixel-oriented values like u and $hair$.

The final line of `cmr10.mf` tells METAFONT to '**generate** roman'. This normally calls in the driver file `roman.mf`, which takes charge of the remaining details of font generation.

Most of the parameter values of `cmr10` are given as multiples of $1/36$ pt. There's no good reason for this, except that the author's original sketches in 1977 were made on graph paper with 36 pixels per point; the same resolution was then used to make proofs throughout most of the development process. When it became desirable to make stems one pixel darker or one pixel lighter on experimental proofsheets, the corresponding parameter was simply increased or decreased by 1/36 of a point.

All of the Computer Modern parameter files look like `cmr10.mf`, except for changes in name and parameter values. Therefore it will suffice to specify the other 73 files in an abbreviated, tabular format.

Computer Modern Roman types appear in eight standard sizes. The largest of these, 17.32 pt, corresponds to a magnification of 10-point type by a factor of '\magstep3' in the conventions of plain TeX.

name	cmr17	cmr12	cmr10	cmr9	cmr8	cmr7	cmr6	cmr5
font_identifier	CMR	CMR	CMR	CMR	CMR	CMR	CMR	CMR
font_size	17.32	12	10	9	8	7	6	5
u	32.5	23.5	20	18.5	17	15.5	14	12.5
width_adj	0	0	0	0	0	0	0	0
serif_fit	0	0	0	0	0	0	0	0
cap_serif_fit	8	5.8	5	4.6	4.1	3.5	2.8	2
letter_fit	−0.1	0	0	0	0	2	3	5
body_height	466	324	270	243	216	189	162	135
asc_height	432	300	250	225	200	175	150	125
cap_height	425	295.2	246	221.4	196.8	172.2	147.6	123
fig_height	401	278.4	232	208.8	185.6	162.4	139.2	116
x_height	267.8	186	155	139.5	124	108.5	93	77.5
math_axis	155.5	108	90	81	72	63	54	45
bar_height	150	104.4	87	78.3	69.6	60.9	52.2	43.5
comma_depth	121	84	70	63	56	49	42	35
desc_depth	121	84	70	63	56	49	42	35
crisp	0	0	0	0	0	0	0	0
tiny	8	8	8	8	8	7	7	6
fine	7	7	7	7	7	6	6	5
thin_join	9	7.5	7	7	7	6	6	5
hair	11	9.5	9	9	9	8.5	8	7.5
stem	33	28	25	24	22	20	18	16
curve	41	33	30	28	25.5	23	20.5	18
ess	35	30	27	25	23	21	17	12
flare	45	36	33	30	27	24	21	19

dot_size	51	42	38	35	32	29	26	22
cap_hair	13	11.5	11	10	9.5	9	8.5	8
cap_stem	40	35	32	29	26.5	24	21.5	19
cap_curve	48	40	37	33	30	27	24	21
cap_ess	43	38	35	31	27	23	19	14
rule_thickness	.60	.44	.40	.38	.36	.34	.31	.28
dish	1	1	1	1	1	.9	.8	.7
bracket	34	24	20	18	16	14	12	10
jut	42	33	28	25	22	19	17	15
cap_jut	50	41	37	33	29	26	23	20
beak_jut	15	11.4	10	9.2	8.4	7.6	6.8	6
beak	121	84	70	63	56	49	42	35
vair	10	8.5	8	8	8	7	7	6
notch_cut	17	12	10	9	8	7	6	5
bar	16	12.5	11	10	9.5	9	8.5	8
slab	16	12.5	11	10	9.5	9	8.5	8
cap_bar	16	12.5	11	10	9.5	9	8.5	8
cap_band	16	12.5	11	10	9.5	9	8.5	8
cap_notch_cut	17	12	10	9	8	7	6	5
serif_drop	17	4.8	4	3.6	3.2	2.8	2.4	2
stem_corr	1	1	1	1	1	.9	.8	.7
vair_corr	1	1	1	1	1	.9	.7	.5
apex_corr	0	0	0	0	0	0	0	0
o	10	9	8	7	6	5	4.5	4
apex_o	10	9	8	7	6	5	4.5	4
slant	0	0	0	0	0	0	0	0
fudge	1	1	1	1	1	1	1	1
math_spread	-0.4	-0.2	0	0.2	0.4	0.6	0.8	1
superness	$1/\sqrt{2}$	$1/\sqrt{2}$	$1/\sqrt{2}$	$1/\sqrt{2}$	$1/\sqrt{2}$	$1/\sqrt{2}$	$1/\sqrt{2}$	$1/\sqrt{2}$
superpull	1/6	1/6	1/6	1/6	1/6	1/6	1/6	1/6
beak_darkness	11/30	11/30	11/30	11/30	11/30	11/30	11/30	11/30
ligs	2	2	2	2	2	2	2	1
square_dots	false	false	false	false	false	false	false	false
hefty	false	false	false	false	false	false	false	false
serifs	**true**	**true**	**true**	**true**	**true**	**true**	**true**	**true**
monospace	false	false	false	false	false	false	false	false
variant_g	false	false	false	false	false	false	false	false
low_asterisk	false	false	false	false	false	false	false	false
math_fitting	false	false	false	false	false	false	false	false
generate	roman	roman	roman	roman	roman	roman	roman	roman

All dimensions in this table represent multiples of $1/36$ pt, except in the cases of **font_size**, *rule_thickness*, *notch_cut*, and *cap_notch_cut*, which are given in pt. (The parameter values for *slant*, . . . , *ligs* are pure numbers, not dimensions.)

The table shows that most of the "vertical" dimensions in `cmr` fonts are scaled in a straightforward way; for example, the *x_height* of `cmr5` is exactly half the *x_height* of `cmr10`. But horizontally the smaller fonts are more extended, and they have relatively heavier weight (especially in hairlines).

Computer Modern Slanted Roman types appear in four standard sizes; the fonts are called `cmsl12`, `cmsl10`, `cmsl9`, and `cmsl8`. The four parameter files need not be shown here, since they are completely identical to their unslanted counterparts `cmr12`–`cmr8`, except that the **font_identifier** is "CMSL" and the *slant* parameter is 1/6.

Computer Modern Bold Extended Roman types appear in seven standard sizes, from 12 pt down to 5 pt; they are called `cmbx12`–`cmbx5`. Vertical dimensions of `cmbx` fonts are similar to the corresponding `cmr` parameters, except that the *x_height* is a bit taller and the *bar_height* is not quite so tall. Bold letters are generated with bolder pen strokes, of course, and the characters are rather more extended; for example, one "em" is 10 pt in `cmr10`, but 11.5 pt in `cmbx10`. A larger value of *superness* makes the bowls larger.

name	cmbx12	cmbx10	cmbx9	cmbx8	cmbx7	cmbx6	cmbx5
font_identifier	CMBX	CMBX	CMBX	CMBX	CMBX	CMBX	CMBX
font_size	12	10	9	8	7	6	5
u	27	23	21.3	19.6	17.9	16.2	14.5
width_adj	13	11	10.2	9.4	8.6	7.8	7
serif_fit	0	0	0	0	0	0	0
cap_serif_fit	8	7	6.2	5.4	4.6	3.8	3
letter_fit	0	0	0	0	1	2	3
body_height	324	270	243	216	189	162	135
asc_height	300	250	225	200	175	150	125
cap_height	296.4	247	222.3	197.6	172.9	148.2	123.5
fig_height	278.4	232	208.8	185.6	162.4	139.2	116
x_height	192	160	144	128	112	96	80
math_axis	108	90	81	72	63	54	45
bar_height	102	85	76	67	58	49	40
comma_depth	84	70	63	56	49	42	35
desc_depth	84	70	63	56	49	42	35
crisp	0	0	0	0	0	0	0
tiny	13	13	13	12	11	10	9
fine	10	10	10	10	9	9	8
thin_join	10.5	10	10	10	9	9	8
hair	18.3	17	16.6	16.2	15.8	15.4	15
stem	47	41	38	35	32	28	24
curve	52	46	43	39	35	31	27
ess	44	38	35	32	29	25	19
flare	51	45	42	39	35	31	27

dot_size	62	56	51	46	41	36	31
cap_hair	20	19	19	19	18	18	17
cap_stem	57	51	47	43	38	33	28
cap_curve	61	55	51	46	41	36	31
cap_ess	59	53	48	43	37	31	24
rule_thickness	.66	.60	.57	.54	.51	.47	.43
dish	1	1	1	1	.9	.8	.7
bracket	12	10	9	8	7	6	5
jut	30	25	22	19	17	15	13
cap_jut	46	39	35	31	27	23	19
beak_jut	12.4	11	10.2	9.4	8.6	7.8	7
beak	84	70	63	55	46	36	25
vair	14.3	13	12.5	12	11.5	11	10
notch_cut	12	10	9	8	7	6	5
bar	18.5	17	16	15	14	13	12
slab	18.5	17	16	15	14	13	12
cap_bar	18.5	17	16	15	14	13	12
cap_band	18.5	17	16	15	14	13	12
cap_notch_cut	12	10	9	8	7	6	5
serif_drop	3.6	3	2.7	2.4	2.1	1.8	1.5
stem_corr	2	2	1.9	1.8	1.7	1.6	1.5
vair_corr	1.5	1.5	1.4	1.3	1.2	1.1	1
apex_corr	0	0	0	0	2	5	9
o	5	4	4	4	3	3	3
apex_o	4	3	3	3	3	3	3
slant	0	0	0	0	0	0	0
fudge	1	1	1	1	1	1	1
math_spread	0.4	0.5	0.7	0.9	1.1	1.3	1.5
superness	8/11	8/11	8/11	8/11	8/11	8/11	8/11
superpull	1/8	1/8	1/8	1/8	1/8	1/8	1/8
beak_darkness	0.4	0.4	0.4	0.4	0.4	0.4	0.4
ligs	2	2	2	2	2	2	2
square_dots	false	false	false	false	false	false	false
hefty	false	false	false	false	false	false	false
serifs	true	true	true	true	true	true	true
monospace	false	false	false	false	false	false	false
variant_g	false	false	false	false	false	false	false
low_asterisk	false	false	false	false	false	false	false
math_fitting	false	false	false	false	false	false	false
generate	roman	roman	roman	roman	roman	roman	roman

Positive values of *apex_corr* are used at small sizes to keep diagonal junctions from filling in, even though these fonts are not '*hefty*'.

Computer Modern Typewriter types have four standard sizes, namely cmtt12, cmtt10, cmtt9, and cmtt8. These fonts have the same *x_height* values as their roman counterparts, but they have shorter ascenders and longer descenders. The stroke weights are almost all identical to the corresponding roman stem weight; there is essentially no contrast between thick and thin. Serifs are rounded and unbracketed. Furthermore, all characters have the same width.

Three standard variations of cmtt10 are also provided, to demonstrate some of the other possibilities: cmsltt10 is slanted; cmvtt10 has characters of variable width; cmtex10 has the TEX extended-ASCII character set.

Since typewriter fonts are quite different from the ordinary roman and bold fonts, the parameter values in the following table are particularly interesting. For example, one of the more subtle points is the unusually high setting of *math_axis*; this raises the mathematical signs so that they blend particularly well with uppercase letters and digits, as desired in applications to computer program listing. Such applications also account for *low_asterisk* being **true**.

name	cmtt12	cmtt10	cmtt9	cmtt8	cmsltt10	cmvtt10	cmtex10
font_identifier	CMTT	CMTT	CMTT	CMTT	CMSLTT	CMVTT	CMTEX
font_size	12	10	9	8	10	10	10
u	24.7	21	18.9	17	21	21	21
width_adj	0	0	0	0	0	0	0
serif_fit	0	0	0	0	0	0	0
cap_serif_fit	0	0	0	0	0	0	0
letter_fit	0	0	0	0	0	0	0
body_height	300	250	225	200	250	250	250
asc_height	264	220	198	176	220	220	220
cap_height	264	220	198	176	220	220	220
fig_height	264	220	198	176	220	220	220
x_height	186	155	139.5	124	155	155	155
math_axis	132	110	99	88	110	110	110
bar_height	95	79	71	63	79	79	79
comma_depth	60	50	45	40	50	50	50
desc_depth	96	80	72	64	80	80	80
crisp	25	22	21	19	22	22	22
tiny	25	22	21	19	22	22	22
fine	22	21	20	18	21	21	21
thin_join	22	21	20	18	21	21	21
hair	28	25	24	22	25	25	25
stem	28	25	24	22	25	25	25
curve	28	25	24	22	25	25	25
ess	25	22	21	19	22	22	22
flare	35	32	30	28	32	32	32

dot_size	39	36	33	31	36	36	36
cap_hair	28	25	24	22	25	25	25
cap_stem	28	25	24	22	25	25	25
cap_curve	28	25	24	22	25	25	25
cap_ess	28	25	24	22	25	25	25
rule_thickness	28/36	25/36	24/36	22/36	25/36	25/36	25/36
dish	0	0	0	0	0	0	0
bracket	0	0	0	0	0	0	0
jut	39	34	31	27	34	34	34
cap_jut	39	34	31	27	34	34	34
beak_jut	0	0	0	0	0	0	0
beak	39	34	31	27	34	34	34
vair	25	22	21	19	22	22	22
notch_cut	28/36	25/36	24/36	22/36	25/36	25/36	25/36
bar	25	22	21	19	22	22	22
slab	25	22	21	19	22	22	22
cap_bar	25	22	21	19	22	22	22
cap_band	25	22	21	19	22	22	22
cap_notch_cut	28/36	25/36	24/36	22/36	25/36	25/36	25/36
serif_drop	0	0	0	0	0	0	0
stem_corr	0	0	0	0	0	0	0
vair_corr	0	0	0	0	0	0	0
apex_corr	11	10	9	8	10	10	10
o	5	4	3.5	3	4	4	4
apex_o	4	3	3	3	3	3	3
slant	0	0	0	0	1/6	0	1/4
fudge	0.86	0.81	0.81	0.81	0.81	0.81	0.81
math_spread	-1	-1	-1	-1	-1	-1	-1
superness	$1/\sqrt{2}$	$1/\sqrt{2}$	$1/\sqrt{2}$	$1/\sqrt{2}$	$1/\sqrt{2}$	$1/\sqrt{2}$	$1/\sqrt{2}$
superpull	0	0	0	0	0	0	0
beak_darkness	0	0	0	0	0	0	0
ligs	0	0	0	0	0	2	0
square_dots	false	false	false	false	false	false	false
hefty	true	true	true	true	true	true	true
serifs	true	true	true	true	true	true	true
monospace	true	true	true	true	true	false	true
variant_g	false	false	false	false	false	false	false
low_asterisk	true	true	true	true	true	true	true
math_fitting	false	false	false	false	false	false	false
generate	roman	roman	roman	roman	roman	roman	texset

Two additional standard fonts, called `cmtex9` and `cmtex8`, are created by modifying `cmtt9` and `cmtt8`, just as `cmtt10` has been changed to make `cmtex10`.

Computer Modern Sans Serif types come in five standard sizes, from 17 pt to 8 pt; the fonts are called cmss17, cmss12, cmss10, cmss9, and cmss8. The parameter settings are analogous in many respects to the corresponding cmr fonts, with which they are supposed to be compatible. For example, the values of u, *asc_height*, *desc_depth* are identical in seriffed and unseriffed fonts.

The main difference between cmss10 and cmr10, besides the fact that cmss10 has *serifs* = **false**, is the "monoline" nature of cmss10. There is almost no contrast between thick and thin strokes, because *hair*, *stem*, and *curve* are all equal to a value that falls between the *stem* and *curve* specifications of a seriffed font. In a monoline font, *hefty* is made **true**, and *notch_cut* is used to reduce heavy junction points.

Computer Modern Slanted Sans Serif types come in the same five sizes. Their names (cmssi17, cmssi12, cmssi10, cmssi9, and cmssi8) are slightly misleading, because the 'i' does not stand for 'italic'; the character shapes follow the roman style. All parameters are the same in corresponding members of the "CMSS" and "CMSSI" families, except that the *slant* values in the latter case are set to produce an angle of 12°.

name	cmss17	cmss12	cmss10	cmss9	cmss8	cmssi10
font_identifier	CMSS	CMSS	CMSS	CMSS	CMSS	CMSSI
font_size	17.32	12	10	9	8	10
u	32.5	23.5	20	18.5	17	20
width_adj	24	17	15	13	12	15
serif_fit	−12	−9	−7	−6.5	−6	−7
cap_serif_fit	−17	−13	−10	−9	−8.5	−10
letter_fit	0	0	0	0	0	0
body_height	466	324	270	243	216	270
asc_height	432	300	250	225	200	250
cap_height	432	300	250	225	200	250
fig_height	408	283	236	236	189	236
x_height	267.8	192	160	144	128	160
math_axis	155.5	108	90	81	72	90
bar_height	136	97	79	71	63	79
comma_depth	78	54	45	41	37	45
desc_depth	121	84	70	63	56	70
crisp	0	0	0	0	0	0
tiny	0	0	0	0	0	0
fine	0	0	0	0	0	0
thin_join	28	20	17	16	15	17
hair	47	33	28	27	25	28
stem	47	33	28	27	25	28
curve	47	33	28	27	25	28
ess	47	33	28	27	25	28
flare	42	30	25	24	22	25

dot_size	50	35	30	28	26	30
cap_hair	47	33	28	27	25	28
cap_stem	52	37	32	31	29	32
cap_curve	52	37	32	31	29	32
cap_ess	52	37	32	31	28	32
rule_thickness	.60	.44	.40	.38	.36	.40
dish	0	0	0	0	0	0
bracket	0	0	0	0	0	0
jut	0	0	0	0	0	0
cap_jut	0	0	0	0	0	0
beak_jut	0	0	0	0	0	0
beak	.8	.6	.5	.5	.4	.5
vair	38	26	22	21	19	22
notch_cut	32/36	22/36	18/36	17/36	16/36	18/36
bar	36	25	21	20	18	21
slab	40	27	23	22	20	23
cap_bar	38	26	22	21	19	22
cap_band	35	24	20	19	17	20
cap_notch_cut	46/36	31/36	25/36	24	22/36	25/36
serif_drop	2	2	2	2	2	2
stem_corr	1	1	1	1	1	1
vair_corr	1	1	1	1	1	1
apex_corr	7	6	5	4.5	4	5
o	10	9	8	7	6	8
apex_o	0	0	0	0	0	0
slant	0	0	0	0	0	sind 12/cosd 12
fudge	1	.98	.96	.95	.93	.96
math_spread	-0.4	-0.2	0	0.2	0.4	0
superness	$1/\sqrt{2}$	$1/\sqrt{2}$	$1/\sqrt{2}$	$1/\sqrt{2}$	$1/\sqrt{2}$	$1/\sqrt{2}$
superpull	1/20	1/20	1/20	1/20	1/20	1/20
beak_darkness	0	0	0	0	0	0
ligs	2	2	2	2	2	2
square_dots	**true**	**true**	**true**	**true**	**true**	**true**
hefty	**true**	**true**	**true**	**true**	**true**	**true**
serifs	**false**	**false**	**false**	**false**	**false**	**false**
monospace	**false**	**false**	**false**	**false**	**false**	**false**
variant_g	**false**	**false**	**false**	**false**	**false**	**false**
low_asterisk	**false**	**false**	**false**	**false**	**false**	**false**
math_fitting	**false**	**false**	**false**	**false**	**false**	**false**
generate	roman	roman	roman	roman	roman	roman

The parameter settings for cmssi17, cmssi12, cmssi9, and cmssi8 are completely analogous to those shown for cmssi10.

Computer Modern Sans Serif Demibold Condensed type, also called `cmssdc10`, is one of several standard fonts that demonstrate additional possibilities for sans-serif typefaces in the Computer Modern family. The chapter titles in this book (and in the entire *Computers and Typesetting* series) have been set in 'cmssdc10 at 40pt', a four-fold magnification of the 10 pt size.

Computer Modern Sans Serif Bold Extended type, also known as `cmssbx10`, is another such "demonstration" font. The big numbers and letters that introduce chapters and appendices in *The TEXbook* and *The META-FONTbook* have been set in a special version of `cmssbx10` called `cminch`; this name reflects the fact that the letters and digits are exactly an inch high. (The parameters for `cminch` are defined just like those for `cmssbx10`, except that `cminch.mf` begins with the line '**numeric** $Pt\#$; ${}^{250}/_{36}Pt\# = 1$ in$\#$'; then Pt is used in place of pt in all the parameter assignments.)

Computer Modern Sans Serif Quotation Style type demonstrates yet another possible variation, used in the quotations and epigraphs of this book. The standard font `cmssq8` has the body size of eight-point type, but its *x_height* is almost the *x_height* of `cmr10`. There is a slanted version called `cmssqi8`.

name	cmssdc10	cmssbx10	cmss10	cmssqi8	cmssq8
font_identifier	CMSSDC	CMSSBX	CMSS	CMSSQI	CMSSQ
font_size	10	10	10	8	8
u	19	22	20	20	20
width_adj	15	22	15	2	2
serif_fit	−8	−9	−7	−10	−10
cap_serif_fit	−9	−11	−10	−14	−14
letter_fit	0	0	0	0	0
body_height	270	270	270	220	220
asc_height	250	250	250	200	200
cap_height	250	250	250	197	197
fig_height	250	250	236	190	190
x_height	170	165	160	150	150
math_axis	95	90	90	80	80
bar_height	95	90	79	80	80
comma_depth	40	38	45	40	40
desc_depth	60	70	70	40	40
crisp	23	26	0	18	18
tiny	23	26	0	18	18
fine	8	9	0	8	8
thin_join	8	9	17	8	8
hair	40	49	28	23	23
stem	40	49	28	23	23
curve	40	49	28	23	23
ess	37	43	28	23	23
flare	31	40	25	21	21

dot_size	38	47	30	28	28
cap_hair	40	49	28	23	23
cap_stem	44	53	32	27	27
cap_curve	44	53	32	27	27
cap_ess	42	51	32	27	27
rule_thickness	25/36	30/36	.40	20/36	20/36
dish	0	0	0	0	0
bracket	0	0	0	0	0
jut	0	0	0	0	0
cap_jut	0	0	0	0	0
beak_jut	0	0	0	0	0
beak	1.5	1.5	.5	0	0
vair	23	26	22	18	18
notch_cut	40/36	49/36	18/36	23/26	23/26
bar	23	26	21	18	18
slab	31	36	23	19	19
cap_bar	29	34	22	19	19
cap_band	27	31	20	19	19
cap_notch_cut	37/36	45/36	25/36	23/26	23/26
serif_drop	2	2	2	0	0
stem_corr	1	1	1	.5	.5
vair_corr	2	2	1	.5	.5
apex_corr	14	18	5	4	4
o	7	8	8	6	6
apex_o	0	0	0	2	2
slant	0	0	0	sind 12/cosd 12	0
fudge	.91	.88	.96	.95	.95
math_spread	0.3	0.5	0	0	0
superness	0.74	0.75	$1/\sqrt{2}$	$1/\sqrt{2}$	$1/\sqrt{2}$
superpull	1/18	1/18	1/20	1/10	1/10
beak_darkness	0	0	0	0	0
ligs	2	2	2	2	2
square_dots	true	true	true	true	true
hefty	true	true	true	true	true
serifs	false	false	false	false	false
monospace	false	false	false	false	false
variant_g	true	false	false	true	true
low_asterisk	false	false	false	false	false
math_fitting	false	false	false	false	false
generate	roman	roman	roman	roman	roman

The parameters of `cmss10` have been repeated here for comparison. The new fonts have "softer" edges, because *crisp*, *tiny*, and *fine* are positive.

Computer Modern Dunhill Roman type demonstrates yet another kind of parameter variation. Font cmdunh10 has the standard parameters of cmr10, except that *body_height*, *asc_height*, *cap_height*, and *fig_height* have been drastically increased, by $^{100}/_{36}$ pt each.

Computer Modern Bold Extended Slanted Roman type, also known as cmbxsl10, is a slanted companion to cmbx10. There's also a standard font called cmb10, which is a non-extended bold roman. Characters have almost the same widths in cmb10 and cmr10, because both fonts have $u = {}^{20}/_{36}$ pt.

Computer Modern Funny Roman type carries the idea of parameter variation to a ridiculous extreme. The author concocted it primarily to test the robustness of his programs, but people have also used cmff10 to typeset party invitations. Its backward slant, large *x_height* and *desc_depth*, small *bar_height*, twiggy stems, diamond-shaped bowls, reverse beaks, and deep notches combine to make rather bizarre effects. Proofmode-size blowups of these freakish characters have a curious property: They convey much of a design's "meta-ness" in a single drawing. More normal settings of the parameters do not do this as well.

name	cmdunh10	cmbxsl10	cmb10	cmff10	cmfib8
font_identifier	CMDUNH	CMBXSL	CMB	CMFF	CMFIB
font_size	10	10	10	10	8
u	20	23	20	16	21
width_adj	0	11	10	-16	0
serif_fit	0	0	0	-3	-2
cap_serif_fit	5	7	6	-4	0
letter_fit	0	0	0	2	0
body_height	370	270	270	240	233
asc_height	350	250	250	220	233
cap_height	346	247	246	225	233
fig_height	332	232	232	210	233
x_height	155	160	160	190	144
math_axis	90	90	90	55	89
bar_height	87	87	85	60	89
comma_depth	70	70	70	70	55
desc_depth	70	70	70	100	55
crisp	0	0	0	10	0
tiny	8	8	13	0	13
fine	7	10	10	0	13
thin_join	7	10	10	14	13
hair	9	17	17	12	21
stem	25	41	41	16	34
curve	30	46	46	20	$34 + 5$
ess	27	38	38	22	34
flare	33	45	45	24	34

dot_size	38	56	56	26	34
cap_hair	11	19	19	16	21
cap_stem	32	51	51	24	43
cap_curve	37	55	55	26	$34+5$
cap_ess	35	53	53	28	34
rule_thickness	.40	.60	.60	.50	$21/36$
dish	1	1	1	5	1
bracket	20	10	10	20	21
jut	28	25	25	3	21
cap_jut	37	39	34	4	21
beak_jut	10	11	11	-8	13
beak	70	70	70	10	55
vair	8	13	13	14	13
notch_cut	10	10	10	$2/36$	8
bar	11	17	17	17	13
slab	11	17	17	20	13
cap_bar	11	17	17	22	13
cap_band	11	17	17	17	13
cap_notch_cut	10	10	10	$3/36$	8
serif_drop	4	3	3	-10	3
stem_corr	1	2	2	-1	1
vair_corr	1	1.5	1.5	-1	1
apex_corr	0	0	0	6	0
o	8	4	4	4	8
apex_o	8	3	3	9	8
slant	0	$1/6$	0	$-.1$	0
fudge	1	1	1	1	1
math_spread	0	0.5	0.5	0.5	$3/8$
superness	$1/\sqrt{2}$	$8/11$	$8/11$	$2/3$	$1/\sqrt{2}$
superpull	$1/6$	$1/8$	$1/8$	$-1/8$	$1/13$
beak_darkness	$11/30$	0.4	0.4	0.5	$5/13$
ligs	2	2	2	2	2
square_dots	**false**	**false**	**false**	**true**	**false**
hefty	**false**	**false**	**false**	**false**	**false**
serifs	**true**	**true**	**true**	**true**	**true**
monospace	**false**	**false**	**false**	**false**	**false**
variant_g	**false**	**false**	**false**	**false**	**false**
low_asterisk	**false**	**false**	**false**	**false**	**false**
math_fitting	**false**	**false**	**false**	**false**	**false**
generate	roman	roman	roman	roman	roman

The fifth column, `cmfib8`, generates a standard font based on the Fibonacci sequence (0, 1, 1, 2, 3, 5, 8, 13, 21, 34, 55, 89, 144, . . .), in hopes that these numbers will yield an especially pleasing alphabet.

Computer Modern Text Italic types come in five standard sizes: cmti12, cmti10, cmti9, cmti8, and cmti7. Uppercase italic letters are generated by the same programs that make uppercase roman letters, but the lowercase letters belong to an entirely different style. Some of the numerals (*1, 2, 3, 4, 7*) are also changed, as are special symbols like question mark and ampersand (*?, &*). The textit driver program controls such stylistic variations.

It is interesting to compare the parameters of cmti12 to those of cmr12, and to compare cmti10 to cmr10, etc.; so cmr12 is repeated in the table below. Text italic letters are slightly condensed (because they have a smaller value of *u*); their stems are slightly lighter, and this makes the total effect lighter even though the hairlines have gained some weight. A significant *letter_fit* is added at the left and right of each character, to keep the letters from bunching up. The slant ratio is 1/4 (compared to 1/6 in slanted roman fonts). The *crisp* parameter is positive, hence text italic serifs have softer edges. These differences all cause *UPPERCASE TEXT ITALIC LETTERS* to be different from *UPPERCASE SLANTED ROMAN LETTERS*.

name	cmr12	cmti12	cmti10	cmti9	cmti8	cmti7
font_identifier	CMR	CMTI	CMTI	CMTI	CMTI	CMTI
font_size	12	12	10	9	8	7
u	23.5	21.6	18.4	17	15.8	14.8
width_adj	0	0	0	0	0	0
serif_fit	0	0	0	0	0	0
cap_serif_fit	5.8	5.8	5	4.6	4.1	3.5
letter_fit	0	10.8	9.2	8.5	7.9	9.4
body_height	324	324	270	243	216	189
asc_height	300	300	250	225	200	175
cap_height	295.2	295.2	246	221.4	196.8	172.2
fig_height	278.4	278.4	232	208.8	185.6	162.4
x_height	186	186	155	139.5	124	108.5
math_axis	108	108	90	81	72	63
bar_height	104.4	104.4	87	78.3	69.6	60.9
comma_depth	84	84	70	63	56	49
desc_depth	84	84	70	63	56	49
crisp	0	8	8	8	8	7
tiny	8	8	8	8	8	7
fine	7	7	7	7	7	6
thin_join	7.5	7.5	7	7	7	6
hair	9.5	12	11	11	11	10.5
stem	28	26	23	22	20	18.5
curve	33	31	28	26	23.5	21.5
ess	30	29	27	25	23	21
flare	36	32	29	26	24	21

dot_size	42	42	38	35	32	29
cap_hair	11.5	11.5	11	11	11	10.5
cap_stem	35	32	29	26	23.5	21.5
cap_curve	40	37	34	30	27	24.5
cap_ess	38	34	31	27	24	21
rule_thickness	.44	.44	.40	.38	.36	.34
dish	1	1	1	1	1	.9
bracket	24	24	20	18	16	14
jut	33	35	30	27	24	21
cap_jut	41	38	34	30.5	27	24
beak_jut	11.4	10.4	9	8.5	7.9	7.4
beak	84	84	70	63	56	49
vair	8.5	8.5	8	8	8	7
notch_cut	12	12	10	9	8	7
bar	12.5	12.5	11	10	9.5	9
slab	12.5	12.5	11	10	9.5	9
cap_bar	12.5	12.5	11	10	9.5	9
cap_band	12.5	12.5	11	10	9.5	9
cap_notch_cut	12	12	10	9	8	7
serif_drop	4.8	4.8	4	3.6	3.2	2.8
stem_corr	1	1	1	1	1	.9
vair_corr	1	1	1	1	1	.9
apex_corr	0	0	0	0	0	0
o	9	9	8	7	6	5
apex_o	9	9	8	7	6	5
slant	0	1/4	1/4	1/4	1/4	1/4
fudge	1	1	1	1	1	1
math_spread	-0.2	-0.2	0	0.2	0.4	0.6
superness	$1/\sqrt{2}$	$1/\sqrt{2}$	$1/\sqrt{2}$	$1/\sqrt{2}$	$1/\sqrt{2}$	$1/\sqrt{2}$
superpull	1/6	1/6	1/6	1/6	1/6	1/6
beak_darkness	11/30	11/30	11/30	11/30	11/30	11/30
ligs	2	2	2	2	2	2
square_dots	false	false	false	false	false	false
hefty	false	false	false	false	false	false
serifs	true	true	true	true	true	true
monospace	false	false	false	false	false	false
variant_g	false	true	true	true	true	true
low_asterisk	false	false	false	false	false	false
math_fitting	false	false	false	false	false	false
generate	roman	textit	textit	textit	textit	textit

The *variant_g* values are **true**, since italic g's are *g*'s; but this parameter is actually irrelevant in fonts generated by textit.

Computer Modern Math Italic types have seven standard sizes, from 12 pt down to 5 pt; the font names are `cmmi12`–`cmmi5`. In this case *math_fitting* is **true**, so the characters are positioned in a special way to enhance their appearance in mathematical formulas. Furthermore, a math italic font has a completely different character set from text italic: The lowercase Greek alphabet is included, and there are special symbols like Weierstrass's 'p' ($\wp$). The `mathit` driver program controls such stylistic variations.

Many of the characters of math italic fonts are unslanted, as if the *slant* parameter had been zero. This includes the numerals, which are in "old style" (0, 1, 2, 3, 4, 5, 6, 7, 8, 9), as well as more than a dozen special symbols like '$\leftharpoonup$', '$\triangleright$', '$\flat$', '$\natural$', '$\sharp$', and '$\star$'. Appendix F of *The T_EXbook* observes that "this portion of the font doesn't deserve the name math italic; it's really a resting place for characters that don't fit anywhere else."

It is interesting to compare the parameters of `cmmi12` to those of `cmr12`, and to compare `cmmi10` to `cmr10`, etc.; so `cmr12` is repeated in the table below. Math italic letters are not condensed as text italic was; and they are not quite as light as text italic. (After all, mathematics is important to mathematicians.)

name	cmr12	cmmi12	cmmi10	cmmi9	cmmi8	cmmi7	cmmi6	cmmi5
font_identifier	CMR	CMMI	CMMI	CMMI	CMMI	CMMI	CMMI	CMMI
font_size	12	12	10	9	8	7	6	5
u	23.5	23.5	20	18.5	17	15.5	14	12.5
width_adj	0	0	0	0	0	0	0	0
serif_fit	0	0	0	0	0	0	0	0
cap_serif_fit	5.8	5.8	5	4.6	4.1	3.5	2.8	2
letter_fit	0	0	0	0	0	4	6	10
body_height	324	324	270	243	216	189	162	135
asc_height	300	300	250	225	200	175	150	125
cap_height	295.2	295.2	246	221.4	196.8	172.2	147.6	123
fig_height	278.4	278.4	232	208.8	185.8	162.4	139.2	116
x_height	186	186	155	139.5	124	108.5	93	77.5
math_axis	108	108	90	81	72	63	54	45
bar_height	104.4	104.4	87	78.3	69.6	60.9	52.2	43.5
comma_depth	84	84	70	63	56	49	42	35
desc_depth	84	84	70	63	56	49	42	35
crisp	0	8	8	8	8	7	6.5	6
tiny	8	8	8	8	8	7	6.5	6
fine	7	7	7	7	7	6	6	5
thin_join	7.5	7.5	7.5	7	7	6	6	5
hair	9.5	9.5	9	9	9	8.5	8	7.5
stem	28	27	24	23	21.5	19.5	17.5	15.5
curve	33	32	29	27	25	22.5	20	17.5
ess	30	30	27	25	23	21	17	12
flare	36	35	32	29	26.5	23.5	20.5	18.5

dot_size	42	42	38	35	32	29	26	22
cap_hair	11.5	11.5	11	10	9.5	9	8.5	8
cap_stem	35	33	30	28	25.5	23.5	21	18.5
cap_curve	40	38	35	32	29	26.5	23.5	20.5
cap_ess	38	32	33	30	26	22.5	18.5	13.5
rule_thickness	.44	.44	.40	.38	.36	.34	.31	.28
dish	1	1	1	1	1	.9	.8	.7
bracket	24	24	20	18	16	14	12	10
jut	33	35	30	27	24	21	19	17
cap_jut	41	41	37	33	29	26	23	20
beak_jut	11.4	11.4	10	9.2	8.4	7.6	6.8	6
beak	84	84	70	63	56	49	42	35
vair	8.5	8.5	8	8	8	7	7	6
notch_cut	12	12	10	9	8	7	6	5
bar	12.5	12.5	11	10	9.5	9	8.5	8
slab	12.5	12.5	11	10	9.5	9	8.5	8
cap_bar	12.5	12.5	11	10	9.5	9	8.5	8
cap_band	12.5	12.5	11	10	9.5	9	8.5	8
cap_notch_cut	12	12	10	9	8	7	6	5
serif_drop	4.8	4.8	4	3.6	3.2	2.8	2.4	2
stem_corr	1	1	1	1	1	.9	.8	.7
vair_corr	1	1	1	1	1	.9	.7	.5
apex_corr	0	0	0	0	0	0	0	0
o	9	9	8	7	6	5	4.5	4
apex_o	9	9	8	7	6	5	4.5	4
slant	0	1/4	1/4	1/4	1/4	1/4	1/4	1/4
fudge	1	1	1	1	1	1	1	1
math_spread	−0.2	−0.2	0	0.2	0.4	0.6	0.8	1
superness	$1/\sqrt{2}$	$1/\sqrt{2}$	$1/\sqrt{2}$	$1/\sqrt{2}$	$1/\sqrt{2}$	$1/\sqrt{2}$	$1/\sqrt{2}$	$1/\sqrt{2}$
superpull	1/6	1/6	1/6	1/6	1/6	1/6	1/6	1/6
beak_darkness	11/30	11/30	11/30	11/30	11/30	11/30	11/30	11/30
ligs	2	2	2	2	2	2	2	1
square_dots	false	false	false	false	false	false	false	false
hefty	false	false	false	false	false	false	false	false
serifs	true	true	true	true	true	true	true	true
monospace	false	false	false	false	false	false	false	false
variant_g	false	true	true	true	true	true	true	true
low_asterisk	false	false	false	false	false	false	false	false
math_fitting	false	true	true	true	true	true	true	true
generate	roman	mathit	mathit	mathit	mathit	mathit	mathit	mathit

The *variant_g* values are **true**, since math g's are *g*'s; but the mathit driver program does not actually look at the parameters *variant_g* or *low_asterisk*.

Computer Modern Bold Extended Text Italic type, also known as
`cmbxti10`, is one of several standard fonts that demonstrate additional possibilities for italic typefaces in the Computer Modern family. There's also a bold math
italic, called `cmmib10`. (Standard font names have been chosen in such a way
that there are no conflicts when names longer than six characters are shortened
by retaining the first three and last three characters. For example, the file names
`cmbxti10.mf` and `cmmib10.mf` can safely become 'cmbi10.mf' and 'cmmb10.mf'
on computer systems that do not allow long file names.)

Computer Modern Italic Typewriter type, also known as `cmitt10`,
is another such "demonstration" font. It is a monospaced text italic, with weights
and spacing compatible with `cmtt10` and `cmsltt10`.

Computer Modern Unslanted Text Italic type, `cmu10`, demonstrates
yet another possible variation. It has italic-style letters, but they are upright
and they have the weights of `cmr10`.

Finally, there's also *Computer Modern Funny Italic* (`cmfi10`), a companion to the funny font `cmff10`. This one is not quite as hilarious as the other.

name	cmbxti10	cmmib10	cmitt10	cmu10	cmfi10
font_identifier	CMBXTI	CMMIB	CMITT	CMU	CMFI
font_size	10	10	10	10	10
u	21.2	23	21	20	21
width_adj	11	11	0	0	−16
serif_fit	0	0	0	0	−3
cap_serif_fit	7	7	0	5	−4
letter_fit	11	0	15	10	2
body_height	270	270	250	270	240
asc_height	250	250	220	250	220
cap_height	247	247	220	247	225
fig_height	232	232	220	232	210
x_height	160	160	155	155	190
math_axis	90	90	110	90	55
bar_height	85	85	79	87	60
comma_depth	70	70	50	70	70
desc_depth	70	70	80	70	100
crisp	13	13	22	0	11
tiny	13	13	22	8	0
fine	10	10	21	7	0
thin_join	10	10	21	7	14
hair	20	17	25	9	11
stem	38	40	25	25	17
curve	43	45	25	30	21
ess	35	36	22	22	23
flare	42	42	32	33	25

dot_size	53	56	36	38	26
cap_hair	22	19	25	11	15
cap_stem	49	50	25	32	25
cap_curve	52	53	25	37	27
cap_ess	50	51	25	32	29
rule_thickness	.60	.60	25/36	.40	.50
dish	1	1	0	1	5
bracket	10	10	0	20	20
jut	27	27	40	28	3
cap_jut	39	39	34	37	4
beak_jut	10	11	0	10	-8
beak	70	70	34	70	10
vair	13	13	22	8	15
notch_cut	10	10	25/36	10	2
bar	17	17	22	11	18
slab	17	17	22	11	21
cap_bar	17	17	22	11	23
cap_band	17	17	22	11	18
cap_notch_cut	10	10	25/36	10	3/36
serif_drop	3	3	0	4	-10
stem_corr	2	2	0	1	-1
vair_corr	1.5	1.5	1.5	1	-1
apex_corr	0	0	10	0	6
o	6	6	4	8	4
apex_o	6	6	3	8	9
slant	1/4	1/4	1/4	0	+.1
fudge	1	1	.81	1	1
math_spread	0.5	0.5	-1	0	0.5
superness	8/11	8/11	$1/\sqrt{2}$	$1/\sqrt{2}$	2/3
superpull	1/8	1/8	0	1/6	$-1/8$
beak_darkness	0.4	0.4	0	11/30	0.5
ligs	2	2	0	2	2
square_dots	**false**	**false**	**false**	**false**	**true**
hefty	**false**	**false**	**true**	**false**	**false**
serifs	**true**	**true**	**true**	**true**	**true**
monospace	**false**	**false**	**true**	**false**	**false**
variant_g	**true**	**true**	**true**	**true**	**true**
low_asterisk	**false**	**false**	**true**	**false**	**false**
math_fitting	**false**	**true**	**false**	**false**	**false**
generate	`textit`	`mathit`	`textit`	`textit`	`textit`

A great many other possibilities for italic parameter settings can, of course, be imagined. For example, a slightly expanded demibold font with a *slant* of 1/8 seems to work well.

COMPUTER MODERN CAPS AND SMALL CAPS TYPES need a different sort of parameter file, because the "lowercase" letters are generated by uppercase programs; two different sets of uppercase parameters are needed.

The problem is solved by giving values to 62 parameters as usual, then giving additional values to 25 parameters with '*lower*' prefixed to their names. For example, *lower.u* is the unit width to use when generating uppercase letters in lowercase positions, and *lower.cap_height* is the height of the small caps. Some of the original 62 parameters apply only to lowercase letters, so they aren't actually used by the csc driver program; but values are given to all parameters, whether they are necessary or not.

There are two standard fonts to demonstrate the possibilities: cmcsc10 is intended to mix well with cmr10, and cmtcsc10 is a "TYPEWRITER CAPS AND SMALL CAPS" font analogous to cmtt10. Many more variations (bold and/or slanted and/or sans-serif) could be tried. The *letter_fit* and *lower.letter_fit* parameters seem to deserve special care.

name	cmcsc10	*lower*	cmtcsc10	*lower*
font_identifier	CMCSC		CMTCSC	
font_size	10		10	
u	21	16	21	21
width_adj	0	0	0	0
serif_fit	0		0	
cap_serif_fit	5	4	0	0
letter_fit	5	2.4	0	3
body_height	270	200	250	190
asc_height	250		220	
cap_height	246	185	220	170
fig_height	232		220	
x_height	155	116	155	120
math_axis	90		110	
bar_height	87	65	79	62
comma_depth	70	52	50	38
desc_depth	70		80	
crisp	0		22	
tiny	8		22	
fine	7		21	
thin_join	7		21	
hair	9		25	
stem	25	21	25	25
curve	30		25	
ess	27		22	
flare	33	25	32	30

dot_size	38		36	
cap_hair	11	9.1	25	25
cap_stem	32	26	25	25
cap_curve	37	31	25	25
cap_ess	35	28	25	25
rule_thickness	.40		25/36	
dish	1		0	
bracket	20		0	
jut	28		34	
cap_jut	37	26	34	26
beak_jut	10	7	0	0
beak	70	52	34	26
vair	8		22	
notch_cut	10		25/36	
bar	11		22	
slab	11	9.1	22	22
cap_bar	11	9.1	22	22
cap_band	11	9.1	22	22
cap_notch_cut	10	10	25/36	24/36
serif_drop	4		0	
stem_corr	1		0	
vair_corr	1		0	
apex_corr	0		10	
o	8	5	4	3
apex_o	8	4	3	2
slant	0		0	
fudge	1	1	0.81	0.85
math_spread	0		−1	
superness	$1/\sqrt{2}$		$1/\sqrt{2}$	
superpull	1/6		0	
beak_darkness	11/30		0	
ligs	1		0	
square_dots	**false**		**false**	
hefty	**false**		**true**	
serifs	**true**		**true**	
monospace	**false**		**true**	
variant_g	**false**		**false**	
low_asterisk	**false**		**true**	
math_fitting	**false**		**false**	
generate	csc		csc	

For example, we have *beak* = $^{70}/_{36}$ pt and *lower.beak* = $^{52}/_{36}$ pt in font cmcsc10. The csc driver file sets *beak* := *lower.beak* before generating the small caps.

The Computer Modern Math Symbol fonts contain 128 characters for use in math formulas. They come in six standard sizes, called `cmsy10`–`cmsy5`, and their 62 parameters are identical to the 62 parameters of the corresponding math italic fonts, `cmmi10`–`cmmi5`.

Besides the 62 parameters needed for font generation, the `cmsy` parameter files also supply 15 '**fontdimen**' parameters that control the way TEX will typeset with these fonts, as explained in *The TEXbook*.

For example, parameter file `cmsy10.mf` begins almost like `cmmi10.mf`, except that it specifies "CMSY" as the **font_identifier**. But where `cmmi10.mf` ends with '**generate** `mathit`', `cmsy10.mf` has the following mumbo jumbo:

% the following font parameters are explained in *The TEXbook*, Appendix G

$subs := {}^7\!/_{10}$;   % subscripts to 10pt will normally be in 7pt type

$rth\# := .4pt\#$;   % assume that rules will come from `cmex10`

fontdimen 8:   % parameters σ_8 through σ_{22} will now be listed

$math\_axis\# + 3.51rth\# + {}^{54}\!/_{36}pt\# + subs * desc\_depth\#$,   % num1

$math\_axis\# + 1.51rth\# + {}^{30}\!/_{36}pt\#$,   % num2

$math\_axis\# + 1.51rth\# + {}^{48}\!/_{36}pt\#$,   % num3

$- (math\_axis\# - 3.51rth\# - subs * fig\_height\# - {}^{124}\!/_{36}pt\#)$,   % denom1

$- (math\_axis\# - 1.51rth\# - subs * fig\_height\# - {}^{30}\!/_{36}pt\#)$,   % denom2

$8.99pt\# - subs * asc\_height\#$,   % sup1

$8.49pt\# - subs * asc\_height\#$,   % sup2

${}^{104}\!/_{36}pt\#$,   % sup3

${}^{54}\!/_{36}pt\#, -(8.49pt\# - 2subs * asc\_height\# - 3.1rth\#)$,   % sub1, sub2

$subs * asc\_height\# - {}^{36}\!/_{36}pt\#, {}^{18}\!/_{36}pt\#$,   % sup_drop, sub_drop

$23.9pt\#, 10.1pt\#$,   % delim1, delim2

$math\_axis\#$;   % axis_height

generate `mathsy`   % switch to the driver file

Similarly, `cmsy9.mf` is like `cmmi9.mf` except that it ends with

$subs := {}^6\!/_9$;   % subscripts to 9pt will normally be in 6pt type

$rth\# := .4pt\#$;   % assume that rules will come from `cmex10`

fontdimen 8:   % parameters σ_8 through σ_{22} will now be listed

$math\_axis\# + 3.51rth\# + {}^{36}\!/_{36}pt\# + subs * desc\_depth\#$,   % num1

$math\_axis\# + 1.51rth\# + {}^{30}\!/_{36}pt\#$,   % num2

$math\_axis\# + 1.51rth\# + {}^{43}\!/_{36}pt\#$,   % num3

$- (math\_axis\# - 3.51rth\# - subs * fig\_height\# - {}^{111}\!/_{36}pt\#)$,   % denom1

$- (math\_axis\# - 1.51rth\# - subs * fig\_height\# - {}^{30}\!/_{36}pt\#)$,   % denom2

$8.49pt\# - subs * asc\_height\#$,   % sup1

$7.99pt\# - subs * asc\_height\#$,   % sup2

${}^{93}\!/_{36}pt\#$,   % sup3

${}^{36}\!/_{36}pt\#, -(7.99pt\# - 2subs * asc\_height\# - 3.1rth\#)$,   % sub1, sub2

$subs * asc\_height\# - {}^{36}\!/_{36}pt\#, {}^{18}\!/_{36}pt\#$,   % sup_drop, sub_drop

$23.9pt\#, 9.1pt\#$,   % delim1, delim2

---

after which comes '$math\_axis$; **generate** `mathsy`' (which we won't bother to mention any more because all symbol font parameter files end this way).

The corresponding lines of `cmsy8.mf` are:

$subs := {}^6\!/_8;$	% subscripts to 8pt will normally be in 6pt type
$rth\# := .4pt\#;$	% assume that rules will come from `cmex10`
fontdimen 8:	% parameters σ_8 through σ_{22} will now be listed
$math\_axis\# + 3.51rth\# + {}^{36}\!/_{36}pt\# + subs * desc\_depth\#,$	% num1
$math\_axis\# + 1.51rth\# + {}^{24}\!/_{36}pt\#,$	% num2
$math\_axis\# + 1.51rth\# + {}^{38}\!/_{36}pt\#,$	% num3
$-(math\_axis\# - 3.51rth\# - subs * fig\_height\# - {}^{98}\!/_{36}pt\#),$	% denom1
$-(math\_axis\# - 1.51rth\# - subs * fig\_height\# - {}^{24}\!/_{36}pt\#),$	% denom2
$7.49pt\# - subs * asc\_height\#,$	% sup1
$6.99pt\# - subs * asc\_height\#,$	% sup2
${}^{82}\!/_{36}pt\#,$	% sup3
${}^{36}\!/_{36}pt\#, {}^{72}\!/_{36}pt\#,$	% sub1, sub2
$subs * asc\_height\# - {}^{36}\!/_{36}pt\#, {}^{18}\!/_{36}pt\#,$	% sup_drop, sub_drop
$11.9pt\#, 9.1pt\#,$	% delim1, delim2

And for `cmsy7.mf` they are:

$subs := {}^5\!/_7;$	% subscripts to 7pt will normally be in 5pt type
$rth\# := .4pt\#;$	% assume that rules will come from `cmex10`
fontdimen 8:	% parameters σ_8 through σ_{22} will now be listed
$math\_axis\# + 3.51rth\# + {}^{36}\!/_{36}pt\# + subs * desc\_depth\#,$	% num1
$math\_axis\# + 1.51rth\# + {}^{12}\!/_{36}pt\#,$	% num2
$math\_axis\# + 1.51rth\# + {}^{34}\!/_{36}pt\#,$	% num3
$-(math\_axis\# - 3.51rth\# - subs * fig\_height\# - {}^{86}\!/_{36}pt\#),$	% denom1
$-(math\_axis\# - 1.51rth\# - subs * fig\_height\# - {}^{12}\!/_{36}pt\#),$	% denom2
$6.99pt\# - subs * asc\_height\#,$	% sup1
$6.49pt\# - subs * asc\_height\#,$	% sup2
${}^{72}\!/_{36}pt\#,$	% sup3
${}^{36}\!/_{36}pt\#, {}^{72}\!/_{36}pt\#,$	% sub1, sub2
$subs * asc\_height\# - {}^{36}\!/_{36}pt\#, {}^{18}\!/_{36}pt\#,$	% sup_drop, sub_drop
$11.9pt\#, 8.1pt\#,$	% delim1, delim2

And for `cmsy6.mf`:

$subs := {}^5\!/_6;$	% subscripts to 6pt will normally be in 5pt type
$rth\# := .4pt\#;$	% assume that rules will come from `cmex10`
fontdimen 8:	% parameters σ_8 through σ_{22} will now be listed
$math\_axis\# + 3.51rth\# + {}^{36}\!/_{36}pt\# + subs * desc\_depth\#,$	% num1
$math\_axis\# + 1.51rth\# + {}^9\!/_{36}pt\#,$	% num2
$math\_axis\# + 1.51rth\# + {}^{29}\!/_{36}pt\#,$	% num3
$-(math\_axis\# - 3.51rth\# - subs * fig\_height\# - {}^{74}\!/_{36}pt\#),$	% denom1
$-(math\_axis\# - 1.51rth\# - subs * fig\_height\# - {}^9\!/_{36}pt\#),$	% denom2
$6.49pt\# - subs * asc\_height\#,$	% sup1
$5.99pt\# - subs * asc\_height\#,$	% sup2
${}^{62}\!/_{36}pt\#,$	% sup3
${}^{36}\!/_{36}pt\#, {}^{72}\!/_{36}pt\#,$	% sub1, sub2
$subs * asc\_height\# - {}^{36}\!/_{36}pt\#, {}^{18}\!/_{36}pt\#,$	% sup_drop, sub_drop
$11.9pt\#, 8.1pt\#,$	% delim1, delim2

Finally, `cmsy5.mf` has these **fontdimen** parameters:

$subs := {}^5\!/_5;$	% subscripts to 5pt will normally be in 5pt type
$rth\# := .4pt\#;$	% assume that rules will come from `cmex10`
fontdimen 8:	% parameters σ_8 through σ_{22} will now be listed
$\quad math\_axis\# + 3.51rth\# + {}^{36}\!/_{36}pt\# + subs * desc\_depth\#,$	% num1
$\quad math\_axis\# + 1.51rth\# + {}^3\!/_{36}pt\#,$	% num2
$\quad math\_axis\# + 1.51rth\# + {}^{24}\!/_{36}pt\#,$	% num3
$\quad -(math\_axis\# - 3.51rth\# - subs * fig\_height\# - {}^{63}\!/_{36}pt\#),$	% denom1
$\quad -(math\_axis\# - 1.51rth\# - subs * fig\_height\# - {}^3\!/_{36}pt\#),$	% denom2
$\quad 5.99pt\# - subs * asc\_height\#,$	% sup1
$\quad 5.49pt\# - subs * asc\_height\#,$	% sup2
$\quad {}^{53}\!/_{36}pt\#,$	% sup3
$\quad {}^{36}\!/_{36}pt\#, {}^{72}\!/_{36}pt\#,$	% sub1, sub2
$\quad subs * asc\_height\# - {}^{36}\!/_{36}pt\#, {}^{18}\!/_{36}pt\#,$	% sup_drop, sub_drop
$\quad 9.9pt\#, 7.1pt\#,$	% delim1, delim2

There's also a bold symbols font, `cmbsy10`, which demonstrates one of many further possibilities. It has the 62 parameters of `cmmib10`, plus this:

$subs := {}^7\!/_{10};$	% subscripts to 10pt will normally be in 7pt type
fontdimen 8:	% parameters σ_8 through σ_{22} will now be listed
$\quad math\_axis\# + 3.51rule\_thickness\# + {}^{54}\!/_{36}pt\# + subs * desc\_depth\#,$	% num1
$\quad math\_axis\# + 1.51rule\_thickness\# + {}^{30}\!/_{36}pt\#,$	% num2
$\quad math\_axis\# + 1.51rule\_thickness\# + {}^{48}\!/_{36}pt\#,$	% num3
$\quad -(math\_axis\# - 3.51rule\_thickness\# - subs * fig\_height\# - {}^{124}\!/_{36}pt\#),$	% denom1
$\quad -(math\_axis\# - 1.51rule\_thickness\# - subs * fig\_height\# - {}^{30}\!/_{36}pt\#),$	% denom2
$\quad 8.99pt\# - subs * asc\_height\#,$	% sup1
$\quad 8.49pt\# - subs * asc\_height\#,$	% sup2
$\quad {}^{104}\!/_{36}pt\#,$	% sup3
$\quad {}^{54}\!/_{36}pt\#, -(8.49pt\# - 2subs * asc\_height\# - 3.1rule\_thickness\#),$	% sub1, sub2
$\quad subs * asc\_height\# - {}^{36}\!/_{36}pt\#, {}^{18}\!/_{36}pt\#,$	% sup_drop, sub_drop
$\quad 23.9pt\#, 10.1pt\#,$	% delim1, delim2

We have now described 74 of the 75 standard font parameter files in the Computer Modern family. The last one is `cmex10.mf`, a so-called "math extension" font that provides the extralarge symbols needed in complicated formulas. It has exactly the parameters of `cmr10.mf`, except that its **font_identifier** is `"CMEX"`; furthermore, where `cmr10.mf` closes with '**generate** roman', the file `cmex10.mf` signs off as follows:

% the following font parameters are explained in *The TEXbook*, Appendix G	
fontdimen 8:	% parameters ξ_8 through ξ_{13} will now be listed
$\quad rule\_thickness\#,$	% default_rule_thickness
$\quad {}^{40}\!/_{36}pt\#,$	% big_op_spacing1
$\quad {}^{60}\!/_{36}pt\#,$	% big_op_spacing2
$\quad {}^{72}\!/_{36}pt\#,$	% big_op_spacing3
$\quad {}^{216}\!/_{36}pt\#,$	% big_op_spacing4
$\quad {}^{36}\!/_{36}pt\#;$	% big_op_spacing5
generate mathex	% switch to the driver file

Let's conclude this chapter by listing all 75 of the standard fonts whose parameters have been defined on the previous pages:

cmr17	cmbx8	cmss10	cmb10	cmbxti10
cmr12	cmbx7*	cmss9	cmff10	cmmib10
cmr10*	cmbx6	cmss8	cmfib8	cmitt10
cmr9	cmbx5*	cmssi17	cmti12	cmu10
cmr8	cmtt12	cmssi12	cmti10*	cmfi10
cmr7*	cmtt10*	cmssi10	cmti9	cmcsc10
cmr6	cmtt9	cmssi9	cmti8	cmtcsc10
cmr5*	cmtt8	cmssi8	cmti7	cmsy10*
cmsl12	cmsltt10	cmssdc10	cmmi12	cmsy9
cmsl10*	cmvtt10	cmssbx10	cmmi10*	cmsy8
cmsl9	cmtex10	cminch	cmmi9	cmsy7*
cmsl8	cmtex9	cmssq8	cmmi8	cmsy6
cmbx12	cmtex8	cmssqi8	cmmi7*	cmsy5*
cmbx10*	cmss17	cmdunh10	cmmi6	cmbsy10
cmbx9	cmss12	cmbxsl10	cmmi5*	cmex10*

The sixteen fonts marked with an asterisk (*) are used in the plain TeX macro package; in some sense they comprise a minimal working set for technical typing.

> 1. *The Stem and other Fat Stroaks of Capital* Romans
>   *is five parts of forty and two (the whole Body:)*
>   *Or, (which is all one) one sixth part of the Heighth*
>   *of an Ascending Letter (as all Capitals are Ascendents) . . .*
>
> 2. *The Stem, and other Fat Stroaks of Capitals* Italick,
>   *is four parts of forty and two, (the Body.)*
>
> 3. *The Stem, and other Fat Stroaks of Lower-Case* Roman,
>   *is three and an half parts of forty and two, (the Body.)*
>
> — JOSEPH MOXON, *Mechanick Exercises* (1683)

> *Variation in width is more essential.*
> *This can be increased till the o becomes almost circular.*
> *The greater this roundness, the clearer the script,*
> *and the greater the capacity for a*
> *significant contrast between thin and thick strokes,*
> *as of light and shade.*
>
> — GIAMBATTISTA BODONI, *Manuale Tipografico* (1818)

Driver Files

The command 'generate roman' in a parameter file tells METAFONT to look at another file, roman.mf, for further instructions. The new file is called a "driver" because it takes charge of the subsequent activities; it makes sure that everything gets done decently and in order.

A driver file starts out by establishing pixel-oriented versions of the parameters. Then it reads in various program files, which actually create the characters of the font. (We will study the program files right after we finish looking at driver files.) Finally it contains a "kerning program" that improves the fit between certain pairs of letters.

There are eight standard driver files in the Computer Modern family, one for each major type of font layout. The most important is roman.mf, which is used by 44 of the 75 standard fonts. Therefore we shall look at the file roman.mf first; here is its complete text:

% The Computer Modern Roman family of fonts (by D. E. Knuth, 1979–1985)

if *ligs* > 1: **font_coding_scheme** := "TeX text";
   spanish_shriek = oct "074"; *spanish_query* = oct "076";
else: **font_coding_scheme** := **if** *ligs* = 0: "TeX typewriter text"
    else: "TeX text without f-ligatures" **fi**;
   spanish_shriek = oct "016"; *spanish_query* = oct "017"; **fi**

mode_setup; **font_setup**;

input romanu;	% upper case (majuscules)
input romanl;	% lower case (minuscules)
input greeku;	% upper case Greek letters
input romand;	% numerals
input romanp;	% ampersand, question marks, currency sign
input romspl;	% lowercase specials (dotless ı, ligature æ, etc.)
input romspu;	% uppercase specials (Æ, Œ, Ø)
input punct;	% punctuation symbols common to roman and italic text
input accent;	% accents common to roman and italic text
if *ligs* > 1: **input** romlig; **fi**	% letter ligatures
if *ligs* > 0: **input** comlig; **fi**	% ligatures common with italic text
if *ligs* ≤ 1: **input** romsub; **fi**	% substitutes for ligatures

ligtable "!": "`" =: *spanish_shriek*;
ligtable "?": "`" =: *spanish_query*;
font_slant *slant*; **font_x_height** *x_height*#;

if *monospace*: **font_normal_space** $9u^\#$;   % no stretching or shrinking
    font_quad $18u^\#$;
    font_extra_space $9u^\#$;
else: **font_normal_space** $6u^\# + 2\mathit{letter\_fit}^\#$;
    font_normal_stretch $3u^\#$; **font_normal_shrink** $2u^\#$;
    font_quad $18u^\# + 4\mathit{letter\_fit}^\#$;
    font_extra_space $2u^\#$;
    $k^\# := -.5u^\#$; $kk^\# := -1.5u^\#$; $kkk^\# := -2u^\#$;   % three degrees of kerning
ligtable "k": **if** *serifs*: "v": "a" kern $-u^\#$, **fi** "w": "e" kern $k^\#$,
    "a" kern $k^\#$, "o" kern $k^\#$, "c" kern $k^\#$;
ligtable "P": "A" kern $kk^\#$,
    "y": "o" kern $k^\#$, "e" kern $k^\#$, "a" kern $k^\#$, "." kern $kk^\#$, "," kern $kk^\#$;
ligtable "F": "V": "W": **if** *serifs*: "o" kern $kk^\#$, "e" kern $kk^\#$, "u" kern $kk^\#$,
        "r" kern $kk^\#$, "a" kern $kk^\#$, "A" kern $kkk^\#$,
    else: "o" kern $k^\#$, "e" kern $k^\#$, "u" kern $k^\#$,
        "r" kern $k^\#$, "a" kern $k^\#$, "A" kern $kk^\#$, **fi**
    "K": "X": "O" kern $k^\#$, "C" kern $k^\#$,
    "G" kern $k^\#$, "Q" kern $k^\#$;
ligtable "T": "y" kern **if** *serifs*: $k^\#$ **else**: $kk^\#$ **fi**,
    "Y": "e" kern $kk^\#$, "o" kern $kk^\#$,
    "r" kern $kk^\#$, "a" kern $kk^\#$, "A" kern $kk^\#$, "u" kern $kk^\#$;
ligtable "O": "D": "X" kern $k^\#$,
    "W" kern $k^\#$, "A" kern $k^\#$,
    "V" kern $k^\#$, "Y" kern $k^\#$;
if *serifs*: **ligtable** "h": "m": "n":
    "t" kern $k^\#$, "u" kern $k^\#$, "b" kern $k^\#$,
    "y" kern $k^\#$, "v" kern $k^\#$, "w" kern $k^\#$;
    ligtable "c": "h" kern $k^\#$, "k" kern $k^\#$; **fi**
ligtable "o": "b": "p": "e" kern $-k^\#$, "o" kern $-k^\#$, "x" kern $k^\#$,
    "d" kern $-k^\#$, "c" kern $-k^\#$, "q" kern $-k^\#$,
    "a": **if** *serifs*: "v" kern $k^\#$, "j" kern $u^\#$, **else**: "r" kern $k^\#$, **fi**
    "t": "y" kern $k^\#$,
    "u": "w" kern $k^\#$;
ligtable "A": **if** *serifs*: "R": **fi** "t" kern $k^\#$,
    "C" kern $k^\#$, "O" kern $k^\#$, "G" kern $k^\#$, "U" kern $k^\#$, "Q" kern $k^\#$,
    "L": "T" kern $kk^\#$, "Y" kern $kk^\#$, "V" kern $kkk^\#$, "W" kern $kkk^\#$;
ligtable "g": "j" kern $-k^\#$;   % logjam
ligtable "I": "I" kern $-k^\#$; **fi**   % Richard III
                    % there are ligature/kern programs for "f" in the `romlig` file
                    % and for "-", "`", and "'" in the `comlig` file
bye.

This driver file generates three different sets of 128 characters, depending on the setting of *ligs*. If *ligs* $= 2$, we get TeX's normal text font layout, and if *ligs* $= 0$ we get the normal typewriter font layout; both of these coding schemes are shown in full in the character indexes at the end of this book. If *ligs* $= 1$, the result is a compromise in which the characters '↑', '↓', '`', '<', and '>' appear instead of the f-ligatures.

The next driver file, `title.mf`, is simply a subset of `roman.mf`; it is used for just one of the standard fonts, namely `cminch`, whose characters have a *cap_height* equal to one inch. Inch-high letters take up a lot of space, and `cminch` is used only for special purposes. So `cminch` has been limited to 36 characters instead of the normal 128.

% This makes a short font (caps and digits only)

font_coding_scheme := "ASCII caps and digits";

mode_setup; **font_setup**;

input romanu;   % upper case (majuscules)
input romand;   % numerals

font_slant *slant*; **font_x_height** *x_height*#;
if *monospace*: **font_normal_space** $9u$#;   % no stretching or shrinking
  font_quad $18u$#;
  font_extra_space $9u$#;
else: **font_normal_space** $6u$# + $2letter\_fit$#;
  font_normal_stretch $3u$#; **font_normal_shrink** $2u$#;
  font_quad $18u$# + $4letter\_fit$#;
  font_extra_space $2u$#;
  k# := $-.5u$#; kk# := $-1.5u$#; kkk# := $-2u$#;   % three degrees of kerning
  ligtable "P": "T": "Y": "A" kern kk#;
  ligtable "F": "V": "W": "A" kern **if** *serifs*: kkk# **else**: kk# **fi**,
    "K": "X": "O" kern k#, "C" kern k#,
      "G" kern k#, "Q" kern k#;
  ligtable "O": "D": "X" kern k#,
      "W" kern k#, "A" kern k#,
      "V" kern k#, "Y" kern k#;
  ligtable "A": **if** *serifs*: "R": **fi**
    "C" kern k#, "O" kern k#, "G" kern k#, "U" kern k#, "Q" kern k#,
    "L": "T" kern kk#, "Y" kern kkk#, "V" kern kk#, "W" kern kkk#;
  ligtable "I": "I" kern $-k$#; **fi**   % Richard III
bye.

Another simple variant of `roman.mf` is `texset.mf`, which produces 128 characters of an extended ASCII code:

% Special version of Computer Modern for TEX's extended ASCII character set

font_coding_scheme := "TeX extended ASCII";

mode_setup; **font_setup**; *mono_charic*# := 0;

input tsetsl;   % special symbols to be slanted

slant := 0;   % the remaining characters will not be slanted
currenttransform := *identity* yscaled *aspect_ratio* scaled *granularity*;

input romanu;   % upper case (majuscules)

```
input roman1;                                        % lower case (minuscules)
input romand;                                                      % numerals
input romanp;                             % ampersand, question marks, currency sign
input punct;                    % punctuation symbols common to roman and italic text
input tset;                           % remaining special symbols of extended ASCII
```

font_x_height $x\_height^\#$;

if *monospace*: **font_normal_space** $9u^\#$;   % no stretching or shrinking
   font_quad $18u^\#$;
   font_extra_space $9u^\#$;
else: **font_normal_space** $6u^\# + 2letter\_fit^\#$;
   font_normal_stretch $3u^\#$; **font_normal_shrink** $2u^\#$;
   font_quad $18u^\# + 4letter\_fit^\#$;
   font_extra_space $2u^\#$;
   $k^\# := -.5u^\#$; $kk^\# := -1.5u^\#$; $kkk^\# := -2u^\#$;   % three degrees of kerning
   ligtable "k": **if** *serifs*: "v": "a" kern $-u^\#$, **fi** "w": "e" kern $k^\#$,
     "a" kern $k^\#$, "o" kern $k^\#$, "c" kern $k^\#$;
   ligtable "P": "A" kern $kk^\#$,
     "y": "o" kern $k^\#$, "e" kern $k^\#$, "a" kern $k^\#$, "." kern $kk^\#$, "," kern $kk^\#$;
   ligtable "F": "V": "W": **if** *serifs*: "o" kern $kk^\#$, "e" kern $kk^\#$, "u" kern $kk^\#$,
       "r" kern $kk^\#$, "a" kern $kk^\#$, "A" kern $kkk^\#$,
     else: "o" kern $k^\#$, "e" kern $k^\#$, "u" kern $k^\#$,
       "r" kern $k^\#$, "a" kern $k^\#$, "A" kern $kk^\#$, **fi**
     "K": "X": "O" kern $k^\#$, "C" kern $k^\#$,
     "G" kern $k^\#$, "Q" kern $k^\#$;
   ligtable "T": "y" kern **if** *serifs*: $k^\#$ **else**: $kk^\#$ **fi**,
     "Y": "e" kern $kk^\#$, "o" kern $kk^\#$,
       "r" kern $kk^\#$, "a" kern $kk^\#$, "A" kern $kk^\#$, "u" kern $kk^\#$;
   ligtable "O": "D": "X" kern $k^\#$,
     "W" kern $k^\#$, "A" kern $k^\#$,
     "V" kern $k^\#$, "Y" kern $k^\#$;
   if *serifs*: **ligtable** "h": "m": "n":
       "t" kern $k^\#$, "u" kern $k^\#$, "b" kern $k^\#$,
       "y" kern $k^\#$, "v" kern $k^\#$, "w" kern $k^\#$;
     ligtable "c": "h" kern $k^\#$, "k" kern $k^\#$; **fi**
   ligtable "o": "b": "p": "e" kern $-k^\#$, "o" kern $-k^\#$, "x" kern $k^\#$,
     "d" kern $-k^\#$, "c" kern $-k^\#$, "q" kern $-k^\#$,
     "a": **if** *serifs*: "v" kern $k^\#$, "j" kern $u^\#$, **else**: "r" kern $k^\#$, **fi**
     "t": "y" kern $k^\#$,
     "u": "w" kern $k^\#$;
   ligtable "A": **if** *serifs*: "R": **fi** "t" kern $k^\#$,
     "C" kern $k^\#$, "O" kern $k^\#$, "G" kern $k^\#$, "U" kern $k^\#$, "Q" kern $k^\#$,
     "L": "T" kern $kk^\#$, "Y" kern $kk^\#$, "V" kern $kkk^\#$, "W" kern $kkk^\#$;
   ligtable "g": "j" kern $-k^\#$;   % logjam
   ligtable "I": "I" kern $-k^\#$;   % Richard III
fi;

bye.

CAPS AND SMALL CAPS FONTS are generated by the driver file `csc.mf`, which is a more interesting variant of `roman.mf` because it has to set up the font parameters twice:

% Caps and Small Caps in Computer Modern Roman

font_coding_scheme := **if** *ligs* = 0: "TeX typewriter text"
  else: "TeX text without f-ligatures" **fi**;
spanish_shriek = oct "016"; *spanish_query* = oct "017";

mode_setup; **font_setup**;
input romanu;   % upper case (majuscules)
input greeku;   % upper case greek letters
input romand;   % numerals
input romanp;   % ampersand, question marks, currency sign
input romspu;   % uppercase specials (Æ, Œ, Ø)
input punct;   % punctuation symbols common to all roman and italic
input accent;   % accents common to roman and italic text
input romsub;   % substitutes for ligatures
if *ligs* > 0: **input** comlig; **fi**   % ligatures common with italic

ligtable "!": "'" =: *spanish_shriek*;
ligtable "?": "'" =: *spanish_query*;
font_slant *slant*; **font_x_height** $x\_height\#$;
if *monospace*: **font_normal_space** $9u\#$;   % no stretching or shrinking
  font_quad $18u\#$;
  font_extra_space $9u\#$;
else: **font_normal_space** $6u\# + 2letter\_fit\#$;
  font_normal_stretch $3u\#$; **font_normal_shrink** $2u\#$;
  font_quad $18u\# + 4letter\_fit\#$;
  font_extra_space $2u\#$;
  $k\# := -.5u\#$; $kk\# := -1.5u\#$; $kkk\# := -2u\#$;   % three degrees of kerning
  ligtable "P": "T": "Y": "a" kern $kk\#$, "A" kern $kk\#$;
  ligtable "F": "V": "W": **if** *serifs*: "a" kern $kkk\#$, "A" kern $kkk\#$,
    else: "a" kern $kk\#$, "A" kern $kk\#$, **fi**
    "K": "X": "o" kern $k\#$, "O" kern $k\#$, "c" kern $k\#$, "C" kern $k\#$,
      "g" kern $k\#$, "G" kern $k\#$, "q" kern $k\#$, "Q" kern $k\#$;
  ligtable "O": "D": "x" kern $k\#$, "X" kern $k\#$,
    "w" kern $k\#$, "W" kern $k\#$, "a" kern $k\#$, "A" kern $k\#$,
    "v" kern $k\#$, "V" kern $k\#$, "y" kern $k\#$, "Y" kern $k\#$;
  ligtable "A": **if** *serifs*: "R": **fi**"c" kern $k\#$, "C" kern $k\#$,
    "o" kern $k\#$, "O" kern $k\#$, "g" kern $k\#$, "G" kern $k\#$,
    "u" kern $k\#$, "U" kern $k\#$, "q" kern $k\#$, "Q" kern $k\#$,
   "L": "T" kern $kk\#$, "t" kern $kk\#$, "Y" kern $kk\#$, "y" kern $kk\#$,
     "V" kern $kkk\#$, "v" kern $kkk\#$, "W" kern $kkk\#$, "w" kern $kkk\#$;
  ligtable "I": "I" kern $-k\#$; **fi**   % Richard III
         % ligature programs for "-", "'", and "'" are in the comlig file

forsuffixes $ = u, \; width_adj, \; cap_serif_fit, \; letter_fit,$
 $body\_height, \; cap\_height, \; x\_height, \; bar\_height, \; comma\_depth,$
 $flare, \; cap\_hair, \; stem, \; cap\_stem, \; cap\_curve, \; cap\_ess,$
 $cap\_jut, \; beak\_jut, \; beak, \; slab, \; cap\_bar, \; cap\_band, \; cap\_notch\_cut,$
 $o, \; apex\_o\colon \$\# := lower.\$\#;$ **endfor**
$fudge := lower.fudge;$
font_setup;   % now try again with *lower* settings
$extra\_endchar := extra\_endchar \; \&$ `"charcode:=charcode+code_offset";`
$code\_offset :=$ ASCII `"a"` $-$ ASCII `"A";`
input `romanu;`   % majuscules (in lowercase positions)
$code\_offset := -3;$
input `romspu;`   % Æ, Œ, Ø (in positions of æ, œ, ø)
$code\_offset := 0;$
input `cscspu;`   % substitutes for the remaining characters of `romspl`
if not *monospace*:
 $k\# := -.5u\#; \quad kk\# := -1.5u\#; \quad kkk\# := -2u\#;$ % three degrees of kerning
 ligtable `"p": "t": "y": "a"` kern $kk\#;$
 ligtable `"f": "v": "w": "a"` kern **if** *serifs*: $kkk\#$ **else**: $kk\#$ **fi**,
  `"k": "x": "o"` kern $k\#,$ `"c"` kern $k\#,$
   `"g"` kern $k\#,$ `"q"` kern $k\#;$
 ligtable `"o": "d": "x"` kern $k\#,$
   `"w"` kern $k\#,$ `"a"` kern $k\#,$
   `"v"` kern $k\#,$ `"y"` kern $k\#;$
 ligtable `"a":` **if** *serifs*: `"r":` **fi**`"c"` kern $k\#,$ `"o"` kern $k\#,$
   `"g"` kern $k\#,$ `"u"` kern $k\#,$ `"q"` kern $k\#,$
   `"l": "'"` kern $kk\#,$ `"t"` kern $kk\#,$ `"y"` kern $kk\#,$ `"v"` kern $kkk\#,$ `"w"` kern $kkk\#;$
 ligtable `"i": "i"` kern $-k\#;$ **fi**   % SKIING
bye.

Computer Modern italic fonts come in two flavors, "text italic" and "math italic." The text italic driver, `textit.mf`, is very much like `roman.mf`:

% The Computer Modern Text Italic family (by D. E. Knuth, 1979–1985)

mode_setup; font_setup;

input `itall;`   % lower case (minuscules)
input `italsp;`   % lowercase specials (dotless ı, ligature æ, etc.)
if $ligs > 1$: **font_coding_scheme** $:=$ `"TeX text";`
 $spanish\_shriek =$ oct `"074";` $spanish\_query =$ oct `"076";`
 input `italig;`   % letter ligatures
else: **font_coding_scheme** $:=$ **if** $ligs = 0$: `"TeX typewriter text"`
  else: `"TeX text without f-ligatures"` **fi**;
 $spanish\_shriek =$ oct `"016";` $spanish\_query =$ oct `"017";` **fi**

font_slant $slant;$ **font_x_height** $x\_height\#;$
if *monospace*: **font_normal_space** $9u\#;$ % no stretching or shrinking
 font_quad $18u\#;$
 font_extra_space $9u\#;$
 $letter\_fit\# := letter\_fit := 0;$

else: font_normal_space $6u^\# + 2letter\_fit^\#$;
  font_normal_stretch $3u^\#$; **font_normal_shrink** $2u^\#$;
  font_quad $18u^\# + 4letter\_fit^\#$;
  font_extra_space $2u^\#$; **fi**

input `romanu`;   % upper case (majuscules)
input `greeku`;   % upper case greek letters
input `itald`;   % numerals
input `italp`;   % ampersand, question marks, currency sign
input `romspu`;   % uppercase specials (Æ, Œ, Ø)
input `punct`;   % punctuation symbols common to roman and italic text
input `accent`;   % accents common to roman and italic text
if *ligs* > 0: **input** `comlig`; **fi**   % ligatures common with roman text
if *ligs* ≤ 1: **input** `romsub`; **fi**   % substitutes for ligatures

ligtable `"!"`: `"‘"` =: *spanish_shriek*;
ligtable `"?"`: `"‘"` =: *spanish_query*;

if not *monospace*:
  $k^\# := -.5u^\#$; $kk^\# := -1.5u^\#$; $kkk^\# := -2u^\#$;   % three degrees of kerning
  ligtable `"d"`: `"w"`: `"l"`: `"l"` kern $+u^\#$;
  ligtable `"F"`: `"V"`: `"o"` kern $kk^\#$, `"e"` kern $kk^\#$,
    `"u"` kern $kk^\#$, `"r"` kern $kk^\#$, `"a"` kern $kk^\#$, `"A"` kern $kkk^\#$,
    `"K"`: `"X"`: `"O"` kern $k^\#$, `"C"` kern $k^\#$,
      `"G"` kern $k^\#$, `"Q"` kern $k^\#$;
  ligtable `"T"`: `"y"` kern $kk^\#$,
    `"Y"`: `"e"` kern $kk^\#$, `"o"` kern $kk^\#$, `"r"` kern $kk^\#$, `"a"` kern $kk^\#$, `"u"` kern $kk^\#$,
    `"P"`: `"W"`: `"A"` kern $kk^\#$;
  ligtable `"O"`: `"D"`: `"X"` kern $k^\#$, `"W"` kern $k^\#$, `"A"` kern $k^\#$,
    `"V"` kern $k^\#$, `"Y"` kern $k^\#$;
  ligtable `"A"`: `"R"`: `"n"` kern $k^\#$, `"l"` kern $k^\#$, `"r"` kern $k^\#$, `"u"` kern $k^\#$,
    `"m"` kern $k^\#$, `"t"` kern $k^\#$, `"i"` kern $k^\#$, `"C"` kern $k^\#$, `"O"` kern $k^\#$, `"G"` kern $k^\#$,
    `"h"` kern $k^\#$, `"b"` kern $k^\#$, `"U"` kern $k^\#$, `"k"` kern $k^\#$, `"v"` kern $k^\#$, `"w"` kern $k^\#$,
    `"Q"` kern $k^\#$, `"L"`: `"T"` kern $kk^\#$, `"Y"` kern $kk^\#$, `"V"` kern $kkk^\#$, `"W"` kern $kkk^\#$,
    `"b"`: `"c"`: `"e"`: `"o"`: `"p"`: `"r"`: `"e"` kern $-u^\#$, `"a"` kern $-u^\#$, `"o"` kern $-u^\#$,
    `"d"` kern $-u^\#$, `"c"` kern $-u^\#$, `"g"` kern $-u^\#$, `"q"` kern $-u^\#$;
  ligtable `"n"`: `"’"` kern $kkk^\#$; **fi**
                    % there are ligature/kern programs for `"f"` in the `italig` file
                    % and for `"-"`, `"‘"`, and `"’"` in the `comlig` file
bye.

  The math italic driver, `mathit.mf`, is quite different. In this case the
kerning program includes provisions for positioning accents over the letters, assuming a \skewchar of '177 (as explained in *The TEXbook*).

% The Computer Modern Math Italic family (by D. E. Knuth, 1979–1985)

font_coding_scheme := `"TeX math italic"`;
mode_setup; **font_setup**;

input `romanu`;   % upper case (majuscules)

```
input itall;                                    % lower case (minuscules)
input greeku;                                   % upper case greek letters
input greekl;                                   % lower case Greek letters
input italms;                                   % special symbols for math italic
```

font_slant *slant*; **font_x_height** *x_height*#;
font_quad $18u^\# + 4letter\_fit^\#$;

slant := *mono_charic*# := 0;   % the remaining characters will not be slanted
currenttransform := *identity* yscaled *aspect_ratio* scaled *granularity*;

```
input olddig;                                   % oldstyle numerals
input romms;                                    % roman math specials
```

skewchar = oct "177"; *skew*# = .5u#;
save *comma*;
period = oct "72"; *comma* = oct "73"; *slash* = oct "75";   % non-ASCII positions
ligtable "h": *skewchar* kern −*skew*#;
ligtable oct "027": oct "034": *comma* kern −u#, *period* kern −u#,   % ν : τ :
  "L": "g": "u": "v": "x": oct "013": oct "026":   % L : g : u : v : x : α : μ :
  oct "035": oct "173": *skewchar* kern *skew*#;   % υ : ι :
ligtable "U": *comma* kern −2u#, *period* kern −2u#,   % U :
  slash kern −u#, *skewchar* kern *skew*#;
ligtable "K": oct "011": *slash* kern −u#,   % K : Ψ :
  oct "016": "r": *comma* kern −u#, *period* kern −u#,   % δ : r :
  "D": "c": "e": "o": "s": "y": "z": oct "017":   % D : c : e : o : s : y : z : ε :
  oct "021": oct "023": oct "037": *skewchar* kern 2*skew*#;   % η : ι : χ :
ligtable oct "007": *slash* kern −u#,   % Υ :
  comma kern −2u#, *period* kern −2u#, *skewchar* kern 2*skew*#;
ligtable oct "005": "H": *slash* kern −u#,   % Π : H :
  comma kern −u#, *period* kern −u#, *skewchar* kern 2*skew*#;
ligtable "N": "X": *slash* kern −1.5u#,   % N : X :
  "C": "T": *slash* kern −.5u#, *comma* kern −u#, *period* kern −u#,   % C : T :
  "B": "E": "G": "O": "Q": "R": oct "174":   % B : E : G : O : Q : R : ɟ :
  "l": "p": "q": "t": "w": oct "002": oct "004":   % l : p : q : t : w : Θ : Ξ :
  oct "006": oct "010": oct "012": oct "014":   % Σ : Φ : Ω : β :
  oct "020": oct "022": oct "032": oct "036":   % ζ : θ : ρ : φ :
  oct "042": oct "043": oct "045":   % ε : ϑ : ϱ :
  oct "046": oct "047": oct "100":   % ς : φ : ∂ :
  skewchar kern 3*skew*#;
ligtable "M": "S": "Z": *slash* kern −u#,   % M : S : Z :
  comma kern −u#, *period* kern −u#, *skewchar* kern 3*skew*#;
ligtable oct "000": "F": "P": *slash* kern −u#,   % Γ : F : P :
  comma kern −2u#, *period* kern −2u#, *skewchar* kern 3*skew*#;
ligtable "I": oct "030": oct "040": oct "140": oct "175":   % I : ξ : ψ : ℓ : ℘ :
  skewchar kern 4*skew*#;
ligtable "A": *skewchar* kern 5*skew*#;   % A :
ligtable "d": "Y" kern u#, "Z" kern −u#, "j" kern −2u#, "f" kern −3u#,   % d :
  oct "001": oct "003": *skewchar* kern 6*skew*#;   % Δ : Λ :
ligtable "f": *comma* kern −u#, *period* kern −u#, *skewchar* kern 6*skew*#;   % f :
```
```

ligtable "J": *slash* kern $-u^\#$,   % *J* :
    comma kern $-2u^\#$, *period* kern $-2u^\#$, *skewchar* kern $6skew^\#$;
ligtable "j": oct "033": *comma* kern $-u^\#$, *period* kern $-u^\#$;   % *j* : σ :
ligtable "V": "W": "Y": *comma* kern $-3u^\#$, *period* kern $-3u^\#$,   % *V* : *W* : *Y* :
    slash kern $-2u^\#$;
ligtable *slash*: oct "001" kern $-u^\#$, **"A"** kern $-u^\#$, **"M"** kern $-u^\#$,   % / :
    "N" kern $-u^\#$, **"Y"** kern $+u^\#$, **"Z"** kern $-u^\#$;

bye.

Fonts that contain 128 math symbols are generated by `mathsy.mf`. This driver file is analogous to `mathit.mf`, but its `\skewchar` is $\acute{0}60$.

% The Computer Modern Symbols family (by D. E. Knuth, 1979–1985)

font_coding_scheme := "TeX math symbols";
mode_setup; **font_setup**;

autorounding := *hair*;
input `calu`;   % upper case calligraphic alphabet
autorounding := 0;

font_slant *slant*; **font_x_height** *x_height*$^\#$;
font_quad $18u^\#$ **if** not *monospace*: $+ 4letter\_fit^\#$ **fi**;
    % (The spacing is zero so that TeX will always add the italic correction.)
    % (The calling file should give the other math symbol font parameters.)

slant := *mono_charic*$^\#$:= 0;   % the remaining characters will not be slanted
currenttransform := *identity* yscaled *aspect_ratio* scaled *granularity*;

input `symbol`;   % the symbols

if not *monospace*:
    skewchar = oct "060"; *skew*$^\#$ = $.5u^\#$;
    ligtable "I": "T": "V": *skewchar* kern *skew*$^\#$;
    ligtable "K": *skewchar* kern $2skew^\#$;
    ligtable "D": "N": "P": "R": "U": "W": "Y": *skewchar* kern $3skew^\#$;
    ligtable "E": "F": "G": "H": "O": "Q": *skewchar* kern $4skew^\#$;
    ligtable "B": "C": "L": "M": "S": "X": "Z": *skewchar* kern $5skew^\#$;
    ligtable "J": *skewchar* kern $6skew^\#$;
    ligtable "A": *skewchar* kern $7skew^\#$;
fi;

bye.

Finally, there's one more driver file, `mathex.mf`. It generates the large math symbols of the standard font `cmex10`.

% The Computer Modern Math-Extension family (by D. E. Knuth, 1979–1985)

font_coding_scheme := "TeX math extension";
mode_setup; **font_setup**;

input `bigdel`;   % large delimiters

input `bigop`;   % large operators
input `bigacc`;   % large accents

font_x_height $x\_height^\#$;
font_quad $18u^\# + 4letter\_fit^\#$;
        % (The calling file should give the other math extension font parameters.)
bye.

The type face that has had the greatest recent vogue
is the one that American founders used to call 'gothic'—
the English more properly calling it by its French name 'sans-serif' . . .
It has been reproduced lately in almost innumerable versions,
none of them fit for the printing of books.
Indeed the lower case, by reason of the principle of its construction,
is unfit for reading anywhere.
— BRUCE ROGERS, *An Address* (1938)

Sans serif, although it is no longer new,
is so simple and clear that it is by far
the best all-purpose type for today
and will remain so for a long time to come.
— JAN TSCHICHOLD, *Typographische Gestaltung* (1935)

[Footnote: This being the author's opinion in 1935.]
— JAN TSCHICHOLD, *Asymmetric Typography* (1967)

American Typewriter type definitely retards speed of reading
and therefore should not be used unless a novelty effect is desired.
— D. G. PATERSON and M. A. TINKER, *How to Make Type Readable* (1940)

Program Files

Now we're ready for the fun part of this book: We get to see the programs that define individual characters. There are more than 500 such programs, grouped into 30 "program files" with names like `accent.mf`, `romanu.mf`, `symbol.mf`. The contents of these 30 files will be listed in the next several hundred pages, in alphabetic order by file name, together with large "proof mode" examples of characters that the programs define.

In many cases a single illustration cannot show the built-in generality of a program, because quite different results will be obtained when the underlying parameters are changed. Therefore two or even three illustrations are provided for the most important character programs. For example, roman letters are each accompanied by three proof diagrams, which show METAFONT's output when the parameters are those of `cmr10` (at a resolution of 72 pixels per point), `cmtt10` (at a resolution of 36 pix/pt), and `cmssbx10` (again at 36 pix/pt). These three illustrations account for the principal variations of the letter designs, since `cmr10` and `cmtt10` have serifs, while `cmtt10` and `cmssbx10` are "hefty."

Accents and certain punctuation marks are illustrated by the results of both `cmr10` and `cmssbx10`, at a resolution of $36\sqrt{2} \approx 52.3$ pixels per point. Italic characters and math symbols are illustrated only once each, at the same resolution; in this case the parameters are those of `cmmi10`, but with *math_fitting* changed to **false**. (A single illustration suffices for italic letters and for math symbols, because these characters have comparatively little "meta-ness.") The largest math symbols are illustrated at a resolution of only 18 pix/pt, since the diagrams must be small enough to fit on a page.

You can tell what resolution is involved in any particular illustration by looking at the vertical grid lines, which are one unit (20/36 pt) apart.

The programs for individual characters are short, but they pack a great deal of information into a small space. Therefore you can't read them in the same way that you would read a novel. Furthermore, you should realize that the order in which individual programs appear in this book is not optimum for expository purposes. If you want to get a deep understanding of what makes things tick, you should start with the simplest characters and work your way up gradually to more complex examples. Here's how: First read the explanation of Computer Modern that appears in Appendix E of *The METAFONTbook*. Then study the programs for characters like '/' and '⊕' that are drawn with a single pen nib. Then try simple lowercase italic letters like '*l*' and '*k*'; these letters will prepare you for '*h*' and '*i*' and '*v*'. Then you'll be ready to understand the uppercase alphabet (looking first at the simplest letters 'O' and 'I'), after which you can safely turn to lowercase roman. The hardest programs of all are those for numeric digits, in file `romand.mf`; read these last!

As you read the programs in this order, you will gradually learn the conventions and subroutines of `cmbase`. (Code that appears at the bottom of a page, below a horizontal line, has been excerpted from the base file `cmbase.mf`.) Each subroutine should be studied when you first encounter it. The index at the back of this book makes it easy to find the definition of a subroutine, together with all places where that subroutine is invoked.

How can you find the program for a specific character? There's a special index at the very end of this book that shows the characters in each font layout, together with the page numbers where the corresponding programs appear.

The best way to study these programs is to use a computer while you're doing it, assuming that you have a working METAFONT system and that you have the Computer Modern files online. Any of the programs on the next pages can be copied into a file called `test.mf`, after which you can use the `rtest` and/or `6test` programs described in Appendix E of *The METAFONTbook*. By making changes to the test file and seeing how your changes affect the resulting shapes, you'll be able to get a good idea of why the programs of Computer Modern do what they do, and you'll be able to change things to suit your own taste.

People who like puzzles may enjoy figuring out how these programs work; the fact that they actually do work (and that they generated all of the letterforms used to typeset this book) is an important clue. On the other hand, it's also fun just to look at the pictures, without comprehending anything about the programs except the fact that they do indeed completely define the characters that are illustrated.

> Curves *do all kinds of queer things when reduced;*
> *and the way lines running together make spots is a thing that will surprise you—*
> *but one or two tries on these points give you the information you need.*
> *I am beginning to get the drift of it and*
> *to foresee from the large drawings what will happen in the type.*
> *I can* modify *in the large outline drawings,*
> *but so far I can't* originate *in that medium.*
>
> — W. A. DWIGGINS, *WAD to RR* (1940)

> *What designer in the development of his drawing*
> *does not know those spooky, stubborn antipathetic shapes*
> *that, maverick-like, will not join the type family?*
>
> — HERMANN ZAPF, *About Alphabets* (1960)

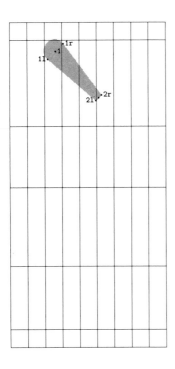

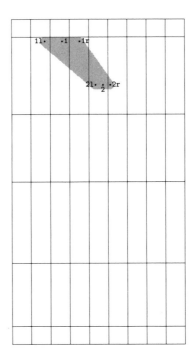

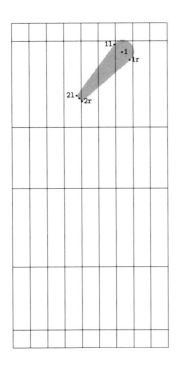

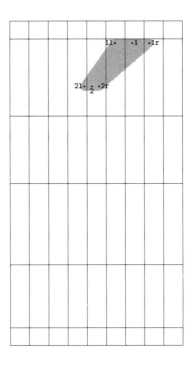

The first program file, in alphabetic order, is `accent.mf`. It begins as follows:

% This file contains accents common to text roman and italic fonts.
% Character codes ´022–´030, ´040, ´136–´137, ´175–´177 are generated.

% (Actually the accents in positions ´040, ´137, and ´175 are not generated
% unless *ligs* > 0, since other symbols are substituted
% for those accents in non-ligature fonts.)

cmchar "Grave accent";
beginchar(oct "022", $9u^\#$, min($asc\_height^\#$, $2x\_height^\#$), 0);
adjust_fit(0, 0);
if *serifs*: **pickup** *crisp.nib*; $x_1 - .5stem = $ hround $2u$; $x_2 = \frac{2}{3}[x_1, w - x_1]$;
  $y_1 + .5stem = h + eps$; $y_2 = \max(\frac{2}{3}[h, x\_height], x\_height + o + hair)$;
  numeric *theta*; *theta* $= $ angle$(z_2 - z_1) + 90$;
  $pos_1(stem, theta)$; $pos_2(hair, theta)$;
  filldraw circ_stroke z_{1e} -- z_{2e};   % diagonal
else: **pickup** *fine.nib*; $pos_1(stem, 0)$; $pos_2(vair, 0)$;
  lft $x_{1l} = $ hround $1.5u$; *rt* $x_{2r} = $ hround$(.5w + .25u + .5vair)$;
  top $y_1 = h$; *bot* $y_2 = $ vround $\frac{2}{3}[h, x\_height]$;
  filldraw stroke z_{1e} -- z_{2e}; **fi**   % diagonal
penlabels(1, 2); **endchar**;

cmchar "Acute accent";
beginchar(oct "023", $9u^\#$, min($asc\_height^\#$, $2x\_height^\#$), 0);
italcorr $h^\# * slant - $ **if** *serifs*: 1.5 **fi** $u^\#$;
adjust_fit(0, 0);
if *serifs*: **pickup** *crisp.nib*; $x_1 + .5stem = $ hround$(w - 2u)$; $x_2 = \frac{2}{3}[x_1, w - x_1]$;
  $y_1 + .5stem = h + eps$; $y_2 = \max(\frac{2}{3}[h, x\_height], x\_height + o + hair)$;
  numeric *theta*; *theta* $= $ angle$(z_2 - z_1) + 90$;
  $pos_1(stem, theta)$; $pos_2(hair, theta)$;
  filldraw circ_stroke z_{1e} -- z_{2e};   % diagonal
else: **pickup** *fine.nib*; $pos_1(stem, 0)$; $pos_2(vair, 0)$;
  rt $x_{1r} = $ hround$(w - 1.5u)$; *lft* $x_{2l} = $ hround$(.5w - .25u - .5vair)$;
  top $y_1 = h$; *bot* $y_2 = $ vround $\frac{2}{3}[h, x\_height]$;
  filldraw stroke z_{1e} -- z_{2e}; **fi**   % diagonal
penlabels(1, 2); **endchar**;

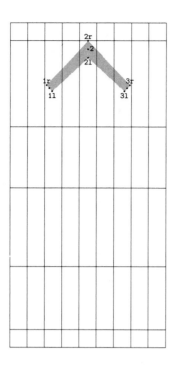

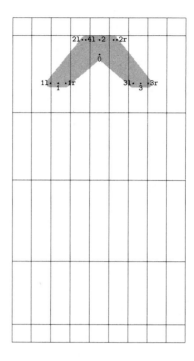

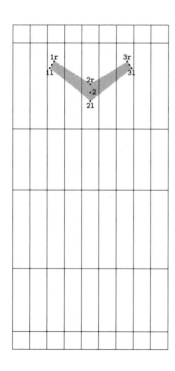

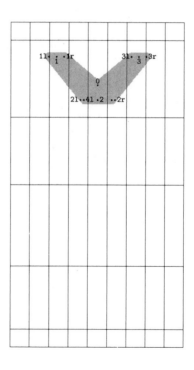

```
cmchar "Circumflex (hat) accent";
```
beginchar(oct "136", $9u^\#$, min($asc\_height^\#$, $2x\_height^\#$), 0);
if *serifs*: **italcorr** $.5[x\_height^\#, h^\#] * slant + .5hair^\# - 1.75u^\#$;
  adjust_fit$(0, 0)$;
  pickup *crisp.nib*; $pos_2(.5[vair, curve], 90)$; top $y_{2r} = h$; $x_2 = .5w$;
  $x_1 = w - x_3 = good.x\ 2.25u$; $y_1 = y_3 = .5[x\_height, y_2]$;
  $pos_1(hair, \text{angle}(z_2 - z_1) + 90)$; $pos_3(hair, \text{angle}(z_3 - z_2) + 90)$;
  filldraw stroke z_{1e} -- z_{2e} -- z_{3e};   % diagonals
else: **italcorr** $^2/_3[x\_height^\#, h^\#] * slant - .5stem^\# + .5vair^\# - .75u^\#$;
  adjust_fit$(0, 0)$;
  pickup *fine.nib*; $pos_1(vair, 0)$; $pos_3(vair, 0)$; $x_1 = w - x_3$;
  $pos_2(stem, 0)$; top $y_2 = h$; $x_2 = .5w$;
  bot $y_1 = $ bot $y_3 = \text{vround}\ ^2/_3[h, x\_height] - eps$;
  lft $x_{1l} = \text{hround}(rt\ x_{2r} - 3.25u - .5vair)$;   % same slope as in the acute accent
  $z_0 = whatever[z_{1r}, z_{2r}] = whatever[z_{2l}, z_{3l}]$;
  $y_{4l} = y_{4r} = y_2$; $x_{4l} = good.x\ .2[x_{2l}, x_2]$; $x_{4r} = w - x_{4l}$;
  filldraw z_{4l} -- z_{1l} -- z_{1r} -- z_0 -- z_{3l} -- z_{3r} -- z_{4r} -- cycle; **fi**   % diagonals
penlabels$(0, 1, 2, 3, 4)$; **endchar**;

```
cmchar "Hachek (check) accent";
```
beginchar(oct "024", $9u^\#$, $.75[x\_height^\#, \text{min}(asc\_height^\#, 2x\_height^\#)]$, 0);
$h' := \text{vround min}(asc\_height, 2x\_height)$;   % height of circumflex being inverted
if *serifs*: **italcorr** $h^\# * slant + .5hair^\# - 1.75u^\#$;
  adjust_fit$(0, 0)$;
  pickup *crisp.nib*; $pos_{2'}(.5[vair, curve], 90)$; top $y_{2'r} = h$;
  $pos_2(.5[vair, curve], 90)$; $x_2 = .5w$;
  $x_1 = w - x_3 = good.x\ 2.25u$; top $y_1 = $ top $y_3 = h$; $y_1 - y_2 = .5(y_{2'} - x\_height)$;
  $pos_1(hair, \text{angle}(z_2 - z_1) + 90)$; $pos_3(hair, \text{angle}(z_3 - z_2) + 90)$;
  filldraw stroke z_{1e} -- z_{2e} -- z_{3e};   % diagonals
else: **italcorr** $h^\# * slant - .5stem^\# + .5vair^\# - .75u^\#$;
  adjust_fit$(0, 0)$;
  pickup *fine.nib*; $pos_1(vair, 0)$; $pos_3(vair, 0)$; $x_1 = w - x_3$;
  $pos_2(stem, 0)$; bot $y_2 = \text{vround}(^1/_{12}[x\_height, h'] + o)$; $x_2 = .5w$;
  top $y_1 = $ top $y_3 = h + o$; lft $x_{1l} = \text{hround}(rt\ x_{2r} - 3.25u - .5vair)$;
  $z_0 = whatever[z_{1r}, z_{2r}] = whatever[z_{2l}, z_{3l}]$;
  $y_{4l} = y_{4r} = y_2$; $x_{4l} = good.x\ .2[x_{2l}, x_2]$; $x_{4r} = w - x_{4l}$;
  filldraw z_{4l} -- z_{1l} -- z_{1r} -- z_0 -- z_{3l} -- z_{3r} -- z_{4r} -- cycle; **fi**   % diagonals
penlabels$(0, 1, 2, 3, 4)$; **endchar**;

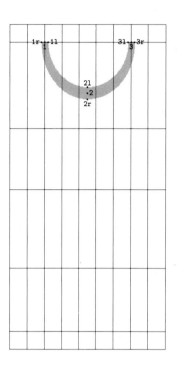

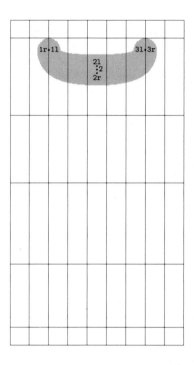

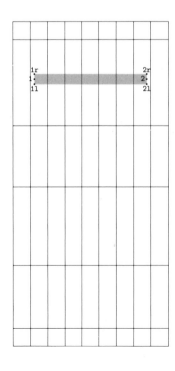

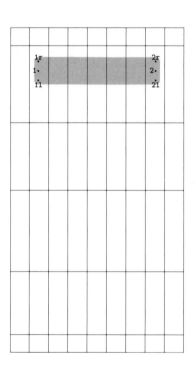

cmchar "Breve accent";
beginchar(oct "025", $9u^\#$, min($asc\_height^\#$, $2x\_height^\#$), 0);
italcorr $h^\# * slant + .5vair^\# - 1.5u^\#$;
adjust_fit(0, 0);
pickup $crisp.nib$; $pos_1(vair, -180)$; $pos_3(vair, 0)$;
$top\ y_1 = top\ y_3 = h$; $lft\ x_{1r} = w - rt\ x_{3r} = \text{hround}(2u - .5vair)$;
numeric $mid\_thickness$; $mid\_thickness = \text{vround}\ ^1/_3[vair, stem]$;
$pos_2(mid\_thickness, -90)$; $x_2 = .5w$;
$bot\ y_{2r} = \text{vround}\max(x\_height + o + tiny, ^1/_3[x\_height, h] + o - .5mid\_thickness)$;
filldraw stroke $z_{1e}\{down\} \ldots z_{2e}\{right\} \ldots \{up\}z_{3e}$;   % stroke
penlabels(1, 2, 3); **endchar**;

cmchar "Macron (bar) accent";
numeric $macron\_breadth^\#$; $macron\_breadth^\# = .2[vair^\#, stem^\#]$;
beginchar(oct "026", $9u^\#$, $.4[x\_height^\#, asc\_height^\#] + macron\_breadth^\#$, 0);
italcorr $h^\# * slant - .75u^\#$;
adjust_fit(0, 0);
numeric $macron\_breadth$; $macron\_breadth := \text{Vround}\ .2[vair, stem]$;
pickup **if** $serifs$: $crisp.nib$ **else**: $fine.nib$ **fi**;
$pos_1(macron\_breadth, 90)$; $pos_2(macron\_breadth, 90)$;
$top\ y_{1r} = top\ y_{2r} = h + o$; $lft\ x_1 = w - rt\ x_2 = \text{hround}\ 1.25u$;
filldraw stroke $z_{1e} \text{ -- } z_{2e}$;   % bar
penlabels(1, 2); **endchar**;

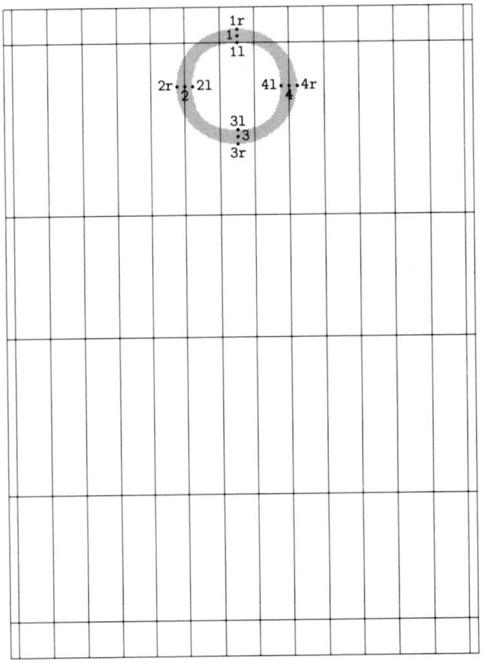
1r
1
1l
2r
2
2l
4l
4
4r
3l
3
3r

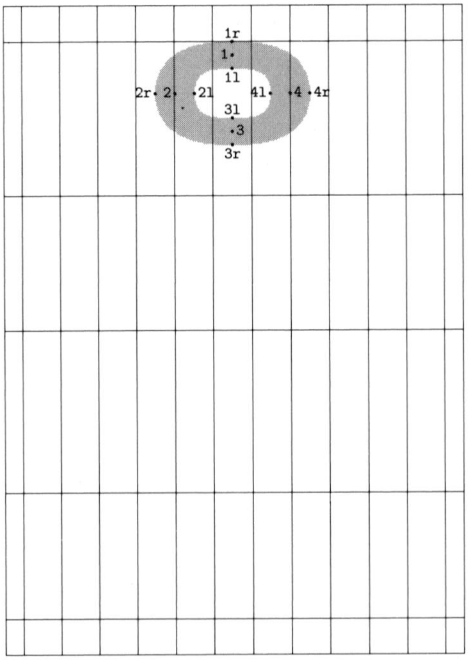
1r
1
1l
2r
2
2l
4l
4
4r
3l
3
3r

cmchar "Scandinavian circle accent";
beginchar(oct "027", $13u\# + \frac{4}{3}(asc\_height\# - x\_height\#) * slant, asc\_height\#, 0$);
adjust_fit($cap\_serif\_fit\#, cap\_serif\_fit\#$);
numeric $circ\_hair, circ\_vair$;
$circ_hair = $ hround $\min(hair, u + .5)$;
$circ_vair = $ vround $\min(vair, (h - x\_height)/6 + .5)$;
$penpos_1(circ\_vair, 90)$; $penpos_3(circ\_vair, -90)$;
$penpos_2(circ\_hair, 180)$; $penpos_4(circ\_hair, 0)$;
$x_{2r} = $ hround$(.5w - 1.5u - .5circ\_hair)$;
$x_{4r} = w - x_{2r}$; $x_1 = x_3 = .5w$; $y_{1r} = h + apex\_o$; $y_2 = y_4 = .5[y_1, y_3]$;
$y_{3r} = $ vround$(\frac{1}{3}[x\_height, h] + apex\_o)$;
penstroke $pulled\_arc_e(1, 2)$ & $pulled\_arc_e(2, 3)$
  & $pulled\_arc_e(3, 4)$ & $pulled\_arc_e(4, 1)$ & cycle;   % bowl
penlabels$(1, 2, 3, 4)$; **endchar**;

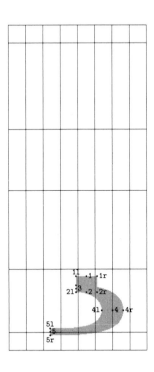

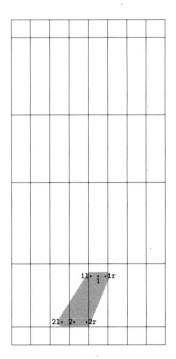

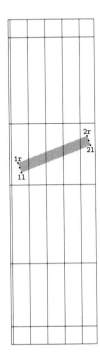

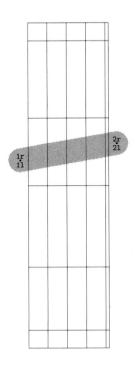

cmchar "Cedilla accent";
beginchar(oct "030", $8u^\#$, 0, $.875desc\_depth^\#$);
adjust_fit$(0, 0)$;
$x_1 = .5w + .5u$;
if *serifs*: **pickup** *crisp.nib*; $pos_1(stem, 0)$; $pos_2(stem, 0)$;
   $pos_3(vair, 90)$; $pos_4(stem, 0)$; $pos_5(vair, -90)$;
   $x_1 = x_2$; $z_{3l} = z_{2l}$; $x_4 = x_2 + 1.5u$; $x_5 = x_3 - 1.5u$;
   bot $y_1 = -o$; *bot* $y_2 = -$ vround $2/7d - o$; $y_4 = .5[y_3, y_5]$;
   bot $y_5 = -d - o$;
   filldraw stroke z_{1e} -- z_{2e};   % stem
   filldraw stroke $z_{3e}\{right\} \ldots z_{4e}\{down\} \ldots \{left\}z_{5e}$;   % hook
else: **pickup** *fine.nib*; $pos_1(vair, 0)$; *top* $y_1 = -o - 2$;
   $pos_2(.5[vair, stem], 0)$; *bot* $y_2 = -d - o$; $x_2 = x_1 - 1.25u$;
   filldraw stroke z_{1e} -- z_{2e}; **fi**   % diagonal
penlabels$(1, 2, 3, 4, 5)$; **endchar**;

iff *ligs* > 0: **cmchar** "Cross for Polish l and L";
if unknown $l\_width^\#$:
   $l\_width^\# := 5u^\# + 2serif\_fit^\#$; **fi**   % nominal width of 'l'
if unknown $L\_stem^\#$:
   $L\_stem^\# := cap\_serif\_fit^\# + \max(2u^\# + .5cap\_stem^\#, 3u^\#)$; **fi** % center of 'L' stem
ligtable oct "040": "l" **kern** $-l\_width^\# - 2letter\_fit^\#$,
   "L" **kern** $-.5l\_width^\# - L\_stem^\# - 2letter\_fit^\#$;
beginchar(oct "040", $l\_width^\#$, $x\_height^\#$, 0);
adjust_fit$(stem\_shift^\#, -stem\_shift^\#)$;
pickup *crisp.nib*; $x_2 - x_1 = \max(4u, 2.8u + stem)$; $.5[x_1, x_2] = .5w$;
$y_1 - .5bar = .2[bar\_height, x\_height]$; $y_2 + .5bar = .8[bar\_height, x\_height]$;
numeric *theta*; $theta = \text{angle}(z_2 - z_1) + 90$;
$pos_1(bar, theta)$; $pos_2(bar, theta)$;
filldraw stroke z_{1e} -- z_{2e};   % diagonal
penlabels$(1, 2)$; **endchar**;

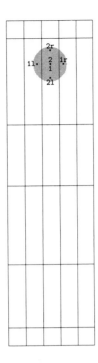

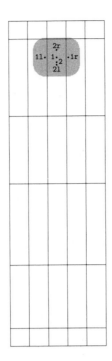

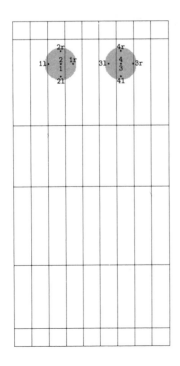

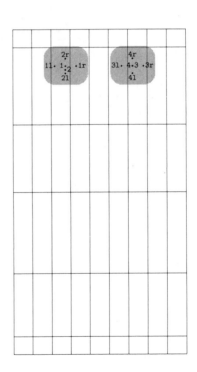

iff *ligs* > 0: **cmchar** "Dot accent";
numeric $dot\_diam\#$; $dot\_diam\# = \max(dot\_size\#, cap\_curve\#)$;
beginchar(oct "137", $5u\#$, $\min(asc\_height\#, {}^{10}/_{7}x\_height\# + .5dot\_diam\#), 0)$;
define_whole_blacker_pixels(dot_diam);
italcorr $h\# * slant + .5dot\_diam\# - 2u\#$;
adjust_fit$(0, 0)$;
pickup $tiny.nib$; $pos_1(dot\_diam, 0)$; $pos_2(dot\_diam, 90)$;
$x_1 = x_2 = .5w$; $top\ y_{2r} = h + 1$;
if $bot\ y_{2l} < x\_height + o + slab$: $y_{2l} := \min(y_{2r} - eps, x\_height + o + slab + .5tiny)$; **fi**
$y_1 = .5[y_{2l}, y_{2r}]$; $dot(1, 2)$;   % dot
penlabels$(1, 2)$; **endchar**;

cmchar "Umlaut (double dot) accent";
numeric $dot\_diam\#$, dot_diam;
$dot\_diam\# = \max(dot\_size\#, cap\_curve\#)$;
beginchar(oct "177", $9u\#$, $\min(asc\_height\#, {}^{10}/_{7}x\_height\# + .5dot\_diam\#), 0)$;
$dot\_diam = \max(tiny.breadth, \mathrm{hround}(\max(dot\_size, cap\_curve) - 2stem\_corr))$;
italcorr $h\# * slant + .5dot\_diam\# - 2.25u\#$;
adjust_fit$(0, 0)$;
pickup $tiny.nib$; $pos_1(dot\_diam, 0)$; $pos_2(dot\_diam, 90)$;
$x_1 = x_2 = 2.75u$; $top\ y_{2r} = h + 1$;
if $bot\ y_{2l} < x\_height + o + slab$: $y_{2l} := \min(y_{2r} - eps, x\_height + o + slab + .5tiny)$; **fi**
$y_1 = .5[y_{2l}, y_{2r}]$; $dot(1, 2)$;   % left dot
$pos_3(dot\_diam, 0)$; $penpos_4(y_{2r} - y_{2l}, 90)$; $y_3 = y_4 = y_1$; $x_3 = x_4 = w - x_1$;
$dot(3, 4)$;   % right dot
penlabels$(1, 2, 3, 4)$; **endchar**;

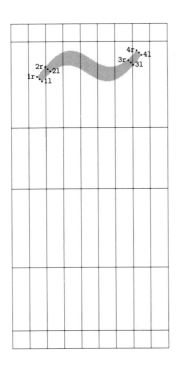

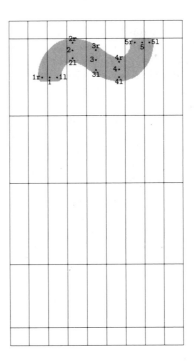

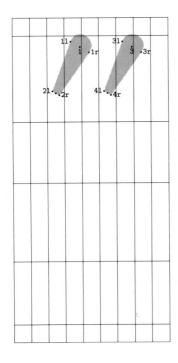

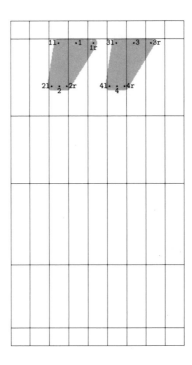

cmchar "Tilde (squiggle) accent";
beginchar(oct "176", $9u^\#$, min($asc\_height^\#$, $^{10}/_7 x\_height^\# + .5dot\_size^\#$), 0);
italcorr $h^\# * slant - u^\#$;
adjust_fit(0, 0);
if *serifs*: **numeric** *theta*; *theta* = angle($^1/_6(6u - vair)$, $^1/_4(h - x\_height)$));
  pickup *crisp.nib*; **numeric** *mid_width*; *mid_width* = $.4[vair, stem]$;
  $pos_1(vair, theta + 90)$; $pos_2(vair, theta + 90)$;
  $pos_3(vair, theta + 90)$; $pos_4(vair, theta + 90)$;
  $z_2 - z_1 = z_4 - z_3 = (mid\_width - crisp) * \text{dir } theta$;
  lft $x_{1r} = w - rt$ x_{4l} = hround $1.5u$; *top* $y_{4r} = h$;
  bot y_{1l} = vround(bot $y_{1l} + \min(^2/_3[x\_height, h], y_{3l} - .25vair) - top$ y_{1r});
  pair *delta*; *ypart delta* = $3(y_{3l} - y_{1l})$; *delta* = *whatever* $* \text{dir } theta$;
  filldraw z_{1l} .. controls$(z_{1l} + delta)$ and $(z_{3l} - delta)$ .. z_{3l} .. z_{4l}
    -- z_{4r} .. controls$(z_{4r} - delta)$ and $(z_{2r} + delta)$ .. z_{2r} .. z_{1r} -- cycle;   % stroke
else: **pickup** *fine.nib*; $pos_1(vair, 180)$; $pos_2(vair, 90)$;
  $pos_3(.5[vair, slab], 90)$; $pos_4(vair, 90)$; $pos_5(vair, 180)$;
  lft $x_{1r} = w - rt$ x_{5l} = hround $1.5u$; $x_2 - x_1 = x_3 - x_2 = x_4 - x_3 = x_5 - x_4$;
  bot y_1 = *bot* y_{4l} = vround($.75[x\_height, h] - vair$);
  top y_{2r} = *top* $y_5 = h$; $y_3 = .5[y_2, y_4]$;
  filldraw stroke $z_{1e}\{up\}$ ... $z_{2e}\{right\}$ .. z_{3e} .. $\{right\}z_{4e}$ ... $\{up\}z_{5e}$; **fi** % stroke
penlabels(1, 2, 3, 4, 5); **endchar**;

iff *ligs* > 0: **cmchar** "Long Hungarian umlaut accent";
beginchar(oct "175", $9u^\#$, min($asc\_height^\#$, $2x\_height^\#$), 0);
italcorr $h^\# * slant - u^\#$;
adjust_fit(0, 0);
$x_3 - x_1 = x_4 - x_2$ = hround $3u$; $y_3 = y_1$; $y_4 = y_2$;
if *serifs*: **pickup** *crisp.nib*; $x_3 + .5stem$ = hround$(w - 1.5u)$; $x_2 = 2.5u$;
  $y_1 + .5stem = h$; $y_2 = \max(^2/_3[h, x\_height], x\_height + o + hair)$;
  numeric *theta*; *theta* = angle$(z_2 - z_1) + 90$;
  $pos_1(stem, theta)$; $pos_2(hair, theta)$;
  $pos_3(stem, theta)$; $pos_4(hair, theta)$;
  filldraw circ_stroke z_{1e} -- z_{2e};   % left diagonal
  filldraw circ_stroke z_{3e} -- z_{4e};   % right diagonal
else: **pickup** *fine.nib*; $pos_1(stem, 0)$; $pos_2(vair, 0)$;
  $pos_3(stem, 0)$; $pos_4(vair, 0)$;
  rt x_{3r} = hround$(w - 1.5u)$; *lft* x_{4l} = hround$(.5w + u - .5vair)$;
  top $y_1 = h$; *bot* y_2 = vround $^2/_3[h, x\_height]$;
  filldraw stroke z_{1e} -- z_{2e};   % left diagonal
  filldraw stroke z_{3e} -- z_{4e}; **fi**   % right diagonal
penlabels(1, 2, 3, 4); **endchar**;

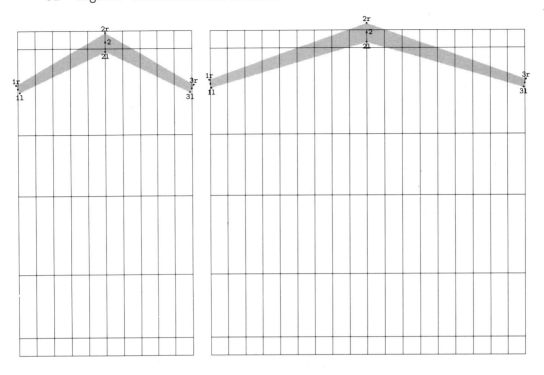

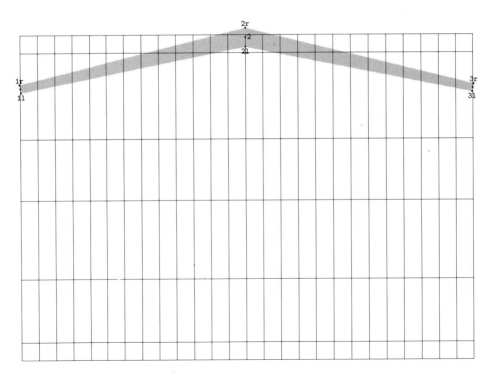

Now we turn to the program file `bigacc.mf`. The idea of this set of programs is to make lists of ever-wider accents, so that TEX can choose the right one when it typesets complex formulas.

The main work of `bigacc` is done by subroutines *big_hat* and *big_tilde* that appear in file `cmbase.mf`. These subroutines are shown "below the line."

% This file contains series of large accents for math extension fonts.

% The sizes are 'wide' ($10u\#$), 'wider' ($18u\#$), and 'widest' ($26u\#$).

% Character codes ´142 – ´147 are generated.

charlist oct "142": oct "143": oct "144";   % circumflexes
charlist oct "145": oct "146": oct "147";   % tildes

cmchar "Wide circumflex (hat) accent";
beginchar(oct "142", $10u\#$, $.5[asc\_height\#, body\_height\#]$, 0);
big_hat; **endchar**;

cmchar "Wider circumflex (hat) accent";
beginchar(oct "143", $18u\#$, $body\_height\#$, 0);
big_hat; **endchar**;

cmchar "Widest circumflex (hat) accent";
beginchar(oct "144", $26u\#$, $body\_height\#$, 0);
big_hat; **endchar**;

---

def *big_hat* $=$
  adjust_fit$(0, 0)$;
  pickup $crisp.nib$; $pos_2(.6[vair, curve], 90)$; $top\ y_{2r} = h + o$; $x_2 = .5w$;
  $x_1 = w - x_3 = good.x - eps$; $y_1 = y_3 = .5[x\_height, y_2]$;
  $pos_1(hair, \text{angle}(z_2 - z_1) + 90)$; $pos_3(hair, \text{angle}(z_3 - z_2) + 90)$;
  filldraw stroke z_{1e} -- z_{2e} -- z_{3e};   % diagonals
  penlabels$(1, 2, 3)$; **enddef**;

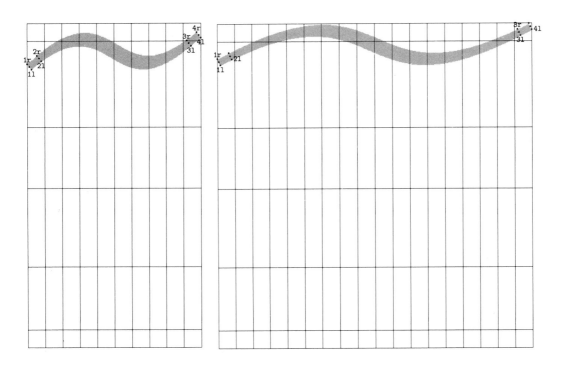

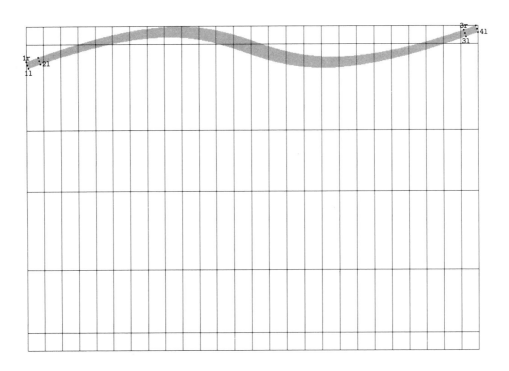

cmchar "Wide tilde (squiggle) accent";
beginchar(oct "145", $10u^\#$, $.5[asc\_height^\#, body\_height^\#]$, 0);
big_tilde; **endchar**;

cmchar "Wider tilde (squiggle) accent";
beginchar(oct "146", $18u^\#$, $body\_height^\#$, 0);
big_tilde; **endchar**;

cmchar "Widest tilde (squiggle) accent";
beginchar(oct "147", $26u^\#$, $body\_height^\#$, 0);
big_tilde; **endchar**;

---

def *big_tilde* =
   adjust_fit$(0, 0)$; **pickup** *crisp.nib*;
   numeric *theta*; $theta = \text{angle}(1/6(w - vair), 1/4(h - x\_height))$;
   numeric *mid_width*; $mid\_width = .4[vair, stem]$;
   $pos_1(vair, theta + 90)$; $pos_2(vair, theta + 90)$;
   $pos_3(vair, theta + 90)$; $pos_4(vair, theta + 90)$;
   $z_2 - z_1 = z_4 - z_3 = (mid\_width - crisp) * \text{dir } theta$;
   lft $x_{1r} = w - rt\ x_{4l} = 0$; *top* $y_{4r} = h$;
   bot $y_{1l} = \text{vround}(bot\ y_{1l} + \min(2/3[x\_height, h], y_{3l} - .25vair) - top\ y_{1r})$;
   pair *delta*; ypart $delta = 3(y_{3l} - y_{1l})$; $delta = whatever * \text{dir } theta$;
   filldraw z_{1l} .. controls$(z_{1l} + delta)$ and $(z_{3l} - delta)$ .. z_{3l} .. z_{4l}
     -- z_{4r} .. controls$(z_{4r} - delta)$ and $(z_{2r} + delta)$ .. z_{2r} .. z_{1r} -- cycle;   % stroke
   penlabels$(1, 2, 3, 4)$; **enddef**;

The program file `bigdel.mf` is responsible for making families of parentheses and brackets of various kinds, linked together in increasing order. Whenever possible, the largest delimiter in a list is made "extensible" by building up arbitrarily large characters from simple parts.

The character lists and extensible specifications are defined at the beginning of the program file. Then come the programs for individual characters, most of which use subroutines from `cmbase` like the *left_paren* and *right_paren* macros shown on the next page.

The delimiters generated by `bigdel` appear almost entirely below the baseline, because this permits TeX to use them with its `\radical` operation. In normal use, TeX will center the delimiters vertically with respect to the *math_axis* of the symbol font it is currently using.

[*Note:* The `bigdel` character illustrations appear at a much smaller scale than usual, because the characters are quite large.]

% This file contains series of large delimiters for math extension fonts.

% The sizes are '\big' ($2dh\#$), '\Big' ($3dh\#$),
% '\bigg' ($4dh\#$), and '\Bigg' ($5dh\#$),
% followed in most cases by an extensible character that can
% grow arbitrarily large in $dh\#$ steps,
% where $dh\#$ is 60% of the font design size.
% (For example, a 10-point font will have large delimiters in sizes
% 12 pt, 18 pt, 24 pt, 30 pt, 36 pt, 42 pt, etc.)

% Character codes $'000$–$'105$ and $'150$–$'177$ are generated.

charlist oct "000": oct "020": oct "022": oct "040": oct "060";   % left parentheses
charlist oct "001": oct "021": oct "023": oct "041": oct "061";   % right parentheses
charlist oct "002": oct "150": oct "024": oct "042": oct "062";   % left brackets
charlist oct "003": oct "151": oct "025": oct "043": oct "063";   % right brackets
charlist oct "004": oct "152": oct "026": oct "044": oct "064";   % left floors
charlist oct "005": oct "153": oct "027": oct "045": oct "065";   % right floors
charlist oct "006": oct "154": oct "030": oct "046": oct "066";   % left ceilings
charlist oct "007": oct "155": oct "031": oct "047": oct "067";   % right ceilings
charlist oct "010": oct "156": oct "032": oct "050": oct "070";   % left braces
charlist oct "011": oct "157": oct "033": oct "051": oct "071";   % right braces
charlist oct "012": oct "104": oct "034": oct "052";   % left angle brackets
charlist oct "013": oct "105": oct "035": oct "053";   % right angle brackets
charlist oct "016": oct "056": oct "036": oct "054";   % slashes
charlist oct "017": oct "057": oct "037": oct "055";   % backslashes
charlist oct "160": oct "161": oct "162": oct "163": oct "164";   % radical signs

extensible oct "014": 0, 0, 0, oct "014";   % vertical line
extensible oct "015": 0, 0, 0, oct "015";   % double vertical line
extensible oct "060": oct "060", 0, oct "100", oct "102";   % left parenthesis
extensible oct "061": oct "061", 0, oct "101", oct "103";   % right parenthesis
extensible oct "062": oct "062", 0, oct "064", oct "066";   % left bracket
extensible oct "063": oct "063", 0, oct "065", oct "067";   % right bracket

extensible oct "064": 0, 0, oct "064", oct "066";   % left floor bracket
extensible oct "065": 0, 0, oct "065", oct "067";   % right floor bracket
extensible oct "066": oct "062", 0, 0, oct "066";   % left ceiling bracket
extensible oct "067": oct "063", 0, 0, oct "067";   % right ceiling bracket
extensible oct "070": oct "070", oct "074", oct "072", oct "076";   % left brace
extensible oct "071": oct "071", oct "075", oct "073", oct "076";   % right brace
extensible oct "072": oct "070", 0, oct "072", oct "076";   % sharp left parenthesis
extensible oct "073": oct "071", 0, oct "073", oct "076";   % sharp right parenthesis
extensible oct "074": 0, 0, 0, oct "077";   % arrow extension modules only
extensible oct "075": 0, 0, 0, oct "167";   % double arrow extension modules only
extensible oct "076": 0, 0, 0, oct "076";   % brace extension modules only
extensible oct "077": oct "170", 0, oct "171", oct "077";   % updownarrow
extensible oct "100": oct "070", 0, oct "073", oct "076";   % left moustache
extensible oct "101": oct "071", 0, oct "072", oct "076";   % right moustache
extensible oct "102": 0, 0, 0, oct "102";   % left parenthesis extension modules only
extensible oct "103": 0, 0, 0, oct "103";   % right parenthesis extension modules only
extensible oct "164": oct "166", 0, oct "164", oct "165";   % radical sign
extensible oct "167": oct "176", 0, oct "177", oct "167";   % double updownarrow
extensible oct "170": oct "170", 0, 0, oct "077";   % uparrow
extensible oct "171": 0, 0, oct "171", oct "077";   % downarrow
extensible oct "176": oct "176", 0, 0, oct "167";   % double uparrow
extensible oct "177": 0, 0, oct "177", oct "167";   % double downarrow

---

def *left_paren*(**expr** *min_breadth*, *max_breadth*) =
  pickup *fine.nib*; pos_1(hround *min_breadth*, 0);
  pos_2(hround *max_breadth*, 0); pos_3(hround *min_breadth*, 0);
  rt x_{1r} = rt x_{3r} = hround($w - 1.25u + .5min\_breadth$); *lft* x_{2l} = hround $1.25u$;
  top $y_1 = h$; $y_2 = .5[y_1, y_3]$; *bot* $y_3 = 1 - d$;
  filldraw stroke $z_{1e}\{3(x_{2e} - x_{1e}), y_2 - y_1\} \ldots z_{2e}$
    $\ldots \{3(x_{3e} - x_{2e}), y_3 - y_2\}z_{3e}$;   % arc
  penlabels(1, 2, 3); **enddef**;

def *right_paren*(**expr** *min_breadth*, *max_breadth*) =
  pickup *fine.nib*; pos_1(hround *min_breadth*, 0);
  pos_2(hround *max_breadth*, 0); pos_3(hround *min_breadth*, 0);
  lft x_{1l} = *lft* x_{3l} = hround($1.25u - .5min\_breadth$); rt x_{2r} = hround($w - 1.25u$);
  top $y_1 = h$; $y_2 = .5[y_1, y_3]$; *bot* $y_3 = 1 - d$;
  filldraw stroke $z_{1e}\{3(x_{2e} - x_{1e}), y_2 - y_1\} \ldots z_{2e}$
    $\ldots \{3(x_{3e} - x_{2e}), y_3 - y_2\}z_{3e}$;   % arc
  penlabels(1, 2, 3); **enddef**;

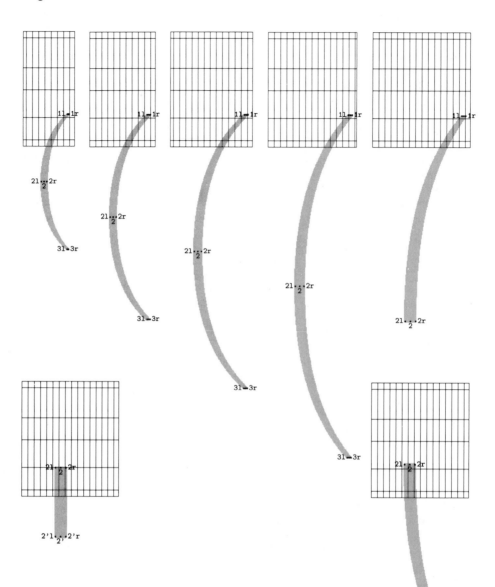

cmchar "\big left parenthesis";
beginchar(oct "000", $7u^\#$, $rule\_thickness^\#$, $2dh^\# - rule\_thickness^\#$);
adjust_fit($1.5u^\#$, $-.25u^\#$); $left\_paren(hair, stem)$; **endchar**;

cmchar "\Big left parenthesis";
beginchar(oct "020", $9u^\#$, $rule\_thickness^\#$, $3dh^\# - rule\_thickness^\#$);
adjust_fit($2u^\#$, $-.25u^\#$); $left\_paren(rule\_thickness, .5[stem, bold])$; **endchar**;

cmchar "\bigg left parenthesis";
beginchar(oct "022", $11u^\#$, $rule\_thickness^\#$, $4dh^\# - rule\_thickness^\#$);
adjust_fit($2.5u^\#$, $-.25u^\#$); $left\_paren(rule\_thickness + .2dw, bold)$; **endchar**;

cmchar "\Bigg left parenthesis";
beginchar(oct "040", $11.5u^\#$, $rule\_thickness^\#$, $5dh^\# - rule\_thickness^\#$);
adjust_fit($3u^\#$, $-.25u^\#$); $left\_paren(rule\_thickness + .4dw, bold + dw)$; **endchar**;

cmchar "Extensible left parenthesis---top";
beginchar(oct "060", $12u^\#$, $rule\_thickness^\#$, $3dh^\# - rule\_thickness^\#$);
adjust_fit($4u^\#$, $-.25u^\#$); **pickup** $fine.nib$;
numeric $min\_breadth$, $max\_breadth$;
$min\_breadth = rule\_thickness + .6dw$; $max\_breadth = bold + 2dw$;
pos_1(hround $min\_breadth$, 0); pos_2(hround $max\_breadth$, 0);
$rt\ x_{1r} =$ hround$(w - 1.25u + .5min\_breadth)$; $lft\ x_{2l} =$ hround $1.25u$;
$top\ y_1 = h - 1$; $y_2 = -d - eps$;
filldraw stroke $z_{1e}\{3(x_{2e} - x_{1e}), y_2 - y_1\} \ldots \{down\}z_{2e}$;   % upper arc
penlabels(1, 2); **endchar**;

cmchar "Extensible left parenthesis---bottom";
beginchar(oct "100", $12u^\#$, $rule\_thickness^\#$, $3dh^\# - rule\_thickness^\#$);
adjust_fit($4u^\#$, $-.25u^\#$); **pickup** $fine.nib$;
numeric $min\_breadth$, $max\_breadth$;
$min\_breadth = rule\_thickness + .6dw$; $max\_breadth = bold + 2dw$;
pos_3(hround $min\_breadth$, 0); pos_2(hround $max\_breadth$, 0);
$rt\ x_{3r} =$ hround$(w - 1.25u + .5min\_breadth)$; $lft\ x_{2l} =$ hround $1.25u$;
$bot\ y_3 = 1 - d$; $y_2 = h + eps$;
filldraw stroke $z_{3e}\{3(x_{2e} - x_{3e}), y_2 - y_3\} \ldots \{up\}z_{2e}$;   % lower arc
penlabels(2, 3); **endchar**;

cmchar "Extensible left parenthesis---extension module";
beginchar(oct "102", $12u^\#$, 0, $dh^\#$);
adjust_fit($4u^\#$, $-.25u^\#$); **pickup** $fine.nib$;
numeric $max\_breadth$; $max\_breadth = bold + 2dw$;
pos_2(hround $max\_breadth$, 0); $pos_{2'}$(hround $max\_breadth$, 0);
$lft\ x_{2l} = lft\ x_{2'l} =$ hround $1.25u$; $y_2 = h + eps$; $y_{2'} = -d - eps$;
filldraw stroke z_{2e} -- $z_{2'e}$;   % link
penlabels(2, 2'); **endchar**;

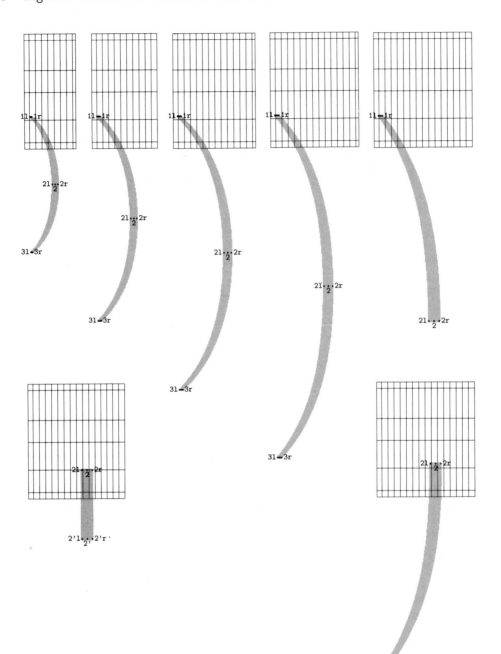

cmchar "\big right parenthesis";
beginchar(oct "001", $7u^\#$, $rule\_thickness^\#$, $2dh^\# - rule\_thickness^\#$);
adjust_fit$(-.25u^\#, 1.5u^\#)$; $right\_paren(hair, stem)$; **endchar**;

cmchar "\Big right parenthesis";
beginchar(oct "021", $9u^\#$, $rule\_thickness^\#$, $3dh^\# - rule\_thickness^\#$);
adjust_fit$(-.25u^\#, 2u^\#)$; $right\_paren(rule\_thickness, .5[stem, bold])$; **endchar**;

cmchar "\bigg right parenthesis";
beginchar(oct "023", $11u^\#$, $rule\_thickness^\#$, $4dh^\# - rule\_thickness^\#$);
adjust_fit$(-.25u^\#, 2.5u^\#)$; $right\_paren(rule\_thickness + .2dw, bold)$; **endchar**;

cmchar "\Bigg right parenthesis";
beginchar(oct "041", $11.5u^\#$, $rule\_thickness^\#$, $5dh^\# - rule\_thickness^\#$);
adjust_fit$(-.25u^\#, 3u^\#)$; $right\_paren(rule\_thickness + .4dw, bold + dw)$; **endchar**;

cmchar "Extensible right parenthesis---top";
beginchar(oct "061", $12u^\#$, $rule\_thickness^\#$, $3dh^\# - rule\_thickness^\#$);
adjust_fit$(-.25u^\#, 4u^\#)$; **pickup** $fine.nib$;
numeric $min\_breadth$, $max\_breadth$;
$min\_breadth = rule\_thickness + .6dw$; $max\_breadth = bold + 2dw$;
$pos_1(\text{hround } min\_breadth, 0)$; $pos_2(\text{hround } max\_breadth, 0)$;
$lft\ x_{1l} = \text{hround}(1.25u - .5min\_breadth)$; $rt\ x_{2r} = \text{hround}(w - 1.25u)$;
$top\ y_1 = h - 1$; $y_2 = -d - eps$;
filldraw stroke $z_{1e}\{3(x_{2e} - x_{1e}), y_2 - y_1\} \ldots \{down\}z_{2e}$;   % upper arc
penlabels$(1, 2)$; **endchar**;

cmchar "Extensible right parenthesis---bottom";
beginchar(oct "101", $12u^\#$, $rule\_thickness^\#$, $3dh^\# - rule\_thickness^\#$);
adjust_fit$(-.25u^\#, 4u^\#)$; **pickup** $fine.nib$;
numeric $min\_breadth$, $max\_breadth$;
$min\_breadth = rule\_thickness + .6dw$; $max\_breadth = bold + 2dw$;
$pos_3(\text{hround } min\_breadth, 0)$; $pos_2(\text{hround } max\_breadth, 0)$;
$lft\ x_{3l} = \text{hround}(1.25u - .5min\_breadth)$; $rt\ x_{2r} = \text{hround}(w - 1.25u)$;
$bot\ y_3 = 1 - d$; $y_2 = h + eps$;
filldraw stroke $z_{3e}\{3(x_{2e} - x_{3e}), y_2 - y_3\} \ldots \{up\}z_{2e}$;   % lower arc
penlabels$(2, 3)$; **endchar**;

cmchar "Extensible right parenthesis---extension module";
beginchar(oct "103", $12u^\#$, 0, $dh^\#$);
adjust_fit$(-.25u^\#, 4u^\#)$; **pickup** $fine.nib$;
numeric $max\_breadth$; $max\_breadth = bold + 2dw$;
$pos_2(\text{hround } max\_breadth, 0)$; $pos_{2'}(\text{hround } max\_breadth, 0)$;
$rt\ x_{2r} = rt\ x_{2'r} = \text{hround}(w - 1.25u)$; $y_2 = h + eps$; $y_{2'} = -d - eps$;
filldraw stroke $z_{2e} \text{ -- } z_{2'e}$;   % link
penlabels$(2, 2')$; **endchar**;

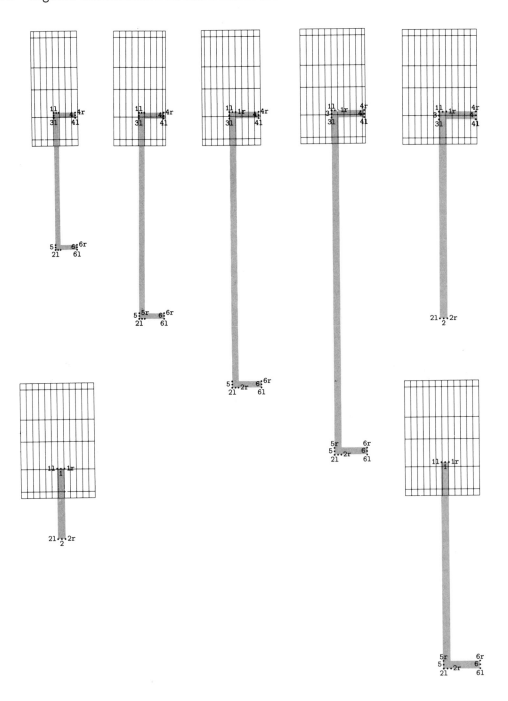

```
cmchar "\big left bracket";
```
beginchar(oct "002", $6u^\#$, *rule_thickness*$^\#$, $2dh^\# - rule\_thickness^\#$);
adjust_fit($1.5u^\#$, 0); *left_bracket*(*rule_thickness*, **true**, **true**); **endchar**;

```
cmchar "\Big left bracket";
```
beginchar(oct "150", $6.5u^\#$, *rule_thickness*$^\#$, $3dh^\# - rule\_thickness^\#$);
adjust_fit($2u^\#$, 0); *left_bracket*($.25[rule\_thickness, stem]$, **true**, **true**); **endchar**;

```
cmchar "\bigg left bracket";
```
beginchar(oct "024", $7u^\#$, *rule_thickness*$^\#$, $4dh^\# - rule\_thickness^\#$);
adjust_fit($2.5u^\#$, 0); *left_bracket*($.5[rule\_thickness, stem]$, **true**, **true**); **endchar**;

```
cmchar "\Bigg left bracket";
```
beginchar(oct "042", $7.5u^\#$, *rule_thickness*$^\#$, $5dh^\# - rule\_thickness^\#$);
adjust_fit($3u^\#$, 0); *left_bracket*($.75[rule\_thickness, stem]$, **true**, **true**); **endchar**;

```
cmchar "Extensible left bracket---top";
```
beginchar(oct "062", $8u^\#$, *rule_thickness*$^\#$, $3dh^\# - rule\_thickness^\#$);
adjust_fit($4u^\#$, 0); **pickup** *crisp.nib*;
$pos_1(stem, 0)$; $pos_2(stem, 0)$;
$top\ y_1 = h - 1$; $y_2 = -d - eps$; $lft\ x_{1l} = lft\ x_{2l} = \text{hround}(2.5u - .5stem)$;
filldraw stroke $z_{1e}\ \text{--}\ z_{2e}$;   % stem
$pos_3(stem, 90)$; $pos_4(stem, 90)$;
$x_3 = x_{1l}$; $rt\ x_4 = \text{hround}(w - .75u + .5stem)$; $y_{3r} = y_{4r} = y_1$;
filldraw stroke $z_{3e}\ \text{--}\ z_{4e}$;   % upper bar
penlabels(1, 2, 3, 4); **endchar**;

```
cmchar "Extensible left bracket---bottom";
```
beginchar(oct "064", $8u^\#$, *rule_thickness*$^\#$, $3dh^\# - rule\_thickness^\#$);
adjust_fit($4u^\#$, 0); **pickup** *crisp.nib*;
$pos_1(stem, 0)$; $pos_2(stem, 0)$;
$y_1 = h + eps$; $bot\ y_2 = 1 - d$; $lft\ x_{1l} = lft\ x_{2l} = \text{hround}(2.5u - .5stem)$;
filldraw stroke $z_{1e}\ \text{--}\ z_{2e}$;   % stem
$pos_5(stem, 90)$; $pos_6(stem, 90)$;
$x_5 = x_{1l}$; $rt\ x_6 = \text{hround}(w - .75u + .5stem)$; $y_{5l} = y_{6l} = y_2$;
filldraw stroke $z_{5e}\ \text{--}\ z_{6e}$;   % lower bar
penlabels(1, 2, 5, 6); **endchar**;

```
cmchar "Extensible left bracket---extension module";
```
beginchar(oct "066", $8u^\#$, 0, $dh^\#$);
adjust_fit($4u^\#$, 0); **pickup** *crisp.nib*;
$pos_1(stem, 0)$; $pos_2(stem, 0)$;
$y_1 = h + 1 + eps$; $bot\ y_2 = -d - 1 - eps$; $lft\ x_{1l} = lft\ x_{2l} = \text{hround}(2.5u - .5stem)$;
filldraw stroke $z_{1e}\ \text{--}\ z_{2e}$;   % stem
penlabels(1, 2); **endchar**;

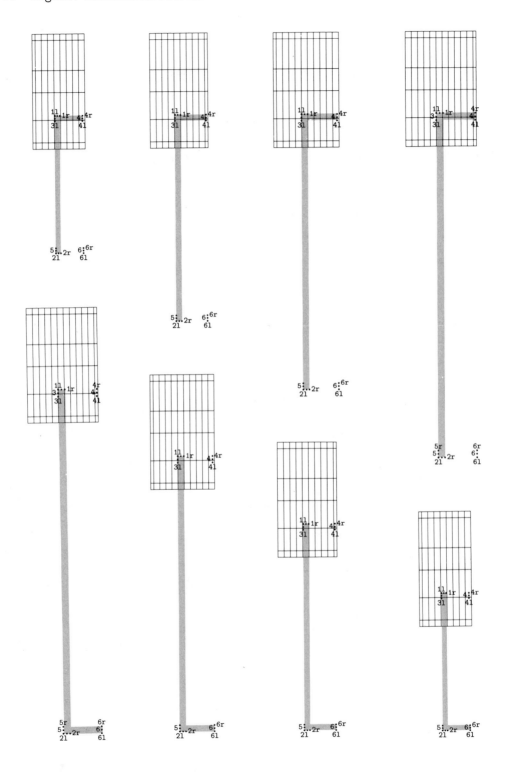

```
cmchar "\big left ceiling bracket";
```
beginchar(oct "006", $7u^\#$, $rule\_thickness^\#$, $2dh^\# - rule\_thickness^\#$);
adjust_fit$(1.5u^\#, 0)$; *left_bracket*($rule\_thickness$, **true**, **false**); **endchar**;

```
cmchar "\Big left ceiling bracket";
```
beginchar(oct "154", $7.5u^\#$, $rule\_thickness^\#$, $3dh^\# - rule\_thickness^\#$);
adjust_fit$(2u^\#, 0)$; *left_bracket*($.25[rule\_thickness, stem]$, **true**, **false**); **endchar**;

```
cmchar "\bigg left ceiling bracket";
```
beginchar(oct "030", $8u^\#$, $rule\_thickness^\#$, $4dh^\# - rule\_thickness^\#$);
adjust_fit$(2.5u^\#, 0)$; *left_bracket*($.5[rule\_thickness, stem]$, **true**, **false**); **endchar**;

```
cmchar "\Bigg left ceiling bracket";
```
beginchar(oct "046", $8.5u^\#$, $rule\_thickness^\#$, $5dh^\# - rule\_thickness^\#$);
adjust_fit$(3u^\#, 0)$; *left_bracket*($.75[rule\_thickness, stem]$, **true**, **false**); **endchar**;

```
cmchar "\big left floor bracket";
```
beginchar(oct "004", $7u^\#$, $rule\_thickness^\#$, $2dh^\# - rule\_thickness^\#$);
adjust_fit$(1.5u^\#, 0)$; *left_bracket*($rule\_thickness$, **false**, **true**); **endchar**;

```
cmchar "\Big left floor bracket";
```
beginchar(oct "152", $7.5u^\#$, $rule\_thickness^\#$, $3dh^\# - rule\_thickness^\#$);
adjust_fit$(2u^\#, 0)$; *left_bracket*($.25[rule\_thickness, stem]$, **false**, **true**); **endchar**;

```
cmchar "\bigg left floor bracket";
```
beginchar(oct "026", $8u^\#$, $rule\_thickness^\#$, $4dh^\# - rule\_thickness^\#$);
adjust_fit$(2.5u^\#, 0)$; *left_bracket*($.5[rule\_thickness, stem]$, **false**, **true**); **endchar**;

```
cmchar "\Bigg left floor bracket";
```
beginchar(oct "044", $8.5u^\#$, $rule\_thickness^\#$, $5dh^\# - rule\_thickness^\#$);
adjust_fit$(3u^\#, 0)$; *left_bracket*($.75[rule\_thickness, stem]$, **false**, **true**); **endchar**;

---

def *left_bracket*(**expr** *breadth*, *do_top*, *do_bot*) =
  pickup *crisp.nib*;
  numeric *thickness*; *thickness* = hround *breadth*;
  $pos_1(thickness, 0)$; $pos_2(thickness, 0)$;
  top $y_1 = h$; *bot* $y_2 = 1 - d$; *lft* $x_{1l} =$ *lft* $x_{2l} =$ hround$(2.5u - .5thickness)$;
  filldraw stroke z_{1e} -- z_{2e};   % stem
  $pos_3(thickness, 90)$; $pos_4(thickness, 90)$;
  $pos_5(thickness, 90)$; $pos_6(thickness, 90)$;
  $x_3 = x_5 = x_{1l}$; *rt* $x_4 =$ *rt* $x_6 =$ hround$(w - .75u + .5thickness)$;
  $y_{3r} = y_{4r} = y_1$; $y_{5l} = y_{6l} = y_2$;
  if *do_top*: **filldraw stroke** z_{3e} -- z_{4e}; **fi**   % upper bar
  if *do_bot*: **filldraw stroke** z_{5e} -- z_{6e}; **fi**   % lower bar
  penlabels$(1, 2, 3, 4, 5, 6)$; **enddef**;

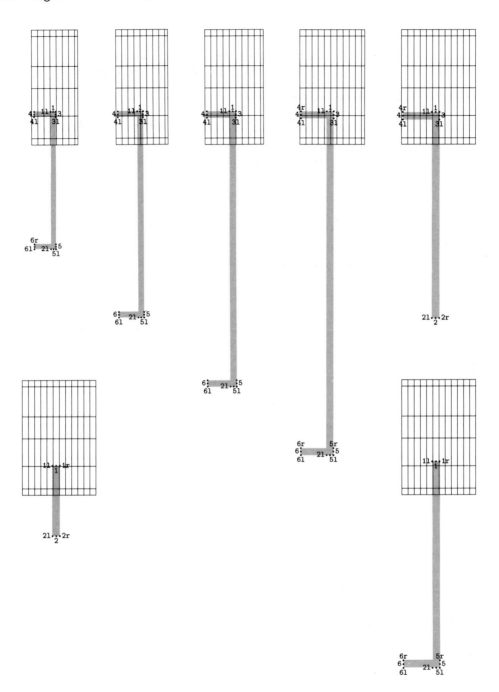

cmchar "\big right bracket";
beginchar(oct "003", $6u\#$, $rule\_thickness\#$, $2dh\# - rule\_thickness\#$);
adjust_fit$(0, 1.5u\#)$; $right\_bracket(rule\_thickness, \textbf{true}, \textbf{true})$; **endchar**;

cmchar "\Big right bracket";
beginchar(oct "151", $6.5u\#$, $rule\_thickness\#$, $3dh\# - rule\_thickness\#$);
adjust_fit$(0, 2u\#)$; $right\_bracket(.25[rule\_thickness, stem], \textbf{true}, \textbf{true})$; **endchar**;

cmchar "\bigg right bracket";
beginchar(oct "025", $7u\#$, $rule\_thickness\#$, $4dh\# - rule\_thickness\#$);
adjust_fit$(0, 2.5u\#)$; $right\_bracket(.5[rule\_thickness, stem], \textbf{true}, \textbf{true})$; **endchar**;

cmchar "\Bigg right bracket";
beginchar(oct "043", $7.5u\#$, $rule\_thickness\#$, $5dh\# - rule\_thickness\#$);
adjust_fit$(0, 3u\#)$; $right\_bracket(.75[rule\_thickness, stem], \textbf{true}, \textbf{true})$; **endchar**;

cmchar "Extensible right bracket---top";
beginchar(oct "063", $8u\#$, $rule\_thickness\#$, $3dh\# - rule\_thickness\#$);
adjust_fit$(0, 4u\#)$; **pickup** $crisp.nib$;
$pos_1(stem, 0)$; $pos_2(stem, 0)$;
$top\ y_1 = h - 1$; $y_2 = -d - eps$; $rt\ x_{1r} = rt\ x_{2r} = \text{hround}(w - 2.5u + .5stem)$;
filldraw stroke z_{1e} -- z_{2e};   % stem
$pos_3(stem, 90)$; $pos_4(stem, 90)$;
$x_3 = x_{1r}$; $lft\ x_4 = \text{hround}(.75u - .5stem)$; $y_{3r} = y_{4r} = y_1$;
filldraw stroke z_{3e} -- z_{4e};   % upper bar
penlabels$(1, 2, 3, 4)$; **endchar**;

cmchar "Extensible right bracket---bottom";
beginchar(oct "065", $8u\#$, $rule\_thickness\#$, $3dh\# - rule\_thickness\#$);
adjust_fit$(0, 4u\#)$; **pickup** $crisp.nib$;
$pos_1(stem, 0)$; $pos_2(stem, 0)$;
$y_1 = h + eps$; $bot\ y_2 = 1 - d$; $rt\ x_{1r} = rt\ x_{2r} = \text{hround}(w - 2.5u + .5stem)$;
filldraw stroke z_{1e} -- z_{2e};   % stem
$pos_5(stem, 90)$; $pos_6(stem, 90)$;
$x_5 = x_{1r}$; $lft\ x_6 = \text{hround}(.75u - .5stem)$; $y_{5l} = y_{6l} = y_2$;
filldraw stroke z_{5e} -- z_{6e};   % lower bar
penlabels$(1, 2, 5, 6)$; **endchar**;

cmchar "Extensible right bracket---extension module";
beginchar(oct "067", $8u\#$, 0, $dh\#$);
adjust_fit$(0, 4u\#)$; **pickup** $crisp.nib$;
$pos_1(stem, 0)$; $pos_2(stem, 0)$;
$y_1 = h + 1 + eps$; $bot\ y_2 = -d - 1 - eps$; $rt\ x_{1r} = rt\ x_{2r} = \text{hround}(w - 2.5u + .5stem)$;
filldraw stroke z_{1e} -- z_{2e};   % stem
penlabels$(1, 2)$; **endchar**;

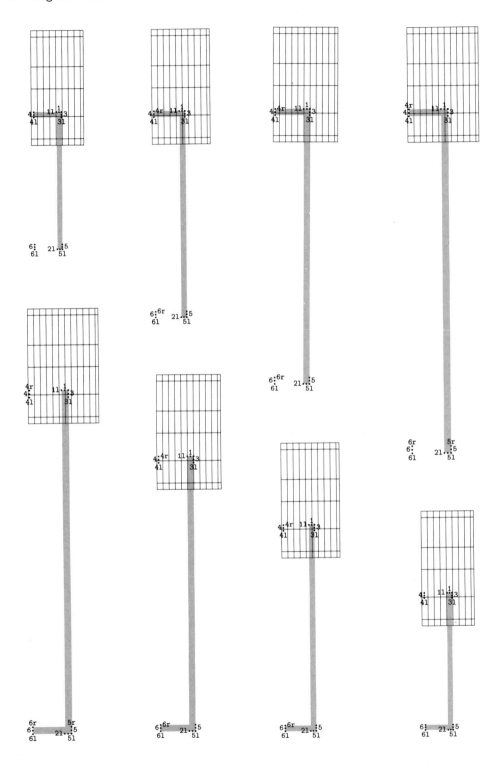

```
cmchar "\big right ceiling bracket";
```
$\textbf{beginchar}(\text{oct }"007", 7u^{\#}, \mathit{rule\_thickness}^{\#}, 2dh^{\#} - \mathit{rule\_thickness}^{\#});$
$\textbf{adjust\_fit}(0, 1.5u^{\#}); \quad \mathit{right\_bracket}(\mathit{rule\_thickness}, \textbf{true}, \textbf{false}); \textbf{ endchar};$

```
cmchar "\Big right ceiling bracket";
```
$\textbf{beginchar}(\text{oct }"155", 7.5u^{\#}, \mathit{rule\_thickness}^{\#}, 3dh^{\#} - \mathit{rule\_thickness}^{\#});$
$\textbf{adjust\_fit}(0, 2u^{\#}); \quad \mathit{right\_bracket}(.25[\mathit{rule\_thickness}, \mathit{stem}], \textbf{true}, \textbf{false}); \textbf{ endchar};$

```
cmchar "\bigg right ceiling bracket";
```
$\textbf{beginchar}(\text{oct }"031", 8u^{\#}, \mathit{rule\_thickness}^{\#}, 4dh^{\#} - \mathit{rule\_thickness}^{\#});$
$\textbf{adjust\_fit}(0, 2.5u^{\#}); \quad \mathit{right\_bracket}(.5[\mathit{rule\_thickness}, \mathit{stem}], \textbf{true}, \textbf{false}); \textbf{ endchar};$

```
cmchar "\Bigg right ceiling bracket";
```
$\textbf{beginchar}(\text{oct }"047", 8.5u^{\#}, \mathit{rule\_thickness}^{\#}, 5dh^{\#} - \mathit{rule\_thickness}^{\#});$
$\textbf{adjust\_fit}(0, 3u^{\#}); \quad \mathit{right\_bracket}(.75[\mathit{rule\_thickness}, \mathit{stem}], \textbf{true}, \textbf{false}); \textbf{ endchar};$

```
cmchar "\big right floor bracket";
```
$\textbf{beginchar}(\text{oct }"005", 7u^{\#}, \mathit{rule\_thickness}^{\#}, 2dh^{\#} - \mathit{rule\_thickness}^{\#});$
$\textbf{adjust\_fit}(0, 1.5u^{\#}); \quad \mathit{right\_bracket}(\mathit{rule\_thickness}, \textbf{false}, \textbf{true}); \textbf{ endchar};$

```
cmchar "\Big right floor bracket";
```
$\textbf{beginchar}(\text{oct }"153", 7.5u^{\#}, \mathit{rule\_thickness}^{\#}, 3dh^{\#} - \mathit{rule\_thickness}^{\#});$
$\textbf{adjust\_fit}(0, 2u^{\#}); \quad \mathit{right\_bracket}(.25[\mathit{rule\_thickness}, \mathit{stem}], \textbf{false}, \textbf{true}); \textbf{ endchar};$

```
cmchar "\bigg right floor bracket";
```
$\textbf{beginchar}(\text{oct }"027", 8u^{\#}, \mathit{rule\_thickness}^{\#}, 4dh^{\#} - \mathit{rule\_thickness}^{\#});$
$\textbf{adjust\_fit}(0, 2.5u^{\#}); \quad \mathit{right\_bracket}(.5[\mathit{rule\_thickness}, \mathit{stem}], \textbf{false}, \textbf{true}); \textbf{ endchar};$

```
cmchar "\Bigg right floor bracket";
```
$\textbf{beginchar}(\text{oct }"045", 8.5u^{\#}, \mathit{rule\_thickness}^{\#}, 5dh^{\#} - \mathit{rule\_thickness}^{\#});$
$\textbf{adjust\_fit}(0, 3u^{\#}); \quad \mathit{right\_bracket}(.75[\mathit{rule\_thickness}, \mathit{stem}], \textbf{false}, \textbf{true}); \textbf{ endchar};$

$\textbf{def } \mathit{right\_bracket}(\textbf{expr } \mathit{breadth}, \mathit{do\_top}, \mathit{do\_bot}) =$
  $\textbf{pickup } \mathit{crisp.nib};$
  $\textbf{numeric } \mathit{thickness}; \quad \mathit{thickness} = \text{hround } \mathit{breadth};$
  $\mathit{pos}_1(\mathit{thickness}, 0); \quad \mathit{pos}_2(\mathit{thickness}, 0);$
  $\mathit{top } y_1 = h; \quad \mathit{bot } y_2 = 1 - d; \quad \mathit{rt } x_{1r} = \mathit{rt } x_{2r} = \text{hround}(w - 2.5u + .5\mathit{thickness});$
  $\textbf{filldraw stroke } z_{1e} \,\text{--}\, z_{2e};$ % stem
  $\mathit{pos}_3(\mathit{thickness}, 90); \quad \mathit{pos}_4(\mathit{thickness}, 90);$
  $\mathit{pos}_5(\mathit{thickness}, 90); \quad \mathit{pos}_6(\mathit{thickness}, 90);$
  $x_3 = x_5 = x_{1r}; \quad \mathit{lft } x_4 = \mathit{lft } x_6 = \text{hround}(.75u - .5\mathit{thickness});$
  $y_{3r} = y_{4r} = y_1; \quad y_{5l} = y_{6l} = y_2;$
  $\textbf{if } \mathit{do\_top}: \textbf{ filldraw stroke } z_{3e} \,\text{--}\, z_{4e}; \textbf{ fi}$ % upper bar
  $\textbf{if } \mathit{do\_bot}: \textbf{ filldraw stroke } z_{5e} \,\text{--}\, z_{6e}; \textbf{ fi}$ % lower bar
  $\textbf{penlabels}(1, 2, 3, 4, 5, 6); \textbf{ enddef};$

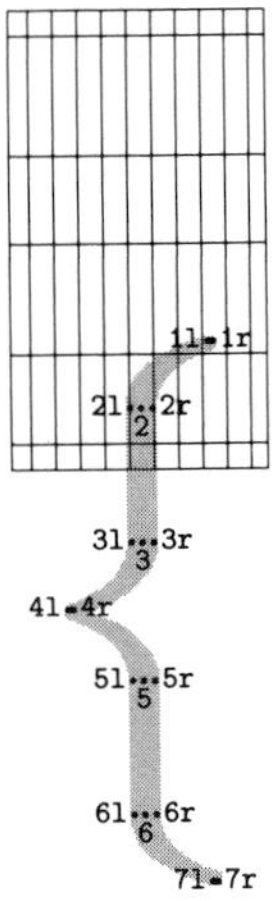
1l 1r
2l 2r
2
3l 3r
3
4l 4r
5l 5r
5
6l 6r
6
7l 7r

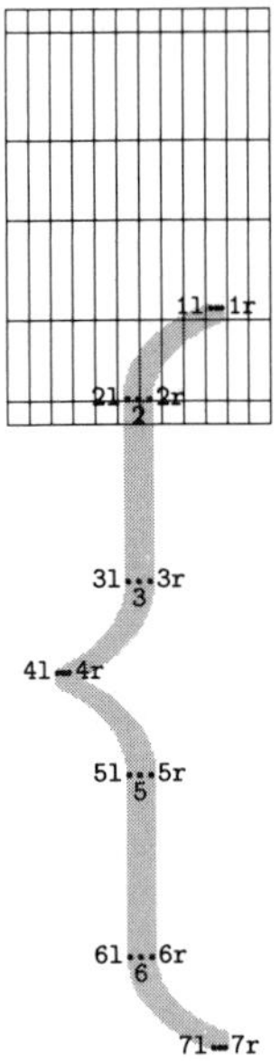
1l 1r
2l 2r
2
3l 3r
3
4l 4r
5l 5r
5
6l 6r
6
7l 7r

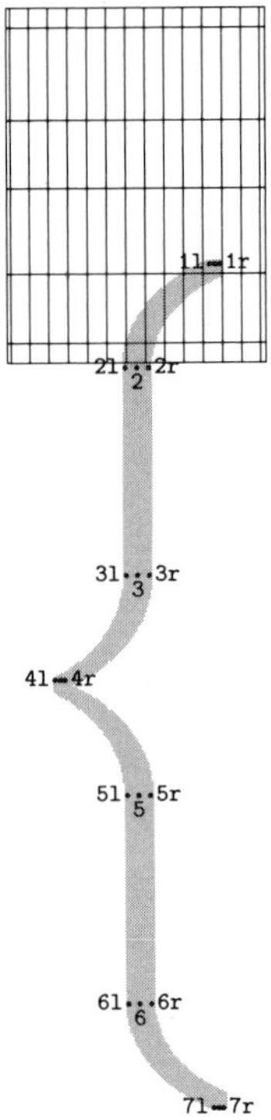
1l 1r
2l 2r
2
3l 3r
3
4l 4r
5l 5r
5
6l 6r
6
7l 7r

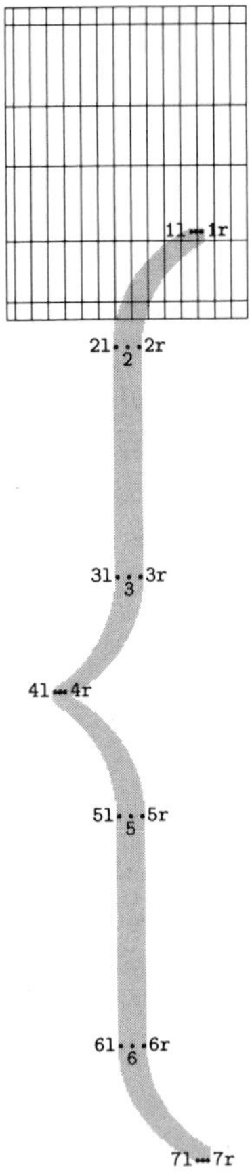
1l 1r
2l 2r
2
3l 3r
3
4l 4r
5l 5r
5
6l 6r
6
7l 7r

```
cmchar "\big left curly brace";
```
beginchar(oct "010", $9u^\#$, *rule_thickness*$^\#$, $2dh^\# - rule\_thickness^\#$);
adjust_fit$(.75u^\#, .75u^\#)$; *left_curly(hair, stem)*; **endchar**;

```
cmchar "\Big left curly brace";
```
beginchar(oct "156", $10u^\#$, *rule_thickness*$^\#$, $3dh^\# - rule\_thickness^\#$);
adjust_fit$(u^\#, u^\#)$; *left_curly(rule_thickness, .5[stem, bold])*; **endchar**;

```
cmchar "\bigg left curly brace";
```
beginchar(oct "032", $11u^\#$, *rule_thickness*$^\#$, $4dh^\# - rule\_thickness^\#$);
adjust_fit$(1.25u^\#, 1.25u^\#)$; *left_curly(rule_thickness + .2dw, bold)*; **endchar**;

```
cmchar "\Bigg left curly brace";
```
beginchar(oct "050", $11.5u^\#$, *rule_thickness*$^\#$, $5dh^\# - rule\_thickness^\#$);
adjust_fit$(1.5u^\#, 1.5u^\#)$; *left_curly(rule_thickness + .4dw, bold + dw)*; **endchar**;

---

def *left_curly*(**expr** *min_breadth, max_breadth*) =
  pickup *fine.nib*;
  forsuffixes \$ = 1, 1', 4, 4', 7, 7': $pos_\$$(hround *min_breadth*, 0); **endfor**
  forsuffixes \$ = 2, 3, 5, 6: $pos_\$$(hround *max_breadth*, 0); **endfor**
  $x_2 = x_3 = x_5 = x_6;$ $x_1 = x_{1'} = x_7 = x_{7'} = w - x_4 = w - x_{4'};$
  lft $x_{4l} =$ hround$(1.5u - .5min\_breadth);$ *lft* $x_{2l} =$ hround$(.5w - .5max\_breadth);$
  top $y_1 = h;$ *bot* $y_7 = 1 - d;$ $.5[y_4, y_{4'}] = .5[y_1, y_7] = .5[y_2, y_6] = .5[y_3, y_5];$
  $y_1 - y_2 = y_3 - y_4 = (y_1 - y_4)/4;$
  $y_1 - y_{1'} = y_4 - y_{4'} = y_{7'} - y_7 =$ vround$(min\_breadth - fine);$
  filldraw $z_{1l}\{3(x_{2l} - x_{1l}), y_2 - y_1\} \ldots z_{2l} --- z_{3l} \ldots \{3(x_{4l} - x_{3l}), y_4 - y_3\}z_{4l}$
    $-- z_{4'l}\{3(x_{5l} - x_{4l}), y_5 - y_{4'}\} \ldots z_{5l} --- z_{6l} \ldots \{3(x_{7l} - x_{6l}), y_7 - y_6\}z_{7l}$
    $-- z_{7r} -- z_{7'r}\{3(x_{6r} - x_{7r}), y_6 - y_{7'}\} \ldots z_{6r} --- z_{5r}$
    $\ldots \{3(x_{4r} - x_{5r}), .5[y_4, y_{4'}] - y_5\}.5[z_{4r}, z_{4'r}]\{3(x_{3r} - x_{4r}), y_3 - .5[y_4, y_{4'}]\}$
    $\ldots z_{3r} --- z_{2r} \ldots \{3(x_{1r} - x_{2r}), y_{1'} - y_2\}z_{1'r} -- z_{1r} --$ cycle;   % stroke
  penlabels$(1, 2, 3, 4, 5, 6, 7)$; **enddef**;
```
```

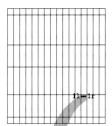

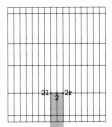

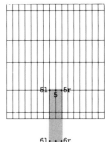

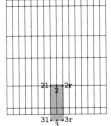

cmchar "Extensible left curly brace---top";
beginchar(oct "070", $12u^\#$, 0, $1.5dh^\#$);
adjust_fit($2u^\#$, $2u^\#$); **pickup** *fine.nib*;
numeric *min_breadth*; *min_breadth* = hround(*rule_thickness* + $.6dw$);
$pos_1(min\_breadth, 0)$; $pos_{1'}(min\_breadth, 0)$;
$pos_2(heavy\_rule\_thickness, 0)$; $pos_3(heavy\_rule\_thickness, 0)$;
$rt\ x_{1r} = rt\ x_{1'r} = $ hround($w - 1.5u + .5min\_breadth$);
$lft\ x_{2l} = lft\ x_{3l} = $ hround($.5w - .5heavy\_rule\_thickness$);
$top\ y_1 = h - 1$; $y_3 = -d - eps$; $y_2 = .5[y_1, y_3]$; $y_1 - y_{1'} = min\_breadth - fine$;
filldraw $z_{1l}\{3(x_{2l} - x_{1l}), y_2 - y_1\} \ldots z_{2l} \text{ --- } z_{3l}$
$\quad \text{ -- } z_{3r} \text{ --- } z_{2r} \ldots \{3(x_{1r} - x_{2r}), y_{1'} - y_2\}z_{1'r} \text{ -- } z_{1r} \text{ -- cycle};$ 　　　　% stroke
penlabels(1, 2, 3); **endchar**;

cmchar "Extensible left curly brace---bottom";
beginchar(oct "072", $12u^\#$, 0, $1.5dh^\#$);
adjust_fit($2u^\#$, $2u^\#$); **pickup** *fine.nib*;
numeric *min_breadth*; *min_breadth* = hround(*rule_thickness* + $.6dw$);
$pos_7(min\_breadth, 0)$; $pos_{7'}(min\_breadth, 0)$;
$pos_5(heavy\_rule\_thickness, 0)$; $pos_6(heavy\_rule\_thickness, 0)$;
$rt\ x_{7r} = rt\ x_{7'r} = $ hround($w - 1.5u + .5min\_breadth$);
$lft\ x_{5l} = lft\ x_{6l} = $ hround($.5w - .5heavy\_rule\_thickness$);
$y_5 = h + eps$; $bot\ y_7 = 1 - d$; $y_6 = .5[y_5, y_7]$; $y_{7'} - y_7 = min\_breadth - fine$;
filldraw $z_{5l} \text{ --- } z_{6l} \ldots \{3(x_{7l} - x_{6l}), y_7 - y_6\}z_{7l}$
$\quad \text{ -- } z_{7r} \text{ -- } z_{7'r}\{3(x_{6r} - x_{7r}), y_6 - y_{7'}\} \ldots z_{6r} \text{ --- } z_{5r} \text{ -- cycle};$ 　　　　% stroke
penlabels(5, 6, 7); **endchar**;

cmchar "Extensible left curly brace---middle";
beginchar(oct "074", $12u^\#$, 0, $3dh^\#$);
adjust_fit($2u^\#$, $2u^\#$); **pickup** *fine.nib*;
numeric *min_breadth*; *min_breadth* = hround(*rule_thickness* + $.6dw$);
$pos_4(min\_breadth, 0)$; $pos_{4'}(min\_breadth, 0)$;
forsuffixes \$ = 2, 3, 5, 6: $pos_{\$}(heavy\_rule\_thickness, 0)$; **endfor**
$lft\ x_{4l} = lft\ x_{4'l} = $ hround($1.5u - .5min\_breadth$);
$x_2 = x_3 = x_5 = x_6$; $lft\ x_{2l} = $ hround($.5w - .5heavy\_rule\_thickness$);
$y_2 = h + eps$; $y_6 = -d - eps$; $.5[y_4, y_{4'}] = .5[y_2, y_6] = .5[y_3, y_5]$;
$y_3 - y_4 = (y_2 - y_6)/4$; $y_4 - y_{4'} = min\_breadth - fine$;
filldraw $z_{2l} \text{ --- } z_{3l} \ldots \{3(x_{4l} - x_{3l}), y_4 - y_3\}z_{4l}$
$\quad \text{ -- } z_{4'l}\{3(x_{5l} - x_{4l}), y_5 - y_{4'}\} \ldots z_{5l} \text{ --- } z_{6l} \text{ -- } z_{6r} \text{ --- } z_{5r}$
$\quad \ldots \{3(x_{4r} - x_{5r}), .5[y_4, y_{4'}] - y_5\}.5[z_{4r}, z_{4'r}]\{3(x_{3r} - x_{4r}), y_3 - .5[y_4, y_{4'}]\}$
$\quad \ldots z_{3r} \text{ --- } z_{2r} \text{ -- cycle};$ 　　　　% stroke
penlabels(2, 3, 4, 5, 6); **endchar**;

cmchar "Extensible curly brace---extension module";
beginchar(oct "076", $12u^\#$, 0, $.5dh^\#$);
adjust_fit($2u^\#$, $2u^\#$); **pickup** *fine.nib*;
$pos_2(heavy\_rule\_thickness, 0)$; $pos_3(heavy\_rule\_thickness, 0)$;
$lft\ x_{2l} = lft\ x_{3l} = $ hround($.5w - .5heavy\_rule\_thickness$); $y_2 = h + eps$; $y_3 = -d - eps$;
filldraw stroke $z_{2e} \text{ -- } z_{3e}$; 　　　　% stem
penlabels(2, 3); **endchar**;

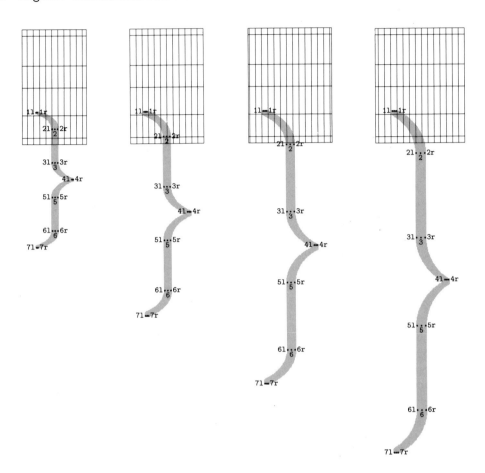

cmchar "\big right curly brace";
beginchar(oct "011", $9u^\#$, $rule\_thickness^\#$, $2dh^\# - rule\_thickness^\#$);
adjust_fit($.75u^\#$, $.75u^\#$); $right\_curly(hair, stem)$; **endchar**;

cmchar "\Big right curly brace";
beginchar(oct "157", $10u^\#$, $rule\_thickness^\#$, $3dh^\# - rule\_thickness^\#$);
adjust_fit($u^\#$, $u^\#$); $right\_curly(rule\_thickness, .5[stem, bold])$; **endchar**;

cmchar "\bigg right curly brace";
beginchar(oct "033", $11u^\#$, $rule\_thickness^\#$, $4dh^\# - rule\_thickness^\#$);
adjust_fit($1.25u^\#$, $1.25u^\#$); $right\_curly(rule\_thickness + .2dw, bold)$; **endchar**;

cmchar "\Bigg right curly brace";
beginchar(oct "051", $11.5u^\#$, $rule\_thickness^\#$, $5dh^\# - rule\_thickness^\#$);
adjust_fit($1.5u^\#$, $1.5u^\#$); $right\_curly(rule\_thickness + .4dw, bold + dw)$; **endchar**;

---

def $right\_curly$(**expr** $min\_breadth$, $max\_breadth$) =
  pickup $fine.nib$;
  forsuffixes $\$ = 1, 1', 4, 4', 7, 7'$: $pos_\$$(hround $min\_breadth$, 0); **endfor**
  forsuffixes $\$ = 2, 3, 5, 6$: $pos_\$$(hround $max\_breadth$, 0); **endfor**
  $x_2 = x_3 = x_5 = x_6$; $x_1 = x_{1'} = x_7 = x_{7'} = w - x_4 = w - x_{4'}$;
  $lft\ x_{1l}$ = hround($1.5u - .5min\_breadth$); $lft\ x_{2l}$ = hround($.5w - .5max\_breadth$);
  $top\ y_1 = h$; $bot\ y_7 = 1 - d$; $.5[y_4, y_{4'}] = .5[y_1, y_7] = .5[y_2, y_6] = .5[y_3, y_5]$;
  $y_1 - y_2 = y_3 - y_4 = (y_1 - y_4)/4$;
  $y_1 - y_{1'} = y_4 - y_{4'} = y_{7'} - y_7 = $ vround($min\_breadth - fine$);
  filldraw $z_{1r}\{3(x_{2r} - x_{1r}), y_2 - y_1\} \dots z_{2r} \text{ --- } z_{3r} \dots \{3(x_{4r} - x_{3r}), y_4 - y_3\}z_{4r}$
    $\text{ -- } z_{4'r}\{3(x_{5r} - x_{4r}), y_5 - y_{4'}\} \dots z_{5r} \text{ --- } z_{6r} \dots \{3(x_{7r} - x_{6r}), y_7 - y_6\}z_{7r}$
    $\text{ -- } z_{7l} \text{ -- } z_{7'l}\{3(x_{6l} - x_{7l}), y_6 - y_{7'}\} \dots z_{6l} \text{ --- } z_{5l}$
    $\dots \{3(x_{4l} - x_{5l}), .5[y_4, y_{4'}] - y_5\}.5[z_{4l}, z_{4'l}]\{3(x_{3l} - x_{4l}), y_3 - .5[y_4, y_{4'}]\}$
    $\dots z_{3l} \text{ --- } z_{2l} \dots \{3(x_{1l} - x_{2l}), y_{1'} - y_2\}z_{1'l} \text{ -- } z_{1l} \text{ -- }$ cycle;   % stroke
  penlabels(1, 2, 3, 4, 5, 6, 7); **enddef**;

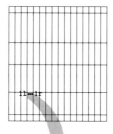

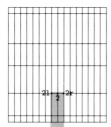

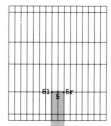

cmchar "Extensible right curly brace---top";
beginchar(oct "071", $12u^\#$, 0, $1.5dh^\#$);
adjust_fit($2u^\#$, $2u^\#$); **pickup** *fine.nib*;
numeric *min_breadth*; *min_breadth* = hround(*rule_thickness* + $.6dw$);
pos_1(*min_breadth*, 0); $pos_{1'}$(*min_breadth*, 0);
pos_2(*heavy_rule_thickness*, 0); pos_3(*heavy_rule_thickness*, 0);
lft x_{1l} = *lft* $x_{1'l}$ = hround($1.5u - .5min\_breadth$);
lft x_{2l} = *lft* x_{3l} = hround($.5w - .5heavy\_rule\_thickness$);
top $y_1 = h - 1$; $y_3 = -d - eps$; $y_2 = .5[y_1, y_3]$; $y_1 - y_{1'} = min\_breadth - fine$;
filldraw $z_{1r}\{3(x_{2r} - x_{1r}), y_2 - y_1\} \ldots z_{2r}$ --- z_{3r}
    -- z_{3l} --- $z_{2l} \ldots \{3(x_{1l} - x_{2l}), y_{1'} - y_2\}z_{1'l}$ -- z_{1l} -- cycle;   % stroke
penlabels(1, 2, 3); **endchar**;

cmchar "Extensible right curly brace---bottom";
beginchar(oct "073", $12u^\#$, 0, $1.5dh^\#$);
adjust_fit($2u^\#$, $2u^\#$); **pickup** *fine.nib*;
numeric *min_breadth*; *min_breadth* = hround(*rule_thickness* + $.6dw$);
pos_7(*min_breadth*, 0); $pos_{7'}$(*min_breadth*, 0);
pos_5(*heavy_rule_thickness*, 0); pos_6(*heavy_rule_thickness*, 0);
lft x_{7l} = *lft* $x_{7'l}$ = hround($1.5u - .5min\_breadth$);
lft x_{5l} = *lft* x_{6l} = hround($.5w - .5heavy\_rule\_thickness$);
$y_5 = h + eps$; *bot* $y_7 = 1 - d$; $y_6 = .5[y_5, y_7]$; $y_{7'} - y_7 = min\_breadth - fine$;
filldraw z_{5r} --- $z_{6r} \ldots \{3(x_{7r} - x_{6r}), y_7 - y_6\}z_{7r}$
    -- z_{7l} -- $z_{7'l}\{3(x_{6l} - x_{7l}), y_6 - y_{7'}\} \ldots z_{6l}$ --- z_{5l} -- cycle;   % stroke
penlabels(5, 6, 7); **endchar**;

cmchar "Extensible right curly brace---middle";
beginchar(oct "075", $12u^\#$, 0, $3dh^\#$);
adjust_fit($2u^\#$, $2u^\#$); **pickup** *fine.nib*;
numeric *min_breadth*; *min_breadth* = hround(*rule_thickness* + $.6dw$);
pos_4(*min_breadth*, 0); $pos_{4'}$(*min_breadth*, 0);
forsuffixes $\$ = 2, 3, 5, 6$: $pos_\$$(*heavy_rule_thickness*, 0); **endfor**
rt x_{4r} = *rt* $x_{4'r}$ = hround($w - 1.5u + .5min\_breadth$);
$x_2 = x_3 = x_5 = x_6$; *lft* x_{2l} = hround($.5w - .5heavy\_rule\_thickness$);
$y_2 = h + eps$; $y_6 = -d - eps$; $.5[y_4, y_{4'}] = .5[y_2, y_6] = .5[y_3, y_5]$;
$y_3 - y_4 = (y_2 - y_6)/4$; $y_4 - y_{4'} = min\_breadth - fine$;
filldraw z_{2r} --- $z_{3r} \ldots \{3(x_{4r} - x_{3r}), y_4 - y_3\}z_{4r}$
    -- $z_{4'r}\{3(x_{5r} - x_{4r}), y_5 - y_{4'}\} \ldots z_{5r}$ --- z_{6r} -- z_{6l} --- z_{5l}
    $\ldots \{3(x_{4l} - x_{5l}), .5[y_4, y_{4'}] - y_5\}.5[z_{4l}, z_{4'l}]\{3(x_{3l} - x_{4l}), y_3 - .5[y_4, y_{4'}]\}$
    $\ldots z_{3l}$ --- z_{2l} -- cycle;   % stroke
penlabels(2, 3, 4, 5, 6); **endchar**;

Most Printing-houses are provided with Middles and Corners,
which answer all the purposes of Braces,
and are preferable to those made of Brass rules.

— PHILIP LUCKOMBE, *The History and Art of Printing* (1770)

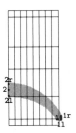

cmchar "Horizontal curly brace tip---down and left";
beginchar(oct "172", $.75dh^\#$, $3rule\_thickness^\#$, 0);
adjust_fit$(0, 0)$; **pickup** *fine.nib*;
numeric *min_breadth*; *min_breadth* = vround(*rule_thickness* + $.6dw$);
$pos_1(min\_breadth, 90)$; $pos_{1'}(min\_breadth, 90)$;
$pos_2(heavy\_rule\_thickness, 90)$;
bot $y_{2l} = 0$; *bot* $y_{1l} =$ *bot* $y_{1'l} =$ vround($y_2 - 4.5u - .5min\_breadth$);
$.5[x_1, x_{1'}] = -eps$; $x_2 = w + shrink\_fit + eps$; $x_{1'} - x_1 = min\_breadth - fine$;
filldraw $z_{1r}\{x_2 - x_1, 3(y_{2r} - y_{1r})\} \ldots \{right\}z_{2r}$
   -- $z_{2l}\{left\} \ldots \{x_{1'} - x_2, 3(y_1 - y_2)\}z_{1'l}$ -- z_{1l} -- cycle;   % stroke
penlabels$(1, 2)$; **endchar**;

cmchar "Horizontal curly brace tip---down and right";
beginchar(oct "173", $.75dh^\#$, $3rule\_thickness^\#$, 0);
adjust_fit$(0, 0)$; **pickup** *fine.nib*;
numeric *min_breadth*; *min_breadth* = vround(*rule_thickness* + $.6dw$);
$pos_1(min\_breadth, 90)$; $pos_{1'}(min\_breadth, 90)$;
$pos_2(heavy\_rule\_thickness, 90)$;
bot $y_{2l} = 0$; *bot* $y_{1l} =$ *bot* $y_{1'l} =$ vround($y_2 - 4.5u - .5min\_breadth$);
$.5[x_1, x_{1'}] = w + shrink\_fit + eps$; $x_2 = -eps$; $x_1 - x_{1'} = min\_breadth - fine$;
filldraw $z_{1r}\{x_2 - x_1, 3(y_{2r} - y_{1r})\} \ldots \{left\}z_{2r}$
   -- $z_{2l}\{right\} \ldots \{x_{1'} - x_2, 3(y_1 - y_2)\}z_{1'l}$ -- z_{1l} -- cycle;   % stroke
penlabels$(1, 2)$; **endchar**;

cmchar "Horizontal curly brace tip---up and left";
beginchar(oct "174", $.75dh^\#$, $3rule\_thickness^\#$, 0);
adjust_fit$(0, 0)$; **pickup** *fine.nib*;
numeric *min_breadth*; *min_breadth* = vround(*rule_thickness* + $.6dw$);
$pos_1(min\_breadth, 90)$; $pos_{1'}(min\_breadth, 90)$;
$pos_2(heavy\_rule\_thickness, 90)$;
bot $y_{2l} = 0$; *top* $y_{1r} =$ *top* $y_{1'r} =$ vround($y_2 + 4.5u + .5min\_breadth$);
$.5[x_1, x_{1'}] = -eps$; $x_2 = w + shrink\_fit + eps$; $x_{1'} - x_1 = min\_breadth - fine$;
filldraw $z_{1l}\{x_2 - x_1, 3(y_{2l} - y_{1l})\} \ldots \{right\}z_{2l}$
   -- $z_{2r}\{left\} \ldots \{x_{1'} - x_2, 3(y_1 - y_2)\}z_{1'r}$ -- z_{1r} -- cycle;   % stroke
penlabels$(1, 2)$; **endchar**;

cmchar "Horizontal curly brace tip---up and right";
beginchar(oct "175", $.75dh^\#$, $3rule\_thickness^\#$, 0);
adjust_fit$(0, 0)$; **pickup** *fine.nib*;
numeric *min_breadth*; *min_breadth* = vround(*rule_thickness* + $.6dw$);
$pos_1(min\_breadth, 90)$; $pos_{1'}(min\_breadth, 90)$;
$pos_2(heavy\_rule\_thickness, 90)$;
bot $y_{2l} = 0$; *top* $y_{1r} =$ *top* $y_{1'r} =$ vround($y_2 + 4.5u + .5min\_breadth$);
$.5[x_1, x_{1'}] = w + shrink\_fit + eps$; $x_2 = -eps$; $x_{1'} - x_1 = min\_breadth - fine$;
filldraw $z_{1l}\{x_2 - x_1, 3(y_{2l} - y_{1l})\} \ldots \{left\}z_{2l}$
   -- $z_{2r}\{right\} \ldots \{x_{1'} - x_2, 3(y_1 - y_2)\}z_{1'r}$ -- z_{1r} -- cycle;   % stroke
penlabels$(1, 2)$; **endchar**;

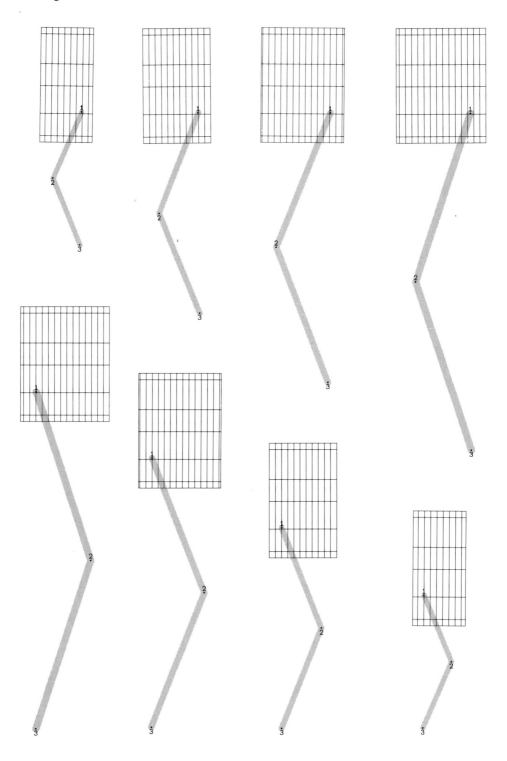

cmchar "\big left angle bracket";
beginchar(oct "012", $7u^\#$, *rule_thickness*$^\#$, $2dh^\# - $ *rule_thickness*$^\#$);
adjust_fit($.75u^\#$, $.75u^\#$); *left_angle*(*rule_thickness*); **endchar**;

cmchar "\Big left angle bracket";
beginchar(oct "104", $9u^\#$, *rule_thickness*$^\#$, $3dh^\# - $ *rule_thickness*$^\#$);
adjust_fit($u^\#$, $u^\#$); *left_angle*($.25[$*rule_thickness*, *stem*$]$); **endchar**;

cmchar "\bigg left angle bracket";
beginchar(oct "034", $11u^\#$, *rule_thickness*$^\#$, $4dh^\# - $ *rule_thickness*$^\#$);
adjust_fit($1.25u^\#$, $1.25u^\#$); *left_angle*($.5[$*rule_thickness*, *stem*$]$); **endchar**;

cmchar "\Bigg left angle bracket";
beginchar(oct "052", $11.5u^\#$, *rule_thickness*$^\#$, $5dh^\# - $ *rule_thickness*$^\#$);
adjust_fit($1.5u^\#$, $1.5u^\#$); *left_angle*($.75[$*rule_thickness*, *stem*$]$); **endchar**;

cmchar "\big right angle bracket";
beginchar(oct "013", $7u^\#$, *rule_thickness*$^\#$, $2dh^\# - $ *rule_thickness*$^\#$);
adjust_fit($.75u^\#$, $.75u^\#$); *right_angle*(*rule_thickness*); **endchar**;

cmchar "\Big right angle bracket";
beginchar(oct "105", $9u^\#$, *rule_thickness*$^\#$, $3dh^\# - $ *rule_thickness*$^\#$);
adjust_fit($u^\#$, $u^\#$); *right_angle*($.25[$*rule_thickness*, *stem*$]$); **endchar**;

cmchar "\bigg right angle bracket";
beginchar(oct "035", $11u^\#$, *rule_thickness*$^\#$, $4dh^\# - $ *rule_thickness*$^\#$);
adjust_fit($1.25u^\#$, $1.25u^\#$); *right_angle*($.5[$*rule_thickness*, *stem*$]$); **endchar**;

cmchar "\Bigg right angle bracket";
beginchar(oct "053", $11.5u^\#$, *rule_thickness*$^\#$, $5dh^\# - $ *rule_thickness*$^\#$);
adjust_fit($1.5u^\#$, $1.5u^\#$); *right_angle*($.75[$*rule_thickness*, *stem*$]$); **endchar**;

---

def *left_angle*(**expr** *breadth*) $=$
  pickup pencircle scaled *breadth*;
  $x_1 = x_3 = good.x(w - u) + eps$; lft $x_2 = $ hround $u - eps$;
  top $y_1 = h + eps$; $.5[y_1, y_3] = y_2 = good.y$ $.5[-d + eps, h]$;
  draw $z_1 -- z_2 -- z_3$;   % diagonals
  labels$(1, 2, 3)$; **enddef**;

def *right_angle*(**expr** *breadth*) $=$
  pickup pencircle scaled *breadth*;
  $x_1 = x_3 = good.x$ $u - eps$; rt $x_2 = $ hround$(w - u) + eps$;
  top $y_1 = h + eps$; $.5[y_1, y_3] = y_2 = good.y$ $.5[-d + eps, h]$;
  draw $z_1 -- z_2 -- z_3$;   % diagonals
  labels$(1, 2, 3)$; **enddef**;

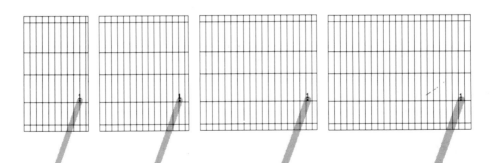

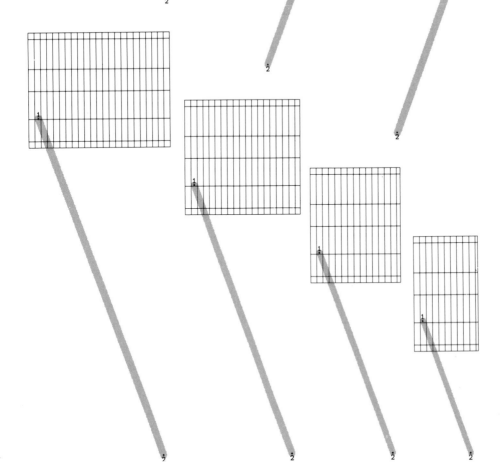

cmchar "\big slash";
beginchar(oct "016", $10.4u^\#$, $rule\_thickness^\#$, $2dh^\# - rule\_thickness^\#$);
$big\_slash(rule\_thickness + .2dw)$; **endchar**;

cmchar "\Big slash";
beginchar(oct "056", $14.6u^\#$, $rule\_thickness^\#$, $3dh^\# - rule\_thickness^\#$);
$big\_slash(rule\_thickness + .6dw)$; **endchar**;

cmchar "\bigg slash";
beginchar(oct "036", $18.8u^\#$, $rule\_thickness^\#$, $4dh^\# - rule\_thickness^\#$);
$big\_slash(rule\_thickness + dw)$; **endchar**;

cmchar "\Bigg slash";
beginchar(oct "054", $23u^\#$, $rule\_thickness^\#$, $5dh^\# - rule\_thickness^\#$);
$big\_slash(rule\_thickness + 1.5dw)$; **endchar**;

cmchar "\big backslash";
beginchar(oct "017", $10.4u^\#$, $rule\_thickness^\#$, $2dh^\# - rule\_thickness^\#$);
$big\_blash(rule\_thickness + .2dw)$; **endchar**;

cmchar "\Big backslash";
beginchar(oct "057", $14.6u^\#$, $rule\_thickness^\#$, $3dh^\# - rule\_thickness^\#$);
$big\_blash(rule\_thickness + .6dw)$; **endchar**;

cmchar "\bigg backslash";
beginchar(oct "037", $18.8u^\#$, $rule\_thickness^\#$, $4dh^\# - rule\_thickness^\#$);
$big\_blash(rule\_thickness + dw)$; **endchar**;

cmchar "\Bigg backslash";
beginchar(oct "055", $23u^\#$, $rule\_thickness^\#$, $5dh^\# - rule\_thickness^\#$);
$big\_blash(rule\_thickness + 1.5dw)$; **endchar**;

---

def $big\_slash(\textbf{expr } breadth) =$
    adjust_fit$(-letter\_fit^\#, -letter\_fit^\#)$; **pickup pencircle** scaled $breadth$;
    $rt\ x_1 = \text{hround}(w - u)$; $lft\ x_2 = \text{hround } u$; $top\ y_1 = h + eps$; $bot\ y_2 = 1 - d - eps$;
    draw $z_1 \text{ -- } z_2$;   % diagonal
    labels$(1, 2)$; **enddef**;

def $big\_blash(\textbf{expr } breadth) =$
    adjust_fit$(-letter\_fit^\#, -letter\_fit^\#)$; **pickup pencircle** scaled $breadth$;
    $lft\ x_1 = \text{hround } u$; $rt\ x_2 = \text{hround}(w - u)$; $top\ y_1 = h + eps$; $bot\ y_2 = 1 - d - eps$;
    draw $z_1 \text{ -- } z_2$;   % diagonal
    labels$(1, 2)$; **enddef**;

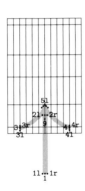

cmchar "Extensible vertical arrow--top";
beginchar(oct "170", $12u^\#$, 0, $dh^\#$);
adjust_fit$(0, 0)$; **pickup** *crisp.nib*;
numeric *thickness*, *barr*;
thickness = hround(*rule_thickness* + $.2dw$); *barr* = Vround $.6[bar, thickness]$;
$pos_1(thickness, 0)$; $pos_2(thickness, 0)$; $pos_3(barr, 90)$; $pos_4(barr, 90)$;
lft x_{1l} = hround$(.5w - .5thickness)$; $y_1 = -d - eps$;
$x_0 = x_1 = x_2$; *top* $y_0 = h$; $x_0 - x_3 = x_4 - x_0 = 4u + eps$;
$y_3 = y_4 = y_0 - .29asc\_height - eps$;
$pos_5(barr, \mathrm{angle}(z_4 - z_0))$; $z_{5l} = z_0$;
$pos_6(barr, \mathrm{angle}(z_3 - z_0))$; $z_{6l} = z_0$;
$z_9 = .381966[.5[z_3, z_4], z_0]$;
numeric t; **path** p; $p = z_{4l}\{z_9 - z_4\} \ldots z_{6r}$;
$t = \mathrm{xpart}(p\ \mathrm{intersectiontimes}\ ((x_{2r}, -d)\ \texttt{--}\ (x_{2r}, h)))$; $y_2 = \mathrm{ypart}$ **point** t **of** p;
filldraw $z_0 \ldots \{z_4 - z_9\}z_{4r}\ \texttt{--}\ \mathbf{subpath}(0, t)\ \mathbf{of}\ (z_{4l}\{z_9 - z_4\} \ldots z_{6r})$
    $\texttt{--}\ z_{2r}\ \texttt{---}\ z_{1r}\ \texttt{--}\ z_{1l}\ \texttt{---}\ z_{2l}\ \texttt{--}\ \mathbf{subpath}(t, 0)\ \mathbf{of}\ (z_{3l}\{z_9 - z_3\} \ldots z_{5r})$
    $\texttt{--}\ z_{3r}\{z_9 - z_3\} \ldots z_0\ \&\ \mathbf{cycle}$;   % arrowhead and stem
penlabels$(0, 1, 2, 3, 4, 5, 6, 9)$; **endchar**;

cmchar "Extensible vertical arrow--bottom";
beginchar(oct "171", $12u^\#$, 0, $dh^\#$);
adjust_fit$(0, 0)$; **pickup** *crisp.nib*;
numeric *thickness*, *barr*;
thickness = hround(*rule_thickness* + $.2dw$); *barr* = Vround $.6[bar, thickness]$;
$pos_1(thickness, 0)$; $pos_2(thickness, 0)$; $pos_3(barr, 90)$; $pos_4(barr, 90)$;
lft x_{1l} = hround$(.5w - .5thickness)$; $y_1 = h + eps$;
$x_0 = x_1 = x_2$; *bot* $y_0 = -d$; $x_0 - x_3 = x_4 - x_0 = 4u + eps$;
$y_3 = y_4 = y_0 + .29asc\_height + eps$;
$pos_5(barr, \mathrm{angle}(z_4 - z_0))$; $z_{5l} = z_0$;
$pos_6(barr, \mathrm{angle}(z_3 - z_0))$; $z_{6l} = z_0$;
$z_9 = .381966[.5[z_3, z_4], z_0]$;
numeric t; **path** p; $p = z_{4r}\{z_9 - z_4\} \ldots z_{6r}$;
$t = \mathrm{xpart}(p\ \mathrm{intersectiontimes}\ ((x_{2r}, -d)\ \texttt{--}\ (x_{2r}, h)))$; $y_2 = \mathrm{ypart}$ **point** t **of** p;
filldraw $z_0 \ldots \{z_4 - z_9\}z_{4l}\ \texttt{--}\ \mathbf{subpath}(0, t)\ \mathbf{of}\ (z_{4r}\{z_9 - z_4\} \ldots z_{6r})$
    $\texttt{--}\ z_{2r}\ \texttt{---}\ z_{1r}\ \texttt{--}\ z_{1l}\ \texttt{---}\ z_{2l}\ \texttt{--}\ \mathbf{subpath}(t, 0)\ \mathbf{of}\ (z_{3r}\{z_9 - z_3\} \ldots z_{5r})$
    $\texttt{--}\ z_{3l}\{z_9 - z_3\} \ldots z_0\ \&\ \mathbf{cycle}$;   % arrowhead and stem
penlabels$(0, 1, 2, 3, 4, 5, 6, 9)$; **endchar**;

"Extensible vertical arrow--extension module";
beginchar(oct "077", $12u^\#$, 0, $dh^\#$);
adjust_fit$(0, 0)$; **pickup** *crisp.nib*;
numeric *thickness*; *thickness* = hround(*rule_thickness* + $.2dw$);
$pos_1(thickness, 0)$; $pos_2(thickness, 0)$;
lft x_{1l} = hround$(.5w - .5thickness)$; $x_2 = x_1$; $y_1 = h + 1 + eps$; $y_2 = -d - 1 - eps$;
filldraw stroke $z_{1e}\ \texttt{--}\ z_{2e}$;   % stem
penlabels$(1, 2)$; **endchar**;

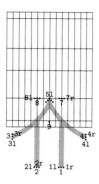

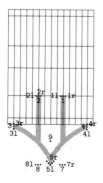

cmchar "Extensible double vertical arrow--top";
beginchar(oct "176", $14u^\#$, 0, $dh^\#$);
adjust_fit$(0, 0)$; **pickup** *crisp.nib*;
numeric *thickness*; *thickness* $=$ Vround($rule\_thickness + .2dw$);
$pos_1(thickness, 0)$; $pos_2(thickness, 0)$; $pos_7(thickness, 0)$; $pos_8(thickness, 0)$;
$y_1 = y_2 = -d - eps$; $y_7 = y_8 = h$; top $y_0 = h + eps$; $x_1 = x_7$; $x_2 = x_8$;
rt $x_{1r} =$ hround$(.5w + 2u + .5thickness)$; $.5[x_1, x_2] = x_0 = good.x\ .5w$;
filldraw stroke z_{1e} -- z_{7e}; **filldraw stroke** z_{2e} -- z_{8e};   % bars
$pos_3(thickness, 90)$; $pos_4(thickness, 90)$;
$x_2 - x_3 = x_4 - x_1 = 4u + eps$; $y_3 = y_4 = y_0 - .48asc\_height - eps$;
$pos_5(thickness, \text{angle}(z_4 - z_0))$; $z_{5l} = z_0$;
$pos_6(thickness, \text{angle}(z_3 - z_0))$; $z_{6l} = z_0$; $z_9 = .381966[.5[z_3, z_4], z_0]$;
erase filldraw $z_0 \ .. \ \{z_3 - z_9\}z_3$ -- (x_3, h)
  -- (x_4, h) -- $z_4\{z_9 - z_4\} \ .. \ z_0$ **& cycle**;   % erase excess
numeric t; **path** p; $p = z_{4l}\{z_9 - z_4\} \ .. \ z_{6r}$;
$t =$ xpart(p intersectiontimes $((x_0, -d)$ -- $(x_0, h)))$;
filldraw $z_0 \ .. \ \{z_4 - z_9\}z_{4r}$ -- **subpath**$(0, t)$ **of** $(z_{4l}\{z_9 - z_4\} \ .. \ z_{6r})$
  -- **subpath**$(t, 0)$ **of** $(z_{3l}\{z_9 - z_3\} \ .. \ z_{5r})$ -- $z_{3r}\{z_9 - z_3\} \ .. \ z_0$ **& cycle**; % arrowhead
penlabels$(0, 1, 2, 3, 4, 5, 6, 7, 8, 9)$; **endchar**;

cmchar "Extensible double vertical arrow--bottom";
beginchar(oct "177", $14u^\#$, 0, $dh^\#$);
adjust_fit$(0, 0)$; **pickup** *crisp.nib*;
numeric *thickness*; *thickness* $=$ Vround($rule\_thickness + .2dw$);
$pos_1(thickness, 0)$; $pos_2(thickness, 0)$; $pos_7(thickness, 0)$; $pos_8(thickness, 0)$;
$y_1 = y_2 = h + eps$; $y_7 = y_8 = -d$; bot $y_0 = -d - eps$; $x_1 = x_7$; $x_2 = x_8$;
rt $x_{1r} =$ hround$(.5w + 2u + .5thickness)$; $.5[x_1, x_2] = x_0 = good.x\ .5w$;
filldraw stroke z_{1e} -- z_{7e}; **filldraw stroke** z_{2e} -- z_{8e};   % bars
$pos_3(thickness, 90)$; $pos_4(thickness, 90)$;
$x_2 - x_3 = x_4 - x_1 = 4u + eps$; $y_3 = y_4 = y_0 + .48asc\_height - eps$;
$pos_5(thickness, \text{angle}(z_4 - z_0))$; $z_{5l} = z_0$;
$pos_6(thickness, \text{angle}(z_3 - z_0))$; $z_{6l} = z_0$; $z_9 = .381966[.5[z_3, z_4], z_0]$;
erase filldraw $z_0 \ .. \ \{z_3 - z_9\}z_3$ -- $(x_3, -d)$
  -- $(x_4, -d)$ -- $z_4\{z_9 - z_4\} \ .. \ z_0$ **& cycle**;   % erase excess
numeric t; **path** p; $p = z_{4r}\{z_9 - z_4\} \ .. \ z_{6r}$;
$t =$ xpart(p intersectiontimes $((x_0, -d)$ -- $(x_0, h)))$;
filldraw $z_0 \ .. \ \{z_4 - z_9\}z_{4l}$ -- **subpath**$(0, t)$ **of** $(z_{4r}\{z_9 - z_4\} \ .. \ z_{6r})$
  -- **subpath**$(t, 0)$ **of** $(z_{3r}\{z_9 - z_3\} \ .. \ z_{5r})$ -- $z_{3l}\{z_9 - z_3\} \ .. \ z_0$ **& cycle**; % arrowhead
penlabels$(0, 1, 2, 3, 4, 5, 6, 7, 8, 9)$; **endchar**;

"Extensible double vertical arrow--extension module";
beginchar(oct "167", $14u^\#$, 0, $dh^\#$);
adjust_fit$(0, 0)$; **pickup** *crisp.nib*;
numeric *thickness*; *thickness* $=$ Vround($rule\_thickness + .2dw$);
$pos_1(thickness, 0)$; $pos_2(thickness, 0)$; $pos_7(thickness, 0)$; $pos_8(thickness, 0)$;
$y_1 = y_2 = h + 1 + eps$; $y_7 = y_8 = -d - 1 - eps$; $x_1 = x_7$; $x_2 = x_8$;
rt $x_{1r} =$ hround$(.5w + 2u + .5thickness)$; $.5[x_1, x_2] = good.x\ .5w$;
filldraw stroke z_{1e} -- z_{7e}; **filldraw stroke** z_{2e} -- z_{8e};   % bars
penlabels$(1, 2, 7, 8)$; **endchar**;

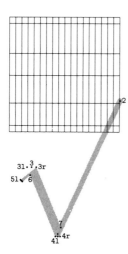

cmchar "\big radical sign";
beginchar(oct "160", $18u^\#$, $rule\_thickness^\#$, $2dh^\# - rule\_thickness^\#$);
big_sqrt; **endchar**;

cmchar "\Big radical sign";
beginchar(oct "161", $18u^\#$, $rule\_thickness^\#$, $3dh^\# - rule\_thickness^\#$);
big_sqrt; **endchar**;

cmchar "\bigg radical sign";
beginchar(oct "162", $18u^\#$, $rule\_thickness^\#$, $4dh^\# - rule\_thickness^\#$);
big_sqrt; **endchar**;

cmchar "\Bigg radical sign";
beginchar(oct "163", $18u^\#$, $rule\_thickness^\#$, $5dh^\# - rule\_thickness^\#$);
big_sqrt; **endchar**;

---

def $big\_sqrt =$
  adjust_fit$(0, -letter\_fit^\#)$; **pickup** $rule.nib$;
  $x_1 = good.x \; ^4/_9 w$; $\quad x_2 = good.x(w + .5)$; $\;\; bot \; y_1 = -d$; $\;\; bot \; y_2 = 0$;
  draw $z_1 \; \texttt{--} \; z_2$;   % diagonal
  pickup $crisp.nib$; $\;\; pos_3(\max(curve, rule\_thickness), 0)$;
  $x_{3l} = 1.5[x_2, x_1]$; $\;\; y_3 = .5[y_1, y_2]$;
  $pos_4(rule\_thickness, 0)$; $\;\; x_4 = x_1$; $\;\; bot \; y_4 = -d$;
  $pos_5(vair, -45)$; $\;\; x_{5l} = good.x(x_{3l} - u)$; $\;\; z_{5l} = whatever[z_{3r}, z_2]$;
  $z_6 = z_{5r} + whatever * (z_2 - z_{3r}) = whatever[z_{3l}, z_{4l}]$;
  $z_7 = whatever[z_1, z_2] = z_{3r} + whatever * (z_{4l} - z_{3l})$;
  filldraw $z_{5r} \; \texttt{--} \; z_6 \; \texttt{--} \; z_{4l} \; \texttt{--} \; z_4 \; \texttt{--} \; z_7 \; \texttt{--} \; z_{3r} \; \texttt{--} \; z_{5l} \; \texttt{--} \; \text{cycle}$;   % left diagonal and serif
  penlabels$(1, 2, 3, 4, 5, 6, 7)$; **enddef**;

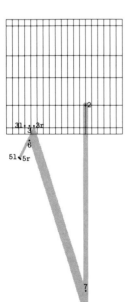

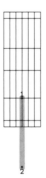

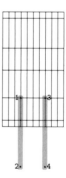

cmchar "Extensible radical sign---bottom";
beginchar(oct "164", $19u^\#$, 0, $3dh^\#$);
adjust_fit$(0, -letter\_fit^\#)$; **pickup** $rule.nib$;
$x_1 = x_2 = good.x(w - 6u)$; $bot\ y_1 = 1 - d$; $y_2 = h + eps$;
draw $z_1 \text{ -- } z_2$; % diagonal
pickup $crisp.nib$; $pos_3(\max(curve, rule\_thickness), 0)$;
$x_{3l} = good.x\ 3u$; $y_3 = .9[y_1, y_2]$;
$pos_4(rule\_thickness, 0)$; $x_4 = x_1$; $bot\ y_4 = -d$;
$pos_5(vair, -45)$; $x_{5l} = good.x(x_{3l} - u)$; $z_{5l} = whatever[z_{3r}, (x_2, body\_height)]$;
$z_6 = z_{5r} + whatever * ((x_2, body\_height) - z_{3r}) = whatever[z_{3l}, z_{4l}]$;
$z_7 = whatever[z_1, z_2] = z_{3r} + whatever * (z_{4l} - z_{3l})$;
filldraw $z_{5r} \text{ -- } z_6 \text{ -- } z_{4l} \text{ -- } z_4 \text{ -- } z_7 \text{ -- } z_{3r} \text{ -- } z_{5l} \text{ -- } \text{cycle}$; % left diagonal and serif
penlabels$(1, 2, 3, 4, 5, 6, 7)$; **endchar**;

cmchar "Extensible radical sign---extension module";
beginchar(oct "165", $19u^\#$, 0, $dh^\#$);
adjust_fit$(0, -letter\_fit^\#)$; **pickup** $rule.nib$;
$x_1 = x_2 = good.x(w - 6u)$; $y_1 = -d - eps$; $y_2 = h + eps$;
draw $z_1 \text{ -- } z_2$; % stem
labels$(1, 2)$; **endchar**;

cmchar "Extensible radical sign---top";
beginchar(oct "166", $19u^\#$, $rule\_thickness^\#$, $dh^\# - rule\_thickness^\#$);
adjust_fit$(0, -letter\_fit^\#)$; **pickup** $rule.nib$;
$x_1 = x_2 = good.x(w - 6u)$; $x_3 = good.x(w + .5)$; $y_1 = -d - eps$; $bot\ y_2 = bot\ y_3 = 0$;
draw $z_1 \text{ -- } z_2 \text{ -- } z_3$; % stem and link
labels$(1, 2, 3)$; **endchar**;

cmchar "Extensible vertical line---extension module";
beginchar(oct "014", $6u^\#$, 0, $dh^\#$);
adjust_fit$(0, 0)$; **pickup** **pencircle** scaled $(rule\_thickness + .2dw)$;
$x_1 = x_2 = good.x\ .5w$; $y_1 = eps$; $y_2 = -d - eps$;
draw $z_1 \text{ -- } z_2$; % stem
labels$(1, 2)$; **endchar**;

cmchar "Extensible double vertical line---extension module";
beginchar(oct "015", $10u^\#$, 0, $dh^\#$);
adjust_fit$(0, 0)$; **pickup** **pencircle** scaled $(rule\_thickness + .2dw)$;
$x_1 = x_2 = good.x\ .3w$; $x_3 = x_4 = w - x_1$; $y_1 = y_3 = eps$; $y_2 = y_4 = -d - eps$;
draw $z_1 \text{ -- } z_2$; **draw** $z_3 \text{ -- } z_4$; % stems
labels$(1, 2, 3, 4)$; **endchar**;

The program file `bigop.mf` makes pairs of "large operator" characters for math formulas. One of the operators is for `\textstyle` formulas, which are embedded in paragraphs; the other (larger) operator is for `\displaystyle` formulas, which are typeset on lines by themselves.

% This file contains pairs of large operators for math extension fonts.

% Each operator has a '`\textstyle`' form, for math in text,
% and a '`\displaystyle`' form, for displayed formulas.

% Character codes '106 – '141 are generated.

charlist oct "106": oct "107";   % square union signs
charlist oct "110": oct "111";   % contour integral signs
charlist oct "112": oct "113";   % circle-dot operators
charlist oct "114": oct "115";   % circle-plus operators
charlist oct "116": oct "117";   % circle-times operators
charlist oct "120": oct "130";   % summation signs
charlist oct "121": oct "131";   % product signs
charlist oct "122": oct "132";   % integral signs
charlist oct "123": oct "133";   % union signs
charlist oct "124": oct "134";   % intersection signs
charlist oct "125": oct "135";   % multiset union signs
charlist oct "126": oct "136";   % lattice infimum signs
charlist oct "127": oct "137";   % lattice supremum signs
charlist oct "140": oct "141";   % coproduct signs

cmchar "\textstyle square set union sign";
beginchar(oct "106", $15u^\#$, 0, $^{10}\!/_6 dh^\#$);
adjust_fit$(0, 0)$; **pickup pencircle** scaled *stem*;
lft $x_1 = $ hround u; $x_2 = x_1$; $x_4 = x_5 = w - x_1$;
top $y_1 = eps$; *bot* $y_2 = -d$; $y_4 = y_2$; $y_5 = y_1$;
draw $z_1 \text{ --- } z_2 \text{ --- } z_4 \text{ --- } z_5$;   % stems and bar
labels$(1, 2, 4, 5)$; **endchar**;

cmchar "\displaystyle square set union sign";
beginchar(oct "107", $20u^\#$, 0, $^{14}\!/_6 dh^\#$); **padded** $^1\!/_6 dh^\#$;
adjust_fit$(0, 0)$; **pickup pencircle** scaled *curve*;
lft $x_1 = $ hround u; $x_2 = x_1$; $x_4 = x_5 = w - x_1$;
top $y_1 = eps$; *bot* $y_2 = -d$; $y_4 = y_2$; $y_5 = y_1$;
draw $z_1 \text{ --- } z_2 \text{ --- } z_4 \text{ --- } z_5$;   % stems and bar
labels$(1, 2, 4, 5)$; **endchar**;

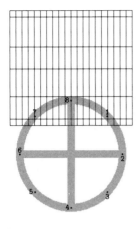
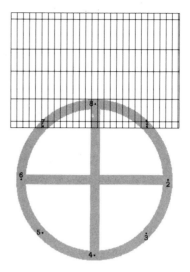
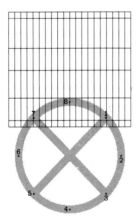
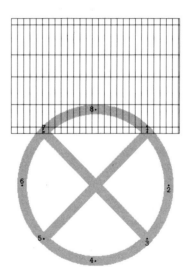

cmchar "\textstyle circle-plus operator";
beginchar(oct "114", $20u^\#$, 0, $^{10}/_6 dh^\#$);
adjust_fit(0, 0); **pickup pencircle** scaled *stem*;
lft x_6 = hround u; $x_2 = w - x_6$; *top* $y_8 = 0$; *bot* $y_4 = -d$;
circle_points; *draw_circle*;   % circle
draw z_2 -- z_6; **draw** z_4 -- z_8;   % plus
labels(1, 2, 3, 4, 5, 6, 7, 8); **endchar**;

cmchar "\displaystyle circle-plus operator";
beginchar(oct "115", $27.2u^\#$, 0, $^{14}/_6 dh^\#$); **padded** $^1/_6 dh^\#$;
adjust_fit(0, 0); **pickup pencircle** scaled *curve*;
lft x_6 = hround u; $x_2 = w - x_6$; *top* $y_8 = 0$; *bot* $y_4 = -d$;
circle_points; *draw_circle*;   % circle
draw z_2 -- z_6; **draw** z_4 -- z_8;   % plus
labels(1, 2, 3, 4, 5, 6, 7, 8); **endchar**;

cmchar "\textstyle circle-times operator";
beginchar(oct "116", $20u^\#$, 0, $^{10}/_6 dh^\#$);
adjust_fit(0, 0); **pickup pencircle** scaled *stem*;
lft x_6 = hround u; $x_2 = w - x_6$; *top* $y_8 = 0$; *bot* $y_4 = -d$;
circle_points; *draw_circle*;   % circle
draw z_1 -- z_5; **draw** z_3 -- z_7;   % times
labels(1, 2, 3, 4, 5, 6, 7, 8); **endchar**;

cmchar "\displaystyle circle-times operator";
beginchar(oct "117", $27.2u^\#$, 0, $^{14}/_6 dh^\#$); **padded** $^1/_6 dh^\#$;
adjust_fit(0, 0); **pickup pencircle** scaled *curve*;
lft x_6 = hround u; $x_2 = w - x_6$; *top* $y_8 = 0$; *bot* $y_4 = -d$;
circle_points; *draw_circle*;   % circle
draw z_1 -- z_5; **draw** z_3 -- z_7;   % times
labels(1, 2, 3, 4, 5, 6, 7, 8); **endchar**;

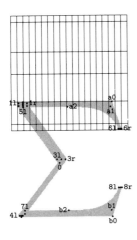
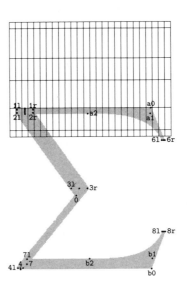

cmchar "\textstyle summation sign";
beginchar(oct "120", $19u^\#$, 0, $^{10}/_6 dh^\#$);
adjust_fit$(0, 0)$; **pickup** $tiny.nib$;
numeric $top\_arm\_thickness$, $bot\_arm\_thickness$;
$top_arm_thickness = $ Vround $rule\_thickness$;
$bot_arm_thickness = $ Vround $.9(.5[rule\_thickness, curve])$;
$lft\ x_{1l} = $ hround u; $x_{1l} = x_{2l} = x_{4l}$; $x_{3l} - x_{1l} = {}^4/_{11}(w - 2u)$;
$top\ y_1 = 0$; $bot\ y_2 = -top\_arm\_thickness - eps$; $bot\ y_4 = -d$; $y_3 = -.5d$;
numeric $alpha[]$; $alpha_1 = ((x_{3l} - x_{1l}) ++ (y_2 - y_3))/(y_2 - y_3)$;
$penpos_1(alpha_1 * (curve - tiny), 0)$; $penpos_2(alpha_1 * (curve - tiny), 0)$;
$penpos_3(alpha_1 * (curve - tiny), 0)$;
$alpha_2 = diag\_ratio(1, rule\_thickness - tiny, y_3 - y_4, x_{3r} - x_{4l})$;
$penpos_4(alpha_2 * (rule\_thickness - tiny), 0)$;
$z_0 = whatever[z_{2l}, z_{3l}] = z_{4l} + whatever * (z_{3r} - z_{4r})$;
filldraw z_{1l} -- z_{2l} -- z_0 -- z_{4l} -- z_{4r} -- z_{3r} -- z_{2r} -- z_{1r} -- cycle;   % diagonals
pickup $crisp.nib$; $pos_5(top\_arm\_thickness, 90)$; $pos_6(hair, 0)$;
$top\ y_{5r} = 0$; $x_5 = x_1$; $rt\ x_{6r} = $ hround$(w - u)$; $y_6 = good.y(y_{5l} - beak) - eps$;
$arm(5, 6, a, .45, {}^{17}/_{11}u)$;   % upper arm and beak
$pos_7(bot\_arm\_thickness, -90)$; $pos_8(hair, 0)$;
$bot\ y_{7r} = -d$; $z_{7l} = whatever[z_4, z_3]$; $x_{7r} := x_4$;
$x_8 = x_6$; $y_8 = good.y(y_{7l} + beak) + eps$;
$arm(7, 8, b, .45, {}^{17}/_{11}u)$;   % lower arm and beak
penlabels$(0, 1, 2, 3, 4, 5, 6, 7, 8)$; **endchar**;

cmchar "\displaystyle summation sign";
beginchar(oct "130", $26u^\#$, 0, $^{14}/_6 dh^\#$); **padded** $^1/_6 dh^\#$;
adjust_fit$(0, 0)$; **pickup** $tiny.nib$;
numeric $top\_arm\_thickness$, $bot\_arm\_thickness$, $thick\_stem$, $thin\_stem$;
$thick\_stem = bold + 4dw$; $thin\_stem = rule\_thickness + dw$;
$top_arm_thickness = $ Vround $.9thin\_stem$;
$bot_arm_thickness = $ Vround $.9(.5[thin\_stem, thick\_stem])$;
$lft\ x_{1l} = $ hround u; $x_{1l} = x_{2l} = x_{4l}$; $x_{3l} - x_{1l} = {}^4/_{11}(w - 2u)$;
$top\ y_1 = 0$; $bot\ y_2 = -top\_arm\_thickness - eps$; $bot\ y_4 = -d$; $y_3 = -.5d$;
numeric $alpha[]$; $alpha_1 = ((x_{3l} - x_{1l}) ++ (y_2 - y_3))/(y_2 - y_3)$;
$penpos_1(alpha_1 * (thick\_stem - tiny), 0)$; $penpos_2(alpha_1 * (thick\_stem - tiny), 0)$;
$penpos_3(alpha_1 * (thick\_stem - tiny), 0)$;
$alpha_2 = diag\_ratio(1, thin\_stem - tiny, y_3 - y_4, x_{3r} - x_{4l})$;
$penpos_4(alpha_2 * (thin\_stem - tiny), 0)$;
$z_0 = whatever[z_{2l}, z_{3l}] = z_{4l} + whatever * (z_{3r} - z_{4r})$;
filldraw z_{1l} -- z_{2l} -- z_0 -- z_{4l} -- z_{4r} -- z_{3r} -- z_{2r} -- z_{1r} -- cycle;   % diagonals
pickup $crisp.nib$; $pos_5(top\_arm\_thickness, 90)$; $pos_6(hair, 0)$;
$top\ y_{5r} = 0$; $x_5 = x_1$; $rt\ x_{6r} = $ hround$(w - u)$; $y_6 = good.y(y_{5l} - 1.2beak) - eps$;
$arm(5, 6, a, .45, {}^{24}/_{11}u)$;   % upper arm and beak
$pos_7(bot\_arm\_thickness, -90)$; $pos_8(hair, 0)$;
$bot\ y_{7r} = -d$; $z_{7l} = whatever[z_4, z_3]$; $x_{7r} := x_4$;
$x_8 = x_6$; $y_8 = good.y(y_{7l} + 1.2beak) + eps$;
$arm(7, 8, b, .45, {}^{24}/_{11}u)$;   % lower arm and beak
penlabels$(0, 1, 2, 3, 4, 5, 6, 7, 8)$; **endchar**;

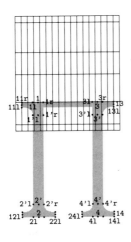

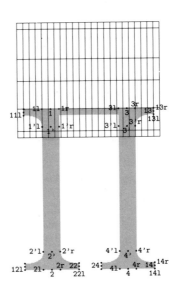

cmchar "\textstyle product sign";

beginchar(oct "121", $17u\#$, 0, $^{10}/_6 dh\#$);

adjust_fit$(0, 0)$; **pickup** *crisp.nib*;

numeric *heavy_stem*, *light_stem*;

heavy_stem = hround($bold + dw$); *light_stem* = *rule_thickness*;

$pos_1(heavy\_stem, 0)$; $pos_2(heavy\_stem, 0)$; $pos_{1'}(heavy\_stem, 0)$; $pos_{2'}(heavy\_stem, 0)$;

$pos_{11}(light\_stem, 90)$; $pos_{12}(light\_stem, 90)$; $pos_{22}(light\_stem, 90)$;

lft x_{11} = hround u; $x_{1l} - x_{11} = x_{2l} - x_{12} = x_{22} - x_{2r}$ = hround *cap_jut*;

$x_1 = x_{1'} = x_2 = x_{2'}$;

top $y_1 = 0$; *bot* $y_2 = -d$; $y_{11r} = y_1$; $y_{12l} = y_{22l} = y_2$;

$y_{11l} - y_{1'} = y_{2'} - y_{12r} = 1.2bracket$;

filldraw z_{1r} -- z_{11r} -- $serif\_arc(11l, 1'l)$ -- reverse $serif\_arc(12r, 2'l)$

     -- z_{12l} -- z_{22l} -- $serif\_arc(22r, 2'r)$ -- cycle;   % left stem and serifs

$pos_3(heavy\_stem, 0)$; $pos_4(heavy\_stem, 0)$; $pos_{3'}(heavy\_stem, 0)$; $pos_{4'}(heavy\_stem, 0)$;

$pos_{13}(light\_stem, 90)$; $pos_{14}(light\_stem, 90)$; $pos_{24}(light\_stem, 90)$;

$x_3 = x_{3'} = x_4 = x_{4'} = w - x_1$; $x_{13} = x_{14} = w - x_{11}$; $x_{24} = w - x_{22}$;

$y_3 = y_{13r} = y_1$; $y_{3'} = y_{1'}$; $y_{4'} = y_{2'}$; $y_4 = y_{14l} = y_{24l} = y_2$;

filldraw z_{3l} -- z_{13r} -- $serif\_arc(13l, 3'r)$ -- reverse $serif\_arc(14r, 4'r)$

     -- z_{14l} -- z_{24l} -- $serif\_arc(24r, 4'l)$ -- cycle;   % right stem and serifs

filldraw stroke z_{11e} -- z_{13e};   % bar

penlabels$(1, 1', 2, 2', 3, 3', 4, 4', 11, 12, 13, 14, 22, 24)$; **endchar**;

cmchar "\displaystyle product sign";

beginchar(oct "131", $23u\#$, 0, $^{14}/_6 dh\#$); **padded** $^1/_6 dh\#$;

adjust_fit$(0, 0)$; **pickup** *crisp.nib*;

numeric *heavy_stem*, *light_stem*;

heavy_stem = hround($bold + 5dw$); *light_stem* = Vround($rule\_thickness + dw$);

$pos_1(heavy\_stem, 0)$; $pos_2(heavy\_stem, 0)$; $pos_{1'}(heavy\_stem, 0)$; $pos_{2'}(heavy\_stem, 0)$;

$pos_{11}(light\_stem, 90)$; $pos_{12}(light\_stem, 90)$; $pos_{22}(light\_stem, 90)$;

lft x_{11} = hround u; $x_{1l} - x_{11} = x_{2l} - x_{12} = x_{22} - x_{2r}$ = hround $1.6cap\_jut$;

$x_1 = x_{1'} = x_2 = x_{2'}$;

top $y_1 = 0$; *bot* $y_2 = -d$; $y_{11r} = y_1$; $y_{12l} = y_{22l} = y_2$;

$y_{11l} - y_{1'} = y_{2'} - y_{12r} = 1.8bracket$;

filldraw z_{1r} -- z_{11r} -- $serif\_arc(11l, 1'l)$ -- reverse $serif\_arc(12r, 2'l)$

     -- z_{12l} -- z_{22l} -- $serif\_arc(22r, 2'r)$ -- cycle;   % left stem and serifs

$pos_3(heavy\_stem, 0)$; $pos_4(heavy\_stem, 0)$; $pos_{3'}(heavy\_stem, 0)$; $pos_{4'}(heavy\_stem, 0)$;

$pos_{13}(light\_stem, 90)$; $pos_{14}(light\_stem, 90)$; $pos_{24}(light\_stem, 90)$;

$x_3 = x_{3'} = x_4 = x_{4'} = w - x_1$; $x_{13} = x_{14} = w - x_{11}$; $x_{24} = w - x_{22}$;

$y_3 = y_{13r} = y_1$; $y_{3'} = y_{1'}$; $y_{4'} = y_{2'}$; $y_4 = y_{14l} = y_{24l} = y_2$;

filldraw z_{3l} -- z_{13r} -- $serif\_arc(13l, 3'r)$ -- reverse $serif\_arc(14r, 4'r)$

     -- z_{14l} -- z_{24l} -- $serif\_arc(24r, 4'l)$ -- cycle;   % right stem and serifs

filldraw stroke z_{11e} -- z_{13e};   % bar

penlabels$(1, 1', 2, 2', 3, 3', 4, 4', 11, 12, 13, 14, 22, 24)$; **endchar**;

---

vardef *serif_arc*(**suffix** \$, \$\$) =

   $z_\$\{x_{\$\$} - x_\$, 0\} \ldots (.75[x_\$, x_{\$\$}], .25[y_\$, y_{\$\$}])\{z_{\$\$} - z_\$\} \ldots \{0, y_{\$\$} - y_\$\}z_{\$\$}$ **enddef**;

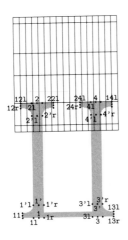

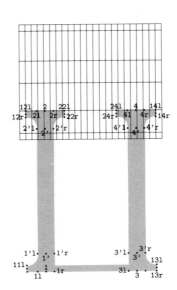

cmchar "\textstyle coproduct sign";
beginchar(oct "140", $17u^\#$, 0, $^{10}/_6 dh^\#$);
adjust_fit$(0, 0)$; **pickup** *crisp.nib*;
numeric *heavy_stem*, *light_stem*;
heavy_stem $=$ hround$(bold + dw)$; *light_stem* $=$ *rule_thickness*;
$pos_1(heavy\_stem, 0)$; $pos_2(heavy\_stem, 0)$; $pos_{1'}(heavy\_stem, 0)$; $pos_{2'}(heavy\_stem, 0)$;
$pos_{11}(light\_stem, -90)$; $pos_{12}(light\_stem, -90)$; $pos_{22}(light\_stem, -90)$;
lft $x_{11} =$ hround u; $x_{1l} - x_{11} = x_{2l} - x_{12} = x_{22} - x_{2r} =$ hround *cap_jut*;
$x_1 = x_{1'} = x_2 = x_{2'}$;
bot $y_1 = -d$; *top* $y_2 = 0$; $y_{11r} = y_1$; $y_{12l} = y_{22l} = y_2$;
$y_{1'} - y_{11l} = y_{12r} - y_{2'} = 1.2 bracket$;
filldraw z_{1r} `--` z_{11r} `--` *serif_arc*$(11l, 1'l)$ `--` reverse *serif_arc*$(12r, 2'l)$
  `--` z_{12l} `--` z_{22l} `--` *serif_arc*$(22r, 2'r)$ `--` cycle; % left stem and serifs
$pos_3(heavy\_stem, 0)$; $pos_4(heavy\_stem, 0)$; $pos_{3'}(heavy\_stem, 0)$; $pos_{4'}(heavy\_stem, 0)$;
$pos_{13}(light\_stem, -90)$; $pos_{14}(light\_stem, -90)$; $pos_{24}(light\_stem, -90)$;
$x_3 = x_{3'} = x_4 = x_{4'} = w - x_1$; $x_{13} = x_{14} = w - x_{11}$; $x_{24} = w - x_{22}$;
$y_3 = y_{13r} = y_1$; $y_{3'} = y_{1'}$; $y_{4'} = y_{2'}$; $y_4 = y_{14l} = y_{24l} = y_2$;
filldraw z_{3l} `--` z_{13r} `--` *serif_arc*$(13l, 3'r)$ `--` reverse *serif_arc*$(14r, 4'r)$
  `--` z_{14l} `--` z_{24l} `--` *serif_arc*$(24r, 4'l)$ `--` cycle; % right stem and serifs
filldraw stroke z_{11e} `--` z_{13e}; % bar
penlabels$(1, 1', 2, 2', 3, 3', 4, 4', 11, 12, 13, 14, 22, 24)$; **endchar**;

cmchar "\displaystyle coproduct sign";
beginchar(oct "141", $23u^\#$, 0, $^{14}/_6 dh^\#$); **padded** $^1/_6 dh^\#$;
adjust_fit$(0, 0)$; **pickup** *crisp.nib*;
numeric *heavy_stem*, *light_stem*;
heavy_stem $=$ hround$(bold + 5dw)$; *light_stem* $=$ Vround$(rule\_thickness + dw)$;
$pos_1(heavy\_stem, 0)$; $pos_2(heavy\_stem, 0)$; $pos_{1'}(heavy\_stem, 0)$; $pos_{2'}(heavy\_stem, 0)$;
$pos_{11}(light\_stem, -90)$; $pos_{12}(light\_stem, -90)$; $pos_{22}(light\_stem, -90)$;
lft $x_{11} =$ hround u; $x_{1l} - x_{11} = x_{2l} - x_{12} = x_{22} - x_{2r} =$ hround *cap_jut*;
$x_1 = x_{1'} = x_2 = x_{2'}$;
bot $y_1 = -d$; *top* $y_2 = 0$; $y_{11r} = y_1$; $y_{12l} = y_{22l} = y_2$;
$y_{1'} - y_{11l} = y_{12r} - y_{2'} = 1.8 bracket$;
filldraw z_{1r} `--` z_{11r} `--` *serif_arc*$(11l, 1'l)$ `--` reverse *serif_arc*$(12r, 2'l)$
  `--` z_{12l} `--` z_{22l} `--` *serif_arc*$(22r, 2'r)$ `--` cycle; % left stem and serifs
$pos_3(heavy\_stem, 0)$; $pos_4(heavy\_stem, 0)$; $pos_{3'}(heavy\_stem, 0)$; $pos_{4'}(heavy\_stem, 0)$;
$pos_{13}(light\_stem, -90)$; $pos_{14}(light\_stem, -90)$; $pos_{24}(light\_stem, -90)$;
$x_3 = x_{3'} = x_4 = x_{4'} = w - x_1$; $x_{13} = x_{14} = w - x_{11}$; $x_{24} = w - x_{22}$;
$y_3 = y_{13r} = y_1$; $y_{3'} = y_{1'}$; $y_{4'} = y_{2'}$; $y_4 = y_{14l} = y_{24l} = y_2$;
filldraw z_{3l} `--` z_{13r} `--` *serif_arc*$(13l, 3'r)$ `--` reverse *serif_arc*$(14r, 4'r)$
  `--` z_{14l} `--` z_{24l} `--` *serif_arc*$(24r, 4'l)$ `--` cycle; % right stem and serifs
filldraw stroke z_{11e} `--` z_{13e}; % bar
penlabels$(1, 1', 2, 2', 3, 3', 4, 4', 11, 12, 13, 14, 22, 24)$; **endchar**;

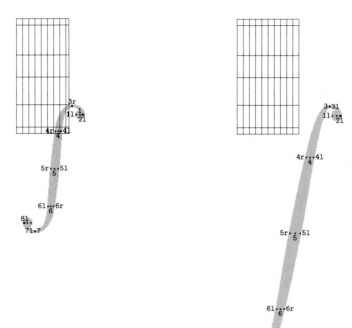

cmchar "\textstyle integral sign";
beginchar(oct "122", $12u^\#$, 0, $^{100}/_{54}dh^\#$);
italcorr $3.5u^\#$;   % TeX kerning between upper limit and lower limit
adjust_fit$(0, -ic^\#)$; **pickup** *fine.nib*;
$pos_1(curve, 0)$; $pos_2(hair, 0)$; $pos_3(vair, 90)$; $pos_4(stem, 180)$;
$pos_5(curve, 180)$; $pos_{5'}(curve, 0)$; $z_{5'} = z_5$; $pos_6(stem, 0)$;
$pos_7(vair, -90)$; $pos_8(hair, -180)$; $pos_9(curve, -180)$;
$rt\ x_{1r} = \text{hround}(w - u)$; $x_9 = w - x_1$; $x_7 = w - x_3 = 3u$;
$x_5 = .5[x_4, x_6]$; $x_4 - x_6 = 1.2u$; $lft\ x_{5r} = \text{hround}(.5w - .5stem)$;
$top\ y_{3r} = 0$; $bot\ y_{7r} = -d$; $y_9 - .5curve = \text{vround}(top\ y_{7l} + .25curve)$;
$y_3 - y_1 = y_9 - y_7$; $y_5 = .5[y_3, y_7] = .5[y_4, y_6]$; $y_4 - y_6 = .6(y_3 - y_7)$;
bulb$(3, 2, 1)$; *bulb*$(7, 8, 9)$;   % bulbs
filldraw stroke $z_{3e}\{left\} \ldots z_{4e}\{(z_{5e} - z_{4e})$ xscaled $1.1\}$
   .. tension atleast 1 and atleast .8 .. $\{z_5 - z_4\}z_{5e}$;   % upper stem
filldraw stroke $z_{5'e}\{z_6 - z_5\}$ .. tension atleast .8 and atleast 1
   .. $\{(z_{6e} - z_{5'e})$ xscaled $1.1\}z_{6e} \ldots \{left\}z_{7e}$;   % lower stem
penlabels$(1, 2, 3, 4, 5, 6, 7, 8, 9)$; **endchar**;

cmchar "\displaystyle integral sign";
beginchar(oct "132", $18u^\#$, 0, $^{200}/_{54}dh^\#$);
italcorr $8u^\#$;   % TeX kerning between upper limit and lower limit
adjust_fit$(0, -ic^\#)$; **pickup** *fine.nib*;
numeric *bulb_size*, *max_size*;
bulb_size $= \text{hround}(bold + dw)$; *max_size* $= \text{hround}(bold + 2dw)$;
$pos_1(bulb\_size, 0)$; $pos_2(hair, 0)$; $pos_3(vair, 90)$; $pos_4(bold, 180)$;
$pos_5(max\_size, 180)$; $pos_{5'}(max\_size, 0)$; $z_{5'} = z_5$; $pos_6(bold, 0)$;
$pos_7(vair, -90)$; $pos_8(hair, -180)$; $pos_9(bulb\_size, -180)$;
$rt\ x_{1r} = \text{hround}(w - u)$; $x_9 = w - x_1$; $x_7 = w - x_3 = 3u$;
$x_5 = .5[x_4, x_6]$; $x_4 - x_6 = 4.8u$; $lft\ x_{5r} = \text{hround}(.5w - .5stem)$;
$top\ y_{3r} = 0$; $bot\ y_{7r} = -d$;
$y_9 - .5bulb\_size = \text{vround}(top\ y_{7l} + .25bulb\_size)$; $y_3 - y_1 = y_9 - y_7$;
$y_5 = .5[y_3, y_7] = .5[y_4, y_6]$; $y_4 - y_6 = .6(y_3 - y_7)$;
bulb$(3, 2, 1)$; *bulb*$(7, 8, 9)$;   % bulbs
filldraw stroke $z_{3e}\{left\} \ldots z_{4e}\{(z_{5e} - z_{4e})$ xscaled $1.1\}$
   .. tension atleast 1 and atleast .8 .. $\{z_5 - z_4\}z_{5e}$;   % upper stem
filldraw stroke $z_{5'e}\{z_6 - z_5\}$ .. tension atleast .8 and atleast 1
   .. $\{(z_{6e} - z_{5'e})$ xscaled $1.1\}z_{6e} \ldots \{left\}z_{7e}$;   % lower stem
penlabels$(1, 2, 3, 4, 5, 6, 7, 8, 9)$; **endchar**;

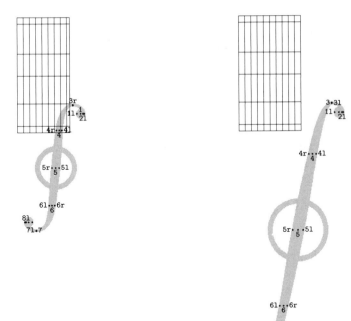

cmchar "\textstyle contour integral sign";
beginchar(oct "110", $12u^\#$, 0, $^{100}/_{54}dh^\#$);
italcorr $3.5u^\#$;   % TEX kerning between upper limit and lower limit
adjust_fit$(0, -ic^\#)$; **pickup** *fine.nib*;
$pos_1(curve, 0)$; $pos_2(hair, 0)$; $pos_3(vair, 90)$; $pos_4(stem, 180)$;
$pos_5(curve, 180)$; $pos_{5'}(curve, 0)$; $z_{5'} = z_5$; $pos_6(stem, 0)$;
$pos_7(vair, -90)$; $pos_8(hair, -180)$; $pos_9(curve, -180)$;
$rt\ x_{1r} = \mathrm{hround}(w - u)$; $x_9 = w - x_1$; $x_7 = w - x_3 = 3u$;
$x_5 = .5[x_4, x_6]$; $x_4 - x_6 = 1.2u$; $lft\ x_{5r} = \mathrm{hround}(.5w - .5stem)$;
$top\ y_{3r} = 0$; $bot\ y_{7r} = -d$; $y_9 - .5curve = \mathrm{vround}(top\ y_{7l} + .25curve)$;
$y_3 - y_1 = y_9 - y_7$; $y_5 = .5[y_3, y_7] = .5[y_4, y_6]$; $y_4 - y_6 = .6(y_3 - y_7)$;
$bulb(3, 2, 1)$; $bulb(7, 8, 9)$;   % bulbs
filldraw stroke $z_{3e}\{left\} \ldots z_{4e}\{(z_{5e} - z_{4e})$ xscaled $1.1\}$
  .. tension atleast 1 and atleast .8 .. $\{z_5 - z_4\}z_{5e}$;   % upper stem
filldraw stroke $z_{5'e}\{z_6 - z_5\}$ .. tension atleast .8 and atleast 1
  .. $\{(z_{6e} - z_{5'e})$ xscaled $1.1\}z_{6e} \ldots \{left\}z_{7e}$;   % lower stem
pickup *rule.nib*; *autorounded*;
draw *fullcircle* scaled $.5w$ shifted z_5;   % contour
penlabels$(1, 2, 3, 4, 5, 6, 7, 8, 9)$; **endchar**;

cmchar "\displaystyle contour integral sign";
beginchar(oct "111", $18u^\#$, 0, $^{200}/_{54}dh^\#$);
italcorr $8u^\#$;   % TEX kerning between upper limit and lower limit
adjust_fit$(0, -ic^\#)$; **pickup** *fine.nib*;
numeric *bulb_size, max_size*;
$bulb\_size = \mathrm{hround}(bold + dw)$; $max\_size = \mathrm{hround}(bold + 2dw)$;
$pos_1(bulb\_size, 0)$; $pos_2(hair, 0)$; $pos_3(vair, 90)$; $pos_4(bold, 180)$;
$pos_5(max\_size, 180)$; $pos_{5'}(max\_size, 0)$; $z_{5'} = z_5$; $pos_6(bold, 0)$;
$pos_7(vair, -90)$; $pos_8(hair, -180)$; $pos_9(bulb\_size, -180)$;
$rt\ x_{1r} = \mathrm{hround}(w - u)$; $x_9 = w - x_1$; $x_7 = w - x_3 = 3u$;
$x_5 = .5[x_4, x_6]$; $x_4 - x_6 = 4.8u$; $lft\ x_{5r} = \mathrm{hround}(.5w - .5stem)$;
$top\ y_{3r} = 0$; $bot\ y_{7r} = -d$;
$y_9 - .5bulb\_size = \mathrm{vround}(top\ y_{7l} + .25bulb\_size)$; $y_3 - y_1 = y_9 - y_7$;
$y_5 = .5[y_3, y_7] = .5[y_4, y_6]$; $y_4 - y_6 = .6(y_3 - y_7)$;
$bulb(3, 2, 1)$; $bulb(7, 8, 9)$;   % bulbs
filldraw stroke $z_{3e}\{left\} \ldots z_{4e}\{(z_{5e} - z_{4e})$ xscaled $1.1\}$
  .. tension atleast 1 and atleast .8 .. $\{z_5 - z_4\}z_{5e}$;   % upper stem
filldraw stroke $z_{5'e}\{z_6 - z_5\}$ .. tension atleast .8 and atleast 1
  .. $\{(z_{6e} - z_{5'e}$ xscaled $1.1\}z_{6e} \ldots \{left\}z_{7e}$;   % lower stem
pickup *rule.nib*; *autorounded*;
draw *fullcircle* scaled $.5w$ shifted z_5;   % contour
penlabels$(1, 2, 3, 4, 5, 6, 7, 8, 9)$; **endchar**;

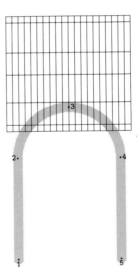

cmchar "\textstyle set intersection sign";
beginchar(oct "124", $15u^\#$, 0, $^{10}/_6 dh^\#$);
adjust_fit$(0, 0)$; **pickup pencircle** scaled *stem*;
lft $x_1 =$ hround u; $x_2 = x_1$; $x_3 = w - x_3$; $x_4 = x_5 = w - x_1$;
top $y_3 = 0$; *bot* $y_1 = -d - eps$; $y_2 = y_4 = ^2/_3[y_1, y_3]$; $y_5 = y_1$;
draw z_1 --- $z_2 \ldots z_3 \ldots z_4$ --- z_5;   % stems and cap
labels$(1, 2, 3, 4, 5)$; **endchar**;

cmchar "\displaystyle set intersection sign";
beginchar(oct "134", $20u^\#$, 0, $^{14}/_6 dh^\#$); **padded** $^1/_6 dh^\#$;
adjust_fit$(0, 0)$; **pickup pencircle** scaled *curve*;
lft $x_1 =$ hround u; $x_2 = x_1$; $x_3 = w - x_3$; $x_4 = x_5 = w - x_1$;
top $y_3 = 0$; *bot* $y_1 = -d - eps$; $y_2 = y_4 = ^2/_3[y_1, y_3]$; $y_5 = y_1$;
draw z_1 --- $z_2 \ldots z_3 \ldots z_4$ --- z_5;   % stems and cap
labels$(1, 2, 3, 4, 5)$; **endchar**;

cmchar "\textstyle set union sign";
beginchar(oct "123", $15u^\#$, 0, $^{10}/_6 dh^\#$);
adjust_fit$(0, 0)$; **pickup pencircle** scaled *stem*;
lft $x_1 =$ hround u; $x_2 = x_1$; $x_3 = w - x_3$; $x_4 = x_5 = w - x_1$;
top $y_1 = eps$; *bot* $y_3 = -d$; $y_2 = y_4 = ^2/_3[y_1, y_3]$; $y_5 = y_1$;
draw z_1 --- $z_2 \ldots z_3 \ldots z_4$ --- z_5;   % stems and cup
labels$(1, 2, 3, 4, 5)$; **endchar**;

cmchar "\displaystyle set union sign";
beginchar(oct "133", $20u^\#$, 0, $^{14}/_6 dh^\#$); **padded** $^1/_6 dh^\#$;
adjust_fit$(0, 0)$; **pickup pencircle** scaled *curve*;
lft $x_1 =$ hround u; $x_2 = x_1$; $x_3 = w - x_3$; $x_4 = x_5 = w - x_1$;
top $y_1 = eps$; *bot* $y_3 = -d$; $y_2 = y_4 = ^2/_3[y_1, y_3]$; $y_5 = y_1$;
draw z_1 --- $z_2 \ldots z_3 \ldots z_4$ --- z_5;   % stems and cup
labels$(1, 2, 3, 4, 5)$; **endchar**;

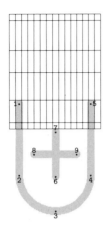

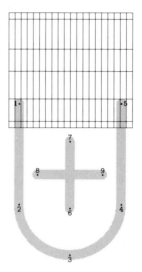

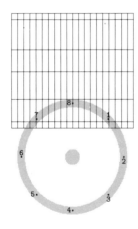

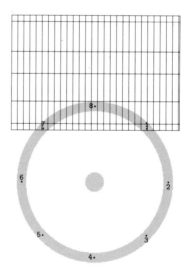

cmchar "\textstyle multiset union sign";
beginchar(oct "125", $15u^\#$, 0, $^{10}/_6 dh^\#$);
adjust_fit$(0, 0)$; **pickup pencircle** scaled *stem*;
lft $x_1 = $ hround u; $x_2 = x_1$; $x_3 = w - x_3$; $x_4 = x_5 = w - x_1$;
top $y_1 = eps$; *bot* $y_3 = -d$; $y_2 = y_4 = {}^2/_3[y_1, y_3]$; $y_5 = y_1$;
draw $z_1 \,\text{---}\, z_2 \ldots z_3 \ldots z_4 \,\text{---}\, z_5$;   % stems and cup
$y_8 = y_9 = .47[y_1, y_3]$; $x_8 = w - x_9 = x_1 + 2stem + eps$; $x_6 = x_7 = x_3$;
$.5[y_6, y_7] = y_8$; $y_7 - y_6 = x_9 - x_8$; **draw** $z_8 \,\text{--}\, z_9$; **draw** $z_6 \,\text{--}\, z_7$;   % enclosed '+'
labels$(1, 2, 3, 4, 5, 6, 7, 8, 9)$; **endchar**;

cmchar "\displaystyle multiset union sign";
beginchar(oct "135", $20u^\#$, 0, $^{14}/_6 dh^\#$); **padded** $^1/_6 dh^\#$;
adjust_fit$(0, 0)$; **pickup pencircle** scaled *curve*;
lft $x_1 = $ hround u; $x_2 = x_1$; $x_3 = w - x_3$; $x_4 = x_5 = w - x_1$;
top $y_1 = eps$; *bot* $y_3 = -d$; $y_2 = y_4 = {}^2/_3[y_1, y_3]$; $y_5 = y_1$;
draw $z_1 \,\text{---}\, z_2 \ldots z_3 \ldots z_4 \,\text{---}\, z_5$;   % stems and cup
$y_8 = y_9 = .47[y_1, y_3]$; $x_8 = w - x_9 = x_1 + 2curve + eps$; $x_6 = x_7 = x_3$;
$.5[y_6, y_7] = y_8$; $y_7 - y_6 = x_9 - x_8$; **draw** $z_8 \,\text{--}\, z_9$; **draw** $z_6 \,\text{--}\, z_7$;   % enclosed '+'
labels$(1, 2, 3, 4, 5, 6, 7, 8, 9)$; **endchar**;

cmchar "\textstyle circle-dot operator";
beginchar(oct "112", $20u^\#$, 0, $^{10}/_6 dh^\#$);
adjust_fit$(0, 0)$; **pickup pencircle** scaled *stem*;
lft $x_6 = $ hround u; $x_2 = w - x_6$; *top* $y_8 = 0$; *bot* $y_4 = -d$;
circle_points; *draw_circle*;   % circle
fill *fullcircle* scaled $(bold + 4dw + eps)$ shifted $(.5[z_4, z_8])$;   % dot
labels$(1, 2, 3, 4, 5, 6, 7, 8)$; **endchar**;

cmchar "\displaystyle circle-dot operator";
beginchar(oct "113", $27.2u^\#$, 0, $^{14}/_6 dh^\#$); **padded** $^1/_6 dh^\#$;
adjust_fit$(0, 0)$; **pickup pencircle** scaled *curve*;
lft $x_6 = $ hround u; $x_2 = w - x_6$; *top* $y_8 = 0$; *bot* $y_4 = -d$;
circle_points; *draw_circle*;   % circle
fill *fullcircle* scaled $(bold + 6dw + eps)$ shifted $(.5[z_4, z_8])$;   % dot
labels$(1, 2, 3, 4, 5, 6, 7, 8)$; **endchar**;

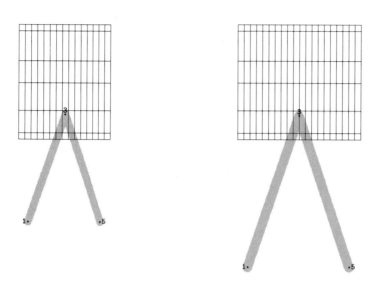

cmchar "\textstyle lattice infimum sign";
beginchar(oct "126", $15u^\#$, 0, $^{10}\!/_6 dh^\#$);
adjust_fit$(0, 0)$; **pickup pencircle** scaled *stem*;
lft $x_1 = $ hround $u - eps$; $x_3 = w - x_3$; $x_5 = w - x_1$;
top $y_3 = 0$; *bot* $y_1 = -d - eps$; $y_5 = y_1$;
draw $z_1 \; \text{--} \; z_3 \; \text{--} \; z_5$;   % diagonals
labels$(1, 3, 5)$; **endchar**;

cmchar "\displaystyle lattice infimum sign";
beginchar(oct "136", $20u^\#$, 0, $^{14}\!/_6 dh^\#$); **padded** $^1\!/_6 dh^\#$;
adjust_fit$(0, 0)$; **pickup pencircle** scaled *curve*;
lft $x_1 = $ hround $u - eps$; $x_3 = w - x_3$; $x_5 = w - x_1$;
top $y_3 = 0$; *bot* $y_1 = -d - eps$; $y_5 = y_1$;
draw $z_1 \; \text{--} \; z_3 \; \text{--} \; z_5$;   % diagonals
labels$(1, 3, 5)$; **endchar**;

cmchar "\textstyle lattice supremum sign";
beginchar(oct "127", $15u^\#$, 0, $^{10}\!/_6 dh^\#$);
adjust_fit$(0, 0)$; **pickup pencircle** scaled *stem*;
lft $x_1 = $ hround $u - eps$; $x_3 = w - x_3$; $x_5 = w - x_1$;
top $y_1 = eps$; *bot* $y_3 = -d$; $y_5 = y_1$;
draw $z_1 \; \text{--} \; z_3 \; \text{--} \; z_5$;   % diagonals
labels$(1, 3, 5)$; **endchar**;

cmchar "\displaystyle lattice supremum sign";
beginchar(oct "137", $20u^\#$, 0, $^{14}\!/_6 dh^\#$); **padded** $^1\!/_6 dh^\#$;
adjust_fit$(0, 0)$; **pickup pencircle** scaled *curve*;
lft $x_1 = $ hround $u - eps$; $x_3 = w - x_3$; $x_5 = w - x_1$;
top $y_1 = eps$; *bot* $y_3 = -d$; $y_5 = y_1$;
draw $z_1 \; \text{--} \; z_3 \; \text{--} \; z_5$;   % diagonals
labels$(1, 3, 5)$; **endchar**;

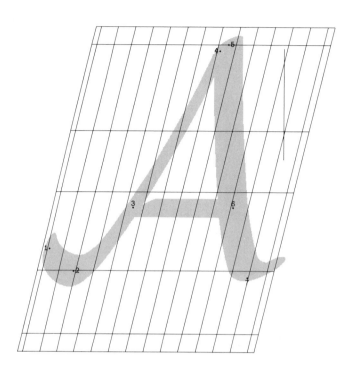

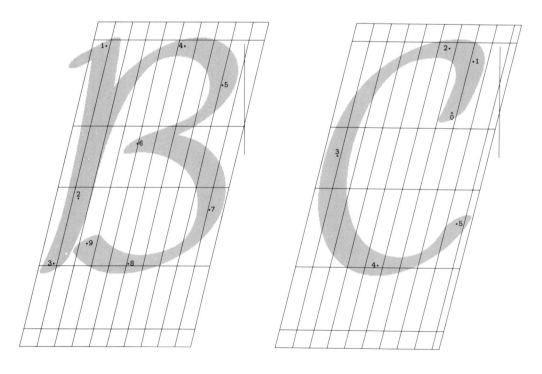

The program file `calu.mf` uses a small number of pen nibs to do all its work, so it presents an interesting contrast to the other programs in this book.

% Calligraphic capitals with 'fixed' pens, by N. N. Billawala (1985).

% These letters are intended for math, hence *math_fitting* is assumed.

% Character codes '*101* through '*132* are generated.

cmchar "Calligraphic A";
beginchar("A", $14.4u^\#$, $cap\_height^\#$, 0);
italcorr $.5u^\#$;
adjust_fit$(-.05w^\#, 0)$; **pickup** $cal.nib$;
lft $x_5 = .54w$; $x_7 = .9w$;
top $y_5 = h + .4cap\_curve$; *bot* $y_7 = bot\_flourish\_line$;
$z_6 = .3[z_7, z_5] - bend$;
pickup $tilted.nib$;
lft $x_1 = .05w$; $x_2 = .2w$; *rt* $x_4 = x_5$;
$y_1 = y_2 + .1h$; *bot* $y_2 = bot\_flourish\_line$; *top* $y_4 = h + .4cap\_curve$;
$y_3 = y_6$; $z_3 = whatever[z_2, z_4] + 2bend$;
draw $(z_1$ .. tension 1.2 .. $\{right\}z_2)$ softjoin flex(z_2, z_3, z_4);   % left diagonal
pickup $cal.nib$;
erase fill $(0, bot\ y_5) \texttt{--} (w, bot\ y_5) \texttt{--} (w, top\ y_5) \texttt{--} (0, top\ y_5) \texttt{--}$ cycle;
draw flex(z_5, z_6, z_7) softjoin $(z_7 \texttt{--} z_7 + cal.extension)$;   % right diagonal
draw *rt* $z_3 \texttt{--} z_6$;   % bar
math_fit$(.5u^\# - .1cap\_height^\# * slant, ic^\#)$; **labels**$(1, 2, 3, 4, 5, 6, 7)$; **endchar**;

cmchar "Calligraphic B";
beginchar("B", $9.9u^\#$, $cap\_height^\#$, 0);
italcorr max$(.8h^\# * slant - .1w^\#, .3h^\# * slant) + .5u^\#$;
adjust_fit$(0, 0)$; **pickup** $cal.nib$;
lft $x_1 = $ *lft* $x_3 = 0$; $x_4 = .6[x_2, x_5]$; *rt* $x_5 = .9w$; $x_6 = .4w$; *rt* $x_7 = w$;
$x_8 = .4[x_9, x_7]$; *lft* $x_9 = $ *rt* x_3;
top $y_1 = h + o$; *bot* $y_3 = -o$; $z_2 = .3[z_3, z_1] + bend$;
$y_4 = y_1$; $y_5 = .6[y_6, y_4]$; $y_6 = .55h$; $y_7 = .45[y_8, y_6]$; *bot* $y_8 = -o$; $y_9 = .1h$;
draw $z_1 - cal.extension \texttt{--}$ flex(z_1, z_2, z_3);   % stem
draw $z_2\{up\} \ldots z_4 \ldots z_5\{down\} \ldots \{$dir 200$\}z_6\{$dir 10$\}$
    $\ldots z_7\{down\} \ldots z_8\{left\} \ldots z_9$;   % lobes
math_fit$(.5u^\#, .3h^\# * slant + .5u^\#)$; **labels**$(1, 2, 3, 4, 5, 6, 7, 8, 9)$; **endchar**;

cmchar "Calligraphic C";
beginchar("C", $9.4u^\#$, $cap\_height^\#$, 0);
italcorr max$(h^\# * slant - .15w^\#, .2h^\# * slant) + .5u^\#$;
adjust_fit$(0, 0)$; **pickup** $cal.nib$;
$x_0 = .7[x_2, x_1]$; *rt* $x_1 = .85w$; $x_2 = .6w$; *lft* $x_3 = 0$; $x_4 = .5w$; *rt* $x_5 = w$;
$y_0 = .7h$; $y_1 = .8[y_0, y_2]$; *top* $y_2 = h + o$; $y_3 = .5h$; *bot* $y_4 = -o$; $y_5 = .2h$;
draw $(z_0\{2(x_1 - x_0), y_1 - y_0\} \ldots z_1)$
    softjoin$(z_1 \ldots z_2\{left\} \ldots . z_3\{down\} \ldots z_4 \ldots z_5)$;   % stroke
math_fit$(.5u^\# - .5h^\# * slant, .2h^\# * slant + .5u^\#)$; **labels**$(0, 1, 2, 3, 4, 5)$; **endchar**;

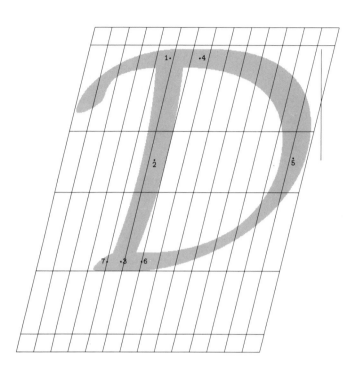

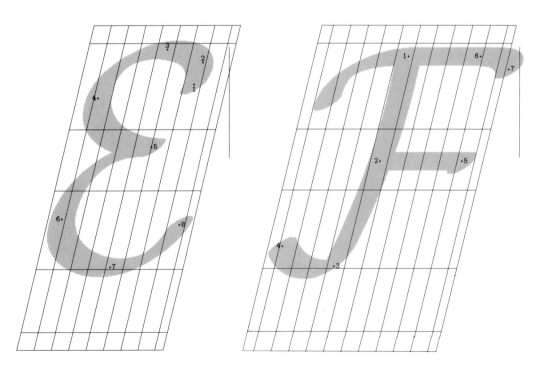

cmchar "Calligraphic D";
beginchar("D", $10u^\#$, $cap\_height^\#$, 0);
italcorr $.6h^\# * slant + .5u^\#$;
adjust_fit($4u^\#$, 0); **pickup** $cal.nib$;
$lft\ x_1 = lft\ x_3 = 0$; $x_4 = .2[x_1, x_5]$; $rt\ x_5 = w$; $x_6 = .2w$; $x_7 = 0$;
$top\ y_1 = top\ y_4 = h$; $bot\ y_3 = 0$; $z_2 = .5[z_3, z_1] + bend$;
$y_5 = .51[y_6, y_4]$; $bot\ y_6 = bot\ y_7 = 0$;
draw flex(z_1, z_2, z_3);   % stem
draw $z_1 \text{ --- } z_4 \text{ .... } z_5\{down\} \ldots z_6 \text{ --- } z_7$;   % lobe
draw $z_1\{left\} \ldots \{down\}z_1 - flourish\_change$;   % swash
math_fit($.5u^\# - .8h^\# * slant$, $ic^\# - .5u^\#$); **labels**($1, 2, 3, 4, 5, 6, 7$); **endchar**;

cmchar "Calligraphic E";
beginchar("E", $8.5u^\#$, $cap\_height^\#$, 0);
italcorr $\max(h^\# * slant - .1w^\#, .2h^\# * slant) + .5u^\#$;
adjust_fit(0, 0); **pickup** $cal.nib$;
$x_1 = .9[x_3, x_2]$; $rt\ x_2 = .9w$; $x_3 = .6[x_4, x_2]$; $lft\ x_4 = .05w$;
$x_5 = .7[x_6, x_2]$; $lft\ x_6 = 0$; $x_7 = .5[x_6, x_8]$; $rt\ x_8 = w$;
$y_1 = y_2 - .1h$; $y_2 = .9h + o$; $top\ y_3 = h + o$; $y_4 = .5[y_5, y_3]$;
$y_5 = .55h$; $y_6 = .6[y_5, y_7]$; $bot\ y_7 = -o$; $y_8 = .2h$;
draw ($z_1\{2(x_2 - x_1), y_2 - y_1\} \ldots z_2$)
   softjoin($z_2 \ldots z_3\{left\} \ldots z_4\{down\} \ldots \{right\}z_5$);   % upper arc
draw $z_5\{left\} \ldots z_6\{down\} \ldots z_7\{right\} \ldots z_8$;   % lower arc
math_fit($.5u^\# - .2h^\# * slant$, $.2h^\# * slant + .5u^\#$);
labels($1, 2, 3, 4, 5, 6, 7, 8$); **endchar**;

cmchar "Calligraphic F";
beginchar("F", $13.5u^\#$, $cap\_height^\#$, 0);
italcorr $h^\# * slant + .5u^\#$;
adjust_fit($-.1w^\#$, $-u^\#$); **pickup** $cal.nib$;
$x_1 = .5w$; $x_3 = .4w$; $lft\ x_4 = .1w$; $x_5 = x_2 + .35w$; $x_6 = .7[x_1, x_7]$; $rt\ x_7 = w$;
$top\ y_1 = top\ y_6 = h$; $z_2 = .5[z_3, z_1] + bend$;
$bot\ y_3 = -o$; $y_4 = .1h$; $y_5 = y_2$; $y_7 = .9h$;
draw flex(z_1, z_2, z_3) softjoin ($z_3 \ldots \{x_4 - x_3, 5(y_4 - y_3)\}z_4$);   % stem
draw $z_1 - flourish\_change\{up\} \ldots z_1 \text{ --- } z_6 \ldots \{down\}z_7$;   % upper bar
draw $z_2 \text{ -- } z_5 \text{ -- } z_5 - (0, .1cap\_curve)$;   % middle bar
math_fit(0, $.5ic^\#$); **labels**($1, 2, 3, 4, 5, 6, 7$); **endchar**;

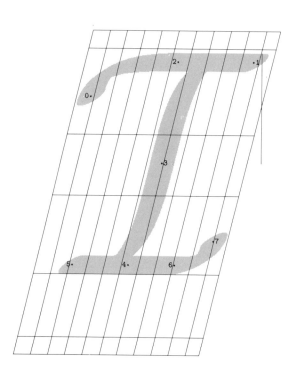

cmchar "Calligraphic G";
beginchar("G", $9.4u^\#$, $cap\_height^\#$, $.5desc\_depth^\#$);
italcorr $\max(h^\# * slant - .05w^\#, .5h^\# * slant) + .5u^\#$;
adjust_fit$(0, 0)$; **pickup** $cal.nib$;
$x_0 = .7[x_2, x_1]$; rt $x_1 = .95w$; $x_2 = .6w$; lft $x_3 = 0$; $x_4 = .5w$;
rt $x_5 = w$; $x_6 = .5[x_7, x_5]$; lft $x_7 = .2w$;
$y_0 = .7h + o$; $y_1 = .8[y_0, y_2]$; top $y_2 = h + o$; $y_3 = .5[y_4, y_2]$; bot $y_4 = .1h$;
$y_5 = .5h$; bot $y_6 = -d - o$; $y_7 = -.5d$;
draw $(z_0\{2(x_1 - x_0), y_1 - y_0\} \ldots z_1)$
    softjoin$(z_1 \ldots z_2\{left\} \ldots z_3\{down\} \ldots z_4 \ldots \{up\}z_5)$;   % arc
draw $z_5\{down\} \ldots z_6\{left\} \ldots z_7$;   % tail
math_fit$(.5u^\# - .4h^\# * slant, .5h^\# * slant + .5u^\#)$;
labels$(0, 1, 2, 3, 4, 5, 6, 7)$; **endchar**;

cmchar "Calligraphic H";
beginchar("H", $12.2u^\#$, $cap\_height^\#$, 0);
italcorr $\max(h^\# * slant - .2w^\#, .15h^\# * slant) + .5u^\#$;
adjust_fit$(4u^\#, 0)$; **pickup** $cal.nib$;
lft $x_1 = lft$ $x_3 = 0$; rt $x_4 = rt$ $x_6 = .8w$; rt $x_9 = w$;
top $y_1 = top$ $y_4 = h$; bot $y_3 = -o$; bot $y_6 = bot\_flourish\_line$; $y_9 = y_6 + .1h$;
$z_2 = .6[z_3, z_1] + bend$; $z_5 = .4[z_6, z_4] - 2bend$;
path $p[]$; $p_1 = \text{flex}(z_1, z_2, z_3)$; $p_2 = \text{flex}(z_4, z_5, z_6)$;
$p_3 = (-w, .55h) \text{ -- } (2w, .55h)$;
lft $z_7 = p_3$ intersectionpoint p_1; rt $z_8 = p_3$ intersectionpoint p_2;
draw$(z_1 - flourish\_change\{up\} \ldots z_1 - (u, 0) \text{ --- } z_1)$ softjoin p_1;   % left stem
draw p_2 softjoin $(z_6\{right\} \ldots \{up\}z_9)$;   % right stem
draw $z_7 \text{ -- } z_8$;   % bar
math_fit$(.5u^\# - .8h^\# * slant, .15h^\# * slant + .5u^\#)$;
labels$(1, 2, 3, 4, 5, 6, 7, 8, 9)$; **endchar**;

cmchar "Calligraphic I";
beginchar("I", $10.8u^\#$, $cap\_height^\#$, 0);
italcorr $\max(h^\# * slant + .5cap\_curve^\# - .2w^\#, .15h^\# * slant) + .5u^\#$;
adjust_fit$(0, 0)$; **pickup** $cal.nib$;
lft $x_0 = 0$; $x_1 = .9w$; $x_2 = x_4 = .5w$; $x_5 = .2w$; $x_6 = .75w$; rt $x_7 = w$;
$y_0 = .8h$; top $y_1 = top$ $y_2 = h$; $z_3 = .5[z_4, z_2] + bend$;
bot $y_4 = bot$ $y_5 = bot$ $y_6 = 0$; $y_7 = .15h$;
draw $z_0\{up\} \ldots z_2 \text{ --- } z_1$;   % upper bar
$z_8 = .5[z_2, z_1]$;
draw $z_8\{left\} \ldots z_3\{down\} \ldots \{left\}.5[z_4, z_5]$;   % stem
draw $z_5 \text{ --- } z_6 \ldots \{up\}z_7$;   % lower bar
math_fit$(.5u^\# - .8h^\# * slant, .15h^\# * slant + .5u^\#)$;
labels$(0, 1, 2, 3, 4, 5, 6, 7)$; **endchar**;

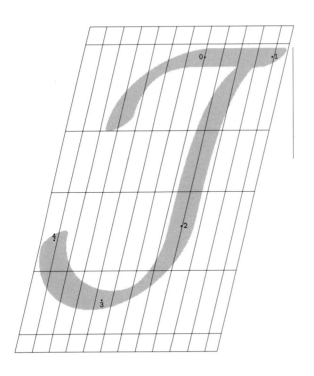

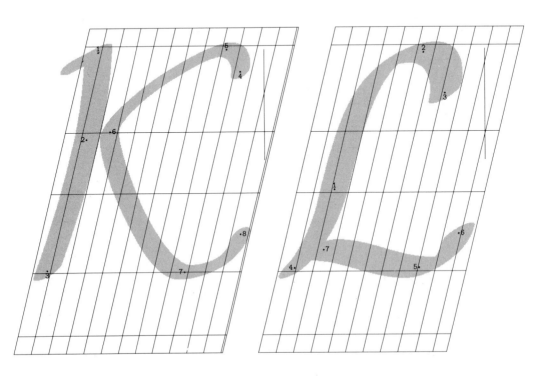

cmchar "Calligraphic J";
beginchar("J", $11.7u^\#$, $cap\_height^\#$, $.5desc\_depth^\#$);
italcorr $h^\# * slant + .25u^\#$;
adjust_fit$(0, 0)$; **pickup** $cal.nib$;
$x_0 = .6w$; $rt\ x_1 = w$; $rt\ x_2 = .75w$; $x_3 = .5[x_4, x_2]$; $lft\ x_4 = 0$;
$top\ y_0 = top\ y_1 = h$; $y_2 = .2h$; $bot\ y_3 = -d - o$; $y_4 = d$;
draw z_1 --- z_0 ... $\{down\}z_0 - (4u, {}^2\!/_7 h)$;   % upper bar
draw $z_1\{left\}$ ... $z_2\{down\}$ ... $z_3\{left\}$ ... $\{up\}z_4$;   % stem and tail
math_fit$(.5u^\#, 0)$; **labels**$(0, 1, 2, 3, 4)$; **endchar**;

cmchar "Calligraphic K";
beginchar("K", $11u^\#$, $cap\_height^\#$, 0);
italcorr $\max(h^\# * slant - .2w^\#, .2h^\# * slant) + .5u^\#$;
adjust_fit$(0, .1w^\#)$; **pickup** $cal.nib$;
$lft\ x_1 = lft\ x_3 = 0$; $top\ y_1 = h + o$; $bot\ y_3 = -o$; $z_2 = .6[z_3, z_1] + bend$;
draw $z_1 - cal.extension$ -- $\mathrm{flex}(z_1, z_2, z_3)$;   % stem
pickup $light\_cal.nib$;
$rt\ x_4 = .9w$; $x_5 = x_4 - .1w$; $x_7 = .8w$; $rt\ x_8 = 1.1w$;
$y_4 = .9h$; $top\ y_5 = h + o$; $bot\ y_7 = -o$; $y_8 = .2h - o$;
$(lft\ z_6)t_- = z_{2t_-} + $ **penoffset** $up\ of\ pen\_[cal.nib]$;
draw $z_4\{up\}$ ... $\{left\}z_5$ .. tension atleast 2 .. $\{down\}z_6$
    .. tension atleast 3 and atleast 2 .. $z_7\{right\}$ ... $\{up\}z_8$;   % diagonals
math_fit$(.5u^\#, .2h^\# * slant + .5u^\#)$; **labels**$(1, 2, 3, 4, 5, 6, 7, 8)$; **endchar**;

cmchar "Calligraphic L";
beginchar("L", $10.8u^\#$, $cap\_height^\#$, 0);
italcorr $.2h^\# * slant + .5u^\#$;
adjust_fit$(0, 0)$; **pickup** $heavy\_cal.nib$;
$x_1 = .2w$; $x_2 = x_1 + .3w$; $rt\ x_3 = x_2 + .25w$; $lft\ x_4 = 0$;
$x_5 = .8[x_4, x_6]$; $rt\ x_6 = w$; $x_7 = .2[x_4, x_5]$;
$y_1 = .4h - o$; $top\ y_2 = h + o$; $y_3 = .8h$; $bot\ y_4 = bot\ y_5 = -o$;
$y_6 = .2h - o$; $y_7 = {}^9\!/_{70}h - o$;
path p; $p = z_4$ ... $z_7\{right\}$ .. $\{right\}z_5$ ... $\{up\}z_6$; **draw** p;   % arm
draw $z_4\{\mathrm{dir}\ .75\ \mathrm{angle}(\mathbf{direction}\ 0\ \mathbf{of}\ p)\}$
    ... $z_1\{up\}$ ... $z_2\{right\}$ ... $\{down\}z_3$;   % stem and flourish
math_fit$(.5u^\#, ic^\#)$; **labels**$(1, 2, 3, 4, 5, 6, 7)$; **endchar**;

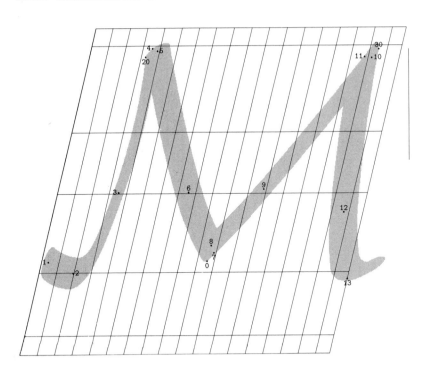

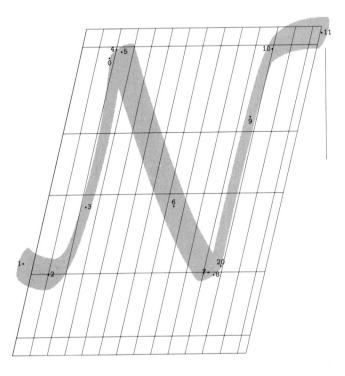

cmchar "Calligraphic M";
beginchar("M", $19.8u^\#$, $cap\_height^\#$, 0);
italcorr $\max(h^\# * slant - u^\#, .75\,cap\_curve^\#) + .5\,cap\_curve^\# + .5u^\#$;
adjust_fit$(-.1w^\#, 0)$; **pickup** $med\_cal.nib$;
$(z_{20})t_- = (z_5)t_- +$ **penoffset** *down* **of** *currentpen*
$\quad = (z_4)t_- +$ **penoffset** *down* **of** $pen\_[tilted.nib]$;
$z_6 = .3[z_7, z_5] - bend$; $z_9 = .3[z_8, z_{10}] + .5bend$; $z_{12} = .3[z_{13}, z_{11}] - bend$;
$x_7 = .5[x_2, x_{13}]$; *bot* $y_7 = .05h$; *top* $y_5 = h + o$;
$(z_0)t_- = (z_7)t_- +$ **penoffset** *right* **of** *currentpen*
$\quad = (z_8)t_- +$ **penoffset** *right* **of** $pen\_[tilted.nib]$;
pickup $cal.nib$; $(z_{30})t_- = (z_{11})t_- +$ **penoffset** *up* **of** *currentpen*
$\quad = (z_{10})t_- +$ **penoffset** *up* **of** $pen\_[tilted.nib]$;
$x_{13} = w$; *bot* $y_{13} = bot\_flourish\_line$;
pickup $tilted.nib$; *lft* $x_1 = .1w$; $x_2 = .2w$; $x_4 = .2[x_2, x_7]$; $x_{10} = .8[x_7, x_{13}]$;
$y_1 = .05h + y_2$; *bot* $y_2 = bot\_flourish\_line$; *top* $y_{10} = h + o$;
$z_3 = whatever[z_2, z_4] + 2bend$; $y_3 = y_6$;
draw $(z_1 \mathbin{..} \text{tension } 1.2 \mathbin{..} \{right\}z_2)$ softjoin flex(z_2, z_3, z_4);   % left stem
erase fill z_{20} -- $(.5w, y_{20})$ -- $(.5w, top\ y_4)$ -- $(x_{20} - 4u, top\ y_4)$ -- cycle;
pickup $med\_cal.nib$; **draw** flex(z_5, z_6, z_7);   % left diagonal
pickup $cal.nib$;
draw flex(z_{11}, z_{12}, z_{13}) softjoin $(z_{13}$ -- $z_{13} + cal.extension)$;   % right stem
pickup $tilted.nib$; **path** p; $p =$ flex(z_8, z_9, z_{10});
erase fill z_0 -- $(x_0, y_0 - .5h)$ -- $(x_9, y_0 - .5h)$ -- **subpath**$(1, 0)$ **of** p -- cycle;
erase fill z_{30} -- $(x_{30}, y_{30} + .5h)$ -- $(x_9, y_{30} + .5h)$ -- **subpath**$(1, 2)$ **of** p -- cycle;
draw p;   % right diagonal
math_fit$(.5u^\# - .05h^\# * slant, ic^\#)$;
labels$(0, 1, 2, 3, 4, 5, 6, 7, 8, 9, 10, 11, 12, 13, 20, 30)$; **endchar**;

cmchar "Calligraphic N";
beginchar("N", $9u^\#$, $cap\_height^\#$, 0);
italcorr $h^\# * slant + .5u^\#$;
adjust_fit$(2u^\#, 2.5u^\#)$; **pickup** $med\_cal.nib$;
$(z_0)t_- = (z_5)t_- +$ **penoffset** *down* **of** *currentpen*
$\quad = (z_4)t_- +$ **penoffset** *down* **of** $pen\_[tilted.nib]$;
$(z_{20})t_- = (z_7)t_- +$ **penoffset** *up* **of** *currentpen*
$\quad = (z_8)t_- +$ **penoffset** *up* **of** $pen\_[tilted.nib]$;
$z_6 = .3[z_7, z_5] - bend$; *rt* $z_7 = (w, 0)$; *top* $y_5 = h + o$;
pickup $tilted.nib$; *lft* $x_1 = x_2 - 2u$; $x_2 = -u$; $x_4 = 0$; $x_{10} = w$; *rt* $x_{11} = w + 3u$;
$y_1 = y_2 + .05h$; *bot* $y_2 = bot\_flourish\_line$; $y_3 = y_6$; $z_3 = whatever[z_2, z_4] + 2bend$;
$y_{10} = h$; $z_9 = .7[z_8, z_{10}] - .5bend$; *bot* $y_{11} = h$;
draw $(z_1 \mathbin{..} \text{tension } 1.2 \mathbin{..} \{right\}z_2)$ softjoin flex(z_2, z_3, z_4);   % left stem
draw flex$(z_8, z_9, z_{10}) \ldots \{right\}z_{11}$;   % right stem
pickup $med\_cal.nib$;
erase fill z_0 -- $(.5w, y_0)$ -- $(.5w, 1.5h)$ -- $(x_0 - 4u, 1.5h)$ -- cycle;
erase fill z_{20} -- $(.5w, y_{20})$ -- $(.5w, -.5h)$ -- $(x_{20} + 4u, -.5h)$ -- cycle;
draw flex(z_5, z_6, z_7);   % diagonal
math_fit$(.5u^\# - .05h^\# * slant, .3h^\# * slant)$;
labels$(0, 1, 2, 3, 4, 5, 6, 7, 8, 9, 10, 11, 20)$; **endchar**;

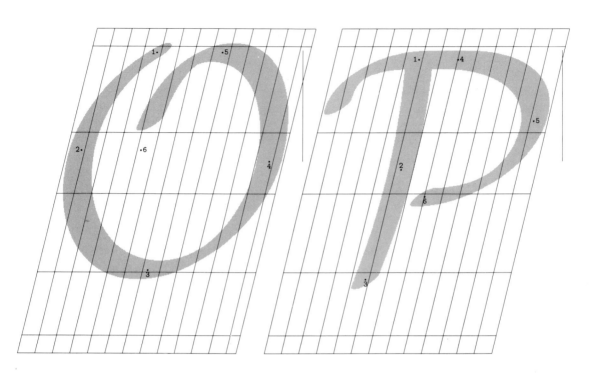

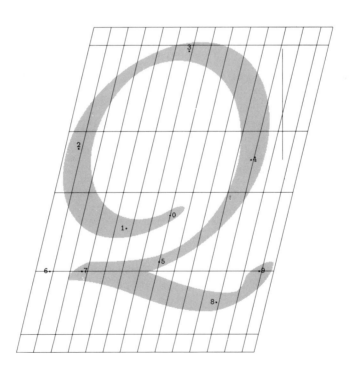

cmchar "Calligraphic O";
beginchar("O", $12.6u^\#$, $cap\_height^\#$, 0);
italcorr $.7h^\# * slant + .5u^\#$;
adjust_fit$(0, 0)$; **pickup** $cal.nib$;
$x_1 = .3w$; $lft\ x_2 = 0$; $x_3 = .5w$; $rt\ x_4 = w$; $x_5 = .6w$; $lft\ x_6 = .27w$;
$top\ y_1 = top\ y_5 = h + o$; $y_2 = .55h$; $bot\ y_3 = -o$; $y_4 = .5h$; $y_6 = y_2$;
path p; $p = z_1 \ldots z_2\{down\} \ldots z_3\{right\} \ldots z_4\{up\} \ldots z_5\{left\} \ldots \{down\}z_6$;
draw subpath$(0, 4.8)$ **of** p;   % bowl
math_fit$(.5u^\# - .3h^\# * slant, ic^\# - .5u^\#)$;
labels$(1, 2, 3, 4, 5, 6)$; **endchar**;

cmchar "Calligraphic P";
beginchar("P", $9u^\#$, $cap\_height^\#$, 0);
italcorr $.8h^\# * slant + .5u^\#$;
adjust_fit$(4u^\#, 0)$; **pickup** $cal.nib$;
$lft\ x_1 = lft\ x_3 = 0$; $x_4 = x_6 = .3[x_1, x_5]$; $rt\ x_5 = w$;
$top\ y_1 = top\ y_4 = h$; $y_3 = -o$; $y_5 = .55[y_6, y_4]$; $bot\ y_6 = .3h$;
$z_2 = .5[z_3, z_1] + bend$;
draw flex(z_1, z_2, z_3);   % stem
draw $z_1\{left\} \ldots \{down\}z_1 - flourish\_change$;   % swash
draw $z_1 \text{---} z_4 \ldots z_5\{down\} \ldots \{left\}z_6$;   % lobe
math_fit$(.5u^\# - .8h^\# * slant, .5ic^\#)$; **labels**$(1, 2, 3, 4, 5, 6)$; **endchar**;

cmchar "Calligraphic Q";
beginchar("Q", $11.7u^\#$, $cap\_height^\#$, $.5desc\_depth^\#$);
italcorr $\max(0, .6h^\# * slant - 2u^\#) + .5u^\#$;
adjust_fit$(0, 2u^\#)$; **pickup** $cal.nib$;
$x_0 = .6w$; $x_1 = .4w$; $lft\ x_2 = 0$; $x_3 = .5w$; $rt\ x_4 = w$; $x_5 = .6w$; $lft\ x_6 = 0$;
$x_7 = .23w$; $rt\ x_8 = w$; $x_9 = x_8 + 2u$;
$y_0 = .25h$; $bot\ y_1 = .15h$; $y_2 = .45[y_1, y_3]$; $top\ y_3 = h + o$; $y_4 = .5h$; $bot\ y_5 = 0$;
$y_6 = y_7 = y_9 = 0$; $y_8 = -d$;
draw $z_0 \ldots z_1\{left\} \ldots z_2\{up\} \ldots z_3\{right\}$
$\quad \ldots z_4\{down\} \ldots z_5 \ldots \{left\}z_7$;   % bowl
draw $z_7\{right\} \ldots z_8\{right\} \ldots \{up\}z_9$;   % tail
math_fit$(.5u^\#, ic^\#)$; **labels**$(0, 1, 2, 3, 4, 5, 6, 7, 8, 9)$; **endchar**;

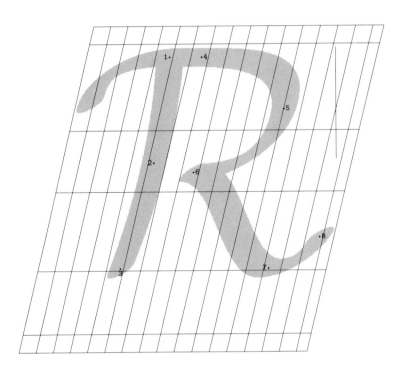

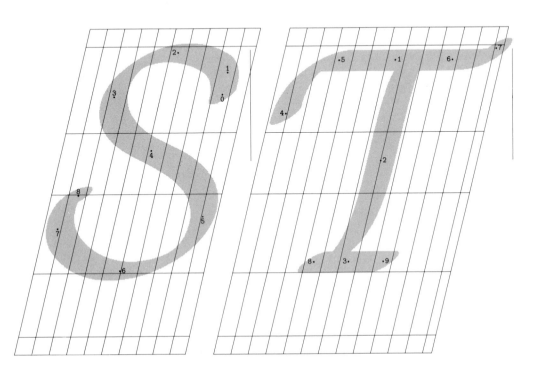

cmchar "Calligraphic R";
beginchar("R", $12.6u^\#$, $cap\_height^\#$, 0);
italcorr $.2h^\# * slant$;
adjust_fit($4u^\#$, 0); **pickup** $cal.nib$;
$lft\ x_1 = lft\ x_3 = 0$; $x_4 = \frac{1}{4}[x_1, x_5]$; $rt\ x_5 = .7w$;
$x_6 = .4[x_1, x_5]$; $rt\ x_7 = .8w$; $rt\ x_8 = w$;
$top\ y_1 = top\ y_4 = h$; $bot\ y_3 = bot\ y_7 = -o$;
$y_5 = .55[y_6, y_4]$; $bot\ y_6 = .4h$; $y_8 = .15h$;
$z_2 = .5[z_3, z_1] + bend$;
draw flex(z_1, z_2, z_3); % stem
draw $z_1\{left\}$ ... $\{down\}z_1 - flourish\_change$; % swash
draw z_1 --- z_4 .... $z_5\{down\}$ ... $\{left\}z_6$; % lobe
draw $z_6\{right\}$ .. tension atleast 1.5 .. $z_7\{right\}$ .. z_8; % tail
math_fit($.5u^\# - .8h^\# * slant, ic^\#$); **labels**($1, 2, 3, 4, 5, 6, 7, 8$); **endchar**;

cmchar "Calligraphic S";
beginchar("S", $9.9u^\#$, $cap\_height^\#$, 0);
italcorr max($.9h^\# * slant - .05w^\#, .3h^\# * slant$) $+ .5u^\#$;
adjust_fit(0, 0); **pickup** $cal.nib$;
$rt\ x_0 = rt\ x_1 = .95w$; $x_2 = .5[x_3, x_1]$; $lft\ x_3 = .15w$; $x_4 = .5[x_6, x_2]$;
$rt\ x_5 = w$; $x_6 = .5w$; $lft\ x_7 = 0$; $lft\ x_8 = .075w$;
$y_0 = .8h$; $y_1 = .9h$; $top\ y_2 = h + o$; $y_3 = .55[y_4, y_2]$; $y_4 = .55[y_6, y_2]$;
$y_5 = .45[y_6, y_4]$; $bot\ y_6 = -o$; $y_7 = .2h$; $y_8 = .35h$;
draw (z_0 -- z_1) softjoin (z_1 ... $z_2\{left\}$ ... $z_3\{down\}$ ... z_4 ... $z_5\{down\}$
    ... $z_6\{left\}$ ... z_7) softjoin ($z_7\{up\}$ ... $\{right\}z_8$); % stroke
math_fit($.5u^\# - .3h^\# * slant, .3h^\# * slant + .5u^\#$);
labels($0, 1, 2, 3, 4, 5, 6, 7, 8$); **endchar**;

cmchar "Calligraphic T";
beginchar("T", $13u^\#$, $cap\_height^\#$, 0);
italcorr $h^\# * slant + .5u^\#$;
adjust_fit(0, $-.5u^\#$); **pickup** $heavy\_cal.nib$;
$x_1 = x_3 = .5w$; $lft\ x_4 = 0$; $x_5 = w - x_6 = .25w$; $rt\ x_7 = w$;
$top\ y_1 = h$; $bot\ y_3 = 0$; $y_4 = \frac{5}{7}h$; $top\ y_5 = top\ y_6 = h$; $top\ y_7 = 1.05h$;
$z_2 = .5[z_3, z_1] + bend$;
$x_1 - x_8 = x_9 - x_1 = 2u$; $y_8 = y_9 = y_3$;
$z_0 = \frac{1}{3}[z_1, z_6]$;
draw $z_0\{left\}$ ... $z_2\{down\}$ ... $\{left\}z_8$; % stem
draw z_8 -- z_9; % foot
draw $z_4\{up\}$ ... $z_5\{right\}$ ... $z_6\{right\}$ ... $\{up\}z_7$; % arms
math_fit($.5u^\# - \frac{5}{7}h^\# * slant, -u^\#$); **labels**($1, 2, 3, 4, 5, 6, 7, 8, 9$); **endchar**;

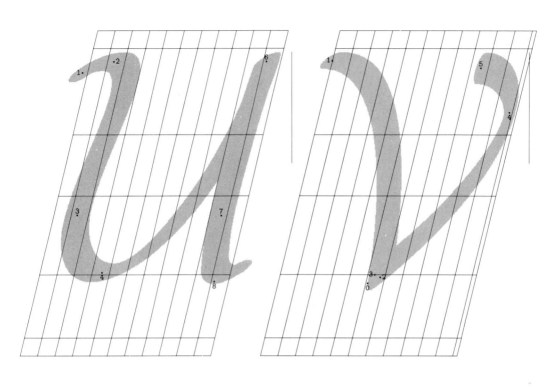

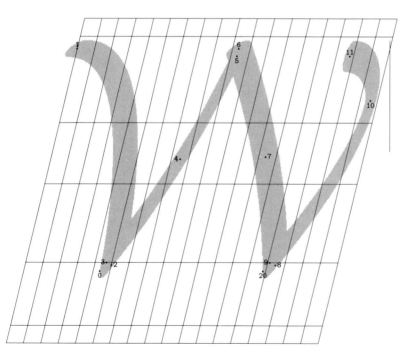

cmchar "Calligraphic U";
beginchar("U", $11u^\#$, $cap\_height^\#$, 0); **italcorr** $h^\# * slant + .5u^\#$;
adjust_fit(0, 0); **pickup** $cal.nib$;
$x_1 = x_2 - .15w$; $lft\ x_2 = .05w$; $x_3 = x_2$; $x_4 = .25[x_3, x_6]$; $rt\ x_6 = rt\ x_8 = w$;
$y_1 = y_2 - .05h$; $top\ y_2 = h$; $y_3 = .3w$; $bot\ y_4 = -o$;
$top\ y_6 = h$; $bot\ y_8 = bot\_flourish\_line$; $z_7 = .3[z_8, z_6] - bend$;
draw $z_1 \ldots z_2\{right\} .. \text{tension 2 and 1} .. z_3\{down\}$
$\quad \ldots \{right\}z_4 .. \text{tension atleast 1.5} .. \{up\}z_6$;   % left stem and arc
draw flex(z_6, z_7, z_8) softjoin $(z_8 -- z_8 + cal.extension)$;   % right stem
math_fit$(.5u^\# - \min(.3h^\# * slant + .1w^\#, .95h^\# * slant), .5ic^\#)$;
labels(1, 2, 3, 4, 6, 7, 8); **endchar**;

cmchar "Calligraphic V";
beginchar("V", $11.25u^\#$, $cap\_height^\#$, 0); **italcorr** $.8h^\# * slant + .5u^\#$;
adjust_fit(0, 0); **pickup** $med\_cal.nib$;
$x_1 = 0$; $top\ y_1 = h$; $z_3 = (.48w, 0)$;
$z_{0t_-} = z_{2t_-} +$ **penoffset** $down$ **of** $currentpen$
$\quad = z_{3t_-} +$ **penoffset** $down$ **of** $pen\_[tilted.nib]$;
draw $z_1\{right\} .. \text{tension atleast 1 and } infinity .. z_2$;   % left diagonal
pickup $tilted.nib$; $rt\ x_4 = w$; $x_5 = x_4 - .2w$; $top\ y_4 = .8h$; $top\ y_5 = h$;
path p; $p = z_3 .. \text{tension atleast 3 and 1} .. \{up\}z_4$;
erase fill $z_0 -- (x_0, y_0 - .5h) -- (x_4, y_0 - .5h) -- (x_4 + eps, y_4) -- \text{reverse } p -- \text{cycle}$;
draw $p \ldots \{left\}z_5$;   % right diagonal
math_fit$(.5u^\# + .5cap\_curve^\# - h^\# * slant, .5ic^\#)$; **labels**(0, 1, 2, 3, 4, 5); **endchar**;

cmchar "Calligraphic W";
beginchar("W", $18u^\#$, $cap\_height^\#$, 0); **italcorr** $.8h^\# * slant + .5u^\#$;
adjust_fit(0, 0); **pickup** $med\_cal.nib$;
$x_1 = 0$; $x_3 = .5[x_1, x_6]$; $x_6 = .52w$; $x_9 = .58[x_6, x_{10}]$;
$y_3 = y_9 = 0$; $top\ y_1 = top\ y_6 = h$;
$z_7 = .5[z_8, z_6] + bend$; $z_4 = .5[z_3, z_5] + bend$;
$(z_0)t_- = (z_2)t_- +$ **penoffset** $down$ **of** $currentpen$
$\quad = (z_3)t_- +$ **penoffset** $down$ **of** $pen\_[tilted.nib]$;
$(z_{20})t_- = (z_8)t_- +$ **penoffset** $down$ **of** $currentpen$
$\quad = (z_9)t_- +$ **penoffset** $down$ **of** $pen\_[tilted.nib]$;
draw $z_1\{right\} .. \text{tension atleast 1 and } infinity .. z_2$;   % first diagonal
pickup $tilted.nib$;
$x_5 = x_6$; $rt\ x_{10} = w$; $x_{11} = x_{10} - .1w$; $top\ y_5 = h$; $top\ y_{10} = .8h$; $top\ y_{11} = h$;
erase fill $z_0 -- (x_0, y_0 - .5h) -- (x_5, y_0 - .5h) -- z_5 .. z_4 .. z_3 -- \text{cycle}$;
draw $z_3 .. z_4 .. z_5$;   % second diagonal
pickup $med\_cal.nib$;
erase fill $(.3w, bot\ y_6) -- (w, bot\ y_6) -- (w, top\ y_6) -- (.3w, top\ y_6) -- \text{cycle}$;
draw $z_6 .. z_7 .. z_8$;   % third diagonal
pickup $tilted.nib$; **path** p; $p = z_9 .. \text{tension atleast 3 and 1} .. \{up\}z_{10}$;
erase fill $z_{20} -- (x_{20}, y_{20} - .5h) -- (x_{10}, y_{20} - .5h) -- (x_{10} + eps, y_{10})$
$\quad -- \text{reverse } p -- \text{cycle}$;
draw $p .. \{left\}z_{11}$;   % fourth diagonal
math_fit$(.5u^\# + .5cap\_curve^\# - h^\# * slant, .5ic^\#)$;
labels(0, 1, 2, 3, 4, 5, 6, 7, 8, 9, 10, 11, 20); **endchar**;

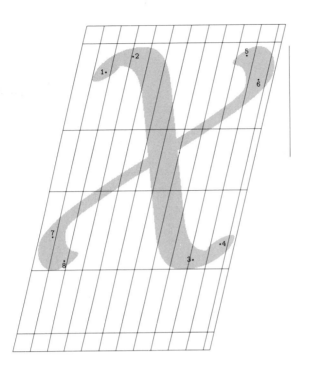

```
cmchar "Calligraphic X";
```
beginchar("X", $11.4u^\#$, $cap\_height^\#$, 0);
italcorr $h^\# * slant + .5u^\#$;
adjust_fit(0, 0); **pickup** $cal.nib$;
$lft\ x_1 = .08w$; $lft\ x_2 = .2w$; $x_4 - x_3 = x_2 - x_1$; $rt\ x_4 = w$;
$h - y_1 = y_4 = {}^1\!/_9 h$; $top\ y_2 = h$; $bot\ y_3 = 0$;
draw $z_1\{up\}$ .... $z_2\{right\}$
     ... $.2[z_2 + (.1w, 0), z_3 - (.1w, 0)]$ --- $.8[z_2 + (.1w, 0), z_3 - (.1w, 0)]$
     ... $\{right\}z_3$ .... $\{up\}z_4$;   % left diagonal
$x_5 = x_6 - u$; $rt\ x_6 = w$; $lft\ x_7 = 0$; $x_8 = x_7 + u$;
$top\ y_5 = h$; $y_6 = .85h$; $y_7 = h - y_6$; $bot\ y_8 = 0$;
draw $z_5\{right\}$ ... $z_6\{down\}$
     .. tension atleast 3 .. $\{down\}z_7$ ... $\{right\}z_8$;   % right diagonal
math_fit($.5u^\#$, ${}^1\!/_7 h^\# * slant + .5u^\#$); **labels**(1, 2, 3, 4, 5, 6, 7, 8); **endchar**;

```
cmchar "Calligraphic Y";
```
beginchar("Y", $11.75u^\#$, $cap\_height^\#$, $.5desc\_depth^\#$);
italcorr $.8h^\# * slant + .5u^\#$;
adjust_fit(0, 0); **pickup** $med\_tilted.nib$;
$rt\ x_5 = w$; $x_6 = x_5 - 2.2u$; $top\ y_5 = .8h$; $top\ y_6 = h$;
$x_4 = .4w$; $lft\ x_3 = .15w$; $y_3 = good.y\ 0$; $y_4 = good.y - d$;
path p; $p = z_3$ .. $z_4\{right\}$ .. tension atleast 3 and 1 .. $z_5\{up\}$ ... $\{left\}z_6$;
pickup $med\_cal.nib$; $x_1 = x_2 - u$; $y_1 = y_2 - .05h$; $lft\ x_2 = .6u$; $top\ y_2 = h$;
draw z_1 ... $z_2\{right\}$ .. tension atleast 1 and $infinity$
     .. rt **point** ${}^4\!/_3$ **of** p;   % left diagonal
erase fill subpath(2, 1) **of** p -- (x_5, y_4) -- $(x_5 + eps, y_5)$ -- **cycle**;
pickup $med\_tilted.nib$; **draw** p;   % right diagonal
math_fit($\max(-1.2u^\#, .9u^\# - .95h^\# * slant)$, $.5ic^\#$); **labels**(1, 2, 3, 4, 5, 6); **endchar**;

```
cmchar "Calligraphic Z";
```
beginchar("Z", $10.4u^\#$, $cap\_height^\#$, 0);
italcorr $h^\# * slant + .5u^\#$;
adjust_fit(0, 0); **pickup** $heavy\_cal.nib$;
$lft\ x_1 = .05w$; $x_2 = .4w$; $rt\ x_3 = w$; $lft\ x_7 = 0$; $x_8 = .8[x_7, x_9]$; $rt\ x_9 = 1.1w$;
$top\ y_1 = {}^{58}\!/_{70}h$; $top\ y_2 = top\ y_3 = h$; $bot\ y_7 = bot\ y_8 = 0$; $bot\ y_9 = {}^{15}\!/_{70}h$;
$z_5 = .55[z_7, z_3] + bend$;
$x_{10} = x_5 - 2.5u$; $x_{11} = x_5 + 2u$; $x_{12} = .2[x_3, x_2]$; $x_{13} = .2[x_7, x_8]$;
$y_{10} = y_5$; $bot\ y_{11} = y_{10} - {}^6\!/_{70}h$; $y_{12} = {}^{64}\!/_{70}h$; $y_{13} = {}^6\!/_{70}h$;
draw $z_1\{up\}$ ... $z_2\{right\}$ ... $\{right\}z_{12}$ ... z_3;   % upper arm
draw flex(z_3, z_5, z_7);   % diagonal
draw z_7 ... $z_{13}\{right\}$ ... $\{right\}z_8$ ... $\{up\}z_9$;   % lower arm
pickup $light\_cal.nib$;
draw z_{10} ... $z_5\{right\}$ ... $\{down\}z_{11}$;   % bar
math_fit($.5u^\#$, $.6ic^\#$); **labels**(1, 2, 3, 5, 7, 8, 9, 10, 11, 12, 13); **endchar**;

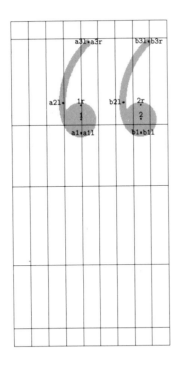

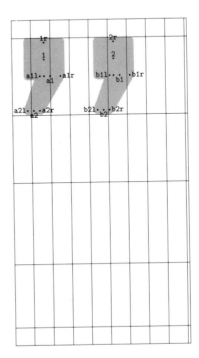

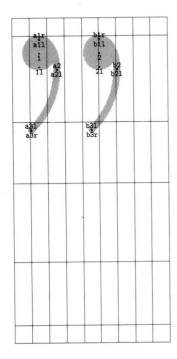

Now we switch to a more mundane program file, `comlig.mf`:

% This file defines characters common to roman and italic text fonts
% that appear only when *ligs* > 0.

% Character codes $'042$, $'055$, $'134$, $'173$, and $'174$ are generated.

ligtable "`‘`": "`‘`" =: oct "134";
ligtable "`’`": "`’`" =: oct "042", "?" kern $2u^\#$, "!" kern $2u^\#$;

ligtable "`-`": "`-`" =: oct "173";
ligtable oct "173": "`-`" =: oct "174";

cmchar "`Opening quotes`";
beginchar(oct "134", $7u^\# + \max(2u^\#, dot\_size^\#)$, $asc\_height^\#$, 0);
italcorr $asc\_height^\# * slant - .1u^\#$;
adjust_fit(0, 0);
$x_2 + .5dot\_size = \text{hround}(w - .6u)$; $y_1 + .5dot\_size = h - comma\_depth$;
$x_2 - x_1 = \text{hround}(1.5u + \max(2u, dot\_size))$; $y_2 = y_1$;
$ammoc(1, a, dot\_size, .25u, comma\_depth)$;   % left dot and tail
$ammoc(2, b, dot\_size, .25u, comma\_depth)$;   % right dot and tail
penlabels(1, 2); **endchar**;

cmchar "`Closing quotes`";
beginchar(oct "042", $7u^\# + \max(2u^\#, dot\_size^\#)$, $asc\_height^\#$, 0);
italcorr $asc\_height^\# * slant + dot\_size^\# - 4.1u^\#$;
adjust_fit(0, 0);
$x_1 - .5dot\_size = \text{hround } .6u$; $y_2 + .5dot\_size = h$;
$x_2 - x_1 = \text{hround}(1.5u + \max(2u, dot\_size))$; $y_2 = y_1$;
$comma(1, a, dot\_size, .25u, comma\_depth)$;   % left dot and tail
$comma(2, b, dot\_size, .25u, comma\_depth)$;   % right dot and tail
penlabels(1, 2); **endchar**;

When English printers did decide to mark quotations,
they refused the French form and made a very awkward substitute
by inverting two commas for the beginning
and using two apostrophes for the ending.

— T. L. DE VINNE, *Correct Composition* (1902)

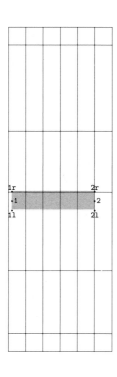

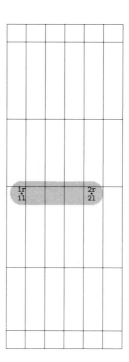

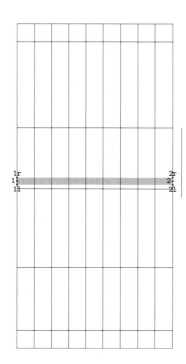

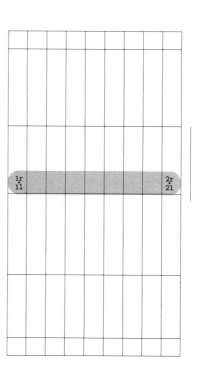

cmchar "Hyphen";
beginchar("-", $6u^\#$, $x\_height^\#$, 0);
italcorr $.5x\_height^\# * slant - .5u^\#$;
adjust_fit(0, 0);
numeric *thickness*; *thickness* = **if** *hefty*: *bar* **else**: $.75[hair, stem]$ **fi**;
pickup *crisp.nib*; $pos_1(thickness, 90)$; $pos_2(thickness, 90)$;
top $y_{1r} = top\ y_{2r} = \text{vround}(.5h + .5thickness)$; *rt* $x_2 = \text{hround}(w - u) + eps$;
if *monospace*: $x_2 = w - x_1$ **else**: *lft* $x_1 = \text{hround}\ .2u - eps$ **fi**;
filldraw stroke z_{1e} -- z_{2e};   % bar
penlabels(1, 2); **endchar**;

cmchar "En dash";
beginchar(oct "173", $9u^\#$, $x\_height^\#$, 0);
italcorr $.61803x\_height^\# * slant + .5u^\#$;
adjust_fit(0, 0);
pickup *crisp.nib*; $pos_1(vair, 90)$; $pos_2(vair, 90)$;
top $y_{1r} = top\ y_{2r} = \text{vround}(.61803h + .5vair)$; *lft* $x_1 = -eps$; *rt* $x_2 = w + eps$;
filldraw stroke z_{1e} -- z_{2e};   % bar
penlabels(1, 2); **endchar**;

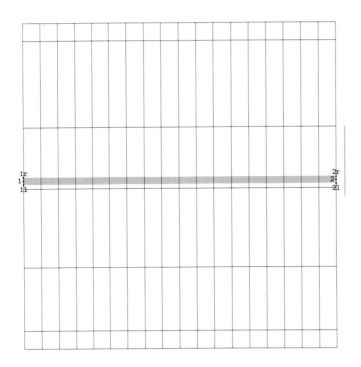

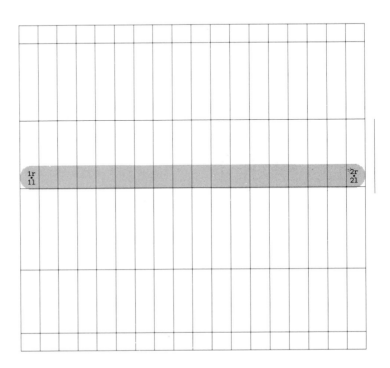

cmchar "Em dash";
beginchar(oct "174", $18u^\#$, $x\_height^\#$, 0);
italcorr $.61803x\_height^\# * slant + .5u^\#$;
adjust_fit($letter\_fit^\#$, $letter\_fit^\#$);
pickup $crisp.nib$; $pos_1(vair, 90)$; $pos_2(vair, 90)$;
$top\ y_{1r} = top\ y_{2r} = \mathrm{vround}(.61803h + .5vair)$; $lft\ x_1 = -eps$; $rt\ x_2 = w + eps$;
filldraw stroke z_{1e} -- z_{2e};   % bar
penlabels(1, 2); **endchar**;

The short program file `cscspu.mf` consists mostly of copies of programs from other files; its purpose is simply to put certain uppercase characters into lowercase positions.

                % This file puts characters into code positions $'020$, $'021$, and $'031$
                        % to take the place of dotless i, dotless j, and sharp s
                                % in caps-and-small-caps fonts

cmchar "The letter I";   % in code position $'020$
beginchar(oct "020", $\max(6u^\#, 4u^\# + cap\_stem^\#)$, $cap\_height^\#$, 0);

    ⋮   (a copy of the program for 'I' in **romanu** comes here)

math_fit(0, $.5ic^\#$); **penlabels**(1, 2); **endchar**;

cmchar "The letter J";   % in code position $'021$
beginchar(oct "021", $9u^\#$, $cap\_height^\#$, 0);

    ⋮   (a copy of the program for 'J' in **romanu** comes here)

math_fit(0, $.5ic^\# - .5u^\#$); **penlabels**(1, 2, 3, 4, 5); **endchar**;

cmchar "Two letters S";
beginchar(oct "031", $10u^\#$, $cap\_height^\#$, 0);

    ⋮   (a copy of the program for 'S' in **romanu** comes here)

  filldraw stroke $term.e(7, 8, left, 1, 4)$; **fi**   % lower arc and terminal
$r := r + w + shrink\_fit$; $charwd := 2charwd$;
addto *currentpicture* **also** *currentpicture* shifted $(w + shrink\_fit, 0)$;
penlabels(0, 1, 1', 2, 3, 4, 5, 6, 7, 8, 8', 9, 10); **endchar**;

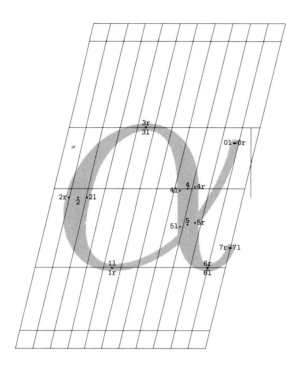

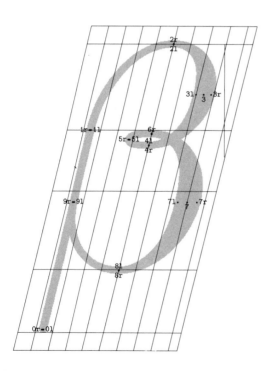

We move now to more ancient letterforms, in program file `greekl.mf`:

% This lowercase Greek alphabet was prepared by D. E. Knuth in December, 1979,
    % inspired by the Monotype faces used in *The Art of Computer Programming*.
            % (It has been designed for math formulas, not Greek texts.)
        % The programs were revised for the new METAFONT conventions in 1985.

                % Character codes $'013$–$'047$ are generated.

cmchar "Lowercase Greek alpha";
beginchar(oct "013", $11u^\#$, $x\_height^\#$, 0);
italcorr max($\frac{1}{3}x\_height^\# * slant + .5hair^\# + .5u^\#$, $x\_height^\# * slant - .5u^\#$);
adjust_fit(0, 0); **pickup** *fine.nib*;
$pos_0(hair, 0)$; $pos_1(vair, -90)$; $pos_2(curve, -180)$; $pos_3(vair, -270)$;
$z_4 = (w - 3.25u, \frac{9}{16}h)$; $z_5 = (w - 2.75u, .5[vair, y_4])$;
numeric *theta*; $theta = angle(z_4 - z_5) - 90$;
$pos_4(stem, theta)$; $pos_5(stem, theta)$;
$pos_6(vair, 90)$; $pos_7(hair, 180)$;
$rt\ x_{0r} = \text{hround}(w - u)$; $x_1 = x_3 = .5w - u$; $lft\ x_{2r} = \text{hround}(1.5u - .5curve)$;
$x_6 = w - u$; $x_7 + .5hair = \text{hround}(w + .5hair - epsilon)$;
$top\ y_0 = \text{vround}\ .8[bar\_height, h]$; $bot\ y_{1r} = bot\ y_{6l} = -oo$;
$y_2 = .5[y_1, y_3]$; $top\ y_{3r} = h + oo$; $y_7 = \frac{1}{4}bar\_height$;
filldraw stroke $z_{0e}\{down\}\ \ldots\ pulled\_arc_e(1, 2)\ \&\ pulled\_arc_e(2, 3)$
        $\ldots\ z_{4e}\ \text{---}\ z_{5e}\ \ldots\ z_{6e}\{right\}\ \ldots\ \{up\}z_{7e}$;   % diagonal, bowl, and hook
math_fit($-.3x\_height^\# * slant + .5curve^\# - u^\#$, $\frac{1}{3}x\_height^\# * slant + .5hair^\# + .5u^\#$);
penlabels(0, 1, 2, 3, 4, 5, 6, 7); **endchar**;

cmchar "Lowercase Greek beta";
beginchar(oct "014", $9.5u^\#$, $asc\_height^\#$, $desc\_depth^\#$);
italcorr $.5[x\_height^\#, asc\_height^\#] * slant - u^\#$;
adjust_fit(0, 0); **pickup** *fine.nib*;
$pos_0(hair, 180)$; $pos_1(hair, 180)$; $pos_2(vair, 90)$;
$pos_3(stem, 0)$; $pos_4(vair, -90)$; $pos_5(hair, -180)$;
$pos_6(vair, -270)$; $pos_7(curve, -360)$; $pos_8(vair, -450)$; $pos_9(hair, -540)$;
$x_0 = x_1 = x_9$; $lft\ x_{0l} = \text{hround}(1.5u - .5hair)$; $x_2 = x_4 = x_6 = x_8 = .5w + .25u$;
$rt\ x_{3r} = \text{hround}(w - 1.5u)$; $rt\ x_{7r} = \text{hround}(w - 1.5u + .5curve)$;
$rt\ x_{5l} = \text{hround}(x_4 - u)$;
$bot\ y_0 = -d$; $y_1 = top\ y_{6r} = x\_height$; $top\ y_{2r} = h + oo$; $y_3 = .5[y_2, y_4]$;
$y_5 = .5[y_4, y_6]$; $top\ y_{6r} - bot\ y_{4r} = vstem + eps$; $bot\ y_8 = -oo$; $y_7 = y_9 = .5[y_6, y_8]$;
if $y_{6l} < y_{4l}$: $y_{6l} := y_{4l} := y_5$; **fi**
filldraw stroke $z_{0e}\ \text{---}\ z_{1e}\ \ldots\ pulled\_arc_e(2, 3)$
        $\&\ pulled\_arc_e(3, 4)\ \ldots\ \{up\}z_{5e}$;   % stem and upper bowl
filldraw stroke $z_{5e}\{up\}\ \ldots\ pulled\_arc_e(6, 7)$
        $\&\ pulled\_arc_e(7, 8)\ \ldots\ \{up\}z_{9e}$;   % lower bowl
math_fit($desc\_depth^\# * slant + .5hair^\# - u^\#$, $.7x\_height^\# * slant + .5curve^\# - 1.5u^\#$);
penlabels(0, 1, 2, 3, 4, 5, 6, 7, 8, 9); **endchar**;

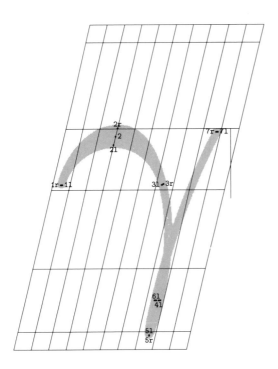

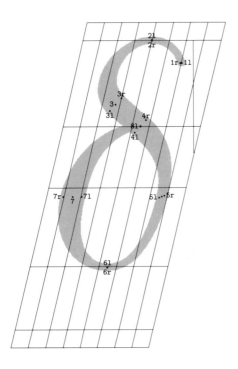

cmchar "Lowercase Greek gamma";
beginchar(oct "015", $10u^\#$, $x\_height^\#$, $desc\_depth^\#$);
italcorr $x\_height^\# * slant - .5u^\#$;
adjust_fit$(0, 0)$; **pickup** *fine.nib*;
$pos_1(hair, 180)$; $pos_2(vstem + dw, 90)$;
$pos_4(hair, 0)$; $pos_5(vair, -90)$; $pos_6(hair, -180)$; $pos_7(hair, -180)$;
$bot\ y_1 = .5772156649h$; $top\ y_{2r} = h + oo$; $y_4 = y_6 = -.5d$;
$bot\ y_{5r} = -d - o$; $top\ y_7 = h$;
$lft\ x_{1r} = \text{hround}(.5u - .5hair)$; $x_2 = 3u$; $rt\ x_{4r} = \text{hround}(w - 2u)$; $x_5 = .5[x_4, x_6]$;
$rt\ x_{4r} - lft\ x_{6r} = \text{hround}\ ^1/_3[hair, stem] + eps$; $rt\ x_{7l} = \text{hround}(w - u)$;
if $x_{4l} < x_{6l}$: $x_{4l} := x_{6l} := x_5$; **fi**
$pos_3(hair, angle(z_4 - z_2) + 90)$; $x_3 = superness[x_2, x_4]$; $y_3 = superness[y_4, y_2]$;
filldraw stroke $z_{1e}\{up\} \ldots z_{2e}\{right\} \ldots z_{3e}\{z_4 - z_2\}$
    $\ldots z_{4e}\{down\} \ldots \{left\}z_{5e}$;   % arc
filldraw stroke $z_{5e}\{left\} \ldots z_{6e}\{up\} \ldots \{2(x_7 - x_6), y_7 - y_6\}z_{7e}$;   % stem
math_fit$(-.5772156649x\_height^\# * slant, ic^\# - u^\#)$;
penlabels$(1, 2, 3, 4, 5, 6, 7)$; **endchar**;

cmchar "Lowercase Greek delta";
beginchar(oct "016", $8u^\#$, $asc\_height^\#$, 0);
italcorr $.9asc\_height^\# * slant + .5hair^\# - 1.5u^\#$;
adjust_fit$(0, 0)$; **pickup** *fine.nib*;
$pos_1(hair, -180)$; $pos_2(vair, -90)$;
numeric $theta$; $theta = angle(18u, -h)$;
$pos_3(stem, theta + 90)$; $pos_4(stem, theta + 90)$; $pos_5(^1/_4[hair, stem], 20)$;
$pos_6(vair, -90)$; $pos_7(curve, -180)$; $pos_8(vair, -270)$;
$rt\ x_{1l} = \text{hround}(w - 2u + .5hair)$; $x_2 = .5w$; $x_{3r} = 3u$; $rt\ x_{5r} = \text{hround}(w - u)$;
$x_4 = x_6 = x_8 = .5w + .5u$; $lft\ x_{7r} = \text{hround}(1.5u - .5curve)$;
$top\ y_{2l} = h + oo$; $y_1 = \min(.9h, y_{2r} - eps)$; $top\ y_{8r} = x\_height + oo$; $y_4 = y_8$;
$z_4 - z_3 = whatever * (18u, -h)$; $y_5 = y_7 = .5[y_6, y_8]$; $bot\ y_6 = -oo$;
filldraw stroke $z_{1e}\{x_2 - x_1, 3(y_2 - y_1)\} \ldots z_{2e}\{left\} \ldots z_{3e} \text{ --- } z_{4e}$
    $\ldots z_{5e}\{down\} \ldots pulled\_arc_e(6, 7) \ \& \ pulled\_arc_e(7, 8)$;   % hook and bowl
math_fit$(-.3x\_height^\# * slant + .5curve^\# - u^\#, .7x\_height^\# * slant - .5u^\#)$;
penlabels$(1, 2, 3, 4, 5, 6, 7, 8)$; **endchar**;

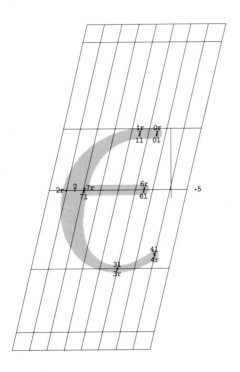

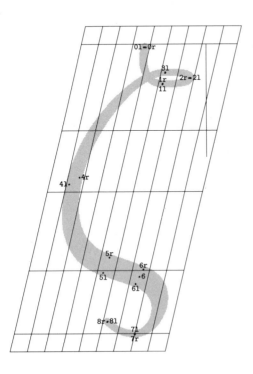

cmchar "Lowercase Greek epsilon";
beginchar(oct "017", $8u^\#$, $x\_height^\#$, 0);
italcorr $x\_height^\# * slant + .5hair^\# - 2u^\#$;
adjust_fit(0, 0);　**pickup** *fine.nib*;
$pos_0(bar, 90)$;　$pos_1(bar, 90)$;　$pos_2(curve, 180)$;
$pos_3(vair, 270)$;　$pos_4(hair, 300)$;　$pos_6(bar, 90)$;　$pos_7(bar, 90)$;
$x_1 = .5w + .5u$;　$x_0 = x_1 + u$;　*lft* $x_{2r} = $ hround$(1.5u - .5curve)$;　$x_3 = .5[x_0, x_1]$;
$x_{4r} = good.x(w - u)$;　$x_5 = w + .5u$;　$x_6 = x_0$;　$z_7 = z_{2l}$;
top $y_{0r} = $ *top* $y_{1r} = h$;　$y_2 = y_5 = y_6 = bar\_height$;　*bot* $y_{3r} = -oo$;
path p;　$p = z_{3r}\{right\} \ldots \{up\}z_5$;
numeric t;　$t = $ ypart$(((x_{4r}, y_{3r}) $ -- $ (x_{4r}, y_5)) $ intersectiontimes $p)$;
$y_{4r} = $ ypart **point** t **of** p;
filldraw circ_stroke $z_{0e} \ldots pulled\_arc_e(1, 2) \& pulled\_arc_e(2, 3)$
　　$\ldots z_{4e}\{$**direction** t **of** $p\}$;　　　　　　　　　　　　% arc
filldraw circ_stroke z_{6e} -- z_{7e};　　　　　　　　　　　　　% bar
math_fit$(-.3x\_height^\# * slant + .5curve^\# - u^\#, ic^\#)$;
penlabels(0, 1, 2, 3, 4, 5, 6, 7);　**endchar**;

cmchar "Lowercase Greek zeta";
beginchar(oct "020", $9u^\#$, $asc\_height^\#$, $desc\_depth^\#$);
italcorr $.75[x\_height^\#, asc\_height^\#] * slant - 1.5u^\#$;
adjust_fit(0, 0);　**pickup** *fine.nib*;
$pos_0(hair, -360)$;　$pos_1(vair, -270)$;　$pos_2(hair, -180)$;　$pos_3(vair, -90)$;
numeric $theta$;　$theta = 90 - $ angle$(25u, x\_height)$;　*slope* $:= -x\_height/25u$;
$pos_6(stem, theta)$;　$pos_7(vair, -90)$;　$pos_8(vair, -135)$;
lft $x_{0l} = $ hround $3.5u$;　$x_1 = x_3 = .5[x_0, x_2]$;
rt $x_{2l} = $ hround max$(rt\ x_{0r}, w - 2u) + eps$;
top $y_0 = h$;　*top* $y_{3l} = $ *bot* $y_{1l} + vstem + eps = $ vround$(y_0 - .25(h - x\_height))$;
$y_2 = .5[y_1, y_3]$;
if $y_{1r} > y_{3r}$: $y_{1r} := y_{3r} := y_2$;　**fi**
lft $x_{4l} = $ hround u;　$x_{4r} - x_{4l} = $ hround $.6[vair, stem] - fine$;
$x_6 + .5u = x_7 = w - 2u$;　$x_8 = .5w + .75u$;
$y_6 = -.1d$;　$y_8 = -3/4d - oo$;　*bot* $y_{7r} = -d - oo$;
ellipse_set$(3l, 4l, 5l, 6l)$;　*ellipse_set*$(3r, 4r, 5r, 6r)$;
$y_{4l} := .9[y_6, y_{4l}]$;　$y_4 = y_{4r} := .9[y_6, y_{4r}]$;
filldraw circ_stroke $z_{0e}\{down\} \ldots z_{1e}\{right\} \ldots \{up\}z_{2e}$;　　% opening hook
filldraw circ_stroke $z_{8e}\{x_7 - x_8, 2(y_7 - y_8)\} \ldots z_{7e}\{right\}$
　　$\ldots z_{6e}$ --- $z_{5e} \ldots . \{up\}z_{4e}$
　　$\ldots$ tension 1 and atleast 1.5 $\ldots \{right\}z_{3e} \ldots \{down\}z_{2e}$;　　% main stroke
math_fit$(-.2asc\_height^\# * slant - .5u^\#, 0)$;
penlabels(0, 1, 2, 3, 4, 5, 6, 7, 8);　**endchar**;

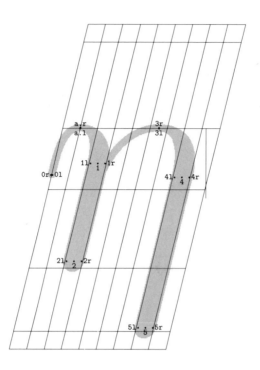

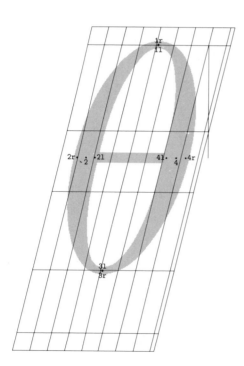

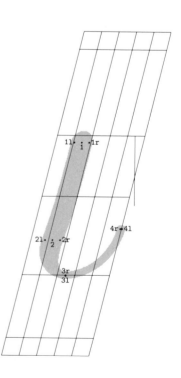

cmchar "Lowercase Greek eta";
beginchar(oct "021", $9u^\#$, $x\_height^\#$, $desc\_depth^\#$);
italcorr $.8x\_height^\# * slant + .5stem^\# - u^\#$;
adjust_fit$(0, 0)$; **pickup** *fine.nib*;
$x_0 = 0$; $x_1 = x_2$; $pos_2(stem, 0)$; *lft* $x_{2l} = \text{hround}(2.5u - .5stem)$; $y_2 - .5stem = -oo$;
$hook\_in(0, a, 1)$;   % opening hook
filldraw circ_stroke $z_{2e} \mathrel{--} z_{1e}$;   % left stem
$x_4 + .5stem = \text{hround}(w - 1.5u + .5stem)$; *ital_arch*$(2, 3, 4)$;   % arch
$pos_5(stem, 0)$; $x_5 = x_4$; $y_5 - .5stem = -d - o$;
filldraw circ_stroke $z_{5e} \mathrel{--} z_{4e}$;   % right stem
math_fit$(-\,^2/_3 x\_height^\# * slant + .5hair^\# + .5u^\#, ic^\# - \,^1/_3 x\_height^\# * slant)$;
penlabels$(0, a, 1, 2, 3, 4, 5)$; **endchar**;

cmchar "Lowercase Greek theta";
beginchar(oct "022", $8.25u^\#$, $asc\_height^\#$, 0);
italcorr $.7asc\_height^\# * slant + .5curve^\# - u^\#$;
adjust_fit$(0, 0)$; **pickup** *fine.nib*;
$pos_1(vair, 90)$; $pos_2(curve, 180)$; $pos_3(vair, 270)$; $pos_4(curve, 360)$;
$x_1 = x_3 = .5w$; *lft* $x_{2r} = \text{hround}(1.5u - .5curve)$; $x_4 = w - x_2$;
top $y_{1r} = h + oo$; $y_2 = y_4 = .5[y_1, y_3]$; *bot* $y_{3r} = -oo$;
filldraw stroke $pulled\_arc_e(1, 2)$ & $pulled\_arc_e(2, 3)$
    & $pulled\_arc_e(3, 4)$ & $pulled\_arc_e(4, 1)$;   % bowl
$pos_{2'}(bar, 90)$; $pos_{4'}(bar, 90)$; $z_{2'} = z_{2l}$; $z_{4'} = z_{4l}$;
filldraw stroke $z_{2'e} \mathrel{--} z_{4'e}$;   % bar
math_fit$(-.3asc\_height^\# * slant - u^\# + .5curve^\#, ic^\# - .5u^\#)$;
penlabels$(1, 2, 3, 4)$; **endchar**;

cmchar "Lowercase Greek iota";
beginchar(oct "023", $5u^\#$, $x\_height^\#$, 0);
italcorr $^1/_3 x\_height^\# * slant + .5hair^\# + .5u^\#$;
adjust_fit(**if** *monospace*: $u^\#$, $u^\#$ **else**: $0, 0$ **fi**); **pickup** *fine.nib*;
$pos_1(stem, 0)$; *lft* $x_{1l} = \text{hround}(1.5u - .5stem)$; $y_1 + .5stem = h + oo$;
$x_2 = x_1 - .25u$; $x_4 = w$; $hook\_out(2, 3, 4)(skewed)$;   % closing hook
filldraw circ_stroke $z_{1e}\{down\} \ldots \{-u, -x\_height\}z_{2e}$;   % stem
math_fit$(0, ic^\#)$; **penlabels**$(1, 2, 3, 4)$; **endchar**;

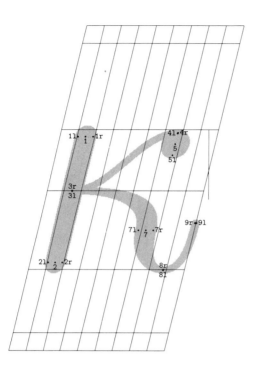

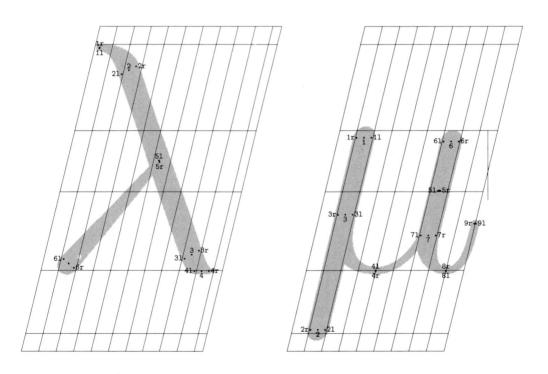

cmchar "Lowercase Greek kappa";
beginchar(oct "024", $9u^\#$, $x\_height^\#$, 0);
italcorr $1/3x\_height^\# * slant + .5hair^\# + .5u^\#$;
adjust_fit(0, 0); **pickup** *fine.nib*;
$pos_1(stem, 0)$; $pos_2(stem, 0)$; $pos_3(vair, 90)$; $pos_4(vair, 90)$; $pos_5(flare, 90)$;
$x_1 = x_2 = x_3$; *lft* $x_{1l} = \text{hround}(1.5u - .5stem)$;
$y_1 + .5stem = h + oo$; $y_2 - .5stem = -oo$;
filldraw $z_{1l} \text{ --- } z_{2l} .. z_{2r} \text{ --- } z_{1r} ..$ cycle;   % stem
$y_3 = bar\_height$; *top* $y_{4r} = h$; $x_4 + .5flare = \text{hround}(w - 1.5u)$; $z_{5r} = z_{4r}$;
path p, q; $p = z_{3l}\{right\} .. \{right\}z_{4l}$; $q = z_{5r}\{right\} .. z_{5l}\{left\} ...$ cycle;
numeric t; $t = \text{ypart}(p \text{ intersectiontimes } q)$;
filldraw stroke $z_{3e}\{right\} .. \{right\}z_{4e}$;   % upper diagonal
filldraw subpath$(0, t)$ **of** q -- cycle;   % bulb
$pos_7(stem, 0)$; $pos_8(vair, 90)$; $pos_9(hair, 180)$;
$x_9 + .5hair = \text{hround}(w + .5hair - epsilon)$; $y_9 = 1/3x\_height$;
lft $x_{7l} = \text{hround}(w - 2.75u - .5stem)$; $y_7 = 1/2y_3$; $x_8 = w - 1.2u$; *bot* $y_{8l} = -oo$;
filldraw stroke $z_{3e}\{right\} ... z_{7e}\{down\}$
$... z_{8e}\{right\} ... \{up\}z_{9e}$;   % lower diagonal
math_fit$(0, ic^\#)$; **penlabels**$(1, 2, 3, 4, 5, 7, 8, 9)$; **endchar**;

cmchar "Lowercase Greek lambda";
beginchar(oct "025", $10.5u^\#$, $asc\_height^\#$, 0); **adjust_fit**(0, 0); **pickup** *fine.nib*;
$pos_1(vair, 90)$; *lft* $x_1 = \text{hround } .1u$; *top* $y_{1r} = h$;
$x_2 = x_1 + 2u$; $y_2 = .7[x\_height, h]$; $x_3 = w - 2u$;
bot $y_4 = -oo$; $y_3 = \max(.07h, y_4 + eps)$;
$z_4 - (.25u, 0) = whatever[z_2, z_3]$; **numeric** *theta*; *theta* $= \text{angle}(z_2 - z_3) - 90$;
$pos_2(stem, theta)$; $pos_3(stem, theta)$; $pos_4(stem, 0)$;
filldraw circ_stroke $z_{1e}\{right\} ... z_{2e} \text{ --- } z_{3e}$
$... \{2(x_{4e} - x_{3e}), y_{4e} - y_{3e}\}z_{4e}$;   % long diagonal
$y_5 = .5[bar\_height, x\_height]$; $z_5 = whatever[z_2, z_3]$;
$x_6 = 1.5u$; $y_6 - .5stem = -oo$; $pos_5(hair, theta - 90)$; $pos_6(stem, \text{angle}(z_5 - z_6) - 90)$;
filldraw circ_stroke z_{6e} -- z_{5e};   % short diagonal
penlabels$(1, 2, 3, 4, 5, 6)$; **endchar**;

cmchar "Lowercase Greek mu";
beginchar(oct "026", $9u^\#$, $x\_height^\#$, $desc\_depth^\#$);
italcorr $1/3x\_height^\# * slant + .5hair^\# + .5u^\#$;
adjust_fit(0, 0); **pickup** *fine.nib*; **interim** *superness* := *more_super*;
$pos_1(stem, -180)$; $pos_2(stem, -180)$; $x_1 = x_2 = x_3$; *lft* $x_{1r} = \text{hround}(1.5u - .5stem)$;
$y_1 + .5stem = h + oo$; $y_2 - .5stem = -d - o$;
filldraw $z_{1r} \text{ --- } z_{2r} .. z_{2l} \text{ --- } z_{1l} ..$ cycle;   % left stem
$pos_3(stem, -180)$; $pos_4(vair, -90)$; $pos_5(hair, 0)$; $x_4 = .5[x_3, x_5]$;
$pos_6(stem, 0)$; *rt* $x_{6r} = \text{hround}(w - 2.5u + .5stem)$;
$x_5 = x_6 = x_7$; $x_9 = w$; *hook_out*(7, 8, 9);   % closing hook
$y_3 = .7[y_4, y_5]$; *bot* $y_{4r} = -oo$; $y_5 = .57h$; $y_6 + .5stem = h$;
filldraw stroke $super\_arc_e(3, 4) ... \{up\}z_{5e}$;   % left stem and arc
filldraw circ_stroke z_{6e} -- z_{7e};   % right stem
math_fit$(desc\_depth^\# * slant + .5stem^\# - u^\#, ic^\#)$;
penlabels$(1, 2, 3, 4, 5, 6, 7, 8, 9)$; **endchar**;

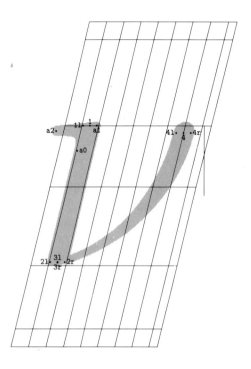

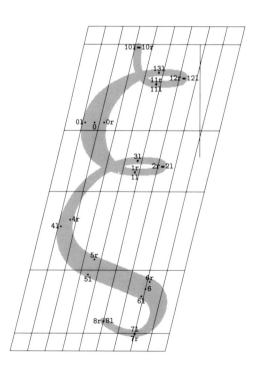

cmchar "Lowercase Greek nu";
beginchar(oct "027", $8.5u^\#$, $x\_height^\#$, 0);
italcorr $x\_height^\# * slant + .5stem^\# - u^\#$;
adjust_fit(0, 0); **pickup** *fine.nib*;
$pos_3(vair, -90)$; $pos_4(stem, 0)$; $bot\ y_{3r} = 0$; $y_4 + .5stem = h + oo$;
$x_3 - .5stem = \text{hround}(1.5u - .5stem)$; $x_4 + .5stem = \text{hround}(w - 1.5u + .5stem)$;
filldraw circ_stroke $z_{4e}\{down\} \ldots \{-36u, -h\}z_{3e}$;   % diagonal
pickup *tiny.nib*; $pos_1(stem, 0)$; $pos_2(stem, 0)$;
$top\ y_1 = h + \min(oo, serif\_drop)$; $bot\ y_2 = 0$; $x_1 = x_2 = x_3$;
$z = ((z_4\{down\} \ldots \{-36u, -h\}z_3)\ \text{intersectionpoint}\ ((x_{2r}, 0) \text{ -- } (x_{2r}, h)))$;
filldraw z_{1l} -- z_{2l} -- z -- z_{1r} -- cycle;   % stem
$sloped\_serif.l(1, 2, a, {}^1\!/_3, jut, serif\_drop)$;   % upper left serif
math_fit$(0, ic^\# - {}^1\!/_3 x\_height^\# * slant - .5u^\#)$; **penlabels**(1, 2, 3, 4); **endchar**;

cmchar "Lowercase Greek xi";
beginchar(oct "030", $9u^\#$, $asc\_height^\#$, $desc\_depth^\#$);
italcorr $.75[x\_height^\#, asc\_height^\#] * slant - 2u^\#$;
adjust_fit(0, 0); **pickup** *fine.nib*;
$pos_{10}(hair, -720)$; $pos_{11}(vair, -630)$; $pos_{12}(hair, -540)$; $pos_{13}(vair, -450)$;
$lft\ x_{10l} = \text{hround}\ {}^1\!/_3 w$; $x_{11} = x_{13} = .5[x_{10}, x_{12}]$; $rt\ x_{12l} = \text{hround}(w - 2.5u)$;
$top\ y_{10} = h$; $top\ y_{13l} = bot\ y_{11l} + vstem + eps = \text{vround}(y_{10} - .25(h - x\_height))$;
$y_{12} = .5[y_{11}, y_{13}]$; **if** $y_{11r} > y_{13r}$: $y_{11r} := y_{13r} := y_{12}$; **fi**
$pos_0(curve, -360)$; $pos_1(vair, -270)$; $pos_2(hair, -180)$; $pos_3(vair, -90)$;
numeric *theta*; $theta = 90 - \text{angle}(22u, x\_height)$; $slope := -x\_height/22u$;
$pos_6(stem, theta)$; $pos_7(vair, -90)$; $pos_8(vair, -135)$;
$lft\ x_{0l} = \text{hround}\ u$; $x_1 = x_3 = x_{11}$; $x_2 = x_{12}$;
$y_0 = .5[y_{13}, y_1]$; $top\ y_{3l} = \text{vround}\ .5h = bot\ y_{1l} + vstem + eps$; $y_2 = .5[y_1, y_3]$;
if $y_{1r} > y_{3r}$: $y_{1r} := y_{3r} := y_2$; **fi**
$lft\ x_{4l} = \text{hround}\ u$; $x_{4r} - x_{4l} = \text{hround}\ .5[vair, stem] - fine$;
$x_6 = x_7 = w - 2u$; $x_8 = .5w + .5u$;
$y_6 = -.3d$; $bot\ y_{7r} = -d - oo$; $y_8 = \max(-{}^3\!/_4 d - oo, y_{7l})$;
$ellipse\_set(3l, 4l, 5l, 6l)$; $ellipse\_set(3r, 4r, 5r, 6r)$;
$y_{4l} := .9[y_6, y_{4l}]$; $y_4 = y_{4r} := .9[y_6, y_{4r}]$;
filldraw circ_stroke $z_{10e}\{down\} \ldots z_{11e}\{right\} \ldots \{up\}z_{12e}$;   % opening hook
filldraw stroke $z_{12e}\{up\} \ldots z_{13e}\{left\} \ldots z_{0e}\{down\}$
   $\ldots z_{1e}\{right\} \ldots \{up\}z_{2e}$;   % upper arc
filldraw circ_stroke $z_{8e}\{x_7 - x_8, 2(y_7 - y_8)\} \ldots z_{7e}\{right\} \ldots z_{6e}$
   --- $z_{5e} \ldots \{up\}z_{4e} \ldots \{right\}z_{3e} \ldots \{down\}z_{2e}$;   % main stroke
math_fit$(-.2asc\_height^\# * slant - .5u^\#, 0)$;
penlabels(0, 1, 2, 3, 4, 5, 6, 7, 8, 10, 11, 12, 13); **endchar**;

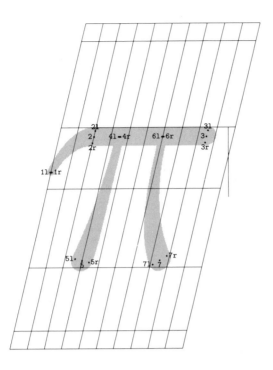

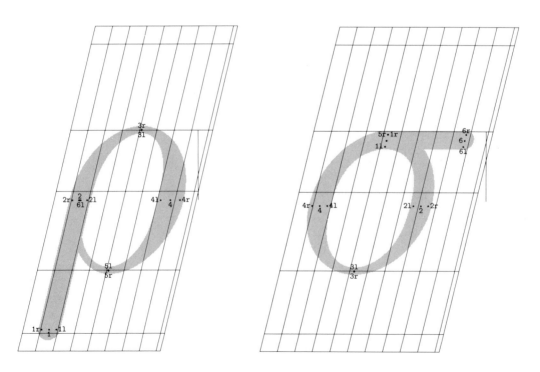

cmchar "Lowercase Greek pi";
beginchar(oct "031", $10u^\#$, $x\_height^\#$, 0);
italcorr $x\_height^\# * slant + .5stem^\# - u^\#$;
adjust_fit(0, 0); pi_stroke;   % hook and bar
$pos_4(hair, 0)$; $pos_6(hair, 0)$; $x_4 = 3.5u$; $x_6 = w - 4u$; $y_4 = y_6 = y_2$;
$x_5 = 3u$; $x_7 = w - 2.5u$; $y_5 = y_7 = .5stem - oo$;
pair $v[]$; $v_1 = (z_4 - z_5)$ xscaled 3.14159; $v_2 = (z_6 - z_7)$ xscaled 3.14159;
$pos_5(stem, \text{angle } v_1 - 90)$; $pos_7(stem, \text{angle } v_2 - 90)$;
filldraw circ_stroke $z_{5e}\{v_1\} \ldots \{up\}z_{4e}$;   % left stem
filldraw circ_stroke $z_{7e}\{v_2\} \ldots \{up\}z_{6e}$;   % right stem
math_fit$(-.7x\_height^\# * slant + .5hair^\# + .5u^\#, ic^\# - \frac{1}{3}x\_height^\# * slant)$;
penlabels(1, 2, 3, 4, 5, 6, 7); **endchar**;

cmchar "Lowercase Greek rho";
beginchar(oct "032", $8.25u^\#$, $x\_height^\#$, $desc\_depth^\#$);
italcorr $.7x\_height^\# * slant + .5curve^\# - u^\#$ **if** $math\_fitting$: $-.5u^\#$ **fi**;
adjust_fit(0, 0); **pickup** $fine.nib$;
$pos_1(stem, 180)$; $pos_2(stem, 180)$; $pos_3(vair, 90)$;
$pos_4(curve, 0)$; $pos_5(vair, -90)$; $pos_6(hair, -180)$;
$lft\ x_{2r} = \text{hround}(1.5u - .5stem)$; $x_1 = x_2 = x_6$; $x_3 = x_5 = .5[x_2, x_4]$;
$rt\ x_{4r} = \text{hround}(w - 1.5u + .5curve)$;
$y_1 - .5stem = -d - o$; $y_2 = y_4 = y_6 = .5[y_3, y_5]$; $top\ y_{3r} = h + oo$; $bot\ y_{5r} = -oo$;
filldraw circ_stroke $z_{1e} \mathbin{..} pulled\_arc_e(2, 3) \mathbin{\&} pulled\_arc_e(3, 4)$
    $\mathbin{\&} pulled\_arc_e(4, 5) \mathbin{\&} pulled\_arc_e(5, 6)$;   % stem and bowl
math_fit$(desc\_depth^\# * slant + .5stem^\# - u^\#, ic^\#)$;
penlabels(1, 2, 3, 4, 5, 6); **endchar**;

cmchar "Lowercase Greek sigma";
beginchar(oct "033", $10.25u^\#$, $x\_height^\#$, 0);
italcorr $x\_height^\# * slant + .5stem^\# - u^\#$;
adjust_fit(0, 0); **pickup** $fine.nib$;
$pos_1(vstem, 90)$; $pos_2(stem, 0)$; $pos_3(vair, -90)$;
$pos_4(stem, -180)$; $pos_5(vstem, -270)$; $pos_6(vstem, -270)$;
$x_1 = x_3 = x_5 = .5[x_2, x_4]$; $rt\ x_{2r} = \text{hround}(w - 2.5u)$;
$lft\ x_{4r} = \text{hround}(1.5u - .5curve)$; $x_6 = w - 1.5u$;
$top\ y_{1r} = h$; $y_2 = y_4 = .5[y_1, y_3]$; $bot\ y_{3r} = -oo$; $y_5 = y_6 = y_1$;
filldraw circ_stroke $z_{6e} \mathbin{..} pulled\_arc_e(5, 4) \mathbin{\&} pulled\_arc_e(4, 3)$
    $\mathbin{\&} pulled\_arc_e(3, 2) \mathbin{\&} pulled\_arc_e(2, 1)$;   % ear and bowl
math_fit$(-.3x\_height^\# * slant + .5curve^\# - u^\#, ic^\# - \frac{1}{3}x\_height^\# * slant)$;
penlabels(1, 2, 3, 4, 5, 6); **endchar**;

---

def $pi_stroke = $ **pickup** $fine.nib$;
   $pos_1(hair, 0)$; $pos_2(vstem, -90)$; $pos_3(vstem, -90)$;
   $x_1 - .5hair = \text{hround} -.5hair$; $x_2 = 2u$; $x_3 = w - 1.5u$;
   $y_1 = x\_height - x\_height/3.141592653589793$; $y_2 = y_3$; $top\ y_{3l} = x\_height$;
   filldraw circ_stroke $z_{3e} \mathbin{---} z_{2e} \ldots \{x_1 - x_2, 3.14159(y_1 - y_2)\}z_{1e}$ **enddef**;

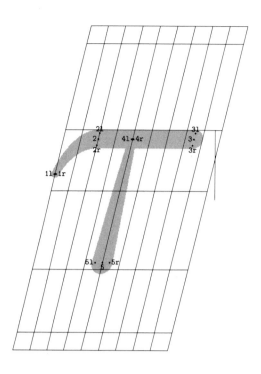

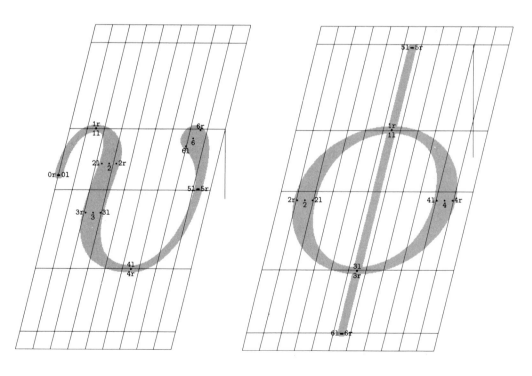

cmchar "Lowercase Greek tau";
beginchar(oct "034", $9u\#$, $x\_height\#$, 0);
italcorr $x\_height\# * slant + .5stem\# - u\#$;
adjust_fit$(0, 0)$; pi_stroke;   % hook and bar
$pos_4(hair, 0)$; $pos_5(stem, 0)$;
$x_4 = x_5$; $x_5 - .5stem = $ hround$(.5w - .5u - .5stem)$; $y_4 = y_2$; $y_5 - .5stem = -oo$;
filldraw circ_stroke z_{5e} -- z_{4e};   % stem
math_fit$(-.7x\_height\# * slant + .5hair\# + .5u\#, -.5u\#)$;
penlabels$(1, 2, 3, 4, 5)$; **endchar**;

cmchar "Lowercase Greek upsilon";
beginchar(oct "035", $9u\#$, $x\_height\#$, 0);
italcorr $x\_height\# * slant$;
adjust_fit$(0, 0)$; **pickup** $fine.nib$; **interim** $superness := more\_super$;
$x_0 = 0$; $x_2 = x_3 + .25u$; $pos_3(stem, -180)$; **lft** $x_{3r} = $ hround$(2.5u - .5stem)$;
$hook\_in(0, 1, 2)(skewed)$;   % opening hook
$pos_{2'}(stem, -180)$; $z_{2'} = z_2$; $pos_4(vair, -90)$; $pos_5(hair, 0)$;
$x_4 = .5w + u$; **rt** $x_{5r} = $ hround$(w - .5u)$; $y_3 = .7[y_4, y_5]$; **bot** $y_{4r} = -oo$; $y_5 = .57h$;
filldraw stroke $z_{2'e}\{-u, -x\_height\} \ldots super\_arc_e(3, 4)$
   $\ldots$ tension atleast $1.05 \ldots \{up\}z_{5e}$;   % left stem and arc
$v\_bulb(5, 6)$;   % closing bulb
math_fit$(-{}^2\!/_3 x\_height\# * slant + .5hair\# + .5u\#, {}^2\!/_3 ic\#)$;
penlabels$(0, 1, 2, 3, 4, 5, 6)$; **endchar**;

cmchar "Lowercase Greek phi";
beginchar(oct "036", $11u\#$, $asc\_height\#$, $desc\_depth\#$);
italcorr $.7x\_height\# * slant + .5curve\# - u\#$ **if** $math\_fitting$: $-.5u\#$ **fi**;
adjust_fit$(0, 0)$; **pickup** $fine.nib$;
numeric $light\_curve$; $light_curve = $ hround$(.5[stem, curve] - 2stem\_corr)$;
$pos_1(vair, 90)$; $pos_2(light\_curve, 180)$; $pos_3(vair, 270)$; $pos_4(light\_curve, 360)$;
$x_1 = x_3 = .5w$; **lft** $x_{2r} = $ hround$(1.5u - .5light\_curve)$; $x_4 = w - x_2$;
top $y_1 = x\_height + oo$; $y_2 = y_4 = .5[y_1, y_3]$; **bot** $y_3 = -oo$;
filldraw stroke $pulled\_arc_e(1, 2)$ & $pulled\_arc_e(2, 3)$
   & $pulled\_arc_e(3, 4)$ & $pulled\_arc_e(4, 1)$;   % bowl
$pos_5(hair, 0)$; $pos_6(hair, 0)$; $x_5 = x_6 = .5w$; **top** $y_5 = h$; **bot** $y_6 = -d - oo$;
filldraw stroke z_{5e} -- z_{6e};   % stem
math_fit$(-.3x\_height\# * slant + .5curve\# - u\#, ic\#)$;
penlabels$(1, 2, 3, 4, 5, 6)$; **endchar**;

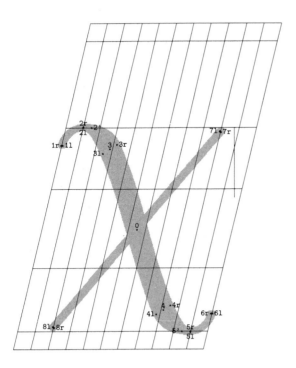

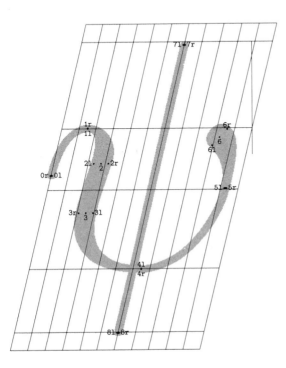

cmchar "Lowercase Greek chi";
beginchar(oct "037", $11u^\#$, $x\_height^\#$, $desc\_depth^\#$);
italcorr $x\_height^\# * slant + .5hair^\# - 1.5u^\#$;
adjust_fit$(0, 0)$; **pickup** $fine.nib$;
$pos_1(hair, 180)$; $pos_2(vair, 80)$; $pos_5(vair, 80)$; $pos_6(hair, 180)$;
$x_1 - .5hair = \text{hround} -.5hair$; $x_6 = w - x_1$; $x_2 = w - x_5 = u$;
$y_1 = y_{2l} - h/8$; top $y_{2r} = h + oo$; bot $y_{5l} = -d - oo$; $y_6 = y_{5r} + h/8$;
$z_0 = .5[z_2, z_5]$; $z_{2'} = z_{2l} + (.5u, 0)$; $z_{5'} = z_{5r} - (.5u, 0)$;
numeric $theta$; $theta = \text{angle}(z_{5'} - z_{2'}) + 90$;
$pos_3(stem, theta)$; $pos_4(stem, theta)$;
$y_{3r} = y_{2r} - h/8$; $y_{4l} = y_{5l} + h/8$; $z_{3l} = whatever[z_{2'}, z_0]$; $z_{4r} = whatever[z_0, z_{5'}]$;
filldraw stroke $z_{1e}\{up\} \ldots z_{2e}\{right\} \ldots z_{3e}\{z_{4r} - z_{3l}\}$
    $.. z_{4e}\{z_{4r} - z_{3l}\} \ldots \{right\}z_{5e} \ldots \{up\}z_{6e}$;   % major diagonal and hooks
$x_8 = w - x_7 = 2u$; $y_7 + .5hair = h$; $y_8 - .5hair = -d$;
numeric $theta$; $theta = \text{angle}(z_7 - z_8) - 90$;
$pos_7(hair, theta)$; $pos_8(hair, theta)$;
filldraw z_{7l} --- z_{8l} .. z_{8r} --- z_{7r} .. cycle;   % minor diagonal
math_fit$((desc\_depth^\# - x\_height^\#) * slant + ic^\#, ic^\#)$;
penlabels$(0, 1, 2, 2', 3, 4, 5', 5, 6, 7, 8)$; **endchar**;

cmchar "Lowercase Greek psi";
beginchar(oct "040", $11u^\#$, $asc\_height^\#$, $desc\_depth^\#$);
italcorr $x\_height^\# * slant$;
adjust_fit$(0, 0)$; **pickup** $fine.nib$; **interim** $superness := more\_super$;
$x_0 = 0$; $x_2 = x_3 + .25u$; $pos_3(stem, -180)$; lft $x_{3r} = \text{hround}(2.5u - .5stem)$;
$hook\_in(0, 1, 2)(skewed)$;   % opening hook
$pos_{2'}(stem, -180)$; $z_{2'} = z_2$; $pos_4(vair, -90)$; $pos_5(hair, 0)$;
$x_4 = .5w + u$; rt $x_{5r} = \text{hround}(w - .5u)$;
$y_3 = .7[y_4, y_5]$; bot $y_{4r} = -oo$; $y_5 = .57x\_height$;
filldraw stroke $z_{2'e}\{-u, -x\_height\} \ldots super\_arc_e(3, 4)$
    $..$ tension atleast $1.05 .. \{up\}z_{5e}$;   % left stem and arc
$v\_bulb(5, 6)$;   % closing bulb
$pos_7(hair, 0)$; $pos_8(hair, 0)$; $x_7 = x_8 = .5w + .5u$; top $y_7 = h$; bot $y_8 = -d - oo$;
filldraw stroke z_{7e} -- z_{8e};   % stem
math_fit$(-{}^2\!/_3 x\_height^\# * slant + .5hair^\# + .5u^\#, {}^2\!/_3 ic^\#)$;
penlabels$(0, 1, 2, 3, 4, 5, 6, 7, 8)$; **endchar**;

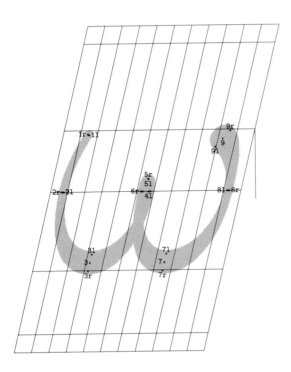

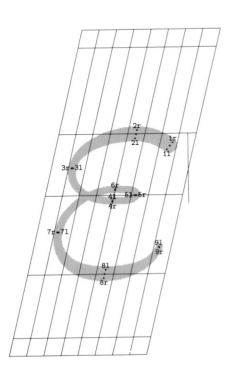

cmchar "Lowercase Greek omega";
beginchar(oct "041", $11u^\#$, $x\_height^\#$, 0);
italcorr $x\_height^\# * slant$;
adjust_fit(0, 0); **pickup** *fine.nib*;
$pos_2(hair, -180)$; $lft\ x_{2r} = $ hround $.5u$; $y_2 = y_4 = y_6 = y_8 = bar\_height$;
$y_1 + .5hair = h$; $x_1 = x_2 + .75u$; $pos_1(hair, angle(2(x_1 - x_2), y_1 - y_2) + 90)$;
$pos_3(vstem + dw, -90)$; $pos_4(hair, 0)$; $pos_5(vair, 90)$;
$pos_6(hair, 180)$; $pos_7(vstem + dw, 270)$; $pos_8(hair, 360)$;
$bot\ y_{3r} = bot\ y_{7r} = -oo$; $top\ y_{5r} = $ vround$(.2[y_4, h] + .5vair)$;
$x_3 = .5[x_2, x_4]$; $x_7 + .25u = .5[x_6, x_8]$; $rt\ x_{8r} = $ hround$(w - .5u)$;
$x_5 + .5stem = $ hround$(.5w + .5stem) + eps$;
$x_5 = .5[x_4, x_6]$; $rt\ x_{4r} - lft\ x_{6r} = \min(stem, 2hair) + 2eps$;
if $x_{4l} < x_{6l}$: $x_{4l} := x_{6l} := x_5$; **fi**
filldraw circ_stroke $z_{1e}\{2(x_2 - x_1), y_2 - y_1\} \ldots z_{2e}\{down\} \ldots z_{3e}\{right\}$
$\ldots \{up\}z_{4e} \ldots \{left\}z_{5e}$;   % left arc
filldraw stroke $z_{5e}\{left\} \ldots z_{6e}\{down\} \ldots z_{7e}\{right\} \ldots \{up\}z_{8e}$;   % right arc
$v\_bulb(8, 9)$;   % closing bulb
math_fit$(-bar\_height^\# * slant, \frac{2}{3}ic^\#)$; **penlabels**(1, 2, 3, 4, 5, 6, 7, 8, 9); **endchar**;

cmchar "Variant lowercase Greek epsilon";
beginchar(oct "042", $8u^\#$, $x\_height^\#$, 0);
italcorr $x\_height^\# * slant - .5u^\#$;
adjust_fit(0, 0); **pickup** *fine.nib*;
numeric *light_vstem*; $light_vstem = $ Vround $\frac{2}{3}[vair, vstem]$;
$pos_2(light\_vstem, 90)$; $x_2 = x_8 = .5w + .5u$; $top\ y_{2r} = h + o$;
$x_1 + .5light_vstem = $ hround$(w - u)$; $y_1 = .2[y_2, bar\_height]$;
$pos_1(light\_vstem, angle(x_1 - x_2, 2(y_1 - y_2)) + 90)$; $pos_3(hair, 180)$; $pos_4(vair, 270)$;
$pos_5(hair, 360)$; $pos_6(vair, 450)$; $pos_7(hair, 540)$; $pos_8(light\_vstem, 630)$;
$lft\ x_{3r} = $ hround u; $x_4 = x_6 = .5w$; $rt\ x_{5r} = $ hround$(w - 2.5u)$; $x_7 = x_3$;
$y_3 = .5[y_2, y_4]$; $y_5 = bar\_height = .5[y_4, y_6]$; $y_7 = .5[y_6, y_8]$; $bot\ y_{8r} = -o$;
$top\ y_{6r} - bot\ y_{4r} = vstem + eps$; **if** $y_{6l} < y_{4l}$: $y_{6l} := y_{4l} := y_5$; **fi**
$x_9 + .5vair = $ hround$(w - .5u)$; $y_9 = \frac{1}{3}[y_8, bar\_height]$;
$pos_9(vair, angle(x_8 - x_9, 2(y_8 - y_9)) + 90)$;
filldraw circ_stroke $z_{1e}\{x_2 - x_1, 2(y_2 - y_1)\} \ldots pulled\_super\_arc_e(2, 3)(.5superpull)$
$\&\ super\_arc_e(3, 4) \ldots \{up\}z_{5e}$;   % upper arc
filldraw circ_stroke $z_{9e}\{x_8 - x_9, 8(y_8 - y_9)\} \ldots pulled\_arc_e(8, 7)$
$\&\ super\_arc_e(7, 6) \ldots \{down\}z_{5e}$;   % lower arc
math_fit$(-.5bar\_height^\# * slant - .5u^\#, ic^\#)$;
penlabels(1, 2, 3, 4, 5, 6, 7, 8, 9); **endchar**;

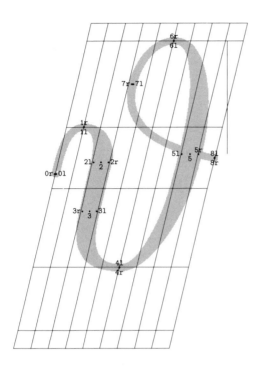

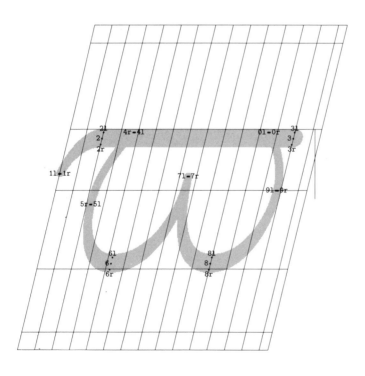

cmchar "Variant lowercase Greek theta";
beginchar(oct "043", $9u^\#$, $asc\_height^\#$, 0);
italcorr $.5[bar\_height^\#, x\_height^\#] * slant + .5vair^\# + .5u^\#$;
adjust_fit$(0, 0)$; **pickup** *fine.nib*;
numeric *light_curve*; $light\_curve = \text{hround } .5[stem, curve]$;
$x_0 = 0$; $x_2 - .5stem = \text{hround}(2.5u - .5stem)$; $hook\_in(0, 1, 2)$;   % opening hook
$pos_{2'}(stem, -180)$; $z_{2'} = z_2$; $pos_3(stem, -180)$; $pos_4(vair, -90)$;
$pos_5(light\_curve, 0)$; $pos_6(vair, 90)$; $pos_7(hair, 180)$; $pos_8(vair, 270)$;
$x_3 = x_2$; $x_4 = x_6 = .5[x_3, x_5]$; $\text{rt } x_{5r} = \text{hround}(w - 1.5u + .5light\_curve)$;
$\text{lft } x_{7r} = \text{hround}(3.25u - .5hair)$; $x_8 + .5vair = \text{hround}(w + .5vair - epsilon)$;
$y_3 = .4x\_height$; $\text{bot } y_{4r} = -oo$; $y_5 = .5[y_4, y_6]$; $\text{top } y_{6r} = h + oo$;
$y_7 = .5[x\_height, h]$; $y_8 = .5[bar\_height, x\_height]$;
filldraw stroke $z_{2'e}$ .. {{ **interim** *superness* := *hein_super*; $super\_arc_e(3, 4)$ }}
     & $pulled\_arc_e(4, 5)$ & $pulled\_arc_e(5, 6)$
     ... $\{down\}z_{7e}$ ... $\{4(x_8 - x_7), y_8 - y_7\}z_{8e}$;   % bowl and loop
math_fit$(-{}^2/_3x\_height^\# * slant + .5hair^\# + .5u^\#, ic^\#)$;
penlabels$(0, a, 1, 2, 3, 4, 5, 6, 7, 8)$; **endchar**;

cmchar "Variant lowercase Greek pi";
beginchar(oct "044", $14.5u^\#$, $x\_height^\#$, 0);
italcorr $x\_height^\# * slant + .5stem^\# - u^\#$;
adjust_fit$(0, 0)$; *pi_stroke*;   % hook and bar
$pos_4(hair, -180)$; $pos_5(hair, -180)$; $pos_6(vstem, -90)$;
$pos_7(hair, 0)$; $pos_{7'}(hair, -180)$; $z_{7'} = z_7$;
$pos_8(vstem, -90)$; $pos_9(hair, 0)$; $pos_0(hair, 0)$;
$x_4 = x_5 + 1.5u$; $\text{lft } x_{5r} = \text{hround } 2u$;
$x_6 = x_4 + .5u$; $\text{lft } x_{7l} = \text{hround}(.5w + .25u - .5hair)$;
$x_8 = w - 4.5u$; $\text{rt } x_{9r} = \text{hround}(w - 1.5u)$; $x_0 = x_9 - 1.25u$;
$\text{top } y_4 = \text{top } y_0 = h$; $y_5 + .1h = y_7 - .1h = y_9 = bar\_height$; $\text{bot } y_{6r} = \text{bot } y_{8r} = -oo$;
filldraw stroke $z_{4e}\{2(x_5 - x_4), y_5 - y_4\}$ ... $z_{5e}\{down\}$
     ... $z_{6e}\{right\}$ ... $z_{7e}\{up\}$;   % left bowl
filldraw stroke $z_{0e}\{2(x_9 - x_0), y_9 - y_0\}$ ... $z_{9e}\{down\}$
     ... $z_{8e}\{left\}$ ... $z_{7'e}\{up\}$;   % right bowl
math_fit$(-.7x\_height^\# * slant + .5hair^\# + .5u^\#, ic^\# - .5u^\#)$;
penlabels$(0, 1, 2, 3, 4, 5, 6, 7, 8, 9)$; **endchar**;

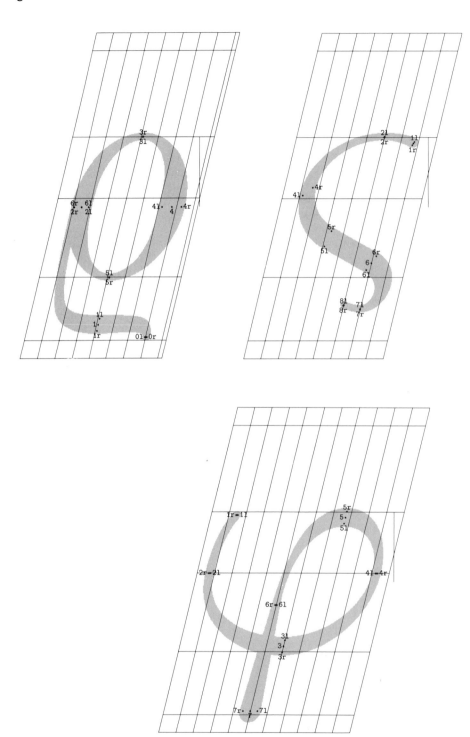

cmchar "Variant lowercase Greek rho";
beginchar(oct "045", $8.25u^\#$, $x\_height^\#$, $desc\_depth^\#$);
italcorr $.7x\_height^\# * slant + .5curve^\# - u^\#$ **if** $math\_fitting$: $-.5u^\#$ **fi**;
adjust_fit$(0, 0)$; **pickup** $fine.nib$;
$pos_2(stem, 180)$; $pos_3(vair, 90)$; $pos_4(curve, 0)$; $pos_5(vair, -90)$; $pos_6(stem, -180)$;
$lft\ x_{2r} = \text{hround}(1.5u - .5stem)$; $x_2 = x_6$; $x_3 = x_5 = .5[x_2, x_4]$;
$rt\ x_{4r} = \text{hround}(w - 1.5u + .5curve)$;
$y_2 = y_4 = y_6 = .5[y_3, y_5]$; $top\ y_{3r} = h + oo$; $bot\ y_{5r} = -oo$;
filldraw circ_stroke $pulled\_arc_e(2, 3)$ & $pulled\_arc_e(3, 4)$
   & $pulled\_arc_e(4, 5)$ & $pulled\_arc_e(5, 6)$;   % bowl
$pos_{2'}(hair, -180)$; $z_{2'r} = z_{2r}$; $pos_1(vstem, -90)$; $pos_{1'}(vstem, 90)$; $z_{1'} = z_1$;
$pos_0(hair, 0)$; $rt\ x_{0r} = \text{hround}(w - u)$; $bot\ y_0 = -d$; $bot\ y_{1r} = \text{vround} -.9d$; $x_1 = x_5$;
interim $superness$:= sqrt $superness$;
filldraw stroke $pulled\_arc_e(0, 1')$; **filldraw stroke** $pulled\_arc_e(1, 2')$;   % tail
math_fit$(desc\_depth^\# * slant + .5stem^\# - u^\#, ic^\#)$;
penlabels$(0, 1, 2, 3, 4, 5, 6)$; **endchar**;

cmchar "Variant lowercase Greek sigma";
beginchar(oct "046", $8u^\#$, $x\_height^\#$, $.5 \min(desc\_depth^\#, .5x\_height^\#))$;
italcorr $x\_height^\# * slant - .5u^\#$;
adjust_fit$(0, 0)$; **pickup** $fine.nib$;
numeric $heavy\_vair$; $heavy\_vair = .25[vair, vstem]$;
$pos_1(heavy\_vair, -110)$; $pos_2(vair, -90)$;
$x_1 + .5heavy\_vair = \text{hround}(w - u)$; $y_1 = .1[y_{2r}, bar\_height]$;
$x_2 = \min(.5w + u, x_{1r} - eps)$; $top\ y_{2l} = h + oo$;
filldraw circ_stroke $z_{1e}\{x_2 - x_1, 2(y_2 - y_1)\} \dots \{left\}z_{2e}$;   % upper bulb
numeric $theta$; $theta = 90 - \text{angle}(16u, x\_height)$; $slope := -x\_height/16u$;
$pos_6(stem, theta)$; $pos_7(vair, -90)$; $pos_8(vair, -135)$;
$lft\ x_{4l} = \text{hround}\ u$; $x_{4r} - x_{4l} = (\text{hround}\ .5[vair, stem]) - fine$;
$x_6 = x_7 = w - 2u$; $x_8 = .5w + u$; $y_6 = .25[y_8, y_2]$; $y_8 = y_7 + \frac{1}{8}d$; $bot\ y_{7r} = -d - oo$;
$ellipse\_set(2l, 4l, 5l, 6l)$; $ellipse\_set(2r, 4r, 5r, 6r)$; $y_4 = y_{4r}$;
filldraw circ_stroke $z_{8e}\{x_7 - x_8, 2(y_7 - y_8)\} \dots z_{7e}\{right\} \dots z_{6e}$
   --- $z_{5e} \dots \{up\}z_{4e} \dots \{right\}z_{2e}$;   % main stroke
math_fit$(-.5x\_height^\# * slant - .5u^\#, 0)$; **penlabels**$(1, 2, 4, 5, 6, 7, 8)$; **endchar**;

cmchar "Variant lowercase Greek phi";
beginchar(oct "047", $11u^\#$, $x\_height^\#$, $desc\_depth^\#$);
italcorr $.7x\_height^\# * slant$;
adjust_fit$(0, 0)$; **pickup** $fine.nib$;
$pos_1(hair, -180)$; $x_1 = x_2 + .75u$; $top\ y_1 = h$;
$pos_2(hair, -180)$; $lft\ x_{2r} = \text{hround}\ .5u$; $y_2 = bar\_height$;
$pos_3(vstem, -90)$; $x_3 = .5(w + u)$; $bot\ y_{3r} = -oo$;
$pos_4(hair, 0)$; $rt\ x_{4r} = \text{hround}(w - .5u)$; $y_4 = y_2$;
$pos_5(vstem, 90)$; $x_5 = .52[x_6, x_4]$; $top\ y_{5r} = h + oo$;
$pos_6(hair, 180)$; $x_6 = x_7$; $y_6 = \frac{1}{3}h$;
$pos_7(stem, 180)$; $lft\ x_{7r} = \text{hround}(.5w - .5u - .5stem)$; $y_7 - .5stem = -d - o$;
filldraw circ_stroke z_{7e} --- $z_{6e} \dots \{right\}z_{5e} \dots \{down\}z_{4e} \dots \{left\}z_{3e}$
   $\dots \{up\}z_{2e} \dots \{3(x_1 - x_2), y_1 - y_2\}z_{1e}$;   % bowl and stem
math_fit$(-.3x\_height^\# * slant, ic^\#)$; **penlabels**$(1, 2, 3, 4, 5, 6, 7)$; **endchar**;

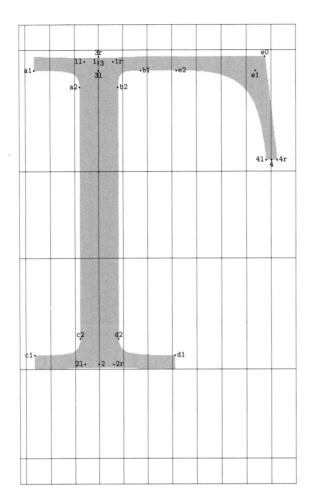

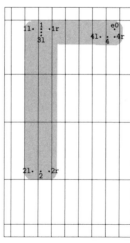

The program file `greeku.mf` is similar to the file `romanu.mf` that we'll see later. These files together contain the characters that have most "meta-ness" in their designs, because uppercase letters are used by six of the eight driver files. Roman text, italic text, typewriter text, and math italic all use the same programs.

% Computer Modern Greek caps, analogous to the uppercase Roman letters.

% Character codes ´000 through ´012 are generated,
% using plain TEX's standard text font layout conventions.

cmchar "Uppercase Greek Gamma";
beginchar(oct "000", $11u\# - width\_adj\#$, $cap\_height\#$, 0);
italcorr $cap\_height\# * slant - beak\_jut\# - .25u\#$;
adjust_fit($cap\_serif\_fit\#$, 0);
$h := \text{vround}(h - stem\_corr)$;
pickup $tiny.nib$; $pos_1(cap\_stem, 0)$; $pos_2(cap\_stem, 0)$;
$lft\ x_{1l} = lft\ x_{2l} = \text{hround max}(2u, 3u - .5cap\_stem)$; $top\ y_1 = h$; $bot\ y_2 = 0$;
filldraw stroke $z_{1e}\ \text{--}\ z_{2e}$;   % stem
pickup $crisp.nib$; $pos_3(slab, 90)$; $pos_4(hair, 0)$;
$top\ y_{3r} = h$; $x_3 = x_1$; $rt\ x_{4r} = \text{hround}(w - .75u)$; $y_4 = good.y(y_{3l} - beak) - eps$;
$arm(3, 4, e, beak\_darkness, beak\_jut)$;   % arm and beak
if *serifs*: $nodish\_serif(1, 2, a, \frac{1}{3}, cap\_jut, b, \frac{1}{3}, .5cap\_jut)$;   % upper serif
     $dish\_serif(2, 1, c, \frac{1}{3}, cap\_jut, d, \frac{1}{3}, 1.25cap\_jut)$; **fi**   % lower serif
math_fit$(0, ic\# - 2.5u\#)$; **penlabels**(1, 2, 3, 4); **endchar**;

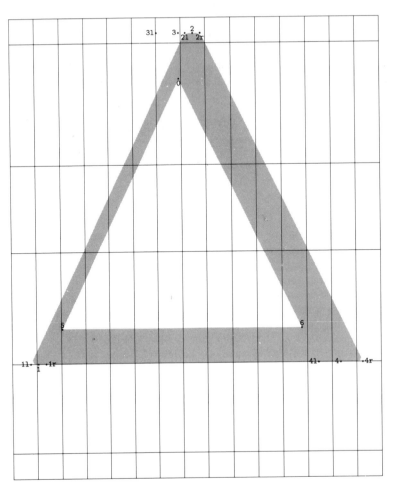

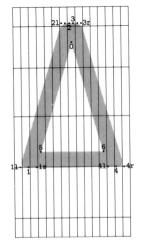

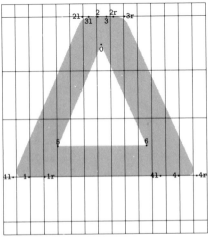

cmchar "Uppercase Greek Delta";
beginchar(oct "001", $15u^\#$, $cap\_height^\#$, 0);
adjust_fit(0, 0);
numeric $left\_stem$, $alpha$;
$left\_stem = cap\_hair$ **if** $hefty$: $-3stem\_corr$ **fi**;
$x_{1l} = w - x_{4r} = .75u$; $y_1 = y_4 = 0$;
$x_2 - x_1 = x_4 - x_3$; $x_{3r} = x_{2r} + apex\_corr$; $y_2 = y_3 = h + apex\_o + apex\_oo$;
$alpha = diag\_ratio(2, left\_stem, y_2 - y_1, x_{4r} - x_{1l} - apex\_corr)$;
$penpos_1(alpha * left\_stem, 0)$; $penpos_2(alpha * left\_stem, 0)$;
$penpos_3(alpha * cap\_stem, 0)$; $penpos_4(alpha * cap\_stem, 0)$;
fill $diag\_end(2l, 1l, 1, 1, 4r, 3r)$ -- $diag\_end(4r, 3r, 1, 1, 2l, 1l)$ -- cycle;   % triangle
$z_0 = whatever[z_{1r}, z_{2r}] = whatever[z_{3l}, z_{4l}]$;
$y_5 = y_6 = cap\_vstem$; $z_5 = whatever[z_{1r}, z_{2r}]$; $z_6 = whatever[z_{3l}, z_{4l}]$;
if $y_0 < h - cap\_notch\_cut$: $y_0 := h - cap\_notch\_cut$;
    unfill $z_0 + .5right\{down\} \ldots \{z_4 - z_3\}z_6$ -- $z_5\{z_2 - z_1\}$
       $\ldots \{up\}z_0 + .5left$ -- cycle;   % counter
else: **unfill** z_0 -- z_5 -- z_6 -- cycle; **fi**   % counter
penlabels(0, 1, 2, 3, 4, 5, 6); **endchar**;

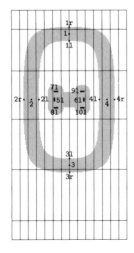
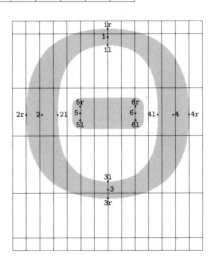

cmchar "Uppercase Greek Theta";
beginchar(oct "002", $14u\#$, $cap\_height\#$, 0);
italcorr $.7cap\_height\# * slant - .5u\#$;
adjust_fit$(0, 0)$;
numeric $light\_curve$; $light\_curve = \text{hround}(cap\_curve - 2stem\_corr)$;
$penpos_1(vair, 90)$; $penpos_3(\text{vround}(vair + .5vair\_corr), -90)$;
$penpos_2(light\_curve, 180)$; $penpos_4(light\_curve, 0)$;
if $monospace$: $x_{2r} = \text{hround } 1.5u$;
    interim $superness := \text{sqrt } superness$;   % make "O", not "0"
else: $x_{2r} = \text{hround } u$; **fi**
$x_{4r} = w - x_{2r}$; $x_1 = x_3 = .5w$; $y_{1r} = h + o$; $y_2 = y_4 = .5h - vair\_corr$; $y_{3r} = -o$;
penstroke $pulled\_super\_arc_e(1, 2)(.5superpull)$
    $\&\ pulled\_super\_arc_e(2, 3)(.5superpull)$
    $\&\ pulled\_super\_arc_e(3, 4)(.5superpull)$
    $\&\ pulled\_super\_arc_e(4, 1)(.5superpull)\ \&\ \text{cycle}$;   % bowl
pickup $crisp.nib$; $pos_5(cap\_vstem, 90)$; $pos_6(cap\_vstem, 90)$;
$lft\ x_5 = w - rt\ x_6 = \text{hround}(x_{2l} + u) + 1$; $y_5 = y_6 = .5[y_{1l}, y_{3l}]$;
filldraw stroke $z_{5e} \text{ -- } z_{6e}$;   % bar
if $serifs$: $pos_7(hair, 0)$; $pos_8(hair, 0)$; $pos_9(hair, 0)$; $pos_{10}(hair, 0)$;
    $x_{7l} = x_{8l} = x_5$; $x_{9r} = x_{10r} = x_6$;
    $y_7 - y_{5r} = y_9 - y_{6r} = y_{5l} - y_8 = y_{6l} - y_{10} = \text{vround } .05h$;
    filldraw stroke $z_{7e} \text{ -- } z_{8e}$;   % left serif
    filldraw stroke $z_{9e} \text{ -- } z_{10e}$; **fi**   % right serif
math_fit$(-.3cap\_height\# * slant - .5u\#, ic\# - .5u\#)$;
penlabels$(1, 2, 3, 4, 5, 6, 7, 8, 9, 10)$; **endchar**;

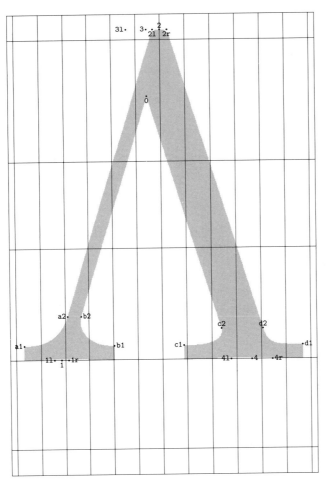

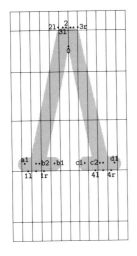

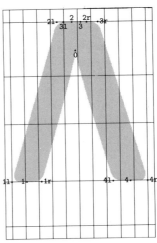

cmchar "Uppercase Greek Lambda";
beginchar(oct "003", $12u^\#$, $cap\_height^\#$, 0);
adjust_fit($cap\_serif\_fit^\#$, $cap\_serif\_fit^\#$);
numeric $left\_stem$, $outer\_jut$, $alpha$;
$left\_stem = cap\_hair$ **if** $hefty$: $-3stem\_corr$ **fi**;
$outer\_jut = .7cap\_jut$; $x_{1l} = w - x_{4r} = l + letter\_fit + outer\_jut + .5u$; $y_1 = y_4 = 0$;
$x_2 - x_1 = x_4 - x_3$; $x_{3r} = x_{2r} + apex\_corr$; $y_2 = y_3 = h + apex\_o + apex\_oo$;
$alpha = diag\_ratio(2, left\_stem, y_2 - y_1, x_{4r} - x_{1l} - apex\_corr)$;
$penpos_1(alpha * left\_stem, 0)$; $penpos_2(alpha * left\_stem, 0)$;
$penpos_3(alpha * cap\_stem, 0)$; $penpos_4(alpha * cap\_stem, 0)$;
$z_0 = whatever[z_{1r}, z_{2r}] = whatever[z_{3l}, z_{4l}]$;
if $y_0 < h - cap\_notch\_cut$: $y_0 := h - cap\_notch\_cut$;
    fill $z_0 + .5right\{down\} \ldots \{z_4 - z_3\}diag\_end(3l, 4l, 1, 1, 4r, 3r)$
        $-- diag\_end(4r, 3r, 1, 1, 2l, 1l) -- diag\_end(2l, 1l, 1, 1, 1r, 2r)\{z_2 - z_1\}$
        $\ldots \{up\}z_0 + .5left$ -- cycle;   % left and right diagonals
else: **fill** $z_0 -- diag\_end(0, 4l, 1, 1, 4r, 3r) -- diag\_end(4r, 3r, 1, 1, 2l, 1l)$
        $-- diag\_end(2l, 1l, 1, 1, 1r, 0) --$ cycle; **fi**   % left and right diagonals
if $serifs$: **numeric** $inner\_jut$; **pickup** $tiny.nib$;
  $prime\_points\_inside(1, 2)$; $prime\_points\_inside(4, 3)$;
  if $rt\ x_{1'r} + cap\_jut + .5u + 1 \le lft\ x_{4'l} - cap\_jut$: $inner\_jut = cap\_jut$;
  else: $rt\ x_{1'r} + inner\_jut + .5u + 1 = lft\ x_{4'l} - inner\_jut$; **fi**
  $dish\_serif(1', 2, a, \frac{1}{2}, outer\_jut, b, .6, inner\_jut)(dark)$;   % left serif
  $dish\_serif(4', 3, c, \frac{1}{2}, inner\_jut, d, \frac{1}{3}, outer\_jut)$; **fi**   % right serif
penlabels(0, 1, 2, 3, 4, 5, 6); **endchar**;

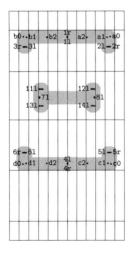

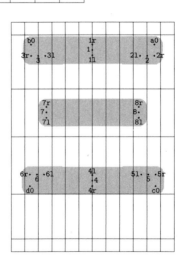

```
cmchar "Uppercase Greek Xi";
```
beginchar(oct "004", $12u^\#$, $cap\_height^\#$, 0);
italcorr $cap\_height^\# * slant - .35u^\#$;
adjust_fit(0, 0);
$h := \text{vround}(h - 2stem\_corr)$;
numeric $shaved\_stem$; $shaved\_stem = \text{hround} .9[vair, .85cap\_stem]$;
pickup $crisp.nib$; $pos_1(shaved\_stem, 90)$; $pos_2(hair, 0)$;
$top\ y_{1r} = h$; $x_1 = .5w$; $rt\ x_{2r} = \text{hround}(w - .85u)$; $y_2 = good.y(y_{1l} - {}^4/_9 beak) - eps$;
$arm(1, 2, a, .4beak\_darkness, .3beak\_jut)$;   % upper right arm and beak
$pos_3(hair, 180)$; $x_3 = w - x_2$; $y_3 = y_2$;
$arm(1, 3, b, .4beak\_darkness, -.3beak\_jut)$;   % upper left arm and beak
$pos_4(shaved\_stem, -90)$; $pos_5(hair, 0)$;
$bot\ y_{4r} = 0$; $x_4 = .5w$; $rt\ x_{5r} = \text{hround}(w - .75u)$; $y_5 = good.y(y_{4l} + .5beak) + eps$;
$arm(4, 5, c, .4beak\_darkness, .3beak\_jut)$;   % lower right arm and beak
$pos_6(hair, 180)$; $x_6 = w - x_5$; $y_6 = y_5$;
$arm(4, 6, d, .4beak\_darkness, -.3beak\_jut)$;   % lower left arm and beak
$pos_7(shaved\_stem, 90)$; $pos_8(shaved\_stem, 90)$;
$lft\ x_7 = w - rt\ x_8 = \text{hround}$ **if** $serifs$: 2.5 **else**: 2 **fi** u;
$top\ y_{7r} = top\ y_{8r} = \text{vround}(.52h + .5shaved\_stem)$;
filldraw stroke $z_{7e}\ \text{--}\ z_{8e}$;   % middle bar
if $serifs$: **numeric** $xjut$;
   if $bot\ y_2 > top\ y_{7r} + .75cap\_jut$: $xjut = .5cap\_jut$;
   else: $bot\ y_2 = top\ y_{7r} + 1.5xjut$; **fi**
   $pos_{11}(hair, 0)$; $pos_{12}(hair, 0)$; $y_{11} = y_{12}$;
   $pos_{13}(hair, 0)$; $pos_{14}(hair, 0)$; $y_{13} = y_{14}$;
   $lft\ x_{11l} = lft\ x_{13l} = w - rt\ x_{12r} = w - rt\ x_{14r} = \text{hround}\ 2.5u$;
   $top\ y_{11} - bot\ y_{13} = shaved\_stem + 2xjut$; $.5[y_{11}, y_{13}] = y_7$;
   filldraw stroke $z_{11e}\ \text{--}\ z_{13e}$; **filldraw stroke** $z_{12e}\ \text{--}\ z_{14e}$; **fi**   % middle serifs
math_fit(0, $.5ic^\#$); **penlabels**(1, 2, 3, 4, 5, 6, 7, 8, 11, 12, 13, 14); **endchar**;

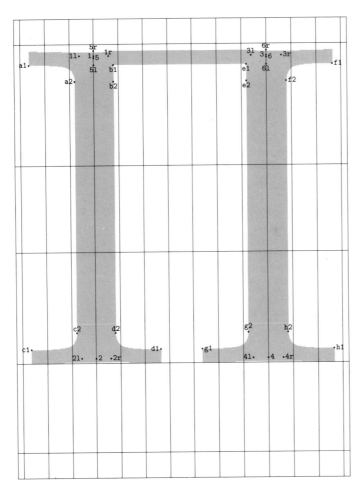

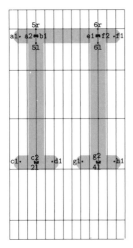

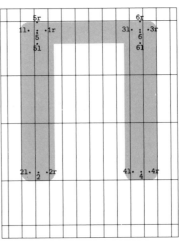

cmchar "Uppercase Greek Pi";

beginchar(oct "005", $13u^\# + width\_adj^\#$, $cap\_height^\#$, 0);

italcorr $cap\_height^\# * slant - cap\_serif\_fit^\# + cap\_jut^\# - 2.5u^\# + \min(.5\,cap\_stem^\#, u^\#)$;

adjust_fit($cap\_serif\_fit^\#$, $cap\_serif\_fit^\#$); **pickup** $tiny.nib$;

$h := \text{vround}(h - stem\_corr)$;

$pos_1(cap\_stem, 0)$; $pos_2(cap\_stem, 0)$; $pos_3(cap\_stem, 0)$; $pos_4(cap\_stem, 0)$;

$lft\ x_{1l} = lft\ x_{2l} = \text{hround} \max(2u, 3u - .5\,cap\_stem)$; $x_3 = x_4 = w - x_1$;

$top\ y_1 = top\ y_3 = h$; $bot\ y_2 = bot\ y_4 = 0$;

filldraw stroke z_{1e} -- z_{2e};   % left stem

filldraw stroke z_{3e} -- z_{4e};   % right stem

$penpos_5(cap\_bar, 90)$; $penpos_6(cap\_bar, 90)$;

$x_5 = x_1$; $x_6 = x_3$; $y_{5r} = y_{6r} = h$;

fill stroke z_{5e} -- z_{6e};   % bar

if $serifs$: **numeric** $inner\_jut$;

  if $rt\ x_{1r} + cap\_jut + .5u + 1 \le lft\ x_{3l} - cap\_jut$: $inner\_jut = cap\_jut$;

  else: $rt\ x_{1r} + inner\_jut + .5u + 1 = lft\ x_{3l} - inner\_jut$; **fi**

  $nodish\_serif(1, 2, a, \frac{1}{3}, cap\_jut, b, \frac{1}{3}, eps)$;   % upper left serif

  $dish\_serif(2, 1, c, \frac{1}{3}, cap\_jut, d, \frac{1}{3}, inner\_jut)$;   % lower left serif

  $nodish\_serif(3, 4, e, \frac{1}{3}, eps, f, \frac{1}{3}, cap\_jut)$;   % upper right serif

  $dish\_serif(4, 3, g, \frac{1}{3}, inner\_jut, h, \frac{1}{3}, cap\_jut)$; **fi** % lower right serif

math_fit$(0, .5ic^\#)$; **penlabels**(1, 2, 3, 4, 5, 6); **endchar**;

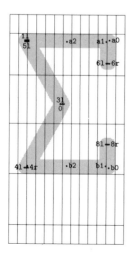

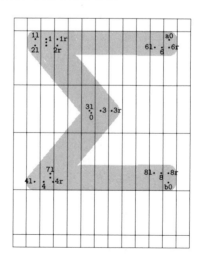

cmchar "Uppercase Greek Sigma";

beginchar(oct "006", $13u^\#$, $cap\_height^\#$, 0);

italcorr $cap\_height^\# * slant - beak\_jut^\# - .5u^\#$;

adjust_fit$(0, 0)$;

numeric $bot\_arm\_thickness$;

$bot_arm_thickness = $ Vround $.25[slab, cap\_vstem]$;

pickup $tiny.nib$; *lft* $x_{1l} = $ hround u; $x_{1l} = x_{2l} = x_{4l}$;

top $y_1 = h$; *bot* $y_2 = h - slab - eps$; *bot* $y_4 = 0$; $x_{3l} - x_{1l} = {}^4\!/_{11}(w - 2u)$; $y_3 = .5h$;

numeric $alpha[]$; $alpha_1 = ((x_{3l} - x_{1l}) ++ (y_2 - y_3))/(y_2 - y_3)$;

$penpos_1(alpha_1 * (cap\_stem - tiny), 0)$; $penpos_2(alpha_1 * (cap\_stem - tiny), 0)$;

$penpos_3(alpha_1 * (cap\_stem - tiny), 0)$;

$alpha_2 = diag\_ratio(1, cap\_hair - tiny, y_3 - y_4, x_{3r} - x_{4l})$;

$penpos_4(alpha_2 * (cap\_hair - tiny), 0)$;

$z_0 = whatever[z_{2l}, z_{3l}] = z_{4l} + whatever * (z_{3r} - z_{4r})$;

filldraw z_{1l} -- z_{2l} -- z_0 -- z_{4l} -- z_{4r} -- z_{3r} -- z_{2r} -- z_{1r} -- cycle;　　　　% diagonals

pickup $crisp.nib$; $pos_5(slab, 90)$; $pos_6(hair, 0)$;

top $y_{5r} = h$; $x_5 = x_1$; *rt* $x_{6r} = $ hround$(w - u)$; $y_6 = good.y(y_{5l} - beak) - eps$;

$arm(5, 6, a, beak\_darkness, beak\_jut)$;　　　　　　% upper arm and beak

$pos_7(bot\_arm\_thickness, -90)$; $pos_8(hair, 0)$;

bot $y_{7r} = 0$; $z_{7l} = whatever[z_4, z_3]$; $x_{7r} := x_4$; $x_8 = x_6$; $y_8 = good.y(y_{7l} + beak) + eps$;

$arm(7, 8, b, beak\_darkness, beak\_jut)$;　　　　　　% lower arm and beak

math_fit$(0, .5ic^\#)$; **penlabels**$(0, 1, 2, 3, 4, 5, 6, 7, 8)$; **endchar**;

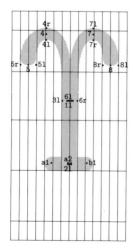

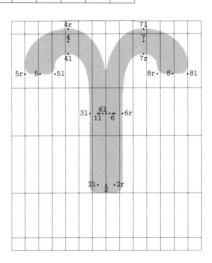

cmchar "Uppercase Greek Upsilon";
beginchar(oct "007", $14u^\#$, $cap\_height^\#$, 0);
italcorr $.8cap\_height^\# * slant - .5u^\#$;
adjust_fit(0, 0);
pickup $tiny.nib$; $pos_1(cap\_stem, 0)$; $pos_2(cap\_stem, 0)$;
$lft\ x_{1l} = lft\ x_{2l} = \text{hround}(.5w - .5cap\_stem)$; $y_1 = .5h$; $bot\ y_2 = 0$;
filldraw stroke z_{1e} -- z_{2e};   % stem
$penpos_3(.6cap\_stem, 0)$; $penpos_4(.75cap\_curve, 90)$; $penpos_5(cap\_hair, 180)$;
$z_{3l} = lft\ z_{1l}$; $x_{5r} = \text{hround}\ u$; $y_5 = bot\ .8h$; $x_4 = .61803[x_{3l}, x_{5l}]$; $y_{4r} = h + o$;
$penpos_{5'}(cap\_hair, 180)$; $x_{5'} = x_5$; $y_{5'} = h$;
fill $z_{3r}\{up\}$ ... $z_{4r}\{left\}$ ... $\{down\}diag\_end(5'r, 5r, 1, 1, 5l, 5'l)\{up\}$
  ... $\{right\}z_{4l}$ ... $\{down\}z_{3l}$ -- cycle;   % left arc
$penpos_6(.6cap\_stem, 0)$; $penpos_7(.75cap\_curve, -90)$; $penpos_8(cap\_hair, -180)$;
$z_{6r} = rt\ z_{1r}$; $x_8 = w - x_5$; $y_8 = y_5$; $x_7 = w - x_4$; $y_7 = y_4$;
$penpos_{8'}(cap\_hair, -180)$; $x_{8'} = x_8$; $y_{8'} = h$;
fill $z_{6r}\{up\}$ ... $z_{7r}\{right\}$ ... $\{down\}diag\_end(8'r, 8r, 1, 1, 8l, 8'l)\{up\}$
  ... $\{left\}z_{7l}$ ... $\{down\}z_{6l}$ -- cycle;   % right arc
if $serifs$: $dish\_serif(2, 1, a, \frac{1}{3}, 1.25cap\_jut, b, \frac{1}{3}, 1.25cap\_jut)$; **fi**   % serif
math_fit$(-.8cap\_height^\# * slant - .5u^\#, ic^\# - 2.5u^\#)$;
penlabels(1, 2, 3, 4, 5, 6, 7, 8); **endchar**;

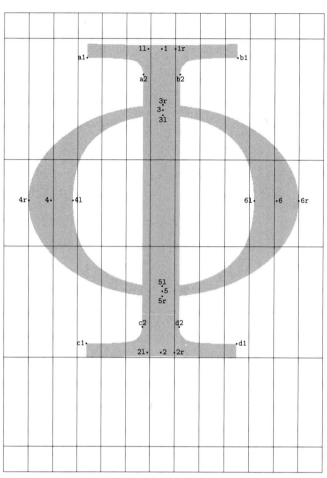

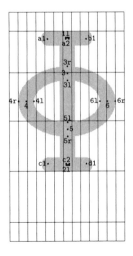

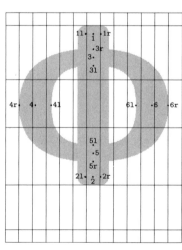

cmchar "Uppercase Greek Phi";
beginchar(oct "010", $13u\#$, $cap\_height\#$, 0);
italcorr $.5cap\_height\# * slant - .5u\#$;
adjust_fit(0, 0);
numeric $shaved\_stem$, $light\_curve$;
$shaved\_stem = cap\_stem - \text{hround } 2stem\_corr$;
$light\_curve = cap\_curve - \text{hround } stem\_corr$;
pickup $tiny.nib$; $pos_1(shaved\_stem, 0)$; $pos_2(shaved\_stem, 0)$;
$lft\ x_{1l} = lft\ x_{2l} = \text{hround}(.5w - .5cap\_stem)$; $top\ y_1 = h$; $bot\ y_2 = 0$;
filldraw stroke $z_{1e} \text{ -- } z_{2e}$;   % stem
$penpos_3(vair, 90)$; $penpos_5(vair, -90)$;
$penpos_4(light\_curve, 180)$; $penpos_6(light\_curve, 0)$;
$x_{4r} = \text{hround } u$; $x_{6r} = w - x_{4r}$; $x_3 = x_5 = .5w$;
$y_{3r} = \text{vround}(.85h \text{ if } serifs: -slab \text{ \bf fi})$; $y_4 = y_6 = .5[y_3, y_5]$;
$y_{5r} = \text{vround}(.15h \text{ if } serifs: +slab \text{ \bf fi})$;
penstroke $pulled\_arc_e(3, 4)$ & $pulled\_arc_e(4, 5)$
    & $pulled\_arc_e(5, 6)$ & $pulled\_arc_e(6, 3)$ & cycle;   % bowl
if $serifs$: $dish\_serif(1, 2, a, \frac{1}{3}, 1.25cap\_jut, b, \frac{1}{3}, 1.25cap\_jut)$;   % upper serif
    $dish\_serif(2, 1, c, \frac{1}{3}, 1.25cap\_jut, d, \frac{1}{3}, 1.25cap\_jut)$; **fi**   % lower serif
math_fit$(-.5cap\_height\# * slant - .5u\#, ic\#)$; **penlabels**(1, 2, 3, 4, 5, 6); **endchar**;

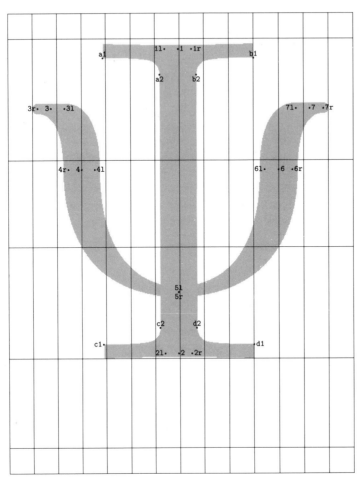

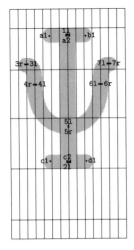

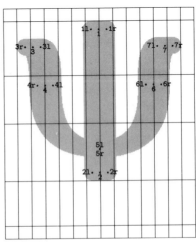

cmchar "Uppercase Greek Psi";
beginchar(oct "011", $14u^\#$, $cap\_height^\#$, 0);
italcorr $.8cap\_height^\# * slant - .5u^\#$;
adjust_fit(0, 0);
numeric $shaved\_stem$;
$shaved\_stem = cap\_stem -$ hround $2stem\_corr$;
pickup $tiny.nib$; $pos_1(shaved\_stem, 0)$; $pos_2(shaved\_stem, 0)$;
$lft\ x_{1l} = lft\ x_{2l} =$ hround$(.5w - .5cap\_stem)$; $top\ y_1 = h$; $bot\ y_2 = 0$;
filldraw stroke $z_{1e}\ \texttt{--}\ z_{2e}$;   % stem
$pos_3(shaved\_stem, -180)$; $pos_4(shaved\_stem, -180)$;
$pos_5(vair, -90)$; $x_5 = x_1$; $bot\ y_{5r} =$ vround$(.15h$ **if** $serifs$: $+slab$ **fi**$)$;
$pos_6(shaved\_stem, 0)$; $pos_7(shaved\_stem, 0)$;
$lft\ x_{3r} =$ hround u; $x_7 = w - x_3$; $lft\ x_{4r} =$ hround$(3u - .5shaved\_stem)$; $x_6 = w - x_4$;
$pos_{3'}(vair, 90)$; $pos_{7'}(vair, 90)$; $z_{3'r} = z_{3r}$; $z_{7'r} = z_{7r}$;
$y_3 = y_7$; $y_4 = y_6 = .6h$; $y_3 = good.y(y_3 + .84h$ **if** $serifs$: $-slab$ **fi** $- y_{3'})$;
interim $superness := more\_super$;
filldraw $z_{3'l}\{right\}\ \ldots\ z_{4r}\{down\}$ & $super\_arc_r(4, 5)$
   & $super\_arc_r(5, 6)$ & $z_{6r}\{up\}\ \ldots\ z_{7'l}\{right\}$
   $\texttt{--}\ z_{7r}\ \texttt{---}\ z_{7l}\ \ldots\ z_{6l}\{down\}$ & $super\_arc_l(6, 5)$ % stroke
   & $super\_arc_l(5, 4)$ & $z_{4l}\{up\}\ \ldots\ z_{3l}\ \texttt{---}\ z_{3r}\ \texttt{--}$ cycle;
if $serifs$: $dish\_serif(1, 2, a, \frac{1}{3}, 1.25cap\_jut, b, \frac{1}{3}, 1.25cap\_jut)$;   % upper serif
   $dish\_serif(2, 1, c, \frac{1}{3}, 1.25cap\_jut, d, \frac{1}{3}, 1.25cap\_jut)$; **fi**   % lower serif
math_fit$(-.8cap\_height^\# * slant - .5u^\#, .4cap\_height^\# * slant - 1.25u^\#)$;
penlabels$(1, 2, 3, 4, 5, 6, 7)$; **endchar**;

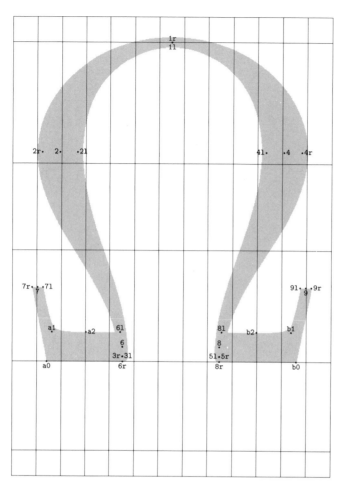

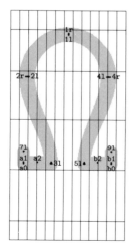

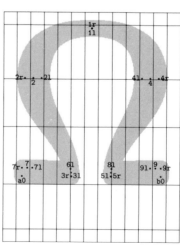

cmchar "Uppercase Greek Omega";
beginchar(oct "012", $13u^\#$, $cap\_height^\#$, 0);
italcorr $.75cap\_height^\# * slant - .5u^\#$;
adjust_fit(0, 0);
pickup $tiny.nib$; $pos_1(vair, 90)$; $pos_2(cap\_curve, 180)$;
$pos_3(vair, 180)$; $pos_4(cap\_curve, 0)$; $pos_5(vair, 0)$;
$x_1 = .5w$; $top\ y_{1r} = h + o$; $lft\ x_{2r} = \text{hround}\ u$; $y_2 = y_4 = {}^2\!/\!_3 h$; $x_4 = w - x_2$;
$rt\ x_{3l} = \text{hround}(^1\!/\!_3(w + .5u) + .5hair)$; $bot\ y_3 = bot\ \acute{y}_5 = 0$; $x_5 = w - x_3$;
filldraw stroke $z_{3e}\{up\} \ldots \{up\}z_{2e}$
    & $pulled\_super\_arc_e(2, 1)(.5superpull)$
    & $pulled\_super\_arc_e(1, 4)(.5superpull)$
    & $z_{4e}\{down\} \ldots \{down\}z_{5e}$;   % bowl
numeric $arm\_thickness$; **path** p; $p = z_3\{up\} \ldots \{up\}z_2$;
$arm\_thickness = \text{Vround}(\textbf{if}\ hefty: slab + 2stem\_corr\ \textbf{else}: .75[slab, cap\_vstem]\ \textbf{fi})$;
pickup $crisp.nib$; $pos_6(arm\_thickness, -90)$; $pos_7(fudged.hair, -180)$;
$bot\ y_{6r} = 0$; $x_6 = x_3$; $lft\ x_{7r} = \text{hround}\ .8u$; $y_7 = good.y(y_{6l} + .5beak) + eps$;
$(x, y) = p\ \text{intersectionpoint}\ ((0, y_{6l}) \texttt{-\,-} (w, y_{6l}))$; $x_{6l} := x$;
$arm(6, 7, a, .5beak\_darkness, -1.2beak\_jut)$;   % left arm and beak
$pos_8(arm\_thickness, -90)$; $pos_9(fudged.hair, 0)$;
$y_8 = y_6$; $y_9 = y_7$; $x_8 + x_6 = x_9 + x_7 = w$; $x_{8l} := w - x_{6l}$;
$arm(8, 9, b, .5beak\_darkness, 1.2beak\_jut)$;   % right arm and beak
math_fit(0, $.5ic^\#$); **penlabels**(1, 2, 3, 4, 5, 6, 7, 8, 9); **endchar**;

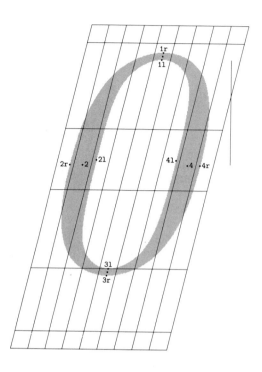

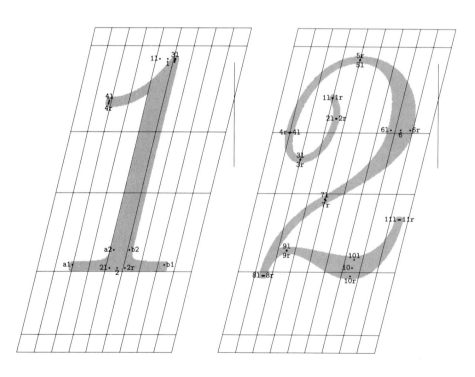

Here is program file `itald.mf`, which makes the numerals *0123456789*.

% This file contains the ten digits in so-called italic style.
% Character codes *'060* through *'071* are generated.

% The characters all have the same italic correction.

cmchar "Italic numeral 0";
beginchar("0", $9u^\#$, *fig_height*$^\#$, 0);

$\vdots$ (a copy of the program for '0' in **romand** comes here)

penlabels(1, 2, 3, 4); **endchar**;

cmchar "Italic numeral 1";
beginchar("1", $9u^\#$, *fig_height*$^\#$, 0);
italcorr *fig_height*$^\#$ $*$ *slant* $-$ $.5u^\#$;
adjust_fit(0, 0); **pickup** *tiny.nib*;
numeric *light_stem*; *light_stem* = hround $.4[stem', cap\_stem']$;
$pos_1(light\_stem, 0)$; $pos_2(light\_stem, 0)$;
lft x_{1l} = *lft* x_{2l} = hround$(.5(w + .5u) - .5cap\_stem')$; *top* $y_1 = h + apex\_o$; *bot* $y_2 = 0$;
filldraw stroke z_{1e} -- z_{2e};   % stem
$dish\_serif(2, 1, a, 1/3, \min(2.25u, lft\ x_{2l} - 1.5u),$
$\quad b, 1/3, \min(2.25u, w - 1.25u - rt\ x_{2r}))$;   % serif
pickup *crisp.nib*; $pos_3(slab, -90)$; $pos_4(bar, -90)$;
top $y_{3l} = h + apex\_o$; *top* $y_{4l} = .8h + apex\_o$;
lft $x_4 = \max(1.25u, tiny.lft\ x_{1l} - 2.35u)$; *tiny.rt* x_{1r} = *lft* $x_3 + .25[tiny, hair]$;
erase fill $z_{3l}\{x_{4l} - x_{3l}, 3(y_{4l} - y_{3l})\} \dots z_{4l}\{left\}$
$\quad$ -- $(x_{4l}, h + apex\_o + 1)$ -- $(x_{3l}, h + apex\_o + 1)$ -- **cycle**;   % erase excess at top
filldraw stroke $z_{3e}\{x_{4e} - x_{3e}, 3(y_{4e} - y_{3e})\} \dots \{left\}z_{4e}$;   % point
penlabels(1, 2, 3, 4); **endchar**;

cmchar "Italic numeral 2";
beginchar("2", $9u^\#$, *fig_height*$^\#$, 0);
italcorr *fig_height*$^\#$ $*$ *slant* $-$ $.5u^\#$;
adjust_fit(0, 0); **pickup** *fine.nib*;
$pos_1(vair, 45)$; $pos_2(vair, 0)$; $pos_3(vair, -90)$; $pos_4(hair, -180)$;
$pos_5(vair, -270)$; $pos_6(curve, -360)$; $pos_7(hair, -405)$; $pos_8(hair, -360)$;
$x_1 = x_2 - .5u$; *rt* x_{2r} = hround$(3.5u + .5vair)$;
$x_3 = .6[x_2, x_4]$; *lft* x_{4r} = hround$(u - .5hair)$;
$x_5 = x_7 = .5w - .5u$; *rt* x_{6r} = hround$(w - u)$; *lft* x_{8l} = hround$(1.5u - .5hair)$;
$y_1 = .5[x\_height, h]$; $y_2 = 1/3[y_1, y_3]$; $y_4 = x\_height$; *bot* y_{3r} = vround $.78y_4$;
top $y_{5r} = h + o$; $y_6 = .5[y_5, y_7]$; $y_7 = .52y_4$; *bot* $y_8 = -o$;
filldraw stroke if not *hefty*: $z_{1e}\{2(x_2 - x_1), y_2 - y_1\} \dots \{down\}z_{2e} \dots \{left\}z_{3e} \dots$ **fi**
$\quad z_{4e}\{up\} \dots pulled\_arc_e(5, 6)$
$\quad\quad \dots z_{7e}\{2(x_7 - x_6), y_7 - y_6\} \dots \{down\}z_{8e}$;   % main stroke
$pos_9(vair, -90)$; $pos_{10}(vstem + curve - stem, -90)$; $pos_{11}(hair, 0)$;
$x_9 = w - x_{10} = 2.5u$; *rt* x_{11r} = hround$(w - .5u + .5hair)$;
$y_9 = .25[y_{10}, y_7]$; *bot* $y_{10r} = -o$; $y_{11} = .38x\_height$;
filldraw stroke $z_{8e}\{up\} \dots z_{9e}\{right\} \dots \{right\}z_{10e} \dots \{up\}z_{11e}$;   % bar
penlabels(1, 2, 3, 4, 5, 6, 7, 8, 9, 10, 11); **endchar**;

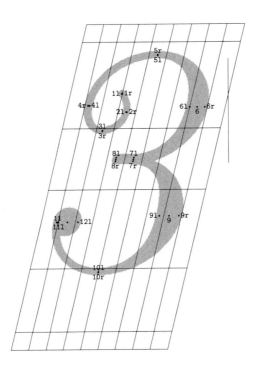

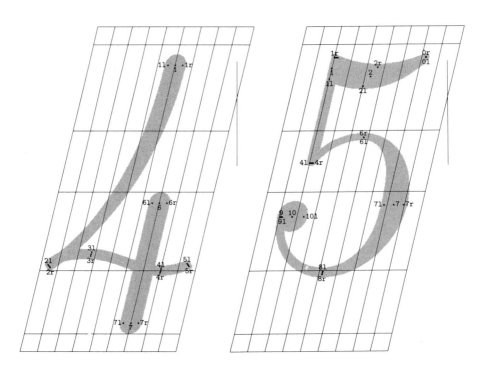

cmchar "Italic numeral 3";
beginchar("3", $9u\#$, $\mathit{fig\_height}\#$, 0);
italcorr $\mathit{fig\_height}\# * \mathit{slant} - .5u\#$;
adjust_fit(0, 0); **pickup** $\mathit{fine.nib}$;
$pos_1(\mathit{vair}, 45)$; $pos_2(\mathit{vair}, 0)$; $pos_3(\mathit{vair}, -90)$; $pos_4(\mathit{hair}, -180)$;
$pos_5(\mathit{vair}, -270)$; $pos_6(\mathit{stem}, -360)$; $pos_7(\mathit{bar}, -450)$; $pos_8(\mathit{bar}, -450)$;
$x_1 = x_2 - .5u$; $rt\ x_{2r} = $ hround$(3.5u + .5\mathit{vair})$; $x_3 = .5[x_2, x_4]$; $lft\ x_{4r} = $ hround u;
$x_5 = x_7 = .5w$; $rt\ x_{6r} = $ hround$(w - u)$; $x_8 = x_7 - u$;
$y_1 = .5[x\_height, h]$; $y_2 = .5[y_1, y_3]$; $y_7 = y_8 = .52h$; $bot\ y_{3r} = $ vround $1/4[y_7, h]$;
$y_4 = 1/3[y_3, y_5]$; $top\ y_{5r} = h + o$; $y_6 = .5[y_5, y_7]$;
filldraw stroke if not *hefty*: $z_{1e}\{2(x_2 - x_1), y_2 - y_1\} \ldots \{down\}z_{2e} \ldots \{left\}z_{3e} \ldots$ **fi**
$\quad z_{4e}\{up\} \ldots pulled\_arc_e(5, 6) \& pulled\_arc_e(6, 7) .. z_{8e}$; $\qquad$ % upper arc
$pos_{7'}(\mathit{vair}, 90)$; $z_{7'l} = z_{7r}$;
$pos_9(\mathit{curve}, 0)$; $pos_{10}(\mathit{vair}, -90)$; $pos_{11}(\mathit{hair}, -180)$; $pos_{12}(\mathit{flare}, -180)$;
$rt\ x_{9r} = $ hround$(w - u)$; $x_{10} = .5w - .5u$; $lft\ x_{11r} = $ hround $.75u$;
$y_9 = .25h$; $bot\ y_{10r} = -o$; $y_{11} = 1/3x\_height$; $bulb(10, 11, 12)$; $\qquad$ % bulb
filldraw stroke $pulled\_arc_e(7', 9) \& pulled\_arc_e(9, 10)$; $\qquad$ % lower arc
penlabels(1, 2, 3, 4, 5, 6, 7, 8, 9, 10, 11, 12); **endchar**;

cmchar "Italic numeral 4";
beginchar("4", $9u\#$, $\mathit{fig\_height}\#$, $\mathit{desc\_depth}\#$);
italcorr $\mathit{fig\_height}\# * \mathit{slant} - .5u\#$;
adjust_fit(0, 0); **pickup** $\mathit{fine.nib}$;
$pos_1(\mathit{stem}, 0)$; $pos_6(\mathit{stem}, 0)$; $pos_7(\mathit{stem}, 0)$;
$pos_2(\mathit{bar}, -45)$; $pos_3(\mathit{bar}, -90)$; $pos_4(\mathit{bar}, -90)$; $pos_5(\mathit{bar}, -45)$;
$rt\ x_{1r} = $ hround$(.5w + .5u + .5\mathit{stem})$; $lft\ x_{2l} = $ hround $.25u$;
$x_3 = 2.75u$; $x_4 = w - 2u$; $rt\ x_{5r} = $ hround$(w - .25u)$;
$rt\ x_{6r} = rt\ x_{7r} = $ hround$(2/3w + .5\mathit{stem})$;
$y_1 + .5\mathit{stem} = h + o$; $bot\ y_{2r} = 0$; $bot\ y_{3r} = $ vround$(.08h - .5\mathit{bar})$;
$bot\ y_{4r} = $ vround $-.5\mathit{bar}$; $bot\ y_{5r} = $ vround$(.03h - .5\mathit{bar})$;
$y_6 + .5\mathit{stem} = \mathit{bar\_height}$; $y_7 - .5\mathit{stem} = -d$;
filldraw circ_stroke $z_{1e}\{down\} \ldots \{3(x_2 - x_1), y_2 - y_1\}z_{2e}$; $\qquad$ % diagonal
filldraw stroke $z_{2e}\{z_1 - z_2\} \ldots z_{3e}\{right\} .. \{right\}z_{4e}$
$\quad \ldots \{x_5 - x_4, 2(y_5 - y_4)\}z_{5e}$; $\qquad$ % bar
filldraw z_{6l} --- $z_{7l} .. z_{7r}$ --- $z_{6r} ..$ cycle; $\qquad$ % stem
penlabels(1, 2, 3, 4, 5, 6, 7); **endchar**;

cmchar "Italic numeral 5";
beginchar("5", $9u\#$, $\mathit{fig\_height}\#$, 0);

$\qquad \vdots \quad$ (a copy of the program for '5' in **romand** comes here)

penlabels(0, 1, 2, 3, 4, 5, 6, 7, 8, 9, 10); **endchar**;

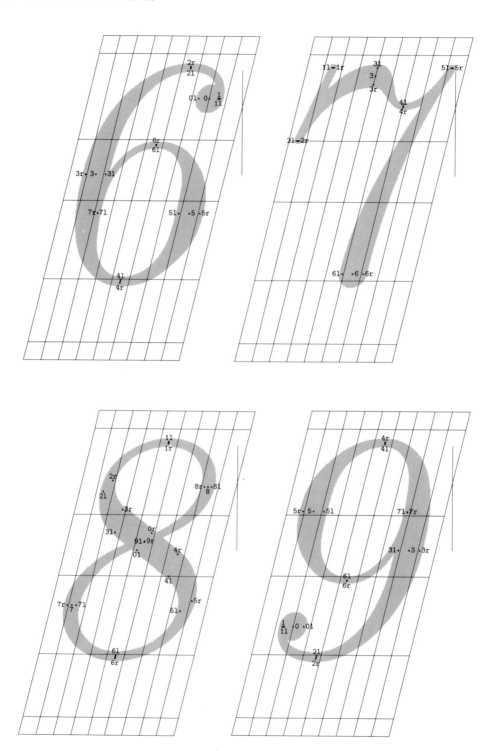

cmchar "Italic numeral 6";
beginchar("6", $9u^\#$, $fig\_height^\#$, 0);

      $\vdots$ (a copy of the program for '6' in **romand** comes here)

penlabels(0, 1, 2, 3, 4, 5, 6, 7); **endchar**;

cmchar "Italic numeral 7";
beginchar("7", $9u^\#$, $fig\_height^\#$, $desc\_depth^\#$);
italcorr $fig\_height^\# * slant - .5u^\#$;
adjust_fit(0, 0); **pickup** $fine.nib$;
numeric fat_curve; $fat\_curve = 1.4[stem, curve]$;
$pos_1(hair, 0)$; $pos_2(hair, 0)$; $pos_3(vstem + curve - stem, -90)$;
$pos_4(vair, -90)$; $pos_5(hair, 0)$; $pos_6(fat\_curve, 0)$;
$top\ y_1 = h + o$; $y_2 = x\_height$; $y_{3l} = y_5 = y_1$;
$bot\ y_{4r} = \text{vround}(.5[y_2, h] - .5vair)$; $y_6 - .5fat\_curve = -o$;
$lft\ x_{2l} = \text{hround}(.5u - .5hair)$; $x_3 = .5w - .5u$; $x_4 = {}^2\!/_3w$;
$rt\ x_{5r} = \text{hround}(w - .75u + .5hair)$; $rt\ x_{6r} = \text{hround}(.5w + u + .5fat\_curve)$;
$z_1 = z_2 + whatever * (z_5 - z_6)$; **filldraw stroke** $z_{1e}\ \text{--}\ z_{2e}$;   % serif
filldraw stroke $z_{2e}\{z_1 - z_2\}\ \ldots\ z_{3e}\{right\}\ ..\ \{right\}z_{4e}$
    $\ldots\ \{2(x_5 - x_6), y_5 - y_6\}z_{5e}$;   % bar
filldraw circ_stroke $z_{6e}\{up\}\ \ldots\ \{2(x_5 - x_6), y_5 - y_6\}z_{5e}$; % diagonal
penlabels(1, 2, 3, 4, 5, 6); **endchar**;

cmchar "Italic numeral 8";
beginchar("8", $9u^\#$, $fig\_height^\#$, 0);

      $\vdots$ (a copy of the program for '8' in **romand** comes here)

penlabels(0, 1, 2, 3, 4, 5, 6, 7, 8, 9); **endchar**;

cmchar "Italic numeral 9";
beginchar("9", $9u^\#$, $fig\_height^\#$, 0);

      $\vdots$ (a copy of the program for '9' in **romand** comes here)

penlabels(0, 1, 2, 3, 4, 5, 6, 7); **endchar**;

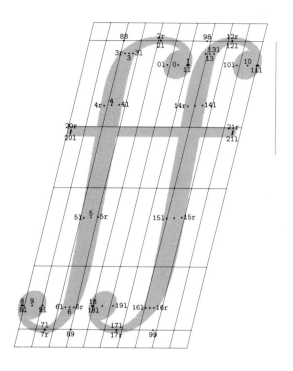

The program file `italig.mf` gives us *ff*, *fi*, *fl*, *ffi*, and *ffl*.

% This file describes five italic ligatures that begin with '*f*'
% and puts them in code positions ´013´–´017´.

numeric *itc*;   % modified italic correction on '*f*' and '*ff*'
itc = (*asc_height#* − *x_height#*) ∗ *slant* + .75*u#*;

ligtable "f": "i" =: oct "014", "f" =: oct "013", "l" =: oct "015",
   "'" **kern** *itc*, "?" **kern** *itc*, "!" **kern** *itc*, ")" **kern** *itc*, "]" **kern** *itc*;
ligtable oct "013": "i" =: oct "016", "l" =: oct "017",
   "'" **kern** *itc*, "?" **kern** *itc*, "!" **kern** *itc*, ")" **kern** *itc*, "]" **kern** *itc*;

cmchar "Italic ligature ff";
beginchar(oct "013", 5*u#* + max(1.5*u#*, *stem#*) + max(3.5*u#*, 2*flare#*) + 2*letter_fit#*,
   asc_height#, *desc_depth#*);
italcorr *asc_height#* ∗ *slant* + .75*u#*;
adjust_fit(0, 0); **pickup** *fine.nib*;
$z_{98} − z_{88} = z_{99} − z_{89} = z_{14} − z_4 = z_{15} − z_5 = (4.8u + 2letter\_fit, 0)$;
$.5[x_{88}, x_{99}] = .5w − .1u$; $x_{89} − x_{88} = u$; $y_{98} = h$; $y_{99} = −d$;
numeric *theta*; *theta* = angle($z_{88} − z_{89}$);
$pos_0(flare, 0)$; $pos_1(hair, 0)$; $pos_2(vair, 90)$; $pos_3(.5[hair, stem], 180)$;
$pos_4(stem, theta + 90)$; $pos_5(stem, theta − 90)$; $pos_6(.5[hair, stem], 0)$;
$pos_7(vair, −90)$; $pos_8(hair, −180)$; $pos_9(flare, −180)$;
rt $x_{1r} = $ hround$(.5w + 1.25u)$; **lft** $x_{8r} = $ hround $−.35u$;
$x_2 = .5[x_1, x_4]$; $x_7 = .6[x_8, x_5]$; $y_9 − .5flare = $ vround $−.85d$; $y_2 − y_0 = y_9 − y_7$;
top $y_{2r} = h + oo$; **bot** $y_{7r} = −d − oo$; $y_4 = .25[x\_height, h]$; $y_5 = .5[−d, y_4]$;
$z_4 = whatever[z_{88}, z_{89}]$; $z_5 = whatever[z_{88}, z_{89}]$;
$x_3 = .8[x_2 + x_4 − x_{88}, x_{88}]$; $x_6 = .8[x_7 + x_5 − x_{89}, x_{89}]$; $y_3 = .8[y_4, y_2]$; $y_6 = .8[y_5, y_7]$;
bulb(2, 1, 0); *bulb*(7, 8, 9);   % left bulbs
filldraw stroke $z_{2e}\{left\} \ldots z_{3e} \ldots \{z_{89} − z_{88}\}z_{4e}$;   % upper middle arc
filldraw z_{4r} -- z_{5l} -- z_{5r} -- z_{4l} -- **cycle**;   % left stem
filldraw stroke $z_{5e}\{z_{89} − z_{88}\} \ldots z_{6e} \ldots \{left\}z_{7e}$;   % lower left arc
$pos_{10}(flare, 0)$; $pos_{11}(hair, 0)$; $pos_{12}(vair, 90)$; $pos_{13}(.5[hair, stem], 180)$;
$pos_{14}(stem, theta + 90)$; $pos_{15}(stem, theta − 90)$; $pos_{16}(.5[hair, stem], 0)$;
$pos_{17}(vair, −90)$; $pos_{18}(hair, −180)$; $pos_{19}(flare, −180)$;
rt $x_{11r} = $ hround$(w + .25u)$; **lft** $x_{18r} = $ hround$(.5w − 1.25u)$;
$x_{12} = .6[x_{11}, x_{14}]$; $x_{17} = .5[x_{18}, x_{15}]$;
$x_{13} = .8[x_{12} + x_{14} − x_{98}, x_{98}]$; $x_{16} = .8[x_{17} + x_{15} − x_{99}, x_{99}]$;
$y_0 = y_{10}$; $y_2 = y_{12}$; $y_3 = y_{13}$; $y_6 = y_{16}$; $y_7 = y_{17}$; $y_9 = y_{19}$;
bulb(12, 11, 10); *bulb*(17, 18, 19);   % right bulbs
filldraw stroke $z_{12e}\{left\} \ldots z_{13e} \ldots \{z_{99} − z_{98}\}z_{14e}$;   % upper right arc
filldraw z_{14r} -- z_{15l} -- z_{15r} -- z_{14l} -- **cycle**;   % right stem
filldraw stroke $z_{15e}\{z_{99} − z_{98}\} \ldots z_{16e} \ldots \{left\}z_{17e}$;   % lower middle arc
pickup *crisp.nib*; $pos_{20}(bar, 90)$; $pos_{21}(bar, 90)$;
top $y_{20r} = $ **top** $y_{21r} = x\_height$;
lft $x_{20} = $ **lft** $x_{4r} − .5stem − u$; **rt** $x_{21} = $ **rt** $x_{14l} + .5stem + 1.5u$;
filldraw stroke z_{20e} -- z_{21e};   % crossbar
penlabels(0, 1, 2, 3, 4, 5, 6, 7, 8, 9, 10, 11, 12, 13, 14, 15, 16, 17, 18, 19,
   20, 21, 88, 89, 98, 99); **endchar**;

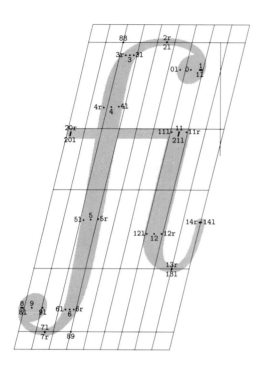

cmchar "Italic ligature fi";
beginchar(oct "014", $6.5u\# + .5 \max(1.5u\#, stem\#) + .5 \max(3.5u\#, 2flare\#)$
$\quad + 2letter\_fit\#, asc\_height\#, desc\_depth\#$);
italcorr $\max(asc\_height\# * slant + .5stem\# - 2u\#, \frac{1}{3}x\_height\# * slant + .5hair\# + .5u\#)$;
adjust_fit$(0, 0)$; **pickup** *fine.nib*;
$.5[x_{88}, x_{89}] = .5(w - 4u - 2letter\_fit)$; $x_{89} - x_{88} = u$; $y_{88} = h$; $y_{89} = -d$;
numeric *theta*; $theta = \text{angle}(z_{88} - z_{89})$;
$pos_0(flare, 0)$; $pos_1(hair, 0)$; $pos_2(vair, 90)$;
$pos_3(.5[hair, stem], 180)$; $pos_4(stem, theta + 90)$;
$pos_5(stem, theta - 90)$; $pos_6(.5[hair, stem], 0)$;
$pos_7(vair, -90)$; $pos_8(hair, -180)$; $pos_9(flare, -180)$;
$pos_{11}(stem, 0)$; $rt\ x_{11r} = \text{hround}(w - 2.5u + .5stem)$;
$x_{12} = x_{11}$; $x_{14} = w$; $hook\_out(12, 13, 14)$;   % closing hook
$x_{1r} = x_{11r}$; $lft\ x_{8r} = \text{hround} -.35u$; $x_2 = .5[x_1, x_4]$; $x_7 = .6[x_8, x_5]$;
$y_9 - .5flare = \text{vround} -.85d$; $bot\ y_{7r} = -d - oo$;
$y_0 + .5flare = \text{vround}(.85[x\_height, h])$; $top\ y_{2r} = h + oo$;
$y_4 = .25[x\_height, h]$; $y_5 = .5[-d, y_4]$;
$z_4 = whatever[z_{88}, z_{89}]$; $z_5 = whatever[z_{88}, z_{89}]$;
$x_3 = .8[x_2 + x_4 - x_{88}, x_{88}]$; $x_6 = .8[x_7 + x_5 - x_{89}, x_{89}]$; $y_3 = .8[y_4, y_2]$; $y_6 = .8[y_5, y_7]$;
$bulb(2, 1, 0)$; $bulb(7, 8, 9)$;   % bulbs
filldraw stroke $z_{2e}\{left\} \ldots z_{3e} \ldots \{z_{89} - z_{88}\}z_{4e}$;   % upper arc
filldraw $z_{4r} -- z_{5l} -- z_{5r} -- z_{4l} -- cycle$;   % left stem
filldraw stroke $z_{5e}\{z_{89} - z_{88}\} \ldots z_{6e} \ldots \{left\}z_{7e}$;   % lower arc
$top\ y_{11} = x\_height$; **filldraw** stroke $z_{11e} -- z_{12e}$;   % right stem
pickup *crisp.nib*; $pos_{20}(bar, 90)$; $pos_{21}(bar, 90)$;
$top\ y_{20r} = top\ y_{21r} = x\_height$;
$lft\ x_{20} = lft\ x_{4r} - .5stem - u$; $x_{21} = x_{11}$;
filldraw stroke $z_{20e} -- z_{21e}$;   % crossbar
penlabels$(0, 1, 2, 3, 4, 5, 6, 7, 8, 9, 10, 11, 12, 13, 14, 20, 21, 88, 89)$; **endchar**;

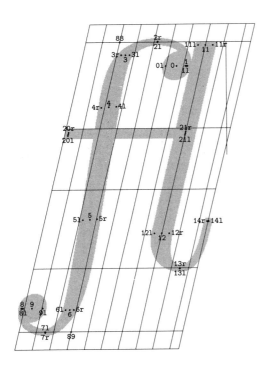

cmchar "Italic ligature fl";
beginchar(oct "015", $7u^\# + .5\max(1.5u^\#, stem^\#) + .5\max(3.5u^\#, 2flare^\#)$
$\qquad + 2letter\_fit^\#, asc\_height^\#, desc\_depth^\#)$;
italcorr $\max(asc\_height^\# * slant + .5stem^\# - 2u^\#, \, 1/3 x\_height^\# * slant + .5hair^\# + .5u^\#)$;
adjust_fit$(0, 0)$; **pickup** *fine.nib*;
$.5[x_{88}, x_{89}] = .5(w - 4.5u - 2letter\_fit)$; $\quad x_{89} - x_{88} = u$; $\quad y_{88} = h$; $\quad y_{89} = -d$;
numeric *theta*; $\quad theta = \text{angle}(z_{88} - z_{89})$;
$pos_0(flare, 0)$; $\quad pos_1(hair, 0)$; $\quad pos_2(vair, 90)$;
$pos_3(.5[hair, stem], 180)$; $\quad pos_4(stem, theta + 90)$;
$pos_5(stem, theta - 90)$; $\quad pos_6(.5[hair, stem], 0)$;
$pos_7(vair, -90)$; $\quad pos_8(hair, -180)$; $\quad pos_9(flare, -180)$;
$pos_{11}(stem, 0)$; $\quad rt\ x_{11r} = \text{hround}(w - 2.5u + .5stem)$; $\quad rt\ x_{1r} = lft\ x_{11l}$;
$x_{12} = x_{11}$; $\quad x_{14} = w$; $\quad hook\_out(12, 13, 14)$; $\hfill$ % closing hook
$lft\ x_{8r} = \text{hround} -.35u$; $\quad x_2 = .5[x_1, x_4]$; $\quad x_7 = .6[x_8, x_5]$;
$y_9 - .5flare = \text{vround} -.85d$; $\quad y_2 - y_0 = y_9 - y_7$; $\quad top\ y_{2r} = h + oo$; $\quad bot\ y_{7r} = -d - oo$;
$y_4 = .25[x\_height, h]$; $\quad y_5 = .5[-d, y_4]$;
$z_4 = whatever[z_{88}, z_{89}]$; $\quad z_5 = whatever[z_{88}, z_{89}]$;
$x_3 = .8[x_2 + x_4 - x_{88}, x_{88}]$; $\quad x_6 = .8[x_7 + x_5 - x_{89}, x_{89}]$; $\quad y_3 = .8[y_4, y_2]$; $\quad y_6 = .8[y_5, y_7]$;
$bulb(2, 1, 0)$; $\quad bulb(7, 8, 9)$; $\hfill$ % bulbs
filldraw stroke $z_{2e}\{left\} \ldots z_{3e} \ldots \{z_{89} - z_{88}\}z_{4e}$; $\hfill$ % upper arc
filldraw $z_{4r} -- z_{5l} -- z_{5r} -- z_{4l} -- \text{cycle}$; $\hfill$ % left stem
filldraw stroke $z_{5e}\{z_{89} - z_{88}\} \ldots z_{6e} \ldots \{left\}z_{7e}$; $\hfill$ % lower arc
$top\ y_{11} = h$; **filldraw stroke** $z_{11e} -- z_{12e}$; $\hfill$ % right stem
pickup *crisp.nib*; $\quad pos_{20}(bar, 90)$; $\quad pos_{21}(bar, 90)$;
$top\ y_{20r} = top\ y_{21r} = x\_height$;
$lft\ x_{20} = lft\ x_{4r} - .5stem - u$; $\quad x_{21} = x_{11}$;
filldraw stroke $z_{20e} -- z_{21e}$; $\hfill$ % crossbar
penlabels$(0, 1, 2, 3, 4, 5, 6, 7, 8, 9, 10, 11, 12, 13, 14, 20, 21, 88, 89)$; **endchar**;

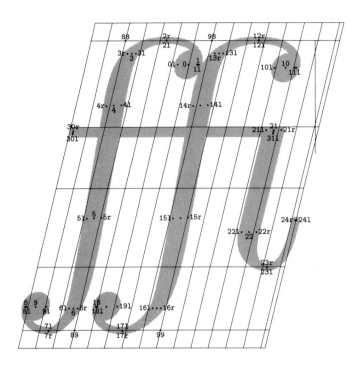

cmchar "Italic ligature ffi";
beginchar(oct "016", $11.75u^\# + .5\max(1.5u^\#, stem^\#) + .5\max(3.5u^\#, 2flare^\#)$
    $+ 4letter\_fit^\#, asc\_height^\#, desc\_depth^\#$);
italcorr $\max(asc\_height^\# * slant + .5stem^\# - 2u^\#, \frac{1}{3}x\_height^\# * slant + .5hair^\# + .5u^\#)$;
adjust_fit$(0, 0)$; **pickup** *fine.nib*;
$z_{98} - z_{88} = z_{99} - z_{89} = z_{14} - z_4 = z_{15} - z_5 = (5u + 2letter\_fit, 0)$;
numeric *theta*, *mid_f*;
$mid\_f = .5[x_{88}, x_{99}] = .5(w - 4.25u - 2letter\_fit)$; $x_{89} - x_{88} = u$;
$y_{98} = h$; $y_{99} = -d$; $theta = \text{angle}(z_{88} - z_{89})$;
$pos_{21}(stem, 0)$; rt $x_{21r} = \text{hround}(w - 2.5u + .5stem)$;
$x_{22} = x_{21}$; $x_{24} = w$; $hook\_out(22, 23, 24)$;   % closing hook
$pos_0(flare, 0)$; $pos_1(hair, 0)$; $pos_2(vair, 90)$;
$pos_3(.5[hair, stem], 180)$; $pos_4(stem, theta + 90)$;
$pos_5(stem, theta - 90)$; $pos_6(.5[hair, stem], 0)$;
$pos_7(vair, -90)$; $pos_8(hair, -180)$; $pos_9(flare, -180)$;
rt $x_{1r} = \text{hround}(mid\_f + 1.75u)$; lft $x_{8r} = \text{hround} -.35u$;
$x_2 = .5[x_1, x_4]$; $x_7 = .6[x_8, x_5]$;
$y_9 - .5flare = \text{vround} -.85d$; $y_2 - y_0 = y_9 - y_7$; top $y_{2r} = h + oo$; bot $y_{7r} = -d - oo$;
$y_4 = .25[x\_height, h]$; $y_5 = .5[-d, y_4]$;
$z_4 = whatever[z_{88}, z_{89}]$; $z_5 = whatever[z_{88}, z_{89}]$;
$x_3 = .8[x_2 + x_4 - x_{88}, x_{88}]$; $x_6 = .8[x_7 + x_5 - x_{89}, x_{89}]$; $y_3 = .8[y_4, y_2]$; $y_6 = .8[y_5, y_7]$;
$bulb(2, 1, 0)$; $bulb(7, 8, 9)$;   % left bulbs
filldraw stroke $z_{2e}\{left\} \ldots z_{3e} \ldots \{z_{89} - z_{88}\}z_{4e}$;   % upper middle arc
filldraw $z_{4r}\,\text{--}\,z_{5l}\,\text{--}\,z_{5r}\,\text{--}\,z_{4l}\,\text{--}\,cycle$;   % left stem
filldraw stroke $z_{5e}\{z_{89} - z_{88}\} \ldots z_{6e} \ldots \{left\}z_{7e}$;   % lower left arc
$pos_{10}(flare, 0)$; $pos_{11}(hair, 0)$; $pos_{12}(vair, 90)$;
$pos_{13}(.5[hair, stem], 180)$; $pos_{14}(stem, theta + 90)$;
$pos_{15}(stem, theta - 90)$; $pos_{16}(.5[hair, stem], 0)$;
$pos_{17}(vair, -90)$; $pos_{18}(hair, -180)$; $pos_{19}(flare, -180)$;
$x_{11r} = x_{21r}$; lft $x_{18r} = \text{hround}(mid\_f - 1.25u)$; $x_{12} = .5[x_{11}, x_{14}]$; $x_{17} = .5[x_{18}, x_{15}]$;
$x_{13} = .8[x_{12} + x_{14} - x_{98}, x_{98}]$; $x_{16} = .8[x_{17} + x_{15} - x_{99}, x_{99}]$;
$y_{10} + .5flare = \text{vround} .85[x\_height, h]$;
$y_2 = y_{12}$; $y_3 = y_{13}$; $y_6 = y_{16}$; $y_7 = y_{17}$; $y_9 = y_{19}$;
$bulb(12, 11, 10)$; $bulb(17, 18, 19)$;   % right bulbs
filldraw stroke $z_{12e}\{left\} \ldots z_{13e} \ldots \{z_{99} - z_{98}\}z_{14e}$;   % upper right arc
filldraw $z_{14r}\,\text{--}\,z_{15l}\,\text{--}\,z_{15r}\,\text{--}\,z_{14l}\,\text{--}\,cycle$;   % middle stem
filldraw stroke $z_{15e}\{z_{99} - z_{98}\} \ldots z_{16e} \ldots \{left\}z_{17e}$;   % lower middle arc
top $y_{21} = x\_height$; **filldraw stroke** $z_{21e}\,\text{--}\,z_{22e}$;   % right stem
pickup *crisp.nib*; $pos_{30}(bar, 90)$; $pos_{31}(bar, 90)$;
top $y_{30r} = $ top $y_{31r} = x\_height$;
lft $x_{30} = $ lft $x_{4r} - .5stem - u$; $x_{31} = x_{21}$;
filldraw stroke $z_{30e}\,\text{--}\,z_{31e}$;   % crossbar
penlabels$(0, 1, 2, 3, 4, 5, 6, 7, 8, 9, 10, 11, 12, 13, 14, 15, 16, 17, 18, 19,$
    $20, 21, 22, 23, 24, 30, 31, 88, 89, 98, 99)$; **endchar**;

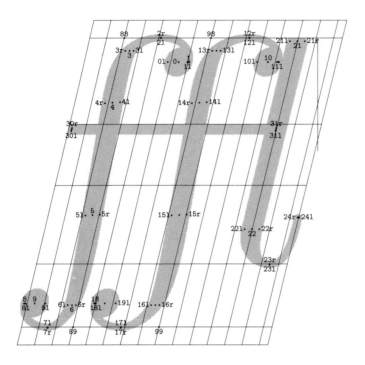

cmchar "Italic ligature ffl";
beginchar(oct "017", $12u^\# + .5\max(1.5u^\#, stem^\#) + .5\max(3.5u^\#, 2flare^\#)$
$+ 4letter\_fit^\#, asc\_height^\#, desc\_depth^\#$);
italcorr $\max(asc\_height^\# * slant + .5stem^\# - 2u^\#, \frac{1}{3}x\_height^\# * slant + .5hair^\# + .5u^\#)$;
adjust_fit$(0, 0)$; **pickup** *fine.nib*;
$z_{98} - z_{88} = z_{99} - z_{89} = z_{14} - z_4 = z_{15} - z_5 = (5u + 2letter\_fit, 0)$;
numeric *theta*, *mid_f*;
$mid\_f = .5[x_{88}, x_{99}] = .5(w - 4.5u - 2letter\_fit)$; $x_{89} - x_{88} = u$;
$y_{98} = h$; $y_{99} = -d$; $theta = angle(z_{88} - z_{89})$;
$pos_{21}(stem, 0)$; $rt\ x_{21r} = \text{hround}(w - 2.5u + .5stem)$;
$x_{22} = x_{21}$; $x_{24} = w$; $hook\_out(22, 23, 24)$;   % closing hook
$pos_0(flare, 0)$; $pos_1(hair, 0)$; $pos_2(vair, 90)$;
$pos_3(.5[hair, stem], 180)$; $pos_4(stem, theta + 90)$;
$pos_5(stem, theta - 90)$; $pos_6(.5[hair, stem], 0)$;
$pos_7(vair, -90)$; $pos_8(hair, -180)$; $pos_9(flare, -180)$;
$rt\ x_{1r} = \text{hround}(mid\_f + 1.25u)$; $lft\ x_{8r} = \text{hround}\ -.35u$;
$x_2 = .5[x_1, x_4]$; $x_7 = .6[x_8, x_5]$;
$y_9 - .5flare = \text{vround}\ -.85d$; $y_2 - y_0 = y_9 - y_7$; $top\ y_{2r} = h + oo$; $bot\ y_{7r} = -d - oo$;
$y_4 = .25[x\_height, h]$; $y_5 = .5[-d, y_4]$;
$z_4 = whatever[z_{88}, z_{89}]$; $z_5 = whatever[z_{88}, z_{89}]$;
$x_3 = .8[x_2 + x_4 - x_{88}, x_{88}]$; $x_6 = .8[x_7 + x_5 - x_{89}, x_{89}]$; $y_3 = .8[y_4, y_2]$; $y_6 = .8[y_5, y_7]$;
$bulb(2, 1, 0)$; $bulb(7, 8, 9)$;   % left bulbs
filldraw stroke $z_{2e}\{left\} \ldots z_{3e} \ldots \{z_{89} - z_{88}\}z_{4e}$;   % upper middle arc
filldraw $z_{4r} -\!\!- z_{5l} -\!\!- z_{5r} -\!\!- z_{4l} -\!\!-$ cycle;   % left stem
filldraw stroke $z_{5e}\{z_{89} - z_{88}\} \ldots z_{6e} \ldots \{left\}z_{7e}$;   % lower left arc
$pos_{10}(flare, 0)$; $pos_{11}(hair, 0)$; $pos_{12}(vair, 90)$;
$pos_{13}(.5[hair, stem], 180)$; $pos_{14}(stem, theta + 90)$;
$pos_{15}(stem, theta - 90)$; $pos_{16}(.5[hair, stem], 0)$;
$pos_{17}(vair, -90)$; $pos_{18}(hair, -180)$; $pos_{19}(flare, -180)$; $rt\ x_{11r} = lft\ x_{21l}$;
$lft\ x_{18r} = \text{hround}(mid\_f - 1.25u)$; $x_{12} = .5[x_{11}, x_{14}]$; $x_{17} = .5[x_{18}, x_{15}]$;
$x_{13} = .8[x_{12} + x_{14} - x_{98}, x_{98}]$; $x_{16} = .8[x_{17} + x_{15} - x_{99}, x_{99}]$;
$y_0 = y_{10}$; $y_2 = y_{12}$; $y_3 = y_{13}$; $y_6 = y_{16}$; $y_7 = y_{17}$; $y_9 = y_{19}$;
$bulb(12, 11, 10)$; $bulb(17, 18, 19)$;   % right bulbs
filldraw stroke $z_{12e}\{left\} \ldots z_{13e} \ldots \{z_{99} - z_{98}\}z_{14e}$;   % upper right arc
filldraw $z_{14r} -\!\!- z_{15l} -\!\!- z_{15r} -\!\!- z_{14l} -\!\!-$ cycle;   % middle stem
filldraw stroke $z_{15e}\{z_{99} - z_{98}\} \ldots z_{16e} \ldots \{left\}z_{17e}$;   % lower middle arc
$top\ y_{21} = h$; **filldraw stroke** $z_{21e} -\!\!- z_{22e}$;   % right stem
pickup *crisp.nib*; $pos_{30}(bar, 90)$; $pos_{31}(bar, 90)$;
$top\ y_{30r} = top\ y_{31r} = x\_height$;
$lft\ x_{30} = lft\ x_{4r} - .5stem - u$; $x_{31} = x_{21}$;
filldraw stroke $z_{30e} -\!\!- z_{31e}$;   % crossbar
penlabels(0, 1, 2, 3, 4, 5, 6, 7, 8, 9, 10, 11, 12, 13, 14, 15, 16, 17, 18, 19,
20, 21, 22, 23, 24, 30, 31, 88, 89, 98, 99); **endchar**;

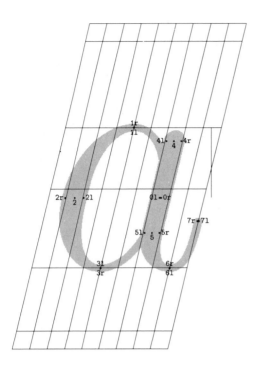

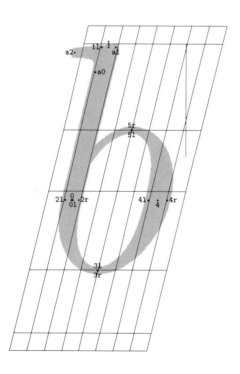

Now we come to program file `itall.mf`, the *abc*'s of italic.

% Computer Modern Italic lower case:

% This lower-case italic alphabet was prepared by D. E. Knuth in December, 1979,

% inspired by the Monotype faces used in *The Art of Computer Programming*.

% The programs were revised for the new METAFONT conventions in 1985.

% Character codes ´141 through ´172 are generated.

cmchar "Italic letter a";
beginchar("a", $9u^\#$, $x\_height^\#$, 0);
italcorr $^1/_3 x\_height^\# * slant + .5hair^\# + .5u^\#$;
adjust_fit(0, 0); **pickup** *fine.nib*;
$pos_0(hair, 0)$; $pos_1(vair, 90)$; $pos_2(curve, 180)$; $pos_3(vair, 270)$;
$pos_4(stem, 0)$; $x_4 = x_0$; $y_4 + .5stem = $ vround $.98h$;
$x_1 = x_3 = .5[x_0, x_2]$; *lft* $x_{2r} = $ hround$(1.5u - .5curve)$;
rt $x_{4r} = $ hround$(w - 2.5u + .5stem)$;
top $y_{1r} = h + oo$; *bot* $y_{3r} = -oo$; $y_0 = y_2 = .5[y_1, y_3]$;
filldraw stroke $super\_arc_e(0, 1)$ & $pulled\_arc_e(1, 2)$
   & $pulled\_arc_e(2, 3)$ & $super\_arc_e(3, 0)$;   % bowl
$x_5 = x_4$; $x_7 = w$; $hook\_out(5, 6, 7)$;   % closing hook
filldraw circ_stroke $z_{4e} -- z_{5e}$;   % stem
math_fit$(-.3x\_height^\# * slant + .5curve^\# - u^\#, ic^\#)$;
penlabels(0, 1, 2, 3, 4, 5, 6, 7); **endchar**;

cmchar "Italic letter b";
beginchar("b", $8u^\#$, $asc\_height^\#$, 0);
italcorr $.7x\_height^\# * slant + .5curve^\# - u^\#$ **if** *math_fitting*: $-.5u^\#$ **fi**;
adjust_fit(0, 0); **pickup** *tiny.nib*;
$pos_1(stem, 0)$; $pos_2(stem, 0)$; $x_1 = x_2$;
lft $x_{1l} = $ hround$(1.5u - .5stem)$; *top* $y_1 = h$; $y_2 = .5x\_height$;
filldraw stroke $z_{1e} -- z_{2e}$;   % stem
sloped_serif.l$(1, 2, a, ^1/_3, jut, serif\_drop)$;   % serif
pickup *fine.nib*; $pos_{2'}(stem, -180)$; $pos_3(vair, -90)$;
$pos_4(curve, 0)$; $pos_5(vair, 90)$; $pos_0(hair, 180)$;
$z_0 = z_2 = z_{2'}$; $x_3 = x_5 = .5[x_2, x_4]$; *rt* $x_{4r} = $ hround$(w - 1.5u + .5curve)$;
bot $y_{3r} = -oo$; *top* $y_{5r} = x\_height + oo$; $y_4 = y_2$;
filldraw stroke $pulled\_arc_e(2', 3)$ & $pulled\_arc_e(3, 4)$
   & $pulled\_arc_e(4, 5)$ & $super\_arc_e(5, 0)$;   % bowl
math_fit$(-.3x\_height^\# * slant + .5curve^\# - u^\#, ic^\#)$;
penlabels(0, 1, 2, 3, 4, 5); **endchar**;

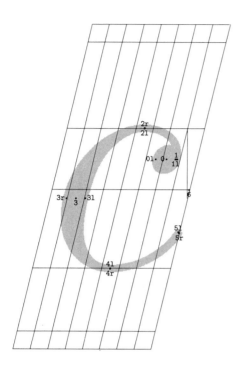

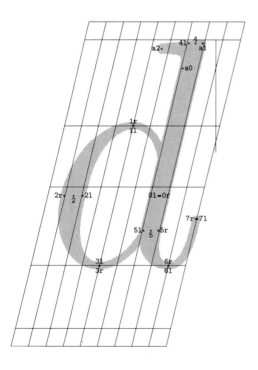

cmchar "Italic letter c";

beginchar("c", $8u\#$, $x\_height\#$, 0);

italcorr if $math\_fitting$: $\frac{1}{3}x\_height\# * slant$ **else**: $x\_height\# * slant - u\#$ **fi**;

adjust_fit$(0, 0)$; **pickup** $fine.nib$;

$pos_0(flare, 0)$; $pos_1(hair, 0)$; $pos_2(vair, 90)$;

$pos_3(curve, 180)$; $pos_4(vair, 270)$; $pos_5(hair, 320)$;

$x_2 = x_4 = .5(w + u)$; $rt\ x_{1r} = \max(rt\ x_2, \text{hround}(w - u)) + eps$;

$lft\ x_{3r} = \text{hround}(1.5u - .5curve)$; $x_{5r} = good.x(w - eps)$; $x_6 = x_5$;

$y_1 = .5[bar\_height, h]$; $top\ y_{2r} = h + oo$; $bulb(2, 1, 0)$;   % bulb

$bot\ y_{4r} = -oo$; $y_3 = .5[y_2, y_4]$; $top\ y_{5l} = $ vround $.5bar\_height$; $y_6 = bar\_height$;

path p; $p = z_4\{right\} .. z_5 .. z_6$;

filldraw stroke $pulled\_arc_e(2, 3)$

    & $pulled\_arc_e(3, 4) \ldots \{$**direction** 1 **of** $p\}z_{5e}$;   % arc

math_fit$(-.3x\_height\# * slant + .5curve\# - u\#, ic\#)$;

penlabels$(0, 1, 2, 3, 4, 5, 6)$; **endchar**;

cmchar "Italic letter d";

beginchar("d", $9u\#$, $asc\_height\#$, 0);

italcorr $\max(\frac{1}{3}x\_height\# * slant + .5hair\# + .5u\#$,

    $h\# * slant + .5stem\# - 2u\#)$ **if** $math\_fitting$: $-.5u\#$ **fi**;

adjust_fit$(0, 0)$; **pickup** $fine.nib$;

$pos_0(hair, 0)$; $pos_1(vair, 90)$; $pos_2(curve, 180)$; $pos_3(vair, 270)$;

$x_0 = x_4$; $x_1 = x_3 = .5[x_0, x_2]$; $lft\ x_{2r} = \text{hround}(1.5u - .5curve)$;

$x_4 + .5stem = \text{hround}(w - 2.5u + .5stem)$;

$top\ y_{1r} = x\_height + oo$; $bot\ y_{3r} = -oo$; $y_0 = y_2 = .5[y_1, y_3]$;

filldraw stroke $super\_arc_e(0, 1)$ & $pulled\_arc_e(1, 2)$

    & $pulled\_arc_e(2, 3)$ & $super\_arc_e(3, 0)$;   % bowl

$x_5 = x_0$; $x_7 = w$; $hook\_out(5, 6, 7)$;   % closing hook

pickup $tiny.nib$; $pos_{5'}(stem, 0)$; $pos_4(stem, 0)$;

$z_{5'} = z_5$; $top\ y_4 = h$; **filldraw stroke** $z_{4e} \,$--$\, z_{5'e}$;   % stem

$sloped\_serif.l(4, 5', a, \frac{1}{3}, jut, serif\_drop)$;   % serif

math_fit$(-.3x\_height\# * slant + .5curve\# - u\#, ic\#)$;

penlabels$(0, 1, 2, 3, 4, 5, 6, 7)$; **endchar**;

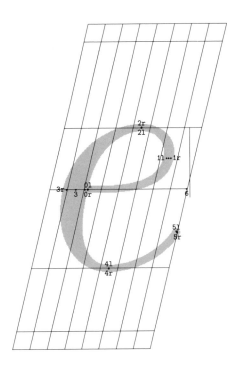

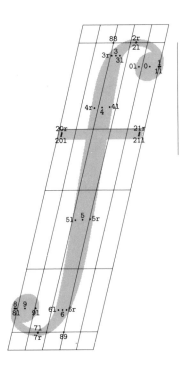

cmchar "Italic letter e";
beginchar("e", $8u^\#$, $x\_height^\#$, 0);
italcorr $\max(\frac{1}{3}x\_height^\# * slant, x\_height^\# * slant + .5(.2[hair^\#, stem^\#]) - u^\#)$;
adjust_fit(0, 0); **pickup** *fine.nib*;
numeric *heavy_hair*; $heavy\_hair = \text{hround } .2[hair, stem]$;
$pos_0(vair, -90)$; $pos_1(heavy\_hair, 0)$; $pos_2(vair, 90)$;
$pos_3(curve, 180)$; $pos_4(vair, 270)$; $pos_5(hair, 320)$;
$x_0 = rt\ x_{3l}$; $rt\ x_{1r} = \text{hround}(w - 1.5u + .5heavy\_hair)$; $x_2 = x_4 = .5(w + u)$;
$lft\ x_{3r} = \text{hround}(1.5u - .5curve)$; $x_{5r} = good.x(w - eps)$; $x_6 = x_5$;
$y_0 = y_3 = y_6 = bar\_height$; $y_1 = .5[y_0, y_2]$; $top\ y_{2r} = h + oo$; $bot\ y_{4r} = -oo$;
$top\ y_{5l} = \text{vround } .5bar\_height$; **path** p; $p = z_4\{right\} \ldots z_5 \ldots z_6$;
filldraw stroke $z_{0e}\{right\} \ldots z_{1e}\{up\} \ldots pulled\_arc_e(2, 3)$
    & $pulled\_arc_e(3, 4) \ldots \{$**direction** 1 **of** $p\}z_{5e}$;   % arc
math_fit$(-.3x\_height^\# * slant + .5curve^\# - u^\#, ic^\#)$;
penlabels(0, 1, 2, 3, 4, 5, 6); **endchar**;

cmchar "Italic letter f";
beginchar("f", $\max(1.5u^\#, stem^\#) + \max(3.5u^\#, 2flare^\#)$, $asc\_height^\#$, $desc\_depth^\#$);
italcorr $asc\_height^\# * slant + .75u^\#$;
adjust_fit(**if** *monospace*: $u^\#$, $u^\#$ **else**: 0, 0 **fi**); **pickup** *fine.nib*;
numeric *theta*; $z_{88} = (.5w - .5u, h)$; $z_{89} = (.5w + .5u, -d)$; $theta = \text{angle}(z_{88} - z_{89})$;
$pos_0(flare, 0)$; $pos_1(hair, 0)$; $pos_2(vair, 90)$;
$pos_3(.5[hair, stem], 180)$; $pos_4(stem, theta + 90)$;
$pos_5(stem, theta - 90)$; $pos_6(.5[hair, stem], 0)$;
$pos_7(vair, -90)$; $pos_8(hair, -180)$; $pos_9(flare, -180)$;
$rt\ x_{1r} = \text{hround}(w + .25u)$; $lft\ x_{8r} = \text{hround } -.35u$; $x_2 = .6[x_1, x_4]$; $x_7 = .6[x_8, x_5]$;
$y_9 - .5flare = \text{vround } -.85d$; $y_2 - y_0 = y_9 - y_7$; $top\ y_{2r} = h + oo$; $bot\ y_{7r} = -d - oo$;
$y_4 = .25[x\_height, h]$; $y_5 = .5[-d, y_4]$;
$z_4 = whatever[z_{88}, z_{89}]$; $z_5 = whatever[z_{88}, z_{89}]$;
$x_3 = .8[x_2 + x_4 - x_{88}, x_{88}]$; $x_6 = .8[x_7 + x_5 - x_{89}, x_{89}]$;
$y_3 = .8[y_4, y_2]$; $y_6 = .8[y_5, y_7]$;
$bulb(2, 1, 0)$; $bulb(7, 8, 9)$;   % bulbs
filldraw stroke $z_{2e}\{left\} \ldots z_{3e} \ldots \{z_{89} - z_{88}\}z_{4e}$;   % upper arc
filldraw z_{4r} -- z_{5l} -- z_{5r} -- z_{4l} -- **cycle**;   % stem
filldraw stroke $z_{5e}\{z_{89} - z_{88}\} \ldots z_{6e} \ldots \{left\}z_{7e}$;   % lower arc
pickup *crisp.nib*; $pos_{20}(bar, 90)$; $pos_{21}(bar, 90)$;
$top\ y_{20r} = top\ y_{21r} = x\_height$;
$lft\ x_{20} = lft\ x_{4r} - .5stem - u$; $rt\ x_{21} = rt\ x_{4l} + .5stem + 1.5u$;
filldraw stroke z_{20e} -- z_{21e};   % crossbar
math_fit$(desc\_depth^\# * slant + u^\#, x\_height^\# * slant)$;
penlabels(0, 1, 2, 3, 4, 5, 6, 7, 8, 9, 20, 21, 88, 89); **endchar**;

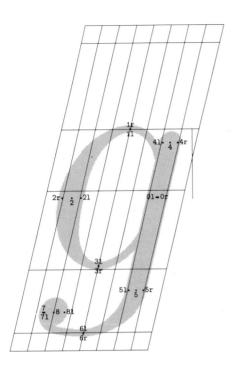

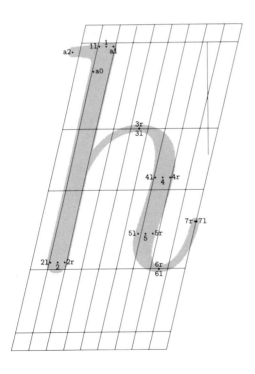

cmchar "Italic letter g";
beginchar("g", $8u^\#$, $x\_height^\#$, $desc\_depth^\#$);
italcorr $x\_height^\# * slant + .5stem^\# - u^\#$;
adjust_fit$(0, 0)$; **pickup** *fine.nib*;
$pos_0(hair, 0)$; $pos_1(vair, 90)$; $pos_2(curve, 180)$; $pos_3(vair, 270)$;
$x_0 = x_4$; $x_1 = x_3 = .5[x_0, x_2]$; *lft* $x_{2r} = \text{hround}(1.5u - .5curve)$;
$x_4 + .5stem = \text{hround}(w - 1.5u + .5stem)$;
top $y_{1r} = h + oo$; *bot* $y_{3r} = 0$; $y_0 = y_2 = .5[y_1, y_3]$;
filldraw stroke $super\_arc_e(0, 1)$ & $pulled\_arc_e(1, 2)$
    & $pulled\_arc_e(2, 3)$ & $super\_arc_e(3, 0)$;   % bowl
$pos_4(stem, 0)$; $y_4 + .5stem = \text{vround } .98h$;
$pos_5(stem, 0)$; $x_5 = x_4$; $y_5 = -^1/_3 d$;
$pos_6(vair, -90)$; $pos_7(hair, -180)$; $pos_8(flare, -180)$;
bot $y_{6r} = -d - oo$; $y_8 - .5flare = \text{vround} -.9d$;
lft $x_{8r} = \text{hround}(2u - .5flare)$; $x_6 = x_1$; $bulb(6, 7, 8)$;   % bulb
filldraw circ_stroke z_{4e} --- z_{5e} ... $\{left\}z_{6e}$;   % stem and arc
math_fit$(- \min(.3x\_height^\# * slant + .5curve^\# - u^\#, 1.5u^\# - desc\_depth^\# * slant),$
    $ic^\# - {}^1/_3 x\_height^\# * slant)$; **penlabels**$(0, 1, 2, 3, 4, 5, 6, 7, 8)$; **endchar**;

cmchar "Italic letter h";
beginchar("h", $9u^\#$, $asc\_height^\#$, 0);
italcorr $^1/_3 x\_height^\# * slant + .5hair^\# + .5u^\#$;
adjust_fit$(0, 0)$; **pickup** *tiny.nib*;
$pos_1(stem, 0)$; $pos_2(stem, 0)$; $x_1 = x_2$;
lft $x_{1l} = \text{hround}(1.5u - .5stem)$; *top* $y_1 = h$; $y_2 - .5stem = -oo$;
filldraw circ_stroke z_{2e} -- z_{1e};   % left stem
$sloped\_serif.l(1, 2, a, {}^1/_3, jut, serif\_drop)$;   % serif
pickup *fine.nib*; $x_4 + .5stem = \text{hround}(w - 2.5u + .5stem)$;
$x_5 = x_4 - .25u$; $ital\_arch(2, 3, 4)$;   % arch
$x_7 = w$; $hook\_out(5, 6, 7)(skewed)$;   % closing hook
filldraw stroke $z_{4e}\{down\}$ .. $\{-u, -x\_height\}z_{5e}$;   % right stem
math_fit$(0, ic^\#)$; **penlabels**$(1, 2, 3, 4, 5, 6, 7)$; **endchar**;

---

def $ital\_arch(\textbf{suffix } \$, \$\$, \$\$\$) =$ % $z_\$$ and $z_{\$\$\$}$ (only) are known
    $pos_{\$'}(hair, 180)$; $z_{\$'} = z_\$$;
    $pos_{\$\$}(vair, 90)$; $pos_{\$\$\$}(stem, 0)$;
    $\{\{$ **interim** $superness := more\_super$; $x_{\$\$} = .6[x_\$, x_{\$\$\$}]$;
    top $y_{\$\$r} = x\_height + oo$; $y_{\$\$\$} = .65x\_height$;
    filldraw stroke $z_{\$'e}\{up\}$ ... $super\_arc_e(\$\$, \$\$\$)$; $\}\}$ **enddef**;   % stroke

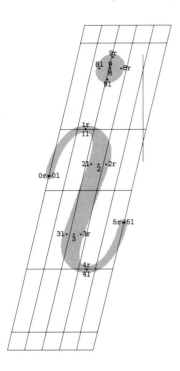

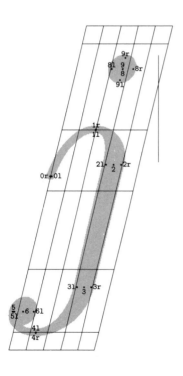

cmchar "Italic letter i";
beginchar("i", $5u^\#$, $\min(asc\_height^\#, {}^{10}/_7 x\_height^\# + .5flare^\#), 0)$;
italcorr $\max({}^1/_3 x\_height^\# * slant + .5hair^\# + .5u^\#, h^\# * slant + .5flare^\# - 2u^\#)$;
adjust_fit(**if** *monospace*: $u^\#, u^\#$ **else**: 0, 0 **fi**); **pickup** *fine.nib*;
$x_0 = 0$; $x_5 = w$; $x_2 = .5w + .25u$; $x_3 = .5w - .25u$;
$hook\_in(0, 1, 2)(skewed)$; $hook\_out(3, 4, 5)(skewed)$;   % hooks
filldraw stroke z_{2e} -- z_{3e};   % stem
$pos_8(flare, 0)$; $pos_9(flare, 90)$;
$x_8 = .5w$ **if** not *monospace*: $-.4(h - x\_height) * slant$ **fi**; *top* $y_{9r} = h + 1$;
if *bot* $y_{9l} - top$ $y_1 < slab$: $y_{9l} := \min(y_{9r} - eps, y_1 + fine + slab)$; **fi**
$x_8 = x_9$; $y_8 = .5[y_{9l}, y_{9r}]$; $dot(8, 9)$;   % dot
math_fit$(-{}^2/_3 x\_height^\# * slant + .5hair^\# + .5u^\#, ic^\#)$;
penlabels(0, 1, 2, 3, 4, 5, 8, 9); **endchar**;

cmchar "Italic letter j";
beginchar("j", $5u^\#$, $\min(asc\_height^\#, {}^{10}/_7 x\_height^\# + .5flare^\#), desc\_depth^\#)$;
italcorr $h^\# * slant + .5stem^\# - u^\#$;
adjust_fit(**if** *monospace*: $2u^\#, .5u^\#$ **else**: 0, 0 **fi**); **pickup** *fine.nib*;
$x_0 = 0$; $x_2 = x_3$; $pos_3(stem, 0)$; *lft* $x_{3l} = \text{hround}(w - 1.5u - .5stem)$;
$hook\_in(0, 1, 2)$;   % opening hook
$pos_4(vair, -90)$; $pos_5(hair, -180)$; $pos_6(flare, -180)$;
bot $y_3 = -{}^1/_3 d$; *bot* $y_{4r} = -d - oo$; $y_6 - .5flare = -$ vround $.9d$;
$x_4 = {}^1/_3(w - u)$; *lft* $x_{5r} = \min(\text{hround} -.5u, lft$ $x_{5r} + x_4 - x_{5l} - eps)$;
filldraw stroke z_{2e} --- z_{3e} ... $\{left\}z_{4e}$;   % stem and arc
$bulb(4, 5, 6)$;   % bulb
$pos_8(flare, 0)$; $pos_9(flare, 90)$;
rt $x_{8r} = rt$ x_{2r} **if** not *monospace*: $-.6(h - x\_height) * slant$ **fi**; *top* $y_{9r} = h + 1$;
if *bot* $y_{9l} - top$ $y_1 < slab$: $y_{9l} := \min(y_{9r} - eps, y_1 + fine + slab)$; **fi**
$x_8 = x_9$; $y_8 = .5[y_{9l}, y_{9r}]$; $dot(8, 9)$;   % dot
math_fit$(desc\_depth^\# * slant, x\_height^\# * slant + .5stem^\# - u^\#)$;
penlabels(0, 1, 2, 3, 4, 5, 6, 8, 9); **endchar**;

---

def $hook\_in$(**suffix** $, $$, $$$) **suffix** *modifier* =   % $x_\$$ and $x_{\$\$\$}$ (only) are known
 $x_\$:= \text{hround}(x_\$ - .5hair) + .5hair$; $pos_\$(hair, 180)$;
 $pos_{\$\$}(vair, 90)$; $pos_{\$\$\$}(stem, 0)$;
 $y_\$ = {}^2/_3 x\_height$; *top* $y_{\$\$r} = x\_height + oo$; $y_{\$\$\$} = {}^3/_4 x\_height$;
 if $skewed_{modifier}$: $x_{\$\$} = x_{\$\$\$} - 1.25u$;
  filldraw stroke $z_{\$e}\{up\}$ ... $z_{\$\$e}\{right\}$ ... $\{-u, -x\_height\}z_{\$\$\$e}$;   % hook
 else: $x_{\$\$} = x_{\$\$\$} - 1.5u$;
  filldraw stroke $z_{\$e}\{x_{\$\$\$} - 2.5u - x_\$, x\_height\}$
   ... $z_{\$\$e}\{right\}$ ... $\{down\}z_{\$\$\$e}$; **fi enddef**;   % hook

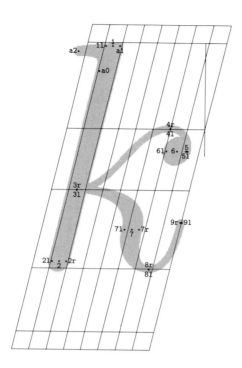

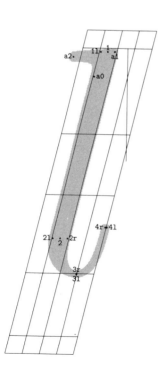

cmchar "Italic letter k";
beginchar("k", $8u^\#$, $asc\_height^\#$, 0);
italcorr $x\_height^\# * slant$;
adjust_fit$(0, 0)$; **pickup** $tiny.nib$;
$pos_1(stem, 0)$; $pos_2(stem, 0)$; $x_1 = x_2$;
$lft\ x_{1l} = \text{hround}(1.5u - .5stem)$; $top\ y_1 = h$; $y_2 - .5stem = -oo$;
filldraw circ_stroke z_{2e} -- z_{1e};   % left stem
$sloped\_serif.l(1, 2, a, \frac{1}{3}, jut, serif\_drop)$;   % serif
pickup $fine.nib$; $pos_3(vair, 90)$; $x_3 = x_1$; $y_3 = bar\_height$;
$pos_4(vair, 90)$; $x_4 = w - 2u$; $top\ y_{4r} = x\_height + oo$;
filldraw stroke $z_{3e}\{right\}$ .. $\{right\}z_{4e}$;   % upper diagonal
$pos_5(hair, 0)$; $pos_6(flare, 0)$;
$rt\ x_{5r} = \text{hround}(w - .5u)$; $y_5 + .5flare = \text{vround}(bot\ y_{4l} - .03x\_height)$;
$bulb(4, 5, 6)$;   % bulb
$pos_7(stem, 0)$; $pos_8(vair, 90)$; $pos_9(hair, 180)$;
$x_9 + .5hair = \text{hround}(w + .5hair - eps)$; $y_9 = \frac{1}{3}x\_height$;
$lft\ x_{7l} = \text{hround}(w - 2.75u - .5stem)$; $y_7 = \frac{1}{2}y_3$; $x_8 = w - 1.2u$; $bot\ y_{8l} = -oo$;
filldraw stroke $z_{3e}\{right\}$ ... $z_{7e}\{down\}$
    ... $z_{8e}\{right\}$ ... $\{up\}z_{9e}$;   % lower diagonal
math_fit$(0, \frac{1}{3}x\_height^\# * slant + .5hair^\# + .5u^\#)$;
penlabels$(1, 2, 3, 4, 5, 6, 7, 8, 9)$; **endchar**;

cmchar "Italic letter l";
beginchar("l", $4u^\#$, $asc\_height^\#$, 0); $l\_width^\# := 4u^\#$;
italcorr $\max(\frac{1}{3}x\_height^\# * slant + .5hair^\# + .5u^\#,$
    $asc\_height^\# * slant + .5stem^\# - 2u^\#)$ **if** $math\_fitting$: $+.5u^\#$ **fi**;
adjust_fit(**if** $monospace$: $u^\#$, $u^\#$ **else**: $0, 0$ **fi**); **pickup** $fine.nib$;
$x_2 - .5stem = \text{hround}(1.5u - .5stem)$; $x_4 = w$; $hook\_out(2, 3, 4)$;   % closing hook
pickup $tiny.nib$; $pos_1(stem, 0)$; $pos_{2'}(stem, 0)$; $z_{2'} = z_2$;
$top\ y_1 = h$; $x_1 = x_2$; **filldraw stroke** z_{1e} -- z_{2e};   % stem
$sloped\_serif.l(1, 2, a, \frac{1}{3}, jut, serif\_drop)$;   % serif
math_fit$(-.5u^\#, \frac{1}{3}x\_height^\# * slant + .5hair^\# + u^\#)$; **penlabels**$(1, 2, 3, 4)$; **endchar**;

---

def $hook\_out$(**suffix** \$, \$\$, \$\$\$) **suffix** $modifier$ =   % $x_\$$ and $x_{\$\$\$}$ (only) are known
    $pos_\$(stem, 0)$; $pos_{\$\$}(vair, 90)$;
    $x_{\$\$\$} := \text{hround}(x_{\$\$\$} + .5hair - eps) - .5hair$; $pos_{\$\$\$}(hair, 180)$;
    $y_\$ = \frac{1}{4}x\_height$; $bot\ y_{\$\$l} = -oo$; $y_{\$\$\$} = \frac{1}{3}x\_height$;
    if $skewed_{modifier}$: $x_{\$\$} = x_\$ + 1.25u$;
        filldraw stroke $z_{\$e}\{-u, -x\_height\}$ ... $z_{\$\$e}\{right\}$ ... $\{up\}z_{\$\$\$e}$;   % hook
    else: $x_{\$\$} = x_\$ + 1.5u$;
        filldraw stroke $z_{\$e}\{down\}$ ... $z_{\$\$e}\{right\}$
            ... $\{x_{\$\$\$} - (x_\$ + 2.5u), x\_height\}z_{\$\$\$e}$; **fi enddef**;   % hook

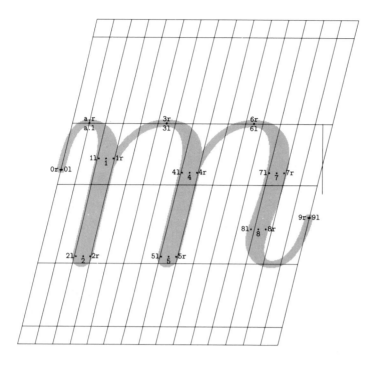

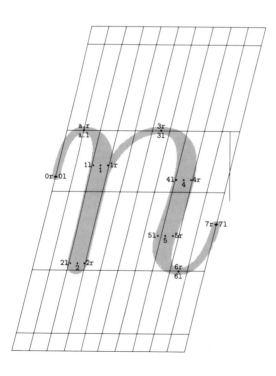

cmchar "Italic letter m";
beginchar("m", $15u^\#$, $x\_height^\#$, 0);
italcorr $1/3x\_height^\# * slant + .5hair^\# + .5u^\#$;
adjust_fit(**if** *monospace*: $-1.5u^\#$, $-2u^\#$ **else**: 0, 0 **fi**); **pickup** *fine.nib*;
numeric *shaved_stem*; *shaved_stem* = *mfudged.stem*;
save *stem*; *stem* = *shaved_stem*;
$pos_2(stem, 0)$; $x_1 = x_2$;
if *monospace*: $pos_1(stem, 0)$; *lft* x_{1l} = hround($2.5u - .5stem$); *top* $y_1 = h$;
else: $x_0 = 0$; *lft* x_{2l} = hround($2.5u - .5stem$);
  $hook\_in(0, a, 1)$; **fi**   % opening hook
$y_2 - .5stem = -oo$; **filldraw circ_stroke** z_{2e} -- z_{1e};   % left stem
$x_4 + .5stem$ = hround($.5w + .5stem$); $ital\_arch(2, 3, 4)$;   % left arch
$pos_5(stem, 0)$; $y_5 = y_2$; $x_5 = x_4$;
filldraw circ_stroke z_{5e} -- z_{4e};   % middle stem
$x_7 + .5stem$ = hround($w - 2.5u + .5stem$);
$x_8 = x_7 - .25u$; $ital\_arch(5, 6, 7)$;   % right arch
if *monospace*: $pos_9(vair, 90)$; $x_9 = good.x \; .5[x_8, w]$; *bot* $y_{9l} = 0$; $y_8 = 1/3h$;
  $pos_8(stem, 0)$; **filldraw stroke** $z_{8e}\{-u, -x\_height\}$ ... $\{right\}z_{9e}$;   % terminal
else: $x_9 = w$; $hook\_out(8, b, 9)(skewed)$; **fi**   % closing hook
filldraw stroke $z_{7e}\{down\}$ .. $\{-u, -x\_height\}z_{8e}$;   % right stem
math_fit($-2/3x\_height^\# * slant + .5hair^\# + .5u^\#$, $ic^\#$);
penlabels(0, a, 1, 2, 3, 4, 5, 6, 7, 8, 9); **endchar**;

cmchar "Italic letter n";
beginchar("n", $10u^\#$, $x\_height^\#$, 0);
italcorr $1/3x\_height^\# * slant + .5hair^\# + .5u^\#$;
adjust_fit(0, 0); **pickup** *fine.nib*;
$x_0 = 0$; $x_1 = x_2$; $pos_2(stem, 0)$; *lft* x_{2l} = hround($2.5u - .5stem$); $y_2 - .5stem = -oo$;
$hook\_in(0, a, 1)$;   % opening hook
filldraw circ_stroke z_{2e} -- z_{1e};   % left stem
$x_4 + .5stem$ = hround($w - 2.5u + .5stem$); $x_5 = x_4 - .25u$; $ital\_arch(2, 3, 4)$; % arch
$x_7 = w$; $hook\_out(5, 6, 7)(skewed)$;   % closing hook
filldraw stroke $z_{4e}\{down\}$ .. $\{-u, -x\_height\}z_{5e}$;   % right stem
math_fit($-2/3x\_height^\# * slant + .5hair^\# + .5u^\#$, $ic^\#$);
penlabels(0, a, 1, 2, 3, 4, 5, 6, 7); **endchar**;

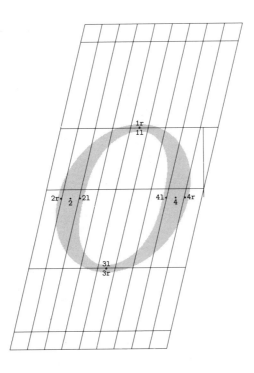

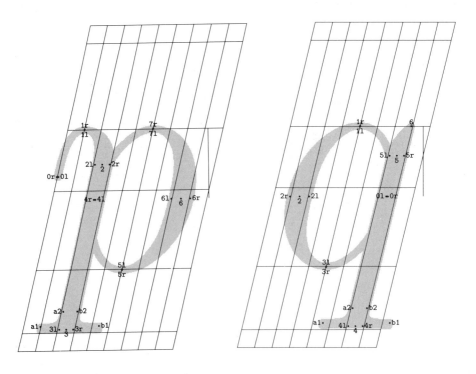

```
cmchar "Italic letter o";
```
beginchar("o", $9u^\#$, $x\_height^\#$, 0);
italcorr $.7x\_height^\# * slant + .5curve^\# - u^\#$ **if** *math_fitting*: $-.5u^\#$ **fi**;
adjust_fit(0, 0); **pickup** *fine.nib*;
$pos_1(vair, 90)$; $pos_2(curve, 180)$; $pos_3(vair, 270)$; $pos_4(curve, 360)$;
$x_1 = x_3 = .5w$; *lft* $x_{2r} = $ hround$(1.5u - .5curve)$; $x_4 = w - x_2$;
top $y_{1r} = h + oo$; $y_2 = y_4 = .5[y_1, y_3]$; *bot* $y_{3r} = -oo$;
filldraw stroke $pulled\_arc_e(1, 2)$ & $pulled\_arc_e(2, 3)$
    & $pulled\_arc_e(3, 4)$ & $pulled\_arc_e(4, 1)$;   % bowl
math_fit$(-.3x\_height^\# * slant + .5curve^\# - u^\#, ic^\#)$; **penlabels**(1, 2, 3, 4); **endchar**;

```
cmchar "Italic letter p";
```
beginchar("p", $9u^\#$, $x\_height^\#$, $desc\_depth^\#$);
italcorr $.7x\_height^\# * slant + .5curve^\# - u^\#$ **if** *math_fitting*: $-.5u^\#$ **fi**;
adjust_fit(0, 0); **pickup** *fine.nib*;
$x_0 = 0$; $x_2 - .5stem = $ hround$(2.5u - .5stem)$; *hook_in*(0, 1, 2);   % opening hook
$pos_4(hair, -180)$; $pos_5(vair, -90)$; $pos_6(curve, 0)$; $pos_7(vair, 90)$;
$x_4 = x_2$; *rt* $x_{6r} = $ hround$(w - 1.5u + .5curve)$; $x_5 = x_7 = .5[x_4, x_6]$;
bot $y_{5r} = -oo$; *top* $y_{7r} = h + oo$; $y_4 = y_6 = .5[y_5, y_7]$;
filldraw stroke $super\_arc_e(4, 5)$ & $pulled\_arc_e(5, 6)$
    & $pulled\_arc_e(6, 7)$ & $super\_arc_e(7, 4)$;   % bowl
pickup *tiny.nib*; $pos_{2'}(stem, 0)$; $pos_3(stem, 0)$;
$z_2 = z_{2'}$; $x_3 = x_2$; *bot* $y_3 = -d$; **filldraw stroke** $z_{2'e} \mathbin{--} z_{3e}$;   % stem
dish_serif$(3, 2', a, 1/3, .75jut, b, 1/3, jut)$;   % serif
math_fit$(-\min(2/3 x\_height^\# * slant - .5hair^\# - .5u^\#,$
  $2u^\# - .5stem^\# - desc\_depth^\# * slant), ic^\#)$;
penlabels(0, 1, 2, 3, 4, 5, 6, 7); **endchar**;

```
cmchar "Italic letter q";
```
beginchar("q", $8u^\#$, $x\_height^\#$, $desc\_depth^\#$);
italcorr $x\_height^\# * slant + .5stem^\# - u^\#$;
adjust_fit(0, 0); **pickup** *fine.nib*;
$pos_0(hair, 0)$; $pos_1(vair, 90)$; $pos_2(curve, 180)$; $pos_3(vair, 270)$;
$x_0 = x_4$; $x_1 = x_3 = .5[x_0, x_2]$; *lft* $x_{2r} = $ hround$(1.5u - .5curve)$;
$x_4 + .5stem = $ hround$(w - 1.5u + .5stem) + eps$;
top $y_{1r} = h + oo$; *bot* $y_{3r} = -oo$; $y_0 = y_2 = .5[y_1, y_3]$;
filldraw stroke $super\_arc_e(0, 1)$ & $pulled\_arc_e(1, 2)$
    & $pulled\_arc_e(2, 3)$ & $super\_arc_e(3, 0)$;   % bowl
pickup *tiny.nib*; $pos_4(stem, 0)$; $pos_5(stem, 0)$;
$x_4 = x_5$; $x_6 = x_{5r}$; *top* $y_6 = h + oo$; *bot* $y_4 = -d$;
$y_5 = $ ypart$(((x_{4l}, 0) \mathbin{--} (x_{4l}, y_6))$ intersectionpoint $super\_arc_r(0, 1))$;
filldraw $z_6\{2(x_{5l} - x_6), y_5 - y_6\} \ldots z_{5l} \mathbin{---} z_{4l} \mathbin{--} z_{4r} \mathbin{--}$ cycle;   % stem
dish_serif$(4, 5, a, 1/3, jut, b, 1/3, jut)$;   % serif
math_fit$(-.3x\_height^\# * slant + .5curve^\# - u^\#, ic^\# - 1/3 x\_height^\# * slant)$;
penlabels(0, 1, 2, 3, 4, 5, 6, 7, 8); **endchar**;

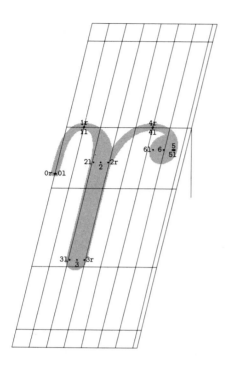

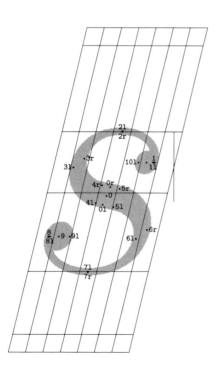

cmchar "Italic letter r";
beginchar("r", $5.5u^\# + \max(1.75u^\#, flare^\#)$, $x\_height^\#$, 0);
italcorr $x\_height^\# * slant$;
adjust_fit(if *monospace*: $.25u^\#, .5u^\#$ **else**: 0, 0 **fi**); **pickup** *fine.nib*;
$x_0 = 0$; $x_2 = x_3$; $pos_3(stem, 0)$; *lft* $x_{3l} = $ hround$(2.5u - .5stem)$; $y_3 - .5stem = -oo$;
hook_in(0, 1, 2); % opening hook
filldraw circ_stroke z_{3e} -- z_{2e}; % left stem
$pos_{3'}(hair, 180)$; $z_{3'} = z_3$; $pos_4(vair, 90)$; $pos_5(hair, 0)$; $pos_6(flare, 0)$;
$x_4 = w - .5u - \max(1.75u, flare)$; *rt* $x_{5r} = $ hround$(r - .5u)$; *top* $y_{4r} = h + oo$;
filldraw stroke $z_{3'e}\{up\} \ldots z_{4e}\{right\}$; % link
$y_6 + .5flare = $ vround$(bot\ y_{4l} - .03x\_height)$; $bulb(4, 5, 6)$; % bulb
math_fit$(-{}^2\!/_3 x\_height^\# * slant + .5hair^\# + .5u^\#, ic^\# - .5u^\#)$;
penlabels(0, 1, 2, 3, 4, 5, 6); **endchar**;

cmchar "Italic letter s";
beginchar("s", $5.25u^\# + \max(1.75u^\#, flare^\#)$, $x\_height^\#$, 0);
italcorr $x\_height^\# * slant - .5u^\#$;
adjust_fit(0, 0); **pickup** *fine.nib*;
numeric *theta*; $theta = 90 - $ angle$(40u, h)$; $slope := -h/40u$; % angle at middle
$pos_2(vair, -90)$; $pos_0(\max(fine.breadth, ess), theta)$; $pos_7(vair, -90)$;
$x_{2l} = x_0 = x_7 = .5w$; *top* $y_{2l} = h + oo$; *bot* $y_{7r} = -oo$;
$y_0 - .5ess = y_{7l} + .55(y_{2r} - y_{7l} - ess)$;
lft $x_{3l} = $ hround $u - eps$; *rt* $x_{6r} = $ hround$(w - .5u) + eps$;
$x_{3r} - x_{3l} = x_{6r} - x_{6l} = $ hround $.5[vair, ess] - fine$;
ellipse_set$(2l, 3l, 4l, 0l)$; *ellipse_set*$(2r, 3r, 4r, 0r)$; $y_3 = y_{3r}$;
ellipse_set$(7l, 6l, 5l, 0l)$; *ellipse_set*$(7r, 6r, 5r, 0r)$; $y_6 = y_{6r}$;
interim *superness* := *more_super*;
filldraw stroke $super\_arc_e(2, 3)\ \&\ z_{3e}\{down\}$
$\ldots z_{4e}$ --- $z_{5e} \ldots z_{6e}\{down\}\ \&\ super\_arc_e(6, 7)$; % main stroke
$pos_1(hair, 0)$; $pos_{10}($hround $.75[hair, flare], 0)$;
$pos_{2'}(vair, 90)$; $z_{2'} = z_2$;
$pos_8(hair, -180)$; $pos_9(flare, -180)$;
rt $x_{10r} = $ hround$(w - u) + 2eps$; *lft* $x_{9r} = $ hround $.5u - 2eps$; $y_{10} = .78h$; $y_9 = .25h$;
$bulb(2', 1, 10)$; $bulb(7, 8, 9)$; % bulbs
math_fit$(0, ic^\#)$; **penlabels**(0, 1, 2, 3, 4, 5, 6, 7, 8, 9, 10); **endchar**;

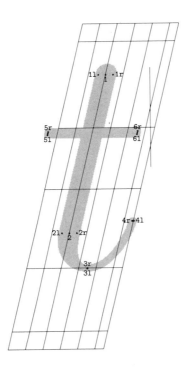

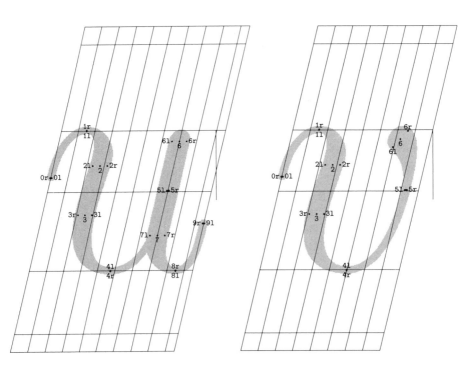

cmchar "Italic letter t";
beginchar("t", $5.5u^\#$, min($asc\_height^\#$, $^{10}/_7 x\_height^\#$), 0);
italcorr max($^1/_3 x\_height^\# * slant + .5hair^\# + .5u^\#$, $x\_height^\# * slant - .25u^\#$);
adjust_fit(**if** *monospace*: $u^\#$, $u^\#$ **else**: 0, 0 **fi**); **pickup** *fine.nib*;
$pos_1(stem, 0)$; *lft* x_{1l} = hround($2u - .5stem$); $y_1 + .5stem = h + oo$;
$x_2 = x_1$; $x_4 = w$; $hook\_out(2, 3, 4)$; % closing hook
filldraw circ_stroke z_{1e} -- z_{2e}; % stem
pickup *crisp.nib*; $pos_5(bar, 90)$; $pos_6(bar, 90)$;
lft x_5 = hround $-.75u$; *rt* x_6 = hround($w - .75u$); *top* y_{5r} = *top* y_{6r} = x_height;
filldraw stroke z_{5e} -- z_{6e}; % crossbar
math_fit($1.25u^\# - x\_height^\# * slant$, $ic^\#$); **penlabels**(1, 2, 3, 4, 5, 6); **endchar**;

cmchar "Italic letter u";
beginchar("u", $9.5u^\#$, $x\_height^\#$, 0);
italcorr $^1/_3 x\_height^\# * slant + .5hair^\# + .5u^\#$;
adjust_fit(0, 0); **pickup** *fine.nib*; **interim** *superness* := *more_super*;
$x_0 = 0$; $x_2 = x_3 + .25u$; $pos_3(stem, -180)$; *lft* x_{3r} = hround($2.5u - .5stem$);
$hook\_in(0, 1, 2)(skewed)$; % opening hook
$pos_{2'}(stem, -180)$; $z_{2'} = z_2$;
$pos_4(vair, -90)$; $pos_5(hair, 0)$; $x_4 = .5[x_3, x_5]$;
$pos_6(stem, 0)$; *rt* x_{6r} = hround($w - 2.5u + .5stem$);
$x_5 = x_6 = x_7$; $x_9 = w$; $hook\_out(7, 8, 9)$; % closing hook
$y_3 = .7[y_4, y_5]$; *bot* $y_{4r} = -oo$; $y_5 = .57h$; $y_6 + .5stem = h$;
filldraw stroke $z_{2'e}\{-u, -x\_height\}$
$\ldots super\_arc_e(3, 4) \ldots \{up\}z_{5e}$; % left stem and arc
filldraw circ_stroke z_{6e} -- z_{7e}; % right stem
math_fit($-^2/_3 x\_height^\# * slant + .5hair^\# + .5u^\#$, $ic^\#$);
penlabels(0, 1, 2, 3, 4, 5, 6, 7, 8, 9); **endchar**;

cmchar "Italic letter v";
beginchar("v", $8u^\#$, $x\_height^\#$, 0);
italcorr $x\_height^\# * slant$;
adjust_fit(0, 0); **pickup** *fine.nib*; **interim** *superness* := *more_super*;
$x_0 = 0$; $x_2 = x_3 + .25u$; $pos_3(stem, -180)$; *lft* x_{3r} = hround($2.5u - .5stem$);
$hook\_in(0, 1, 2)(skewed)$; % opening hook
$pos_{2'}(stem, -180)$; $z_{2'} = z_2$; $pos_4(vair, -90)$; $pos_5(hair, 0)$;
$x_4 = .5w + u$; *rt* x_{5r} = hround($w - .5u$); $y_3 = .7[y_4, y_5]$; *bot* $y_{4r} = -oo$; $y_5 = .57h$;
filldraw stroke $z_{2'e}\{-u, -x\_height\} \ldots super\_arc_e(3, 4)$
.. tension atleast 1.05 .. $\{up\}z_{5e}$; % left stem and arc
$v\_bulb(5, 6)$; % closing bulb
math_fit($-^2/_3 x\_height^\# * slant + .5hair^\# + .5u^\#$, $^2/_3 ic^\#$);
penlabels(0, 1, 2, 3, 4, 5, 6); **endchar**;

---

def v_bulb(**suffix** \$, \$\$) = % $pos_\$$ is known
  $y_{\$\$} + .5curve = x\_height + oo$; $x_{\$\$} + .5curve = w - u$;
  numeric *theta*; *theta* = angle($4(x_\$ - x_{\$\$})$, $y_\$ - y_{\$\$}$); $pos_{\$\$}(curve, theta + 90)$;
  filldraw $z_{\$\$l}\{\text{dir } theta\}$ .. tension atleast 1 and 1 .. $\{down\}z_{\$l}$
    -- $z_{\$r}\{up\} \ldots \{-\text{dir } theta\}z_{\$\$r}$ .. cycle; % bulb
  enddef;

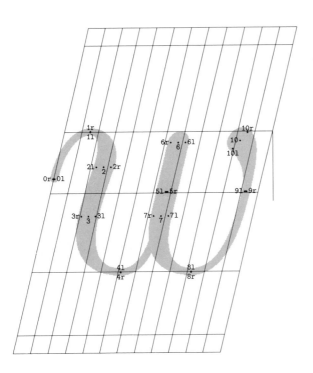

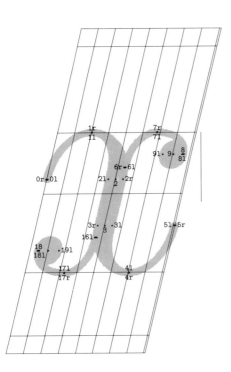

cmchar "Italic letter w";
beginchar("w", $12u^\#$, $x\_height^\#$, 0);
italcorr $x\_height^\# * slant$;
adjust_fit(if *monospace*: $-1.5u^\#$, $-u^\#$ else: 0, 0 **fi**);
pickup *fine.nib*; **interim** *superness* := *more_super*; **begingroup**
forsuffixes $ = *hair*, *stem*: *shaved*$_\$$:= *mfudged*.$; **save** $; $ = *shaved*$_\$$; **endfor**
$x_0 = 0$; $x_2 = x_3 + .25u$; $pos_3(stem, -180)$; *lft* $x_{3r} = $ hround$(2.5u - .5stem)$;
if *monospace*: $pos_1(vair, 90)$; $x_1 = good.x$ $.5[x_0, x_2]$; *top* $y_{1r} = h$; $y_2 = {}^2\!/_3 h$;
$\quad pos_2(stem, 0)$; **filldraw stroke** $z_{1e}\{right\} \ldots \{-u, -x\_height\}z_{2e}$;
else: *hook_in*$(0, 1, 2)(skewed)$; **fi** $\hfill$ % opening hook
$pos_{2'}(stem, -180)$; $z_{2'} = z_2$;
$pos_4(vair, -90)$; $pos_5(hair, 0)$;
$x_4 = .6[x_2, x_5]$; $x_5 = x_6 = x_7$; $pos_6(stem, -180)$; $pos_7(stem, -180)$;
$y_3 = .7[y_4, y_5]$; *bot* $y_{4r} = -oo$; $y_5 = .57h$;
rt $x_{6l} = $ hround$(rt\ x_{6l} + .5w + .75u - x_6)$; $y_6 + .5stem = h$; $y_7 = y_3$;
$pos_8(vair, -90)$; $pos_9(hair, 0)$;
$x_8 = w - 2.75u$; *rt* $x_{9r} = $ hround$(w - .5u)$; *bot* $y_{8r} = -oo$; $y_9 = y_5$;
filldraw stroke $z_{2'e}\{-u, -x\_height\}$
$\quad \ldots super\_arc_e(3, 4) \ldots \{up\}z_{5e}$; $\hfill$ % left stem and arc
filldraw circ_stroke $z_{6e} \ldots super\_arc_e(7, 8) \ldots \{up\}z_{9e}$; $\hfill$ % middle stem and arc
v_bulb$(9, 10)$; $\hfill$ % closing bulb
endgroup; **math_fit**$(-{}^2\!/_3 x\_height^\# * slant + .5hair^\# + .5u^\#, {}^3\!/_4 ic^\#)$;
penlabels$(0, 1, 2, 3, 4, 5, 6, 7, 8, 9, 10)$; **endchar**;

cmchar "Italic letter x";
beginchar("x", $6.5u^\# + \max(1.5u^\#, flare^\#)$, $x\_height^\#$, 0);
italcorr $\max({}^1\!/_3 x\_height^\# * slant + .5hair^\# + .5u^\#, x\_height^\# * slant + .25u^\#)$;
adjust_fit$(0, 0)$; **pickup** *fine.nib*;
$pos_0(hair, 180)$; $pos_1(vair, 90)$; $pos_2(stem, 0)$;
$pos_3(stem, -180)$; $pos_4(vair, -90)$; $pos_5(hair, 0)$;
$y_0 = y_2 = {}^2\!/_3 h$; $y_3 = y_5 = {}^1\!/_3 h$; *top* $y_{1r} = h + oo$; *bot* $y_{4r} = -oo$;
rt $x_{2r} = $ hround$(.5w + .5stem - eps)$; $x_2 = x_3$;
$x_0 - .5hair = $ hround $-.5hair$; $x_5 + .5hair = $ hround$(w + .5hair - eps)$;
$x_1 = .5[x_0, x_2]$; $x_4 = .5[x_3, x_5]$;
filldraw stroke $z_{0e}\{up\} \ldots pulled\_arc_e(1, 2)$; $\hfill$ % opening hook
filldraw z_{2l} -- z_{3r} -- z_{3l} -- z_{2r} -- *cycle*; $\hfill$ % stem
filldraw stroke $pulled\_arc_e(3, 4) \ldots \{up\}z_{5e}$; $\hfill$ % closing hook
$pos_{3'}(hair, 180)$; $pos_6(hair, 180)$; $pos_7(vair, 90)$;
$pos_8(hair, 0)$; $pos_9(flare, 0)$;
$x_{3'l} = x_{6l} = x_{3l}$; $y_{3'} = y_3$; $y_6 = {}^3\!/_4 h$; $x_7 = .5[x_8, x_2]$; *top* $y_{7r} = h + oo$;
rt $x_{8r} = $ hround$(w - .25u)$; $y_8 + .5flare = $ vround$(bot\ y_{7l} - .03x\_height)$;
filldraw stroke $z_{3'e}$ --- $z_{6e} \ldots \{right\}z_{7e}$; *bulb*$(7, 8, 9)$; $\hfill$ % upper link and bulb
$pos_{2'}(hair, 0)$; $pos_{16}(hair, 0)$; $pos_{17}(vair, -90)$;
$pos_{18}(hair, -180)$; $pos_{19}(flare, -180)$;
$x_{2'l} = x_{16l} = x_{2l}$; $y_{2'} = y_2$; $y_{16} = {}^1\!/_4 h$; $x_{17} = .5[x_{18}, x_3]$; *bot* $y_{17r} = -oo$;
lft $x_{18r} = $ hround $.25u$; $y_{18} - .5flare = $ vround$(top\ y_{17l} + .03x\_height)$;
filldraw stroke $z_{2'e}$ --- $z_{16e} \ldots \{left\}z_{17e}$; *bulb*$(17, 18, 19)$; $\hfill$ % lower link and bulb
math_fit$(0, ic^\#)$; **penlabels**$(0, 1, 2, 3, 4, 5, 6, 7, 8, 9, 16, 17, 18, 19)$; **endchar**;

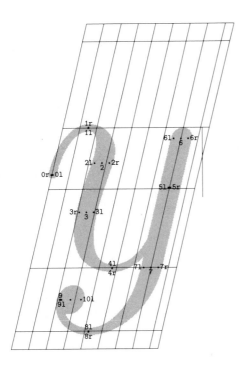

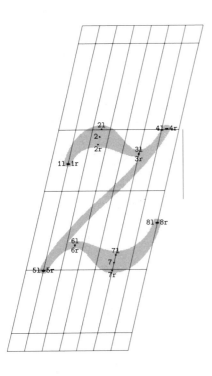

cmchar "Italic letter y";
beginchar("y", $8.5u^\#$, $x\_height^\#$, $desc\_depth^\#$);
italcorr $x\_height^\# * slant + .5stem^\# - u^\#$;
adjust_fit$(0, 0)$; **pickup** $fine.nib$; **interim** $superness := more\_super$;
$x_0 = 0$; $x_2 = x_3 + .25u$; $pos_3(stem, -180)$; $lft\ x_{3r} = \mathrm{hround}(2.5u - .5stem)$;
$hook\_in(0, 1, 2)(skewed)$;   % opening hook
$pos_{2'}(stem, -180)$; $z_{2'} = z_2$;
$pos_4(vair, -90)$; $pos_5(hair, 0)$; $x_4 = .5[x_3, x_5]$;
$pos_6(stem, 0)$; $rt\ x_{6r} = \mathrm{hround}(w - 1.5u + .5stem)$;
$pos_7(stem, 0)$; $pos_8(vair, -90)$;
$y_3 = .7[y_4, y_5]$; $bot\ y_{4r} = -oo$; $y_5 = .57h$; $y_6 + .5stem = h$;
$y_7 = 0$; $bot\ y_{8r} = -d - oo$; $x_5 = x_6 = x_7$; $x_8 = .5w$;
$pos_9(hair, -180)$; $pos_{10}(flare, -180)$; $y_9 = -.5d$;
$lft\ x_{9r} = \mathrm{hround}(2.75u - .5flare)$; $bulb(8, 9, 10)$;   % bulb
filldraw stroke $z_{2'e}\{-u, -x\_height\}$
$\ldots super\_arc_e(3, 4) \ldots \{up\}z_{5e}$;   % left stem and arc
filldraw circ_stroke $z_{6e} \dashdash z_{7e} \ldots \{left\}z_{8e}$;   % right stem and link
math_fit$(-{}^2\!/\!_3 x\_height^\# * slant + .5hair^\# + .5u^\#, ic^\# - {}^1\!/\!_3 x\_height^\# * slant)$;
penlabels$(0, 1, 2, 3, 4, 5, 6, 7, 8, 9, 10)$; **endchar**;

cmchar "Italic letter z";
beginchar("z", $5.5u^\# + \max(1.5u^\#, stem^\#)$, $x\_height^\#$, 0);
italcorr $x\_height^\# * slant + .5hair^\#$;
adjust_fit(**if** $monospace$: $.5u^\#$, $.5u^\#$ **else**: $0, 0$ **fi**); **pickup** $fine.nib$;
$pos_1(hair, 0)$; $pos_2(stem, -90)$; $pos_3(vair, -90)$; $pos_4(hair, 0)$;
$lft\ x_{1l} = \mathrm{hround}(u - .5hair)$; $x_2 = 2.5u$; $x_3 = w - 2u$; $rt\ x_{4r} = \mathrm{hround}(w - .5u)$;
$top\ y_1 = .78h$; $top\ y_{2l} = top\ y_4 = h + oo$; $y_3 = .825h$;
$pos_5(hair, 0)$; $pos_6(vair, -90)$; $pos_7(stem, -90)$; $pos_8(hair, 0)$;
$x_5 = x_1$; $x_6 = 2.5u$; $x_7 = w - 2u$; $x_8 + .5hair = \mathrm{hround}(w + .5hair - eps)$;
$bot\ y_5 = bot\ y_{7r} = -oo$; $y_6 = .175h$; $bot\ y_8 = .31h$;
pair p; $p = (z_4 - z_5)$ yscaled 2;
filldraw stroke $z_{1e}\{up\} \ldots z_{2e}\{right\} \dotdot z_{3e}\{right\} \ldots \{p\}z_{4e}$;   % upper bar
filldraw stroke $z_{5e}\{p\} \ldots z_{6e}\{right\} \dotdot \{right\}z_{7e} \ldots \{up\}z_{8e}$;   % lower bar
filldraw stroke $z_{5e}\{p\} \dotdot \{p\}z_{4e}$;   % diagonal
math_fit$(0, {}^1\!/\!_3 x\_height^\# * slant + .5hair^\# + .5u^\#)$;
penlabels$(1, 2, 3, 4, 5, 6, 7, 8)$; **endchar**;

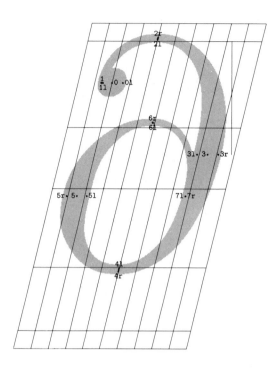

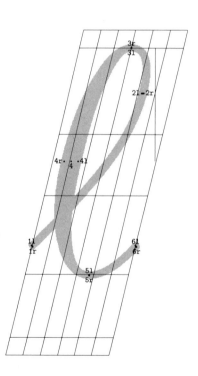

The program file `italms.mf` gives us symbols dear to the heart of Karl Weierstraß (who once taught calligraphy but was much better as a mathematician!).

% This file contains miscellaneous symbols of math italic fonts.
% The character codes are $'100$, $'140$, and $'173$–$'177$.

cmchar "Partial differential sign";
beginchar(oct "100", $10u^\#$, $asc\_height^\#$, 0);
italcorr $.7asc\_height^\# * slant + .5curve^\# - 1.5u^\#$;
adjust_fit(0, 0);
numeric $top\_thickness$, $bot\_thickness$, $side\_thickness$, $pull$;
$top\_thickness = \max(fine.breadth, \text{vround}(slab - 2vair\_corr))$;
$bot\_thickness = \max(fine.breadth, \text{vround}(slab - vair\_corr))$;
$side\_thickness = \max(fine.breadth, \text{hround } ^1\!/_3[curve, cap\_curve])$;
$pull = \min(.25, 1.5superpull)$;
pickup $fine.nib$; $pos_2(top\_thickness, 90)$;
$pos_3(side\_thickness, 0)$; $pos_4(bot\_thickness, -90)$;
$pos_5(side\_thickness, -180)$; $pos_6(vair, -270)$;
$lft\ x_{5r} = w - rt\ x_{3r} = \text{hround} \max(.75u, 1.5u - .5side\_thickness)$;
$x_4 = x_6 + .1u = x_2 + u = .5w$;
$top\ y_{2r} = h + o$; $y_3 = .5[y_2, y_4]$; $bot\ y_{4r} = -o$;
$y_5 = .5[y_4, y_6]$; $top\ y_6 = \text{vround } ^5\!/_8 h + o$;
path p; $p = pulled\_super\_arc_l(3, 4)(pull)$;
numeric t; $t = \text{xpart}(p \text{ intersectiontimes } ((x_{3r}, y_5) \text{ -- } (x_4, y_5)))$;
$pos_7(thin\_join, 0)$; $z_{7l} = $ **point** t **of** p;
$(x, y_{6r}) = \text{whatever}[z_{7l}, z_{6l}]$; $x_{6r} := \max(x, .5[x_{5r}, x_6])$;
filldraw stroke $pulled\_super\_arc_e(2, 3)(pull)$
    & {{ **interim** $superness := more\_super$; $pulled\_super\_arc_e(3, 4)(pull)$ }}
    & {{$less\_tense$; $pulled\_super\_arc_e(4, 5)(pull)$ & $pulled\_super\_arc_e(5, 6)(pull)$ }}
    & $z_{6e}\{right\} \dots \{$**direction** t **of** $p\}z_{7e}$;   % arc and bowl
$pos_1(hair, 180)$; $pos_0(flare, 180)$;
$lft\ x_{0r} = \min(lft\ x_2 - eps, \text{hround } 1.2u)$;
$y_0 = \text{vround} \min(.85h - .5flare, .8h + .5flare) + o$;
$\{\{less\_tense; bulb(2, 1, 0)\}\}$;   % arc and bulb
math_fit$(-.3x\_height^\# * slant + .5curve^\# - u^\#, ic^\# - u^\#)$;
penlabels(0, 1, 2, 3, 4, 5, 6, 7); **endchar**;

cmchar "Lowercase italic script l";
beginchar(oct "140", $4.5u^\# + \max(1.5u^\#, stem^\#)$, $asc\_height^\#$, 0);
italcorr $.8asc\_height^\# * slant - u^\#$;
adjust_fit(**if** $monospace$: $u^\#$, $u^\#$ **else**: 0, 0 **fi**); **pickup** $fine.nib$;
$pos_1(hair, -45)$; $pos_2(hair, 0)$; $pos_3(vair, 90)$;
$pos_4(stem, 180)$; $pos_5(vair, 270)$; $pos_6(hair, 315)$;
$lft\ x_{1l} = \text{hround}(lft\ x_{1l} - x_1)$; $rt\ x_{2r} = \text{hround}(w - 1.5u)$; $x_3 = .5w$;
$lft\ x_{4r} = \text{hround } .5u$; $x_5 = x_3 + .75u$; $x_6 = x_1 + w + 1$;
$y_1 = y_6 = .125h$; $y_2 = .8h$; $top\ y_{3r} = h + oo$; $y_4 = .5[y_3, y_5]$; $bot\ y_5 = -oo$;
filldraw stroke $z_{1e}\{10u, asc\_height\} \dots z_{2e}\{up\} \dots pulled\_arc_e(3, 4)$
    & $pulled\_arc_e(4, 5) \dots z_{6e}\{10u, asc\_height\}$;   % bowl and hook
math_fit$(0, ic^\#)$; **penlabels**(1, 2, 3, 4, 5, 6); **endchar**;

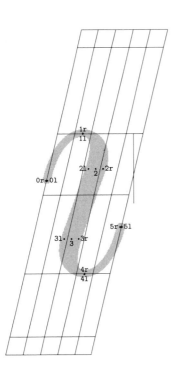

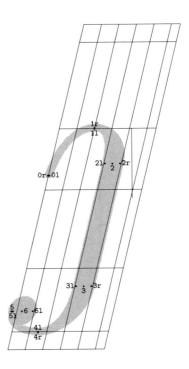

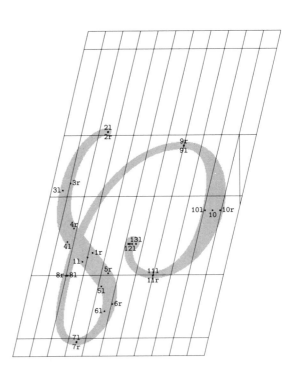

cmchar "Dotless italic letter i";
beginchar(oct "173", $5u\#$, $x\_height\#$, 0);
italcorr $^1/_3x\_height\# * slant + .5hair\# + .5u\#$;
adjust_fit(**if** *monospace*: $u\#$, $u\#$ **else**: 0, 0 **fi**); **pickup** *fine*.*nib*;
$x_0 = 0$; $x_5 = w$; $x_2 = .5w + .25u$; $x_3 = .5w - .25u$;
$hook\_in(0, 1, 2)(skewed)$; $hook\_out(3, 4, 5)(skewed)$;   % hooks
filldraw stroke z_{2e} -- z_{3e};   % stem
math_fit$(-^2/_3x\_height\# * slant + .5hair\# + .5u\#, ic\#)$;
penlabels(0, 1, 2, 3, 4, 5); **endchar**;

cmchar "Dotless italic letter j";
beginchar(oct "174", $5.5u\#$, $x\_height\#$, $desc\_depth\#$);
italcorr $x\_height\# * slant + .5stem\# - 2u\#$;
adjust_fit(**if** *monospace*: $2u\#$ **else**: 0 **fi**, 0); **pickup** *fine*.*nib*;
$x_0 = 0$; $x_2 = x_3$; $pos_3(stem, 0)$; $lft\ x_{3l} = \mathrm{hround}(w - 2u - .5stem)$;
$hook\_in(0, 1, 2)$;   % opening hook
$pos_4(vair, -90)$; $pos_5(hair, -180)$; $pos_6(flare, -180)$;
$bot\ y_3 = -^1/_3d$; $bot\ y_{4r} = -d - oo$; $y_6 - .5flare = -\mathrm{vround}\ .9d$;
$x_4 = ^1/_3(w - u)$; $lft\ x_{5r} = \min(\mathrm{hround} -.5u, lft\ x_{5r} + x_4 - x_{5l} - eps)$;
filldraw stroke z_{2e} --- z_{3e} ... $\{left\}z_{4e}$;   % stem and arc
$bulb(4, 5, 6)$;   % bulb
math_fit$(desc\_depth\# * slant, ic\#)$; **penlabels**(0, 1, 2, 3, 4, 5, 6); **endchar**;

cmchar "Weierstrass p";
beginchar(oct "175", $11u\#$, $x\_height\#$, $desc\_depth\#$);
italcorr $.7x\_height\# * slant + .5stem\# - u\#$ **if** *math_fitting*: $- .5u\#$ **fi**;
adjust_fit(0, 0); **pickup** *fine*.*nib*;
numeric *theta*; $theta = 90 - \mathrm{angle}(8u, h)$; $slope := -h/8u$;   % angle at middle
$pos_2(vair, -90)$; $pos_1(vstem, theta)$; $pos_7(vair, -90)$;
$x_2 + .5u = x_1 = x_7 - .5u = 3u$; $top\ y_{2l} = h + o$; $bot\ y_{7r} = -d - o$; $y_1 = .4[-d, h]$;
$lft\ x_{3l} = \mathrm{hround}\ .5u$; $rt\ x_{6r} = \mathrm{hround}\ \max(rt\ x_7 + .5, .5w - .25u)$;
$x_{3r} - x_{3l} = x_{6r}' - x_{6l} = \mathrm{hround}\ .5[vair, vstem] - fine$;
$ellipse\_set(2l, 3l, 4l, 1l)$; $ellipse\_set(2r, 3r, 4r, 1r)$; $y_3 = y_{3r}$;
$ellipse\_set(7l, 6l, 5l, 1l)$; $ellipse\_set(7r, 6r, 5r, 1r)$; $y_6 = y_{6r}$;
filldraw stroke $super\_arc_e(2, 3)$ & $z_{3e}\{down\}$
    .. z_{4e} --- z_{5e} .. $z_{6e}\{down\}$ & $super\_arc_e(6, 7)$;   % flourish
$pos_8(hair, 180)$; $pos_9(vair, 90)$; $pos_{10}(stem, 0)$;
$pos_{11}(vair, -90)$; $pos_{12}(hair, -180)$; $pos_{13}(.3[hair, flare], -180)$;
$rt\ x_{10r} = \mathrm{hround}(w - 1.5u + .5stem)$; $lft\ x_{12r} = \mathrm{hround}(.5w - .5u)$;
$rt\ x_{8l} = \mathrm{hround}\ 2.25u$; $x_9 = x_{11} = \max(x_{12l} + eps, .5w + 1.5u)$;
$y_8 = 0$; $top\ y_{9r} = \mathrm{vround}(.9h + o)$; $y_{10} = .5[y_9, y_{11}]$; $bot\ y_{11r} = -oo$;
filldraw stroke $z_{7e}\{left\}$ ... $z_{8e}\{up\}$ ... $pulled\_arc_e(9, 10)$
    & $pulled\_arc_e(10, 11)$;   % stem and bowl
$y_{13} - .5(.6[hair, flare]) = .15h$; $bulb(11, 12, 13)$;   % bulb
math_fit$(0, ic\#)$; **penlabels**(1, 2, 3, 4, 5, 6, 7, 8, 9, 10, 11, 12, 13); **endchar**;

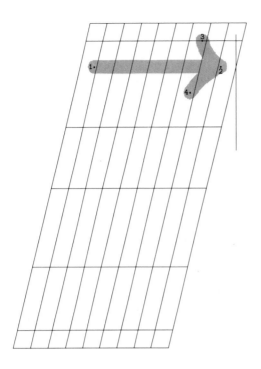

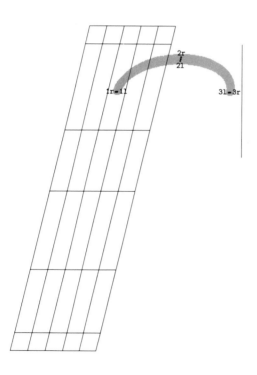

cmchar "Arrow (vector) accent";
beginchar(oct "176", $9u^\#$, $asc\_height^\# + .5rule\_thickness^\#$, 0);
italcorr $.7[x\_height^\#, asc\_height^\#] * slant$;
adjust_fit$(0, 0)$; **pickup** $rule.nib$;
$lft\ x_1 =$ hround $.5u$; $\ x_2 = w - x_1$; $\ y_1 = y_2 = good.x\ .7[x\_height, asc\_height]$;
draw $z_1 \mathbin{--} z_2$;   % bar
$rt\ x_3 = rt\ x_4 =$ hround$(x_2 - u)$;
$y_3 = y_2 + .3(asc\_height - x\_height)$; $\ y_4 = y_2 - .3(asc\_height - x\_height)$;
draw $z_3\{x_2 - x_3, 2(y_2 - y_3)\} \ldots \{2(x_2 - x_3), y_2 - y_3\}z_2$;   % upper point
draw $z_4\{x_2 - x_4, 2(y_2 - y_4)\} \ldots \{2(x_2 - x_4), y_2 - y_4\}z_2$;   % lower point
labels$(1, 2, 3, 4)$; **endchar**;

cmchar "Tie accent";
beginchar(oct "177", $5u^\#$, $asc\_height^\#$, 0);
italcorr $^4\!/_9[x\_height^\#, asc\_height^\#] * slant + 4.5u^\# + 2letter\_fit^\# + .5hair^\#$;
adjust_fit(**if** *monospace*: $2u^\#, 2u^\#$ **else**: $serif\_fit^\#, serif\_fit^\#$ **fi**);
pickup $fine.nib$; $pos_1(hair, 180)$; $\ pos_2(\text{vround }^1\!/_5[vair, stem], 90)$; $\ pos_3(hair, 0)$;
$lft\ x_{1r} =$ hround$(.5w - .5hair)$; $\ x_2 = .5[x_1, x_3]$;
$rt\ x_{3r} =$ hround$(w + 4u + 2letter\_fit + .5hair)$;
$y_1 = y_3 =\ ^4\!/_9[x\_height, asc\_height]$; $\ top\ y_{2r} =$ vround $^8\!/_9[x\_height, asc\_height]$;
filldraw stroke $super\_arc_e(1, 2)$ & $super\_arc_e(2, 3)$;   % arc
penlabels$(1, 2, 3)$; **endchar**;

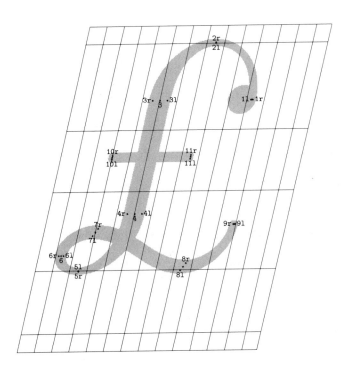

Program file `italp.mf` makes the debatable claim that '£' is an italic dollar sign. Less controversial ampersand and query marks are also generated here.

% This file contains '$' and '&' and '?' in the so-called italic style.

% Codes '044', '046', and '077' are generated, as well as code *spanish_query*
% (for a Spanish question mark) if that code value is known.

cmchar "Sterling sign";
beginchar("$", $12u^\#$, $asc\_height^\#$, 0);
adjust_fit(0, $.75asc\_height^\# * slant - .5u^\#$); **pickup** *fine.nib*;
$pos_0(flare, 0)$; $pos_1(hair, 0)$; $pos_2(vair, 90)$; $pos_3(stem, 180)$;
$pos_4(stem, 180)$; $pos_{4'}(stem, 0)$; $pos_5(vair, -90)$; $z_{4'} = z_4$;
$x_2 = {}^2\!/_3 w - .5u$; $rt\ x_{3l} = rt\ x_{4l} = \text{hround}(.5w - u + .5stem)$; $x_5 = 2.5u$;
$y_1 = y_3 = .75h$; $top\ y_2 = h + oo$; $y_4 = .25h$; $bot\ y_{5r} = -oo$;
$rt\ x_{1r} = \text{hround}(w - 1.5u)$; $bulb(2, 1, 0)$;   % bulb
filldraw stroke $pulled\_arc_e(2, 3) .. z_{4e}$;   % stem
numeric *light_stem*; $light\_stem = {}^2\!/_3[vair, vstem]$;
$pos_6(.5[hair, light\_stem], -180)$; $pos_7(light\_stem, -300)$;
$pos_8(light\_stem, -300)$; $pos_9(hair, -180)$;
$lft\ x_{6r} = \text{hround}\ u$; $x_7 = 3u$; $x_8 = w - 3.5u$; $rt\ x_{9r} = \text{hround}(w - u)$;
$y_6 = .4[y_5, y_7]$; $top\ y_{7r} = \text{vround}\ .2h$; $bot\ y_{8l} = -oo$; $y_9 = good.y\ .2h$;
filldraw stroke $pulled\_arc_e(4', 5) \ldots z_{6e}\{up\} \ldots z_{7e}\{right\}$
    $.. \{right\}z_{8e} \ldots \{up\}z_{9e}$;   % loop and arm
$pos_{10}(bar, 90)$; $pos_{11}(bar, 90)$; $x_{10} = 3u$; $x_{11} = w - 4.5u$;
$top\ y_{10r} = top\ y_{11r} = \text{vround}(.5h + .5bar)$; **filldraw stroke** $z_{10e} \text{--} z_{11e}$;   % bar
penlabels(1, 2, 3, 4, 5, 6, 7, 8, 9, 10, 11); **endchar**;

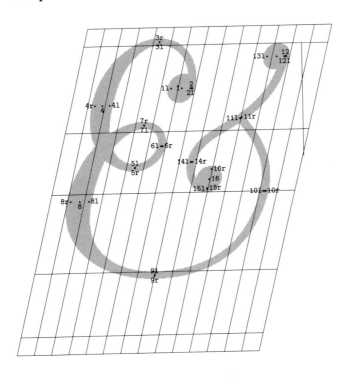

cmchar "Italic ampersand";
beginchar("&", $14u^\#$, $asc\_height^\#$, 0);
italcorr $asc\_height^\# * slant - 1.5u^\#$;
adjust_fit(**if** *monospace*: $-u^\#$, $-2u^\#$ **else**: 0, 0 **fi**); **pickup** *fine.nib*;
$pos_1(flare, 0)$; $pos_2(hair, 0)$; $pos_3(vair, 90)$;
$rt\ x_{2r} = $ hround $.5w$; $x_3 = \frac{1}{3}(w - u)$;
$top\ y_{3r} = h + o$; $y_2 = .5[x\_height, h]$; $bulb(3, 2, 1)$;   % left bulb
$pos_4(stem, 180)$; $pos_5(vair, 270)$; $pos_6(hair, 360)$; $pos_7(vair, 450)$;
$pos_8(curve, 540)$; $pos_9(vair, 630)$; $pos_{10}(hair, 720)$;
$lft\ x_{4r} = $ hround $1.25u$; $x_5 = x_7 = x_3 + \frac{1}{6}u$; $rt\ x_{6r} = $ hround$(x_5 + 1.5u)$;
$lft\ x_{8r} = $ hround u; $x_9 = .5w$; $rt\ x_{10r} = $ hround$(w - 1.5u)$;
$y_4 = .5[y_3, y_5]$; $top\ y_{5l} = $ vround $.77x\_height$; $y_6 = .5[y_5, y_7]$;
$y_{7l} = good.y\ \frac{1}{3}[y_5, y_3]$; $y_8 = .5[y_7, y_9]$; $bot\ y_{9r} = -o$; $y_{10} = bar\_height$;
$pos_{12}(hair, 0)$; $pos_{13}(curve, 0)$; $pos_{14}(hair, 0)$; $pos_{15}(vair, 90)$; $pos_{16}(curve, 90)$;
$rt\ x_{12r} = rt\ x_{13r} = $ hround$(w - 2u)$; $lft\ x_{14l} = $ hround$(.5w + .5u)$;
$x_{15} = x_{16} = rt\ x_{14r} + u$;
$y_{12} = y_{13} = h - .5curve$; $y_{14} = .5[bar\_height, x\_height]$;
$bot\ y_{15l} = bot\ y_{16l} = $ vround y_{10};
numeric *theta*; $theta = $ angle$((z_{12} - z_{14})$ xscaled $2)$;
$pos_{11}(hair, theta)$; $x_{11} = w - 4u$; $y_{11} = .5[y_{13}, y_{16}]$;
filldraw stroke $pulled\_arc_e(3, 4)$ & $pulled\_arc_e(4, 5)$ & $pulled\_arc_e(5, 6)$
  & $pulled\_arc_e(6, 7)$ & $pulled\_arc_e(7, 8)$ & $pulled\_arc_e(8, 9)$
  & {{ **interim** *superness* := $more\_super$; $pulled\_arc_e(9, 10)$ }}
  .. tension .9 and 1 .. {dir$(theta + 100)$}z_{11e};   % bowls, loop, and stem
$pos_{11'}(hair, theta - 90)$; $z_{11'} = z_{11}$;
forsuffixes $ = l, r$: **path** $p_\$$;
  $p_\$ = z_{12\$}\{down\}$ .. $z_{11'\$}\{-$ dir $theta\}$ .. $\{down\}z_{14\$}$ ... $\{right\}z_{15\$}$; **endfor**
filldraw p_l -- reverse p_r -- cycle;   % arms
path $q[]$; $q_1 = z_{13r}\{up\}$ .. $z_{13l}\{down\}$ .. cycle;
$q_2 = z_{16l}\{right\}$ .. $z_{16r}\{left\}$ .. cycle;
filldraw subpath$(0, $ ypart$(p_l$ intersectiontimes $q_1))$ **of** q_1 -- cycle;   % upper bulb
filldraw subpath$(0, $ ypart$(p_r$ intersectiontimes $q_2))$ **of** q_2 -- cycle;   % lower bulb
penlabels$(1, 2, 3, 4, 5, 6, 7, 8, 9, 10, 11, 12, 13, 14, 15, 16)$; **endchar**;

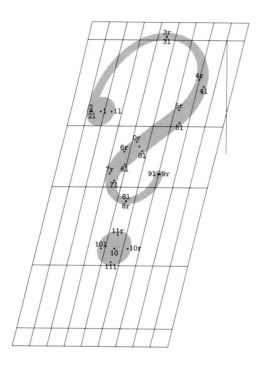

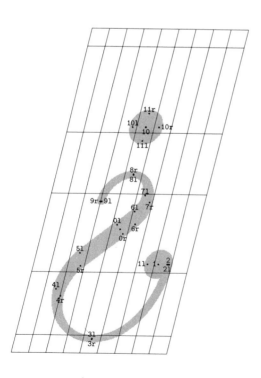

cmchar "Italic question mark";
beginchar("?", $9u^\#$, $asc\_height^\#$, 0);
italcorr $asc\_height^\# * slant - u^\#$;
adjust_fit(0, 0); **pickup** $tiny.nib$; $pos_{10}(dot\_size, 0)$; $pos_{11}(dot\_size, 90)$;
$lft\ x_{10l} = \text{hround}(.5w - .5dot\_size)$; $bot\ y_{11l} = 0$; $z_{10} = z_{11}$; $dot(10, 11)$; % dot
pickup $fine.nib$; $pos_1(flare, 180)$; $pos_2(hair, 180)$; $pos_3(vair, 90)$;
$lft\ x_{1r} = \text{hround}\ u$; $x_3 = .5w$;
$y_1 - .5flare = x\_height$; $top\ y_{3r} = h + o$; $bulb(3, 2, 1)$; % bulb
$pos_8(vair, -90)$; $x_8 = .5w$; $bot\ y_{8r} = .25[top\ y_{11r}, x\_height] + 1$;
numeric $theta$; $theta = 90 + \text{angle}(10u, y_3 - y_8)$; $slope := (y_3 - y_8)/10u$;
$pos_{3'}(vair, -90)$; $z_{3'} = z_3$; $pos_0(vstem, theta)$; $x_0 = x_3$; $y_0 = {}^{1}/_{3}[y_8, y_3]$;
$rt\ x_{4l} = \text{hround}(w - 1.5u)$; $lft\ x_{7r} = \text{hround}\ {}^{1}/_{3}w$;
$x_{4l} - x_{4r} = x_{7l} - x_{7r} = \text{hround}\ .5[vair, vstem] - fine$;
$ellipse\_set(3'l, 4l, 5l, 0l)$; $ellipse\_set(3'r, 4r, 5r, 0r)$; $y_4 = y_{4r}$;
$ellipse\_set(8l, 7l, 6l, 0l)$; $ellipse\_set(8r, 7r, 6r, 0r)$; $y_7 = y_{7r}$;
$pos_9(hair, 0)$; $rt\ x_{9r} = \text{hround}({}^{2}/_{3}w + .5hair)$; $y_9 = good.y\ .5[y_8, y_0]$;
filldraw stroke $super\_arc_e(3', 4)\ \&\ z_{4e}\{down\}$
 $.. z_{5e}\ \text{---}\ z_{6e} .. z_{7e}\{down\}\ \&\ super\_arc_e(7, 8) ... \{up\}z_{9e}$; % main stroke
penlabels(0, 1, 2, 3, 4, 5, 6, 7, 8, 9, 10, 11); **endchar**;

iff known $spanish\_query$: **cmchar** "Spanish open italic question mark";
beginchar($spanish\_query$, $9u^\#$, $asc\_height^\# - desc\_depth^\#$, $desc\_depth^\#$);
adjust_fit(0, 0); **pickup** $tiny.nib$; $pos_{10}(dot\_size, 0)$; $pos_{11}(dot\_size, 90)$;
$lft\ x_{10l} = \text{hround}(.5w - .5dot\_size)$; $top\ y_{11r} = h$; $z_{10} = z_{11}$; $dot(10, 11)$; % dot
pickup $fine.nib$; $pos_1(flare, 0)$; $pos_2(hair, 0)$; $pos_3(vair, -90)$;
$rt\ x_{1r} = \text{hround}(w - u)$; $x_3 = .5w$; $y_1 + .5flare = asc\_height - x\_height - d$;
$bot\ y_{3r} = -d - o$; $bulb(3, 2, 1)$; % bulb
$pos_8(vair, 90)$; $x_8 = .5w$; $top\ y_{8r} = .25[bot\ y_{11l}, y_1 + .5flare] - 1$;
numeric $theta$; $theta = \text{angle}(10u, y_8 - y_3) - 90$; $slope := (y_8 - y_3)/10u$;
$pos_{3'}(vair, 90)$; $z_{3'} = z_3$; $pos_0(vstem, theta)$; $x_0 = x_3$; $y_0 = {}^{1}/_{3}[y_8, y_3]$;
$lft\ x_{4l} = \text{hround}\ 1.5u$; $rt\ x_{7r} = \text{hround}\ {}^{2}/_{3}w$;
$x_{4r} - x_{4l} = x_{7r} - x_{7l} = \text{hround}\ .5[vair, vstem] - fine$;
$ellipse\_set(3'l, 4l, 5l, 0l)$; $ellipse\_set(3'r, 4r, 5r, 0r)$; $y_4 = y_{4r}$;
$ellipse\_set(8l, 7l, 6l, 0l)$; $ellipse\_set(8r, 7r, 6r, 0r)$; $y_7 = y_{7r}$;
$pos_9(hair, 180)$; $lft\ x_{9r} = \text{hround}({}^{1}/_{3}w - .5hair)$; $y_9 = good.y\ .5[y_8, y_0]$;
filldraw stroke $super\_arc_e(3', 4)\ \&\ z_{4e}\{up\}$
 $.. z_{5e}\ \text{---}\ z_{6e} .. z_{7e}\{up\}\ \&\ super\_arc_e(7, 8) ... \{down\}z_{9e}$; % main stroke
penlabels(0, 1, 2, 3, 4, 5, 6, 7, 8, 9, 10, 11); **endchar**;

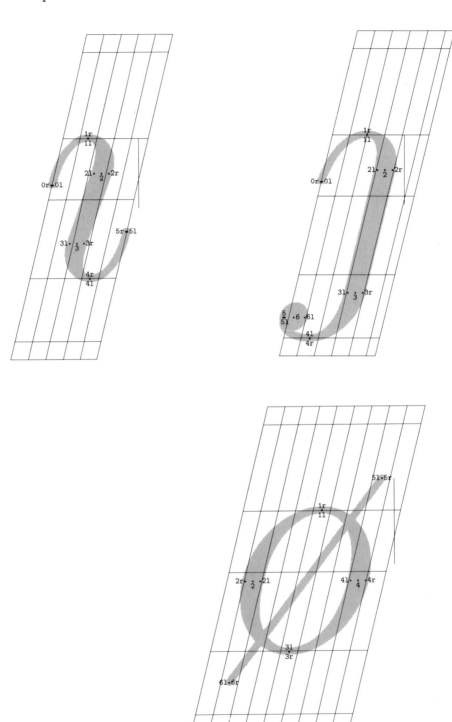

Program file `italsp.mf` generates six italic letters whose roman equivalents are generated by `romspl.mf`.

% This file contains special letters and letter combinations,
% compatible with the alphabet 'itall'.

% Codes '020 – '021 and '031 – '034 are generated.

cmchar "Dotless italic letter i";
beginchar(oct "020", $5u^\#$, $x\_height^\#$, 0);

⋮   (a copy of the program for '$\imath$' in **italms** comes here)

penlabels(0, 1, 2, 3, 4, 5); **endchar**;

cmchar "Dotless italic letter j";
beginchar(oct "021", $5.5u^\#$, $x\_height^\#$, $desc\_depth^\#$);

⋮   (a copy of the program for '$\jmath$' in **italms** comes here)

penlabels(0, 1, 2, 3, 4, 5, 6); **endchar**;

cmchar "Italic Scandinavian letter o/slash";
beginchar(oct "034", $9u^\#$, $x\_height^\# + .5desc\_depth^\#$, $.5desc\_depth^\#$);
italcorr $h^\# * slant - u^\# + .5vair^\#$;
adjust_fit(0, 0); **pickup** $fine.nib$;
$pos_1(vair, 90)$; $pos_2(fudged.stem, 180)$;
$pos_3(vair, 270)$; $pos_4(fudged.stem, 360)$;
$x_1 = x_3 = .5w$; *lft* $x_{2r} =$ hround$(1.5u - .5fudged.stem)$; $x_4 = w - x_2$;
top $y_1 = x\_height + oo$; $y_2 = y_4 = .5[y_1, y_3]$; *bot* $y_3 = -oo$;
filldraw stroke $pulled\_arc_e(1, 2)$ & $pulled\_arc_e(2, 3)$
   & $pulled\_arc_e(3, 4)$ & $pulled\_arc_e(4, 1)$;   % bowl
$x_5 = x_4$; $x_6 = x_2$; $y_5 = h$; $y_6 = -d$;
numeric $theta$; $theta =$ angle$(z_5 - z_6) - 90$;
pickup $crisp.nib$; $pos_5(vair, theta)$; $pos_6(vair, theta)$;
filldraw stroke z_{5e} -- z_{6e};   % diagonal
penlabels(1, 2, 3, 4, 5, 6); **endchar**;

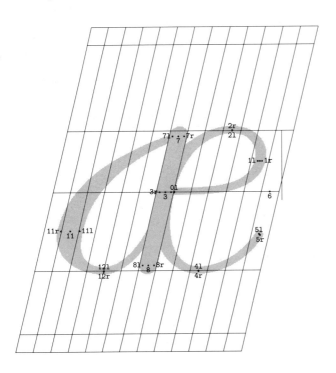

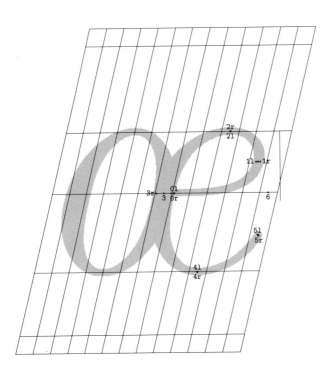

cmchar "Italic ligature ae";
beginchar(oct "032", $13u^\#$, $x\_height^\#$, 0);
italcorr $\max(\frac{1}{3}x\_height^\# * slant, x\_height^\# * slant + .5(.2[hair^\#, stem^\#]) - u^\#)$;
adjust_fit(**if** *monospace*: $-u^\#$, $-u^\#$ **else**: 0, 0 **fi**); **pickup** *fine.nib*;
forsuffixes $\$ = hair, stem$: *shaved*$_\$$:= *mfudged*.$\$$; **save** $\$$; $\$ = shaved_\$$; **endfor**
numeric *heavy_hair*; *heavy_hair* = hround $.2[hair, stem]$;
numeric *light_stem*; *light_stem* = hround $.75[hair, stem]$;
$pos_0(vair, -90)$; $pos_1(heavy\_hair, 0)$; $pos_2(vair, 90)$;
$pos_3(light\_stem, 180)$; $pos_4(vair, 270)$; $pos_5(hair, 320)$;
$x_0 = rt\ x_{3l}$; $rt\ x_{1r} = $ hround$(w - 1.5u + .5heavy\_hair)$; $x_2 = x_4 = .5(w + 6u)$;
$lft\ x_{3r} = $ hround$(.5w - .5light\_stem)$; $x_{5r} = good.x(w - .5u)$; $x_6 = x_5$;
$y_0 = y_3 = y_6 = bar\_height$; $y_1 = .5[y_0, y_2]$; $top\ y_{2r} = h + oo$; $bot\ y_{4r} = -oo$;
$top\ y_{5l} = $ vround$(.5bar\_height + .5)$; **path** p; $p = z_4\{right\} .. z_5 .. z_6$;
filldraw stroke $z_{0e}\{right\} \ldots z_{1e}\{up\} \ldots pulled\_arc_e(2, 3)$
    & $pulled\_arc_e(3, 4) \ldots \{$**direction** 1 **of** $p\}z_{5e}$;   % arc of e
$pos_7(light\_stem, 0)$; $pos_8(light\_stem, 0)$;
$x_7 = x_8 = x_3$; $y_7 + .5light\_stem = h + oo$; $y_8 - .5light\_stem = -oo$;
$pos_{7'}(vair, -225)$; $pos_{11}(curve, -180)$; $z_{7'} = z_7$;
$pos_{12}(vair, -90)$; $pos_{3'}(hair, 0)$; $z_{3'} = z_3$;
$lft\ x_{11r} = $ hround$(1.5u - .5curve)$; $x_{12} = .5[x_{11}, x_3]$;
$y_{11} = .3[y_{12}, y_7]$; $bot\ y_{12r} = -oo$;
filldraw stroke $z_{7'e}\{3(x_{11} - x_7), y_{11} - y_7\} \ldots pulled\_arc_e(11, 12)$
    & $pulled\_arc_e(12, 3')$;   % bowl of a
filldraw $z_{7l} --- z_{8l} .. z_{8r} --- z_{7r} ..$ **cycle**;   % stem
penlabels(0, 1, 2, 3, 4, 5, 6, 7, 8, 11, 12); **endchar**;

cmchar "Italic ligature oe";
beginchar(oct "033", $13u^\#$, $x\_height^\#$, 0);
italcorr $\max(\frac{1}{3}x\_height^\# * slant, x\_height^\# * slant + .5(.2[hair^\#, stem^\#]) - u^\#)$;
adjust_fit(**if** *monospace*: $-u^\#$, $-u^\#$ **else**: 0, 0 **fi**); **pickup** *fine.nib*;
forsuffixes $\$ = hair, stem$: *shaved*$_\$$:= *mfudged*.$\$$; **save** $\$$; $\$ = shaved_\$$; **endfor**
numeric *heavy_hair*; *heavy_hair* = hround $.2[hair, stem]$;
$pos_0(vair, -90)$; $pos_1(heavy\_hair, 0)$; $pos_2(vair, 90)$;
$pos_3(stem, 180)$; $pos_4(vair, 270)$; $pos_5(hair, 320)$;
$x_0 = rt\ x_{3l}$; $rt\ x_{1r} = $ hround$(w - 1.5u + .5heavy\_hair)$; $x_2 = x_4 = .5(w + 6u)$;
$lft\ x_{3r} = $ hround$(.5w - .5stem)$; $x_{5r} = good.x(w - .5u)$; $x_6 = x_5$;
$y_0 = y_3 = y_6 = bar\_height$; $y_1 = .5[y_0, y_2]$; $top\ y_{2r} = h + oo$; $bot\ y_{4r} = -oo$;
$top\ y_{5l} = $ vround$(.5bar\_height + .5)$; **path** p; $p = z_4\{right\} .. z_5 .. z_6$;
filldraw stroke $z_{0e}\{right\} \ldots z_{1e}\{up\} \ldots pulled\_arc_e(2, 3)$
    & $pulled\_arc_e(3, 4) \ldots \{$**direction** 1 **of** $p\}z_{5e}$;   % arc of e
$pos_{11}(vair, 90)$; $pos_{12}(curve, 180)$; $pos_{13}(vair, 270)$; $pos_{14}(stem, 360)$;
$x_{11} = x_{13} = .5[x_{12}, x_{14}]$; $lft\ x_{12r} = $ hround$(1.5u - .5curve)$; $x_{14} = x_3$;
$top\ y_{11} = h + oo$; $y_{12} = y_{14} = .5[y_{11}, y_{13}]$; $bot\ y_{13} = -oo$;
filldraw stroke $pulled\_arc_e(11, 12)$ & $pulled\_arc_e(12, 13)$
    & $pulled\_arc_e(13, 14)$ & $pulled\_arc_e(14, 11)$;   % bowl
penlabels(0, 1, 2, 3, 4, 5, 6); **endchar**;

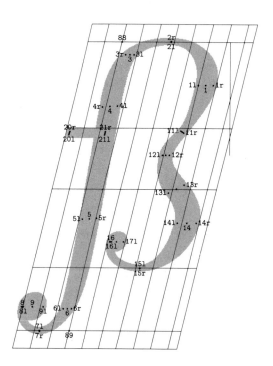

cmchar "Italic German letter es-zet (sharp s)";

beginchar(oct "031", $4.5u^\# + \max(1.5u^\#, stem^\#) + \max(3.5u^\#, 2flare^\#)$,
$\quad asc\_height^\#, desc\_depth^\#$);

italcorr $.9asc\_height^\# * slant - u^\#$;

adjust_fit(**if** *monospace*: $u^\#$ **else**: 0 **fi**, 0); **pickup** *fine.nib*;

$z_{88} = (.5w - 2.75u, h);\ z_{89} = (.5w - 1.75u, -d);$

numeric *theta*; $theta = \text{angle}(z_{88} - z_{89});$

$pos_1(stem, 0);\ pos_2(vair, 90);\ pos_3(.5[hair, stem], 180);$

$pos_4(stem, theta + 90);\ pos_5(stem, theta - 90);\ pos_6(.5[hair, stem], 0);$

$pos_7(vair, -90);\ pos_8(hair, -180);\ pos_9(flare, -180);$

$rt\ x_{1r} = \text{hround}(w - 1.5u);\ lft\ x_{8r} = \text{hround} -.25u;\ x_2 = .5[x_1, x_4];\ x_7 = .5[x_8, x_5];$

$y_9 - .5flare = \text{vround} -.85d;\ bot\ y_{7r} = -d - oo;\ y_1 = .5[x\_height, h];\ top\ y_{2r} = h + oo;$

$y_4 = .25[x\_height, h];\ y_5 = .5[-d, y_4];$

$z_4 = whatever[z_{88}, z_{89}];\ z_5 = whatever[z_{88}, z_{89}];$

$x_3 = .8[x_2 + x_4 - x_{88}, x_{88}];\ x_6 = .8[x_7 + x_5 - x_{89}, x_{89}];\ y_3 = .8[y_4, y_2];\ y_6 = .8[y_5, y_7];$

$bulb(7, 8, 9);$ % left bulb

filldraw stroke $z_{1e}\{up\} \ldots z_{2e}\{left\} \ldots z_{3e} \ldots \{z_{89} - z_{88}\}z_{4e};$ % upper arc

filldraw $z_{4r} -- z_{5l} -- z_{5r} -- z_{4l} --$ cycle; % stem

filldraw stroke $z_{5e}\{z_{89} - z_{88}\} \ldots z_{6e} \ldots \{left\}z_{7e};$ % lower arc

$pos_{11}(.1[hair, curve], -30);\ x_{11l} = {}^2/_3[x_{12l}, x_{1l}];\ y_{11} = {}^2/_3[y_1, y_{12}];$

$pos_{12}(.3[hair, curve], 0);\ rt\ x_{12r} = \text{hround}(w - 3u);\ y_{12} = .5h;$

$pos_{13}(.8[hair, curve], 30);\ x_{13} = .5[x_{12}, x_{14}];\ y_{13} = .5[y_{12}, y_{14}];$

$pos_{14}(curve, 0);\ rt\ x_{14r} = \text{hround}(w - .5u);\ y_{14} = .2h;$

$pos_{15}(vair, -90);\ x_{15} = .5[x_{14}, x_{16}];\ bot\ y_{15r} = -oo;$

$pos_{16}(hair, -180);\ pos_{17}(.6[hair, flare], -180);$

$lft\ x_{16r} = \text{hround}(rt\ x_{5r} + .75u);\ y_{17} - .5(.6[hair, flare]) = .07h;$

filldraw stroke $z_{1e}\{down\} \ldots z_{11e}\{1.5(x_{12e} - x_{11e}), y_{12e} - y_{11e}\}$
$\quad \ldots \{down\}z_{12e} \ldots \{2(x_{13} - x_{12}), y_{13} - y_{12}\}z_{13e}$
$\quad \ldots \{down\}z_{14e} \ldots \{left\}z_{15e};$ % stroke

$bulb(15, 16, 17);$ % inner bulb

pickup *crisp.nib*; $pos_{20}(bar, 90);\ pos_{21}(bar, 90);$

$top\ y_{20r} = top\ y_{21r} = x\_height;$

$lft\ x_{20} = lft\ x_{4r} - .5stem - u;\ z_{21} = whatever[z_4, z_5];$

filldraw stroke $z_{20e} -- z_{21e};$ % bar

penlabels(1, 2, 3, 4, 5, 6, 7, 8, 9, 11, 12, 13, 14, 15, 16, 17, 20, 21, 88, 89); **endchar**;

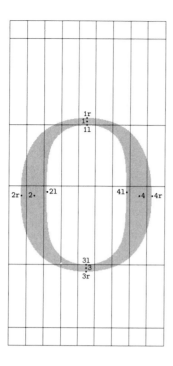

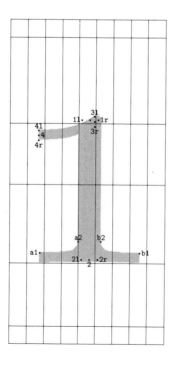

Here is program file `olddig.mf`, which makes the numerals 0123456789.

% This file contains the ten digits in so-called old style.
% Character codes *'060* through *'071* are generated.

cmchar "Oldstyle numeral 0";
beginchar("0", $9u^\#$, $x\_height^\#$, 0);
italcorr $.7x\_height^\# * slant - \max(.2u^\#, .95u^\# - .5curve^\#)$;
adjust_fit(0, 0);
$penpos_1(vair, 90)$; $penpos_3(vair, -90)$; $penpos_2(curve, 180)$; $penpos_4(curve, 0)$;
if not *monospace*: **interim** *superness* := $\text{sqrt}(more\_super * hein\_super)$; **fi**
$x_{2r} = \text{hround} \max(.7u, 1.45u - .5curve)$;
$x_{4r} = w - x_{2r}$; $x_1 = x_3 = .5w$; $y_{1r} = h + o$; $y_{3r} = -o$;
$y_2 = y_4 = .5h - vair\_corr$; $y_{2l} := y_{4l} := .52h$;
penstroke $pulled\_arc_e(1, 2)$ & $pulled\_arc_e(2, 3)$
   & $pulled\_arc_e(3, 4)$ & $pulled\_arc_e(4, 1)$ & cycle;   % bowl
penlabels(1, 2, 3, 4); **endchar**;

cmchar "Oldstyle numeral 1";
beginchar("1", $9u^\#$, $x\_height^\#$, 0);
italcorr $x\_height^\# * slant + .5cap\_stem^\# - 4.25u^\#$;
adjust_fit(0, 0);
numeric *light_stem*; $light\_stem = \text{hround} .4[stem', cap\_stem']$;
pickup *tiny.nib*;
$pos_1(light\_stem, 0)$; $pos_2(light\_stem, 0)$;
$lft\ x_{1l} = lft\ x_{2l} = \text{hround}(.5(w + .5u) - .5cap\_stem')$; $top\ y_1 = h + apex\_o$; $bot\ y_2 = 0$;
filldraw stroke $z_{1e}\ \text{--}\ z_{2e}$;   % stem
if not *serifs*: **save** *slab*; $slab = bar$; **fi**
$dish\_serif(2, 1, a, \frac{1}{3}, \min(2.25u, lft\ x_{2l} - 1.5u)$,
     $b, \frac{1}{3}, \min(2.25u, w - 1.25u - rt\ x_{2r}))$;   % serif
pickup *crisp.nib*; $pos_3(slab, -90)$; $pos_4(bar, -90)$;
$top\ y_{3l} = h + apex\_o$; $top\ y_{4l} =$ **if** *monospace*: .8 **else**: .9 **fi** $h + apex\_o$;
$lft\ x_4 = \max(1.25u, tiny.lft\ x_{1l} - 2.35u)$;
$tiny.rt\ x_{1r} = lft\ x_3 + .25[tiny, hair]$;
erase fill $z_{3l}\{x_{4l} - x_{3l}, 3(y_{4l} - y_{3l})\}\ \ldots\ z_{4l}\{left\}$
   -- $(x_{4l}, h + apex\_o + 1)$ -- $(x_{3l}, h + apex\_o + 1)$ -- cycle;   % erase excess at top
filldraw stroke $z_{3e}\{x_{4e} - x_{3e}, 3(y_{4e} - y_{3e})\}\ ..\ z_{4e}\{left\}$;   % point
penlabels(1, 2, 3, 4); **endchar**;

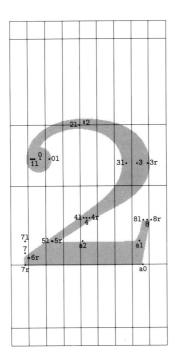

cmchar "Oldstyle numeral 2";
beginchar("2", $9u^\#$, $x\_height^\#$, 0);
italcorr $.8x\_height^\# * slant - .4u^\#$;
adjust_fit(0, 0);
numeric $arm\_thickness$, $hair\_vair$; $hair\_vair = .25[vair, hair]$;
$arm\_thickness = \text{Vround}(\textbf{if } hefty: slab + 2stem\_corr \textbf{ else}: .75[vair, cap\_stem] \textbf{ fi})$;
pickup $crisp.nib$; $pos_7(arm\_thickness, -90)$; $pos_8(hair, 0)$;
$bot\ y_{7r} = 0$; $lft\ x_7 = \text{hround } .8u$;
$rt\ x_{8r} = \text{hround}(w - .9u)$; $y_8 = good.y(y_{7l} + beak/3) + eps$;
$arm(7, 8, a, .3beak\_darkness, beak\_jut)$;   % arm and beak
pickup $fine.nib$; $pos_2(slab, 90)$; $pos_3(.4[curve, cap\_curve], 0)$;
$top\ y_{2r} = h + o$; $x_2 = .5(w - .5u)$; $rt\ x_{3r} = \text{hround}(w - .9u)$; $y_3 + .5vair = .75h$;
if $serifs$: **numeric** $bulb\_diam$; $bulb\_diam = \text{hround } .8[hair, flare]$;
  $pos_0(bulb\_diam, 180)$; $pos_1(cap\_hair, 180)$;
  $lft\ x_{1r} = \text{hround } u$; $y_1 - .5bulb\_diam = {}^2\!/3h$;
  $(x, y_{2l}) = whatever[z_{1l}, z_{2r}]$; $x_{2l} := x$; $bulb(2, 1, 0)$;   % bulb and arc
else: $x_{2l} := x_{2l} - .25u$; $pos_1(flare, angle(-9u, h))$;
  $lft\ x_{1r} = \text{hround } .75u$; $bot\ y_{1l} = \text{vround } .7h$;
  $y_{1r} := good.y\ y_{1r} + eps$; $x_{1l} := good.x\ x_{1l}$;
  filldraw stroke $term.e(2, 1, left, .9, 4)$; **fi**   % terminal and arc
$pos_4(.25[hair\_vair, cap\_stem], 0)$;
$pos_5(hair\_vair, 0)$; $pos_6(hair\_vair, 0)$;
$y_5 = arm\_thickness$; $y_4 = .3[y_5, y_3]$; $top\ y_6 = \min(y_5, slab, top\ y_{7l})$;
$lft\ x_{6l} = crisp.lft\ x_7$; $z_{4l} = whatever[z_{6l}, (x_{3l}, bot\ .58h)]$; $z_{5l} = whatever[z_{6l}, z_{4l}]$;
erase fill z_{4l} -- z_{6l} -- $lft\ z_{6l}$ -- $(lft\ x_{6l}, y_{4l})$ -- cycle;   % erase excess at left
filldraw stroke $z_{2e}\{right\}$ .. tension atleast .9 and atleast 1
  .. $z_{3e}\{down\}$ .. z_{4e} --- z_{5e} -- z_{6e};   % stroke
penlabels(0, 1, 2, 3, 4, 5, 6, 7, 8); **endchar**;

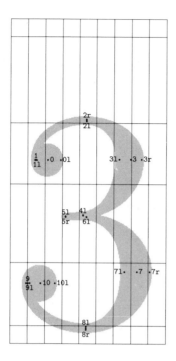

cmchar "Oldstyle numeral 3";
beginchar("3", $9u\#$, $x\_height\#$, $desc\_depth\#$);
italcorr $.8x\_height\# * slant - .4u\#$;
adjust_fit$(0, 0)$;
numeric $top\_thickness$, $mid\_thickness$, $bot\_thickness$;
$top\_thickness = \max(fine.breadth, \text{vround}(slab - 2vair\_corr))$;
$mid\_thickness = \max(fine.breadth, \text{vround } 2/3vair)$;
$bot\_thickness = \max(fine.breadth, \text{vround}(slab - vair\_corr))$;
pickup $fine.nib$; $pos_2(top\_thickness, 90)$; $top\ y_{2r} = h + o$;
$pos_3(\max(fine.breadth, .6[curve, cap\_curve] - stem\_corr), 0)$;
$rt\ x_{3r} = \text{hround}(w - 1.25u)$;
$pos_4(vair, -90)$; $pos_5(vair, -90)$;
$pos_6(mid\_thickness, 90)$; $x_2 = x_6 = x_8 = .5[1.5u, x_7]$;
$pos_7(cap\_curve, 0)$; $rt\ x_{7r} = \text{hround}(w - .75u)$; $lft\ x_5 = \min(\text{hround } 3u, lft\ x_6)$;
$pos_8(bot\_thickness, -90)$; $bot\ y_{8r} = -d - o$;
$y_3 = .6[top\ y_{4l}, bot\ y_{2l}]$; $y_7 = .5[bot\ y_{6l}, top\ y_{8l}]$;
$top\ y_{5l} = \text{vround}(.54[-d, h] + .5vair)$; $y_{5r} = y_{6l}$;
$x_4 = 1/3[x_5, x_{3l}]$; $z_4 = z_5 + whatever * (150u, h + d)$;
filldraw stroke $pulled\_super\_arc_e(2, 3)(.5superpull)$
   & $z_{3e}\{down\} \ldots z_{4e} \text{ --- } z_{5e}$;   % upper bowl
filldraw $z_{5r} \text{ -- } z_{6l} \text{ -- } z_{6r} \text{ -- } z_{5l} \text{ --- cycle}$;   % middle tip
filldraw stroke $pulled\_super\_arc_e(6, 7)(.5superpull)$
   & $pulled\_super\_arc_e(7, 8)(.5superpull)$;   % lower bowl
if $serifs$: **numeric** $bulb\_diam[]$;
  $bulb\_diam_1 = flare + .5(cap\_stem - stem)$; $bulb\_diam_2 = flare + cap\_stem - stem$;
  $pos_0(bulb\_diam_1, 180)$; $pos_1(hair, 180)$;
  $lft\ x_{0r} = \text{hround } 1.25u$;
  $y_0 = \min(.9[-d, h] - .5bulb\_diam_1, .75[-d, h] + .5bulb\_diam_1)$;
  $bulb(2, 1, 0)$;   % upper bulb
  $pos_{10}(bulb\_diam_2, -180)$; $pos_9(cap\_hair, -180)$;
  $lft\ x_{10r} = \text{hround } .75u$;
  $y_{10} = \max(.1[-d, h] + .5bulb\_diam_2, .3[-d, h] - .5bulb\_diam_2)$;
  $bulb(8, 9, 10)$;   % lower bulb
else: $pos_1(.5[vair, flare], \text{angle}(-8u, h + d))$; $lft\ x_{1r} = \text{hround } u$;
  $bot\ y_{1l} = (\text{vround } .75[-d, h]) + o$; $y_{1r} := good.y\ y_{1r} + eps$; $x_{1l} := good.x\ x_{1l}$;
  $pos_9(bot\_thickness, \text{angle}(-2u, -h - d))$;
  $lft\ x_{9r} = \text{hround } .75u$; $top\ y_{9l} = (\text{vround } .25[-d, h]) - o$;
  $y_{9r} := good.y\ y_{9r} - eps$; $x_{9l} := good.x\ x_{9l}$;
  filldraw stroke $term.e(2, 1, left, 1, 4)$;   % upper terminal
  filldraw stroke $term.e(8, 9, left, 1, 4)$; **fi**   % lower terminal
penlabels$(0, 1, 2, 3, 4, 5, 6, 7, 8, 9, 10)$; **endchar**;

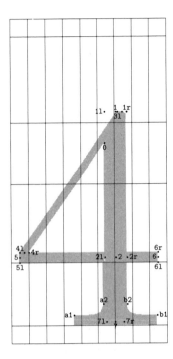

```
cmchar "Oldstyle numeral 4";
```
beginchar("4", $9u^\#$, $x\_height^\#$, $desc\_depth^\#$);
italcorr $x\_height^\# * slant + .5stem^\# - 2.5u^\#$;
adjust_fit$(0, 0)$;
numeric $light\_stem$, $light\_stem'$, $diag\_stem$, $alpha$, cut; $cut = .75notch\_cut$;
$light_stem = $ hround $.4[fudged.stem, fudged.cap\_stem]$;
$light_stem' = $ hround $\max(tiny.breadth, light\_stem - 2stem\_corr)$;
$diag\_stem = \max(tiny.breadth, .4[vair, fudged.hair])$;
pickup $crisp.nib$; $pos_5(cap\_bar, 90)$; $pos_6(cap\_bar, 90)$;
$lft\ x_5 = $ hround $.5u$; $rt\ x_6 = $ hround$(w - .5u)$; $bot\ y_{5l} = 0$;
$z_{4l} = top\ lft\ z_{5r}$; $y_2 = y_{2'} = y_5 = y_6$; $x_{1r} = x_{2r} = $ hround$(w - 3u + .5light\_stem)$;
$penpos_1(light\_stem', 0)$; $penpos_2(light\_stem', 0)$; $y_1 = y_3 = h + apex\_o + apex\_oo$;
$x_{3r} + apex\_corr = x_{1r}$; $alpha = diag\_ratio(1, diag\_stem, y_3 - y_{4l}, x_{3r} - x_{4l})$;
$penpos_3(alpha * diag\_stem, 0)$; $penpos_4(alpha * diag\_stem, 0)$;
$x_0 = x_{1l}$; $z_0 = whatever[z_{3r}, z_{4r}]$;
$x_{5'} = x_5$; $z_{5''} = z_{5'} + $ **penoffset** $z_4 - z_3$ of $currentpen = whatever[z_{4l}, z_{3l}]$;
fill $diag\_end(2r, 1r, 1, .5, 3l, 4l)$ --- $z_{5''}$ ... $lft\ z_{5'}$
    --- $lft\ z_{5l}$ -- (x_{4r}, y_{5l}) -- z_{4r}
    if $y_0 < h - cut$: $\{z_{3r} - z_{4r}\}$ ... $\{up\}(x_{1l} - 1, h - cut)$
      -- $(x_{1l}, h - cut)$ **else**: -- z_0 **fi**
    -- z_{2l} -- z_{2r} -- **cycle**;   % diagonal and upper stem

filldraw stroke z_{5e} -- z_{6e};   % bar

pickup $tiny.nib$; $pos_7(light\_stem, 0)$; $pos_{2'}(light\_stem, 0)$; $x_{2'} = x_7$;
$rt\ x_{7r} = x_{1r}$; $bot\ y_7 = -d$ **if not** $serifs$: $-o$ **fi**;
filldraw stroke $z_{2'e}$ -- z_{7e};   % lower stem
if $serifs$: $dish\_serif(7, 2', a, 1/3, 1.75u$,
     $b, 1/3, \min(1.75u, w - .5u - rt\ x_{7r}))$; **fi**   % serif
penlabels$(0, 1, 2, 3, 4, 5, 6, 7)$; **endchar**;

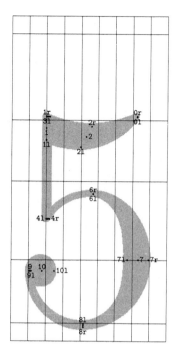

```
cmchar "Oldstyle numeral 5";
```
beginchar(`"5"`, $9u^\#$, $x\_height^\#$, $desc\_depth^\#$);
italcorr $x\_height^\# * slant - u^\#$;
adjust_fit$(0, 0)$;
numeric $bot\_thickness$, $light\_hair$;
$bot\_thickness = \max(fine.breadth, \text{vround}(slab - vair\_corr))$;
$light\_hair = \text{hround}(cap\_hair \textbf{ if } hefty\text{: } -2stem\_corr \textbf{ fi})$;
pickup $tiny.nib$; $pos_5(vair, 180)$; $pos_6(vair, 90)$;
$bot\ y_5 = \text{vround}(.53[-d, h] - vair)$;
$top\ y_{6r} = \max((\text{vround }.61803[-d, h]) + o, top\ y_{6r} + y_5 + eps - y_{6l})$;
$pos_3(light\_hair, 0)$; $pos_4(light\_hair, 0)$;
$lft\ x_{3l} = \max(1.35u, 2.1u - .5light\_hair)$; $x_3 = x_4 = x_5$; $y_4 = y_5$;
$top\ y_3 = h \textbf{ if not } hefty\text{: } + o \textbf{ fi}$;
filldraw stroke z_{3e} -- z_{4e};   % thin stem
$penpos_7(cap\_stem - fine, 0)$; $penpos_8(bot\_thickness - fine, -90)$;
$fine.rt\ x_{7r} = \text{hround}(w - .9u)$; $x_8 = .5[u, x_7]$; $x_6 = .5[x_5, x_7]$;
erase fill z_5 -- $bot\ z_5$ -- $(x_6, bot\ y_5)$ -- $z_6\{left\}$
    .. tension .9 and 1 .. $\{x_5 - x_6, 3(y_5 - y_6)\}$ cycle;   % erase excess in middle
filldraw stroke $z_{6e}\{left\}$ .. tension .9 and 1 .. $\{x_5 - x_6, 3(y_5 - y_6)\}z_{5e}$;   % link
pickup $fine.nib$; $pos_{6'}(vair, 90)$; $z_{6'} = z_6$;
$y_7 = .5[y_6, y_8]$; $bot\ y_{8r} = -d - o$;
filldraw stroke $pulled\_arc_e(6', 7)$ & $pulled\_arc_e(7, 8)$;   % bowl
if $serifs$: $pos_9(hair, -180)$; $y_9 = .5[-d, y_5]$; $lft\ x_{9r} = \text{hround }.9u$;
    $pos_{10}(flare + \tfrac{1}{3}(cap\_stem - stem), -180)$; $bulb(8, 9, 10)$;   % bulb
else: $pos_9(\tfrac{3}{7}[bot\_thickness, flare], angle(-7u, -h - d))$;
    $lft\ x_{9r} = \text{hround }.9u$; $bot\ y_{9r} = (\text{vround }.15[-d, h]) - o$;
    $x_{9l} := good.x\ x_{9l}$; $y_{9l} := good.y\ y_{9l}$;
    filldraw stroke $term.e(8, 9, left, 1, 4)$; **fi**   % terminal
if $hefty$: **pickup** $crisp.nib$; $pos_1(slab, 90)$; $pos_2(hair, 0)$;
    $top\ y_{1r} = h$; $x_1 = x_4$; $rt\ x_{2r} = \text{hround}(w - 1.5u)$;
    $y_2 = y_{1l} - eps$; $arm(1, 2, a, 0, 0)$;   % arm
else: **numeric** $flag\_breadth$; $flag\_breadth = \tfrac{7}{8}[vair, cap\_curve]$;
    $pos_1(flag\_breadth, 90)$; $pos_2(flag\_breadth, 60)$;
    $pos_0(vair, 90)$; $top\ y_{1r} = tiny.top\ y_3$; $top\ y_{2r} = (\text{vround }.95[-d, h]) + o$; $y_{0r} = y_{1r}$;
    $lft\ x_1 = tiny.lft\ x_{3l}$; $x_{2r} = .5[x_1, x_0]$; $rt\ x_0 = \text{hround}(w - 1.6u)$;
    erase fill $top\ z_{1r}$ -- z_{1r} ... $\{right\}z_{2r}$
        -- $(x_{2r}, top\ y_{1r})$ -- cycle;   % erase excess at top
    filldraw stroke z_{1e} ... $\{right\}z_{2e}$ ... z_{0e}; **fi**   % flag
penlabels$(0, 1, 2, 3, 4, 5, 6, 7, 8, 9, 10)$; **endchar**;

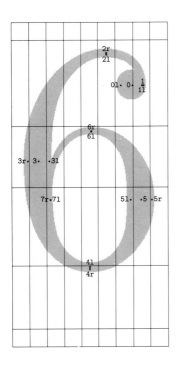

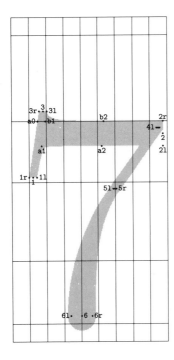

cmchar "Oldstyle numeral 6";
beginchar("6", $9u^\#$, $\mathit{fig\_height}^\#$, 0);
italcorr $\mathit{fig\_height}^\# * slant - u^\#$;

      ⋮   (a copy of the program for '6' in **romand** comes here)

penlabels(0, 1, 2, 3, 4, 5, 6, 7); **endchar**;

cmchar "Oldstyle numeral 7";
beginchar("7", $9u^\#$, $\mathit{x\_height}^\#$, $\mathit{desc\_depth}^\#$);
italcorr $\mathit{x\_height}^\# * slant$;
adjust_fit(0, 0);
numeric $\mathit{arm\_thickness}$, $\mathit{bot\_width}$, $\mathit{top\_shift}$, $\mathit{top\_hair}$;
if *hefty*: $\mathit{arm\_thickness} = \text{Vround}(\mathit{slab} + 2\mathit{stem\_corr})$; $\mathit{top\_shift} = 0$;
    $\mathit{bot\_width} = \text{hround } .51[\mathit{curve}, \mathit{cap\_curve}]$; $\mathit{top\_hair} = .4[\mathit{thin\_join}, \mathit{bot\_width}]$;
else: $\mathit{arm\_thickness} = \text{Vround } .4[\mathit{stem}, \mathit{cap\_stem}]$; $\mathit{top\_shift} = .5u$;
    $\mathit{bot\_width} = \mathit{flare}$; $\mathit{top\_hair} = \mathit{cap\_hair}$; **fi**
if $\mathit{top\_hair} < \mathit{tiny.breadth}$: $\mathit{top\_hair} := \mathit{tiny.breadth}$; **fi**
pickup $\mathit{crisp.nib}$; $\mathit{pos}_2(\mathit{arm\_thickness}, 90)$; $\mathit{pos}_1(\mathit{hair}, 180)$;
$\mathit{top}\ y_{2r} = h$; $\mathit{rt}\ x_2 = \text{hround}(w - .75u + \mathit{top\_shift})$;
$\mathit{lft}\ x_{1r} = \text{hround}(.75u + .5\mathit{top\_shift})$; $y_1 = \mathit{good.y}(y_{2l} - \mathit{beak}/2) - \mathit{eps}$;
$\mathit{arm}(2, 1, a, .3\mathit{beak\_darkness}, -\mathit{beak\_jut})$;   % arm and beak
$\mathit{pos}_3(\mathit{hair}, 180)$; $y_3 = \mathit{good.y}(y_{2r} + \mathit{beak}/6) + \mathit{eps}$; $z_{3r} = \mathit{whatever}[z_{1r}, z_{a0}]$;
$\mathit{penpos}_{2'}(2\mathit{epsilon}, -90)$; $z_{2'} = z_{2r}$;
$\mathit{arm}(2', 3, b, \mathit{beak\_darkness}, x_{3r} - x_{a0})$;   % upward extension of beak
pickup $\mathit{tiny.nib}$; $\mathit{pos}_4(\mathit{top\_hair}, 0)$; $\mathit{pos}_6(\mathit{bot\_width}, 0)$;
$\mathit{bot}\ y_4 = \max(h - \mathit{arm\_thickness}, h - \mathit{slab}, \mathit{bot}\ y_{2l})$; $\mathit{rt}\ x_{4r} = \mathit{crisp.rt}\ x_2$;
$\mathit{lft}\ x_{6l} = \text{hround}(3.5u + \mathit{top\_shift} - .5\mathit{bot\_width})$;
if *serifs*: $y_6 - .5\mathit{bot\_width} = -d - o$; **filldraw** $z_{6l}\{\mathit{down}\}$ .. $\{\mathit{up}\}z_{6r}$ -- cycle; % bulb
else: $\mathit{bot}\ y_6 = -d - \mathit{oo}$; **fi**
if *hefty*: **erase fill** $\mathit{rt}\ z_{4r}$ -- z_{4r} ... $\{\mathit{down}\}z_{6r}$
    -- $(\mathit{rt}\ x_{4r}, y_6)$ -- cycle;   % erase excess at top
    filldraw stroke z_{4e} ... $\{\mathit{down}\}z_{6e}$;   % stroke
else: $\mathit{pos}_5(\mathit{top\_hair}, 0)$; $y_5 = \frac{2}{3}[-d, h]$; $z_5 = \mathit{whatever}[z_4, (.75u, y_6)]$;
    erase fill $\mathit{rt}\ z_{4r}$ -- z_{4r} -- z_{5r} -- $(\mathit{rt}\ x_{4r}, y_5)$ -- cycle;   % erase excess at top
    filldraw stroke z_{4e} --- z_{5e} ... $\{\mathit{down}\}z_{6e}$; **fi**   % stroke
penlabels(1, 2, 3, 4, 5, 6); **endchar**;

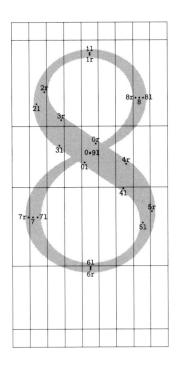

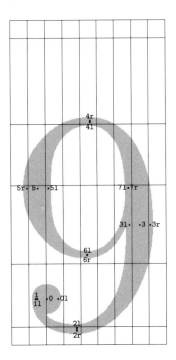

cmchar "Oldstyle numeral 8";
beginchar("8", $9u\#$, $fig\_height\#$, 0);

      $\vdots$ (a copy of the program for '8' in **romand** comes here)

penlabels(0, 1, 2, 3, 4, 5, 6, 7, 8, 9); **endchar**;

cmchar "Oldstyle numeral 9";
beginchar("9", $9u\#$, $x\_height\#$, $desc\_depth\#$);
italcorr $x\_height\# * slant - u\#$;
adjust_fit$(0, 0)$;
numeric $top\_thickness$, $bot\_thickness$, $side\_thickness$, $pull$;
$top\_thickness = \max(fine.breadth, \mathrm{vround}(slab - 2vair\_corr))$;
$bot\_thickness = \max(fine.breadth, \mathrm{vround}(slab - vair\_corr))$;
$side\_thickness = \max(fine.breadth, \mathrm{hround}\ 1/3[curve, cap\_curve])$;
$pull = \min(.25, 1.5superpull)$;
pickup $fine.nib$; $pos_2(bot\_thickness, -90)$;
$pos_3(side\_thickness, 0)$; $pos_4(top\_thickness, 90)$;
$pos_5(side\_thickness, 180)$; $pos_6(vair, 270)$;
$w - rt\ x_{3r} = lft\ x_{5r} = \mathrm{hround}\ \max(.75u, 1.5u - .5side\_thickness)$;
$x_4 - .1u = x_6 + .1u = x_2 + .75u = .5w$;
$bot\ y_{2r} = -d - o$; $y_3 = .5[y_2, y_4]$; $top\ y_{4r} = h + o$;
$y_5 = .5[y_4, y_6]$; $bot\ y_6 = (\mathrm{vround}\ 3/8[-d, h]) - o$;
path p; $p = pulled\_super\_arc_l(3, 4)(pull)$;
numeric t; $t = \mathrm{xpart}(p\ \mathrm{intersectiontimes}\ ((x_{3r}, y_5)\ \text{-{}-}\ (x_4, y_5)))$;
$pos_7(thin\_join, 360)$; $z_{7l} = $ **point** t **of** p;
$(x, y_{6r}) = whatever[z_{7l}, z_{6l}]$; $x_{6r} := \max(x, .5[x_{5r}, x_6])$;
filldraw stroke $pulled\_super\_arc_e(2, 3)(pull)$
    & {{ **interim** $superness := more\_super$; $pulled\_super\_arc_e(3, 4)(pull)$ }}
    & {{$less\_tense$; $pulled\_super\_arc_e(4, 5)(pull)$ & $pulled\_super\_arc_e(5, 6)(pull)$ }}
    & $z_{6e}\{right\}\ \ldots\ \{\textbf{direction}\ t\ \textbf{of}\ p\}z_{7e}$;   % arc and bowl
if $serifs$: $pos_1(hair, -180)$; $pos_0(flare, -180)$;
    $lft\ x_{0r} = \min(lft\ x_2 - eps, \mathrm{hround}\ 1.2u)$;
    $y_0 = \mathrm{vround}\ \max(.1[-d, h] + .5flare, .15[-d, h] - .5flare) - o$;
    {{$less\_tense$; $bulb(2, 1, 0)$ }};   % arc and bulb
else: $pos_1(.1[bot\_thickness, flare], -120)$;
    $bot\ y_{1r} = (\mathrm{vround}\ .07[-d, h]) - o$; $lft\ x_{1r} = \mathrm{hround}\ 1.3u$;
    filldraw stroke $term.e(2, 1, left, .9, 4)$; **fi**   % terminal
penlabels(0, 1, 2, 3, 4, 5, 6, 7); **endchar**;

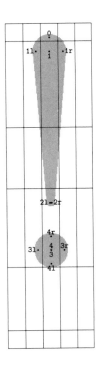

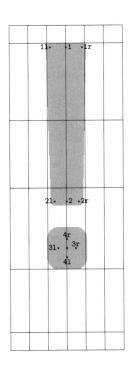

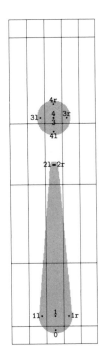

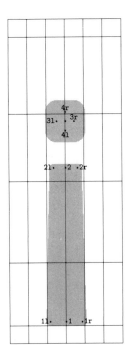

Although program file punct.mf deals with some of the simplest characters in a font, the programs reveal that a surprising amount of subtlety is involved.

% This file contains punctuation marks common to roman and italic styles.

% Codes ´041, ´043, ´045, ´047–´054, ´056, ´057, ´072, ´073, ´075, ´100,
% ´133, ´135, and ´140 are generated, as well as code *spanish_shriek*
% (for a Spanish exclamation point) if that code value is known.

cmchar "Exclamation point";
beginchar("!", $5u\# + width\_adj\#$, $asc\_height\#$, 0);
italcorr $asc\_height\# * slant - 2u\# - .5width\_adj\# + .5dot\_size\#$;
adjust_fit(0, 0);
pickup *tiny.nib*; $pos_3(dot\_size, 0)$; $pos_4(dot\_size, 90)$;
lft x_{3l} = hround($.5w - .5dot\_size$); *bot* $y_{4l} = 0$; $z_3 = z_4$; $dot(3, 4)$;   % dot
numeric *bot_width*;
bot_width = **if** *hefty*: max(hround $.8dot\_size$, *fine.breadth*) **else**: *hair* **fi**;
pickup *fine.nib*; $pos_1(dot\_size, 0)$; $pos_2(bot\_width, 0)$;
$x_1 = x_2 = x_3$; *bot* $y_2 = .25[$*top* $y_{4r}, x\_height] + 1$;
if *square_dots*: *top* $y_1 = h$;
    filldraw stroke z_{1e} -- z_{2e};   % stem
else: *top* $z_0 = (x_1, h + o)$; $y_1 + .5dot\_size = h + o$;
    filldraw $z_{1r} \ldots z_0 \ldots z_{1l}$ --- z_{2l} -- z_{2r} --- cycle; **fi**   % stem and bulb
penlabels(0, 1, 2, 3, 4); **endchar**;

iff known *spanish_shriek*: **cmchar** "Spanish open exclamation point";
beginchar(*spanish_shriek*, $5u\#+width\_adj\#$, $asc\_height\#-desc\_depth\#$, $desc\_depth\#$);
italcorr $h\# * slant - 2u\# - .5width\_adj\# + .5dot\_size\#$;
adjust_fit(0, 0);
pickup *tiny.nib*; $pos_3(dot\_size, 0)$; $pos_4(dot\_size, 90)$;
lft x_{3l} = hround($.5w - .5dot\_size$); *top* $y_{4r} = h$; $z_3 = z_4$; $dot(3, 4)$;   % dot
numeric *top_width*;
top_width = **if** *hefty*: max(hround $.8dot\_size$, *fine.breadth*) **else**: *hair* **fi**;
pickup *fine.nib*; $pos_1(dot\_size, 0)$; $pos_2(top\_width, 0)$;
$x_1 = x_2 = x_3$; *top* $y_2 = .25[$*bot* $y_{4l}, h - x\_height] - 1$;
if *square_dots*: *bot* $y_1 = -d$;
    filldraw stroke z_{1e} -- z_{2e};   % stem
else: *bot* $z_0 = (x_1, -d - o)$; $y_1 - .5dot\_size = -d - o$;
    filldraw $z_{1l} \ldots z_0 \ldots z_{1r}$ --- z_{2r} -- z_{2l} --- cycle; **fi**   % stem and bulb
penlabels(0, 1, 2, 3, 4); **endchar**;

---

def *dot*(**suffix** \$, \$\$) =
    filldraw if *square_dots*: $(x_{\$l}, y_{\$\$l})$ -- $(x_{\$r}, y_{\$\$l})$
        -- $(x_{\$r}, y_{\$\$r})$ -- $(x_{\$l}, y_{\$\$r})$ -- cycle   % squarish dot
        else: $z_{\$l} \ldots z_{\$\$l} \ldots z_{\$r} \ldots z_{\$\$r} \ldots$ cycle **fi**   % roundish dot
    enddef;

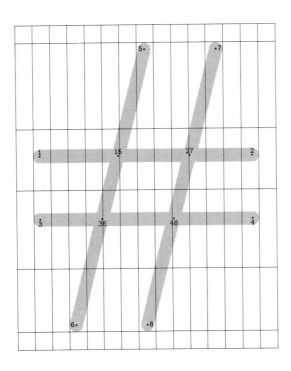

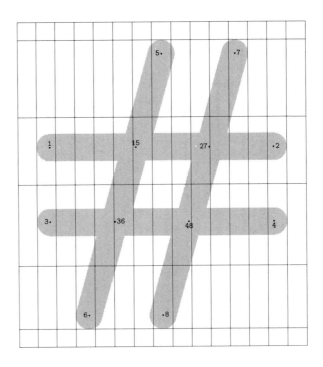

cmchar "Hash mark (number sign)";
if *monospace*: *compute_spread*$(.6x\_height\#, .7x\_height\#)$;
else: *compute_spread*$(.45x\_height\#, .55x\_height\#)$; **fi**
beginchar("#", $15u\#$, *asc_height*$\#$, *asc_depth*$\#$);
italcorr$(math\_axis\# + .5(spread\# + rule\_thickness\#)) * slant - .5u\#$;
adjust_fit$(0, 0)$;
pickup *rule.nib*; *lft* $x_1 = $ hround $u - eps$; $x_3 = x_1$; $x_2 = x_4 = w - x_1$;
$y_1 = y_2$; $y_3 = y_4$; $y_1 - y_3 = spread$; $.5[y_1, y_3] = math\_axis$;
draw z_1 -- z_2;   % upper bar
draw z_3 -- z_4;   % lower bar
lft $x_6 = $ hround $3u$; *rt* $x_7 = $ hround$(w - 3u)$; $x_5 - x_6 = x_7 - x_8$;
$x_8 = good.x$ **if** *monospace*: $.6$ **else**: $.5$ **fi** w;
top $y_5 = $ *top* $y_7 = h + eps$; *bot* $y_6 = $ *bot* $y_8 = -d - eps$;
$y_{15} = y_1$; $z_{15} = whatever[z_5, z_6]$; $y_{36} = y_3$; $z_{36} = whatever[z_5, z_6]$;
$y_{27} = y_2$; $z_{27} = whatever[z_7, z_8]$; $y_{48} = y_4$; $z_{48} = whatever[z_7, z_8]$;
draw z_5 -- **if** $x_5 > x_6 + 1$: $(good.x(x_{15} + .5), y_1)$ -- $(good.x(x_{15} - .5), y_1)$
  -- $(good.x(x_{36} + .5), y_3)$ -- $(good.x(x_{36} - .5), y_3)$ -- **fi** z_6;   % left diagonal
draw z_7 -- **if** $x_7 > x_8 + 1$: $(good.x(x_{27} + .5), y_2)$ -- $(good.x(x_{27} - .5), y_2)$
  -- $(good.x(x_{48} + .5), y_4)$ -- $(good.x(x_{48} - .5), y_4)$ -- **fi** z_8;   % right diagonal
labels$(1, 2, 3, 4, 5, 6, 7, 8, 15, 27, 36, 48)$; **endchar**;

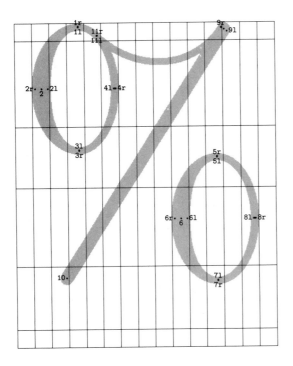

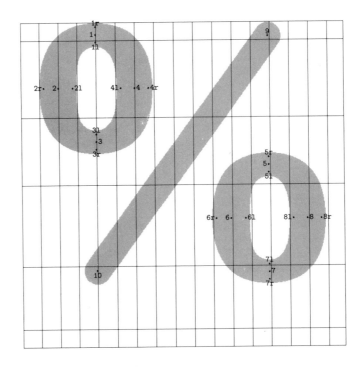

cmchar "Per cent sign";
beginchar("%", $9u\# + \max(6u\#, 2fudge * (hair\# + stem\#))$,
    $body\_height\#, body\_height\# - asc\_height\#$);
italcorr **if** *hefty*: $.4asc\_height\# * slant - .5u\#$ **else**: $h\# * slant - u\#$ **fi**;
adjust_fit$(0, 0)$; **pickup** *fine.nib*;
numeric *left_curve, right_curve*;
$left\_curve = \text{hround } {}^5\!/\!_6[fudged.hair, fudged.stem]$;
$right\_curve = \max(fine.breadth, \text{hround}(fudged.hair \text{ **if** } hefty: -2stem\_corr \text{ **fi**}))$;
$pos_1(vair, 90)$; $pos_2(left\_curve, 180)$; $pos_3(vair, 270)$; $pos_4(right\_curve, 360)$;
$top\ y_{1r} = h$; $lft\ x_{2r} = \text{hround } u$; $rt\ x_{4r} = \text{hround}(.5w - 1.5u)$;
$bot\ y_{3r} = \text{floor}(\text{**if** } monospace: .7 \text{ **else**: } .5 \text{ **fi** } asc\_height)$;
$x_1 = x_3 = .5[x_2, x_4]$; $y_2 = y_4 = .5[y_1, y_3]$;
filldraw stroke $pulled\_super\_arc_e(1, 2)(superpull)$
    & $pulled\_super\_arc_e(2, 3)(superpull)$;   % left half of upper bowl
filldraw stroke $super\_arc_e(3, 4)$ & $super\_arc_e(4, 1)$;   % right half of upper bowl
$pos_5(vair, 90)$; $pos_6(left\_curve, 180)$; $pos_7(vair, 270)$; $pos_8(right\_curve, 360)$;
$bot\ y_{7r} = -d$; $rt\ x_{8r} = \text{hround}(w - u)$; $lft\ x_{6r} = \text{hround}(.5w + 1.5u)$;
$top\ y_{5r} = \text{vround}(\text{**if** } monospace: .3 \text{ **else**: } .5 \text{ **fi** } asc\_height)$;
$x_5 = x_7 = .5[x_6, x_8]$; $y_6 = y_8 = .5[y_5, y_7]$;
filldraw stroke $pulled\_super\_arc_e(5, 6)(superpull)$
    & $pulled\_super\_arc_e(6, 7)(superpull)$;   % left half of lower bowl
filldraw stroke $super\_arc_e(7, 8)$ & $super\_arc_e(8, 5)$;   % right half of lower bowl
pickup *rule.nib*; $top\ y_9 = h$; $bot\ y_{10} = -d$;
if *hefty*: $x_9 = good.x(x_5 - eps)$; $x_{10} = good.x(x_1 + eps)$;
    draw $z_9 -\!\!- z_{10}$;   % diagonal
else: $rt\ x_9 = \text{hround}(w - 2.5u)$; $lft\ x_{10} = \text{hround } 2.5u$; **draw** $z_9 -\!\!- z_{10}$;   % diagonal
    pickup *fine.nib*; $pos_9(rule\_thickness, \text{angle}(z_9 - z_{10}) + 90)$;
    $pos_{11}(vair, \text{angle}(z_{1r} - z_{4r}) - 90)$; $pos_{12}(vair, \text{angle}(z_9 - z_{10}) + 90)$;
    path p; $p = super\_arc_r(1, 4)$; $z_{11r} = \textbf{point } {}^2\!/\!_3 \textbf{ of } p$; $z_{12r} = z_{9r}$;
    filldraw stroke $z_{11e}\{\textbf{direction } {}^2\!/\!_3 \textbf{ of } p\} \ldots \{z_9 - z_{10}\}z_{12e}$; **fi**   % link
penlabels$(1, 2, 3, 4, 5, 6, 7, 8, 9, 10, 11, 12)$; **endchar**;

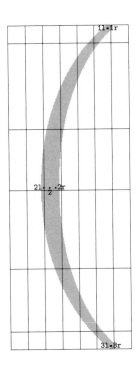

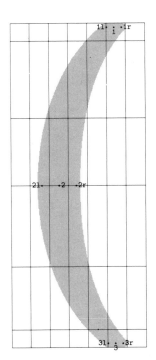

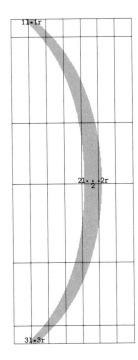

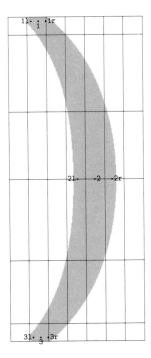

cmchar `"Left parenthesis"`;
beginchar(`"("`, $7u\#$ **if** *monospace*: $-u\#$ **fi**, *body_height*$\#$, *paren_depth*$\#$);
italcorr *body_height*$\# * slant - .5u\#$;
adjust_fit$(0, 0)$; **pickup** *fine.nib*;
$pos_1(vair, 0)$; $pos_2(.75[hair, stem], 0)$; $pos_3(vair, 0)$;
$rt\ x_{1r} = rt\ x_{3r} = $ hround$(w - u)$; $lft\ x_{2l} = $ hround$(x_1 - 4u$ **if** *monospace*: $+ {}^4\!/_3 u$ **fi**$)$;
$top\ y_1 = h$; $y_2 = .5[y_1, y_3] = math\_axis$;
filldraw stroke $z_{1e}\{3(x_{2e} - x_{1e}), y_2 - y_1\} \ldots z_{2e}$
$\qquad \ldots \{3(x_{3e} - x_{2e}), y_3 - y_2\}z_{3e}$; % arc
penlabels$(1, 2, 3)$; **endchar**;

cmchar `"Right parenthesis"`;
beginchar(`")"`, $7u\#$ **if** *monospace*: $-u\#$ **fi**, *body_height*$\#$, *paren_depth*$\#$);
italcorr *math_axis*$\# * slant - .5u\#$;
adjust_fit$(0, 0)$; **pickup** *fine.nib*;
$pos_1(vair, 0)$; $pos_2(.75[hair, stem], 0)$; $pos_3(vair, 0)$;
$lft\ x_{1l} = lft\ x_{3l} = $ hround u; $rt\ x_{2r} = $ hround$(x_1 + 4u$ **if** *monospace*: $- {}^4\!/_3 u$ **fi**$)$;
$top\ y_1 = h$; $y_2 = .5[y_1, y_3] = math\_axis$;
filldraw stroke $z_{1e}\{3(x_{2e} - x_{1e}), y_2 - y_1\} \ldots z_{2e}$
$\qquad \ldots \{3(x_{3e} - x_{2e}), y_3 - y_2\}z_{3e}$; % arc
penlabels$(1, 2, 3)$; **endchar**;

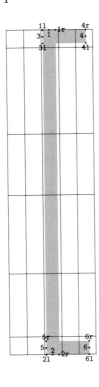

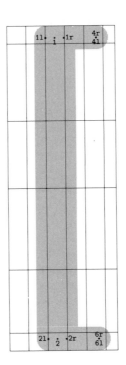

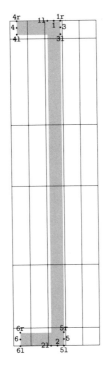

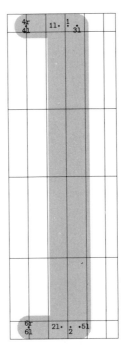

```
cmchar "Left bracket";
```
numeric $wd\#$; $\quad wd\# = \max(5u\#, 4.5u\# + .5$ **if** *hefty*: *stem*# **else**: *rule_thickness*# **fi**);
beginchar("[", $wd\#$, *body_height*#, *paren_depth*#);
italcorr *body_height*# $*$ *slant*;
adjust_fit$(0, 0)$;
numeric *top_thickness*, *side_thickness*;
if *hefty*: *top_thickness* = *vair*;
$\quad$ *side_thickness* = $\max($*crisp.breadth*, *stem* $- 2$*stem_corr*$)$;
else: *top_thickness* = *side_thickness* = *rule_thickness*; **fi**;
pickup *crisp.nib*; $pos_1($*side_thickness*, $0)$; $pos_2($*side_thickness*, $0)$;
top $y_1 = h$; *bot* $y_2 = -d$;
lft x_{1l} = *lft* x_{2l} = hround$(2.5u - .5$*side_thickness*$) - 1 - eps$;
filldraw stroke z_{1e} -- z_{2e}; $\hfill$ % stem
$pos_3($*top_thickness*, $90)$; $pos_4($*top_thickness*, $90)$;
$pos_5($*top_thickness*, $90)$; $pos_6($*top_thickness*, $90)$;
$x_3 = x_5 = x_{1l}$; *rt* x_4 = *rt* x_6 = ceiling$(w-.4u)+eps$; $y_{3r} = y_{4r} = y_1$; $y_{5l} = y_{6l} = y_2$;
filldraw stroke z_{3e} -- z_{4e}; $\hfill$ % upper bar
filldraw stroke z_{5e} -- z_{6e}; $\hfill$ % lower bar
penlabels$(1, 2, 3, 4, 5, 6)$; **endchar**;

```
cmchar "Right bracket";
```
numeric $wd\#$; $\quad wd\# = \max(5u\#, 4.5u\# + .5$ **if** *hefty*: *stem*# **else**: *rule_thickness*# **fi**);
beginchar("]", $wd\#$, *body_height*#, *paren_depth*#);
italcorr *body_height*# $*$ *slant* $- 2u\# + .5$ **if** *hefty*: *stem*# **else**: *rule_thickness*# **fi**;
adjust_fit$(0, 0)$;
numeric *top_thickness*, *side_thickness*;
if *hefty*: *top_thickness* = *vair*;
$\quad$ *side_thickness* = $\max($*crisp.breadth*, *stem* $- 2$*stem_corr*$)$;
else: *top_thickness* = *side_thickness* = *rule_thickness*; **fi**;
pickup *crisp.nib*; $pos_1($*side_thickness*, $0)$; $pos_2($*side_thickness*, $0)$;
top $y_1 = h$; *bot* $y_2 = -d$;
rt x_{1r} = *rt* x_{2r} = hround$(w - 2.5u + .5$*side_thickness*$) + 1 + eps$;
filldraw stroke z_{1e} -- z_{2e}; $\hfill$ % stem
$pos_3($*top_thickness*, $90)$; $pos_4($*top_thickness*, $90)$;
$pos_5($*top_thickness*, $90)$; $pos_6($*top_thickness*, $90)$;
$x_3 = x_5 = x_{1r}$; *lft* x_4 = *lft* x_6 = floor $.4u - eps$; $y_{3r} = y_{4r} = y_1$; $y_{5l} = y_{6l} = y_2$;
filldraw stroke z_{3e} -- z_{4e}; $\hfill$ % upper bar
filldraw stroke z_{5e} -- z_{6e}; $\hfill$ % lower bar
penlabels$(1, 2, 3, 4, 5, 6)$; **endchar**;

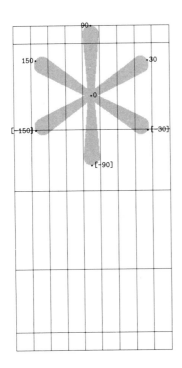
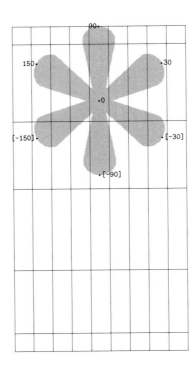
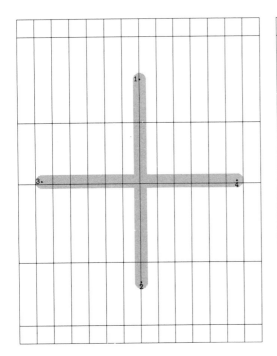
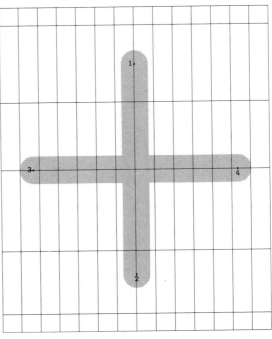

cmchar "Asterisk";
beginchar("*", $9u^\#$,
  if *low_asterisk*: $math\_axis^\# + .5x\_height^\#$ else: $body\_height^\#$ fi, 0);
italcorr $h^\# * slant - .75u^\#$;
adjust_fit(0, 0);
numeric *ast_flare*; ast_flare = hround $.7[thin\_join, stem]$;
$x_0 = .5w$; $y_0 = h - .5x\_height$;
for $d = -150$ step 60 until 150: $z[d] = z_0 + .5$ dir d xscaled $7.5u$ yscaled x_height;
 numeric *theta*; $theta$ = angle($z[d] - z_0$);
 fill $z_0 + .5(0, -thin\_join)$ rotated *theta*
  $\cdots z[d] + .5(-ast\_flare, -ast\_flare)$ rotated *theta*
  $\cdot\cdot z[d] \cdot\cdot z[d] + .5(-ast\_flare, ast\_flare)$ rotated *theta*
  $\cdots z_0 + .5(0, thin\_join)$ rotated *theta* -- cycle;   **endfor**   % diagonal at angle d
labels(0, $[-150]$, $[-90]$, $[-30]$, 30, 90, 150);   endchar;

cmchar "Plus sign";
beginarithchar("+");   pickup *rule.nib*;
$x_1 = x_2 = good.x \ .5w$;   top $y_1 = h + eps$; $.5[y_1, y_2] = math\_axis$;
lft x_3 = hround $u - eps$; $x_4 = w - x_3$; $y_3 = y_4 = math\_axis$;
draw $z_1 \text{ -- } z_2$;   % stem
draw $z_3 \text{ -- } z_4$;   % crossbar
labels(1, 2, 3, 4);   endchar;

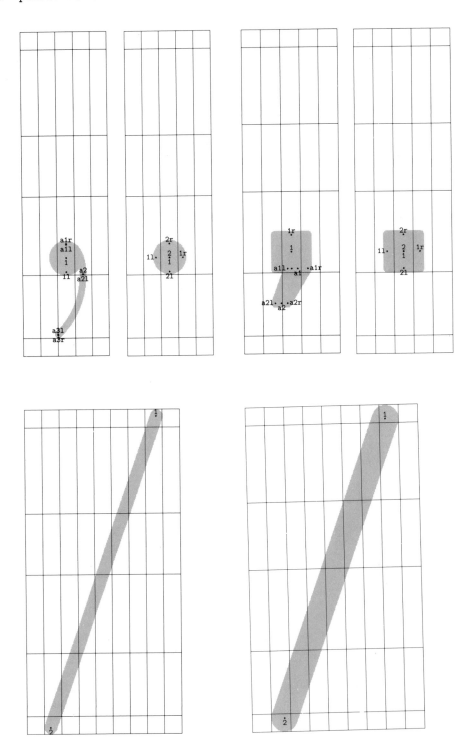

cmchar "Comma";
numeric $dot\_diam^\#$; $dot_diam^\# = $ **if** $monospace$: $^5/_4$ **fi** $dot\_size^\#$;
define_whole_blacker_pixels(dot_diam);
beginchar(",", $5u^\#$, $dot\_diam^\#$, $comma\_depth^\#$);
adjust_fit$(0, 0)$;
$x_1 - .5dot_diam = $ hround$(.5w - .5dot\_diam)$; $\ y_1 - .5dot\_diam = 0$;
$comma(1, a, dot\_diam, .2u, comma\_depth)$;   % dot and tail
penlabels(1); **endchar**;

cmchar "Period";
numeric $dot\_diam^\#$; $dot_diam^\# = $ **if** $monospace$: $^5/_4$ **fi** $dot\_size^\#$;
define_whole_blacker_pixels(dot_diam);
beginchar(".", $5u^\#$, $dot\_diam^\#$, 0);
adjust_fit$(0, 0)$; **pickup** $fine.nib$;
$pos_1(dot\_diam, 0)$; $\ pos_2(dot\_diam, 90)$;
$lft\ x_{1l} = $ hround$(.5w - .5dot\_diam)$; $\ bot\ y_{2l} = 0$; $\ z_1 = z_2$; $\ dot(1, 2)$;   % dot
penlabels$(1, 2)$; **endchar**;

cmchar "Virgule (slash)";
beginchar("/", $9u^\#$, $body\_height^\#$, $paren\_depth^\#$);
italcorr $body\_height^\# * slant - .5u^\#$;
adjust_fit$(0, 0)$; **pickup** $rule.nib$;
$rt\ x_1 = $ hround$(w - u) + eps$; $\ top\ y_1 = h + eps$;
$lft\ x_2 = $ hround $u - eps$; $\ bot\ y_2 = -d - eps$;
draw $z_1 \ \text{--} \ z_2$;   % diagonal
penlabels$(1, 2)$; **endchar**;

---

def $comma$(**suffix** \$, @)(**expr** $dot\_size, jut, depth$) =
  pickup $fine.nib$; $\ pos_\$(dot\_size, 90)$;
  if $square\_dots$: $pos_{\$'}(dot\_size, 0)$; $\ z_{\$'} = z_\$$; $\ dot(\$', \$)$;   % squarish dot
    $comma\_join\_ := \max(fine.breadth, \text{floor } .7dot\_size)$;
    $comma\_bot\_ := \max(fine.breadth, \text{floor } .5dot\_size)$;
    $pos_{@0}(comma\_join\_, 0)$; $\ pos_{@1}(comma\_join\_, 0)$;
    $pos_{@2}(comma\_bot\_, 0)$; $\ y_{@0} = y_\$$; $\ y_{@1} = y_{\$l}$; $\ y_{@2} = y_{@1} - depth$;
    $x_{@0r} = x_{@1r} = x_{\$'r}$; $\ rt\ x_{@2r} = good.x(x_\$ - eps)$;
    filldraw stroke $z_{@0e} \ \text{--} \ z_{@1e} \ .. \ z_{@2e}$;   % tail
  else: $pos_{@1}(vair, 90)$; $\ pos_{@2}(vair, 0)$; $\ pos_{@3}(vair, -45)$;
    $z_{@1r} = z_{\$r}$; $\ rt\ x_{@2r} = $ hround$(x_\$ + .5dot\_size + jut) + 2eps$; $\ x_{@3} = x_\$ - .5u$;
    $y_{@2} = {}^1/_3[y_{@1}, y_{@3}]$; $\ bot\ y_{@3r} = $ vround$(y_\$ - .5dot\_size - depth)$;
    $y\_ := \text{ypart}((z_{@1}\{right\} \ ... \ z_{@2}\{down\} \ ... \ z_{@3})$
        intersectiontimes $(z_{\$l}\{right\} \ .. \ \{left\}z_{\$r}))$; **if** $y\_ < 0$: $y\_ := 1$; **fi**
    filldraw $z_{\$r}\{left\} \ .. \ $**subpath**$(0, y_)$ **of**$(z_{\$l}\{right\} \ .. \ \{left\}z_{\$r}) \ \text{--} \ $cycle;   % dot
    filldraw stroke $z_{@1e}\{right\} \ ... \ z_{@2e}\{down\} \ ... \ z_{@3e}$; **fi**   % tail
  penlabels$(@1, @2, @3)$; **enddef**;

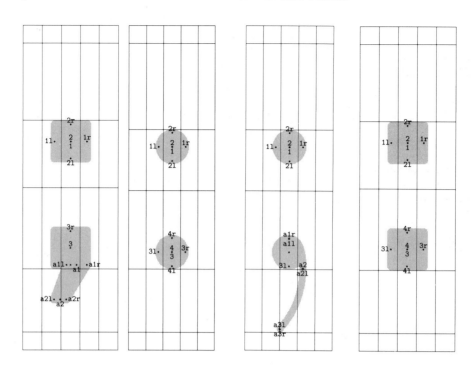

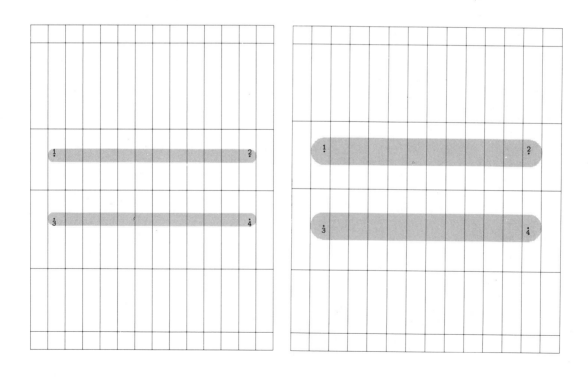

cmchar "Semicolon";
numeric $dot\_diam\#$; $dot_diam\# = $ **if** *monospace*: $5/4$ **fi** $dot\_size\#$;
define_whole_blacker_pixels(dot_diam);
beginchar(";", $5u\#$, $x\_height\#$, $comma\_depth\#$);
italcorr $x\_height\# * slant + .5dot\_diam\# - 2u\#$;
adjust_fit$(0, 0)$; **pickup** *fine.nib*;
$pos_1(dot\_diam, 0)$; $pos_2(dot\_diam, 90)$;
lft $x_{1l} = $ hround$(.5w - .5dot\_diam)$; *top* $y_{2r} = h$; $z_1 = z_2$; $dot(1, 2)$;   % upper dot
$x_3 - .5dot_diam = $ hround$(.5w - .5dot\_diam)$; $y_3 - .5dot\_diam = 0$;
$comma(3, a, dot\_diam, .05u, comma\_depth)$;   % lower dot and tail
penlabels$(1, 2, 3)$; **endchar**;

cmchar "Colon";
numeric $dot\_diam\#$; $dot_diam\# = $ **if** *monospace*: $5/4$ **fi** $dot\_size\#$;
define_whole_blacker_pixels(dot_diam);
beginchar(":", $5u\#$, $x\_height\#$, 0);
italcorr $x\_height\# * slant + .5dot\_diam\# - 2u\#$;
adjust_fit$(0, 0)$; **pickup** *fine.nib*;
$pos_1(dot\_diam, 0)$; $pos_2(dot\_diam, 90)$;
lft $x_{1l} = $ hround$(.5w - .5dot\_diam)$; *top* $y_{2r} = h$; $z_1 = z_2$; $dot(1, 2)$;   % upper dot
$pos_3(dot\_diam, 0)$; $pos_4(dot\_diam, 90)$;
$x_3 = x_1$; *bot* $y_{4l} = 0$; $z_3 = z_4$; $dot(3, 4)$;   % lower dot
penlabels$(1, 2, 3, 4)$; **endchar**;

cmchar "Equals sign";
$compute\_spread(.45x\_height\#, .55x\_height\#)$;
beginchar("=", $14u\#$, $v\_center(spread\# + rule\_thickness\#)$);
italcorr $h\# * slant - .5u\#$;
adjust_fit$(0, 0)$; **pickup** *rule.nib*;
lft $x_1 = $ hround $u - eps$; $x_3 = x_1$; $x_2 = x_4 = w - x_1$;
$y_1 = y_2$; $y_3 = y_4$; $y_1 - y_3 = spread$; $.5[y_1, y_3] = math\_axis$;
draw $z_1 -- z_2$;   % upper bar
draw $z_3 -- z_4$;   % lower bar
labels$(1, 2, 3, 4)$; **endchar**;

> *She admitted herself that it was her style,*
> *sonorous yet racy, polished yet eloquent,*
> *which was her strong point;*
> *and it was only in her prose that she had occasion to exhibit*
> *that delicious but restrained humor which her readers found so irresistible.*
> *It was not a humor of ideas, nor even a humor of words;*
> *it was much more subtle than that, it was a humor of punctuation:*
> *in a flash of inspiration she had discovered*
> *the comic possibilities of the semicolon,*
> *and of this she had made abundant and exquisite use.*
>
> — W. SOMERSET MAUGHAM, *The Creative Impulse* (1926)

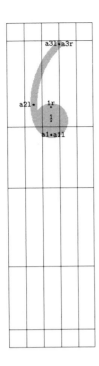

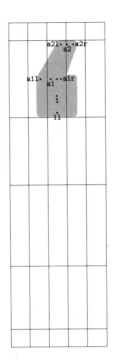

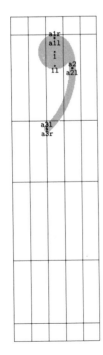

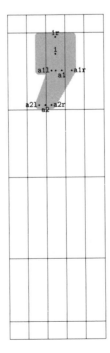

cmchar "Reverse apostrophe";
beginchar("`", $5u^\#$, $asc\_height^\#$, 0);
italcorr $asc\_height^\# * slant + .5dot\_size^\# - 2u^\#$;
adjust_fit$(0, 0)$;
$x_1 - .5dot\_size = \text{hround}(.5w - .5dot\_size)$; $y_1 + .5dot\_size = h - comma\_depth$;
if *monospace*: $ammoc(1, a, dot\_size, .28u, \text{vround } 1.5comma\_depth)$;   % large ammoc
else: $ammoc(1, a, dot\_size, .25u, comma\_depth)$; **fi**   % normal ammoc
penlabels(1); **endchar**;

cmchar "Apostrophe";
beginchar("'", $5u^\#$, $asc\_height^\#$, 0);
italcorr $asc\_height^\# * slant + .5dot\_size^\# - 2u^\#$;
adjust_fit$(0, 0)$;
$x_1 - .5dot\_size = \text{hround}(.5w - .5dot\_size)$; $y_1 + .5dot\_size = h$;
if *monospace*: $comma(1, a, dot\_size, .28u, \text{vround } 1.5comma\_depth)$;   % large comma
else: $comma(1, a, dot\_size, .25u, comma\_depth)$; **fi**   % comma with increased jut
penlabels(1); **endchar**;

---

def $ammoc$(**suffix** \$, @)(**expr** dot_size, jut, $depth$) =   % reversed comma
  pickup $fine.nib$; $pos_\$(dot\_size, 90)$;
  if $square\_dots$: $pos_{\$'}(dot\_size, 0)$; $z_{\$'} = z_\$$; $dot(\$', \$)$;   % squarish dot
    $comma\_join_- := \max(fine.breadth, \text{floor } .7dot\_size)$;
    $comma\_top_- := \max(fine.breadth, \text{floor } .5dot\_size)$;
    $pos_{@0}(comma\_join_-, 0)$; $pos_{@1}(comma\_join_-, 0)$;
    $pos_{@2}(comma\_top_-, 0)$; $y_{@0} = y_\$$; $y_{@1} = y_{\$r}$; $y_{@2} = y_{@1} + depth$;
    $x_{@0l} = x_{@1l} = x_{\$'l}$; $\text{lft } x_{@2l} = good.x(x_\$ + eps)$;
    filldraw stroke $z_{@0e} \text{ -- } z_{@1e} .. z_{@2e}$;   % tail
  else: $pos_{@1}(vair, 90)$; $pos_{@2}(vair, 0)$; $pos_{@3}(vair, -45)$;
    $z_{@1l} = z_{\$l}$; $\text{lft } x_{@2l} = \text{hround}(x_\$ - .5dot\_size - jut) - 2eps$; $x_{@3} = x_\$ + .5u$;
    $y_{@2} = \frac{1}{3}[y_{@1}, y_{@3}]$; $\text{top } y_{@3l} = \text{vround}(y_\$ + .5dot\_size + depth)$;
    $y_- := \text{ypart}((z_{@1}\{left\} \ldots z_{@2}\{up\} \ldots z_{@3})$
      $\text{intersectiontimes } (z_{\$r}\{left\} .. \{right\}z_{\$l}))$; **if** $y_- < 0$: $y_- := 1$; **fi**
    filldraw $z_{\$l}\{right\} .. \textbf{subpath}(0, y_-) \textbf{ of}(z_{\$r}\{left\} .. \{right\}z_{\$l}) \text{ -- cycle}$;   % dot
    filldraw stroke $z_{@1e}\{left\} \ldots z_{@2e}\{up\} \ldots z_{@3e}$; **fi**   % tail
  penlabels(@1, @2, @3); **enddef**;

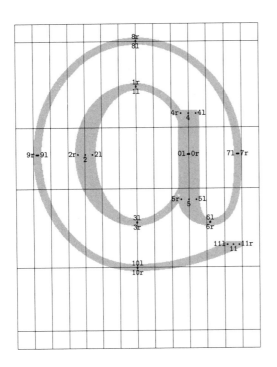

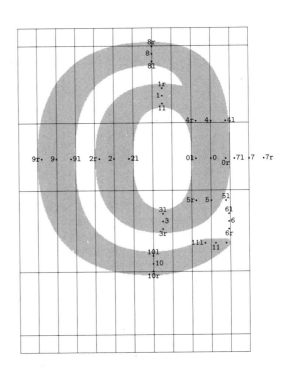

cmchar "At sign";
beginchar("@", $14u^\#$, $asc\_height^\#$, 0);
italcorr $.7asc\_height^\# * slant - .5u^\#$;
adjust_fit(0, **if** *hefty* or *monospace*: $-2u^\#$ **else**: 0 **fi**);
pickup *fine.nib*; $pos_0(fudged.hair, 0)$; $pos_1(vair, 90)$;
$pos_2(fudged.stem, 180)$; $pos_3(vair, 270)$;
$pos_4(fudged.stem, -180)$; $pos_5(fudged.stem, -180)$;
$pos_6(vair, -90)$; $pos_7(fudged.hair, 0)$;
$pos_8(vair, 90)$; $pos_9(fudged.hair, 180)$;
$pos_{10}(vair, 270)$; $pos_{11}(.5[vair, flare], 360)$;
$x_1 = x_3 = .5[x_0, x_2]$; $y_0 = y_2 = .5[y_1, y_3]$;
$x_8 = x_{10} = .5w$; $y_7 = y_9 = .5[y_8, y_{10}]$;
lft $x_{9r} =$ hround u; $x_7 = w - x_9$; *top* $y_{8r} = h + oo$; *bot* $y_{10r} = -oo$;
top $y_{1r} =$ vround$(.8[y_{10}, y_8] + .5vair)$; *bot* $y_{3r} =$ vround$(.2[y_{10}, y_8] - .5vair)$;
$x_{6l} = \frac{1}{3}[x_{5l}, x_{7l}]$; $y_6 = y_3$; $y_{11} = good.y(.1[y_{10}, y_8] - .5)$;
$x_0 = x_4 = x_5$; $y_4 = .8[y_3, y_1]$; $y_5 = \frac{2}{3}[y_7, y_6]$;
if *hefty* or *monospace*: *lft* $x_{2r} =$ hround$(5u - .5fudged.stem)$;
   rt $x_{0r} =$ hround$(w - 3u)$; $x_{11r} = x_{0r}$;
else: *lft* $x_{2r} =$ hround $3.4u$; $x_0 = w - x_2$; $x_{11r} = x_{7r}$; **fi**
filldraw stroke $super\_arc_e(1, 2)$ & $super\_arc_e(2, 3)$;   % left inner bowl
filldraw stroke $super\_arc_e(3, 0)$ & $super\_arc_e(0, 1)$;   % right inner bowl
filldraw stroke $super\_arc_e(8, 9)$ & $super\_arc_e(9, 10)$
   & $term.e(10, 11, right, 1, 4)$;   % left outer bowl and terminal
if *hefty* or *monospace*: {{ **interim** *superness* := *hein_super*;
    filldraw stroke $super\_arc_e(0, 8)$ }};   % link
else: $(x, y_{6r}) = whatever[z_{6l}, z_{7l}]$; $x_{6r} := x$;
    filldraw stroke z_{4e} --- $z_{5e} \ldots z_{6e}\{right\} \ldots \{up\}z_{7e}$
    & $super\_arc_e(7, 8)$; **fi**   % stem and link
penlabels($0, 1, 2, 3, 4, 5, 6, 7, 8, 9, 10, 11$); **endchar**;

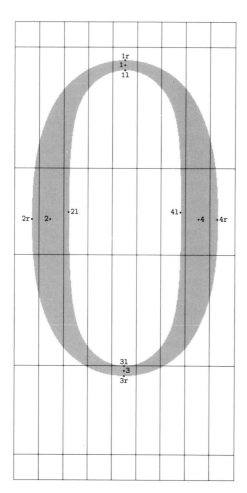

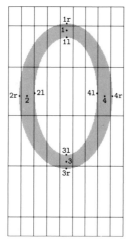

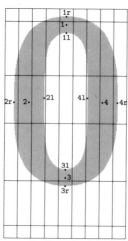

Here is program file `romand.mf`, which makes the numerals 0123456789. (Incidentally, it's curious that computer scientists always place 0 before the 1, while printers always place it after the 9.)

```
% Computer Modern Roman digits:
% This file contains the ten digits in so-called roman style.
% Character codes '060 through '071 are generated.
```

% All digits have the same height, width, depth, and italic correction.

cmchar "The numeral 0";
beginchar("0", $9u^\#$, $fig\_height^\#$, 0);
italcorr $fig\_height^\# * slant - .5u^\#$;
adjust_fit(0, 0);
$penpos_1(vair, 90)$; $penpos_3(vair, -90)$; $penpos_2(curve, 180)$; $penpos_4(curve, 0)$;
if not *monospace*: **interim** *superness* := sqrt($more\_super * hein\_super$); **fi**
$x_{2r} =$ hround max$(.7u, 1.45u - .5curve)$; $x_{4r} = w - x_{2r}$; $x_1 = x_3 = .5w$;
$y_{1r} = h + o$; $y_{3r} = -o$; $y_2 = y_4 = .5h - vair\_corr$; $y_{2l} := y_{4l} := .52h$;
penstroke $pulled\_arc_e(1, 2)$ & $pulled\_arc_e(2, 3)$
    & $pulled\_arc_e(3, 4)$ & $pulled\_arc_e(4, 1)$ & cycle;   % bowl
penlabels(1, 2, 3, 4); **endchar**;

*[Numbers] are the only characters which can actually be "read"
by all people of this earth, regardless of language.*

— HERMANN ZAPF, *The Changes in Letterforms
due to Technical Developments* (1968)

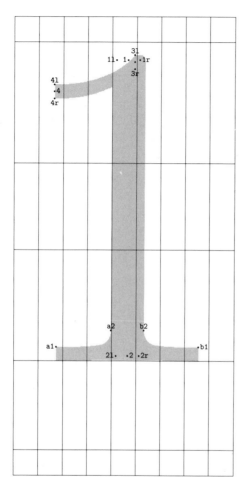

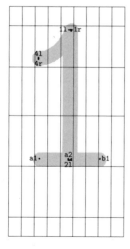

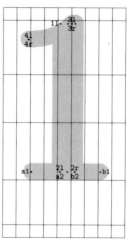

cmchar "The numeral 1";
beginchar("1", $9u^\#$, $\mathit{fig\_height}^\#$, 0);
italcorr $\mathit{fig\_height}^\# * slant - .5u^\#$;
adjust_fit$(0, 0)$;
numeric $\mathit{light\_stem}$; $\mathit{light_stem} = $ hround $.4[stem', cap\_stem']$;
pickup $tiny.nib$;
$\mathrm{pos}_1(\mathit{light\_stem}, 0)$; $\mathrm{pos}_2(\mathit{light\_stem}, 0)$;
$\mathit{lft}\ x_{1l} = \mathit{lft}\ x_{2l} = $ hround$(.5(w + .5u) - .5cap\_stem')$; $\mathit{top}\ y_1 = h + o$; $\mathit{bot}\ y_2 = 0$;
filldraw stroke z_{1e} -- z_{2e}; %% stem
if not $serifs$: **save** $slab$; $slab = bar$; **fi**
$\mathit{dish\_serif}(2, 1, a, \tfrac{1}{3}, \min(2.25u, \mathit{lft}\ x_{2l} - 1.5u)$,
    $b, \tfrac{1}{3}, \min(2.25u, w - 1.25u - \mathit{rt}\ x_{2r}))$; %% serif
pickup $crisp.nib$; $\mathrm{pos}_3(slab, -90)$; $\mathrm{pos}_4(bar, -90)$;
$\mathit{top}\ y_{3l} = h + o$; $\mathit{top}\ y_{4l} = $ **if** $monospace$: $.8$ **else**: $.9$ **fi** $h + o$;
$\mathit{lft}\ x_4 = \max(1.25u, tiny.\mathit{lft}\ x_{1l} - 2.35u)$;
$tiny.\mathit{rt}\ x_{1r} = \mathit{lft}\ x_3 + .25[tiny, hair]$;
erase fill $z_{3l}\{x_{4l} - x_{3l}, 3(y_{4l} - y_{3l})\} \ldots z_{4l}\{left\}$
    -- $(x_{4l}, h + o + 1)$ -- $(x_{3l}, h + o + 1)$ -- cycle; %% erase excess at top
filldraw stroke $z_{3e}\{x_{4e} - x_{3e}, 3(y_{4e} - y_{3e})\} \mathrel{..} z_{4e}\{left\}$; %% point
penlabels$(1, 2, 3, 4)$; **endchar**;

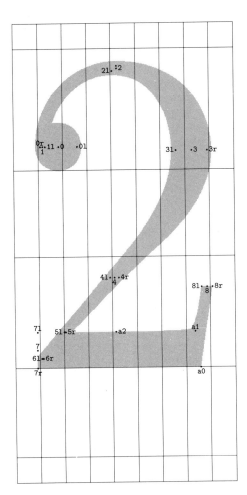

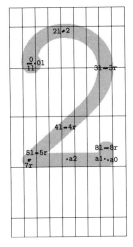

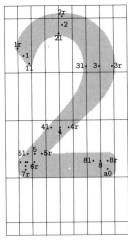

cmchar "The numeral 2";
beginchar("2", $9u\#$, $\mathit{fig\_height}\#$, 0);
italcorr $\mathit{fig\_height}\# * slant - .5u\#$;
adjust_fit$(0, 0)$;
numeric $\mathit{arm\_thickness}$, $\mathit{hair\_vair}$; $\mathit{hair\_vair} = .25[\mathit{vair}, \mathit{hair}]$;
$\mathit{arm\_thickness} = \mathrm{Vround}(\mathbf{if}\ \mathit{hefty}\colon \mathit{slab} + 2\mathit{stem\_corr}\ \mathbf{else}\colon .4[\mathit{stem}, \mathit{cap\_stem}]\ \mathbf{fi})$;
pickup $\mathit{crisp.nib}$; $\mathit{pos}_7(\mathit{arm\_thickness}, -90)$; $\mathit{pos}_8(\mathit{hair}, 0)$;
$\mathit{bot}\ y_{7r} = 0$; $\mathit{lft}\ x_7 = \mathrm{hround}\ .9u$;
$\mathit{rt}\ x_{8r} = \mathrm{hround}(w - .9u)$; $y_8 = \mathit{good.y}(y_{7l} + \mathit{beak}/2) + \mathit{eps}$;
$\mathrm{arm}(7, 8, a, .3\mathit{beak\_darkness}, \mathit{beak\_jut})$;   % arm and beak
pickup $\mathit{fine.nib}$; $\mathit{pos}_2(\mathit{slab}, 90)$; $\mathit{pos}_3(.4[\mathit{curve}, \mathit{cap\_curve}], 0)$;
$\mathit{top}\ y_{2r} = h + o$; $x_2 = .5(w - .5u)$; $\mathit{rt}\ x_{3r} = \mathrm{hround}(w - .9u)$; $y_3 + .5\mathit{vair} = .75h$;
if serifs: **numeric** $\mathit{bulb\_diam}$; $\mathit{bulb\_diam} = \mathrm{hround}(\mathit{flare} + {}^2\!/_3(\mathit{cap\_stem} - \mathit{stem}))$;
$\quad \mathit{pos}_0(\mathit{bulb\_diam}, 180)$; $\mathit{pos}_1(\mathit{cap\_hair}, 180)$;
$\quad \mathit{lft}\ x_{1r} = \mathrm{hround}\ .9u$; $y_1 - .5\mathit{bulb\_diam} = {}^2\!/_3h$;
$\quad (x, y_{2l}) = \mathit{whatever}[z_{1l}, z_{2r}]$; $x_{2l} := x$; $\mathrm{bulb}(2, 1, 0)$;   % bulb and arc
else: $x_{2l} := x_{2l} - .25u$; $\mathit{pos}_1(\mathit{flare}, \mathrm{angle}(-9u, h))$;
$\quad \mathit{lft}\ x_{1r} = \mathrm{hround}\ .75u$; $\mathit{bot}\ y_{1l} = \mathrm{vround}\ .7h$;
$\quad y_{1r} := \mathit{good.y}\ y_{1r} + \mathit{eps}$; $x_{1l} := \mathit{good.x}\ x_{1l}$;
$\quad$ **filldraw stroke** $\mathit{term.e}(2, 1, \mathit{left}, .9, 4)$; **fi**   % terminal and arc
$\mathit{pos}_4(.25[\mathit{hair\_vair}, \mathit{cap\_stem}], 0)$;
$\mathit{pos}_5(\mathit{hair\_vair}, 0)$; $\mathit{pos}_6(\mathit{hair\_vair}, 0)$;
$y_5 = \mathit{arm\_thickness}$; $y_4 = .3[y_5, y_3]$; $\mathit{top}\ y_6 = \min(y_5, \mathit{slab}, \mathit{top}\ y_{7l})$;
$\mathit{lft}\ x_{6l} = \mathit{crisp.lft}\ x_7$; $z_{4l} = \mathit{whatever}[z_{6l}, (x_{3l}, \mathit{bot}\ .58h)]$; $z_{5l} = \mathit{whatever}[z_{6l}, z_{4l}]$;
erase fill z_{4l} -- z_{6l} -- $\mathit{lft}\ z_{6l}$ -- $(\mathit{lft}\ x_{6l}, y_{4l})$ -- cycle;   % erase excess at left
filldraw stroke $z_{2e}\{\mathit{right}\}$ .. tension atleast .9 and atleast 1
$\quad$ .. $z_{3e}\{\mathit{down}\}$ .. z_{4e} --- z_{5e} -- z_{6e};   % stroke
penlabels$(0, 1, 2, 3, 4, 5, 6, 7, 8)$; **endchar**;

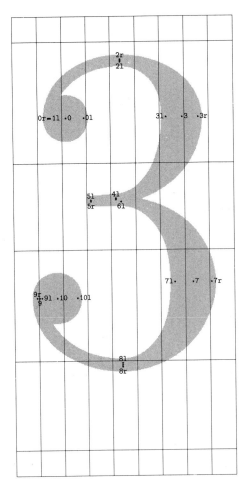

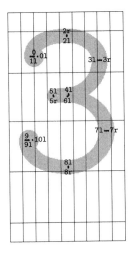

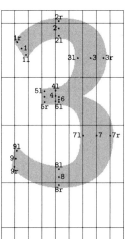

cmchar "The numeral 3";
beginchar("3", $9u^\#$, $\mathit{fig\_height}^\#$, 0);
italcorr $\mathit{fig\_height}^\# * \mathit{slant} - .5u^\#$;
adjust_fit(0, 0);
numeric $\mathit{top\_thickness}$, $\mathit{mid\_thickness}$, $\mathit{bot\_thickness}$;
$\mathit{top\_thickness} = \max(\mathit{fine.breadth}, \mathrm{vround}(\mathit{slab} - 2\mathit{vair\_corr}))$;
$\mathit{mid\_thickness} = \max(\mathit{fine.breadth}, \mathrm{vround}\ \tfrac{2}{3}\mathit{vair})$;
$\mathit{bot\_thickness} = \max(\mathit{fine.breadth}, \mathrm{vround}(\mathit{slab} - \mathit{vair\_corr}))$;
pickup $\mathit{fine.nib}$; $\mathit{pos}_2(\mathit{top\_thickness}, 90)$; $\mathit{top}\ y_{2r} = h + o$;
$\mathit{pos}_3(\max(\mathit{fine.breadth}, .6[\mathit{curve}, \mathit{cap\_curve}] - \mathit{stem\_corr}), 0)$;
$\mathit{rt}\ x_{3r} = \mathrm{hround}(w - 1.25u)$;
$\mathit{pos}_4(\mathit{vair}, -90)$; $\mathit{pos}_5(\mathit{vair}, -90)$;
$\mathit{pos}_6(\mathit{mid\_thickness}, 90)$; $x_2 = x_6 = x_8 = .5[1.5u, x_7]$;
$\mathit{pos}_7(\mathit{cap\_curve}, 0)$; $\mathit{rt}\ x_{7r} = \mathrm{hround}(w - .75u)$; $\mathit{lft}\ x_5 = \min(\mathrm{hround}\ 3u, \mathit{lft}\ x_6) - \mathit{eps}$;
$\mathit{pos}_8(\mathit{bot\_thickness}, -90)$; $\mathit{bot}\ y_{8r} = -o$;
$y_3 = .6[\mathit{top}\ y_{4l}, \mathit{bot}\ y_{2l}]$; $y_7 = .5[\mathit{bot}\ y_{6l}, \mathit{top}\ y_{8l}]$;
$\mathit{top}\ y_{5l} = \mathrm{vround}(.54h + .5\mathit{vair})$; $y_{5r} = y_{6l}$;
$x_4 = \tfrac{1}{3}[x_5, x_{3l}]$; $z_4 = z_5 + \mathit{whatever} * (150u, h)$;
filldraw stroke $\mathit{pulled\_super\_arc}_e(2, 3)(.5\mathit{superpull})$
    & $z_{3e}\{\mathit{down}\} \ldots z_{4e} \mathrel{-\!-\!-} z_{5e}$;   % upper bowl
filldraw $z_{5r} \mathrel{-\!-} z_{6l} \mathrel{-\!-} z_{6r} \mathrel{-\!-} z_{5l} \mathrel{-\!-\!-} \mathrm{cycle}$;   % middle tip
filldraw stroke $\mathit{pulled\_super\_arc}_e(6, 7)(.5\mathit{superpull})$
    & $\mathit{pulled\_super\_arc}_e(7, 8)(.5\mathit{superpull})$;   % lower bowl
if *serifs*: **numeric** $\mathit{bulb\_diam}[\,]$;
   $\mathit{bulb\_diam}_1 = \mathit{flare} + .5(\mathit{cap\_stem} - \mathit{stem})$; $\mathit{bulb\_diam}_2 = \mathit{flare} + \mathit{cap\_stem} - \mathit{stem}$;
   $\mathit{pos}_0(\mathit{bulb\_diam}_1, 180)$; $\mathit{pos}_1(\mathit{hair}, 180)$;
   $\mathit{lft}\ x_{0r} = \mathrm{hround}\ 1.25u$; $y_0 = \min(.9h - .5\mathit{bulb\_diam}_1, .75h + .5\mathit{bulb\_diam}_1)$;
   $\mathit{bulb}(2, 1, 0)$;   % upper bulb
   $\mathit{pos}_{10}(\mathit{bulb\_diam}_2, -180)$; $\mathit{pos}_9(\mathit{cap\_hair}, -180)$;
   $\mathit{lft}\ x_{10r} = \mathrm{hround}\ .75u$; $y_{10} = \max(.1h + .5\mathit{bulb\_diam}_2, .3h - .5\mathit{bulb\_diam}_2)$;
   $\mathit{bulb}(8, 9, 10)$;   % lower bulb
else: $\mathit{pos}_1(.5[\mathit{vair}, \mathit{flare}], \mathrm{angle}(-8u, h))$;
   $\mathit{lft}\ x_{1r} = \mathrm{hround}\ u$; $\mathit{bot}\ y_{1l} = \mathrm{vround}\ .75h + o$;
   $y_{1r} := \mathit{good.y}\ y_{1r} + \mathit{eps}$; $x_{1l} := \mathit{good.x}\ x_{1l}$;
   $\mathit{pos}_9(\mathit{bot\_thickness}, \mathrm{angle}(-2u, -h))$;
   $\mathit{lft}\ x_{9r} = \mathrm{hround}\ .75u$; $\mathit{top}\ y_{9l} = \mathrm{vround}\ .25h - o$;
   $y_{9r} := \mathit{good.y}\ y_{9r} - \mathit{eps}$; $x_{9l} := \mathit{good.x}\ x_{9l}$;
   filldraw stroke $\mathit{term.e}(2, 1, \mathit{left}, 1, 4)$;   % upper terminal
   filldraw stroke $\mathit{term.e}(8, 9, \mathit{left}, 1, 4)$; **fi**   % lower terminal
penlabels(0, 1, 2, 3, 4, 5, 6, 7, 8, 9, 10); **endchar**;

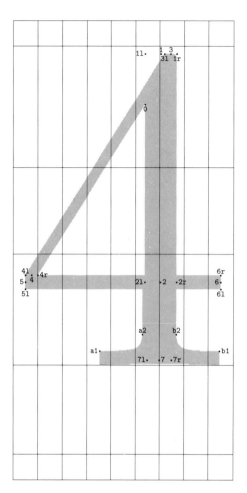

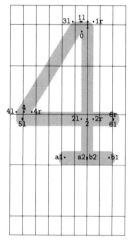

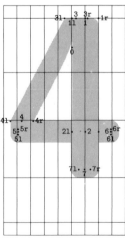

cmchar "The numeral 4";
beginchar("4", $9u^\#$, $\textit{fig\_height}^\#$, 0);
italcorr $\textit{fig\_height}^\# * slant - .5u^\#$;
adjust_fit(0, 0);
numeric $\textit{light\_stem}$, $\textit{light\_stem}'$, $\textit{diag\_stem}$, $\textit{alpha}$, $\textit{cut}$; $\textit{cut} = .75\textit{notch\_cut}$;
$\textit{light_stem} = $ hround $.4[\textit{fudged.stem}, \textit{fudged.cap\_stem}]$;
$\textit{light_stem}' = $ hround $\max(\textit{tiny.breadth}, \textit{light\_stem} - 2\textit{stem\_corr})$;
$\textit{diag\_stem} = \max(\textit{tiny.breadth}, .4[\textit{vair}, \textit{fudged.hair}])$;
pickup $\textit{crisp.nib}$; $\textit{pos}_5(\textit{cap\_bar}, 90)$; $\textit{pos}_6(\textit{cap\_bar}, 90)$;
$\textit{lft } x_5 = $ hround $.5u$; $\textit{rt } x_6 = $ hround$(w - .5u)$;
$\textit{top } y_{5r} = $ vround(**if** $\textit{serifs}$: $5/18[\textit{slab}, h - \textit{light\_stem}] + 1$
   else: $.35(h - \textit{light\_stem})$ **fi** $+ .5\textit{cap\_bar}$);
$z_{4l} = \textit{top lft } z_{5r}$; $y_2 = y_{2'} = y_5 = y_6$; $x_{1r} = x_{2r} = $ hround$(w - 3u + .5\textit{light\_stem})$;
$\textit{penpos}_1(\textit{light\_stem}', 0)$; $\textit{penpos}_2(\textit{light\_stem}', 0)$; $y_1 = y_3 = h + \textit{apex\_o} + \textit{apex\_oo}$;
$x_{3r} + \textit{apex\_corr} = x_{1r}$; $\textit{alpha} = \textit{diag\_ratio}(1, \textit{diag\_stem}, y_3 - y_{4l}, x_{3r} - x_{4l})$;
$\textit{penpos}_3(\textit{alpha} * \textit{diag\_stem}, 0)$; $\textit{penpos}_4(\textit{alpha} * \textit{diag\_stem}, 0)$;
$x_0 = x_{1l}$; $z_0 = \textit{whatever}[z_{3r}, z_{4r}]$;
$x_{5'} = x_5$; $z_{5''} = z_{5'} + $ **penoffset** $z_4 - z_3$ **of** $\textit{currentpen} = \textit{whatever}[z_{4l}, z_{3l}]$;
fill $\textit{diag\_end}(2r, 1r, 1, .5, 3l, 4l)$ `---` $z_{5''}$ $\ldots$ $\textit{lft } z_{5'}$
   `---` $\textit{lft } z_{5l}$ `--` (x_{4r}, y_{5l}) `--` z_{4r}
   if $y_0 < h - \textit{cut}$: $\{z_{3r} - z_{4r}\}$ $\ldots$ $\{up\}(x_{1l} - 1, h - \textit{cut})$
      `--` $(x_{1l}, h - \textit{cut})$ **else**: `--` z_0 **fi**
   `--` z_{2l} `--` z_{2r} `--` cycle;   % diagonal and upper stem
filldraw stroke z_{5e} `--` z_{6e};   % bar
pickup $\textit{tiny.nib}$; $\textit{pos}_7(\textit{light\_stem}, 0)$; $\textit{rt } x_{7r} = x_{1r}$; $\textit{bot } y_7 = 0$;
$\textit{pos}_{2'}(\textit{light\_stem}, 0)$; $x_{2'} = x_7$;
filldraw stroke $z_{2'e}$ `--` z_{7e};   % lower stem
if $\textit{serifs}$: $\textit{dish\_serif}(7, 2', a, 1/3, 1.75u,$
      $b, 1/3, \min(1.75u, w - .5u - \textit{rt } x_{7r}))$; **fi**   % serif
penlabels(0, 1, 2, 3, 4, 5, 6, 7); **endchar**;

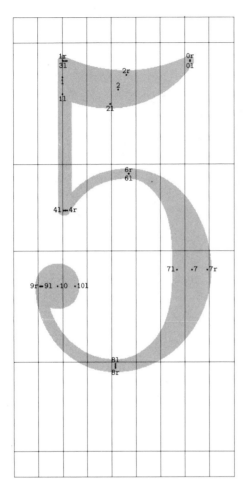

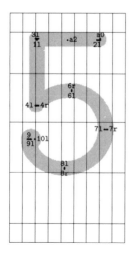

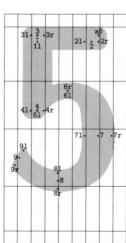

cmchar "The numeral 5";
beginchar("5", $9u^\#$, $fig\_height^\#$, 0);
italcorr $fig\_height^\# * slant - .5u^\#$;
adjust_fit$(0, 0)$;
numeric $bot\_thickness$, $light\_hair$;
$bot\_thickness = \max(fine.breadth, \text{vround}(slab - vair\_corr))$;
$light\_hair = \text{hround}(cap\_hair$ **if** $hefty: -2stem\_corr$ **fi**$)$;
pickup $tiny.nib$; $pos_5(vair, 180)$; $pos_6(vair, 90)$;
$bot\ y_5 = \text{vround}(.53h - vair)$;
$top\ y_{6r} = \max(\text{vround } .61803h + o, top\ y_{6r} + y_5 + eps - y_{6l})$;
$pos_3(light\_hair, 0)$; $pos_4(light\_hair, 0)$;
$lft\ x_{3l} = \max(1.35u, 2.1u - .5light\_hair)$; $x_3 = x_4 = x_5$; $y_4 = y_5$;
$top\ y_3 = h$ **if** not $hefty: + o$ **fi**;
filldraw stroke z_{3e} `--` z_{4e};   % thin stem
$penpos_7(cap\_stem - fine, 0)$; $penpos_8(bot\_thickness - fine, -90)$;
$fine.rt\ x_{7r} = \text{hround}(w - .9u)$; $x_8 = .5[u, x_7]$; $x_6 = .5[x_5, x_7]$;
erase fill z_5 `--` $bot\ z_5$ `--` $(x_6, bot\ y_5)$ `--` $z_6\{left\}$
   `..` tension .9 and 1 `..` $\{x_5 - x_6, 3(y_5 - y_6)\}$ cycle;   % erase excess in middle
filldraw stroke $z_{6e}\{left\}$ `..` tension .9 and 1 `..` $\{x_5 - x_6, 3(y_5 - y_6)\}z_{5e}$;   % link
pickup $fine.nib$; $pos_{6'}(vair, 90)$; $z_{6'} = z_6$;
$y_7 = .5[y_6, y_8]$; $bot\ y_{8r} = -o$;
filldraw stroke $pulled\_arc_e(6', 7)$ & $pulled\_arc_e(7, 8)$;   % bowl
if $serifs$: $pos_9(hair, -180)$; $y_9 = .5y_5$; $lft\ x_{9r} = \text{hround } .9u$;
   $pos_{10}(flare + \frac{1}{3}(cap\_stem - stem), -180)$; $bulb(8, 9, 10)$;   % bulb
else: $pos_9(\frac{3}{7}[bot\_thickness, flare], angle(-7u, -h))$;
   $lft\ x_{9r} = \text{hround}(tiny.lft\ x_{3l} - .75u)$; $bot\ y_{9r} = \text{vround } .15h - o$;
   $x_{9l} := good.x\ x_{9l}$; $y_{9l} := good.y\ y_{9l}$;
   filldraw stroke $term.e(8, 9, left, 1, 4)$; **fi**   % terminal
if $hefty$: **pickup** $crisp.nib$; $pos_1(slab, 90)$; $pos_2(hair, 0)$;
   $top\ y_{1r} = h$; $x_1 = x_4$; $rt\ x_{2r} = \text{hround}(w - 1.5u)$; $y_2 = y_{1l} - eps$;
   $arm(1, 2, a, 0, 0)$;   % arm
else: **numeric** $flag\_breadth$; $flag\_breadth = \frac{7}{8}[vair, cap\_curve]$;
   $pos_1(flag\_breadth, 90)$; $pos_2(flag\_breadth, 60)$;
   $pos_0(vair, 90)$; $top\ y_{1r} = tiny.top\ y_3$; $top\ y_{2r} = \text{vround } .95h + o$; $y_{0r} = y_{1r}$;
   $lft\ x_1 = tiny.lft\ x_{3l}$; $x_{2r} = .5[x_1, x_0]$; $rt\ x_0 = \text{hround}(w - 1.6u)$;
   erase fill $top\ z_{1r}$ `--` z_{1r} `...` $\{right\}z_{2r}$
      `--` $(x_{2r}, top\ y_{1r})$ `--` cycle;   % erase excess at top
   filldraw stroke z_{1e} `...` $\{right\}z_{2e}$ `...` z_{0e}; **fi**   % flag
penlabels$(0, 1, 2, 3, 4, 5, 6, 7, 8, 9, 10)$; **endchar**;

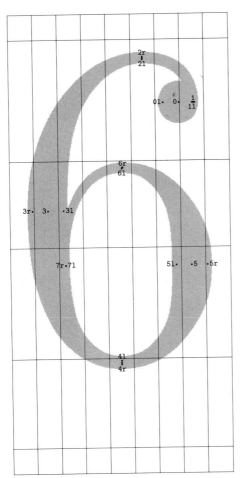

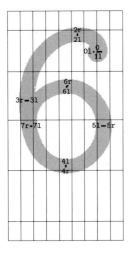

```
cmchar "The numeral 6";
```
beginchar("6", $9u^\#$, $fig\_height^\#$, 0);

italcorr $fig\_height^\# * slant - .5u^\#$;

adjust_fit(0, 0);

numeric $top\_thickness$, $bot\_thickness$, $side\_thickness$, $pull$;

$top\_thickness = \max(fine.breadth, \mathrm{vround}(slab - 2vair\_corr))$;

$bot\_thickness = \max(fine.breadth, \mathrm{vround}(slab - vair\_corr))$;

$side\_thickness = \max(fine.breadth, \mathrm{hround}\ \frac{1}{3}[curve, cap\_curve])$;

$pull = \min(.25, 1.5superpull)$;

pickup $fine.nib$; $pos_2(top\_thickness, -270)$;

$pos_3(side\_thickness, -180)$; $pos_4(bot\_thickness, -90)$;

$pos_5(side\_thickness, 0)$; $pos_6(vair, 90)$;

$lft\ x_{3r} = w - rt\ x_{5r} = \mathrm{hround}\ \max(.75u, 1.5u - .5side\_thickness)$;

$x_4 = x_6 - .1u = x_2 - u = .5w$;

$top\ y_{2r} = h + o$; $y_3 = .5[y_2, y_4]$; $bot\ y_{4r} = -o$;

$y_5 = .5[y_4, y_6]$; $top\ y_6 = \mathrm{vround}\ \frac{5}{8}h + o$;

path p; $p = pulled\_super\_arc_l(3, 4)(pull)$;

numeric t; $t = \mathrm{xpart}(p\ \mathrm{intersectiontimes}\ ((x_{3r}, y_5)\ \text{-{}-}\ (x_4, y_5)))$;

$pos_7(thin\_join, 180)$; $z_{7l} = \textbf{point } t \textbf{ of } p$;

$(x, y_{6r}) = whatever[z_{7l}, z_{6l}]$; $x_{6r} := \min(x, .5[x_{5r}, x_6])$;

filldraw stroke $pulled\_super\_arc_e(2, 3)(pull)$

    & {{ **interim** $superness := more\_super$; $pulled\_super\_arc_e(3, 4)(pull)$ }}

    & {{$less\_tense$; $pulled\_super\_arc_e(4, 5)(pull)$ & $pulled\_super\_arc_e(5, 6)(pull)$ }}

    & $z_{6e}\{left\}\ \dots\ \{\textbf{direction } t \textbf{ of } p\}z_{7e}$;   % arc and bowl

if $serifs$: $pos_1(hair, -360)$; $pos_0(flare, -360)$;

    $rt\ x_{0r} = \max(rt\ x_2 + eps, \mathrm{hround}(w - 1.2u))$;

    $y_0 = \mathrm{vround}\ \min(.9h - .5flare, .85h + .5flare) + o$;

    {{$less\_tense$; $bulb(2, 1, 0)$ }};   % arc and bulb

else: $pos_1(\mathrm{vround}\ .1[top\_thickness, flare], 90)$;

    $top\ y_{1r} = \mathrm{vround}\ .97h + o$; $rt\ x_1 = \mathrm{hround}(x_5 - .5)$;

    filldraw stroke $term.e(2, 1, right, .9, 4)$; **fi**   % terminal

penlabels(0, 1, 2, 3, 4, 5, 6, 7); **endchar**;

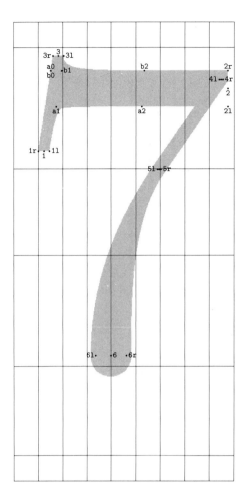

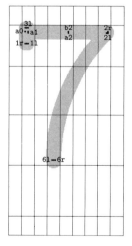

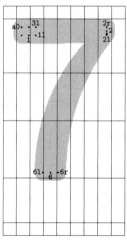

cmchar "The numeral 7";
beginchar("7", $9u^{\#}$, $fig\_height^{\#}$, 0);
italcorr $fig\_height^{\#} * slant - .5u^{\#}$;
adjust_fit$(0, 0)$;
numeric $arm\_thickness$, bot_width, top_shift, top_hair;
if *hefty*: $arm\_thickness = \mathrm{Vround}(slab + 2stem\_corr)$; $top\_shift = 0$;
  $bot\_width = \mathrm{hround}\ .51[curve, cap\_curve]$; $top\_hair = .4[thin\_join, bot\_width]$;
else: $arm\_thickness = \mathrm{Vround}\ .4[stem, cap\_stem]$; $top\_shift = .5u$;
  $bot\_width = flare$; $top\_hair = cap\_hair$; **fi**
if $top\_hair < tiny.breadth$: $top\_hair := tiny.breadth$; **fi**
pickup $crisp.nib$; $pos_2(arm\_thickness, 90)$; $pos_1(hair, 180)$;
$top\ y_{2r} = h$; $rt\ x_2 = \mathrm{hround}(w - .75u + top\_shift)$;
$lft\ x_{1r} = \mathrm{hround}(.75u + .5top\_shift)$; $y_1 = good.y(y_{2l} - beak/2) - eps$;
$arm(2, 1, a, .3beak\_darkness, -beak\_jut)$;   % arm and beak
$pos_3(hair, 180)$; $y_3 = good.y(y_{2r} + beak/6) + eps$; $z_{3r} = whatever[z_{1r}, z_{a0}]$;
$penpos_{2'}(eps, -90)$; $z_{2'} = z_{2r}$;
$arm(2', 3, b, beak\_darkness, x_{3r} - x_{a0})$;   % upward extension of beak
pickup $tiny.nib$; $pos_4(top\_hair, 0)$; $pos_6(bot\_width, 0)$;
$bot\ y_4 = \max(h - arm\_thickness, h - slab, bot\ y_{2l})$; $rt\ x_{4r} = crisp.rt\ x_2$;
$lft\ x_{6l} = \mathrm{hround}(3.5u + top\_shift - .5bot\_width)$;
if *serifs*: $y_6 - .5bot\_width = -o$; **filldraw** $z_{6l}\{down\} \mathbin{..} \{up\}z_{6r}$ -- cycle;   % bulb
else: $bot\ y_6 = -oo$; **fi**
if *hefty*: **erase fill** $rt\ z_{4r}$ -- $z_{4r} \ldots \{down\}z_{6r}$
     -- $(rt\ x_{4r}, y_6)$ -- cycle;   % erase excess at top
  filldraw stroke $z_{4e} \ldots \{down\}z_{6e}$;   % stroke
else: $pos_5(top\_hair, 0)$; $y_5 = {}^2\!/_3 h$; $z_5 = whatever[z_4, (.75u, y_6)]$;
  erase fill $rt\ z_{4r}$ -- z_{4r} -- z_{5r} -- $(rt\ x_{4r}, y_5)$ -- cycle;   % erase excess at top
  filldraw stroke z_{4e} --- $z_{5e} \ldots \{down\}z_{6e}$; **fi**   % stroke
penlabels$(1, 2, 3, 4, 5, 6)$; **endchar**;

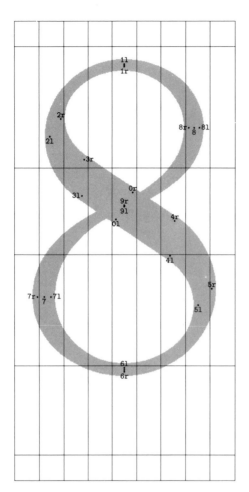

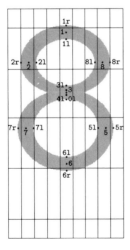

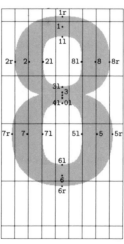

cmchar "The numeral 8";
beginchar("8", $9u^\#$, *fig_height*$^\#$, 0);
italcorr *fig_height*$^\#$ $* slant - .5u^\#$;
adjust_fit(0, 0);
numeric *top_thickness*, *mid_thickness*, *bot_thickness*, *upper_side*, *lower_side*, *theta*;
top_thickness = max(*fine.breadth*, vround(*slab* $- 2vair\_corr$));
bot_thickness = max(*fine.breadth*, vround(*slab* $- vair\_corr$));
$x_0 = .5w$; $y_0 = .54h$;
if *hefty*: *mid_thickness* = vround $^2/_3 vair$; *upper_side* = hround(*stem* $- 3stem\_corr$);
   lower_side = hround min(.5[*curve*, *cap_curve*] $- stem\_corr$, *upper_side* $+ .25u$);
   $penpos_1(top\_thickness, 90)$; $penpos_2(upper\_side, 180)$;
   $penpos_3(mid\_thickness, 270)$; $penpos_8(upper\_side, 360)$;
   $penpos_4(mid\_thickness, 90)$; $penpos_7(lower\_side, 180)$;
   $penpos_6(bot\_thickness, 270)$; $penpos_5(lower\_side, 360)$;
   $penpos_0(vair, 90)$; $z_{3l} = z_{0r}$; $z_{4l} = z_{0l}$;
   $x_1 = x_6 = .5w$; $x_{2r} = w - x_{8r} = $ hround u; $x_{7r} = w - x_{5r} = $ hround $.75u$;
   top $y_{1r} = h + o$; bot $y_{6r} = -o$; $y_2 = y_8 = .5[y_{1l}, y_{3l}]$; $y_7 = y_5 = .5[y_{4l}, y_{6l}]$;
   filldraw stroke $pulled\_arc_e(1, 2)$
      & $pulled\_arc_e(2, 3)$;   % left half of upper bowl
   filldraw stroke $pulled\_arc_e(4, 5)$
      & $pulled\_arc_e(5, 6)$;   % right half of lower bowl
   filldraw stroke $pulled\_arc_e(6, 7)$
      & $pulled\_arc_e(7, 4)$;   % left half of lower bowl
   filldraw stroke $pulled\_arc_e(3, 8)$
      & $pulled\_arc_e(8, 1)$;   % right half of upper bowl
else: pickup *fine.nib*; *theta* = $90 - $ angle($18u$, h); *slope* := $-h/18u$;
   upper_side = max(*fine.breadth*, hround(.5[*hair*, *stem*] $- stem\_corr$));
   lower_side = hround(.5[*hair*, *stem*] $+ stem\_corr$);
   $pos_1(top\_thickness, -90)$; $pos_6(bot\_thickness, -90)$;
   $x_1 = x_6 = .5w$; top $y_{1l} = h + o$; bot $y_{6r} = -o$; $pos_0(cap\_stem, theta)$;
   lft $x_{2l} = w - $ rt $x_{8l} = $ hround $1.25u$; lft $x_{7r} = w - $ rt $x_{5r} = $ hround $.75u$;
   $x_{2r} - x_{2l} = upper\_side - fine$; $x_{5r} - x_{5l} = lower\_side - fine$;
   ellipse_set($1l$, $2l$, $3l$, $0l$); *ellipse_set*($1r$, $2r$, $3r$, $0r$);
   ellipse_set($6l$, $5l$, $4l$, $0l$); *ellipse_set*($6r$, $5r$, $4r$, $0r$);
   numeric *tau*; *tau* = max(.8, $.20710678/(superness - .5)$);
   filldraw stroke $z_{1e}\{left\}$ .. tension atleast *tau* .. $z_{2e}\{down\}$
      .. z_{3e} --- z_{4e} .. $z_{5e}\{down\}$ .. tension atleast *tau* .. $z_{6e}\{left\}$;   % S stroke
   $pos_7(lower\_side, 180)$; $pos_8(upper\_side, 180)$;
   $y_7 = .5[y_{5l}, y_{5r}]$; $y_8 = .5[y_{2l}, y_{2r}]$; $pos_9(vair, 90)$; $z_9 = z_0$;
   filldraw stroke $z_{1e}\{right\}$ .. tension atleast *tau* .. $z_{8e}\{down\}$
      .. tension atleast *tau* and atleast 1 .. $\{-18u, -.618h\}z_{9e}$;   % upper right stroke
   filldraw stroke $z_{6e}\{left\}$ .. tension atleast *tau* .. $z_{7e}\{up\}$
      .. tension atleast *tau* and atleast 1 .. $\{18u, .5h\}z_{9e}$; **fi**   % lower left stroke
penlabels(0, 1, 2, 3, 4, 5, 6, 7, 8, 9); **endchar**;

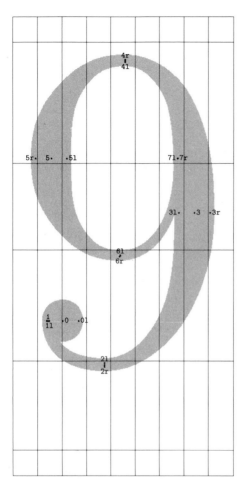

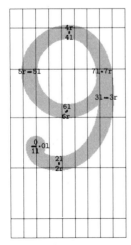

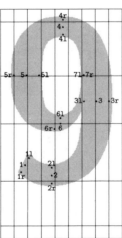

cmchar "The numeral 9";
beginchar("9", $9u^\#$, $\mathit{fig\_height}^\#$, 0);
italcorr $\mathit{fig\_height}^\# * \mathit{slant} - .5u^\#$;
adjust_fit(0, 0);
numeric $\mathit{top\_thickness}$, $\mathit{bot\_thickness}$, $\mathit{side\_thickness}$, pull;
$\mathit{top\_thickness} = \max(\mathit{fine.breadth}, \mathrm{vround}(\mathit{slab} - 2\mathit{vair\_corr}))$;
$\mathit{bot\_thickness} = \max(\mathit{fine.breadth}, \mathrm{vround}(\mathit{slab} - \mathit{vair\_corr}))$;
$\mathit{side\_thickness} = \max(\mathit{fine.breadth}, \mathrm{hround}\ ^1\!/_3[\mathit{curve}, \mathit{cap\_curve}])$;
$\mathit{pull} = \min(.25, 1.5\mathit{superpull})$;
pickup $\mathit{fine.nib}$; $\mathit{pos}_2(\mathit{bot\_thickness}, -90)$;
$\mathit{pos}_3(\mathit{side\_thickness}, 0)$; $\mathit{pos}_4(\mathit{top\_thickness}, 90)$;
$\mathit{pos}_5(\mathit{side\_thickness}, 180)$; $\mathit{pos}_6(\mathit{vair}, 270)$;
$w - \mathit{rt}\ x_{3r} = \mathit{lft}\ x_{5r} = \mathrm{hround}\max(.75u, 1.5u - .5\mathit{side\_thickness})$;
$x_4 - .1u = x_6 + .1u = x_2 + .75u = .5w$;
$\mathit{bot}\ y_{2r} = -o$; $y_3 = .5[y_2, y_4]$; $\mathit{top}\ y_{4r} = h + o$;
$y_5 = .5[y_4, y_6]$; $\mathit{bot}\ y_6 = \mathrm{vround}\ ^3\!/_8h - o$;
path p; $p = \mathit{pulled\_super\_arc}_l(3, 4)(\mathit{pull})$;
numeric t; $t = \mathrm{xpart}(p\ \mathrm{intersectiontimes}\ ((x_{3r}, y_5) \mathbin{--} (x_4, y_5)))$;
$\mathit{pos}_7(\mathit{thin\_join}, 360)$; $z_{7l} = \textbf{point } t \textbf{ of } p$;
$(x, y_{6r}) = \mathit{whatever}[z_{7l}, z_{6l}]$; $x_{6r} := \max(x, .5[x_{5r}, x_6])$;
filldraw stroke $\mathit{pulled\_super\_arc}_e(2, 3)(\mathit{pull})$
    & {{ **interim** $\mathit{superness} := \mathit{more\_super}$; $\mathit{pulled\_super\_arc}_e(3, 4)(\mathit{pull})$ }}
    & {{$\mathit{less\_tense}$; $\mathit{pulled\_super\_arc}_e(4, 5)(\mathit{pull})$ & $\mathit{pulled\_super\_arc}_e(5, 6)(\mathit{pull})$}}
    & $z_{6e}\{\mathbf{right}\} \ldots \{\textbf{direction } t \textbf{ of } p\}z_{7e}$;   % arc and bowl
if serifs: $\mathit{pos}_1(\mathit{hair}, -180)$; $\mathit{pos}_0(\mathit{flare}, -180)$;
   $\mathit{lft}\ x_{0r} = \min(\mathit{lft}\ x_2 - \mathit{eps}, \mathrm{hround}\ 1.2u)$;
   $y_0 = \mathrm{vround}\max(.1h + .5\mathit{flare}, .15h - .5\mathit{flare}) - o$;
   {{$\mathit{less\_tense}$; $\mathit{bulb}(2, 1, 0)$}};   % arc and bulb
else: $\mathit{pos}_1(.1[\mathit{bot\_thickness}, \mathit{flare}], -120)$;
   $\mathit{bot}\ y_{1r} = \mathrm{vround}\ .07h - o$; $\mathit{lft}\ x_{1r} = \mathrm{hround}\ 1.3u$;
   filldraw stroke $\mathit{term.e}(2, 1, \mathit{left}, .9, 4)$; **fi**   % terminal
penlabels(0, 1, 2, 3, 4, 5, 6, 7); **endchar**;

cmr10

cmtt10

cmssbx10

The program file `roman1.mf` was hardest of all to prepare, because the lowercase alphabet is the real workhorse of a font. These characters are used most often, so they deserve the most attention. Three examples of each character will be illustrated, for three rather different settings of the parameters, as indicated on the opposite page.

Several subroutines that are used frequently in the character programs of `roman1` appear below. The *super_arc$_l$* and *super_arc$_r$* macros define the inside and outside edges of one-fourth of a superellipse; this makes many of the bowl shapes. The *term.l* and *term.r* routines define the inside and outside edges of sans-serif terminal strokes.

% Computer Modern Roman lower case:
% These letters were originally coded by D. E. Knuth in November, 1979,
% inspired by the Monotype faces used in *The Art of Computer Programming.*
% Sans serif designs by Richard Southall were added in April, 1982.
% The programs were revised for the new METAFONT conventions in 1985.

% Character codes '141 through '172 are generated.

---

vardef *super_arc$_l$*(**suffix** \$, \$\$) = %% inside of super-ellipse
  pair *center*, *corner*;
  if $y_\$ = y_{\$r}$: *center* $= (x_{\$\$l}, y_{\$l})$; *corner* $= (x_{\$l}, y_{\$\$l})$;
  else: *center* $= (x_{\$l}, y_{\$\$l})$; *corner* $= (x_{\$\$l}, y_{\$l})$; **fi**
  $z_{\$l}\{corner - z_{\$l}\} \ldots superness[center, corner]\{z_{\$\$l} - z_{\$l}\}$
    $\ldots \{z_{\$\$l} - corner\}z_{\$\$l}$ **enddef**;

vardef *super_arc$_r$*(**suffix** \$, \$\$) = %% outside of super-ellipse
  pair *center*, *corner*;
  if $y_\$ = y_{\$r}$: *center* $= (x_{\$\$r}, y_{\$r})$; *corner* $= (x_{\$r}, y_{\$\$r})$;
  else: *center* $= (x_{\$r}, y_{\$\$r})$; *corner* $= (x_{\$\$r}, y_{\$r})$; **fi**
  $z_{\$r}\{corner - z_{\$r}\} \ldots superness[center, corner]\{z_{\$\$r} - z_{\$r}\}$
    $\ldots \{z_{\$\$r} - corner\}z_{\$\$r}$ **enddef**;

vardef *term.l*(**suffix** \$, \$\$)(**expr** d, t, s) = %% "robust" sans-serif terminal
  path p_-; $p_- = z_{\$l}\{d\} \ldots$ tension $t \ldots z_{\$\$l}$;
  pair d_-; $d_- = (x_{\$\$l} - x_{\$l}, s * (y_{\$\$l} - y_{\$l}))$;
  if(abs angle **direction** 1 **of** $p_- <$ abs angle $d_-) \neq (x_{\$l} < x_{\$\$l})$:
    $p_- := z_{\$l}\{d\} \ldots$ tension atleast $t \ldots \{d_-\}z_{\$\$l}$; **fi**
  p_- **enddef**;
vardef *term.r*(**suffix** \$, \$\$)(**expr** d, t, s) =
  path p_-; $p_- = z_{\$r}\{d\} \ldots$ tension $t \ldots z_{\$\$r}$;
  pair d_-; $d_- = (x_{\$\$r} - x_{\$r}, s * (y_{\$\$r} - y_{\$r}))$;
  if(abs angle **direction** 1 **of** $p_- <$ abs angle $d_-) \neq (x_{\$r} < x_{\$\$r})$:
    $p_- := z_{\$r}\{d\} \ldots$ tension atleast $t \ldots \{d_-\}z_{\$\$r}$; **fi**
  p_- **enddef**;
def *rterm* = reverse *term* **enddef**;

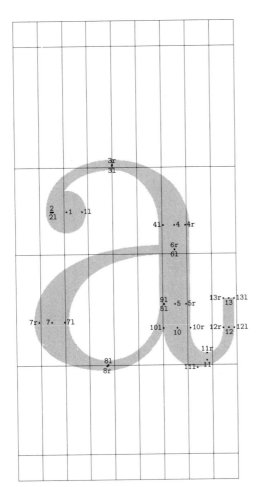

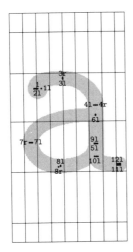

cmchar "The letter a";
beginchar("a", $9u^\#$, $x\_height^\#$, 0);
$bh^\# := \min(bar\_height^\#, 1.14x\_height^\# - bar\_height^\#)$; **define_pixels**($bh$);
italcorr $^1\!/_3[bh^\#, x\_height^\#] * slant + .5stem^\# - serif\_fit^\# - 2u^\#$;
adjust_fit(0, $serif\_fit^\#$ if *serifs*: **if** $hair^\# + .5stem^\# > 1.5u^\#$: $-.25u^\#$ **fi fi**);
pickup *fine.nib*; $top\ y_{3r} = h + $ vround $1.5oo$;
if *serifs*: $pos_1(flare, 180)$; $pos_2(hair, 180)$;
   $pos_3(vair, 90)$; $lft\ x_{1r} = $ hround $\max(u, 2.1u - .5flare)$; $x_3 = .5w - .5u$;
   $y_1 = \min(bh + .5flare + 2vair + 2, .9[bh, h] - .5flare)$;
   $bulb(3, 2, 1)$;   % bulb
else: $pos_1(^5\!/_7[vair, flare], 95)$; $x_{1l} = good.x\ 1.5u$; $x_{1r} := good.x\ x_{1r}$;
   $pos_3(^1\!/_8[vair, thin\_join], 90)$;
   $x_3 = .5w - .2u$; $top\ y_{1r} = $ vround $.82[bh, top\ y_{3r}]$;
   filldraw stroke $term.e(3, 1, left, .9, 4)$; **fi**   % terminal
$pos_4(stem, 0)$; $rt\ x_{4r} = $ hround$(w - 2.5u + .5stem)$; $y_4 = {}^1\!/_3[bh, h]$;
$pos_5(stem, 0)$; $x_5 = x_4$; $y_5 = \max(.55bh, 2vair)$;
filldraw stroke $super\_arc_e(3, 4)\ \&\ z_{4e}\ ..\ z_{5e}$;   % arc and stem
$pos_6(.3[thin\_join, vair], 90)$; $x_6 = x_4$; $bot\ y_6 = bh$;
$pos_7($hround$(curve - 2stem\_corr), 180)$;
$lft\ x_{7r} = $ hround $\max(.5u, 1.5u - .5curve)$; $y_7 = {}^1\!/_3[top\ y_{8l}, top\ y_{6r}]$;
$pos_8(vair, 270)$; $x_{8l} = .5w - .75u$; $bot\ y_{8r} = -oo$;
$pos_9(thin\_join, 360)$; $z_{9l} = z_{5l}$;
$(x, y_{8r}) = whatever[z_{8l}, z_{9l}]$; $x_{8r} := \max(x, x_8 - u)$;
$\{\{$ **interim** *superness* := *more_super*;
   filldraw stroke $z_{9e}\{down\}\ ...\ z_{8e}\{left\}\ ...\ \{up\}z_{7e}\ \&\ super\_arc_e(7, 6)\}\}$;   % bowl
if *serifs*: **numeric** *shaved_stem*; $shaved_stem = $ hround$(stem - 3stem\_corr)$;
  if $hair^\# + .5stem^\# > 1.5u^\#$: **pickup** *tiny.nib*;
   $pos_{5'}(shaved\_stem, 0)$; $rt\ x_{5'r} = fine.rt\ x_{5r}$; $y_{5'} = y_5$;
   $pos_{10}(shaved\_stem, 0)$; $x_{10} = x_{5'}$; $y_{10} = .2[.5tiny, bh]$;
   $pos_{11}(shaved\_stem, 0)$; $rt\ x_{11r} = $ hround$(w - .25u)$; $bot\ y_{11} = 0$;
   $pos_{12}(shaved\_stem, 0)$; $x_{11} = x_{12}$; $top\ y_{12} = slab + eps$;
   filldraw $z_{5'l}\ ---\ z_{10l}\ ...\ z_{11l}\{right\}\ --\ z_{11r}$
      $--\ z_{12r}\{left\}\ ...\ z_{10r} + .75(z_{12} - z_{11})\ ---\ z_{5'r}\ --\ $cycle;   % foot
  else: **pickup** *crisp.nib*; $pos_{5'}(shaved\_stem, 0)$; $rt\ x_{5'r} = fine.rt\ x_{5r}$; $y_{5'} = y_5$;
   $pos_{10}(shaved\_stem, 0)$; $x_{10} = x_{5'}$; $y_{10} = {}^1\!/_3bh$;
   $pos_{11}(.2[vair, stem], 90)$; $x_{11r} = .5[x_{10r}, x_{12r}]$; $bot\ y_{11l} = - $ vround $.5oo$;
   $pos_{12}(hair, 180)$; $rt\ x_{12l} = $ hround$(w - .1u)$; $y_{12} = \max(y_{10}, y_{11} + vair)$;
   $pos_{13}(hair, 180)$; $x_{13} = x_{12}$; $top\ y_{13} = \max($vround $.6bh, top\ y_{12})$;
   $(x', y_{11l}) = whatever[z_{11r}, z_{12r}]$; $x_{11l} := \max(x', x_{10})$;
   filldraw stroke $z_{5'e}\ ---\ z_{10e}\ ...\ z_{11e}\{right\}\ ...\ z_{12e}\ ---\ z_{13e}$; **fi**   % hook
else: **numeric** *shaved_stem*; $shaved_stem = $ hround$(stem - stem\_corr)$;
  pickup *tiny.nib*; $pos_{5'}(shaved\_stem, 0)$; $rt\ x_{5'r} = fine.rt\ x_{5r}$; $y_{5'} = y_5$;
  $pos_{10}(shaved\_stem, 0)$; $x_{10} = x_{5'}$; $bot\ y_{10} = 0$;
  filldraw stroke $z_{5'e}\ --\ z_{10e}$; **fi**   % base of stem
penlabels(1, 2, 3, 4, 5, 6, 7, 8, 9, 10, 11, 12, 13); **endchar**;

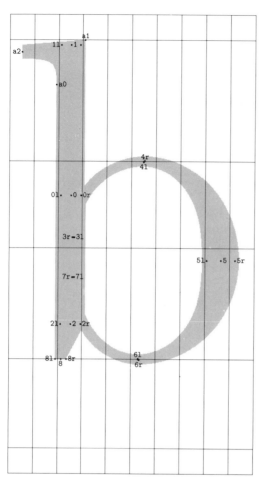

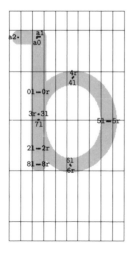

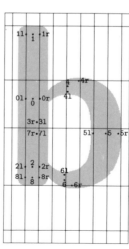

cmchar `"The letter b"`;
beginchar(`"b"`, $10u\# + \mathit{serif\_fit}\# , \mathit{asc\_height}\#, 0$);
italcorr $.5x\_height\# * slant + \min(.5curve\# - u\#, -.25u\#)$;
adjust_fit($\mathit{serif\_fit}\#, 0$);
pickup $tiny.nib$; $pos_1(stem', 0)$; $pos_2(stem, 0)$;
$pos_{0'}(stem', 0)$; $pos_0(stem, 0)$; $z_{0l} = z_{0'l}$; $x_{0'} = x_1$; $x_0 = x_2$;
$lft\ x_{1l} = \mathrm{hround}(2.5u - .5stem')$; $top\ y_1 = h$;
numeric $edge$; $edge = rt\ x_{2r}$;
pickup $fine.nib$; $pos_3(\textbf{if}\ hefty{:}\ thin\_join\ \textbf{else}{:}\ hair\ \textbf{fi}, 180)$;
$pos_4(vair, 90)$; $pos_5(curve, 0)$; $pos_6(vair, -90)$; $penpos_7(x_{3l} - x_{3r}, -180)$;
$rt\ x_{3l} = \max(rt\ x_{3l} - (lft\ x_{3r} - tiny.lft\ x_{2l}), \ \tfrac{1}{3}[rt\ x_2, edge])$;
$y_3 = \tfrac{1}{8}[bar\_height, x\_height]$;
$x_{4l} = w - .5(w - serif\_fit) + .5u$; $top\ y_{4r} = x\_height + oo$;
$rt\ x_{5r} = \mathrm{hround}\min(w - 1.35u + .5curve, w - .6u)$; $y_5 = .5x\_height$;
$x_{6l} = x_{4l} - .2u$; $bot\ y_{6r} = -oo$;
$x_7 = x_3$; $y_7 = \min(y_3, y_6 + y_4 - y_3 + .6vair)$;
$(x, y_{4r}) = whatever[z_{3l}, z_{4l}]$; $x_{4r} := \min(x, .5[x_4, x_{5r}])$;
$(x', y_{6r}) = whatever[z_{7l}, z_{6l}]$; $x_{6r} := \min(x', .5[x_6, x_{5r}])$;
filldraw stroke $z_{3e}\{up\} \ldots pulled\_arc_e(4, 5)\ \&\ pulled\_arc_e(5, 6) \ldots \{up\}z_{7e}$;   % bowl
$y_0 = \mathrm{ypart}(((edge, h) \text{ -- } (edge, 0))\ \mathrm{intersectionpoint}\ (z_{3l}\{up\} \ldots \{right\}z_{4l}))$;
$y_2 = \mathrm{ypart}(((edge, h) \text{ -- } (edge, 0))\ \mathrm{intersectionpoint}\ (z_{6l}\{left\} \ldots \{up\}z_{7l}))$;
pickup $tiny.nib$; **filldraw stroke** $z_{1e} \text{ -- } z_{0'e} \text{ -- } z_{0e} \text{ -- } z_{2e}$;   % stem
pickup $crisp.nib$; $pos_8(hair, 0)$; $pos_{7'}(stem, 0)$;
$z_{7'} = z_2$; $x_{8l} = x_{7'l}$; $bot\ y_8 = 0$;
filldraw stroke $z_{7'e} \text{ -- } z_{8e}$;   % point
if $serifs$: $sloped\_serif.l(1, 0', a, \tfrac{1}{3}, jut, serif\_drop)$; **fi**   % upper serif
penlabels(0, 1, 2, 3, 4, 5, 6, 7, 8); **endchar**;

---

vardef $sloped\_serif.l(\textbf{suffix}\ \$, \$\$, @)(\textbf{expr}\ darkness, jut, drop) =$
  pickup $crisp.nib$; $pos_{@2}(slab, 90)$;
  $lft\ x_{@0} = tiny.lft\ x_{\$l}$; $rt\ x_{@1} = tiny.rt\ x_{\$r}$; $top\ y_{@1} = tiny.top\ y_{\$r}$;
  $lft\ x_{@2} = lft\ x_{@0} - jut$; $y_{@2r} = y_{@1} - drop$;
  $y_{@0} = \max(y_{@2l} - bracket, y_{\$\$}) - eps$;
  if $drop > 0$: **erase fill** $z_{@1} \text{ -- } top\ z_{@1}$
    $\text{ -- } (x_{@2r}, top\ y_{@1}) \text{ -- } z_{@2r} \text{ -- } \mathrm{cycle}$; **fi**   % erase excess at top
  filldraw $z_{@1} \text{ -- } z_{@2r} \text{ -- } z_{@2l}\{right\}$
    $\ldots darkness[(x_{@0}, y_{@2l}), .5[z_{@2l}, z_{@0}]]\{z_{@0} - z_{@2l}\}$
    $\ldots \{down\}z_{@0} \text{ -- } (x_{@1}, y_{@0}) \text{ -- } \mathrm{cycle}$;   % sloped serif
  labels(@0, @1, @2); **enddef**;

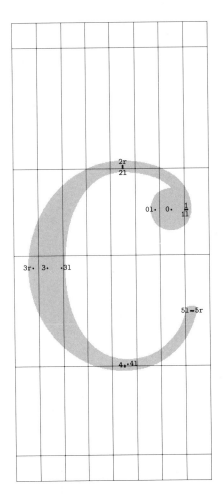

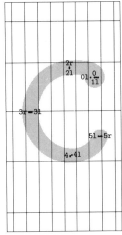

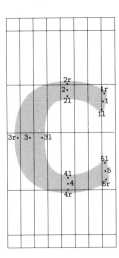

cmchar "The letter c";
beginchar("c", $8u^\#$, $x\_height^\#$, 0);
italcorr $x\_height^\# * slant - .2u^\#$;
adjust_fit(**if** *monospace*: $.5u^\#$, $.5u^\#$ **else**: 0, 0 **fi**);
pickup *fine.nib*; $pos_2(vair', 90)$; $pos_4(vair', 270)$;
$x_2 = x_4 = .5(w + u)$; *top* $y_{2r} = \text{vround}(h + 1.5oo)$; *bot* $y_{4r} = -oo$;
$pos_3(curve, 180)$; *lft* $x_{3r} = \text{hround max}(.6u, 1.35u - .5curve)$; $y_3 = .5h$;
if *serifs*: $pos_1(hair, 0)$; $pos_0(flare, 0)$;
   $y_1 = \min(bar\_height + .5flare + 2vair' + 2, .9[bar\_height, h] - .5flare)$;
   rt $x_{1r} = \text{hround}(w - .7u)$; *bulb*$(2, 1, 0)$;   % bulb
   $pos_5(hair, 0)$; *rt* $x_{5r} = \text{hround}(w - .5u)$;
   $y_5 = \max(good.y(.5bar\_height - .9), y_{4l} + vair')$;
   $(x, y_{4l}) = whatever[z_{4r}, z_{5l}]$; $x_{4l} := \min(x, x_{4l} + .5u)$;
   filldraw stroke $pulled\_super\_arc_e(2, 3)(.7superpull)$
      & $pulled\_super\_arc_e(3, 4)(.5superpull)$
      .. tension .9 and 1 .. $\{x_5 - x_4, 5(y_5 - y_4)\}z_{5e}$;   % arc and lower terminal
else: $pos_1(\,^4/_7[vair', flare], 80)$;
   rt $x_{1r} = \text{hround}(w - .6u)$; *top* $y_{1r} = \text{vround } .82[bar\_height, top\ y_{2r}]$;
   filldraw stroke $term.e(2, 1, right, .8, 4)$;   % upper terminal
   $pos_5(.6[vair', flare], 275)$; *rt* $x_{5r} = \text{hround}(w - .5u)$;
   $y_{5r} = good.y(y_{5r} + \,^1/_3 bar\_height - y_5)$; $y_{5l} := good.y\ y_{5l}$; $x_{5l} := good.x\ x_{5l}$;
   forsuffixes $e = l, r$: **path** p_e; $p_e = z_{4e}\{right\}$ .. tension .9 and 1 .. z_{5e};
      if angle **direction** 1 **of** $p_e > 75$:
         $p_e := z_{4e}\{right\}$ .. tension atleast .9 and 1 .. $\{\text{dir } 75\}z_{5e}$; **fi endfor**
   filldraw stroke $pulled\_super\_arc_e(2, 3)(.7superpull)$
      & $pulled\_super\_arc_e(3, 4)(.5superpull)$ & p_e; **fi**   % arc and lower terminal
penlabels(0, 1, 2, 3, 4, 5); **endchar**;

---

vardef $pulled\_super\_arc_l(\textbf{suffix } \$, \$\$)(\textbf{expr } superpull) =$
  pair *center, corner, outer_point*;
  if $y_\$ = y_{\$r}$: $center = (x_{\$\$l}, y_{\$l})$; $corner = (x_{\$l}, y_{\$\$l})$;
    $outer\_point = superness[(x_{\$\$r}, y_{\$r}), (x_{\$r}, y_{\$\$r})]$;
  else: $center = (x_{\$l}, y_{\$\$l})$; $corner = (x_{\$\$l}, y_{\$l})$;
    $outer\_point = superness[(x_{\$r}, y_{\$\$r}), (x_{\$\$r}, y_{\$r})]$; **fi**
  $z_{\$l}\{corner - z_{\$l}\}$
    ... $superpull[superness[center, corner], outer\_point]\{z_{\$\$l} - z_{\$l}\}$
    ... $\{z_{\$\$l} - corner\}z_{\$\$l}$ **enddef**;

vardef $pulled\_super\_arc_r(\textbf{suffix } \$, \$\$)(\textbf{expr } superpull) =$
  pair *center, corner*;
  if $y_\$ = y_{\$r}$: $center = (x_{\$\$r}, y_{\$r})$; $corner = (x_{\$r}, y_{\$\$r})$;
  else: $center = (x_{\$r}, y_{\$\$r})$; $corner = (x_{\$\$r}, y_{\$r})$; **fi**
  $z_{\$r}\{corner - z_{\$r}\}$ ... $superness[center, corner]\{z_{\$\$r} - z_{\$r}\}$
    ... $\{z_{\$\$r} - corner\}z_{\$\$r}$ **enddef**;

vardef $pulled\_arc_{@\#}(\textbf{suffix } \$, \$\$) =$
  $pulled\_super\_arc_{@\#}(\$, \$\$)(superpull)$ **enddef**;

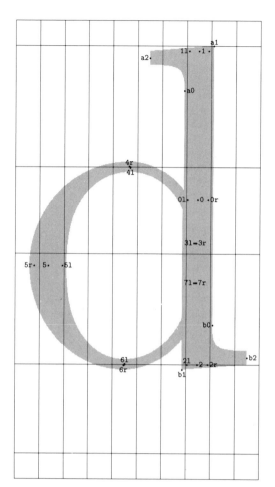

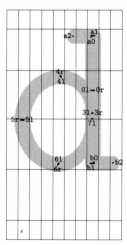

cmchar "The letter d";

beginchar("d", $10u\# + serif\_fit\#$, $asc\_height\#$, 0);

italcorr $asc\_height\# * slant - serif\_fit\# + .5stem\# - 2u\#$;

adjust_fit(0, $serif\_fit\#$);

pickup $tiny.nib$; $pos_1(stem', 0)$; $pos_2(stem, 0)$;

$pos_{0'}(stem', 0)$; $pos_0(stem, 0)$; $z_{0r} = z_{0'r}$; $x_{0'} = x_1$; $x_0 = x_2$;

$rt\ x_{1r} = \mathrm{hround}(w - 2.5u + .5stem')$; $top\ y_1 = h$;

numeric $edge$; $edge = lft\ x_{2l}$;

pickup $fine.nib$; $pos_3(\textbf{if}\ hefty:\ thin\_join\ \textbf{else}:\ hair\ \textbf{fi}, 0)$;

$pos_4(vair, 90)$; $pos_5(curve, 180)$; $pos_6(vair, 270)$; $penpos_7(x_{3r} - x_{3l}, 360)$;

$lft\ x_{3l} = \min(lft\ x_{3l} - (rt\ x_{3r} - tiny.rt\ x_{2r}), \frac{1}{3}[lft\ x_2, edge])$;

$y_3 = \frac{1}{8}[bar\_height, x\_height]$;

$x_{4l} = .5(w - serif\_fit) - .3u$; $top\ y_{4r} = x\_height + oo$;

$lft\ x_{5r} = \mathrm{hround}\max(1.35u - .5curve, .6u)$; $y_5 = .5x\_height$;

$x_{6l} = x_{4l} - .2u$; $bot\ y_{6r} = -oo$;

$x_7 = x_3$; $y_7 = \min(y_3, y_6 + y_4 - y_3 + .6vair)$;

$(x, y_{4r}) = whatever[z_{3l}, z_{4l}]$; $x_{4r} := \max(x, .5[x_{5r}, x_4])$;

$(x', y_{6r}) = whatever[z_{7l}, z_{6l}]$; $x_{6r} := \max(x', .5[x_{5r}, x_6])$;

filldraw stroke $z_{3e}\{up\} \ldots pulled\_arc_e(4, 5)$

    & $pulled\_arc_e(5, 6) \ldots \{up\}z_{7e}$;   % bowl

$y_0 = \mathrm{ypart}(((edge, h) -- (edge, 0))\ \mathrm{intersectionpoint}\ (z_{3l}\{up\} \ldots \{left\}z_{4l}))$;

pickup $tiny.nib$; $bot\ y_2 = \textbf{if}\ serifs: -\min(oo, serif\_drop)\ \textbf{else}:\ 0\ \textbf{fi}$;

filldraw stroke $z_{1e} -- z_{0'e} -- z_{0e} -- z_{2e}$;   % stem

if $serifs$: $sloped\_serif.l(1, 0', a, \frac{1}{3}, jut, serif\_drop)$;   % upper serif

    $sloped\_serif.r(2, 0, b, \frac{1}{3}, jut, \min(oo, serif\_drop))$; **fi**   % lower serif

penlabels($0, 1, 2, 3, 4, 5, 6, 7$); **endchar**;

---

vardef $sloped\_serif.r(\textbf{suffix}\ \$, \$\$, @)(\textbf{expr}\ darkness, jut, drop) =$

    pickup $crisp.nib$; $pos_{@2}(slab, -90)$;

    $rt\ x_{@0} = tiny.rt\ x_{\$r}$; $lft\ x_{@1} = tiny.lft\ x_{\$l}$; $bot\ y_{@1} = tiny.bot\ y_{\$l}$;

    $rt\ x_{@2} = rt\ x_{@0} + jut$; $y_{@2r} = y_{@1} + drop$;

    $y_{@0} = \min(y_{@2l} + bracket, y_{\$\$}) + eps$;

if $drop > 0$: **erase fill** $z_{@1} -- bot\ z_{@1}$

    $-- (x_{@2r}, bot\ y_{@1}) -- z_{@2r} -- \mathrm{cycle}$; **fi**   % erase excess at bottom

    filldraw $z_{@1} -- z_{@2r} -- z_{@2l}\{left\}$

        $\ldots darkness[(x_{@0}, y_{@2l}), .5[z_{@2l}, z_{@0}]]\{z_{@0} - z_{@2l}\}$

        $\ldots \{up\}z_{@0} -- (x_{@1}, y_{@0}) -- \mathrm{cycle}$;   % sloped serif

    labels(@0, @1, @2); **enddef**;

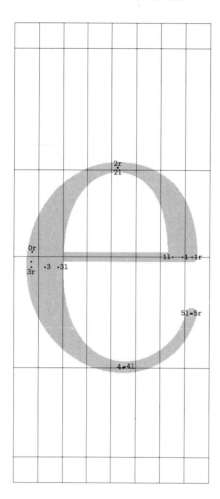

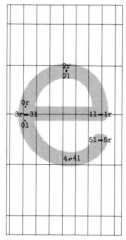
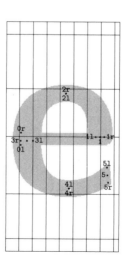

cmchar "The letter e";

beginchar("e", $7.25u^\# + \max(.75u^\#, .5curve^\#)$, $x\_height^\#$, 0);

italcorr $.5[bar\_height^\#, x\_height^\#] * slant + .5\min(curve^\# - 1.5u^\#, 0)$;

adjust_fit(**if** $monospace$: $.25u^\#$, $.5u^\#$ **else**: $0, 0$ **fi**);

numeric $left\_curve, right\_curve$;

$left\_curve = right\_curve + 6stem\_corr = curve$ **if not** $serifs$: $-3stem\_corr$ **fi**;

if $right\_curve < tiny.breadth$: $right\_curve := tiny.breadth$; **fi**

if $left\_curve < tiny.breadth$: $left\_curve := tiny.breadth$; **fi**

pickup $tiny.nib$; $pos_1(right\_curve, 0)$;

$pos_2(vair, 90)$; $pos_3(left\_curve, 180)$;

$y_1 = good.y\ bar\_height$; $top\ y_{2r} = h + \text{vround } 1.5oo$; $y_{0l} = bot\ y_1$;

$rt\ x_{1r} = \text{hround} \min(w - .5u, w - u + .5right\_curve)$;

$lft\ x_{3r} = \text{hround} \max(.5u, 1.25u - .5left\_curve)$; $x_2 = .5w + .25u$;

$\{\{$ **interim** $superness := more\_super$;

   filldraw stroke $super\_arc_e(1, 2)\}\}$;   % right bowl

$y_3 = .5[y_2, y_4]$; $bot\ y_{4r} = -oo$; $x_4 = x_2 + .25u$;

if $serifs$: $pos_4(vair', 270)$; $pos_5(hair, 360)$;

   $y_5 = \max(good.y(.5bar\_height - .9), y_{4l} + vair)$; $x_{5r} = x_{1r}$;

   $(x, y_{4l}) = whatever[z_{4r}, z_5]$; $x_{4l} := \min(x, x_{4l} + .5u)$;

   filldraw stroke $pulled\_arc_e(2, 3)$ & $pulled\_arc_e(3, 4)$

      ... $\{x_5 - x_4, 5(y_5 - y_4)\}z_{5e}$;   % left bowl, arc, and terminal

else: $pos_4(vair, 270)$;

   filldraw stroke $super\_arc_e(2, 3)$ & $super\_arc_e(3, 4)$;   % left bowl and arc

   pickup $fine.nib$; $pos_{4'}(vair, 270)$; $z_4 = z_{4'}$;

   $pos_5(.5[vair, flare], 275)$; $rt\ x_{5r} = \text{hround}(w - .6u)$;

   $y_{5r} = good.y(y_{5r} + \frac{1}{3}bar\_height - y_5)$; $y_{5l} := good.y\ y_{5l}$; $x_{5l} := good.x\ x_{5l}$;

   filldraw stroke $term.e(4', 5, right, 1, 4)$; **fi**   % terminal

path $testpath$; $testpath = super\_arc_r(2, 3)$ & $super\_arc_r(3, 4)$;

$y_{1'r} = y_{0r} = y_{0l} + .6[thin\_join, vair]$; $y_{1'l} = y_{0l}$; $x_{1'l} = x_{1'r} = x_1$;

forsuffixes $\$ = l, r$:

   $x_{0\$} = \text{xpart}(((0, y_{0\$}) -\!\!- (x_1, y_{0\$}))$ intersectionpoint $testpath$); **endfor**

fill stroke $z_{0e} -\!\!- z_{1'e}$;   % crossbar

penlabels$(0, 1, 2, 3, 4, 5)$; **endchar**;

Our work also has cryptographic and linguistic applications.
... It is shown by an actual construction that
grammatical constraints do not imply statistical constraints.
In particular our writing contains only 25 symbols:
A, B, C, D, F, G, H, I, J, K, L, M, N, O, P, Q, R, S, T, U, V, W, X, Y and Z.
Thus a symbol of maximum probability in ordinary writing is missing from ours.

— E. N. GILBERT, *A Capacity Formula for a Binary Communication Link*
in which Wrong Output Digits Occur in Bursts (1959)

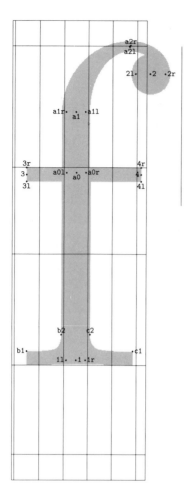

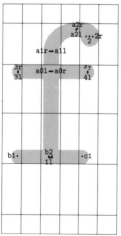

cmchar "The letter f";

beginchar("f", $5.5u\#$, $asc\_height\#$, 0);

italcorr $asc\_height\# * slant +$ **if** $serifs$: $flare\# - .25u\#$ **else**: $1.25u\#$ **fi**;

adjust_fit($stem\_shift\#$, **if** $monospace$: $.5u\#$ **else**: $-stem\_shift\#$ **fi**);

pickup $tiny.nib$; $pos_1(stem', 0)$; $lft\ x_{1l} = \text{hround}(2.5u - .5stem')$;

pickup $fine.nib$; **numeric** $bulb\_diam$;

if $serifs$: $bulb\_diam = \text{hround}\ .8[stem, flare]$;

$\quad pos_2(bulb\_diam, 0)$; $y_2 + .5bulb\_diam = .9[x\_height, h + oo]$;

$\quad$ **if** $monospace$: $rt\ x_{2r} = \text{hround}(w - .5u) + 1$ **else**: $lft\ x_{2l} = \text{hround}(w - .75u + .5)$ **fi**;

else: $pos_2(\frac{5}{7}[vair, flare], 90)$; $top\ y_{2r} = h$;

$\quad rt\ x_2 = \text{hround}(\textbf{if}\ monospace$: $w - .5u\ \textbf{else}$: $w + .75u\ \textbf{fi})$; **fi**

$f\_stroke(1, 2, a, b, c, jut, \textbf{if not}\ monospace$: $1.25\ \textbf{fi}\ jut)$; $\qquad$ % stem, terminal, serif

pickup $crisp.nib$; $top\ y_{3r} = top\ y_{4r} = x\_height$; $lft\ x_3 = \text{hround}\ .5u - 1$;

$pos_3(bar, 90)$; $pos_4(bar, 90)$;

$rt\ x_4 = \text{hround}(w - \textbf{if}\ monospace$: $.75u + 1\ \textbf{else}$: $\frac{1}{3}u\ \textbf{fi})$;

filldraw stroke $z_{3e}\ \text{--}\ z_{4e}$; $\qquad\qquad$ % bar

penlabels(1, 2, 3, 4); **endchar**;

---

def $f\_stroke(\textbf{suffix}\ \$, \$\$, @, left\_serif, right\_serif)(\textbf{expr}\ left\_jut, right\_jut) =$

$\quad$ **pickup** $tiny.nib$; $bot\ y_\$ = 0$;

$\quad penpos_{@0}(x_{\$r} - x_{\$l}, 0)$; $x_{@0l} = x_{\$l}$; $top\ y_{@0} = x\_height$;

$\quad$ **filldraw stroke** $z_{\$e}\ \text{--}\ z_{@0e}$; $\qquad\qquad$ % stem

$\quad$ **pickup** $fine.nib$; $pos_{@0'}(x_{\$r} - x_{\$l} - (\text{hround}\ stem\_corr) + tiny, 180)$;

$\quad y_{@0'} = y_{@0}$; $lft\ x_{@0'r} = tiny.lft\ x_{\$l}$;

$\quad penpos_{@1}(x_{@0'l} - x_{@0'r}, 180)$; $x_{@1} = x_{@0'}$; $y_{@1} + .5vair = .5[x\_height, h]$;

$\quad pos_{@2}(vair, 90)$; $top\ y_{@2r} = h + oo$;

$\quad$ **if** $serifs$: $x_{@2} = .6[x_{@1}, x_{\$\$r}]$; $(x_@, y_{@2r}) = whatever[z_{@2l}, z_{@1l}]$;

$\qquad x_{@2r} := \min(x_@, .5[x_{@2}, x_{\$\$r}])$; $pos_{@3}(hair, 0)$; $bulb(@2, @3, \$\$)$; $\qquad$ % bulb

$\qquad$ **filldraw stroke** $z_{@0'e}\ \text{--}\ z_{@1e}\ \&\ super\_arc_e(@1, @2)$; $\qquad$ % arc

$\qquad dish\_serif(\$, @0, left\_serif, \frac{1}{3}, left\_jut, right\_serif, \frac{1}{3}, right\_jut)$; $\qquad$ % serif

$\quad$ **else**: $x_{@2} = .6[x_{@1}, x_{\$\$}]$; $y_{@1l} := \frac{1}{3}[y_{@1l}, y_{@2l}]$;

$\qquad$ **filldraw stroke** $z_{@0'e}\ \text{--}\ z_{@1e}\ \&\ super\_arc_e(@1, @2)$

$\qquad\quad \&\ term.e(@2, \$\$, right, .9, 4)$; **fi** $\qquad\qquad$ % arc and terminal

$\quad$ **penlabels**(@0, @1, @2); **enddef**;

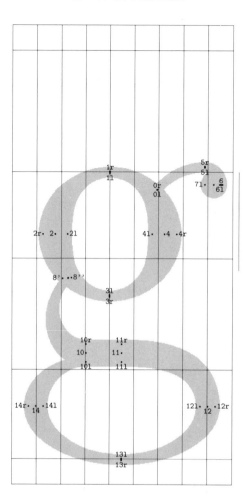

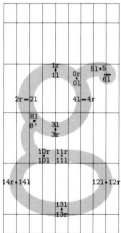

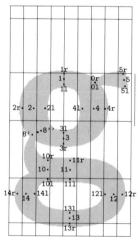

iff not *variant_g*: **cmchar** "The letter g";
beginchar("g", $9u\#$, $x\_height\#$, $desc\_depth\#$);
italcorr $x\_height\# * slant + .25u\#$;
adjust_fit$(0, 0)$;
numeric *light_vair*, *light_curve*, *loop_top*, *loop_side*;
$light\_vair = \text{Vround}(.5[thin\_join, vair] + vair\_corr)$;
$light\_curve = \max(fine.breadth, \text{hround}(curve - 3stem\_corr))$;
$loop\_top = \text{Vround } .77[vair, fudged.stem]$;
$loop\_side = \text{hround } .64[vair, fudged.stem]$;
pickup *fine.nib*; $pos_1(light\_vair, 90)$;
$pos_2(light\_curve, 180)$; $pos_3(light\_vair, 270)$;
$pos_4(light\_curve, 360)$; $pos_{11}(loop\_top, 90)$;
$y_{11r} = good.y(y_{11r} + .15bar\_height - y_{11})$; $x_1 = x_3 = .5[x_2, x_4]$; $y_2 = y_4 = .5[y_1, y_3]$;
lft $x_{2r} = \text{hround}(1.75u - .5light\_curve)$; *rt* $x_{4r} = \text{hround}(w - 2.75u + .5light\_curve)$;
top $y_{1r} = h + oo$; $y_{3r} = good.y(y_{3r} + .27[top\ y_{11r}, bot\ y_{1l}] - y_3)$;
filldraw stroke $pulled\_arc_e(1, 2)$ & $pulled\_arc_e(2, 3)$;   % left half of bowl
filldraw stroke $pulled\_arc_e(3, 4)$ & $pulled\_arc_e(4, 1)$;   % right half of bowl
$x_0 = superness[x_{1r}, x_{4r}]$; $y_0 = superness[y_{4r}, y_{1r}]$;   % NE point on the super bowl
$x_{8'} = superness[x_{3r}, x_{2r}]$; $y_{8'} = superness[y_{2r}, y_{3r}]$;   % SW point on the super bowl
$x_{8''} = superness[x_3, x_2]$; $y_{8''} = superness[y_2, y_3]$;
$pos_0(thin\_join, \text{angle}(z_0 - z_{8'}) + 90)$;
$pos_8(thin\_join, \text{angle}(z_0 - z_{8'}) - 90)$; $z_8 = .618[z_{8'}, z_{8''}]$;
if *serifs*: $pos_5(vair, 90)$;
    $pos_6(hair, 0)$; $pos_7(.5[hair, flare], 0)$; $x_5 = .75[x_0, x_6]$; *top* $y_{5r} = h + o$;
    rt $x_{6r} = \text{hround}(w - .25u)$; $y_6 + (.5[hair, flare])/2 = .95[bar\_height, h] + oo$;
    filldraw stroke $z_{0e} \mathrel{..} \{right\}z_{5e}$; *bulb*(5, 6, 7);   % ear
else: $pos_5(vair', 100)$; *top* $y_{5r} = h + oo$;
    rt $x_{5l} = \text{hround}(w - .25u)$; $y_{5l} := good.y\ y_{5l}$;
    filldraw $z_{0l}\{z_5 - z_0\} \mathrel{..} z_{5l} \mathrel{--} z_{5r}\{left\} \mathrel{..} \{curl\ 1\}z_{0r} \mathrel{--} cycle$; **fi**   % ear
$pos_{10}(loop\_top, 90)$; $x_{10} = x_8 + .75u$; $y_{10} = y_{11}$;
$pos_{12}(loop\_side, 0)$; $pos_{13}(light\_vair, -90)$;
$pos_{14}(loop\_side, -180)$; $pos_{10'}(.5[thin\_join, vair], -270)$;
rt $x_{12r} = \text{hround} \max(w - 1.25u + .5loop\_side, w - .5u)$; $y_{12} = y_{14} = .5[y_{11}, y_{13}]$;
$x_{11} = x_{13} = \max(.5w, x_{10} + eps)$; *bot* $y_{13r} = -d - oo - 1$; $x_{14} = w - x_{12}$; $z_{10'l} = z_{10l}$;
filldraw stroke $z_{8e}\{z_8 - z_0\} \mathrel{..} z_{10e} \mathrel{---} z_{11e}$;   % link
filldraw stroke {{ **interim** *superness* := *hein_super*; $super\_arc_e(11, 12)$ }}
   & $super\_arc_e(12, 13)$ & $super\_arc_e(13, 14)$ & $super\_arc_e(14, 10')$;   % loop
penlabels(0, 1, 2, 3, 4, 5, 6, 7, 8, 10, 11, 12, 13, 14); **labels**(8', 8''); **endchar**;

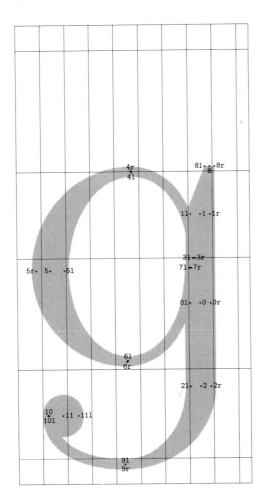

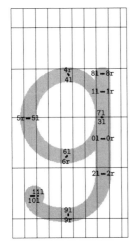

iff *variant_g*: **cmchar** "Variant letter g";
beginchar("g", $10u\# + serif\_fit\#$, $x\_height\#$, $desc\_depth\#$);
italcorr $x\_height\# * slant - serif\_fit\# + .5stem\# - 2u\#$ **if** *serifs*: $+.5u\#$ **fi**;
adjust_fit$(0, serif\_fit\#$ **if** *serifs*: $-.5u\#$ **fi**$)$;
pickup *tiny.nib*; $pos_1(stem', 0)$; $pos_2(stem, 0)$;
$pos_{0'}(stem', 0)$; $pos_0(stem, 0)$; $z_{0r} = z_{0'r}$; $x_{0'} = x_1$; $x_0 = x_2$;
rt $x_{1r} = \text{hround}(w - 2.5u + .5stem')$;
numeric *edge*; $edge = \text{lft } x_{2l}$;
path *edge_path*; $edge\_path = (edge, h) \text{ -- } (edge, 0)$;
pickup *fine.nib*; $pos_3(\textbf{if } hefty\text{: } thin\_join \textbf{ else: } hair \textbf{ fi}, 0)$;
$pos_4(vair, 90)$; $pos_5(curve, 180)$; $pos_6(vair, 270)$; $penpos_7(x_{3r} - x_{3l}, 360)$;
lft $x_{3l} = \min(\text{lft } x_{3l} - (\text{rt } x_{3r} - tiny.\text{rt } x_{2r}), \text{ }^2\!/_3[\text{lft } x_2, edge])$; $y_3 = bar\_height$;
$x_{4l} = .5(w - serif\_fit) - .3u$; **top** $y_{4r} = x\_height + oo$;
lft $x_{5r} = \text{hround} \max(1.35u - .5curve, .6u)$; $y_5 = .5x\_height$;
$x_{6l} = x_{4l} - .2u$; **bot** $y_{6r} = \text{vround } ^1\!/_3vair$;
lft $x_{7l} = edge$; $y_7 = \min(y_3, y_6 + y_4 - y_3 + .6vair)$;
$(x, y_{4r}) = whatever[z_{3l}, z_{4l}]$; $x_{4r} := \max(x, .5[x_{5r}, x_4])$;
$(x', y_{6r}) = whatever[z_{7l}, z_{6l}]$; $x_{6r} := \max(x', .5[x_{5r}, x_6])$;
filldraw stroke $z_{3e}\{up\} \ldots \{left\}z_{4e}$ & $super\_arc_e(4, 5)$
    & $super\_arc_e(5, 6)$ & $z_{6e}\{right\} \ldots \{up\}z_{7e}$;   % bowl
$y_1 = \text{ypart}(edge\_path \text{ intersectionpoint } (z_{3l}\{up\} \ldots \{left\}z_{4l}))$;
$y_0 = \text{ypart}(edge\_path \text{ intersectionpoint } (z_{7l}\{down\} \ldots \{left\}z_{6l}))$;
pickup *tiny.nib*; **bot** $y_2 = $ **if** *serifs*: $-.25d$ **else**: 0 **fi**;
filldraw stroke $z_{1e} \text{ -- } z_{0'e} \text{ -- } z_{0e} \text{ -- } z_{2e}$;   % stem
pickup *crisp.nib*;
$pos_8(\text{hround}(hair - stem\_corr), 0)$; $pos_{7'}(stem', 0)$;
$z_{7'} = z_1$; $x_{8r} = x_{7'r}$; **top** $y_8 = h + oo$;
filldraw stroke $z_{7'e} \text{ -- } z_{8e}$;   % point
if *serifs*: **pickup** *tiny.nib*;
    $pos_9(vair, -90)$; $x_9 = .5[x_2, x_{10}]$; **bot** $y_{9r} = -d - o - 1$;
    $pos_{10}(hair, -180)$; **lft** $x_{10r} = \text{hround } u$; $y_{10} = -.75d + .5flare$;
    $pos_{11}(flare, -180)$; $z_{11r} = z_{10r}$;
    $bulb(9, 10, 11)$; **filldraw stroke** $super\_arc_e(2, 9)$;   % tail
else: **pickup** *fine.nib*; $pos_{2'}(stem, 0)$; $z_{2'} = z_2$;
    $z_{2''r} = z_{2'r}$; $z_{2''} = z_{2'}$; $z_{2''l} = (x_{2'l}, 0)$;
    $pos_9(vair, -90)$; $x_9 = 4.5u$; **bot** $y_{9r} = -d - o - 1$;
    $pos_{10}(.5[vair, flare], -90)$; **lft** $x_{10} = \text{hround } 1.25u$;
    $y_{10r} = good.y - \,^5\!/_6d$; $y_{10l} := good.y \; y_{10l}$;
    filldraw stroke $z_{2'e} \ldots z_{2''e}$ & $super\_arc_e(2'', 9)$
        & $term.e(9, 10, left, .9, 4)$; **fi**   % tail
penlabels$(0, 1, 2, 3, 4, 5, 6, 7, 8, 9, 10, 11)$; **endchar**;

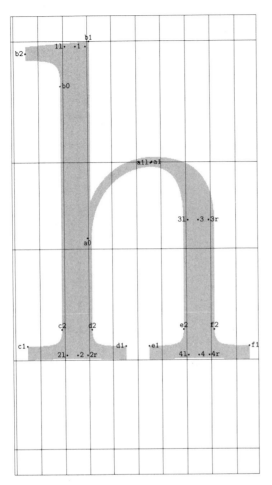

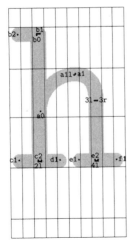

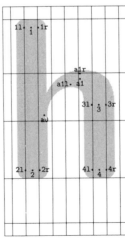

```
cmchar "The letter h";
beginchar("h", 10u#, asc_height#, 0);
italcorr .5[bar_height#, x_height#] * slant − serif_fit# + .5stem# − 2u#;
adjust_fit(serif_fit# + stem_shift#, serif_fit# − stem_shift#);
pickup tiny.nib; pos₁(stem, 0); pos₂(stem, 0);
```

$pos_{1'}(stem', 0); \ pos_{2'}(stem', 0); \ pos_3(stem, 0);$

$lft \ x_{1l} = hround(2.5u − .5stem); \ x_{1l} = x_{1'l} = x_{2l} = x_{2'l}; \ x_3 = w − x_1;$

$top \ y_1 = h; \ bot \ y_2 = 0; \ y_1 = y_{1'}; \ y_2 = y_{2'};$

filldraw stroke $z_{1'e} \ \text{--} \ z_{2'e};$ % left stem

$h\_stroke(2, a, 3, 4);$ % arch and right stem

if $serifs$: $sloped\_serif.l(1', 2', b, \frac{1}{3}, jut, serif\_drop);$ % upper left serif

     numeric $inner\_jut$; **pickup** $tiny.nib$;

     if $rt \ x_{2r} + jut + .5u + 1 \leq lft \ x_{4l} − jut$: $inner\_jut = jut;$

     else: $rt \ x_{2r} + jut + .5u + 1 = lft \ x_{4l} − inner\_jut;$ **fi**

     $dish\_serif(2, 1, c, \frac{1}{3}, jut, d, \frac{1}{3}, jut);$ % lower left serif

     $dish\_serif(4, 3, e, \frac{1}{3}, inner\_jut, f, \frac{1}{3}, jut);$ **fi**   % lower right serif

penlabels(1, 2, 3, 4); **endchar**;

---

def $h\_stroke($**suffix** $\$, @, @@, \$\$) =$

     $penpos_{\$\$}(x_{@@r} − x_{@@l}, 0); \ x_{\$\$} = x_{@@}; \ bot \ y_{\$\$} = 0;$

     $y_{@@} = \frac{1}{3}[bar\_height, x\_height];$

     $penpos_{\$''}(x_{\$r} − x_{\$l}, 0); \ x_{\$''} = x_{\$}; \ y_{\$''} = \frac{1}{8}[bar\_height, x\_height];$

     filldraw stroke $z_{\$''e} \ \text{--} \ z_{\$e};$ % thicken the lower left stem

     $penpos_{@0}(\min(rt \ x_{\$r} − lft \ x_{\$l}, thin\_join) − fine, 180);$ **pickup** $fine.nib;$

     $rt \ x_{@0l} = tiny.rt \ x_{\$r}; \ y_{@0} = y_{\$''};$

     $pos_{@1}(vair, 90); \ pos_{@@'}(x_{@@r} − x_{@@l} + tiny, 0); \ z_{@@'} = z_{@@};$

     $x_{@1} = .5[rt \ x_{@0l}, rt \ x_{@@'r}]; \ top \ y_{@1r} = x\_height + oo;$

     $(x_@, y_{@1l}) = whatever[z_{@1r}, z_{@0l}]; \ x_{@1l} := x_@;$

     filldraw stroke $z_{@0e}\{up\} \ldots \{right\}z_{@1e}$

         & {{ **interim** $superness := hein\_super; \ super\_arc_e(@1, @@')$ }};   % arch

     pickup $tiny.nib$; **filldraw stroke** $z_{@@e} \ \text{--} \ z_{\$\$e};$ % right stem

     labels(@0); **penlabels**(@1); **enddef**;

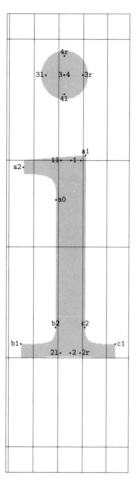

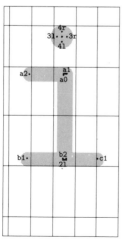

cmchar "The letter i";
numeric $dot\_diam\#$; $dot\_diam\# = \max(dot\_size\#, cap\_curve\#)$;
beginchar("i", $5u\#$, $\min(asc\_height\#, {}^{10}\!/_{7}x\_height\# + .5dot\_diam\#)$, 0);
define_whole_blacker_pixels(dot_diam);
italcorr $h\# * slant - serif\_fit\# + .5dot\_diam\# - 2u\#$;
adjust_fit($serif\_fit\# + stem\_shift\#$ **if** $monospace$: $+.25u\#$ **fi**, $serif\_fit\# - stem\_shift\#$);
pickup $tiny.nib$; $pos_1(stem', 0)$; $pos_2(stem', 0)$;
if odd$(w - stem')$: $change\_width$; **fi**
lft $x_{1l} = \text{hround}(.5w - .5stem')$; $x_1 = x_2$;
top $y_1 = x\_height$ **if** $serifs$: $+ \min(oo, serif\_drop)$ **fi**; *bot* $y_2 = 0$;
filldraw stroke z_{1e} -- z_{2e};   % stem
$pos_3(dot\_diam, 0)$; $pos_4(dot\_diam, 90)$;
if $serifs$: $x_{3r} = \max(x_{1r}, x_1 + .5(dot\_diam - tiny) - .2jut)$ **else**: $x_3 = x_1 - .5$ **fi**;
top $y_{4r} = h + 1$;
if *bot* $y_{4l} - top$ $y_1 < slab$: $y_{4l} := \min(y_{4r} - eps, y_1 + tiny + slab)$; **fi**
$x_3 = x_4$; $y_3 = .5[y_{4l}, y_{4r}]$; $dot(3, 4)$;   % dot
if $serifs$: $sloped\_serif.l(1, 2, a, {}^{1}\!/_{3}, .95jut, serif\_drop)$;   % upper serif
    $dish\_serif(2, 1, b, {}^{1}\!/_{3}, jut, c, {}^{1}\!/_{3}, .9jut)$; **fi**   % lower serif
penlabels$(1, 2, 3, 4)$; **endchar**;

---

def $dish\_serif$(**suffix** \$, \$\$, @)(**expr** $left\_darkness, left\_jut$)
    (**suffix** @@)(**expr** $right\_darkness, right\_jut$) **suffix** $modifier =$
    $serif(\$, \$\$, @, left\_darkness, -left\_jut)modifier$;
    $serif(\$, \$\$, @@, right\_darkness, right\_jut)modifier$;
    if $dish > 0$: **pickup** $tiny.nib$; **numeric** $dish\_out, dish\_in$;
        if $y_{\$} < y_{\$\$}$: $dish\_out = bot$ $y_{\$}$; $dish\_in = dish\_out + dish$; **let** $rev_ = $ reverse;
        else: $dish\_out = top$ $y_{\$}$; $dish\_in = dish\_out - dish$; **let** $rev_ = $ **relax**; **fi**
        erase fill $rev\_$
            $((x_{@1}, dish\_out) .. (x_{\$}, dish\_in)\{right\} .. (x_{@@1}, dish\_out) \text{ -- cycle})$;
    fi enddef;

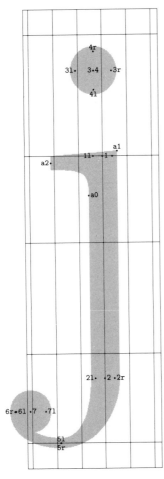

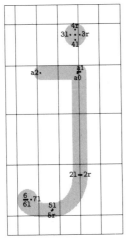

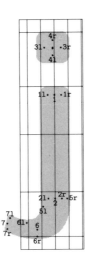

```
cmchar "The letter j";
```
numeric $dot\_diam\#$; $dot\_diam\# = \max(dot\_size\#, cap\_curve\#)$;

beginchar("j", $5.5u\#$, $\min(asc\_height\#, {}^{10}\!/_7 x\_height\# + .5dot\_diam\#)$, $desc\_depth\#$);

define_whole_blacker_pixels(dot_diam);

italcorr $h\# * slant - serif\_fit\# + .5stem\# - 2u\#$;

adjust_fit($serif\_fit\# + 2stem\_shift\#$ **if** $monospace$: $+ .5u\#$ **fi**,

    $serif\_fit\# - 2stem\_shift\#$ **if** $monospace$: $-.5u\#$ **fi**);

pickup $tiny.nib$; $pos_1(stem', 0)$; $pos_2(stem', 0)$;

$rt\ x_{1r} = \text{hround}(.5w + .25u + .5stem')$; $x_1 = x_2$;

$top\ y_1 = x\_height$ **if** $serifs$: $+ \min(oo, serif\_drop)$ **fi**; $bot\ y_2 = -{}^1\!/_3 d$;

filldraw stroke z_{1e} -- z_{2e};   % stem

$pos_3(dot\_diam, 0)$; $pos_4(dot\_diam, 90)$;

$x_{3r} = x_{1r}$; $top\ y_{4r} = h + 1$;

if $bot\ y_{4l} - top\ y_1 < slab$: $y_{4l} := \min(y_{4r} - eps, y_1 + tiny + slab)$; **fi**

$x_3 = x_4$; $y_3 = .5[y_{4l}, y_{4r}]$; $dot(3, 4)$;   % dot

if $serifs$: $sloped\_serif.l(1, 2, a, {}^1\!/_3, 1.1jut, serif\_drop)$;   % upper serif

    pickup $tiny.nib$; $pos_5(vair, -90)$; $pos_6(hair, -180)$; $pos_7(flare, -180)$;

    $x_5 = .5[x_2, x_{6r}]$; $bot\ y_{5r} = -d - oo$; $y_6 - .5flare = -.88d$;

    if $monospace$: $lft\ x_{6r} = 0$ **else**: $z_{6r} = z_{7r}$; $rt\ x_{7l} = \text{floor} .75u$ **fi**;

    $(x, y_{5r}) = whatever[z_{5l}, z_{2l}]$; $x_{5r} := \max(x, .5[x_{6r}, x_5])$;

    filldraw stroke $z_{2e}\{down\} \ldots z_{5e}\{left\}$; $bulb(5, 6, 7)$;   % arc and bulb

else: **pickup** $fine.nib$; $pos_{2'}(stem', 0)$; $z_{2'} = z_2$;

    $pos_6(.2[vair, stem'], -90)$; $pos_7(vair, -90)$;

    $lft\ x_{7r} = \text{hround} -.75u$; $bot\ y_{7r} = \text{vround}\ {}^5\!/_6(-d - oo)$;

    $(x, y_{7l}) = whatever[z_{7r}, z_3]$; $x_{7l} := x$;

    $z_{5r} = z_{2'r}$; $(x_{2'l}, y_{5l}) = whatever[z_{7l}, z_{5r}]$; $x_{5l} = x_{2'l}$; $y_5 = y_{5r}$;

    $x_{6r} = .5[x_{7r}, x_{5r}]$; $x_{6l} := .5[x_{7l}, x_{5l}]$; $bot\ y_{6r} = -d - oo$;

    filldraw stroke $z_{2'e} \ldots \{down\}z_{5e}\ \&\ super\_arc_e(5, 6)$

       $\&\ z_{6e}\{left\} \ldots z_{7e}$; **fi**   % arc and terminal

penlabels(1, 2, 3, 4, 5, 6, 7);   **endchar**;

---

def $bulb(\textbf{suffix}\ \$, \$\$, \$\$\$) =$

    $z_{\$\$\$r} = z_{\$\$r}$;

    $path_{-l} := z_{\$l}\{x_{\$\$r} - x_{\$r}, 0\} \ldots \{0, y_{\$\$r} - y_{\$r}\}z_{\$\$l}$;

    filldraw $path_{-l}$ -- $z_{\$\$r}\{0, y_{\$r} - y_{\$\$r}\} \ldots \{x_{\$r} - x_{\$\$r}, 0\}z_{\$r}$ -- cycle;   % link

    $path_{-r} := z_{\$\$\$l}\{0, y_{\$r} - y_{\$\$r}\} \ldots z_{\$\$\$r}\{0, y_{\$\$r} - y_{\$r}\}$;   % near-circle

    filldraw subpath$(0, \text{xpart}(path_{-r}\ \text{intersectiontimes}\ path_{-l}))$ **of** $path_{-r}$

      -- $z_{\$\$r}\{0, y_{\$\$r} - y_{\$r}\} \ldots$ cycle;   % bulb

    enddef;

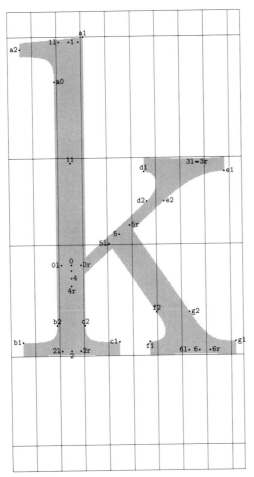

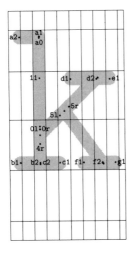

cmchar "The letter k";
beginchar("k", $9.5u^\#$, $asc\_height^\#$, 0);
italcorr $x\_height^\# * slant - .2u^\#$;
adjust_fit($serif\_fit^\#$, $serif\_fit^\#$); **pickup** $tiny.nib$;
numeric $right\_jut$, $stem[]$, $alpha[]$;
$stem_1 = \max(tiny.breadth, \text{hround}(fudged.stem - stem\_corr))$;
$stem_2 = \max(tiny.breadth, \text{hround}(fudged.stem - 2stem\_corr))$;
$stem_3 = \max(tiny.breadth, \text{hround}(fudged.hair \textbf{ if } hefty\text{: } -4stem\_corr \textbf{ fi}))$;
$stem_4 = \max(tiny.breadth, \text{hround}(fudged.stem - 3stem\_corr))$;
if $serifs$: $right\_jut = .6jut$; **else**: $right\_jut = .4tiny$; **fi**
$pos_1(stem_1, 0)$; $pos_2(stem_2, 0)$; **top** $y_1 = h$; **bot** $y_2 = 0$;
lft $x_{1l} = $ **lft** $x_{2l} = \text{hround}(2.5u - .5stem_1)$;
top $y_3 = x\_height$; **rt** $x_{3r} = \text{hround}(r - letter\_fit - .7u - right\_jut) + eps$;
bot $y_6 = 0$; **rt** $x_{6r} = \text{hround}(r - letter\_fit - .3u - right\_jut) + eps$;
$x_4 = x_{11} = x_1$; $y_4 = .7bar\_height$; $y_{11} = y_3$;
$alpha_1 = diag\_ratio(1, .5(stem_3 - tiny), y_3 - y_4, x_{3r} - x_4)$;
$alpha_2 = diag\_ratio(1, .5(stem_4 - tiny), y_{11} - y_6, x_{6r} - x_1)$;
$penpos_3(alpha_1 * (stem_3 - tiny), 0)$; $penpos_4(whatever, -90)$;
$z_5 = .5[z_{5l}, z_{5r}]$; $penpos_6(alpha_2 * (stem_4 - tiny), 0)$;
forsuffixes \$ $= l, r$: $y_{3'\$} = x\_height$; $y_{6'\$} = 0$; $z_{4\$} = z_{3'\$} + whatever * (z_3 - z_4)$;
  $z_{5\$} = z_{6'\$} + whatever * (z_{11} - z_6) = whatever[z_3, z_4]$; **endfor**
$z_{3'r} = z_{3r} + $ **penoffset** $z_3 - z_4$ **of** $currentpen + whatever * (z_3 - z_4)$;
% we have also $z_{3'l} = z_{3l} + $ **penoffset** $z_4 - z_3$ **of** $currentpen + whatever * (z_3 - z_4)$;
$z_{6'r} = z_{6r} + $ **penoffset** $z_{11} - z_6$ **of** $currentpen + whatever * (z_{11} - z_6)$;
$z_{6'l} = z_{6l} + $ **penoffset** $z_6 - z_{11}$ **of** $currentpen + whatever * (z_{11} - z_6)$;
fill z_{4r} -- $diag\_end(4r, 3'r, 1, .5, 3'l, 4l)$ -- z_{4l} -- **cycle**;   % upper diagonal
fill z_{5l} -- $diag\_end(5l, 6'l, .5, 1, 6'r, 5r)$ -- z_{5r} -- **cycle**;   % lower diagonal
$pos_0(stem_1, 0)$; $pos_{0'}(stem_2, 0)$; $y_0 = y_{0'}$; $x_0 = x_1$; $x_{0'} = x_2$;
rt $z_{0r} = whatever[z_3, z_4]$; **filldraw stroke** $z_{1e} .. z_{0e}$ -- $z_{0'e} .. z_{2e}$;   % stem
if $serifs$: **numeric** $inner\_jut$;
  if rt $x_{2r} + jut + .5u + 1 \leq$ **lft** $x_{6l} - jut$: $inner\_jut = jut$;
  else: **rt** $x_{2r} + inner_jut + .5u + 1 = $ **lft** $x_{6l} - inner\_jut$; **fi**
  $sloped\_serif.l(1, 0, a, \frac{1}{3}, jut, serif\_drop)$;   % upper stem serif
  $dish\_serif(2, 0', b, \frac{1}{3}, jut, c, \frac{1}{3}, inner\_jut)$;   % lower stem serif
  $dish\_serif(3, 4, d, \frac{2}{3}, 1.4jut, e, \frac{1}{2}, right\_jut)(dark)$;   % upper diagonal serif
  $dish\_serif(6, 5, f, \frac{1}{2}, inner\_jut, g, \frac{1}{3}, right\_jut)(dark)$; **fi**   % lower diagonal serif
penlabels(0, 1, 2, 3, 4, 5, 6, 11); **endchar**;

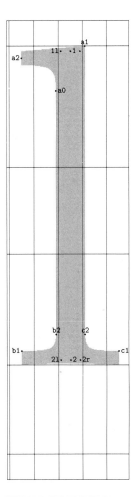

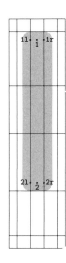

cmchar "The letter l";
beginchar("l", $5u^\#$, $asc\_height^\#$, 0); $l\_width^\# := 5u^\# + 2serif\_fit^\#$;
italcorr $asc\_height^\# * slant - serif\_fit^\# + .5stem^\# - 2u^\#$;
adjust_fit($serif\_fit^\# + stem\_shift^\#$, $serif\_fit^\# - stem\_shift^\#$);
pickup $tiny.nib$; $pos_1(stem', 0)$; $pos_2(stem', 0)$;
if odd$(w - stem')$: $change\_width$; **fi**
$lft\ x_{1l} = $ hround$(.5w - .5stem')$; $x_1 = x_2$; $top\ y_1 = h$; $bot\ y_2 = 0$;
filldraw stroke z_{1e} -- z_{2e};   % stem
if $serifs$: $sloped\_serif.l(1, 2, a, \frac{1}{3}, jut, serif\_drop)$;   % upper serif
   $dish\_serif(2, 1, b, \frac{1}{3}, jut, c, \frac{1}{3}, jut)$; **fi**   % lower serif
penlabels(1, 2); **endchar**;

---

vardef $serif$(**suffix** \$, \$\$, @)   % serif at $z_\$$ for stroke from $z_{\$\$}$
       (**expr** $darkness, jut$) **suffix** $modifier$ =
pickup $crisp.nib$; **numeric** $bracket\_height$; **pair** $downward$;
$bracket_height = $ **if** $dark_{modifier}$: 1.5 **fi** $bracket$;
if $y_\$ < y_{\$\$}$: $y_{@2} = \min(y_\$ + bracket\_height, y_{\$\$})$;
   $top\ y_{@1} - slab = bot\ y_{@0} + eps = tiny.bot\ y_\$$; $downward = z_\$ - z_{\$\$}$;
   if $y_{@1} > y_{@2}$: $y_{@2} := y_{@1}$; **fi**
else: $y_{@2} = \max(y_\$ - bracket\_height, y_{\$\$})$;
   $bot\ y_{@1} + slab = top\ y_{@0} - eps = tiny.top\ y_\$$; $downward = z_{\$\$} - z_\$$;
   if $y_{@1} < y_{@2}$: $y_{@2} := y_{@1}$; **fi fi**
$y_{@3} = y_{@2}$; $z_{@3} = whatever[z_\$, z_{\$\$}]$;
if $jut < 0$: $z_{@2} + $ **penoffset** $downward$ **of** $currentpen =$
     $z_{\$l} + $ **penoffset** $downward$ **of** $pen\_[tiny.nib] + whatever * downward$;
   $lft\ x_{@0} = lft\ x_{@1} = tiny.lft\ x_{\$l} + jut$;
   if $x_{@3} < x_{@2} + eps$: $x_{@3} := x_{@2} + eps$; **fi**
else: $z_{@2} - $ **penoffset** $downward$ **of** $currentpen =$
     $z_{\$r} - $ **penoffset** $downward$ **of** $pen\_[tiny.nib] + whatever * downward$;
   $rt\ x_{@0} = rt\ x_{@1} = tiny.rt\ x_{\$r} + jut$;
   if $x_{@3} > x_{@2} - eps$: $x_{@3} := x_{@2} - eps$; **fi fi**
pair $corner$; $ypart\ corner = y_{@1}$; $corner = z_{@2} + whatever * downward$;
filldraw $z_{@2}\{z_\$ - z_{\$\$}\}$
   $... darkness[corner, .5[z_{@1}, z_{@2}]]\{z_{@1} - z_{@2}\}$
   $... \{jut, 0\}z_{@1}$ -- $z_{@0}$ -- $(x_\$, y_{@0})$ -- $z_{@3}$ -- **cycle**;   % the serif
labels(@1, @2); **enddef**;

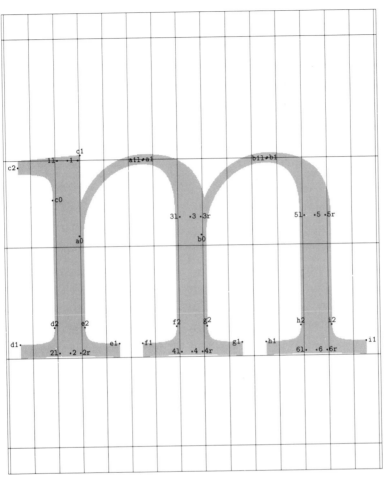

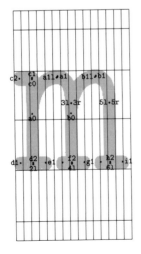

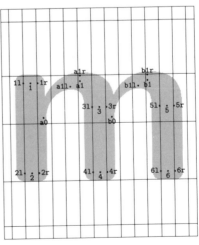

```
cmchar "The letter m";
```
beginchar("m", $15u\#$, $x\_height\#$, 0);

italcorr $.5[bar\_height\#, x\_height\#] * slant - serif\_fit\# + .5stem\# - 2u\#$;

adjust_fit($serif\_fit\# + stem\_shift\#$, $serif\_fit\# - stem\_shift\#$);

numeric $shaved\_stem$; $shaved\_stem = \text{hround}(mfudged.stem - 2stem\_corr)$;

pickup $tiny.nib$; $pos_1(mfudged.stem, 0)$; $pos_2(mfudged.stem, 0)$;

$pos_{1'}(shaved\_stem, 0)$; $pos_{2'}(shaved\_stem, 0)$;

$pos_3(mfudged.stem, 0)$; $pos_5(mfudged.stem, 0)$;

lft $x_{1l} = \text{hround}(2.5u - .5stem)$; $x_{1l} = x_{1'l} = x_{2l} = x_{2'l}$;

lft $x_{3l} = \text{hround}(.5w - .5stem)$; $x_5 - x_3 = x_3 - x_1$;

if not *monospace*: $r := \text{hround}(x_5 + x_1) - l$; **fi**   % change width for better fit

top $y_1 = h + \min(oo, serif\_drop)$; *bot* $y_2 = 0$; $y_1 = y_{1'}$; $y_2 = y_{2'}$;

filldraw stroke $z_{1'e}$ -- $z_{2'e}$;   % left stem

$h\_stroke(2, a, 3, 4)$;   % left arch and middle stem

$h\_stroke(4, b, 5, 6)$;   % right arch and right stem

if *serifs*: $sloped\_serif.l(1', 2', c, \frac{1}{3}, jut, serif\_drop)$;   % upper left serif

   numeric $inner\_jut$; **pickup** $tiny.nib$;

   if *rt* $x_{2r} + jut + .5u + 1 \le$ *lft* $x_{4l} - jut$: $inner\_jut = jut$;

   else: *rt* $x_{2r} + jut + .5u + 1 =$ *lft* $x_{4l} - inner\_jut$; **fi**

   $dish\_serif(2, 1, d, \frac{1}{3}, jut, e, \frac{1}{3}, jut)$;   % lower left serif

   $dish\_serif(4, 3, f, \frac{1}{3}, inner\_jut, g, \frac{1}{3}, jut)$;   % lower middle serif

   $dish\_serif(6, 5, h, \frac{1}{3}, inner\_jut, i, \frac{1}{3}, jut)$; **fi**   % lower right serif

penlabels($1, 2, 3, 4, 5, 6$); **endchar**;

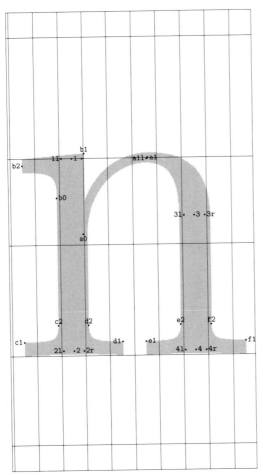

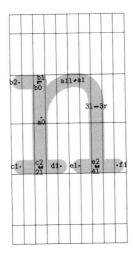

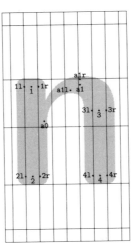

cmchar "The letter n";

beginchar("n", $10u^\#$, $x\_height^\#$, 0);

italcorr $.5[bar\_height^\#, x\_height^\#] * slant - serif\_fit^\# + .5stem^\# - 2u^\#$;

adjust_fit($serif\_fit^\# + stem\_shift^\#$, $serif\_fit^\# - stem\_shift^\#$);

pickup $tiny.nib$; $pos_1(stem, 0)$; $pos_2(stem, 0)$;

numeric $shaved\_stem$; $shaved\_stem = \mathrm{hround}(stem - 2stem\_corr)$;

$pos_{1'}(shaved\_stem, 0)$; $pos_{2'}(shaved\_stem, 0)$; $pos_3(stem, 0)$;

$lft\ x_{1l} = \mathrm{hround}(2.5u - .5stem)$; $x_{1l} = x_{1'l} = x_{2l} = x_{2'l}$; $x_3 = w - x_1$;

$top\ y_1 = h + \min(oo, serif\_drop)$; $bot\ y_2 = 0$; $y_1 = y_{1'}$; $y_2 = y_{2'}$;

filldraw stroke $z_{1'e} \, \text{--} \, z_{2'e}$;   % left stem

$h\_stroke(2, a, 3, 4)$;   % arch and right stem

if $serifs$: $sloped\_serif.l(1', 2', b, \tfrac{1}{3}, jut, serif\_drop)$;   % upper left serif

   numeric $inner\_jut$; pickup $tiny.nib$;

   if $rt\ x_{2r} + jut + .5u + 1 \le lft\ x_{4l} - jut$: $inner\_jut = jut$;

   else: $rt\ x_{2r} + jut + .5u + 1 = lft\ x_{4l} - inner\_jut$; fi

   $dish\_serif(2, 1, c, \tfrac{1}{3}, jut, d, \tfrac{1}{3}, jut)$;   % lower left serif

   $dish\_serif(4, 3, e, \tfrac{1}{3}, inner\_jut, f, \tfrac{1}{3}, jut)$; fi   % lower right serif

penlabels($1, 2, 3, 4$); endchar;

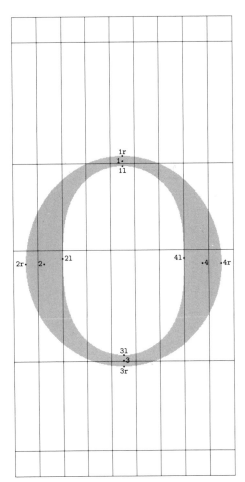

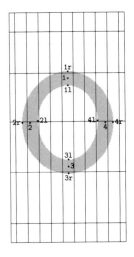

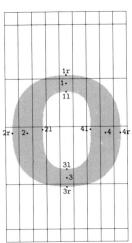

```
cmchar "The letter o";
```
beginchar("o", $9u\#$, $x\_height\#$, 0);

italcorr $.7x\_height\# * slant$;

adjust_fit(**if** $monospace$: $.5u\#$, $.5u\#$ **else**: $0, 0$ **fi**);

$penpos_1(vair, 90)$; $penpos_3(vair', -90)$;

$penpos_2(curve, 180)$; $penpos_4(curve, 0)$;

$x_{2r} = \text{hround max}(.5u, 1.25u - .5curve)$;

$x_{4r} = w - x_{2r}$; $x_1 = x_3 = .5w$; $y_{1r} = h + \text{vround } 1.5oo$; $y_{3r} = -oo$;

$y_2 = y_4 = .5h - vair\_corr$; $y_{2l} := y_{4l} := .52h$;

penstroke $pulled\_arc_e(1, 2)$ & $pulled\_arc_e(2, 3)$

   & $pulled\_arc_e(3, 4)$ & $pulled\_arc_e(4, 1)$ & cycle;   % bowl

penlabels$(1, 2, 3, 4)$; **endchar**;

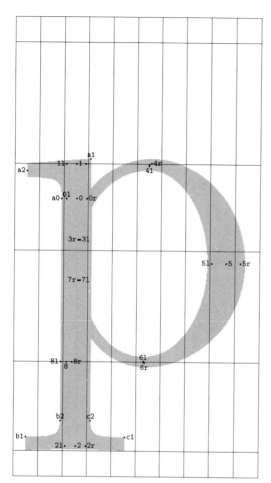

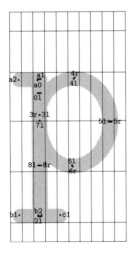

cmchar "The letter p";

beginchar("p", $10u^\# + serif\_fit^\#, x\_height^\#, desc\_depth^\#$);

italcorr $.5x\_height^\# * slant + \min(.5curve^\# - .85u^\#, -.1u^\#)$;

adjust_fit($serif\_fit^\#, 0$);

pickup $tiny.nib$; $pos_1(stem', 0)$; $pos_2(stem, 0)$;

$pos_{0'}(stem', 0)$; $pos_0(stem, 0)$; $z_{0l} = z_{0'l}$; $x_{0'} = x_1$; $x_0 = x_2$;

$lft\ x_{1l} = \text{hround}(2.5u - .5stem')$; $top\ y_1 = h$ **if** $serifs$: $+ \min(oo, serif\_drop)$ **fi**;

numeric $edge$; $edge = rt\ x_{2r}$;

pickup $fine.nib$; $pos_3(\textbf{if}\ hefty\text{: } thin\_join\ \textbf{else: } hair\ \textbf{fi}, 180)$;

$pos_4(vair', 90)$; $pos_5(curve, 0)$; $pos_6(vair, -90)$; $penpos_7(x_{3l} - x_{3r}, -180)$;

$rt\ x_{3l} = \max(rt\ x_{3l} - (lft\ x_{3r} - tiny.lft\ x_{2l}), \frac{1}{3}[rt\ x_2, edge])$;

$y_3 = \frac{1}{8}[bar\_height, x\_height]$;

$x_{4l} = w - .5(w - serif\_fit) + .5u$; $top\ y_{4r} = x\_height + oo$;

$rt\ x_{5r} = \text{hround}\min(w - 1.35u + .5curve, w - .6u)$; $y_5 = .5x\_height$;

$x_{6l} = x_{4l} - .2u$; $bot\ y_{6r} = -oo$;

$x_7 = x_3$; $y_7 = \min(y_3, y_6 + y_4 - y_3 + .6vair)$;

$(x, y_{4r}) = whatever[z_{3l}, z_{4l}]$; $x_{4r} := \min(x, .5[x_{5r}, x_4])$;

$(x', y_{6r}) = whatever[z_{7l}, z_{6l}]$; $x_{6r} := \min(x', .5[x_{5r}, x_6])$;

filldraw stroke $z_{3e}\{up\} \ldots \{right\}z_{4e}$ & $super\_arc_e(4, 5)$

     & $super\_arc_e(5, 6)$ & $z_{6e}\{left\} \ldots \{up\}z_{7e}$;   % bowl

$y_0 = \text{ypart}(((edge, h) \text{ -- } (edge, 0))\ \text{intersectionpoint}\ (z_{3l}\{up\} \ldots \{right\}z_{4l}))$;

pickup $tiny.nib$; $bot\ y_2 = -d$;

filldraw stroke $z_{1e} \text{ -- } z_{0'e} \text{ -- } z_{0e} \text{ -- } z_{2e}$;   % stem

pickup $crisp.nib$; $pos_8(hair, 0)$; $pos_{7'}(stem, 0)$;

$z_{7'} = z_2$; $x_{8l} = x_{7'l}$; $bot\ y_8 = 0$;

filldraw stroke $z_{7'e} \text{ -- } z_{8e}$;   % point

if $serifs$: $sloped\_serif.l(1, 0', a, \frac{1}{3}, jut, serif\_drop)$;   % upper serif

     $dish\_serif(2, 0, b, \frac{1}{3}, jut, c, \frac{1}{3}, jut)$; **fi**   % lower serif

penlabels(0, 1, 2, 3, 4, 5, 6, 7, 8); **endchar**;

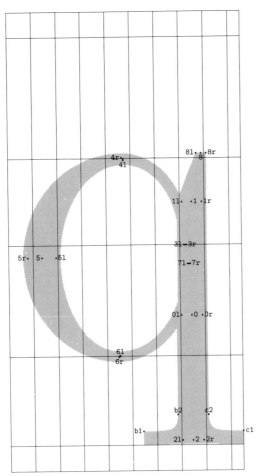

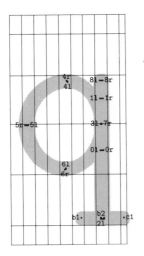

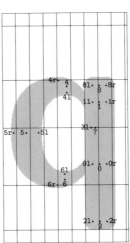

cmchar "The letter q";
beginchar("q", $10u\# + \mathit{serif\_fit}\# , \mathit{x\_height}\#, \mathit{desc\_depth}\#$);
italcorr $\mathit{x\_height}\# * \mathit{slant} - \mathit{serif\_fit}\# + .5\mathit{stem}\# - 2u\#$ **if** *serifs*: $+.5u\#$ **fi**;
adjust_fit$(0, \mathit{serif\_fit}\#$ **if** *serifs*: $-.5u\#$ **fi**);
pickup *tiny.nib*; $pos_1(\mathit{stem}', 0)$; $pos_2(\mathit{stem}, 0)$;
$pos_{0'}(\mathit{stem}', 0)$; $pos_0(\mathit{stem}, 0)$; $z_{0r} = z_{0'r}$; $x_{0'} = x_1$; $x_0 = x_2$;
$rt \; x_{1r} = \mathrm{hround}(w - 2.5u + .5\mathit{stem}')$;
numeric *edge*; $\mathit{edge} = \mathit{lft} \; x_{2l}$;
pickup *fine.nib*; $pos_3($**if** *hefty*: $\mathit{thin\_join}$ **else**: *hair* **fi**$, 0)$;
$pos_4(\mathit{vair}', 90)$; $pos_5(\mathit{curve}, 180)$; $pos_6(\mathit{vair}, 270)$; $\mathit{penpos}_7(x_{3r} - x_{3l}, 360)$;
$\mathit{lft} \; x_{3l} = \min(\mathit{lft} \; x_{3l} - (rt \; x_{3r} - \mathit{tiny}.rt \; x_{2r}), \tfrac{2}{3}[\mathit{lft} \; x_2, \mathit{edge}])$; $y_3 = \mathit{bar\_height}$;
$x_{4l} = .5(w - \mathit{serif\_fit}) - .3u$; $top \; y_{4r} = \mathit{x\_height} + oo$;
$\mathit{lft} \; x_{5r} = \mathrm{hround} \max(1.35u - .5\mathit{curve}, .6u)$; $y_5 = .5\mathit{x\_height}$;
$x_{6l} = x_{4l} - .2u$; $bot \; y_{6r} = -oo$; $y_7 = \min(y_3, y_6 + y_4 - y_3 + .6\mathit{vair})$;
$\mathit{lft} \; x_{7l} = \min(\mathit{lft} \; x_{7l} - (rt \; x_{7r} - \mathit{tiny}.rt \; x_{2r}), \tfrac{1}{3}[\mathit{lft} \; x_2, \mathit{edge}])$;
$(x, y_{4r}) = \mathit{whatever}[z_{3l}, z_{4l}]$; $x_{4r} := \max(x, .5[x_{5r}, x_4])$;
$(x', y_{6r}) = \mathit{whatever}[z_{7l}, z_{6l}]$; $x_{6r} := \max(x', .5[x_{5r}, x_6])$;
filldraw stroke $z_{3e}\{up\} \ldots \{left\}z_{4e}$ & $\mathit{super\_arc}_e(4, 5)$
  & $\mathit{super\_arc}_e(5, 6)$ & $z_{6e}\{right\} \ldots \{up\}z_{7e}$; % bowl
$y_1 = \mathrm{ypart}(((\mathit{edge}, h) -- (\mathit{edge}, 0)) \; \mathrm{intersectionpoint} \; (z_{3l}\{up\} \ldots \{left\}z_{4l}))$;
$y_0 = \mathrm{ypart}(((\mathit{edge}, h) -- (\mathit{edge}, 0)) \; \mathrm{intersectionpoint} \; (z_{6l}\{right\} \ldots \{up\}z_{7l}))$;
pickup *tiny.nib*; $bot \; y_2 = -d$;
filldraw stroke $z_{1e} -- z_{0'e} -- z_{0e} -- z_{2e}$; % stem
pickup *crisp.nib*;
$pos_8(\mathrm{hround}(\mathit{hair} - \mathit{stem\_corr}), 0)$; $pos_{7'}(\mathit{stem}', 0)$;
$z_{7'} = z_1$; $x_{8r} = x_{7'r}$; $top \; y_8 = h + oo$;
filldraw stroke $z_{7'e} -- z_{8e}$; % point
if *serifs*: $\mathit{dish\_serif}(2, 0, b, \tfrac{1}{3}, \mathit{jut}, c, \tfrac{1}{3}, \mathit{jut})$; **fi** % lower serif
penlabels$(0, 1, 2, 3, 4, 5, 6, 7, 8)$; **endchar**;

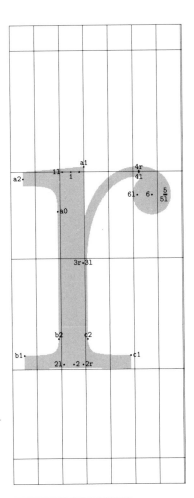

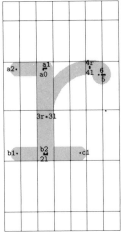

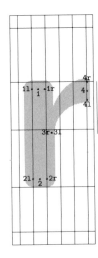

cmchar "The letter r";

numeric $r\_flare\#$; $\ r\_flare\# = .75[\mathbf{if}\ serifs:\ stem\#\ \mathbf{else}:\ vair\#\ \mathbf{fi},\ flare\#]$;

define_whole_blacker_pixels(r_flare);

beginchar("r", **if** $serifs: \max(7u\#, 5.5u\# + r\_flare\#)$ **else**: $6.5u\#$ **fi**, $x\_height\#, 0)$;

italcorr $x\_height\# * slant$ **if** not $serifs: +.25u\#$ **fi**;

adjust_fit$(serif\_fit\#, 0)$;

pickup $fine.nib$; $\ top\ y_{4r} = h + oo$;

if $serifs:\ pos_4(vair, 90)$; $\ pos_5(hair, 0)$;

$\quad x_4 = w - \max(1.75u, .25u + r\_flare)$;

$\quad rt\ x_{5r} = \mathrm{hround}(w - .5u + .5)$; $\ y_5 + .5r\_flare = .9[bar\_height, h] + oo$;

$\quad pos_6(r\_flare, 0)$; $\ bulb(4, 5, 6)$; $\hfill \%\ \text{bulb}$

else: $pos_4(r\_flare, 90)$; $\ rt\ x_4 = \mathrm{hround}(w - .25u)$; **fi**

$pos_3(thin\_join, 180)$; $\ rt\ x_{3l} = \mathrm{hround}(2.5u - .5stem') + stem'$; $\ top\ y_3 = bar\_height$;

filldraw stroke $z_{3e}\{up\} \ldots \{right\}z_{4e}$; $\hfill \%\ \text{arc}$

pickup $tiny.nib$; $\ pos_0(stem', 0)$; $\ pos_2(stem', 0)$;

$pos_1(\mathrm{hround}(stem - 3stem\_corr), 0)$; $\ top\ y_1 = h + \min(oo, serif\_drop)$;

$pos_{0'}(\mathrm{hround}(stem - 3stem\_corr), 0)$; $\ y_0 = y_{0'} = y_3$; $\ x_{1l} = x_{0l} = x_{0'l} = x_{2l}$;

$lft\ x_{1l} = \mathrm{hround}(2.5u - .5stem')$; $\ bot\ y_2 = 0$;

filldraw stroke $z_{1e}\ \texttt{--}\ z_{0'e}\ \texttt{--}\ z_{0e}\ \texttt{--}\ z_{2e}$; $\hfill \%\ \text{stem}$

if $serifs:\ sloped\_serif.l(1, 0', a, \tfrac{1}{3}, jut, serif\_drop)$; $\hfill \%\ \text{upper serif}$

$\quad dish\_serif(2, 0, b, \tfrac{1}{3}, jut, c, \tfrac{1}{3}, 1.25jut)$; **fi** $\hfill \%\ \text{lower serif}$

penlabels$(1, 2, 3, 4, 5, 6)$; **endchar**;

The good type designer knows that,
for a new fount to be successful,
it has to be so good that only very few recognize its novelty.
. . . If my friends think that the tail of my lower-case r
or the lip of my lower-case e is rather jolly,
you may know that the fount would have been better
had neither been made.

— STANLEY MORISON, *First Principles of Typography* (1930)

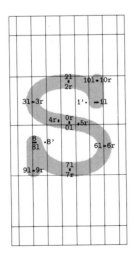

cmchar "The letter s";
beginchar("s", $7.1u\#$, $x\_height\#$, 0);
italcorr $x\_height\# * slant -$ **if** $serifs$: $.55u\#$ **else**: $.3u\#$ **fi**;
adjust_fit(**if** $monospace$: $.5u\#$, $.4u\#$ **else**: 0, **if** $serifs$: 0 **else**: $-.2u\#$ **fi fi**);
numeric $theta$; $theta = 90 - \text{angle}(40u, h)$; $slope := -h/40u$;   % angle at middle
numeric s_slab; $s\_slab =$ **if** $serifs$: $vair$ **else**: Vround $.1[vair, stem]$ **fi**;
numeric ess'; $ess' = \max(fine.breadth, ess)$;
pickup $fine.nib$; $pos_2(\max(fine.breadth, s\_slab - \text{vround } vair\_corr), -100)$;
$pos_0(ess', theta)$; $pos_7(s\_slab, -90)$; $x_{2l} = x_0 = x_7 = .5w$;
$top\ y_{2l} = h + \text{vround } 1.5oo$; $bot\ y_{7r} = -oo$;
$y_0 - .5ess' = y_{7l} +$ **if** $serifs$: $.54$ **else**: $.52$ **fi** $(y_{2r} - y_{7l} - ess')$;
$lft\ x_{3l} = \text{hround } .6u$; $rt\ x_{6r} = \text{hround}(w - .6u)$;
$x_{3r} - x_{3l} = x_{6r} - x_{6l} = \text{hround } .5[s\_slab, ess'] - fine$;
$ellipse\_set(2l, 3l, 4l, 0l)$; $ellipse\_set(2r, 3r, 4r, 0r)$; $y_3 = y_{3r}$;
$ellipse\_set(7l, 6l, 5l, 0l)$; $ellipse\_set(7r, 6r, 5r, 0r)$; $y_6 = y_{6r}$;
interim $superness := more\_super$;
filldraw stroke $super\_arc_e(2, 3)$ & $z_{3e}\{down\}$
    .. z_{4e} --- z_{5e} .. $z_{6e}\{down\}$ & $super\_arc_e(6, 7)$;   % main stroke
if $serifs$: $pos_1(hair, 180)$; $pos_8(hair, 180)$;
    $rt\ x_{1l} = \text{hround}(w - 1.05u)$; $lft\ x_{8r} = \text{hround } .6u$;
    $bot\ y_1 = \min(bot\ y_{2r}, \text{vround } 1/5[top\ y_{5r}, h])$;
    $top\ y_8 = \max(top\ y_{7l}, \text{vround } 5/6 bot\ y_{4l})$;
    filldraw stroke $z_{1e}\{up\}$ .... $\{left\}z_{2e}$;   % upper arc
    filldraw stroke $z_{7e}\{left\}$ .... $\{x_8 - x_7, 5(y_8 - y_7)\}z_{8e}$;   % lower arc
    path $upper\_arc, lower\_arc$;
    $upper\_arc = z_1\{up\}$ .... $\{left\}z_2$; $lower\_arc = z_7\{left\}$ .... $\{x_8 - x_7, 5(y_8 - y_7)\}z_8$;
    $pos_{10}(.3[fine.breadth, cap\_hair], 0)$; $pos_9(.3[fine.breadth, cap\_hair], 0)$;
    $x_{10r} = x_{1l}$; $top\ y_{10} = top\ y_{2l}$; $x_{9l} = x_{8r}$; $bot\ y_9 = bot\ y_{7r}$;
    $x_{1l} - x_{1'} = x_{8'} - x_{8r} = 1.6cap\_curve - fine$; $y_{1'} = y_1$; $y_{8'} = y_8$;
    numeric t; $t = \text{xpart}(upper\_arc \text{ intersectiontimes } (z_{10l} \text{ -- } z_{1'}))$;
    filldraw z_{1l} -- z_{10r} -- z_{10l} -- **subpath**$(t, 0)$ **of** $upper\_arc$ -- **cycle**;   % upper barb
    $t := \text{xpart}(lower\_arc \text{ intersectiontimes } (z_{9r} \text{ -- } z_{8'}))$;
    filldraw z_{8r} -- z_{9l} -- z_{9r} -- **subpath**$(t, 1)$ **of** $lower\_arc$ -- **cycle**;   % lower barb
else: $pos_1(4/7[s\_slab, flare], -100)$; $pos_8(flare, -100)$;
    $x_{1l} = good.x(x_{1l} + w - u - rt\ x_1)$; $lft\ x_{8r} = \text{hround } .5u$;
    $top\ y_{1l} = \text{vround}(.93h + 1.5oo)$; $bot\ y_{8r} = \text{vround } .1h - oo$;
    filldraw stroke $term.e(2, 1, right, .9, 4)$;   % upper arc and terminal
    filldraw stroke $term.e(7, 8, left, 1, 4)$; **fi**   % lower arc and terminal
penlabels(0, 1, 1', 2, 3, 4, 5, 6, 7, 8, 8', 9, 10); **endchar**;

---

def $ellipse\_set($**suffix** $\$, @, @@, \$\$) =$ % given $z_\$$, $x_@$, $z_{\$\$}$, find $y_@$ and $z_{@@}$
                  % such that the path $z_\$\{x_@ - x_\$, 0\}$ .. $z_@\{0, y_@ - y_\$\}$ .. $\{z_{\$\$} - z_{@@}\}z_{@@}$
                  % is consistent with an ellipse
                  % and such that the line $z_{@@}$ -- $z_{\$\$}$ has a given $slope$
$alpha\_ := slope * (x_@ - x_\$)$; $beta\_ := y_{\$\$} - y_\$ - slope * (x_{\$\$} - x_\$)$;
$gamma\_ := alpha\_/beta\_$;
$y_@ - y_\$ = .5(beta\_ - alpha\_ * gamma\_)$;
$x_{@@} - x_\$ = -2gamma\_ * (x_@ - x_\$)/(1 + gamma\_ * gamma\_)$;
$y_{@@} - y_{\$\$} = slope * (x_{@@} - x_{\$\$})$ **enddef**;

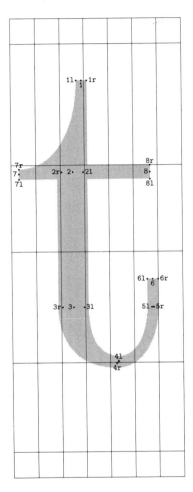

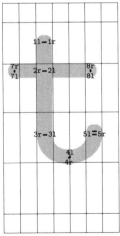

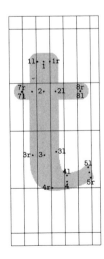

cmchar "The letter t";

beginchar("t", $6u\# + \max(u\#, .5stem\#)$,

$\quad \min(asc\_height\#, \text{ if } hefty: {}^{9}\!/_{7} \text{ else: } {}^{10}\!/_{7} \text{ fi } x\_height\#), 0)$;

italcorr $x\_height\# * slant$ **if** $serifs: -.9u\#$ **else:** $-.4u\#$ **fi**;

adjust_fit$(0, \text{ if } serifs: 0 \text{ else: } -.5u\# \text{ fi})$;

numeric $shaved\_stem$; $shaved\_stem = \text{hround}(stem \text{ if } hefty: -2stem\_corr \text{ fi})$;

pickup $fine.nib$; $pos_2(shaved\_stem, 180)$; $pos_3(shaved\_stem, 180)$;

$lft \ x_{2r} = lft \ x_{3r} = \text{hround}(2.5u - .5shaved\_stem)$;

$y_2 = y_8$; $y_3 = \max(.5bar\_height, 2vair)$;

pickup $crisp.nib$; $pos_8(bar, 90)$;

$rt \ x_8 = \text{hround}(w - 1.3u)$; $top \ y_{8r} = x\_height$; $lft \ x_7 = \text{hround} \ {}^{1}\!/_{3}u$; $y_{7l} = y_{8l}$;

if $hefty: pos_7(bar, 90)$;

$\quad$ **filldraw stroke** $z_{7e} \ \text{--} \ z_{8e}$; $\hfill \%$ crossbar

$\quad$ **pickup** $tiny.nib$; $pos_1(\text{hround}(shaved\_stem - stem\_corr), 0)$;

$\quad rt \ x_{1r} = fine.rt \ x_{2l}$; $top \ y_1 = h$;

$\quad penpos_{2'}(x_{1r} - x_{1l}, 0)$; $x_{2'} = x_1$; $y_{2'} = y_2$;

$\quad$ **filldraw stroke** $z_{1e} \ \text{--} \ z_{2'e}$; $\hfill \%$ upper terminal

else: $pos_7(vair, 90)$; $pos_1(hair, 0)$;

$\quad rt \ x_{1r} = fine.rt \ x_{2l}$; $top \ y_1 = h$;

$\quad$ **filldraw** $z_{1l}\{down\} \ \ldots \ \{left\}z_{7r} \ \text{--} \ z_{7l} \ \text{--} \ z_{8l}$

$\quad\quad \text{--} \ z_{8r} \ \text{--} \ (x_{1r}, y_{8r}) \ \text{--} \ z_{1r} \ \text{--} \ $cycle$;$ **fi** $\hfill \%$ upper terminal and crossbar

pickup $fine.nib$; **interim** $superness := more\_super$;

$pos_4(vair', -90)$; $bot \ y_{4r} = -oo$; $rt \ x_{5r} = \text{hround}(w - u)$;

if $serifs: pos_5(hair, 0)$; $y_5 = y_3$; $x_{4l} = .5[x_{3l}, x_{5l}]$;

$\quad (x, y_{4r}) = whatever[z_{4l}, z_{5l}]$; $x_{4r} := \max(x, .5[x_{3r}, x_4])$;

$\quad$ **filldraw stroke** $z_{2e} \ .. \ super\_arc_e(3, 4) \ \ldots \ \{up\}z_{5e}$; $\hfill \%$ stem and hook

$\quad$ **pickup** $crisp.nib$; $pos_6(hair, 0)$; $pos_{5'}(hair, 0)$;

$\quad x_6 = x_5 = x_{5'}$; $top \ y_6 = \max(\text{vround} \ .75bar\_height, top \ y_5)$; $y_5 = y_{5'}$;

$\quad$ **filldraw stroke** $z_{5'e} \ \text{--} \ z_{6e}$; $\hfill \%$ terminal

else: $pos_5(vair, -75)$; $top \ y_{5l} = \text{vround} \ .2[top \ y_{4l}, bar\_height]$;

$\quad x_{5l} := good.x \ x_{5l}$; $x_{4l} = {}^{1}\!/_{3}[x_{3l}, x_{5l}]$; $x_{4r} := {}^{1}\!/_{3}[x_{3r}, x_{5r}]$; $y_{3l} := y_{3l} + .2vair$;

$\quad$ **filldraw stroke** $z_{2e} \ .. \ super\_arc_e(3, 4)$; $\hfill \%$ stem and hook

$\quad$ **path** p; $p = $ **stroke** $z_{4e}\{right\} \ .. \ $tension$ .9$ and atleast$ 1 \ .. \ z_{5e}$; $\hfill \%$ terminal

$\quad$ **if**$(\text{xpart}(z_{5l} - \text{\textbf{precontrol} 1 \textbf{of} } p) < 0)$ **or** $(\text{xpart}(z_{5r} - \text{\textbf{postcontrol} 2 \textbf{of} } p) < 0)$:

$\quad\quad$ **filldraw stroke** $z_{4e}\{right\} \ \ldots \ \{up\}z_{5e}$;

$\quad$ **else: filldraw** p; **fi fi**;

penlabels$(1, 2, 3, 4, 5, 6, 7, 8)$; **endchar**;

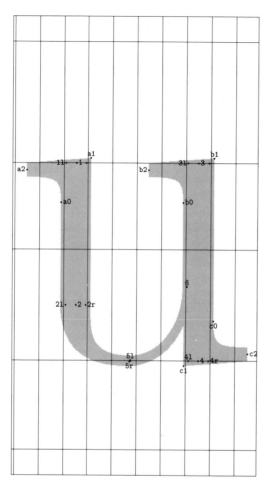

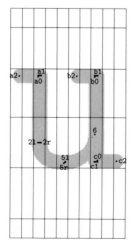

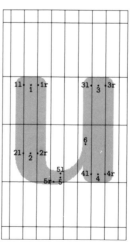

cmchar "The letter u";
beginchar("u", $10u^\#$, $x\_height^\#$, 0);
italcorr $x\_height^\# * slant - serif\_fit^\# + .5stem^\# - 2u^\#$;
adjust_fit($serif\_fit^\# + stem\_shift^\#$, $serif\_fit^\# - stem\_shift^\#$);
numeric $light\_vair$; $light\_vair = vair$ **if** $hefty$: $-$ vround $2vair\_corr$ **fi**;
if $light\_vair < fine.breadth$: $light\_vair := fine.breadth$; **fi**
pickup $tiny.nib$; $pos_1(stem, 0)$; $pos_2(stem, 0)$;
$pos_3(stem, 0)$; $pos_4(stem', 0)$;
$lft\ x_{1l} = \text{hround}(2.5u - .5stem)$; $x_1 = x_2$; $x_3 = w - x_1$; $x_{3r} = x_{4r}$;
if $serifs$: $top\ y_1 = h + \min(oo, serif\_drop)$; $bot\ y_4 = -\min(oo, serif\_drop)$;
else: $top\ y_1 = h$; $bot\ y_4 = 0$; **fi**
$pos_0(stem, 0)$; $pos_{0'}(stem', 0)$; $x_0 = x_3$; $x_{0'} = x_4$; $y_0 = y_{0'}$;
$penpos_{2'}(stem - fine, -180)$; $z_{2'} = z_2$; $y_3 = y_1$; $y_2 = .5bar\_height$;
$penpos_5(\max(eps, light\_vair - fine), -90)$; $penpos_6(thin\_join - fine, 0)$;
$y_6 = y_0 = {}^2\!/\!_3 bar\_height$;
filldraw stroke $z_{1e}\ \text{--}\ z_{2e}$;   % left stem
filldraw stroke $z_{3e}\ ..\ z_{0e}\ \text{--}\ z_{0'e}\ ..\ z_{4e}$;   % right stem
pickup $fine.nib$; $bot\ y_{5r} = -oo$; $x_{5l} = .5w - .25u$; $lft\ x_{6l} = tiny.lft\ x_{0l}$;
$(x, y_{5r}) = whatever[z_{5l}, z_{6l}]$; $x_{5r} := \max(x, .5[x_5, x_{2'r}])$;
filldraw stroke {{ **interim** $superness := hein\_super$;
    $pulled\_arc_e(2', 5)$ }} & $z_{5e}\{right\}\ \ldots\ \{up\}z_{6e}$;   % arc
if $serifs$: $sloped\_serif.l(1, 2, a, {}^1\!/\!_3, jut, serif\_drop)$;   % upper left serif
    $sloped\_serif.l(3, 0, b, {}^1\!/\!_3, jut, serif\_drop)$;   % upper right serif
    $sloped\_serif.r(4, 0', c, {}^1\!/\!_3, jut, \min(oo, serif\_drop))$; **fi**   % lower right serif
penlabels($1, 2, 3, 4, 5$); **labels**(6); **endchar**;

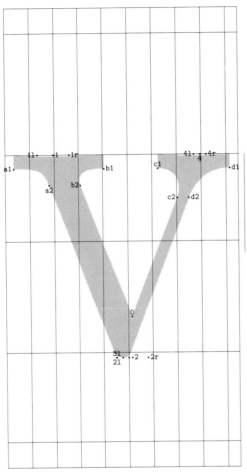

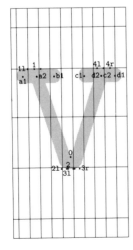

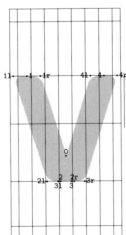

```
cmchar "The letter v";
```
beginchar(`"v"`, **if** *serifs*: 9.5u# **else**: 9u# **fi**, *x_height*#, 0);
italcorr *x_height*# * *slant* + .25u#;
adjust_fit(*serif_fit*# **if** *monospace*: + .5u#, .5u# + **else**: , **fi** *serif_fit*#);
numeric *left_stem*, *right_stem*, *outer_jut*, *alpha*;
left_stem = *fudged*.*stem* − *stem_corr*;
right_stem = min(*fudged*.*hair* **if** *hefty*: −2*stem_corr* **fi**, *left_stem*);
outer_jut = .75*jut*; $x_{1l} = w - x_{4r} = l + letter\_fit + outer\_jut + .25u$; $y_1 = y_4 = h$;
$x_2 - x_1 = x_4 - x_3$; $x_{2l} + apex\_corr = x_{3l}$; $y_2 = y_3 = -apex\_oo$;
alpha = *diag_ratio*(2, *right_stem*, $y_1 - y_2$, $x_{4r} - x_{1l} - apex\_corr$);
$penpos_1$(*alpha* * *left_stem*, 0); $penpos_2$(*alpha* * *left_stem*, 0);
$penpos_3$(*alpha* * *right_stem*, 0); $penpos_4$(*alpha* * *right_stem*, 0);
$z_0 = whatever[z_{1r}, z_{2r}] = whatever[z_{3l}, z_{4l}]$;
if $y_0 > notch\_cut$: $y_0 := notch\_cut$;
    fill $z_0 + .5right\{up\}$ ... $\{z_4 - z_3\}$ *diag_end*(3l, 4l, 1, 1, 4r, 3r)
        -- *diag_end*(4r, 3r, 1, 1, 2l, 1l) -- *diag_end*(2l, 1l, 1, 1, 1r, 2r)$\{z_2 - z_1\}$
        ... $\{down\}z_0 + .5left$ -- **cycle**;   % left and right diagonals
else: **fill** z_0 -- *diag_end*(0, 4l, 1, 1, 4r, 3r) -- *diag_end*(4r, 3r, 1, 1, 2l, 1l)
        -- *diag_end*(2l, 1l, 1, 1, 1r, 0) -- **cycle**; **fi**   % left and right diagonals
if *serifs*: **numeric** *inner_jut*; **pickup** *tiny.nib*;
  prime_points_inside(1, 2); *prime_points_inside*(4, 3);
  if *rt* $x_{1'r}$ + *jut* + .5u + 1 ≤ *lft* $x_{4'l}$ − *jut*: *inner_jut* = *jut*;
  else: *rt* $x_{1'r}$ + *inner_jut* + .5u + 1 = *lft* $x_{4'l}$ − *inner_jut*; **fi**
  dish_serif(1′, 2, a, 1/3, *outer_jut*, b, 1/2, *inner_jut*);   % left serif
  dish_serif(4′, 3, c, .6, *inner_jut*, d, 1/2, *outer_jut*)(*dark*); **fi**   % right serif
penlabels(0, 1, 2, 3, 4); **endchar**;

There is no set rule governing the relative weight of thick and thin lines
in characters having vertical and diagonal strokes, such as k, v, w, etc.
The stem of the 'k' should be the same as that of the 'h';
the heavy strokes of v, w, x, and y, should be
the same as those of the lower case 'm' and other smaller characters;
the thin strokes should have about the same weight as
the horizontal line in the lower case 'e'.

— C. H. GRIFFITH, *Letter to W. A. Dwiggins* (1931)

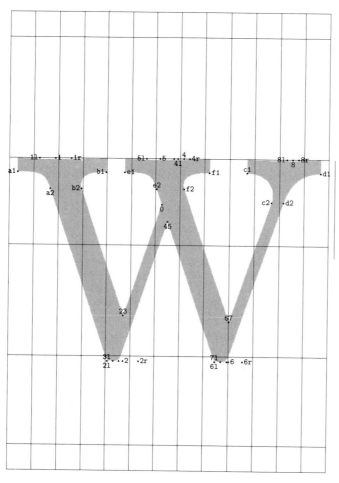

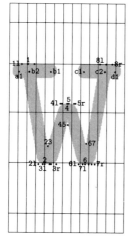

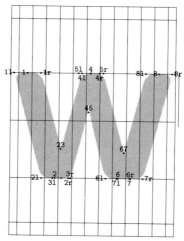

```
cmchar "The letter w";
```
beginchar("w", $13u^\#$, $x\_height^\#$, 0);
italcorr $x\_height^\# * slant + .25u^\#$;
adjust_fit($serif\_fit^\#$, $serif\_fit^\#$);
numeric $stem[\,]$, $outer\_jut$, $upper\_notch$, $alpha$, mid_corr;
$outer\_jut = .7jut$; $x_{1l} = w - x_{8r} = l + letter\_fit + outer\_jut + .25u$;
$stem_1 = fudged.stem - stem\_corr$;
$stem_4 = \min(fudged.hair$ **if** $hefty: -2stem\_corr$ **fi**, $stem_1)$;
$stem_2 =$ **if** $hefty: .1[vair, stem_4]$ **else**: $stem_4$ **fi**;
$stem_3 = \max(stem_2, stem_1 - 3stem\_corr)$;
$x_2 - x_1 = x_4 - x_3 = x_6 - x_5 \doteq x_8 - x_7$; $x_{2l} + apex\_corr = x_{3l}$; $x_{6l} + apex\_corr = x_{7l}$;
$y_1 = y_8 = h$; $y_2 = y_3 = y_6 = y_7 = -apex\_oo$;
$y_4 = y_5 =$ **if** $monospace$: vround $.6$ **fi** h; $upper\_notch = y_4 - notch\_cut$;
$mid\_corr =$ **if** $monospace$ or $hefty$: $-.3apex\_corr$ **else**: $.5jut$ **fi**;
$alpha = diag\_ratio(4, stem_2 - stem_3 + stem_4, y_1 - y_2, x_{8r} - x_{1l} + mid\_corr - 2apex\_corr)$;
$penpos_1(alpha * stem_1, 0)$; $penpos_2(alpha * stem_1, 0)$;
$penpos_3(alpha * stem_2, 0)$; $penpos_4(alpha * stem_2, 0)$;
$penpos_5(alpha * stem_3, 0)$; $penpos_6(alpha * stem_3, 0)$;
$penpos_7(alpha * stem_4, 0)$; $penpos_8(alpha * stem_4, 0)$;
$x_{4l} - x_{1l} =$ floor$(x_{4l} - x_{1l} + .5(x_{5r} + mid\_corr - x_{4r}))$;   % $x_{5r} \approx x_{4r} + mid\_corr$
$z_{23} = whatever[z_{1r}, z_{2r}] = whatever[z_{3l}, z_{4l}]$;
$z_{45} = whatever[z_{3r}, z_{4r}] = whatever[z_{5l}, z_{6l}]$;
$z_{67} = whatever[z_{5r}, z_{6r}] = whatever[z_{7l}, z_{8l}]$;
fill $diag\_end(1l, 2l, 1, 1, 3r, 4r)\{z_4 - z_3\}$
  ... **if** $y_{45} < upper\_notch$: $(x_{45}, upper\_notch) + .5left\{up\}$
    -- $(x_{45}, upper\_notch) + .5right\{down\}$ **else**: z_{45} & z_{45} **fi**
  ... $\{z_6 - z_5\}diag\_end(5l, 6l, 1, 1, 7r, 8r)$ -- $diag\_end(7r, 8r, 1, 1, 8l, 7l)\{z_7 - z_8\}$
  ... **if** $y_{67} > notch\_cut$: $(x_{67}, notch\_cut) + .5right\{down\}$
    -- $(x_{67}, notch\_cut) + .5left\{up\}$ **else**: z_{67} & z_{67} **fi**
  ... $\{z_5 - z_6\}special\_diag\_end(6, 5, 4, 3)\{z_3 - z_4\}$
  ... **if** $y_{23} > notch\_cut$: $(x_{23}, notch\_cut) + .5right\{down\}$
    -- $(x_{23}, notch\_cut) + .5left\{up\}$ **else**: z_{23} & z_{23} **fi**
  ... $\{z_1 - z_2\}diag\_end(2r, 1r, 1, 1, 1l, 2l)$ -- cycle;   % diagonals
if $serifs$: **numeric** $inner\_jut[\,]$; **pickup** $tiny.nib$;
  $prime\_points\_inside(1, 2)$; $prime\_points\_inside(5, 6)$; $prime\_points\_inside(8, 7)$;
  if $monospace$: $inner\_jut_1 = inner\_jut_4 = 1.5jut$;
  elseif $hefty$: $inner\_jut_1 = inner\_jut_4 = jut$;
  else: **fill** $diag\_end(6r, 5r, 1, 1, 5l, 6l)$ -- $.5[z_{5l}, z_{6l}]$
    -- $.5[z_{5r}, z_{6r}]$ -- cycle;   % middle stem
    $inner\_jut_2 = .7inner\_jut_1$; $inner\_jut_4 = 1.1inner\_jut_3$;
    if rt $x_{1'r} + jut + .5u + 1 \leq$ lft $x_{5'l} - .7jut$: $inner\_jut_1 = jut$;
    else: rt $x_{1'r} + inner\_jut_1 + .5u + 1 =$ lft $x_{5'l} - inner\_jut_2$; **fi**
    if rt $x_{5'r} + jut + .5u + 1 \leq$ lft $x_{8'l} - 1.1jut$: $inner\_jut_3 = jut$;
    else: rt $x_{5'r} + inner\_jut_3 + .5u + 1 =$ lft $x_{8'l} - inner\_jut_4$; **fi**
    $dish\_serif(5', 6, e, \frac{1}{3}, inner\_jut_2, f, \frac{1}{2}, inner\_jut_3)$; **fi**   % middle serif
  $dish\_serif(1', 2, a, \frac{1}{3}, outer\_jut, b, \frac{1}{2}, inner\_jut_1)$;   % left serif
  $dish\_serif(8', 7, c, .6, inner\_jut_4, d, \frac{1}{2}, outer\_jut)(dark)$; **fi**   % right serif
penlabels($0, 1, 2, 3, 4, 5, 6, 7, 8, 23, 45, 67$); **endchar**;

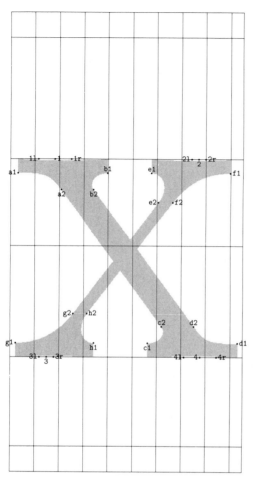

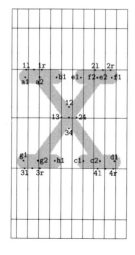
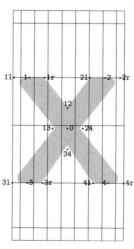

```
cmchar "The letter x";
```
beginchar("x", **if** *serifs*: 9.5$u^\#$ **else**: 9$u^\#$ **fi**, *x_height*$^\#$, 0);
italcorr *x_height*$^\#$ * *slant* $-$ .05$u^\#$;
adjust_fit(*serif_fit*$^\#$ **if** *monospace*: $+$ .5$u^\#$, .5$u^\#$ $+$ **else**: , **fi** *serif_fit*$^\#$);
numeric *stem*[], *outer_jut*, *xjut*, *alpha*[];
$stem_1 = fudged.stem - 4stem\_corr$; $stem_2 = \min(fudged.hair, stem_1)$;
$outer\_jut = .75jut$; $xjut = $ **if** *serifs*: $(stem_1 - stem_2)/4$ **else**: 0 **fi**;
$x_{1l} = l + letter\_fit + .1u + outer\_jut$; $x_{2r} = r - letter\_fit - .3u - outer\_jut - xjut$;
$x_{3l} = l + letter\_fit + outer\_jut + xjut$; $x_{4r} = r - letter\_fit - outer\_jut$;
$y_1 = y_2 = h$; $y_3 = y_4 = 0$;
$alpha_1 = diag\_ratio(1, stem_1, h, x_{4r} - x_{1l})$;
$alpha_2 = diag\_ratio(1, stem_2, h, x_{2r} - x_{3l})$;
$penpos_1(alpha_1 * stem_1, 0)$; $penpos_2(alpha_2 * stem_2, 0)$;
$penpos_3(alpha_2 * stem_2, 0)$; $penpos_4(alpha_1 * stem_1, 0)$;
if *hefty*: $z_0 = whatever[z_1, z_4] = whatever[z_2, z_3]$;
  $x_{12} = x_{34} = x_0$; $y_{13} = y_{24} = y_0$;
  $z_{12} = whatever[z_{2l}, z_{3l}]$; $z_{13} = whatever[z_{2l}, z_{3l}]$;
  $z_{24} = whatever[z_{2r}, z_{3r}]$; $z_{34} = whatever[z_{2r}, z_{3r}]$;
  forsuffixes $\$ = 13, 24, 34$: $z_{\$'} = .2[z_\$, z_0]$; **endfor**
  fill $diag\_end(12, 1r, .5, 1, 1l, 13') -- z_{13'} -- diag\_end(13', 3l, 1, .5, 3r, 34') -- z_{34'}$
    $-- diag\_end(34', 4l, .5, 1, 4r, 24') -- z_{24'}$
    $-- diag\_end(24', 2r, 1, .5, 2l, 12) -- z_{12} --$ **cycle**;   % diagonals
else: **fill** $diag\_end(4r, 1r, .5, 1, 1l, 4l)$
    $-- diag\_end(1l, 4l, .5, 1, 4r, 1r) --$ **cycle**;   % left diagonal
  fill $diag\_end(2l, 3l, .5, 1, 3r, 2r)$
    $-- diag\_end(3r, 2r, .5, 1, 2l, 3l) --$ **cycle**; **fi**   % right diagonal
if *serifs*: **numeric** *inner_jut*[]; **pickup** *tiny.nib*;
  $prime\_points\_inside(1, 4)$; $prime\_points\_inside(2, 3)$;
  $prime\_points\_inside(3, 2)$; $prime\_points\_inside(4, 1)$;
  if *rt* $x_{1'r} + jut + .5u + 1 \leq$ *lft* $x_{2'l} - jut - xjut$: $inner\_jut_1 = jut$;
  else: *rt* $x_{1'r} + inner_jut_1 + .5u + 1 = $ *lft* $x_{2'l} - inner\_jut_1 - xjut$; **fi**
  if *rt* $x_{3'r} + jut + .5u + 1 \leq$ *lft* $x_{4'l} - jut - xjut$: $inner\_jut_2 = jut$;
  else: *rt* $x_{3'r} + inner_jut_2 + .5u + 1 = $ *lft* $x_{4'l} - inner\_jut_2 - xjut$; **fi**
  $dish\_serif(1', 4, a, \frac{1}{3}, outer\_jut, b, \frac{2}{3}, inner\_jut_1)$;   % upper left serif
  $dish\_serif(4', 1, c, \frac{2}{3}, inner\_jut_2, d, \frac{1}{3}, outer\_jut)$;   % lower right serif
  $dish\_serif(2', 3, e, \frac{2}{3}, inner\_jut_1 + xjut,$
    $f, \frac{1}{2}, outer\_jut + xjut)(dark)$;   % upper right serif
  $dish\_serif(3', 2, g, \frac{1}{2}, outer\_jut + xjut,$
    $h, \frac{2}{3}, inner\_jut_2 + xjut)(dark)$; **fi**   % lower left serif
penlabels(0, 1, 2, 3, 4, 12, 13, 24, 34); **endchar**;

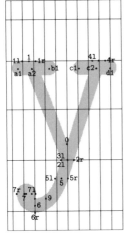

`cmchar "The letter y";`
beginchar(`"y"`, **if** *serifs*: $9.5u\#$ **else**: $9u\#$ **fi**, $x\_height\#$, $desc\_depth\#$);
italcorr $x\_height\# * slant + .25u\#$;
adjust_fit($serif\_fit\#$ **if** *monospace*: $+ .5u\#$, $.5u\# +$ **else**: , **fi** $serif\_fit\#$);
numeric $left\_stem$, $right\_stem$, bot_stem, bot_vair, $outer\_jut$;
$left\_stem = fudged.stem - stem\_corr$;
$right\_stem = fudged.hair$ **if** *hefty*: $-2stem\_corr$ **fi**;
$bot\_stem = fudged.hair$ **if** *hefty*: $-8stem\_corr$ **fi**;
$bot\_vair = \mathrm{Vround}($**if** *serifs*: $vair$ **else**: $.5[vair, bot\_stem]$ **fi**$)$;
$outer\_jut = .75jut$;
$x_{1l} = w - x_{4r} = l + letter\_fit + outer\_jut + .25u$; $y_1 = y_{4r} = h$; $y_2 = y_3 = 0$; $x_{2l} = x_{3l}$;
numeric $alpha$, $alpha[\,]$; $x_9 = 3u$; $y_9 = bot\_vair - d - oo$;
$alpha_1 = diag\_ratio(2, bot\_stem, y_1 - y_3, x_{4r} - x_{1l} - apex\_corr)$;
$alpha_2 = diag\_ratio(1, bot\_stem, y_1 - y_9, x_{4r} - x_9)$;
if $alpha_1 < alpha_2$: $x_{2l} - x_{1l} = x_{4r} - x_{3r} + apex\_corr$; $alpha = alpha_1$;
else: $alpha = alpha_2$; $z_{3l} = whatever[z_9, z_{4r} - (alpha * bot\_stem, 0)]$; **fi**
$penpos_3(alpha * bot\_stem, 0)$; $penpos_4(alpha * right\_stem, 0)$;
$alpha_3 = (y_1 ++ (x_{2l} - x_{1l}))/y_1$;
$penpos_1(alpha_3 * left\_stem, 0)$; $penpos_2(alpha_3 * left\_stem, 0)$;
$z_0 = whatever[z_{1r}, z_{2r}] = z_{4l} + whatever * (z_{3r} - z_{4r})$;
if $y_0 > notch\_cut$: $y_0 := notch\_cut$;
  fill $z_0 + .5right\{up\}$ ... $\{z_{4r} - z_{3r}\} diag\_end(0, 4l, 1, 1, 4r, 3r)$
   $-- z_{3r} -- z_{2l} -- diag\_end(2l, 1l, 1, 1, 1r, 2r)\{z_2 - z_1\}$
    ... $\{down\}z_0 + .5left$ -- cycle;   % left and right diagonals
else: **fill** $z_0 -- diag\_end(0, 4l, 1, 1, 4r, 3r) -- z_{3r} -- z_{2l}$
   $-- diag\_end(2l, 1l, 1, 1, 1r, 0)$ -- cycle; **fi**   % left and right diagonals
$penpos_5(alpha * bot\_stem, 0)$; $z_{5r} = whatever[z_{3r}, z_{4r}]$; $y_5 - .5vair = -.5d$;
if *serifs*: **numeric** $light\_bulb$; $light\_bulb = \mathrm{hround}\,{}^7\!/_8[hair, flare]$; **clearpen**;
 $penpos_6(vair, -90)$; $penpos_7(hair, -180)$; $penpos_8(light\_bulb, -180)$;
 $x_6 = 2u$; $y_{6r} = -d - oo$; $y_8 - .5light\_bulb = -.85d$; $x_{8r} = \mathrm{hround}\,.35u$;
 fill stroke $z_{3e} \mathbin{-\!\!-\!\!-} z_{5e}$ ... $\{left\}z_{6e}$; $bulb(6, 7, 8)$;   % arc and bulb
 numeric $inner\_jut$; **pickup** $tiny.nib$;
 $prime\_points\_inside(1, 2)$; $prime\_points\_inside(4, 3)$;
 if $rt\; x_{1'r} + jut + .5u + 1 \le lft\; x_{4'l} - jut$: $inner\_jut = jut$;
 else: $rt\; x_{1'r} + inner\_jut + .5u + 1 = lft\; x_{4'l} - inner\_jut$; **fi**
 $dish\_serif(1', 2, a, {}^1\!/_3, outer\_jut, b, {}^1\!/_2, inner\_jut)$;   % left serif
 $dish\_serif(4', 3, c, .6, inner\_jut, d, {}^1\!/_2, outer\_jut)(dark)$; % right serif
else: $penpos_6(bot\_vair, -90)$; $x_6 = 2.5u$; $y_{6r} = -d - oo$;
 fill stroke $z_{3e} \mathbin{-\!\!-\!\!-} z_{5e}$ ... $\{left\}z_{6e}$;   % arc
 pickup $fine.nib$; $pos_{6'}(bot\_vair, -90)$; $z_{6'} = z_6$;
 $pos_7({}^2\!/_3[bot\_vair, flare], -85)$;
 $lft\; x_{7l} = \mathrm{hround}\,u$; $bot\; y_{7r} = \mathrm{vround}\,{-.96d} - oo$; $y_{7l} := good.y\; y_{7l}$;
 filldraw stroke $term.e(6', 7, left, 1, 4)$; **fi**   % arc and terminal
penlabels(0, 1, 2, 3, 4, 5, 6, 7, 8, 9); **endchar**;

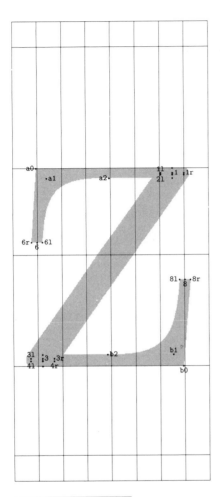

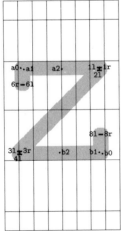

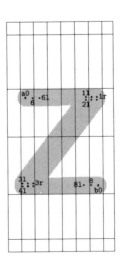

cmchar "The letter z";
beginchar("z", $8u^\#$, $x\_height^\#$, 0);
italcorr $x\_height^\# * slant - .5serif\_fit^\# - .3u^\#$;
adjust_fit$(0, .5serif\_fit^\#)$;
numeric $arm\_thickness[\,]$, z_stem;
if *hefty*: $arm\_thickness_1 = \text{Vround}(vair - vair\_corr)$; $arm\_thickness_2 = vair$;
$\quad z\_stem = .6[vair, stem]$;
else: $arm\_thickness_1 = vair$; $arm\_thickness_2 = vair'$; $z\_stem = .9[vair, stem]$; **fi**
pickup *tiny.nib*; $rt\ x_{1r} = rt\ x_{2r} = \text{hround}(w - .8u)$; $lft\ x_{3l} = lft\ x_{4l} = \text{hround}\ .5u$;
$top\ y_1 = h$; $y_2 = \min(y_1, h - {}^2\!/_3 arm\_thickness_1)$;
$bot\ y_4 = 0$; $y_3 = \max(y_4, {}^2\!/_3 arm\_thickness_2)$;
numeric $alpha$; $alpha = diag\_ratio(1, z\_stem - tiny, y_2 - y_3, x_{2r} - x_{3l} - slant*(y_2 - y_3))$;
$penpos_1(alpha * (z\_stem - tiny), 0)$; $penpos_2(alpha * (z\_stem - tiny), 0)$;
$penpos_3(alpha * (z\_stem - tiny), 0)$; $penpos_4(alpha * (z\_stem - tiny), 0)$;
pair *delta*; $delta = $ **penoffset** $z_3 - z_2$ **of** *currentpen*;
fill $top\ lft\ z_{1l}$ -- $z_{2l} + delta$ --- $z_{3l} + delta$ .. $lft\ z_{3l}$ --- $lft\ z_{4l}$ .. $bot\ z_{4l}$
$\quad$ --- $bot\ rt\ z_{4r}$ -- $z_{3r} - delta$ --- $z_{2r} - delta$ .. $rt\ z_{2r}$ --- $rt\ z_{1r}$ .. $top\ z_{1r}$
$\quad$ --- **cycle**; $\hspace{8cm}$ % diagonal
pickup *crisp.nib*; $pos_5(arm\_thickness_1, 90)$; $pos_6(hair, 180)$;
$top\ y_{5r} = h$; $x_5 = x_1$; $lft\ x_{6r} = \text{hround}\ .75u$; $y_6 = good.y(y_{5l} - beak/1.4) - eps$;
$arm(5, 6, a, beak\_darkness, -.4beak\_jut)$; $\hspace{3cm}$ % upper arm and beak
$pos_7(arm\_thickness_2, -90)$; $pos_8(hair, 0)$;
$bot\ y_{7r} = 0$; $x_7 = x_4$; $rt\ x_{8r} = \text{hround}(w - .75u)$; $y_8 = good.y(y_{7l} + beak/1.2) + eps$;
$arm(7, 8, b, beak\_darkness, .6beak\_jut)$; $\hspace{3cm}$ % lower arm and beak
penlabels$(1, 2, 3, 4, 5, 6, 7, 8)$; **endchar**;

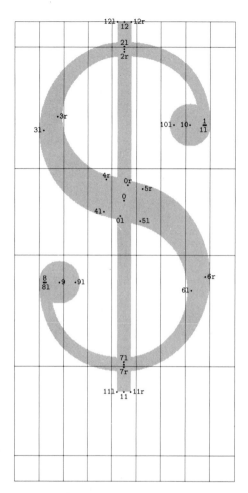

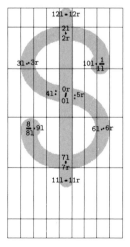

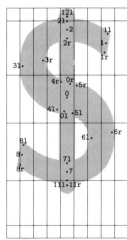

Program file `romanp.mf` gives us the characters whose italic variants were in `italp.mf`.

% This file contains '$' and '&' and '?' in the so-called roman style.

% Codes '044, '046, and '077 are generated, as well as code *spanish_query*
% (for a Spanish question mark) if that code value is known.

cmchar "Dollar sign";
beginchar("$", $9u^\#$, $body\_height^\#$, $body\_height^\# - asc\_height^\#$);
italcorr $fig\_height^\# * slant - .5u^\#$;   % same as for digits
adjust_fit$(0, 0)$;
numeric *theta*; $theta = 90 - \text{angle}(50u, asc\_height)$; $slope := -asc\_height/50u$;
pickup *fine.nib*; $pos_2(slab, -90)$;
$pos_0(cap\_stem, theta)$; $pos_7(slab, -90)$;
$x_2 = x_0 = x_7 = .5w$; $top\ y_{2l} = asc\_height + oo$; $bot\ y_{7r} = -oo$;
$y_0 = .52asc\_height$; $lft\ x_{3l} = \text{hround}\ u$; $rt\ x_{6r} = \text{hround}(w - u)$;
$x_{3r} - x_{3l} = x_{6r} - x_{6l} = \text{hround}\ .35[slab, cap\_stem] - fine$;
ellipse_set$(2l, 3l, 4l, 0l)$; *ellipse_set*$(2r, 3r, 4r, 0r)$; $y_3 = y_{3r}$;
ellipse_set$(7l, 6l, 5l, 0l)$; *ellipse_set*$(7r, 6r, 5r, 0r)$; $y_6 = y_{6r}$;
filldraw stroke $super\_arc_e(2, 3)$ & $z_{3e}\{down\}$
    .. z_{4e} --- z_{5e} .. $z_{6e}\{down\}$ & $super\_arc_e(6, 7)$;   % main stroke
if *serifs*: $pos_1(hair, 0)$; $pos_8(hair, 180)$;
    $pos_{10}(flare, 0)$; $pos_9(flare, 180)$;
    $rt\ x_{1r} = \text{hround}(w - u)$; $lft\ x_{8r} = \text{hround}\ u$; $y_1 = .5[y_0, y_2]$; $y_8 = .5[y_0, y_7]$;
    $\{\{less\_tense;\ pos_{2'}(slab, 90);\ z_{2'} = z_2;\ bulb(2', 1, 10)$;   % upper arc and bulb
    $bulb(7, 8, 9)\}\}$;   % lower arc and bulb
else: $pos_1(.6[slab, flare], -100)$; $pos_8(flare, -100)$;
    $rt\ x_{1l} = \text{hround}(w - 1.3u)$; $lft\ x_{8r} = \text{hround}\ .8u$;
    $top\ y_{1l} = \text{vround}\ .92asc\_height + oo$; $bot\ y_{8r} = \text{vround}\ .1asc\_height - oo$;
    filldraw stroke $term.e(2, 1, right, .9, 4)$;   % upper arc and terminal
    filldraw stroke $term.e(7, 8, left, 1, 4)$; **fi**   % lower arc and terminal
pickup *crisp.nib*; $pos_{12}(bar, 0)$; $pos_{11}(bar, 0)$;
$lft\ x_{12l} = lft\ x_{11l} = \text{hround}(.5w - .5bar)$; $top\ y_{12} = h$; $bot\ y_{11} = -d$;
filldraw stroke z_{12e} -- z_{11e};   % vertical crossbar
penlabels$(0, 1, 2, 3, 4, 5, 6, 7, 8, 9, 10, 11, 12)$; **endchar**;

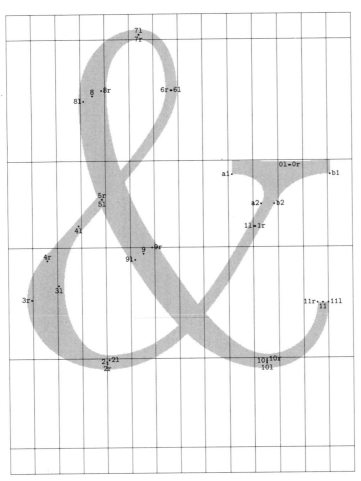

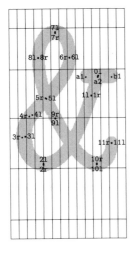

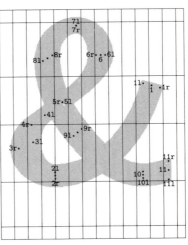

cmchar "Ampersand";
beginchar("&", $14u^\#$, $asc\_height^\#$, 0);
italcorr $x_height^\# * slant - serif_fit^\# - $ **if** $serifs$: $.4u^\#$ **else**: $1.5u^\#$ **fi**;
adjust_fit(0, $serif\_fit^\#$);
pickup $tiny.nib$; $pos_2(slab, -90)$; $x_2 = 4u$; $bot\ y_{2r} = -o$;
if not $hefty$: $(x, y_{2l}) = whatever[z_{2r}, (w - 5u, x\_height)]$; $x_{2l} := x$; **fi**
if $serifs$: $pos_0(fudged.hair, 0)$;
   $rt\ x_{0r} + jut = $ hround$(w - .9u)$; $top\ y_0 = x\_height$;
   $pos_1(fudged.hair, 0)$; $z_1 = whatever[z_0, (.6[x_0, x_2], 0)]$;
   $y_1 = \max(y_0 - 1.5bracket - .2x\_height, {}^2/_3 x\_height)$;
   filldraw stroke z_{0e} --- $z_{1e} \ldots \{left\}z_{2e}$;   % short diagonal
else: **pickup** $fine.nib$; $pos_1(.25[slab, flare], -15)$; $rt\ x_{1r} = $ hround$(w - 2u)$;
   $y_{1r} = good.y\ .75[bar\_height, x\_height]$; $x_{1l} := good.x\ x_{1l}$; $y_{1l} := good.y\ y_{1l}$;
   $top\ z_{2'l} = (x_{2l}, tiny.top\ y_{2l})$; $bot\ z_{2'r} = (x_{2r}, tiny.bot\ y_{2r})$;
   filldraw stroke $term.e(2', 1, right, 1, 4)$; **fi**   % short diagonal and terminal
pickup $tiny.nib$; **numeric** $slope$, $theta$, $reduced\_hair$;
$slope = (h - 2vair - slab)/10.5u$; $theta = $ angle$(-slope, 1)$;
$reduced_hair = \max(tiny.breadth, $ hround$(fudged.hair$ **if** $hefty$: $-2stem\_corr$ **fi**$))$;
$lft\ x_{3r} = $ hround $.75u$; $x_5 = .5[x_{3r}, x_{6l}]$; $lft\ x_{6r} = $ hround $.5(w - u)$;
$x_{3l} - x_{3r} = curve - tiny$; $pos_6(reduced\_hair, 180)$;
$pos_5(vair, theta)$; $y_5 = .5h$;
$ellipse\_set(2l, 3l, 4l, 5l)$; $ellipse\_set(2r, 3r, 4r, 5r)$;
$pos_7(vair, 270)$; $top\ y_{7l} = h + o$; $x_7 = .45[x_{6r}, x_{8r}]$;
$pos_8(fudged.stem, 30)$; $x_{8l} = good.x(x_{8l} + 3.5u - x_8)$; $y_{8r} = y_6$;
$ellipse\_set(7l, 6l, 5', 5l)$;
filldraw stroke $z_{2e}\{left\} \ldots z_{3e}\{up\} \ldots z_{4e}$ --- $z_{5e} \ldots \{up\}z_{6e}$
   $\ldots z_{7e}\{left\} \ldots z_{8e}\{down\}$;   % bowls
$pos_{10}(slab, 90)$; $x_{10} = w - 3.5u$; $bot\ y_{10l} = -o$;
$pos_9(fudged.stem, $ angle$(z_8 - z_{10}) - 90)$;
$z_9 = .5[z_8, z_{10}] + (1.75u, 0)$ rotated (angle$(z_8 - z_{10}) + 90)$;
filldraw stroke $z_{8e}\{down\} \ldots z_{9e}\{z_{10} - z_8\} \ldots \{right\}z_{10e}$;   % long diagonal
if $serifs$: **pickup** $crisp.nib$; $pos_{10'}(slab, 90)$; $z_{10'} = z_{10}$;
   $pos_{11}(fudged.hair, 180)$; $rt\ x_{11l} = $ hround$(w - u)$; $y_{11} = .5bar\_height$;
   filldraw stroke $z_{10'e}\{right\} \ldots \{up\}z_{11e}$;   % terminal
   numeric $inner\_jut$; **if** $rt\ x_{6l} + .5u < lft\ x_{0l} - 1.5jut$: $inner\_jut = 1.5jut$;
   else: $rt\ x_{6l} + .5u = lft\ x_{0l} - inner\_jut$; **fi**
   $dish\_serif(0, 1, a, .6, inner\_jut, b, .5, jut)(dark)$;   % serif
else: **pickup** $fine.nib$; $pos_{10'}(slab, 90)$; $z_{10'} = z_{10}$;
   $pos_{11}(\text{Vround } .5[slab, flare], 90)$;
   $rt\ x_{11} = $ hround$(r - letter\_fit - u)$; $bot\ y_{11l} = $ vround $.07bar\_height - o$;
   filldraw stroke $term.e(10', 11, right, 1, 4)$; **fi**   % terminal
penlabels($0, 1, 2, 3, 4, 5, 6, 7, 8, 9, 10, 11$); **endchar**;

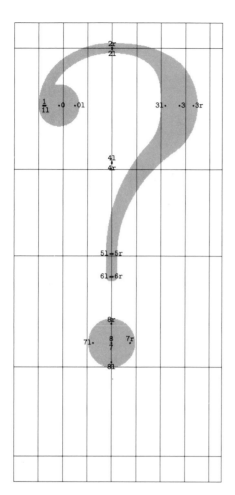

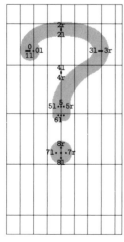
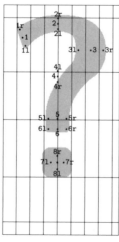

cmchar "Question mark";
beginchar("?", $8.5u^\#$, $asc\_height^\#$, 0);
italcorr $.8asc\_height^\# * slant$;
adjust_fit$(0, 0)$;
pickup $tiny.nib$; $pos_7(dot\_size, 0)$; $pos_8(dot\_size, 90)$;
lft $x_{7l} = $ hround$(.5w - .25u - .5dot\_size)$; *bot* $y_{8l} = 0$; $z_7 = z_8$; $dot(7, 8)$; % dot
numeric bot_width;
$bot_width = $ **if** $hefty$: max(hround $.8dot\_size$, $fine.breadth)$ **else**: $hair$ **fi**;
pickup $fine.nib$; $pos_2(vair, 90)$; $pos_3(curve, 0)$;
$pos_4(vair, -90)$; $pos_5(bot\_width, 0)$; $pos_6(bot\_width, 0)$;
$x_2 = x_4 = x_5 = x_6 = x_7$; *rt* $x_{3r} = $ hround$(w - u)$; *bot* $y_6 = 1 + .25[top\ y_{8r}, x\_height]$;
top $y_{2r} = h + oo$; $y_3 = .75[y_6, y_2]$; $y_4 = .5[y_6, y_2]$; $y_5 = .1[y_6, y_2]$;
$\{\{$ **interim** $superness := more\_super$;
filldraw stroke $pulled\_super\_arc_e(2, 3)(superpull)$
  & **subpath**$(0, 1)$ **of** $super\_arc_e(3, 4) .. z_{5e} \text{---} z_{6e} \}\}$; % arc and stem
if $serifs$: $pos_1(hair, 180)$; $pos_0(flare, 180)$;
  lft $x_{1r} = $ hround u; $y_1 = y_3$; $bulb(2, 1, 0)$; % bulb
else: $pos_1($Vround $^5/_7[vair, flare], 110)$;
  lft $x_{1r} = $ hround u; *top* $y_{1r} = $ vround $.9[y_6, top\ y_{2r}]$;
  filldraw stroke $term.e(2, 1, left, 1, 4)$; **fi** % terminal
penlabels$(0, 1, 2, 3, 4, 5, 6, 7, 8)$; **endchar**;

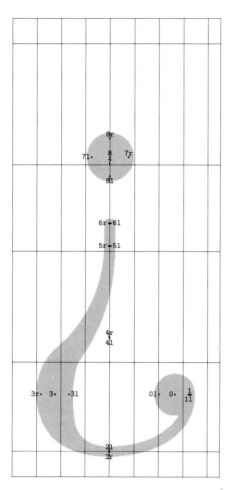

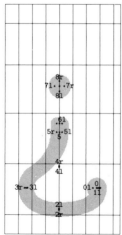

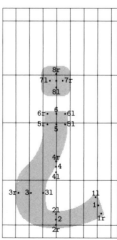

iff known *spanish_query*: **cmchar** "Spanish open question mark";
beginchar(*spanish_query*, $8.5u^\#$, *asc_height*$^\#$ − *desc_depth*$^\#$, *desc_depth*$^\#$);
adjust_fit(0, 0);
pickup *tiny.nib*; $pos_7(dot\_size, 0)$; $pos_8(dot\_size, 90)$;
lft x_{7l} = hround(.5w − .25u − .5dot_size); *top* $y_{8r} = h$; $z_7 = z_8$; *dot*(7, 8);   % dot
numeric *top_width*;
top_width = **if** *hefty*: max(hround .8*dot_size*, *fine.breadth*) **else**: *hair* **fi**;
pickup *fine.nib*; $pos_2(vair, 270)$; $pos_3(curve, 180)$;
$pos_4(vair, 90)$; $pos_5(top\_width, 180)$; $pos_6(top\_width, 180)$;
$x_2 = x_4 = x_5 = x_6 = x_7$; *lft* x_{3r} = hround u; *top* y_6 = .25[*bot* y_{8l}, h − x_height] − 1;
bot y_{2r} = −d − *oo*; $y_3 = .75[y_6, y_2]$; $y_4 = .5[y_6, y_2]$; $y_5 = .1[y_6, y_2]$;
{{ **interim** *superness* := *more_super*;
filldraw stroke *pulled_super_arc$_e$*(2, 3)(*superpull*)
    & **subpath**(0, 1) **of** *super_arc$_e$*(3, 4) .. z_{5e} --- z_{6e} }};   % arc and stem
if *serifs*: $pos_1(hair, 0)$; $pos_0(flare, 0)$;
    rt x_{1r} = hround(w − u); $y_1 = y_3$; *bulb*(2, 1, 0);   % bulb
else: pos_1(Vround ⁵⁄₇[*vair*, *flare*], −70);
    rt x_{1r} = hround(w − u); *bot* y_{1r} = vround .9[y_6, *bot* y_{2r}];
    filldraw stroke *term.e*(2, 1, *right*, 1, 4); **fi**   % terminal
penlabels(0, 1, 2, 3, 4, 5, 6, 7, 8); **endchar**;

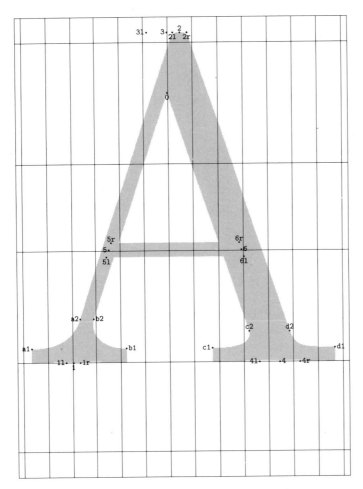

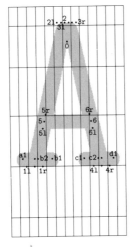

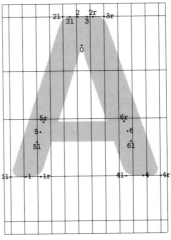

Now we come to program file `romanu.mf`, whose letters are used in all fonts except those containing nothing but math symbols. In fact, `romanu` is used twice in the caps-and-small-caps fonts.

% Computer Modern Roman upper case:
% These letters were originally coded by D. E. Knuth in November, 1979,
% inspired by the Monotype faces used in *The Art of Computer Programming*.
% Sans serif designs by Richard Southall were added in April, 1982.
% The programs were revised for the new METAFONT conventions in 1985.

% Character codes '101 through '132 are generated.

cmchar "The letter A";
beginchar("A", $13u^\#$, $cap\_height^\#$, 0);
adjust_fit($cap\_serif\_fit^\#$, $cap\_serif\_fit^\#$);
numeric $left\_stem$, $right\_stem$, $outer\_jut$, $alpha$;
$right\_stem = cap\_stem - stem\_corr$;
$left\_stem = \min(cap\_hair$ **if** $hefty$: $-3stem\_corr$ **fi**, $right\_stem$);
$outer\_jut = .8cap\_jut$; $x_{1l} = w - x_{4r} = l + letter\_fit + outer\_jut + .5u$; $y_1 = y_4 = 0$;
$x_2 - x_1 = x_4 - x_3$; $x_{3r} = x_{2r} + apex\_corr$; $y_2 = y_3 = h + apex\_o + apex\_oo$;
$alpha = diag\_ratio(2, left\_stem, y_2 - y_1, x_{4r} - x_{1l} - apex\_corr)$;
penpos$_1$($alpha * left\_stem$, 0); **penpos**$_2$($alpha * left\_stem$, 0);
penpos$_3$($alpha * right\_stem$, 0); **penpos**$_4$($alpha * right\_stem$, 0);
$z_0 = whatever[z_{1r}, z_{2r}] = whatever[z_{3l}, z_{4l}]$;
if $y_0 < h - cap\_notch\_cut$: $y_0 := h - cap\_notch\_cut$;
    fill $z_0 + .5right\{down\}$ ... $\{z_4 - z_3\}diag\_end(3l, 4l, 1, 1, 4r, 3r)$
    $-- diag\_end(4r, 3r, 1, 1, 2l, 1l) -- diag\_end(2l, 1l, 1, 1, 1r, 2r)\{z_2 - z_1\}$
    ... $\{up\}z_0 + .5left -- $ cycle;   % left and right diagonals
else: **fill** $z_0 -- diag\_end(0, 4l, 1, 1, 4r, 3r) -- diag\_end(4r, 3r, 1, 1, 2l, 1l)$
    $-- diag_end(2l, 1l, 1, 1, 1r, 0) -- $ cycle; **fi**   % left and right diagonals
penpos$_5$($whatever$, $angle(z_2 - z_1)$); $z_5 = whatever[z_1, z_2]$;
penpos$_6$($whatever$, $angle(z_3 - z_4)$); $z_6 = whatever[z_3, z_4]$; $y_6 = y_5$;
if $hefty$: y_{5r} **else**: y_5 **fi** $= {}^{5/12}y_0$;
$y_{5r} - y_{5l} = y_{6r} - y_{6l} = cap\_band$; **penstroke** $z_{5e} -- z_{6e}$;   % bar line
if $serifs$: **numeric** $inner\_jut$; **pickup** $tiny.nib$;
    $prime\_points\_inside(1, 2)$; $prime\_points\_inside(4, 3)$;
    if **rt** $x_{1'r} + cap\_jut + .5u + 1 \le$ **lft** $x_{4'l} - cap\_jut$: $inner\_jut = cap\_jut$;
    else: **rt** $x_{1'r} + inner_jut + .5u + 1 = $ **lft** $x_{4'l} - inner\_jut$; **fi**
    $dish\_serif(1', 2, a, {}^{1/2}, outer\_jut, b, .6, inner\_jut)(dark)$;   % left serif
    $dish\_serif(4', 3, c, {}^{1/2}, inner\_jut, d, {}^{1/3}, outer\_jut)$; **fi**   % right serif
penlabels(0, 1, 2, 3, 4, 5, 6); **endchar**;

> On the breast of her gown, in fine red cloth,
> surrounded with an elaborate embroidery
> and fantastic flourishes of gold-thread,
> appeared the letter A.
>
> — NATHANIEL HAWTHORNE, *The Scarlet Letter* (1850)

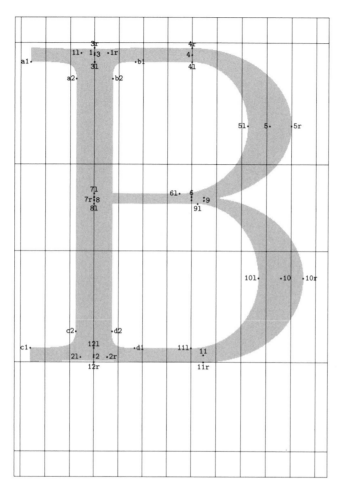

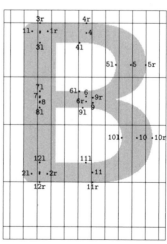

cmchar "The letter B";

beginchar("B", $12.5u^\#$, $cap\_height^\#$, 0);

italcorr $.75cap\_height^\# * slant - .5u^\#$;

adjust_fit($cap\_serif\_fit^\#$, 0);

numeric $left\_stem$, $right\_curve$, $middle\_weight$;

$left\_stem = cap\_stem -$ hround $2stem\_corr$; $middle\_weight = .6vair + .5$;

pickup $tiny.nib$; $pos_1(left\_stem, 0)$; $pos_2(left\_stem, 0)$;

$lft\ x_{1l} = lft\ x_{2l} =$ hround $\max(2u, 3u - .5left\_stem)$; $top\ y_1 = h$; $bot\ y_2 = 0$;

filldraw stroke z_{1e} -- z_{2e};   % stem

$penpos_3(cap\_band, 90)$; $penpos_4(cap\_band, 90)$;

$penpos_6(middle\_weight, -90)$; $penpos_7(middle\_weight, -90)$;

$penpos_8(middle\_weight, 90)$; $penpos_9(middle\_weight, 90)$;

$penpos_5(right\_curve - stem\_corr, 0)$; $penpos_{10}(right\_curve, 0)$;

$penpos_{11}(cap\_band, -90)$; $penpos_{12}(cap\_band, -90)$;

$z_{3r} = top\ z_1$; $y_4 = y_3$; $y_5 = .5[y_4, y_6]$; $y_6 = y_7$; $y_{7l} - y_{8l} = vair$;

$z_{12r} = bot\ z_2$; $y_{11} = y_{12}$; $y_{10} = .5[y_{11}, y_9]$; $y_8 = y_9$; $.5[y_{7l}, y_{8l}] = .52h$;

$x_4 = x_6$; $x_9 = x_{11} = x_4 + .5u$; $x_7 = x_8 = x_1$; $x_{9l} := x_4 + .25u$;

$x_{5r} =$ hround$(w - 1.5u)$; $x_{10r} =$ hround$(w - u)$;

if $serifs$: $right\_curve = cap\_curve - stem\_corr$; $x_4 = .5[x_1, w - 1.5u]$;

else: $right\_curve = cap\_curve - 3stem\_corr$; $x_4 = .5[x_1, w - 2.5u]$;

    $x_{4l} := x_{4l} - .5u$; $x_{9l} := x_{9l} - .5u$; **fi**

$x_{6l} := x_{6l} - .5u$; $x_{11l} := x_{11l} - .5u$;

fill stroke z_{3e} .. $super\_arc_e(4, 5)$ & $super\_arc_e(5, 6)$ .. z_{7e};   % upper lobe

fill stroke z_{8e} .. $super\_arc_e(9, 10)$ & $super\_arc_e(10, 11)$ .. z_{12e};   % lower lobe

if $serifs$: $nodish\_serif(1, 2, a, ⅓, cap\_jut, b, ⅓, .5cap\_jut)$;   % upper serif

    $nodish\_serif(2, 1, c, ⅓, cap\_jut, d, ⅓, .5cap\_jut)$; **fi**   % lower serif

math_fit$(0, .5ic^\#)$; **penlabels**$(1, 2, 3, 4, 5, 6, 7, 8, 9, 10, 11, 12)$; **endchar**;

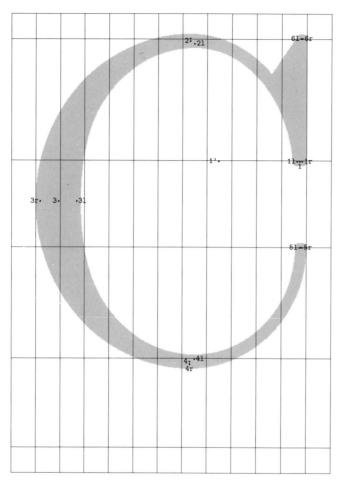

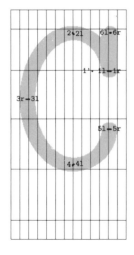

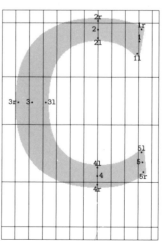

cmchar "The letter C";
if *serifs*: **beginchar**("C", $13u^\#$, $cap\_height^\#$, 0);
   italcorr $cap\_height^\# * slant - .5u^\#$;
   adjust_fit(0, 0);
   pickup *fine.nib*; $pos_1(cap\_hair, 0)$; $pos_2(cap\_band, 90)$;
   $pos_3(cap\_curve, 180)$; $pos_4(cap\_band, 270)$; $pos_5(hair, 360)$;
   $rt\ x_{1r} = rt\ x_{5r} = \text{hround}(w - u)$; $lft\ x_{3r} = \text{hround}\ u$; $x_2 = x_4 = .55[x_3, x_1]$;
   $top\ y_{2r} = h + o$; $bot\ y_{4r} = -o$; $y_3 = .5[y_2, y_4]$;
   $bot\ y_1 = \min(\text{vround} \max(.6h, x\_height - .5vair), bot\ y_{2l} - eps)$;
   $y_5 = \max(good.y\ .95(h - y_1), y_{4l} + eps)$;
   $(x_{2l'}, y_{2l}) = whatever[z_{2r}, z_{1l}]$; $x_{2l} := \min(x_{2l'}, x_{2l} + .5u)$;
   $(x_{4l'}, y_{4l}) = whatever[z_{4r}, z_{5l}]$; $x_{4l} := \min(x_{4l'}, x_{4l} + .5u)$;
   filldraw stroke $z_{1e}\{x_2 - x_1, 10(y_2 - y_1)\}$
     $\ldots pulled\_arc_e(2, 3)\ \&\ pulled\_arc_e(3, 4) \ldots \{up\}z_{5e}$;   % arc
   $pos_6(.3[fine.breadth, cap\_hair], 0)$; $x_{6r} = x_{1r}$; $top\ y_6 = h + o$;
   $x_{1r} - x_{1'} = 2cap\_curve - fine$; $y_{1'} = y_1$;
   path *upper_arc*; $upper\_arc = z_1\{x_2 - x_1, 10(y_2 - y_1)\} .. z_2\{left\}$;
   numeric t; $t = \text{xpart}(upper\_arc \text{ intersectiontimes } (z_{6l} \text{ -- } z_{1'}))$;
   filldraw z_{1r} -- z_{6r} -- z_{6l} -- **subpath**$(t, 0)$ **of** $upper\_arc$ -- **cycle**;   % barb
else: **beginchar**("C", $11.5u^\#$, $cap\_height^\#$, 0);
   italcorr $cap\_height^\# * slant - .5u^\#$;
   adjust_fit(0, 0);
   pickup *fine.nib*; $pos_1(1.2flare, 80)$; $pos_2(slab, 90)$;
   $pos_3(cap\_curve, 180)$; $pos_4(slab, 270)$; $pos_5(flare, 275)$;
   $rt\ x_{1r} = \text{hround}(w - 1.1u)$; $x_2 = x_4 = .5w + 1.25u$;
   $lft\ x_{3r} = \text{hround} \max(u, 2u - .5cap\_curve)$; $rt\ x_{5r} = \text{hround}(w - .9u)$;
   $top\ y_{1r} = \text{vround}\ .95h + o$; $top\ y_{2r} = h + o$; $y_3 = .5h$;
   $bot\ y_{4r} = -o$; $bot\ y_{5r} = \text{vround}\ .08h - o$; $y_{5l} := good.y\ y_{5l}$; $x_{5l} := good.x\ x_{5l}$;
   filldraw stroke $rterm_e(2, 1, right, .9, 4)\ \&\ super\_arc_e(2, 3)$
     $\&\ super\_arc_e(3, 4)\ \&\ term.e(4, 5, right, .8, 4)$; **fi**   % arc and terminals
math_fit$(-.3cap\_height^\# * slant - .5u^\#, .5ic^\#)$;
penlabels$(1, 1', 2, 3, 4, 5, 6)$; **endchar**;

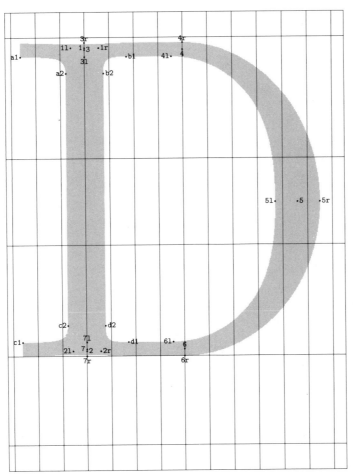

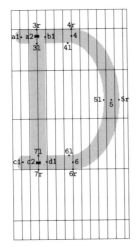

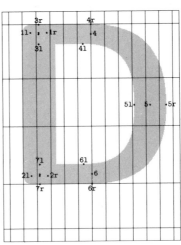

cmchar "The letter D";
beginchar("D", $13.5u^{\#}$, $cap\_height^{\#}$, 0);
italcorr $.7cap\_height^{\#} * slant - .5u^{\#}$;
adjust_fit($cap\_serif\_fit^{\#}$, 0);
pickup $tiny.nib$; $pos_1(cap\_stem', 0)$; $pos_2(cap\_stem', 0)$;
$lft\ x_{1l} = lft\ x_{2l} = \text{hround}\max(2u, 3u - .5cap\_stem')$; $top\ y_1 = h$; $bot\ y_2 = 0$;
filldraw stroke z_{1e} -- z_{2e};   % stem
$penpos_3(cap\_band, 90)$; $penpos_4(cap\_band, 90)$;
$penpos_5(cap\_curve - stem\_corr, 0)$;
$penpos_6(cap\_band, -90)$; $penpos_7(cap\_band, -90)$;
$z_{3r} = top\ z_1$; $y_4 = y_3$; $y_5 = .51[y_4, y_6]$; $y_6 = y_7$;
$z_{7r} = bot\ z_2$; $x_4 = x_6 = .5w + .25u$; $x_{5r} = \text{hround}(w - u)$;
$x_{4l} := x_{6l} := x_4 - .25cap\_curve$;
fill stroke z_{3e} .. $pulled\_arc_e(4, 5)$ & $pulled\_arc_e(5, 6)$ .. z_{7e};   % lobe
if $serifs$: $nodish\_serif(1, 2, a, \frac{1}{3}, cap\_jut, b, \frac{1}{3}, .5cap\_jut)$;   % upper serif
    $nodish\_serif(2, 1, c, \frac{1}{3}, cap\_jut, d, \frac{1}{3}, .5cap\_jut)$; **fi**   % lower serif
math_fit$(0, ic^{\#} - .5u^{\#})$; **penlabels**$(1, 2, 3, 4, 5, 6, 7)$; **endchar**;

---

def $nodish\_serif(\textbf{suffix}\ \$, \$\$, @)(\textbf{expr}\ left\_darkness, left\_jut)$
    $(\textbf{suffix}\ @@)(\textbf{expr}\ right\_darkness, right\_jut)\ \textbf{suffix}\ modifier =$
  $serif(\$, \$\$, @, left\_darkness, -left\_jut)modifier$;
  $serif(\$, \$\$, @@, right\_darkness, right\_jut)modifier$; **enddef**;

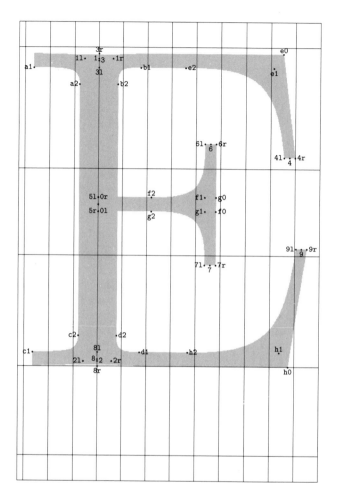

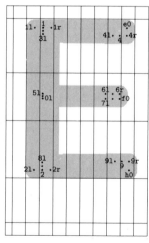

```
cmchar "The letter E";
```
beginchar("E", $12u\# - width\_adj\#$, $cap\_height\#$, 0);
italcorr $cap\_height\# * slant - beak\_jut\# - .5u\#$;
adjust_fit($cap\_serif\_fit\#$, 0);
$h := \text{vround}(h - stem\_corr)$;
pickup $tiny.nib$; $pos_1(cap\_stem, 0)$; $pos_2(cap\_stem, 0)$;
$lft\ x_{1l} = lft\ x_{2l} = \text{hround max}(2u, 3u - .5cap\_stem)$; $top\ y_1 = h$; $bot\ y_2 = 0$;
filldraw stroke z_{1e} -- z_{2e};   % stem
pickup $crisp.nib$; $pos_3(slab, 90)$; $pos_4(hair, 0)$;
$top\ y_{3r} = h$; $x_3 = x_1$; $rt\ x_{4r} = \text{hround}(w - u)$; $y_4 = good.y(y_{3l} - beak) - eps$;
$arm(3, 4, e, beak\_darkness, beak\_jut)$;   % upper arm and beak
$pos_5(cap\_bar, -90)$; $pos_6(hair, 0)$;
$top\ y_{5l} = \text{vround}(.52[y_2, y_1] + .5cap\_bar)$; $x_5 = x_1$;
$pos_0(cap\_bar, 90)$; $pos_7(hair, 0)$;
$z_0 = z_5$; $x_6 = x_7$; $y_6 - y_{5l} = y_{0l} - y_7$;
if $serifs$: $rt\ x_{6r} = \text{hround}(w - 4.4u + .5hair)$; $y_6 = good.y(y_{5l} + .6beak) + eps$;
    $rt\ x_{9r} = \text{hround}(w - .5u)$;
else: $rt\ x_{6r} = \text{hround}(w - 1.5u)$; $y_6 = y_{5l} + eps$; $rt\ x_{9r} = \text{hround}(w - .75u)$; **fi**
$arm(5, 6, f, beak\_darkness, 0)$; $arm(0, 7, g, beak\_darkness, 0)$; % middle arm and serif
$pos_8(slab\ \textbf{if not}\ serifs:\ +2stem\_corr\ \textbf{fi}, -90)$; $pos_9(hair, 0)$;
$bot\ y_{8r} = 0$; $x_8 = x_2$; $y_9 = good.y(y_{8l} + {}^7\!/_6 beak) + eps$;
$arm(8, 9, h, beak\_darkness, 1.5beak\_jut)$;   % lower arm and beak
if $serifs$: $nodish\_serif(1, 2, a, {}^1\!/_3, cap\_jut, b, {}^1\!/_3, .5cap\_jut)$;   % upper serif
    $nodish\_serif(2, 1, c, {}^1\!/_3, cap\_jut, d, {}^1\!/_3, .5cap\_jut)$; **fi**   % lower serif
math_fit(0, $.5ic\#$); **penlabels**(0, 1, 2, 3, 4, 5, 6, 7, 8, 9); **endchar**;

---

vardef $arm(\textbf{suffix}\ \$, \$\$, @)(\textbf{expr}\ darkness, jut) =$ % arm from $z_\$$ to $z_{\$\$}$
  $x_{@0} = good.x(x_{\$\$r} - jut)$; $y_{@0} = y_{\$r}$;
  if $serifs$: $y_{@1} = y_{\$l}$; $z_{@1} = z_{\$\$l} + whatever * (z_{\$\$r} - z_{@0})$;
    $z_{@2} = .5[z_{\$l}, z_{@1}]$;
    filldraw $z_{\$\$l}\{z_{@1} - z_{\$\$l}\} \ldots darkness[z_{@1}, .5[z_{@2}, z_{\$\$l}]] \ldots z_{@2}$
      --- $z_{\$l}$ -- $z_{\$r}$ -- $z_{@0}$ -- $z_{\$\$r}$ -- cycle;   % arm and beak
    else: filldraw $z_{\$l}$ -- $z_{\$r}$ -- $z_{@0}$ -- $z_{\$\$r}$ -- cycle; **fi**   % sans-serif arm
  penlabels(@0, @1, @2); **enddef**;

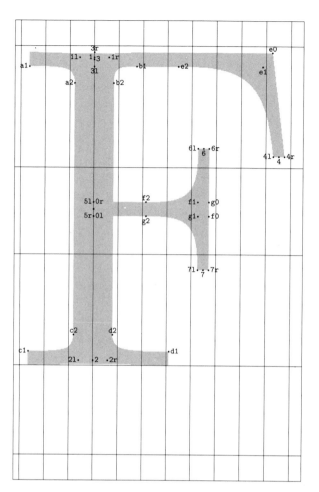

cmchar "The letter F";

beginchar("F", $11.5u\# - width\_adj\#, cap\_height\#, 0$);

italcorr $cap\_height\# * slant - beak\_jut\# - .25u\#$;

adjust_fit($cap\_serif\_fit\#, 0$);

$h := \text{vround}(h - stem\_corr)$;

pickup $tiny.nib$; $pos_1(cap\_stem, 0)$; $pos_2(cap\_stem, 0)$;

$lft\ x_{1l} = lft\ x_{2l} = \text{hround max}(2u, 3u - .5cap\_stem)$; $top\ y_1 = h$; $bot\ y_2 = 0$;

filldraw stroke $z_{1e} \text{ -- } z_{2e}$;   % stem

pickup $crisp.nib$; $pos_3(slab, 90)$; $pos_4(hair, 0)$;

$top\ y_{3r} = h$; $x_3 = x_1$; $rt\ x_{4r} = \text{hround}(w - .75u)$; $y_4 = good.y(y_{3l} - beak) - eps$;

$arm(3, 4, e, beak\_darkness, beak\_jut)$;   % upper arm and beak

$pos_5(cap\_bar, -90)$; $pos_6(hair, 0)$;

$top\ y_{5l} = \text{vround}(.5[y_2, y_1] + .5cap\_bar)$; $x_5 = x_1$;

$pos_0(cap\_bar, 90)$; $pos_7(hair, 0)$;

$z_0 = z_5$; $x_6 = x_7$; $y_6 - y_{5l} = y_{0l} - y_7$;

if *serifs*: $rt\ x_{6r} = \text{hround}(w - 4u + .5hair)$; $y_6 = good.y(y_{5l} + .6beak) + eps$;

$\quad rt\ x_{9r} = \text{hround}(w - .5u)$;

else: $rt\ x_{6r} = \text{hround}(w - 1.5u)$; $y_6 = y_{5l} + eps$; $rt\ x_{9r} = \text{hround}(w - .75u)$; **fi**

$arm(5, 6, f, beak\_darkness, 0)$; $arm(0, 7, g, beak\_darkness, 0)$; % middle arm and serif

if *serifs*: $nodish\_serif(1, 2, a, \frac{1}{3}, cap\_jut, b, \frac{1}{3}, .5cap\_jut)$;   % upper serif

$\quad dish\_serif(2, 1, c, \frac{1}{3}, cap\_jut, d, \frac{1}{3}, 1.25cap\_jut)$; **fi**   % lower serif

math_fit($0, ic\# - 2.5u\#$); **penlabels**($0, 1, 2, 3, 4, 5, 6, 7, 8, 9$); **endchar**;

F is a letter wherewith felons, &c. are branded
and marked with an hot iron,
on their being admitted to the benefit of clergy.
— T. E. TOMLINS, *Law Dictionary* (1797)

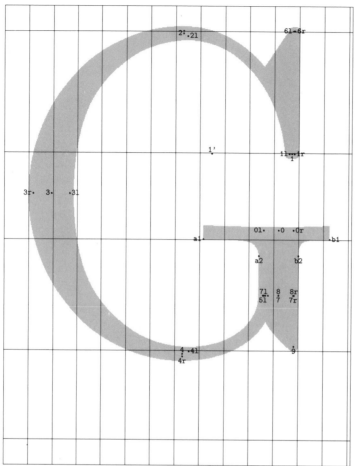

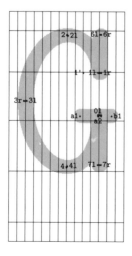

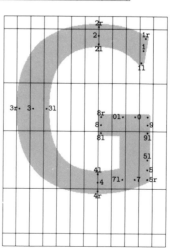

cmchar "The letter G";
if *serifs*: **beginchar**("G", $14u^\#$, $cap\_height^\#$, 0);
   italcorr $cap\_height^\# * slant - 1.5u^\# - .5cap\_serif\_fit^\#$;
   adjust_fit$(0, .5cap\_serif\_fit^\#)$;
   pickup *tiny.nib*; $pos_0(cap\_stem, 0)$; $pos_7(cap\_stem, 0)$;
   rt $x_{0r} = $ hround$(w - 2u)$; $y_0 = good.y(.1[bar\_height, x\_height] + 1)$; $x_7 = x_0$;
   pickup *fine.nib*;
   if *hefty*: bot $y_7 = 0$; $pos_5(cap\_stem, 0)$; $x_5 = x_0$; top $y_5 = tiny.top\ y_0$;
   else: $pos_5(cap\_hair, 0)$; $pos_8(cap\_stem, 0)$;
      $y_7 = .5bar\_height$; $z_{5l} = z_{8l}$; $z_8 = z_7$; $x_9 = x_{8r}$; bot $y_9 = 0$;
      filldraw $z_{8l}\{down\}$ .. $\{4(x_9 - x_8), y_9 - y_8\}z_9$ -- z_{8r} -- cycle; **fi**   % spur
   $pos_1(cap\_hair, 0)$; $pos_2(cap\_band, 90)$;
   $pos_3(cap\_curve, 180)$; $pos_4(cap\_band, 270)$;
   rt $x_{1r} = $ hround$(w - 2u)$; lft $x_{3r} = $ hround u; $x_2 = x_4 = .55[x_3, x_1]$;
   top $y_{2r} = h + o$; bot $y_{4r} = -o$; $y_3 = .5[y_2, y_4]$;
   bot $y_1 = \min($vround $\max(.6h, x\_height - .5vair)$, bot $y_{2l} - eps)$;
   $(x_{2l'}, y_{2l}) = whatever[z_{2r}, z_{1l}]$; $x_{2l} := \min(x_{2l'}, x_{2l} + .5u)$;
   $(x_{4l'}, y_{4l}) = whatever[z_{4r}, z_{5l}]$; $x_{4l} := \min(x_{4l'}, x_{4l} + .5u)$;
   filldraw stroke $z_{1e}\{x_2 - x_1, 10(y_2 - y_1)\}$
      ... $pulled\_arc_e(2, 3)\ \&\ pulled\_arc_e(3, 4)$ ... $z_{5e}\{up\}$;   % arc
   $pos_6(.3[fine.breadth, cap\_hair], 0)$; $x_{6r} = x_{1r}$; top $y_6 = h + o$;
   $x_{1r} - x_{1'} = 2cap\_curve - fine$; $y_{1'} = y_1$;
   path *upper_arc*; $upper\_arc = z_1\{x_2 - x_1, 10(y_2 - y_1)\}$ .. $z_2\{left\}$;
   numeric t; $t = $ xpart$(upper\_arc$ intersectiontimes $(z_{6l}$ -- $z_{1'}))$;
   filldraw z_{1r} -- z_{6r} -- z_{6l} -- **subpath**$(t, 0)$ of *upper_arc* -- cycle;   % barb
   pickup *tiny.nib*; **filldraw stroke** z_{0e} -- z_{7e};   % stem
   $dish\_serif(0, 7, a, \frac{1}{3}, \max(cap\_jut, 2.25u), b, \frac{1}{3}, 1.25u)$;   % serif
   math_fit$(-.3cap\_height^\# * slant - .5u^\#, ic^\#)$;
else: **beginchar**("G", $12u^\#$, $cap\_height^\#$, 0);
   italcorr $cap\_height^\# * slant - .5u^\#$;
   adjust_fit$(0, 0)$;
   pickup *fine.nib*; $pos_1(1.2flare, 80)$; $pos_2(slab, 90)$;
   $pos_3(cap\_curve, 180)$; $pos_4(slab, 270)$; $pos_5(flare, 270)$;
   rt $x_{1r} = $ hround$(w - 1.35u)$; $x_2 = x_4 = .5w + u$;
   lft $x_{3r} = $ hround $\max(u, 2u - .5cap\_curve)$; rt $x_{5l} = $ hround$(w - 1.2u)$;
   top $y_{1r} = $ vround $.93h + o$; top $y_{2r} = h + o$; $y_3 = .5h$;
   bot $y_{4r} = -o$; bot $y_{5r} = $ vround $.07h - o$;
   filldraw stroke $rterm_e(2, 1, right, .9, 4)\ \&\ super\_arc_e(2, 3)$
      $\&\ super\_arc_e(3, 4)\ \&\ term.e(4, 5, right, 1, 4)$;   % arc and terminals
   $pos_0(stem, 0)$; $pos_7(stem, 0)$;
   $z_{7r} = z_{5r}$; $x_0 = x_7$; top $y_0 = 1 + $ vround $.35[bar\_height, x\_height]$;
   filldraw stroke z_{0e} -- z_{7e};   % stem
   $pos_8(cap\_bar, 90)$; $pos_9(cap\_bar, 90)$;
   $z_{0r} = z_{9r}$; $y_8 = y_9$; lft $x_8 = $ hround x_4;
   filldraw stroke z_{8e} -- z_{9e};   % bar
   math_fit$(-.3cap\_height^\# * slant - .5u^\#, .5ic^\#)$; **fi**
penlabels$(0, 1, 1', 2, 3, 4, 5, 6, 7, 8, 9)$; **endchar**;

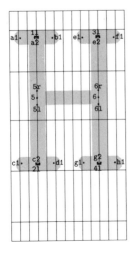

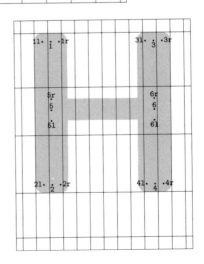

cmchar "The letter H";

beginchar("H", $13u^\# + width\_adj^\#$, $cap\_height^\#$, 0);

italcorr $cap\_height^\# * slant - cap\_serif\_fit^\# + cap\_jut^\# - 2.5u^\# + \min(.5cap\_stem^\#, u^\#)$;

adjust_fit($cap\_serif\_fit^\#$, $cap\_serif\_fit^\#$);

pickup $tiny.nib$; $pos_1(cap\_stem, 0)$; $pos_2(cap\_stem, 0)$;

$pos_3(cap\_stem, 0)$; $pos_4(cap\_stem, 0)$;

$lft\ x_{1l} = lft\ x_{2l} = $ hround $\max(2u, 3u - .5cap\_stem)$; $x_3 = x_4 = w - x_1$;

$top\ y_1 = top\ y_3 = h$; $bot\ y_2 = bot\ y_4 = 0$;

filldraw stroke z_{1e} -- z_{2e};   % left stem

filldraw stroke z_{3e} -- z_{4e};   % right stem

$penpos_5(cap\_bar, 90)$; $penpos_6(cap\_bar, 90)$;

$x_5 = x_1$; $x_6 = x_3$; $y_5 = y_6 = .52h$;

fill stroke z_{5e} -- z_{6e};   % bar

if $serifs$: **numeric** $inner\_jut$;

  if $rt\ x_{1r} + cap\_jut + .5u + 1 \leq lft\ x_{3l} - cap\_jut$: $inner\_jut = cap\_jut$;

  else: $rt\ x_{1r} + inner\_jut + .5u + 1 = lft\ x_{3l} - inner\_jut$; **fi**

  $dish\_serif(1, 2, a, \frac{1}{3}, cap\_jut, b, \frac{1}{3}, inner\_jut)$;   % upper left serif

  $dish\_serif(2, 1, c, \frac{1}{3}, cap\_jut, d, \frac{1}{3}, inner\_jut)$;   % lower left serif

  $dish\_serif(3, 4, e, \frac{1}{3}, inner\_jut, f, \frac{1}{3}, cap\_jut)$;   % upper left serif

  $dish\_serif(4, 3, g, \frac{1}{3}, inner\_jut, h, \frac{1}{3}, cap\_jut)$; **fi**   % lower left serif

math_fit($0, .5ic^\#$); **penlabels**(1, 2, 3, 4, 5, 6); **endchar**;

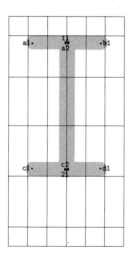

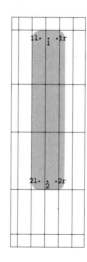

```
cmchar "The letter I";
```
beginchar("I", max($6u^\#$, $4u^\# + cap\_stem^\#$), $cap\_height^\#$, 0);
italcorr $cap\_height^\# * slant - .25u^\#$;
adjust_fit($cap\_serif\_fit^\#$, $cap\_serif\_fit^\#$);
pickup $tiny.nib$; $pos_1(cap\_stem, 0)$; $pos_2(cap\_stem, 0)$;
$lft\ x_{1l} = lft\ x_{2l} = $ hround($.5w - .5cap\_stem$); $top\ y_1 = h$; $bot\ y_2 = 0$;
filldraw stroke z_{1e} -- z_{2e};   % stem
if $serifs$: $dish\_serif(1, 2, a, \frac{1}{3}, 1.05cap\_jut, b, \frac{1}{3}, 1.05cap\_jut)$;   % upper serif
   $dish\_serif(2, 1, c, \frac{1}{3}, 1.05cap\_jut, d, \frac{1}{3}, 1.05cap\_jut)$; **fi**   % lower serif
math_fit($0, .5ic^\#$); **penlabels**(1, 2); **endchar**;

For some strange reason the letter I
is one of the more difficult letters to cut.
Perhaps, there being so little of it, its symmetry is over-exposed.
Kindersley used to make us come to terms with this letter
before tackling anything else.

— WILL CARTER, *Carter's Caps* (1982)

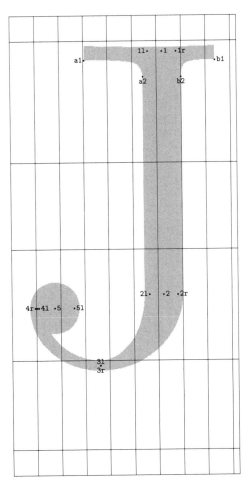

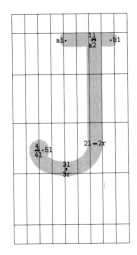

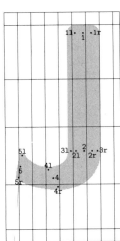

cmchar "The letter J";
beginchar("J", $9u^\#$, $cap\_height^\#$, 0);
italcorr $cap\_height^\# * slant - cap\_serif\_fit^\#$
$\qquad + .75cap\_jut^\# - 2.5u^\# + \min(.5cap\_stem^\#, u^\#)$;
adjust_fit(0, $cap\_serif\_fit^\#$);
pickup $tiny.nib$; $pos_1(cap\_stem', 0)$; $pos_2(cap\_stem', 0)$;
$top\ y_1 = h$; $rt\ x_{1r} = \text{hround}(w - 2u)$; $x_2 = x_1$; $y_2 = .21h$;
if $serifs$: $pos_3(vair, -90)$; $pos_4(cap\_hair, -180)$;
$\quad pos_5(flare + (cap\_stem - stem), -180)$;
$\quad bot\ y_{3r} = -o$; $x_3 = .5[x_4, x_2]$; $y_5 = \frac{1}{6}h$; $rt\ x_{5l} = \text{hround}\ 2.75u$; $z_{5r} = z_{4r}$;
$\quad$ **filldraw stroke** $z_{1e}\ \texttt{-{}-}\ z_{2e}$ & $super\_arc_e(2, 3)$; $\qquad\qquad$ % stem and arc
$\quad dish\_serif(1, 2, a, \frac{1}{3}, 1.3cap\_jut, b, \frac{1}{3}, .75cap\_jut)$; $\qquad\qquad$ % serif
$\quad bulb(3, 4, 5)$; $\qquad\qquad$ % bulb
else: **filldraw stroke** $z_{1e}\ \texttt{-{}-}\ z_{2e}$; $\qquad\qquad$ % stem
$\quad$ **pickup** $fine.nib$; $pos_3(cap\_stem', 0)$; $z_3 = z_2$;
$\quad pos_4(flare, \text{angle}(6.5u, -h))$; $pos_5(1.1flare, -100)$;
$\quad bot\ y_{4r} = -o$; $x_{4r} = .5[x_{5r}, x_{3r}]$; $lft\ x_{5r} = \text{hround}\ .75u$; $bot\ y_{5r} = \text{vround}\ .06h - o$;
$\quad$ **filldraw stroke** $z_{3e}\{down\}\ \texttt{....}\ term.e(4, 5, left, 1, 4)$; **fi** $\qquad$ % arc and terminal
math_fit(0, $.5ic^\# - .5u^\#$); **penlabels**(1, 2, 3, 4, 5); **endchar**;

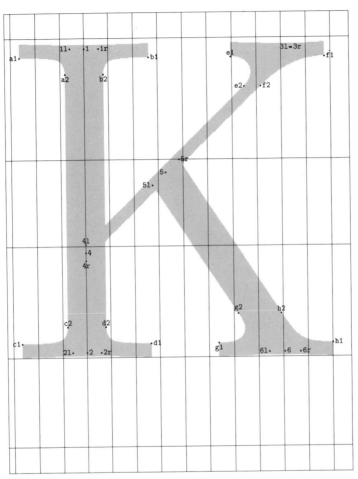

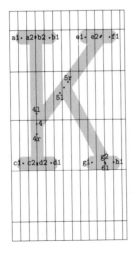

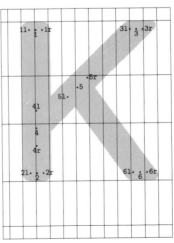

```
cmchar "The letter K";
```
beginchar("K", $13.5u^\#$, $cap\_height^\#$, 0);
italcorr $cap\_height^\# * slant - .5u^\#$;
adjust_fit($cap\_serif\_fit^\#$, $cap\_serif\_fit^\#$);
numeric $right\_jut$, $stem[\,]$, $alpha[\,]$;
if $serifs$: $right\_jut = .6cap\_jut$;
else: $right\_jut = .4tiny$; **fi**
pickup $tiny.nib$; $pos_1(fudged.cap\_stem, 0)$; $pos_2(fudged.cap\_stem, 0)$;
$lft\ x_{1l} = lft\ x_{2l} = $ hround $\max(2u, 3u - .5fudged.cap\_stem)$; $top\ y_1 = h$; $bot\ y_2 = 0$;
filldraw stroke $z_{1e} \text{ -- } z_{2e}$;   % stem
$stem_2 = \max(tiny.breadth, fudged.cap\_stem - 3stem\_corr)$;
$stem_1 = \max(tiny.breadth, fudged.hair$ **if** $hefty: -3stem\_corr$ **fi**$)$;
$top\ y_3 = h$; $rt\ x_{3r} = $ hround$(r - letter\_fit - u - right\_jut)$;
$bot\ y_6 = 0$; $rt\ x_{6r} = $ hround$(r - letter\_fit - .75u - right\_jut)$;
$x_4 = x_1$; $y_4 = \frac{1}{3}h$;
$alpha_1 = diag\_ratio(1, .5(stem_1 - tiny), y_3 - y_4, x_{3r} - x_4)$;
$penpos_3(alpha_1 * (stem_1 - tiny), 0)$; $penpos_4(whatever, -90)$;
$alpha_2 = diag\_ratio(1, .5(stem_2 - tiny), y_1 - y_6, x_{6r} - x_1)$;
$penpos_6(alpha_2 * (stem_2 - tiny), 0)$;
forsuffixes $\$ = l, r$: $y_{3'\$} = h$; $y_{6'\$} = 0$; $z_{4\$} = z_{3'\$} + whatever * (z_3 - z_4)$;
     $z_{5\$} = z_{6'\$} + whatever * (z_1 - z_6) = whatever[z_3, z_4]$; **endfor**
$z_5 = .5[z_{5l}, z_{5r}]$;
$z_{3'r} = z_{3r} + $ **penoffset** $z_3 - z_4$ **of** $currentpen + whatever * (z_3 - z_4)$;
% we have also $z_{3'l} = z_{3l} + $ **penoffset** $z_4 - z_3$ **of** $currentpen + whatever * (z_3 - z_4)$;
$z_{6'r} = z_{6r} + $ **penoffset** $z_1 - z_6$ **of** $currentpen + whatever * (z_1 - z_6)$;
$z_{6'l} = z_{6l} + $ **penoffset** $z_6 - z_1$ **of** $currentpen + whatever * (z_1 - z_6)$;
fill $z_{4r} \text{ -- } diag\_end(4r, 3'r, 1, .5, 3'l, 4l) \text{ -- } z_{4l} \text{ -- }$ cycle;   % upper diagonal
fill $z_{5l} \text{ -- } diag\_end(5l, 6'l, .5, 1, 6'r, 5r) \text{ -- } z_{5r} \text{ -- }$ cycle;   % lower diagonal
if $serifs$: **numeric** $inner\_jut$;
    if $rt\ x_{2r} + cap\_jut + .5u + 1 \leq lft\ x_{6l} - cap\_jut$: $inner\_jut = cap\_jut$;
    else: $rt\ x_{2r} + cap\_jut + .5u + 1 = lft\ x_{6l} - inner\_jut$; **fi**
    $dish\_serif(1, 2, a, \frac{1}{3}, cap\_jut, b, \frac{1}{3}, cap\_jut)$;   % upper stem serif
    $dish\_serif(2, 1, c, \frac{1}{3}, cap\_jut, d, \frac{1}{3}, cap\_jut)$;   % lower stem serif
    $dish\_serif(3, 4, e, \frac{2}{3}, 1.2cap\_jut, f, \frac{1}{2}, right\_jut)(dark)$;   % upper diagonal serif
    $dish\_serif(6, 5, g, \frac{1}{2}, inner\_jut, h, \frac{1}{3}, right\_jut)(dark)$; **fi**   % lower diagonal serif
math_fit$(0, .5ic^\#)$; **penlabels**$(1, 2, 3, 4, 5, 6)$; **endchar**;

---

vardef $diag_ratio(\textbf{expr}\ a, b, y, c) = $ % assuming that $a > |b/y|$,
                       % compute the value $\alpha = (x ++ y)/y$ such that $ax + b\alpha = c$
   numeric a_-, b_-; $b_- = b/y$; $a_- = a * a - b_- * b_-$;
   $(a * (c ++ y * \text{sqrt}\ a_-) - b_- * c)/a_-/y$ **enddef**;

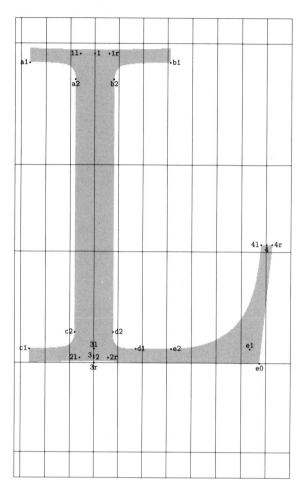

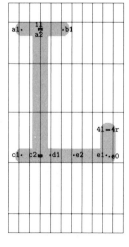

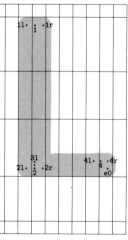

cmchar "The letter L";

beginchar("L", $11u^{\#} - width\_adj^{\#}$, $cap\_height^{\#}$, 0);

adjust_fit($cap\_serif\_fit^{\#}$, 0);

pickup $tiny.nib$; $pos_1(cap\_stem, 0)$; $pos_2(cap\_stem, 0)$;

$lft\ x_{1l} = lft\ x_{2l} = \text{hround max}(2u, 3u - .5cap\_stem)$; $top\ y_1 = h$; $bot\ y_2 = 0$;

filldraw stroke $z_{1e} \text{ -- } z_{2e}$;   % stem

pickup $crisp.nib$; $pos_3(slab, -90)$; $pos_4(hair, 0)$;

$bot\ y_{3r} = 0$; $x_3 = x_2$; $y_4 = y_{3l} + {}^7/_6 beak + eps$; $rt\ x_{4r} = \text{hround}(w - .75u)$;

$arm(3, 4, e, 1.2beak\_darkness, beak\_jut)$;   % lower arm and beak

if $serifs$: $dish\_serif(1, 2, a, {}^1/_3, cap\_jut, b, {}^1/_3, 1.25cap\_jut)$;   % upper serif

   $nodish\_serif(2, 1, c, {}^1/_3, cap\_jut, d, {}^1/_3, .5cap\_jut)$; **fi**   % lower serif

math_fit(0, $u^{\#}$); **penlabels**(1, 2, 3, 4); **endchar**;

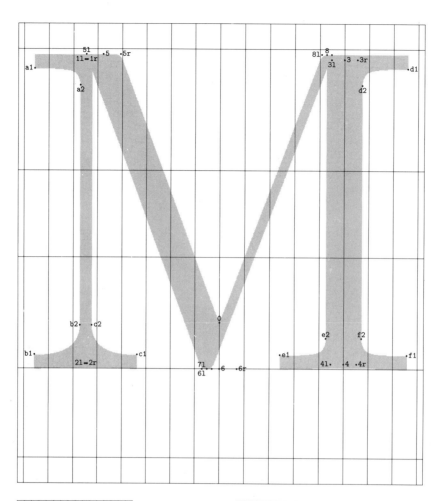

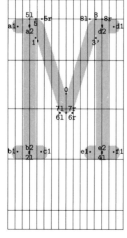

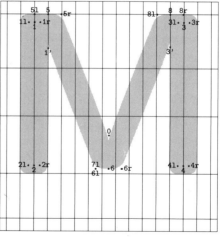

cmchar "The letter M";
beginchar("M", $16u\# + width\_adj\#$, $cap\_height\#$, 0);
italcorr $cap\_height\# * slant - cap\_serif\_fit\# + cap\_jut\# - 2.5u\# + \min(.5cap\_stem\#, u\#)$;
adjust_fit($cap\_serif\_fit\#$, $cap\_serif\_fit\#$);
numeric $stem[\,]$;   % thicknesses of the four strokes
$stem_1 = \text{hround}(fudged.hair + stem\_corr)$;
$stem_2 = \text{hround}(fudged.cap\_stem - 4stem\_corr)$;
$stem_3 = \text{hround}(fudged.hair - stem\_corr)$;
$stem_4 = \text{hround}(fudged.cap\_stem - 3stem\_corr)$;
if $stem_4 < stem_1$: $stem_4 := stem_1$; **fi**
pickup $tiny.nib$; $pos_1(stem_1, 0)$; $pos_2(stem_1, 0)$; $pos_3(stem_4, 0)$; $pos_4(stem_4, 0)$;
$x_1 = x_2$; $x_3 = x_4$; $x_{1l} = w - x_{3r}$; $rt\ x_{3r} = \text{hround}\min(w - 2u, w - 3u + .5stem_4)$;
$top\ y_1 = top\ y_3 = h$; $bot\ y_2 = bot\ y_4 = 0$;
filldraw stroke z_{1e} -- z_{2e};   % left stem
filldraw stroke z_{3e} -- z_{4e};   % right stem
$penpos_5(stem_2, 0)$; $penpos_6(stem_2, 0)$; $penpos_7(stem_3, 0)$; $penpos_8(stem_3, 0)$;
$x_{5l} = x_1$; $x_{6l} = x_{7l}$; $x_8 = lft\ x_{3l}$; $x_6 - x_5 = x_8 - x_7$; $y_5 = y_8 = h$; $y_6 = y_7$;
if $hefty$: $y_6 = $ **if** $monospace$: vround $1/3h$ **else**: o **fi**;
   numeric $upper\_notch$, $lower\_notch$;
   $upper\_notch = h - cap\_notch\_cut$; $lower\_notch = y_6 + cap\_notch\_cut$;
   $x_{1'} = rt\ x_{1r}$; $z_{1'} = whatever[z_{5l}, z_{6l}]$; $x_{3'} = lft\ x_{3l}$; $z_{3'} = whatever[z_{7r}, z_{8r}]$;
   $z_0 = whatever[z_{5r}, z_{6r}] = whatever[z_{7l}, z_{8l}]$;
   fill z_{5l} .. **if** $y_{1'} < upper\_notch$: $\{right\}(x_{1'} + 1, upper\_notch)\{down\}$ ... **fi**
      $\{z_6 - z_5\}diag\_in(5l, 6l, 1, 6r)$ .. $diag\_out(7l, 1, 7r, 8r)\{z_8 - z_7\}$
      if $y_{3'} < upper\_notch$: ... $\{up\}(x_{3'} - 1, upper\_notch)\{right\}$ **fi**
      .. z_{8r} -- $diag\_out(8r, 1, 8l, 7l)\{z_7 - z_8\}$
      if $y_0 \leq lower\_notch$: .. $\{z_7 - z_8\}z_0\{z_5 - z_6\}$ ..
      else: ... $\{down\}(x_0 + .5, lower\_notch)$ -- $(x_0 - .5, lower\_notch)\{up\}$ ... **fi**
      $\{z_5 - z_6\}diag\_in(6r, 5r, 1, 5l)$ -- cycle;   % diagonals
else: $y_6 = 0$; $z_0 = whatever[z_{5r}, z_{6r}] = whatever[z_{7l}, z_{8l}]$;
   fill z_{5l} .. $\{z_6 - z_5\}diag\_in(5l, 6l, 1, 6r)$ .. $diag\_out(7l, 1, 7r, 8r)\{z_8 - z_7\}$
      .. z_{8r} -- $diag\_out(8r, 1, 8l, 7l)\{z_7 - z_8\}$ .. $\{z_7 - z_8\}z_0\{z_5 - z_6\}$
      .. $\{z_5 - z_6\}diag\_in(6r, 5r, 1, 5l)$ -- cycle; **fi**   % diagonals
if $serifs$: $serif(1, 2, a, 1/3, -cap\_jut)$;   % upper left serif
   $dish\_serif(2, 1, b, 1/2, cap\_jut, c, 1/2, cap\_jut)(dark)$;   % lower left serif
   $serif(3, 4, d, 1/3, cap\_jut)$;   % upper right serif
   $dish\_serif(4, 3, e, 1/3, cap\_jut, f, 1/3, cap\_jut)$; **fi**   % lower right serif
math_fit(0, $\max(.5ic\# - .5u\#, 0)$);
penlabels(0, 1, $1'$, 2, 3, $3'$, 4, 5, 6, 7, 8); **endchar**;

Midnight wags are diligently studying the alphabet
to see how many of the letters are susceptible
to mutation into something new and strange. ...
There are two schools of M-sters;
when their warfare is accomplished we shall know
whether that letter is to figure henceforth as
two sides of a triangle or three sides of a square.

— AMBROSE BIERCE, *The Opinionator. Alphabêtes* (1911)

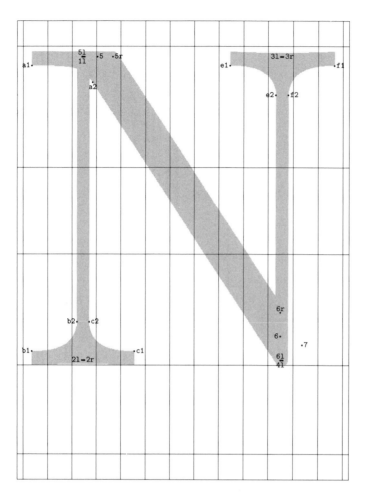

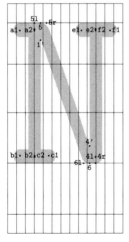

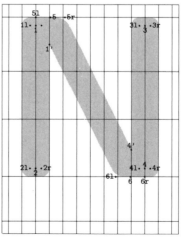

cmchar "The letter N";
beginchar("N", $13u\# + width\_adj\#$, $cap\_height\#$, 0);
italcorr $cap\_height\# * slant - cap\_serif\_fit\# + cap\_jut\# - 2.5u\# + \min(.5\,cap\_stem\#, u\#)$;
adjust_fit($cap\_serif\_fit\#$, $cap\_serif\_fit\#$);
numeric $thin\_stem$; $thin\_stem = \mathrm{hround}(fudged.hair + stem\_corr)$;
pickup $tiny.nib$; $pos_1(thin\_stem, 0)$; $pos_2(thin\_stem, 0)$;
$pos_3(thin\_stem, 0)$; $pos_4(thin\_stem, 0)$;
pickup $tiny.nib$; $top\ y_1 = top\ y_3 = h$; $bot\ y_2 = bot\ y_4 = 0$;
$x_1 = x_2$; $x_3 = x_4$; $x_{1l} = w - x_{3r}$;
$rt\ x_{3r} = \mathrm{hround}\min(w - 2u, w - 3u + .5\,fudged.cap\_stem)$;
filldraw stroke z_{1e} `--` z_{2e};   % left stem
filldraw stroke z_{3e} `--` z_{4e};   % right stem
if *hefty*: $penpos_5(fudged.cap\_stem, 0)$; $penpos_6(fudged.cap\_stem, 0)$;
   $x_{5l} = x_1$; $x_{6r} = x_4$; $y_5 = h$; $y_6 = 0$;
   numeric $upper\_notch$, $lower\_notch$;
   $upper\_notch = h - cap\_notch\_cut$; $lower\_notch = cap\_notch\_cut$;
   $x_{1'} = rt\ x_{1r}$; $z_{1'} = whatever[z_{5l}, z_{6l}]$; $x_{4'} = lft\ x_{4l}$; $z_{4'} = whatever[z_{5r}, z_{6r}]$;
   fill z_{5l} `..`
     if $y_{1'} < upper\_notch$: $\{right\}(x_{1'} + 1, upper\_notch)\{down\}$ ... **fi**
     $\{z_6 - z_5\}diag\_in(5l, 6l, 1, 6r)$ `--` z_{6r} `..`
     if $y_{4'} > lower\_notch$: $\{left\}(x_{4'} - 1, lower\_notch)\{up\}$ ... **fi**
     $\{z_5 - z_6\}diag\_in(6r, 5r, 1, 5l)$ `--` cycle;   % diagonal
else: $penpos_5(whatever, 0)$; $penpos_6(whatever, 90)$;
   $z_{5l} = z_{1l}$; $z_{6l} = z_{4l}$;
   $z_7 = z_{6l} + (\max(eps, cap\_stem - 3\,stem\_corr - tiny), 0)\,\mathrm{rotated}\,(\mathrm{angle}(z_{5l} - z_{6l}) - 90)$;
   $z_{5r} = z_7 + whatever * (z_{5l} - z_{6l})$; $z_{6r} = z_7 + whatever * (z_{5l} - z_{6l})$;
   filldraw stroke z_{5e} `..` z_{6e}; **fi**   % diagonal
if *serifs*: **if** *hefty*: $serif(1, 2, a, ⅓, -cap\_jut)$;   % upper left serif
   else: $serif(5, 6, a, ⅓, -cap\_jut)$; **fi**   % upper left serif
   $dish\_serif(2, 1, b, ½, cap\_jut, c, ½, cap\_jut)(dark)$;   % lower left serif
   $dish\_serif(3, 4, e, ½, cap\_jut, f, ½, cap\_jut)(dark)$; **fi**   % upper right serif
math_fit$(0, \max(.5ic\# - .5u\#, 0))$; **penlabels**$(1, 1', 2, 3, 4, 4', 5, 6, 7)$; **endchar**;

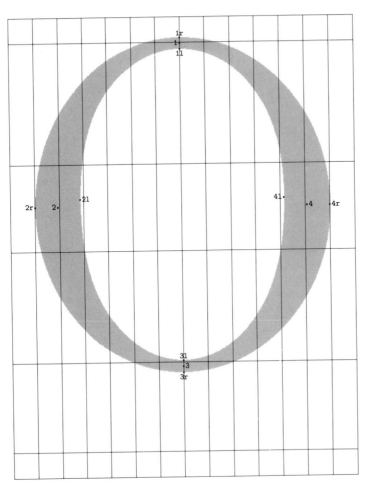

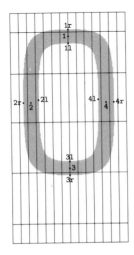

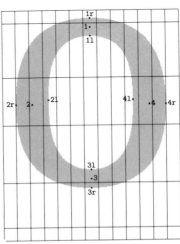

cmchar "The letter O";
beginchar("O", $14u\# - width\_adj\#$, $cap\_height\#$, 0);
italcorr $.7cap\_height\# * slant - .5u\#$;
adjust_fit(0, 0);
$penpos_1(vair', 90)$; $penpos_3(\mathrm{vround}(vair + 1.5vair\_corr), -90)$;
$penpos_2(cap\_curve, 180)$; $penpos_4(cap\_curve, 0)$;
if $monospace$: $x_{2r} = \mathrm{hround}\, 1.5u$;
　　interim $superness := \mathrm{sqrt}\, superness$;　　　　　　% make "O", not "0"
else: $x_{2r} = \mathrm{hround}\, u$; **fi**
$x_{4r} = w - x_{2r}$; $x_1 = x_3 = .5w$; $y_{1r} = h + o$; $y_{3r} = -o$;
$y_2 = y_4 = .5h - vair\_corr$; $y_{2l} := y_{4l} := .52h$;
penstroke $pulled\_super\_arc_e(1, 2)(.5superpull)$
　　& $pulled\_super\_arc_e(2, 3)(.5superpull)$
　　& $pulled\_super\_arc_e(3, 4)(.5superpull)$
　　& $pulled\_super\_arc_e(4, 1)(.5superpull)$ & cycle;　　　　　　% bowl
math_fit$(-.3cap\_height\# * slant - .5u\#, ic\# - .5u\#)$; **penlabels**(1, 2, 3, 4); **endchar**;

"I'll get rid of O, in upper case and lower," cried the man in black.
"I'll issue an edict. All words in books or signs with an O in them
shall have the O erased or painted out.
We'll print new books and paint new signs without an O in them."
— JAMES THURBER, *The Wonderful O* (1957)

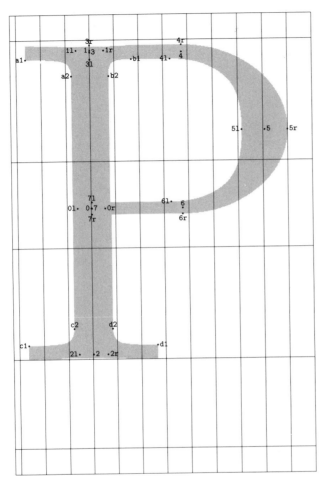

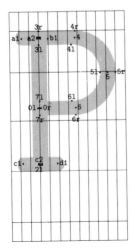

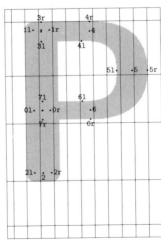

cmchar "The letter P";
beginchar("P", $12u^\#$, $cap\_height^\#$, 0);
italcorr $.75cap\_height^\# * slant - .5u^\#$;
adjust_fit($cap\_serif\_fit^\#$, 0);
pickup $tiny.nib$; $penpos_1(cap\_stem' - tiny, 0)$; $penpos_2(cap\_stem - tiny, 0)$;
$pos_0(cap\_stem', 0)$; $pos_{0'}(cap\_stem, 0)$;
lft $x_{1l} = $ hround max$(2u, 3u - .5cap\_stem')$; *top* $y_1 = h$; *bot* $y_2 = 0$;
$x_{1l} = x_{2l} = x_{0l} = x_{0'l}$; $y_0 = y_{0'} = y_7$;
$penpos_3(cap\_band, 90)$; $penpos_4(cap\_band, 90)$;
$penpos_5(cap\_curve$ **if** *hefty*: $-3stem\_corr$ **fi**, $0)$;
$penpos_6(.5[vair, cap\_band], -90)$; $penpos_7(.5[vair, cap\_band], -90)$;
$z_{3r} = $ *top* z_1; $y_4 = y_3$; $y_5 = .5[y_{4l}, y_{6l}]$; $y_6 = y_7$;
$x_7 = x_2$; $y_{7l} = $ vround $.5h$; $x_4 = x_6 = .5w + .75u$; $x_{5r} = $ hround$(w - u)$;
$x_{4l} := x_{6l} := x_4 - .25cap\_curve$;
filldraw stroke z_{1e} -- z_{0e} -- $z_{0'e}$ -- z_{2e};   % stem
fill stroke z_{3e} .. $pulled\_arc_e(4, 5)$ & $pulled\_arc_e(5, 6)$ .. z_{7e};   % lobe
if *serifs*: $nodish\_serif(1, 0, a, ⅓, cap\_jut, b, ⅓, .5cap\_jut)$;   % upper serif
$\quad dish\_serif(2, 0', c, ⅓, cap\_jut, d, ⅓, cap\_jut)$; **fi**   % lower serif
math_fit(0, $ic^\# - 2.5u^\#$); **penlabels**($0, 1, 2, 3, 4, 5, 6, 7$); **endchar**;

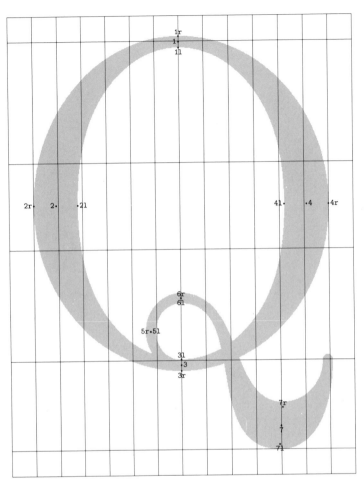

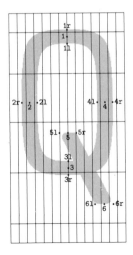

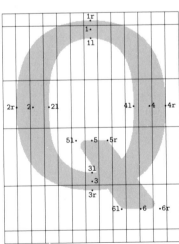

cmchar "The letter Q";
beginchar("Q", $14u\# - width\_adj\#$, $cap\_height\#$, $comma\_depth\#$);
italcorr $.7cap\_height\# * slant - .5u\#$;
adjust_fit$(0, 0)$;
numeric $light\_curve$; $light_curve = cap_curve - $ hround $stem\_corr$;
$penpos_1(vair', 90)$; $penpos_3(vair', -90)$;
$penpos_2(light\_curve, 180)$; $penpos_4(light\_curve, 0)$;
if $monospace$: $x_{2r} = $ hround $1.5u$;
    interim $superness := $ sqrt $superness$;   % make "Q" like "O"
else: $x_{2r} = $ hround u; **fi**
$x_{4r} = w - x_{2r}$; $x_1 = x_3 = .5w$; $y_{1r} = h + o$; $y_2 = y_4 = .5h - vair\_corr$; $y_{3r} = -o$;
penstroke $pulled\_super\_arc_e(1, 2)(.5superpull)$
    & $pulled\_super\_arc_e(2, 3)(.5superpull)$
    & $pulled\_super\_arc_e(3, 4)(.5superpull)$
    & $pulled\_super\_arc_e(4, 1)(.5superpull)$ & cycle;   % bowl
pickup $tiny.nib$;
if $hefty$: $penpos_5(1.2(.5[cap\_bar, light\_curve]), 0)$; $penpos_6(1.2light\_curve, 0)$;
    $x_5 = .5w$; $x_{6r} = $ hround$(w - 1.5u)$;
    $y_5 = $ vround $.28h$; $y_6 = -d$;
    fill $diag\_end(6r, 5r, .25, 1, 5l, 6l)$ -- $diag\_end(5l, 6l, .5, 1, 6r, 5r)$ -- cycle;   % tail
else: $pos_{3'}(vair, 270)$; $pos_5(vair, 180)$; $pos_6(vair, 90)$;
    $pos_7(cap\_curve, 85)$; $penpos_8(eps, 180)$;
    $z_{3'} = z_3$; $x_6 = x_3$; top $y_{6r} = $ vround$(.2h + .5vair)$;
    lft $x_{5r} = $ hround$(.5w - 1.25u - .5vair)$; $y_5 = .5[y_3, y_6]$;
    bot $y_{7l} = -d$; $x_{7l} = \frac{2}{3}[x_6, x_8]$; $y_8 = 0$; rt $x_8 = $ hround$(x_{4r} + .1u)$;
    filldraw stroke $z_{3'e}\{left\} \ldots z_{5e}\{up\} \ldots z_{6e}\{right\}$
      $.. z_{7e}\{right\} \ldots z_{8e}\{up\}$; **fi**   % tail
math_fit$(-.3cap\_height\# * slant - .5u\#, ic\#)$; **penlabels**$(1, 2, 3, 4, 5, 6, 7)$; **endchar**;

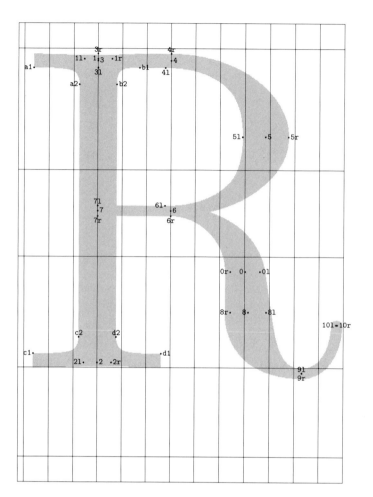

cmchar "The letter R";
beginchar("R", **if** *serifs*: $12u\# + .5 \max(2u\#, cap\_curve\#)$
   else: $12.5u\# - .5width\_adj\#$ **fi**, $cap\_height\#$, 0);
italcorr $.75cap\_height\# * slant -$ **if** *serifs*: 1.75 **else**: .5 **fi** $u\#$;
adjust_fit($cap\_serif\_fit\#$, 0);
pickup $tiny.nib$; $pos_1(cap\_stem', 0)$; $pos_2(cap\_stem', 0)$;
$lft\ x_{1l} = lft\ x_{2l} = $ hround $\max(2u, 3u - .5cap\_stem')$; $top\ y_1 = h$; $bot\ y_2 = 0$;
filldraw stroke $z_{1e} -- z_{2e}$;   % stem
$penpos_3(cap\_band, 90)$; $penpos_4(cap\_band, 90)$;
$penpos_5(cap\_curve$ **if** *hefty*: $-3stem\_corr$ **fi**, 0);
$penpos_6(vair, -90)$; $penpos_7(vair, -90)$;
$z_{3r} = top\ z_1$; $y_4 = y_3$; $y_5 = .5[y_{4l}, y_{6l}]$; $y_6 = y_7$;
$x_7 = x_2$; $y_{7l} = $ vround$(.5h + .5vair)$; $x_4 = x_6$;
if *serifs*: $x_4 = .5w - .5u$; $x_{5r} = $ hround$(w - 2.25u)$;
else: $x_4 = .5w + .5u$; $x_{5r} = $ hround$(w - u)$; **fi**
$x_{4l} := x_{6l} := x_4 - .125cap\_curve$;
fill stroke $z_{3e} .. pulled\_arc_e(4, 5) \& pulled\_arc_e(5, 6) .. z_{7e}$;   % lobe
if *serifs*: $pos_{6'}(vair, -90)$; $pos_0(cap\_stem, 180)$;
   $pos_8(cap\_curve, 180)$; $pos_9(vair, -90)$; $pos_{10}(hair, 0)$;
   $z_{6'} = z_6$; $lft\ x_{0r} = lft\ x_{8r} = $ hround$(x_5 - {}^2/3u - .5cap\_curve)$;
   $y_8 = {}^1/3[y_2, y_7]$; $y_0 = {}^3/5[y_2, y_7]$; $x_9 = .5[x_{8l}, x_{10r}]$;
   $bot\ y_{9r} = -o$; $rt\ x_{10r} = $ hround$(w - .05u)$; $y_{10} = {}^1/4[y_2, y_7]$;
   filldraw stroke $z_{6'e}\{right\} .. z_{0e} --- z_{8e} .... z_{9e}\{right\} .. z_{10e}\{up\}$;   % tail
   $nodish\_serif(1, 2, a, {}^1/3, cap\_jut, b, {}^1/3, .5cap\_jut)$;   % upper serif
   $dish\_serif(2, 1, c, {}^1/3, cap\_jut, d, {}^1/3, cap\_jut)$;   % lower serif
else: $penpos_8(cap\_stem - 2stem\_corr, 0)$; $penpos_9(cap\_stem, 0)$;
   $x_8 = x_6 + .5u$; $y_8 = y_6$; $x_{9r} = $ hround$(w - .5u)$; $y_9 = 0$;
   fill $z_{8l} -- diag\_end(8l, 9l, .5, 1, 9r, 8r) -- z_{8r} --$ cycle; **fi**   % tail
math_fit$(0, .75ic\#)$; **penlabels**$(0, 1, 2, 3, 4, 5, 6, 7, 8, 9, 10)$; **endchar**;

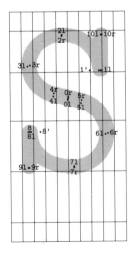

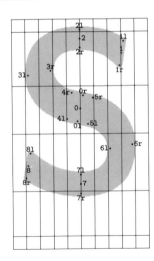

cmchar "The letter S";
beginchar("S", $10u^\#$, $cap\_height^\#$, 0);
italcorr $cap\_height^\# * slant - u^\#$;
adjust_fit(0, 0);
numeric $theta$; $theta = 90 - angle(50u, h)$; $slope := -h/50u$;   % angle at middle
numeric s_slab; $s\_slab =$ **if** $serifs$: $slab$ **else**: $vround\ .2[slab, cap\_stem]$ **fi**;
numeric ess'; $ess' = max(fine.breadth, cap\_ess)$;
pickup $fine.nib$; $pos_2(max(fine.breadth, s\_slab - vround\ vair\_corr), -90)$;
$pos_0(ess', theta)$; $pos_7(s\_slab, -90)$;
$x_2 + x_7 = 2x_0 = w$; $x_7 - x_2 =$ **if** $serifs$: u **else**: 0 **fi**; $top\ y_{2l} = h + o$; $bot\ y_{7r} = -o$;
$y_0 = .52h$; $lft\ x_{3l} = hround\ u$; $rt\ x_{6r} = hround(w - u)$;
$x_{3r} - x_{3l} = x_{6r} - x_{6l} = hround\ .5[s\_slab, ess'] - fine$;
$ellipse\_set(2l, 3l, 4l, 0l)$; $ellipse\_set(2r, 3r, 4r, 0r)$; $y_3 = y_{3r}$;
$ellipse\_set(7l, 6l, 5l, 0l)$; $ellipse\_set(7r, 6r, 5r, 0r)$; $y_6 = y_{6r}$;
filldraw stroke $super\_arc_e(2, 3)$ & $z_{3e}\{down\}$
    .. z_{4e} --- z_{5e} .. $z_{6e}\{down\}$ & $super\_arc_e(6, 7)$;   % main stroke
if $serifs$: $pos_1(hair, 180)$; $pos_8(hair, 180)$;
    $rt\ x_{1l} = hround(w - 1.5u)$; $lft\ x_{8r} = hround\ u$;
    $bot\ y_1 = vround\ 2/3h + 1$; $top\ y_8 = vround\ 1/3h - 1$;
    filldraw stroke $z_{1e}\{x_2 - x_1, 10(y_2 - y_1)\}$ .... $\{left\}z_{2e}$;   % upper arc
    filldraw stroke $z_{7e}\{left\}$ .... $\{up\}z_{8e}$;   % lower arc
    path $upper\_arc$, $lower\_arc$;
    $upper\_arc = z_1\{x_2 - x_1, 10(y_2 - y_1)\}$ .... $\{left\}z_2$;
    $lower\_arc = z_7\{left\}$ .... $\{up\}z_8$;
    $pos_{10}(.3[fine.breadth, cap\_hair], 0)$; $pos_9(.3[fine.breadth, cap\_hair], 0)$;
    $x_{10r} = x_{1l}$; $top\ y_{10} = top\ y_{2l}$; $x_{9l} = x_{8r}$; $bot\ y_9 = bot\ y_{7r}$;
    $x_{1l} - x_{1'} = x_{8'} - x_{8r} = 1.6cap\_curve - fine$; $y_{1'} = y_1$; $y_{8'} = y_8$;
    numeric t; $t = xpart(upper\_arc\ intersectiontimes\ (z_{10l} -- z_{1'}))$;
    filldraw z_{1l} -- z_{10r} -- z_{10l} -- **subpath**$(t, 0)$ **of** $upper\_arc$ -- **cycle**;   % upper barb
    $t := xpart(lower\_arc\ intersectiontimes\ (z_{9r} -- z_{8'}))$;
    filldraw z_{8r} -- z_{9l} -- z_{9r} -- **subpath**$(t, 1)$ **of** $lower\_arc$ -- **cycle**;   % lower barb
else: $pos_1(1.2flare, -100)$; $pos_8(1.2flare, -100)$;
    $x_{1l} = good.x(x_{1l} + w - 1.75u - rt\ x_1)$; $lft\ x_{8r} = hround\ .8u$;
    $top\ y_{1l} = vround\ .93h + o$; $bot\ y_{8r} = vround\ .1h - o$;
    filldraw stroke $term.e(2, 1, right, .9, 4)$;   % upper arc and terminal
    filldraw stroke $term.e(7, 8, left, 1, 4)$; **fi**   % lower arc and terminal
math_fit(0, $.5ic^\#$); **penlabels**(0, 1, $1'$, 2, 3, 4, 5, 6, 7, 8, $8'$, 9, 10); **endchar**;

> *Messala Corvinus, a Great Man, and a*
> *famos Orator amongst the Romans,*
> *Writ a Book concerning the Letter S.*
> — JOHN WILKINS, *Towards a Real Character* (1668)

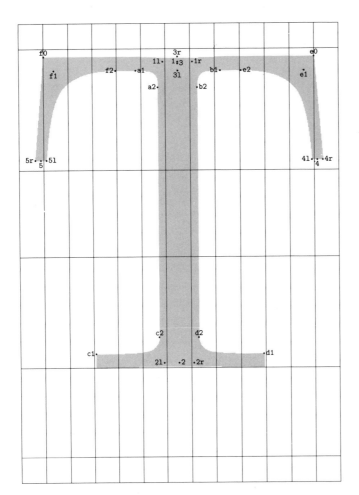

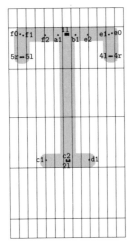

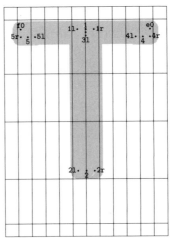

cmchar "The letter T";
beginchar("T", $13u\# - width\_adj\#$, $cap\_height\#$, 0);
italcorr $cap\_height\# * slant - beak\_jut\# - .25u\#$;
adjust_fit(0, 0);
$h :=$ vround($h - 2stem\_corr$);
pickup $tiny.nib$; $pos_1(cap\_stem, 0)$; $pos_2(cap\_stem, 0)$;
$lft\ x_{1l} = lft\ x_{2l} =$ hround($.5w - .5cap\_stem$); $top\ y_1 = h$; $bot\ y_2 = 0$;
filldraw stroke z_{1e} -- z_{2e};   % stem
pickup $crisp.nib$; $pos_3(slab, 90)$; $pos_4(hair, 0)$;
$top\ y_{3r} = h$; $x_3 = x_1$; $rt\ x_{4r} =$ hround($w - .65u$); $y_4 = good.y(y_{3l} - beak) - eps$;
$arm(3, 4, e, beak\_darkness, .7beak\_jut)$;   % right arm and beak
$pos_5(hair, 180)$; $x_5 = w - x_4$; $y_5 = y_4$;
$arm(3, 5, f, beak\_darkness, -.7beak\_jut)$;   % left arm and beak
if $serifs$: $dish\_serif(2, 1, c, 1/3, 1.414cap\_jut, d, 1/3, 1.414cap\_jut)$;   % lower serif
    $nodish\_serif(1, 2, a, 1/3, .5cap\_jut, b, 1/3, .5cap\_jut)$; **fi**   % upper bracketing
math_fit($-.75cap\_height\# * slant, ic\# - 2.5u\#$); **penlabels**(1, 2, 3, 4, 5, 6); **endchar**;

I do not presume to criticise your Italic Capitals;
they are generally perfect:
I would only beg leave to say,
that to me the form of the T *in the word* LETTRE
on the Title Page seems preferable to that of
the T *in the word* Typographie *in the next Page.*
— BENJAMIN FRANKLIN, *Letter to Bodoni* (1787)

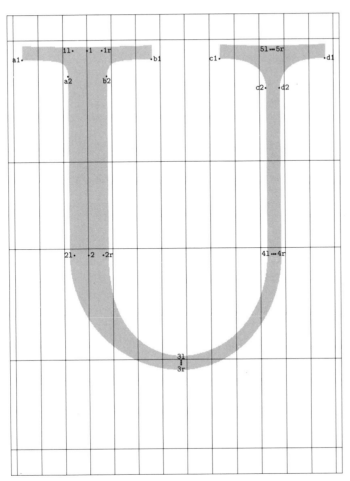

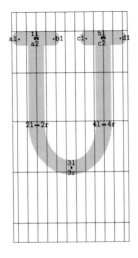

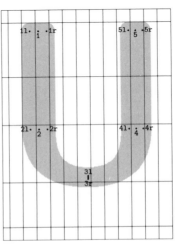

cmchar "The letter U";

beginchar("U", $13u^\# + .5width\_adj^\#$, $cap\_height^\#$, 0);

italcorr $cap\_height^\# * slant - cap\_serif\_fit^\# + cap\_jut^\# - 2.5u^\# + \min(.5cap\_stem^\#, u^\#)$;

if *monospace*: **adjust_fit**($cap\_serif\_fit^\# - .5u^\#$, $cap\_serif\_fit^\# - .5u^\#$)

else: **adjust_fit**($cap\_serif\_fit^\#$, $cap\_serif\_fit^\#$) **fi**;

pickup *tiny.nib*; $pos_1(cap\_stem, 0)$; $pos_2(cap\_stem, 0)$;

$pos_{2'}(cap\_stem, 180)$; $z_{2'} = z_2$;

$pos_3(cap\_band, -90)$;

$pos_4(cap\_hair, 0)$; $pos_5(cap\_hair, 0)$;

$x_1 = x_2$; $x_3 = .5[x_1, x_5]$; $x_4 = x_5$; $x_{1l} = w - x_{5r}$;

$top\ y_1 = top\ y_5 = h$; $y_2 = y_4 = \frac{1}{3}h$; $bot\ y_{3r} = -o$;

$lft\ x_{1l} =$ hround $\max(2u, 3u - .5cap\_stem)$;

filldraw stroke z_{1e} -- z_{2e};   % left stem

filldraw stroke $pulled\_arc_e(2', 3)$

    & $pulled\_arc_e(3, 4)$ & z_{4e} -- z_{5e};   % arc and right stem

if *serifs*: *dish_serif*$(1, 2, a, \frac{1}{3}, cap\_jut, b, \frac{1}{3}, cap\_jut)$;   % left serif

    dish_serif$(5, 4, c, \frac{1}{2}, cap\_jut, d, \frac{1}{2}, cap\_jut)(dark)$; **fi**   % right serif

math_fit$(-cap\_serif\_fit^\# - .3cap\_height^\# * slant - \min(cap\_height^\# * slant, u^\#)$,

    $\max(.5ic^\# - .5u^\#, 0))$; **penlabels**(1, 2, 3, 4, 5); **endchar**;

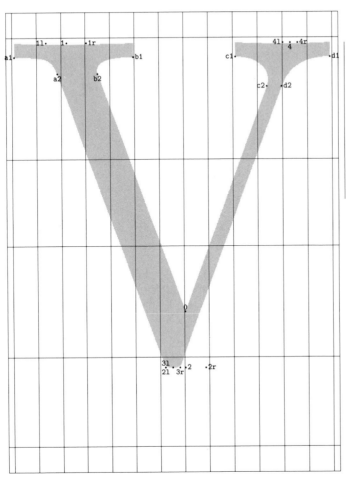

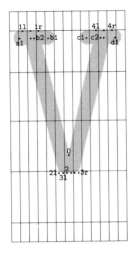

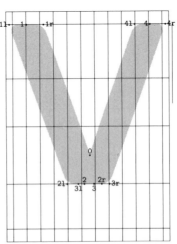

cmchar "The letter V";
beginchar("V", $13u\#$, $cap\_height\#$, 0);
italcorr $cap\_height\# * slant + .25u\#$;
adjust_fit($cap\_serif\_fit\#$, $cap\_serif\_fit\#$);
numeric $left\_stem$, $right\_stem$, $outer\_jut$, $alpha$;
$left\_stem = cap\_stem - stem\_corr$;
$right\_stem = \min(cap\_hair$ **if** $hefty$: $-2stem\_corr$ **fi**, $left\_stem$);
$outer\_jut = .75cap\_jut$; $x_{1l} = w - x_{4r} = l + letter\_fit + outer\_jut + .25u$; $y_1 = y_4 = h$;
$x_2 - x_1 = x_4 - x_3$; $x_{2l} + apex\_corr = x_{3l}$; $y_2 = y_3 = -apex\_o$;
$alpha = diag\_ratio(2, right\_stem, y_1 - y_2, x_{4r} - x_{1l} - apex\_corr)$;
$penpos_1(alpha * left\_stem, 0)$; $penpos_2(alpha * left\_stem, 0)$;
$penpos_3(alpha * right\_stem, 0)$; $penpos_4(alpha * right\_stem, 0)$;
$z_0 = whatever[z_{1r}, z_{2r}] = whatever[z_{3l}, z_{4l}]$;
if $y_0 > cap\_notch\_cut$: $y_0 := cap\_notch\_cut$;
      fill $z_0 + .5right\{up\} \ldots \{z_4 - z_3\}diag\_end(3l, 4l, 1, 1, 4r, 3r)$
          $-- diag\_end(4r, 3r, 1, 1, 2l, 1l) -- diag\_end(2l, 1l, 1, 1, 1r, 2r)\{z_2 - z_1\}$
          $\ldots \{down\}z_0 + .5left$ -- **cycle**;   % left and right diagonals
else: **fill** $z_0 -- diag\_end(0, 4l, 1, 1, 4r, 3r) -- diag\_end(4r, 3r, 1, 1, 2l, 1l)$
          $-- diag\_end(2l, 1l, 1, 1, 1r, 0) --$ **cycle**; **fi**   % left and right diagonals
if $serifs$: **numeric** $inner\_jut$; **pickup** $tiny.nib$;
  $prime\_points\_inside(1, 2)$; $prime\_points\_inside(4, 3)$;
  if $rt\ x_{1'r} + cap\_jut + .5u + 1 \leq lft\ x_{4'l} - cap\_jut$: $inner\_jut = cap\_jut$;
  else: $rt\ x_{1'r} + inner\_jut + .5u + 1 = lft\ x_{4'l} - inner\_jut$; **fi**
  $dish\_serif(1', 2, a, 1/3, outer\_jut, b, 1/2, inner\_jut)$;   % left serif
  $dish\_serif(4', 3, c, .6, inner\_jut, d, 1/2, outer\_jut)(dark)$; **fi**   % right serif
math_fit($.75u\# - cap\_height\# * slant$, $ic\# - 4u\#$); **penlabels**($0, 1, 2, 3, 4$); **endchar**;

---

def $prime\_points\_inside(\textbf{suffix}\ \$, \$\$) =$
  $theta_- := \text{angle}(z_{\$r} - z_{\$l})$;
  $penpos_{\$'}(whatever, theta_-)$;
  if $y_{\$\$} > y_\$$: $z_{\$'} = (0, pen\_top)$ rotated $theta_- + whatever[z_{\$l}, z_{\$r}]$;
    $theta_- := \text{angle}(z_{\$\$} - z_\$) - 90$;
  else: $z_{\$'} = (0, pen\_bot)$ rotated $theta_- + whatever[z_{\$l}, z_{\$r}]$;
    $theta_- := \text{angle}(z_{\$\$} - z_\$) + 90$; **fi**
  $z_{\$'l} + (pen\_lft, 0)$ rotated $theta_- = z_{\$l} + whatever * (z_\$ - z_{\$\$})$;
  $z_{\$'r} + (pen\_rt, 0)$ rotated $theta_- = z_{\$r} + whatever * (z_\$ - z_{\$\$})$; **enddef**;

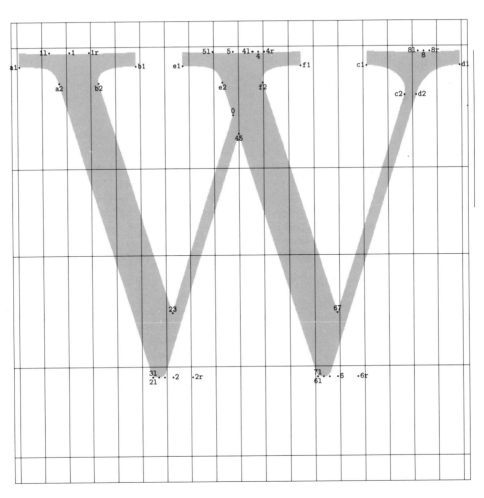

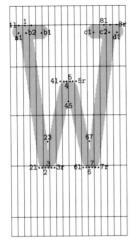

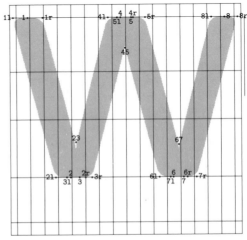

cmchar "The letter W";
beginchar("W", $18u^\#$, $cap\_height^\#$, 0);
italcorr $cap\_height^\# * slant + .25u^\#$;
adjust_fit($cap\_serif\_fit^\#$, $cap\_serif\_fit^\#$);
numeric $stem[]$, $outer\_jut$, $upper\_notch$, $alpha$, mid_corr;
$outer\_jut = .7cap\_jut$; $x_{1l} = w - x_{8r} = l + letter\_fit + outer\_jut + .25u$;
$stem_1 = fudged.cap\_stem - stem\_corr$;
$stem_4 = \min(fudged.hair$ **if** $hefty$: $-2stem\_corr$ **fi**, $stem_1)$;
$stem_2 = stem_4$ **if** $hefty$: $-2stem\_corr$ **fi**;
$stem_3 = stem_1$ **if** $hefty$: $-2stem\_corr$ **fi**;
$x_2 - x_1 = x_4 - x_3 = x_6 - x_5 = x_8 - x_7$; $x_{2l} + apex\_corr = x_{3l}$; $x_{6l} + apex\_corr = x_{7l}$;
$y_1 = y_8 = h$; $y_2 = y_3 = y_6 = y_7 = -apex\_o$; $y_4 = y_5 =$ **if** $monospace$: vround $.6$ **fi** h;
$mid\_corr =$ **if** $monospace$ or $hefty$: $-apex\_corr$ **else**: $1/3jut$ **fi**;
$alpha = diag\_ratio(4, stem_2 - stem_3 + stem_4, y_1 - y_2, x_{8r} - x_{1l} + mid\_corr - 2apex\_corr)$;
$penpos_1(alpha * stem_1, 0)$; $penpos_2(alpha * stem_1, 0)$;
$penpos_3(alpha * stem_2, 0)$; $penpos_4(alpha * stem_2, 0)$;
$penpos_5(alpha * stem_3, 0)$; $penpos_6(alpha * stem_3, 0)$;
$penpos_7(alpha * stem_4, 0)$; $penpos_8(alpha * stem_4, 0)$;
$x_{4l} - x_{1l} = \text{floor}(x_{4l} - x_{1l} + .5(x_{5r} + mid\_corr - x_{4r}))$;   % $x_{5r} + mid\_corr \approx x_{4r}$
$z_{23} = whatever[z_{1r}, z_{2r}] = whatever[z_{3l}, z_{4l}]$;
$z_{45} = whatever[z_{3r}, z_{4r}] = whatever[z_{5l}, z_{6l}]$;
$z_{67} = whatever[z_{5r}, z_{6r}] = whatever[z_{7l}, z_{8l}]$; $upper\_notch = y_4 - cap\_notch\_cut$;
fill $diag\_end(1l, 2l, 1, 1, 3r, 4r)\{z_4 - z_3\}$
        $\ldots$ **if** $y_{45} < upper\_notch$: $(x_{45}, upper\_notch) + .5left\{up\}$
            $-- (x_{45}, upper\_notch) + .5right\{down\}$ **else**: z_{45} & z_{45} **fi**
        $\ldots \{z_6 - z_5\}diag\_end(5l, 6l, 1, 1, 7r, 8r) -- diag\_end(7r, 8r, 1, 1, 8l, 7l)\{z_7 - z_8\}$
        $\ldots$ **if** $y_{67} > cap\_notch\_cut$: $(x_{67}, cap\_notch\_cut) + .5right\{down\}$
            $-- (x_{67}, cap\_notch\_cut) + .5left\{up\}$ **else**: z_{67} & z_{67} **fi**
        $\ldots \{z_5 - z_6\}special\_diag\_end(6, 5, 4, 3)\{z_3 - z_4\}$
        $\ldots$ **if** $y_{23} > cap\_notch\_cut$: $(x_{23}, cap\_notch\_cut) + .5right\{down\}$
            $-- (x_{23}, cap\_notch\_cut) + .5left\{up\}$ **else**: z_{23} & z_{23} **fi**
        $\ldots \{z_1 - z_2\}diag\_end(2r, 1r, 1, 1, 1l, 2l) --$ cycle;   % diagonals
if $serifs$: **numeric** $inner\_jut[]$; **pickup** $tiny.nib$;
    $prime\_points\_inside(1, 2)$; $prime\_points\_inside(5, 6)$; $prime\_points\_inside(8, 7)$;
    if $monospace$: $inner\_jut_1 = inner\_jut_4 = 1.5cap\_jut$;
    elseif $hefty$: $inner\_jut_1 = inner\_jut_4 = cap\_jut$;
    else: **fill** $diag\_end(6r, 5r, 1, 1, 5l, 6l)$
        $-- .5[z_{5l}, z_{6l}] -- .5[z_{5r}, z_{6r}] --$ cycle;   % middle stem
        $inner\_jut_2 = .7inner\_jut_1$; $inner\_jut_4 = 1.1inner\_jut_3$;
        if $rt\ x_{1'r} + cap\_jut + .5u + 1 \leq lft\ x_{5'l} - .7cap\_jut$: $inner\_jut_1 = cap\_jut$;
        else: $rt\ x_{1'r} + inner\_jut_1 + .5u + 1 = lft\ x_{5'l} - inner\_jut_2$; **fi**
        if $rt\ x_{5'r} + cap\_jut + .5u + 1 \leq lft\ x_{8'l} - 1.1cap\_jut$: $inner\_jut_3 = cap\_jut$;
        else: $rt\ x_{5'r} + inner\_jut_3 + .5u + 1 = lft\ x_{8'l} - inner\_jut_4$; **fi**
        $dish\_serif(5', 6, e, 1/3, inner\_jut_2, f, 1/2, inner\_jut_3)$; **fi**   % middle serif
    $dish\_serif(1', 2, a, 1/3, outer\_jut, b, 1/2, inner\_jut_1)$;   % left serif
    $dish\_serif(8', 7, c, .6, inner\_jut_4, d, 1/2, outer\_jut)(dark)$; **fi**   % right serif
math_fit($.75u^\# - cap\_height^\# * slant$, $ic^\# - 2.5u^\#$);
penlabels(0, 1, 2, 3, 4, 5, 6, 7, 8, 23, 45, 67); **endchar**;

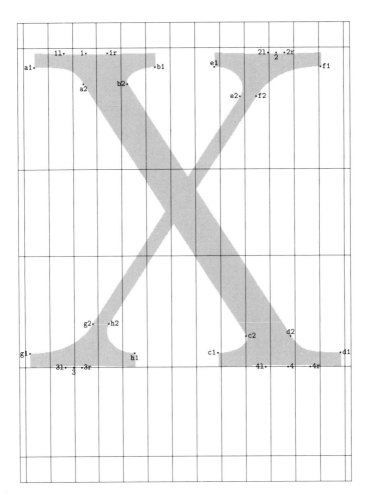

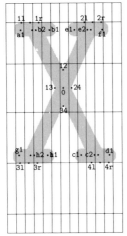

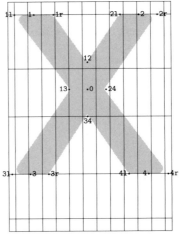

cmchar "The letter X";
beginchar("X", $13u^\#$, $cap\_height^\#$, 0);
italcorr $cap\_height^\# * slant - .25u^\#$;
adjust_fit($cap\_serif\_fit^\#$, $cap\_serif\_fit^\#$);
numeric $stem[]$, $outer\_jut$, $xjut$, $alpha[]$;
$stem_1 = cap\_stem - 2stem\_corr$; $stem_2 = \min(cap\_hair, stem_1)$;
$outer\_jut = .75cap\_jut$; $xjut = $ **if** $serifs$: $(stem_1 - stem_2)/4$ **else**: 0 **fi**;
$x_{1l} = l + letter\_fit + .5u + outer\_jut$; $x_{2r} = r - letter\_fit - u - outer\_jut - xjut$;
$x_{3l} = l + letter\_fit + .25u + outer\_jut + xjut$; $x_{4r} = r - letter\_fit - .25u - outer\_jut$;
$y_1 = y_2 = h$; $y_3 = y_4 = 0$;
$alpha_1 = diag\_ratio(1, stem_1, h, x_{4r} - x_{1l})$;
$alpha_2 = diag\_ratio(1, stem_2, h, x_{2r} - x_{3l})$;
$penpos_1(alpha_1 * stem_1, 0)$; $penpos_2(alpha_2 * stem_2, 0)$;
$penpos_3(alpha_2 * stem_2, 0)$; $penpos_4(alpha_1 * stem_1, 0)$;
if $hefty$: $z_0 = whatever[z_1, z_4] = whatever[z_2, z_3]$;
  $x_{12} = x_{34} = x_0$; $y_{13} = y_{24} = y_0$;
  $z_{12} = whatever[z_{2l}, z_{3l}]$; $z_{13} = whatever[z_{2l}, z_{3l}]$;
  $z_{24} = whatever[z_{2r}, z_{3r}]$; $z_{34} = whatever[z_{2r}, z_{3r}]$;
  forsuffixes $\$ = 13, 24, 34$: $z_{\$'} = .1[z_\$, z_0]$; **endfor**
  fill $diag\_end(12, 1r, .5, 1, 1l, 13')$ -- $z_{13'}$ -- $diag\_end(13', 3l, 1, .5, 3r, 34')$ -- $z_{34'}$
    -- $diag\_end(34', 4l, .5, 1, 4r, 24')$ -- $z_{24'}$
    -- $diag\_end(24', 2r, 1, .5, 2l, 12)$ -- z_{12} -- **cycle**;   % diagonals
else: **fill** $diag\_end(4r, 1r, .5, 1, 1l, 4l)$
    -- $diag\_end(1l, 4l, .5, 1, 4r, 1r)$ -- **cycle**;   % left diagonal
  fill $diag\_end(2l, 3l, .5, 1, 3r, 2r)$
    -- $diag\_end(3r, 2r, .5, 1, 2l, 3l)$ -- **cycle**; **fi**   % right diagonal
if $serifs$: **numeric** $inner\_jut[]$; **pickup** $tiny.nib$;
  $prime\_points\_inside(1, 4)$; $prime\_points\_inside(2, 3)$;
  $prime\_points\_inside(3, 2)$; $prime\_points\_inside(4, 1)$;
  if $rt\ x_{1'r} + cap\_jut + .5u + 1 \leq lft\ x_{2'l} - cap\_jut - xjut$: $inner\_jut_1 = cap\_jut$;
  else: $rt\ x_{1'r} + inner\_jut_1 + .5u + 1 = lft\ x_{2'l} - inner\_jut_1 - xjut$; **fi**
  if $rt\ x_{3'r} + cap\_jut + .5u + 1 \leq lft\ x_{4'l} - cap\_jut - xjut$: $inner\_jut_2 = cap\_jut$;
  else: $rt\ x_{3'r} + inner\_jut_2 + .5u + 1 = lft\ x_{4'l} - inner\_jut_2 - xjut$; **fi**
  $dish\_serif(1', 4, a, \frac{1}{3}, outer\_jut, b, \frac{2}{3}, inner\_jut_1)$;   % upper left serif
  $dish\_serif(4', 1, c, \frac{2}{3}, inner\_jut_2, d, \frac{1}{3}, outer\_jut)$;   % lower right serif
  $dish\_serif(2', 3, e, \frac{2}{3}, inner\_jut_1 + xjut,$
    $f, \frac{1}{2}, outer\_jut + xjut)(dark)$;   % upper right serif
  $dish\_serif(3', 2, g, \frac{1}{2}, outer\_jut + xjut,$
    $h, \frac{2}{3}, inner\_jut_2 + xjut)(dark)$; **fi**   % lower left serif
math_fit(0, $.5ic^\#$); **penlabels**($0, 1, 2, 3, 4, 12, 13, 24, 34$); **endchar**;

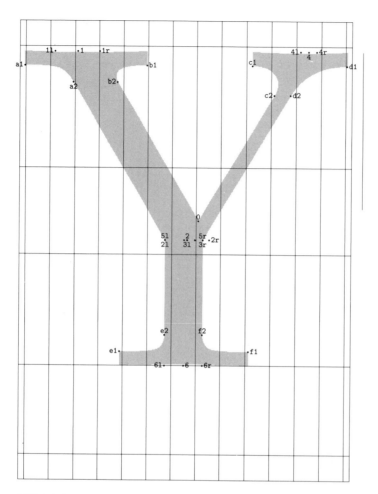

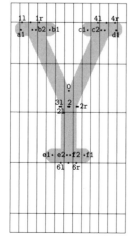

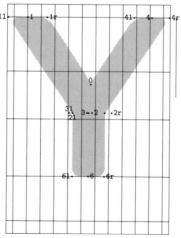

cmchar "The letter Y";
beginchar("Y", $13u^\#$, $cap\_height^\#$, 0);
italcorr $cap\_height^\# * slant + .45u^\#$;
adjust_fit($cap\_serif\_fit^\#$, $cap\_serif\_fit^\#$);
numeric $left\_stem$, $right\_stem$, $outer\_jut$, dy, $alpha$;
$left\_stem = cap\_stem - stem\_corr$;
$right\_stem = \min(cap\_hair$ **if** $hefty$: $-2stem\_corr$ **fi**, $left\_stem$);
$outer\_jut = .75cap\_jut$; $x_{1l} = w - x_{4r} = l + letter\_fit + outer\_jut + .05u$;
$x_{2l} = x_{5l} = \text{hround}(.5w - .5left\_stem)$; $x_{3r} = x_{5r}$; $y_1 = y_4 = h$; $y_2 = y_3 = y_5 = .4h$;
$dy = y_1 - y_2$; $alpha = ((x_{2l} - x_{1l}) + \!\!+ dy)/dy$;
$penpos_1(alpha * left\_stem, 0)$; $penpos_2(alpha * left\_stem, 0)$;
$penpos_3(alpha * right\_stem, 0)$; $penpos_4(alpha * right\_stem, 0)$;
$penpos_5(left\_stem, 0)$; $penpos_6(left\_stem, 0)$; $x_5 = x_6$; $y_6 = 0$;
$z_0 = whatever[z_{1r}, z_{2r}] = whatever[z_{3l}, z_{4l}]$;
if $y_0 > y_2 + cap\_notch\_cut$: $y_0 := y_2 + cap\_notch\_cut$;
    fill $z_0 + .5right\{up\} \ldots \{z_4 - z_3\}diag\_end(3l, 4l, 1, 1, 4r, 3r)$ -- z_{5r}
        -- $diag\_end(5r, 6r, 1, 1, 6l, 5l)$ -- z_{5l} -- $diag\_end(2l, 1l, 1, 1, 1r, 2r)\{z_2 - z_1\}$
        $\ldots \{down\}z_0 + .5left$ -- cycle;   % diagonals and stem
else: fill z_0 -- $diag\_end(0, 4l, 1, 1, 4r, 3r)$ -- z_{5r}
        -- $diag\_end(5r, 6r, 1, 1, 6l, 5l)$ -- z_{5l}
        -- $diag\_end(2l, 1l, 1, 1, 1r, 0)$ -- cycle; **fi**   % diagonals and stem
if $serifs$: **numeric** $inner\_jut$; **pickup** $tiny.nib$;
  $prime\_points\_inside(1, 2)$; $prime\_points\_inside(4, 3)$; $prime\_points\_inside(6, 5)$;
  if rt $x_{1'r} + cap\_jut + .5u + 1 \leq lft$ $x_{4'l} - cap\_jut$: $inner\_jut = cap\_jut$;
  else: rt $x_{1'r} + inner\_jut + .5u + 1 = lft$ $x_{4'l} - inner\_jut$; **fi**
  $dish\_serif(1', 2, a, \frac{1}{3}, outer\_jut, b, \frac{1}{2}, inner\_jut)$;   % upper left serif
  $dish\_serif(4', 3, c, .6, inner\_jut, d, \frac{1}{2}, outer\_jut)(dark)$;   % upper right serif
  $dish\_serif(6', 5, e, \frac{1}{3}, cap\_jut, f, \frac{1}{3}, cap\_jut)$; **fi**   % lower serif
math_fit($.5u^\# - cap\_height^\# * slant$, $ic^\# - 4u^\#$);
penlabels(0, 1, 2, 3, 4, 5, 6); **endchar**;

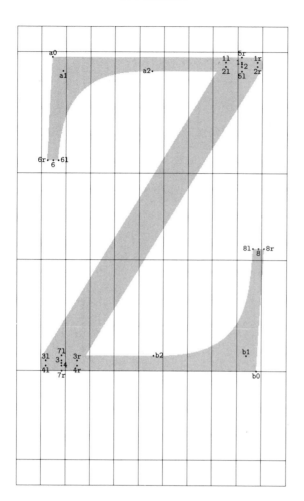

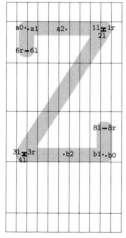

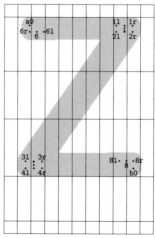

cmchar "The letter Z";

beginchar("Z", $11u^\#$, $cap\_height^\#$, 0);

italcorr $cap\_height^\# * slant - .5u^\#$;

adjust_fit(0, 0);

numeric $arm\_thickness[]$, z_stem;

if $hefty$: $arm\_thickness_1 = \text{Vround}(slab - vair\_corr)$; $arm\_thickness_2 = slab$;

  $z\_stem = .8[vair, cap\_stem]$;

else: $arm\_thickness_1 = slab$; $arm\_thickness_2 = \text{vround}(slab + vair\_corr)$;

  $z\_stem = .9[vair, cap\_stem]$; **fi**

pickup $tiny.nib$; $x_{3l} = x_{4l} = w - x_{1r} = w - x_{2r}$; $lft\ x_{3l} = \text{hround } u$;

$top\ y_1 = h$; $y_2 = \min(y_1, h - {}^2\!/_3 arm\_thickness_1)$;

$bot\ y_4 = 0$; $y_3 = \max(y_4, {}^2\!/_3 arm\_thickness_2)$;

numeric $alpha$; $alpha = diag\_ratio(1, z\_stem - tiny, y_2 - y_3, x_{2r} - x_{3l})$;

$penpos_1(alpha * (z\_stem - tiny), 0)$; $penpos_2(alpha * (z\_stem - tiny), 0)$;

$penpos_3(alpha * (z\_stem - tiny), 0)$; $penpos_4(alpha * (z\_stem - tiny), 0)$;

pair $delta$; $delta = $ **penoffset** $z_3 - z_2$ **of** $currentpen$;

fill $top\ lft\ z_{1l}\ \text{-- } z_{2l} + delta\ \text{---}\ z_{3l} + delta\ \text{.. } lft\ z_{3l}\ \text{---}\ lft\ z_{4l}\ \text{.. } bot\ z_{4l}$

  $\text{--- } bot\ rt\ z_{4r}\ \text{-- } z_{3r} - delta\ \text{---}\ z_{2r} - delta\ \text{.. } rt\ z_{2r}\ \text{---}\ rt\ z_{1r}\ \text{.. } top\ z_{1r}$

  --- cycle;   % diagonal

pickup $crisp.nib$; $pos_5(arm\_thickness_1, 90)$; $pos_6(hair, 180)$;

$top\ y_{5r} = h$; $x_5 = x_1$; $lft\ x_{6r} = \text{hround } 1.25u$; $y_6 = good.y(y_{5l} - beak) - eps$;

$arm(5, 6, a, beak\_darkness ** .8, -.4beak\_jut)$;   % upper arm and beak

$pos_7(arm\_thickness_2, -90)$; $pos_8(hair, 0)$;

$bot\ y_{7r} = 0$; $x_7 = x_4$; $rt\ x_{8r} = \text{hround}(w - .9u)$; $y_8 = good.y(y_{7l} + 1.2beak) + eps$;

$arm(7, 8, b, beak\_darkness ** .9, .6beak\_jut)$;   % lower arm and beak

math_fit(0, $.5ic^\#$); **penlabels**(1, 2, 3, 4, 5, 6, 7, 8); **endchar**;

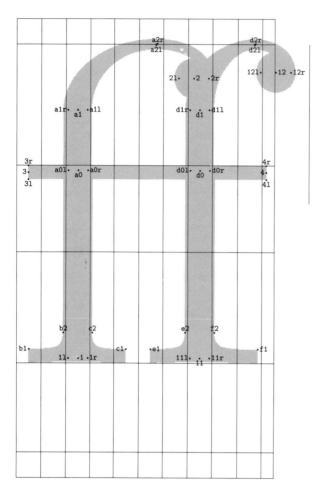

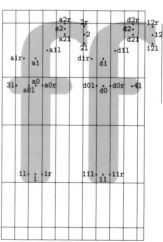

The program file `romlig.mf` gives us ff, fi, fl, ffi, and ffl. For obvious reasons, these characters do not appear in the monospaced font `cmtt10`.

> % This file describes five roman ligatures that begin with 'f'
> % and puts them in code positions '013–'017.

numeric *itc#*;   % modified italic correction on 'f' and 'ff'
itc# = **if** *serifs*: max(0, *flare#* − .25*u#*) **else**: 1.25*u#* **fi**;

ligtable "f": "i" =: oct "014", "f" =: oct "013", "l" =: oct "015",
  "'" **kern** *itc#*, "?" **kern** *itc#*, "!" **kern** *itc#*, ")" **kern** *itc#*, "]" **kern** *itc#*;
ligtable oct "013": "i" =: oct "016", "l" =: oct "017",
  "'" **kern** *itc#*, "?" **kern** *itc#*, "!" **kern** *itc#*, ")" **kern** *itc#*, "]" **kern** *itc#*;

cmchar "The ligature ff";
beginchar(oct "013", 10.5*u#* + 2*letter_fit#*, *asc_height#*, 0);
italcorr *asc_height#* ∗ *slant* + **if** *serifs*: *flare#* − .25*u#* **else**: 1.25*u#* **fi**;
adjust_fit(0, 0);
pickup *tiny.nib*; $pos_1(stem', 0)$; *lft* x_{1l} = hround(2.5*u* − .5*stem'*);
$pos_{11}(stem', 0)$; *rt* x_{11r} = hround(*w* − 3*u* + .5*stem'*);
pickup *fine.nib*; **numeric** *bulb_diam*, *inner_jut*;
if *serifs*: *bulb_diam* = hround .8[*stem*, *flare*];
  $pos_2(bulb\_diam, 0)$; $pos_{12}(bulb\_diam, 0)$;
  rt x_{2r} = hround(*rt* x_{11r} − *stem_corr*); *lft* x_{12l} = hround(*w* − .75*u* + .5);
  y_2 + .5*bulb_diam* = .85[*x_height*, *h* + *oo*]; y_{12} + .5*bulb_diam* = .9[*x_height*, *h* + *oo*];
  if *rt* x_{1r} + *jut* + .5*u* + 2 ≤ *lft* x_{11l} − *jut*: *inner_jut* = *jut*;
  else: *rt* x_{1r} + *inner_jut* + .5*u* + 2 = *lft* x_{11l} − *inner_jut*; **fi**
else: $pos_2(5/7[vair, flare], 90)$; *top* y_{2r} = *h*; *rt* x_2 = hround 6.25*u*;
  $pos_{12}(5/7[vair, flare], 90)$; y_{12} = y_2; *rt* x_{12} = hround(*w* + .75*u*); **fi**
f_stroke(1, 2, *a*, *b*, *c*, *jut*, *inner_jut*);   % left stem, arc, terminal, serif
f_stroke(11, 12, *d*, *e*, *f*, *inner_jut*, 1.25*jut*);   % right stem, arc, terminal, serif
pickup *crisp.nib*; *top* y_{3r} = *top* y_{4r} = *x_height*; *lft* x_3 = hround .5*u* − 1;
$pos_3(bar, 90)$; $pos_4(bar, 90)$;
rt x_4 = hround(*w* − 1/3*u*);
if *hefty*: $pos_{3'}(bar, 90)$; $x_{3'} − x_1 = x_4 − x_{11}$; $x_{3'} = y_3$;
  $pos_{4'}(bar, 90)$; $x_{4'} = x_{11}$; $y_{4'} = y_4$;
  filldraw stroke z_{3e} -- $z_{3'e}$; **filldraw stroke** $z_{4'e}$ -- z_{4e};   % bars
else: **filldraw stroke** z_{3e} -- z_{4e}; **fi**   % bar
penlabels(1, 2, 3, 4, 11, 12); **endchar**;

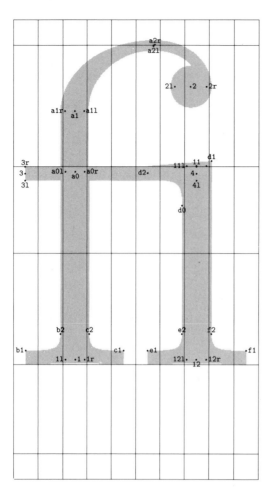

cmchar "The ligature fi";
beginchar(oct "014", $10u\# + 2letter\_fit\#$, $asc\_height\#$, 0);
italcorr $asc\_height\# * slant - serif\_fit\# + .5$ **if** $serifs$: $stem\#$ **else**: $dot\_size\#$ **fi** $- 2u\#$;
adjust_fit(0, $serif\_fit\#$);
pickup $tiny.nib$; $pos_1(stem', 0)$; $lft\ x_{1l} = \text{hround}(2.5u - .5stem')$;
$pos_{11}(stem', 0)$; $rt\ x_{11r} = \text{hround}(w - 2.5u + .5stem')$;
$pos_{12}(stem', 0)$; $x_{11} = x_{12}$; $bot\ y_{12} = 0$;
pickup $fine.nib$; **numeric** $bulb\_diam$, $inner\_jut$;
if $serifs$: $bulb\_diam = \text{hround}\ ^1/_4[.8[stem, flare], dot\_size]$;
  $pos_2(bulb\_diam, 0)$; $x_{2r} = x_{12r}$;
  $y_2 + .5bulb\_diam = .8[x\_height, h + oo]$; $top\ y_{11} = x\_height + \min(oo, serif\_drop)$;
  if $rt\ x_{1r} + jut + .5u + 2 \leq lft\ x_{11l} - jut$: $inner\_jut = jut$;
  else: $rt\ x_{1r} + inner\_jut + .5u + 2 = lft\ x_{11l} - inner\_jut$; **fi**
else: $bulb\_diam = \max(stem, dot\_size)$;
  $pos_2(^6/_7[vair, flare], 90)$; $top\ y_{2r} = h$; $rt\ x_2 = \text{hround}\ 5.3u$;
  pickup $tiny.nib$; $pos_{13}(bulb\_diam, 0)$; $pos_{14}(bulb\_diam, 90)$;
  $x_{13} = x_{11} - .5$; $top\ y_{14r} = \min(2x\_height, h + 1)$; $top\ y_{11} = x\_height$;
  if $bot\ y_{14l} - x\_height < tiny$: $y_{14l} := \min(y_{14r} - eps, y_{11} + 2tiny)$; **fi**
  $x_{13} = x_{14}$; $y_{13} = .5[y_{14l}, y_{14r}]$; $dot(13, 14)$; % dot
fi;   % this is the ligature we're drawing
$f\_stroke(1, 2, a, b, c, jut, inner\_jut)$;   % left stem, arc, terminal, serif
pickup $tiny.nib$; **filldraw stroke** $z_{11e} -- z_{12e}$; % right stem
pickup $crisp.nib$; $top\ y_{3r} = top\ y_{4r} = x\_height$; $lft\ x_3 = \text{hround}\ .5u - 1$;
$pos_3(bar, 90)$; $pos_4(bar, 90)$;
if $serifs$: $x_4 = x_{11}$;   % bar will overlap upper right serif
  $sloped\_serif.l(11, 12, d, ^1/_3, jut, \min(oo, serif\_drop))$; % upper right serif
  $dish\_serif(12, 11, e, ^1/_3, inner\_jut, f, ^1/_3, jut)$; % lower right serif
else: $rt\ x_4 = \text{hround}\ 5.3u$; **fi**
pickup $crisp.nib$; **filldraw stroke** $z_{3e} -- z_{4e}$; % bar
penlabels(1, 2, 3, 4, 11, 12, 13, 14); **endchar**;

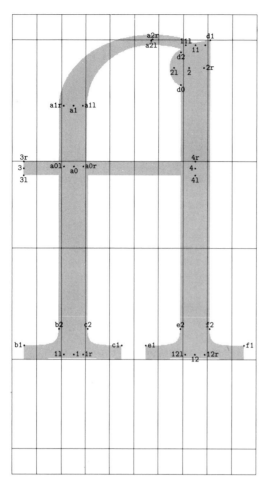

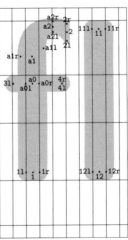

cmchar "The ligature fl";
beginchar(oct "015", $10u\# + 2letter\_fit\#$, $asc\_height\#$, 0);
italcorr $asc\_height\# * slant - serif\_fit\# + .5stem\# - 2u\#$;
adjust_fit(0, $serif\_fit\#$);
pickup $tiny.nib$; $pos_1(stem', 0)$; lft x_{1l} = hround($2.5u - .5stem'$);
$pos_{11}(stem', 0)$; rt x_{11r} = hround($w - 2.5u + .5stem'$);
$pos_{12}(stem', 0)$; $x_{11} = x_{12}$; bot $y_{12} = 0$; top $y_{11} = h$;
filldraw stroke $z_{11e} \; {-}{-} \; z_{12e}$;   % right stem
pickup $fine.nib$; **numeric** $bulb\_diam$, $inner\_jut$;
if $serifs$: $bulb\_diam$ = hround $.8[stem, flare]$;
$\quad pos_2(bulb\_diam, 0)$; $x_{2r} = x_{11r} - stem\_corr$;
$\quad y_2 + .5bulb\_diam = .9[x\_height, h + oo]$;
$\quad sloped\_serif.l(11, 12, d, \frac{1}{3}, eps, \max(serif\_drop, oo))$;   % erase excess at top
$\quad$ **if** rt $x_{1r} + jut + .5u + 2 \leq$ lft $x_{11l} - jut$: $inner\_jut = jut$;
$\quad$ **else:** rt $x_{1r} + inner\_jut + .5u + 2 =$ lft $x_{11l} - inner\_jut$; **fi**
else: $pos_2(\frac{5}{7}[vair, flare], 90)$; top $y_{2r} = h$; rt x_2 = hround $5.3u$; **fi**
$f\_stroke(1, 2, a, b, c, jut, inner\_jut)$;   % left stem, arc, terminal, serif
pickup $crisp.nib$; top $y_{3r} =$ top $y_{4r} = x\_height$; lft x_3 = hround $.5u - 1$;
$pos_3(bar, 90)$; $pos_4(bar, 90)$;
if $serifs$: $x_4 = x_{11}$;
$\quad dish\_serif(12, 11, e, \frac{1}{3}, inner\_jut, f, \frac{1}{3}, jut)$;   % lower right serif
else: rt x_4 = hround $5.3u$; **fi**
pickup $crisp.nib$; **filldraw stroke** $z_{3e} \; {-}{-} \; z_{4e}$;   % bar
penlabels(1, 2, 3, 4, 11, 12); **endchar**;

Top diagram labels: a2r, a21, d2r, d21, 21, ·2, ·2r, 121·, ·12, ·12r, a1r, a1, ·a11, d1r, d1, ·d11, g1, 3r, 3·, 31, a01·, a0, ·a0r, d01·, d0, ·d0r, g2·, 211·, ·21, 4·, 41, g0, b2, ·2, e2, f2, h2, ·2, b1·, c1·, ·e1, f1·, ·h1, ·i1, 11·, ·1, ·1r, 111·, ·11r, 11, 221·, ·22r, 22

Bottom diagram labels: a2r, 2r, d2r, ·12r, 24r, a2·, d2·, ·12, ·23r, a21, d21, ·121, 241, a1r·, a1, ·a11, 21, d1r·, d1, ·d11, ·2, 31·, a0, ·a0r, d01·, d0, ·d0r, 4r, 211·, ·21, ·21r, a01, 41, 11·, ·1r, 111·, ·11r, 221·, ·22r, i, 11, 22

cmchar "The ligature ffi";

beginchar(oct "016", $15u\# + 4letter\_fit\#$, $asc\_height\#$, 0);

italcorr $asc\_height\# * slant - serif\_fit\# + .5$ **if** $serifs$: $stem\#$ **else**: $dot\_size\#$ **fi** $- 2u\#$;

adjust_fit(0, $serif\_fit\#$);

pickup $tiny.nib$; $pos_1(stem', 0)$; $lft\ x_{1l} = \mathrm{hround}(2.5u - .5stem')$;

$pos_{11}(stem', 0)$; $lft\ x_{11l} = \mathrm{hround}(.5w - .5stem')$;

$pos_{21}(stem', 0)$; $rt\ x_{21r} = \mathrm{hround}(w - 2.5u + .5stem')$;

$pos_{22}(stem', 0)$; $x_{21} = x_{22}$; $bot\ y_{22} = 0$;

pickup $fine.nib$; **numeric** $bulb\_diam$, $inner\_jut$;

if $serifs$: $bulb\_diam = \mathrm{hround}\ ^1/_4[.8[stem, flare], dot\_size]$;

  $pos_2(bulb\_diam, 0)$; $x_{2r} = x_{11r} - stem\_corr$;

  $pos_{12}(bulb\_diam, 0)$; $x_{12r} = x_{21r}$;

  $top\ y_{21} = x\_height + \min(oo, serif\_drop)$;

  $y_2 + .5bulb\_diam = .8[x\_height, h + oo]$; $y_{12} = y_2$;

  if $rt\ x_{1r} + jut + .5u + 2 \leq lft\ x_{11l} - jut$: $inner\_jut = jut$;

  else: $rt\ x_{1r} + inner\_jut + .5u + 2 = lft\ x_{11l} - inner\_jut$; **fi**

else: $bulb\_diam = \max(stem, dot\_size)$;

  $pos_2(^5/_7[vair, flare], 90)$; $top\ y_{2r} = h$; $rt\ x_2 = \mathrm{hround}\ 5.75u$;

  $pos_{12}(^6/_7[vair, flare], 90)$; $y_{12} = y_2$; $rt\ x_{12} = \mathrm{hround}(.5w + 2.8u)$;

  pickup $tiny.nib$; $pos_{23}(bulb\_diam, 0)$; $pos_{24}(bulb\_diam, 90)$;

  $x_{23} = x_{21} - .5$; $top\ y_{24r} = \min(2x\_height, h + 1)$; $top\ y_{21} = x\_height$;

  if $bot\ y_{24l} - x\_height < tiny$: $y_{24l} := \min(y_{24r} - eps, y_{21} + 2tiny)$; **fi**

  $x_{23} = x_{24}$; $y_{23} = .5[y_{24l}, y_{24r}]$; $dot(23, 24)$; **fi**   % dot

$f\_stroke(1, 2, a, b, c, jut, inner\_jut)$;   % left stem, arc, terminal, serif

$f\_stroke(11, 12, d, e, f, inner\_jut, inner\_jut)$;   % middle ditto

pickup $tiny.nib$; **filldraw stroke** $z_{21e}\ \texttt{--}\ z_{22e}$;   % right stem

pickup $crisp.nib$; $top\ y_{3r} = top\ y_{4r} = x\_height$; $lft\ x_3 = \mathrm{hround}\ .5u - 1$;

$pos_3(bar, 90)$; $pos_4(bar, 90)$;

if $serifs$: $x_4 = x_{21}$;   % bar will overlap upper right serif

  $sloped\_serif.l(21, 22, g, ^1/_3, jut, \min(oo, serif\_drop))$;   % upper right serif

  $dish\_serif(22, 21, h, ^1/_3, inner\_jut, i, ^1/_3, jut)$;   % lower right serif

else: $rt\ x_4 = \mathrm{hround}(.5w + 2.8u)$; **fi**

pickup $crisp.nib$;

if $hefty$: $pos_{3'}(bar, 90)$; $x_{3'} - x_1 = x_4 - x_{11}$; $y_{3'} = y_3$;

  $pos_{4'}(bar, 90)$; $x_{4'} = x_{11}$; $y_{4'} = y_4$;

  filldraw stroke $z_{3e}\ \texttt{--}\ z_{3'e}$; **filldraw stroke** $z_{4'e}\ \texttt{--}\ z_{4e}$;   % bars

else: **filldraw stroke** $z_{3e}\ \texttt{--}\ z_{4e}$; **fi**   % bar

penlabels(1, 2, 3, 4, 11, 12, 21, 22, 23, 24); **endchar**;

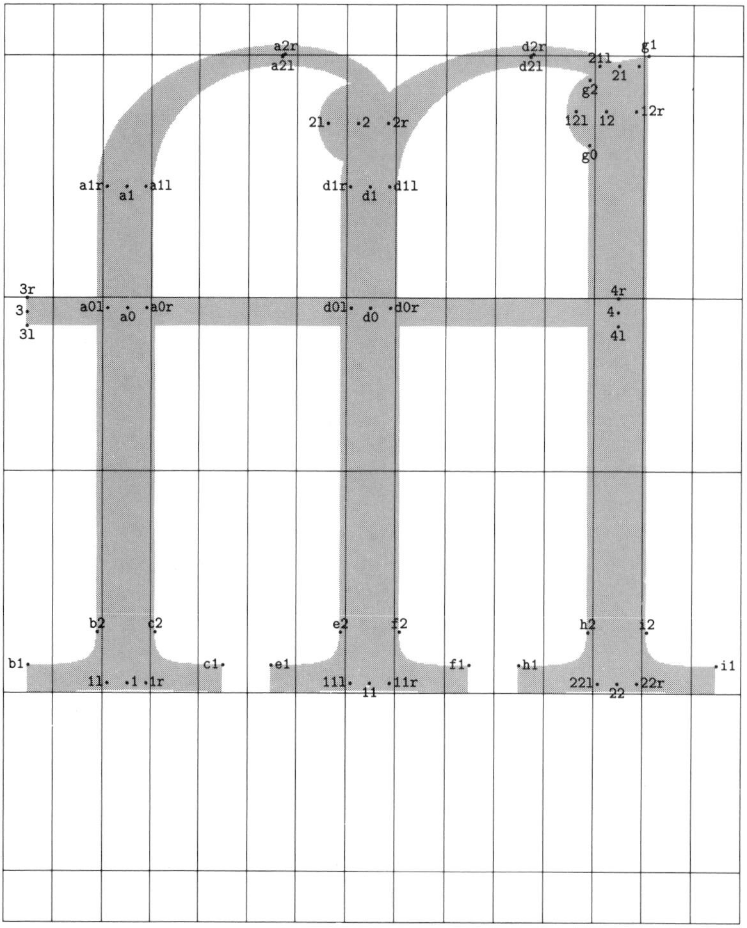
a2r
a21
d2r
d21
211
g1
21
g2
121
12
12r
21
2
2r
g0
a1r
a1
a11
d1r
d1
d11
3r
3
31
a01
a0
a0r
d01
d0
d0r
4r
4
41
b2
c2
e2
f2
h2
i2
b1
c1
e1
f1
h1
i1
11
1
1r
111
11
11r
221
22
22r

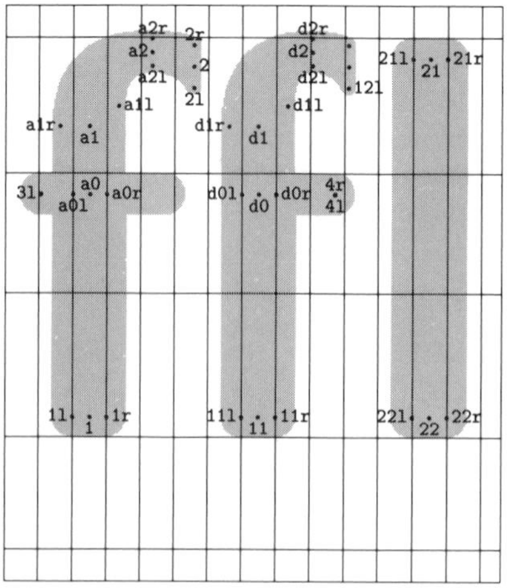
a2r
2r
d2r
a2
2
d2
211
21
21r
a21
d21
121
a11
21
d11
a1r
a1
d1r
d1
31
a0
a01
a0r
d01
d0
d0r
4r
41
11
1
1r
111
11
11r
221
22
22r

cmchar "The ligature ffl";
beginchar(oct "017", $15u\# + 4letter\_fit\#$, $asc\_height\#$, 0);
italcorr $asc\_height\# * slant - serif\_fit\# + .5stem\# - 2u\#$;
adjust_fit(0, $serif\_fit\#$);
pickup $tiny.nib$; $pos_1(stem', 0)$; lft $x_{1l} = $ hround$(2.5u - .5stem')$;
$pos_{11}(stem', 0)$; lft $x_{11l} = $ hround$(.5w - .5stem')$;
$pos_{21}(stem', 0)$; rt $x_{21r} = $ hround$(w - 2.5u + .5stem')$;
$pos_{22}(stem', 0)$; $x_{21} = x_{22}$; bot $y_{22} = 0$; top $y_{21} = h$;
filldraw stroke z_{21e} -- z_{22e};   % right stem
pickup $fine.nib$; **numeric** $bulb\_diam$, $inner\_jut$;
if $serifs$: $bulb_diam = $ hround $.8[stem, flare]$;
   $pos_2(bulb\_diam, 0)$; $x_{2r} = x_{11r} - stem\_corr$;
   $pos_{12}(bulb\_diam, 0)$; $x_{12r} = x_{21r} - stem\_corr$;
   $y_2 + .5bulb\_diam = .85[x\_height, h + oo]$; $y_{12} + .5bulb\_diam = .9[x\_height, h + oo]$;
   $sloped\_serif.l(21, 22, g, \frac{1}{3}, eps, \max(serif\_drop, oo))$;   % erase excess at top
   if rt $x_{1r} + jut + .5u + 2 \leq$ lft $x_{11l} - jut$: $inner\_jut = jut$;
   else: rt $x_{1r} + inner_jut + .5u + 2 = $ lft $x_{11l} - inner\_jut$; **fi**
else: $pos_2(\frac{5}{7}[vair, flare], 90)$; top $y_{2r} = h$; rt $x_2 = $ hround $5.75u$;
   $pos_{12}(\frac{5}{7}[vair, flare], 90)$; $y_{12} = y_2$; rt $x_{12} = $ hround$(.5w + 2.8u)$; **fi**
$f\_stroke(1, 2, a, b, c, jut, inner\_jut)$;   % left stem, arc, terminal, serif
$f\_stroke(11, 12, d, e, f, inner\_jut, inner\_jut)$;   % middle ditto
pickup $crisp.nib$; top $y_{3r} = $ top $y_{4r} = x\_height$; lft $x_3 = $ hround $.5u - 1$;
$pos_3(bar, 90)$; $pos_4(bar, 90)$;
if $serifs$: $dish\_serif(22, 21, h, \frac{1}{3}, inner\_jut, i, \frac{1}{3}, jut)$;   % lower right serif
   pickup $crisp.nib$; $x_4 = x_{21}$;
else: rt $x_4 = $ hround$(.5w + 2.8u)$; **fi**
if $hefty$: $pos_{3'}(bar, 90)$; $x_{3'} - x_1 = x_4 - x_{11}$; $y_{3'} = y_3$;
   $pos_{4'}(bar, 90)$; $x_{4'} = x_{11}$; $y_{4'} = y_4$;
   filldraw stroke z_{3e} -- $z_{3'e}$; **filldraw stroke** $z_{4'e}$ -- z_{4e};   % bars
else: **filldraw stroke** z_{3e} -- z_{4e}; **fi**   % bar
penlabels(1, 2, 3, 4, 11, 12, 21, 22); **endchar**;

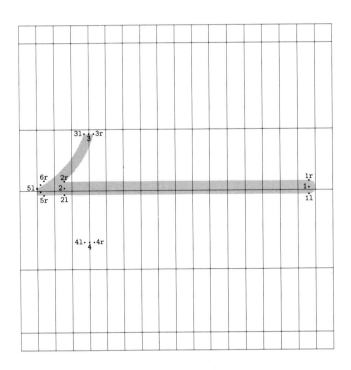

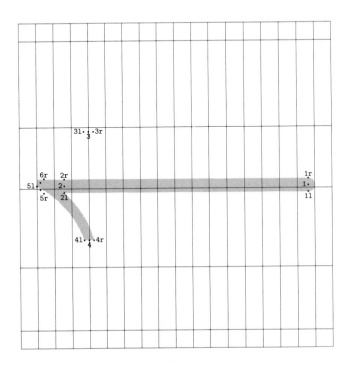

Now we switch gears abruptly: The program file `romms.mf` generates miscellaneous mathematical and musical symbols.

% This file contains special characters of "math italic" fonts
% that actually are not supposed to be slanted.
% Codes $'050-'057$, $'072-'077$, and $'133-'137$ are generated.

% The italic corrections are zero in all of these characters.

cmchar "Leftward top half arrow";
$compute\_spread(.45x\_height^\#, .55x\_height^\#)$;
beginchar(oct "050", $18u^\#$, $v\_center(spread^\# + rule\_thickness^\#)$);
adjust_fit$(0,0)$; **pickup** $crisp.nib$;
$pos_1(rule\_thickness, 90)$; $pos_2(rule\_thickness, 90)$; $pos_3(bar, 0)$; $pos_4(bar, 0)$;
$y_0 = y_1 = y_2 = math\_axis$; $x_1 + .5rule_thickness = $ hround$(w-u)$; lft $x_0 = $ hround u;
$y_3 - y_0 = y_0 - y_4 = .24asc\_height + eps$; $x_3 = x_4 = x_0 + 3u + eps$;
$pos_5(bar, $ angle$(z_4 - z_0))$; $z_{5l} = z_0$; $pos_6(bar, $ angle$(z_3 - z_0))$; $z_{6l} = z_0$;
numeric t; **path** p; $p = z_{4r} .. \{2(x_0 - x_4), y_0 - y_4\}z_{6r}$;
$t = $ xpart$(p$ intersectiontimes $((0, y_{2l}) -- (w, y_{2l})))$; $x_2 = $ xpart **point** t **of** p;
filldraw $z_0 -- (x_0, y_{2l}) --- z_{1l} .. z_{1r} --- z_{2r}$
   .. **subpath**$(t, 0)$ **of** $(z_{3r} .. \{2(x_0 - x_3), y_0 - y_3\}z_{5r})$
   $-- z_{3l} .. \{2(x_0 - x_3), y_0 - y_3\}$ cycle;   % arrowhead and stem
penlabels$(0, 1, 2, 3, 4, 5, 6)$; **endchar**;

cmchar "Leftward bottom half arrow";
$compute\_spread(.45x\_height^\#, .55x\_height^\#)$;
beginchar(oct "051", $18u^\#$, $v\_center(spread^\# + rule\_thickness^\#)$);
adjust_fit$(0,0)$; **pickup** $crisp.nib$;
$pos_1(rule\_thickness, 90)$; $pos_2(rule\_thickness, 90)$; $pos_3(bar, 0)$; $pos_4(bar, 0)$;
$y_0 = y_1 = y_2 = math\_axis$; $x_1 + .5rule_thickness = $ hround$(w-u)$; lft $x_0 = $ hround u;
$y_3 - y_0 = y_0 - y_4 = .24asc\_height + eps$; $x_3 = x_4 = x_0 + 3u + eps$;
$pos_5(bar, $ angle$(z_4 - z_0))$; $z_{5l} = z_0$; $pos_6(bar, $ angle$(z_3 - z_0))$; $z_{6l} = z_0$;
numeric t; **path** p; $p = z_{4r} .. \{2(x_0 - x_4), y_0 - y_4\}z_{6r}$;
$t = $ xpart$(p$ intersectiontimes $((0, y_{2l}) -- (w, y_{2l})))$; $x_2 = $ xpart **point** t **of** p;
filldraw $z_0\{2(x_4 - x_0), y_4 - y_0\} .. z_{4l}$
   $--$ **subpath**$(0, t)$ **of** $(z_{4r} .. \{2(x_0 - x_4), y_0 - y_4\}z_{6r})$
   $.. z_{2l} --- z_{1l} .. z_{1r} --- (x_0, y_{2r}) --$ cycle;   % arrowhead and stem
penlabels$(0, 1, 2, 3, 4, 5, 6)$; **endchar**;

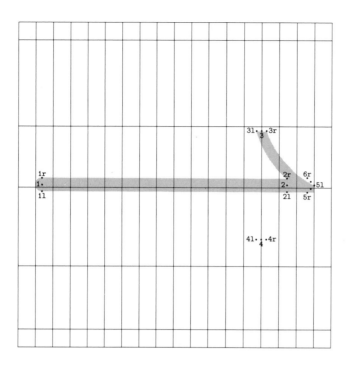

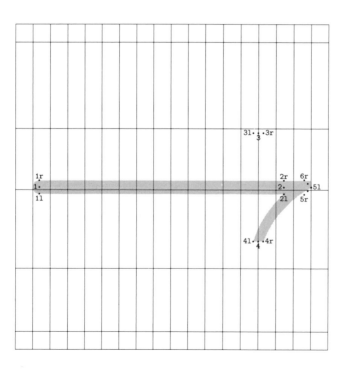

cmchar "Rightward top half arrow";
compute_spread(.45*x_height*#, .55*x_height*#);
beginchar(oct "052", 18*u*#, *v_center*(*spread*# + *rule_thickness*#));
adjust_fit(0, 0); **pickup** *crisp.nib*;
$pos_1(rule\_thickness, 90)$; $pos_2(rule\_thickness, 90)$; $pos_3(bar, 0)$; $pos_4(bar, 0)$;
$y_0 = y_1 = y_2 = math\_axis$; $x_1 - .5rule\_thickness =$ hround u; rt $x_0 =$ hround$(w - u)$;
$y_3 - y_0 = y_0 - y_4 = .24asc\_height + eps$; $x_3 = x_4 = x_0 - 3u - eps$;
$pos_5(bar, \text{angle}(z_4 - z_0))$; $z_{5l} = z_0$; $pos_6(bar, \text{angle}(z_3 - z_0))$; $z_{6l} = z_0$;
numeric t; **path** p; $p = z_{4l} .. \{2(x_0 - x_4), y_0 - y_4\}z_{6r}$;
$t = $ xpart(p intersectiontimes $((0, y_{2l}) -- (w, y_{2l}))$); $x_2 = $ xpart **point** t **of** p;
filldraw $z_0 -- (x_0, y_{2l}) --- z_{1l} .. z_{1r} --- z_{2r}$
   .. **subpath**$(t, 0)$ **of** $(z_{3l} .. \{2(x_0 - x_3), y_0 - y_3\}z_{5r})$
   $-- z_{3r} .. \{2(x_0 - x_3), y_0 - y_3\}$ cycle;   % arrowhead and stem
penlabels(0, 1, 2, 3, 4, 5, 6); **endchar**;

cmchar "Rightward bottom half arrow";
compute_spread(.45*x_height*#, .55*x_height*#);
beginchar(oct "053", 18*u*#, *v_center*(*spread*# + *rule_thickness*#));
adjust_fit(0, 0); **pickup** *crisp.nib*;
$pos_1(rule\_thickness, 90)$; $pos_2(rule\_thickness, 90)$; $pos_3(bar, 0)$; $pos_4(bar, 0)$;
$y_0 = y_1 = y_2 = math\_axis$; $x_1 - .5rule\_thickness =$ hround u; rt $x_0 =$ hround$(w - u)$;
$y_3 - y_0 = y_0 - y_4 = .24asc\_height + eps$; $x_3 = x_4 = x_0 - 3u - eps$;
$pos_5(bar, \text{angle}(z_4 - z_0))$; $z_{5l} = z_0$; $pos_6(bar, \text{angle}(z_3 - z_0))$; $z_{6l} = z_0$;
numeric t; **path** p; $p = z_{4l} .. \{2(x_0 - x_4), y_0 - y_4\}z_{6r}$;
$t = $ xpart(p intersectiontimes $((0, y_{2l}) -- (w, y_{2l}))$); $x_2 = $ xpart **point** t **of** p;
filldraw $z_0\{2(x_4 - x_0), y_4 - y_0\} .. z_{4r}$
   $--$ **subpath**$(0, t)$ **of** $(z_{4l} .. \{2(x_0 - x_4), y_0 - y_4\}z_{6r})$
   $.. z_{2l} --- z_{1l} .. z_{1r} --- (x_0, y_{2r}) --$ cycle;   % arrowhead and stem
penlabels(0, 1, 2, 3, 4, 5, 6); **endchar**;

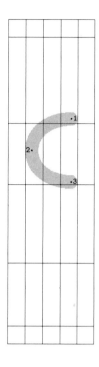

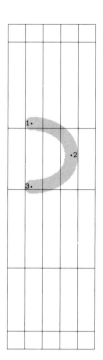

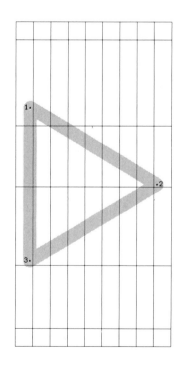

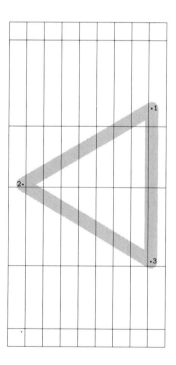

cmchar "Left hook";
compute_spread(.45x_height#, .55x_height#);
beginchar(oct "054", 5u#, v_center(2spread# + rule_thickness#));
adjust_fit(0, 0); **pickup** *rule.nib*; *autorounded*;
lft x_2 = hround $u - eps$; $x_1 = x_3 = w - x_2$;
$y_1 - y_3$ = *spread*; $y_2 = .5[y_1, y_3]$; y_3 = *math_axis*;
draw $z_1\{left\} \ldots z_2\{down\} \ldots z_3\{right\}$;   % hook
labels(1, 2, 3); **endchar**;

cmchar "Right hook";
compute_spread(.45x_height#, .55x_height#);
beginchar(oct "055", 5u#, v_center(2spread# + rule_thickness#));
adjust_fit(0, 0); **pickup** *rule.nib*; *autorounded*;
rt x_2 = hround($w - u$) + eps; $x_1 = x_3 = w - x_2$;
$y_1 - y_3$ = *spread*; $y_2 = .5[y_1, y_3]$; y_3 = *math_axis*;
draw $z_1\{right\} \ldots z_2\{down\} \ldots z_3\{left\}$;   % hook
labels(1, 2, 3); **endchar**;

cmchar "Triangle pointing right";
beginchar(oct "056", 9u#, v_center(x_height#));
adjust_fit(0, 0); **pickup** *rule.nib*;
numeric a, b; a = sqrt(3.14159 / sqrt 3);   % triangle area = circle area
$b = .5w - (rt$ hround $u)$; $.5[x_{1'}, x_{2'}] = .5w$; $x_{2'} - x_{1'} = a * b *$ sqrt 3;
$x_1 = x_3$ = *good.x* $x_{1'}$; x_2 = *good.x* $x_{2'}$;
$y_2 = .5[y_1, y_3]$ = *math_axis*; y_1 = *good.y*$(y_2 + a * b)$;
draw z_1 -- z_2 -- z_3 -- cycle;   % triangle
labels(1, 2, 3); **endchar**;

cmchar "Triangle pointing left";
beginchar(oct "057", 9u#, v_center(x_height#));
adjust_fit(0, 0); **pickup** *rule.nib*;
numeric a, b; a = sqrt(3.14159 / sqrt 3);   % triangle area = circle area
$b = .5w - (rt$ hround $u)$; $.5[x_{1'}, x_{2'}] = .5w$; $x_{1'} - x_{2'} = a * b *$ sqrt 3;
$x_1 = x_3$ = *good.x* $x_{1'}$; x_2 = *good.x* $x_{2'}$;
$y_2 = .5[y_1, y_3]$ = *math_axis*; y_1 = *good.y*$(y_2 + a * b)$;
draw z_1 -- z_2 -- z_3 -- cycle;   % triangle
labels(1, 2, 3); **endchar**;

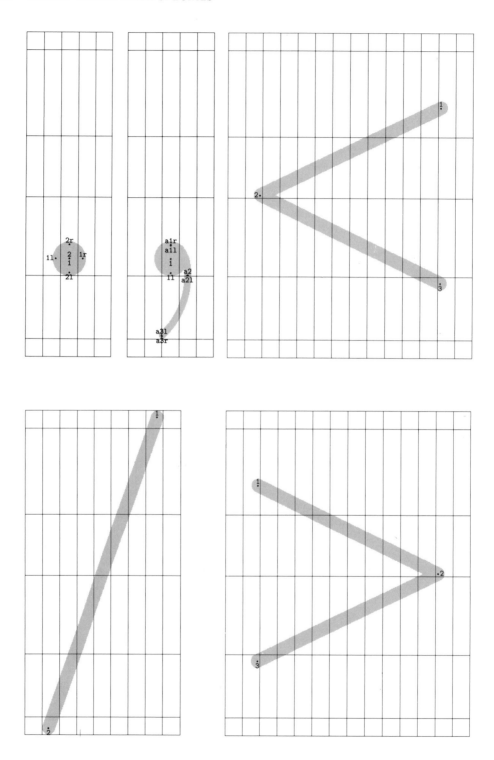

Five characters from other fonts are duplicated in math italic so that TEX can provide better spacing for them within formulas.

cmchar "Period";
numeric *dot_diam*#; *dot_diam*# = **if** *monospace*: ⁵⁄₄ **fi** *dot_size*#;
define_whole_blacker_pixels(*dot_diam*);
beginchar(oct "072", 5*u*#, *dot_diam*#, 0);   % non-ASCII position

    ⋮   (a copy of the program for '.' in **punct** comes here)

penlabels(1, 2); **endchar**;

cmchar "Comma";
numeric *dot_diam*#; *dot_diam*# = **if** *monospace*: ⁵⁄₄ **fi** *dot_size*#;
define_whole_blacker_pixels(*dot_diam*);
beginchar(oct "073", 5*u*#, *dot_diam*#, *comma_depth*#);   % non-ASCII position

    ⋮   (a copy of the program for ',' in **punct** comes here)

penlabels(1); **endchar**;

cmchar "Less than sign";
compute_spread(⁵⁄₄*x_height*#, ³⁄₂*x_height*#);
beginchar("<", 14*u*#, *v_center*(*spread*# + *rule_thickness*#));

    ⋮   (a copy of the program for '<' in **sym** comes here)

labels(1, 2, 3); **endchar**;

cmchar "Virgule (slash)";
beginchar(oct "075", 9*u*#, *body_height*#, *paren_depth*#);   % non-ASCII position

    ⋮   (a copy of the program for '/' in **punct** comes here)

penlabels(1, 2); **endchar**;

cmchar "Greater than sign";
compute_spread(⁵⁄₄*x_height*#, ³⁄₂*x_height*#);
beginchar(">", 14*u*#, *v_center*(*spread*# + *rule_thickness*#));

    ⋮   (a copy of the program for '>' in **sym** comes here)

labels(1, 2, 3); **endchar**;

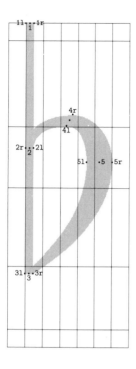

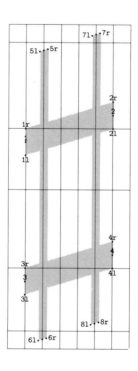

cmchar "Musical flat sign";
beginchar(oct "133", $7u^{\#}$, $body\_height^{\#}$, 0);
adjust_fit$(0, 0)$; **pickup** $crisp.nib$;
numeric $light\_hair$; $light\_hair =$ **if** $hefty$: $vair$ **else**: $hair$ **fi**;
$pos_1(light\_hair, 0)$; $pos_2(light\_hair, 180)$; $pos_3(light\_hair, 0)$; $x_1 = x_2 = x_3$;
$pos_4(.25[light\_hair, curve], 60)$; $pos_5(curve, 0)$;
$lft\ x_{1l} = $ hround u; $x_4 = .5w$; $rt\ x_{5r} = $ hround$(w - u)$;
$top\ y_1 = h$; $bot\ y_3 = -o$; $top\ y_4 = x\_height + o$;
$y_2 = y_4 - .2x\_height$; $y_5 = {}^3\!/_4 x\_height$;
filldraw stroke z_{1e} -- z_{3e};   % stem
filldraw stroke $z_{2e}\{up\}$ ... $z_{4e}\{right\}$ ... $z_{5e}\{down\}$
 ... $\{2(x_3 - x_{5e}), y_3 - y_{5e}\}z_{3e}$;   % bowl
penlabels$(1, 2, 3, 4, 5)$; **endchar**;

cmchar "Musical natural sign";
beginchar(oct "134", $7u^{\#}$, $asc\_height^{\#}$, $desc\_depth^{\#}$);
adjust_fit$(0, 0)$; **pickup** $crisp.nib$;
numeric $light\_hair$; $light\_hair =$ **if** $hefty$: $vair$ **else**: $hair$ **fi**;
$pos_1(light\_hair, 0)$; $pos_2(curve, 90)$; $pos_3(curve, 90)$;
$pos_4(curve, 90)$; $pos_5(curve, 90)$; $pos_6(light\_hair, 0)$;
$rt\ x_{1r} = $ hround ${}^{15}\!/_8 u$; $x_2 = x_4 = x_{1l}$; $x_3 = x_5 = x_{6r} = w - x_2$;
$y_1 = h + o$; $top\ y_{2r} = 0$; $.5[y_2, y_3] = 0$; $y_4 - y_2 = y_5 - y_3 = x\_height$; $bot\ y_6 = -d - o$;
$x_{2'} = x_{1r}$; $z_{2'} = whatever[z_{2r}, z_{3r}]$; $x_{5'} = x_{6l}$; $z_{5'} = whatever[z_{4l}, z_{5l}]$;
$(x_{1r}, y) = z_{1l} + whatever * (z_5 - z_4)$; $y_{6l} := y_{6l} - (y - y_{1r})$; $y_{1r} := y$;
filldraw z_{1l} -- z_{2l} -- z_{3l} -- z_{3r} -- $z_{2'}$ -- z_{1r} -- **cycle**;   % left stem and lower bar
filldraw z_{6r} -- z_{5r} -- z_{4r} -- z_{4l} -- $z_{5'}$ -- z_{6l} -- **cycle**;   % right stem and upper bar
penlabels$(1, 2, 3, 4, 5, 6)$; **endchar**;

cmchar "Musical sharp sign";
beginchar(oct "135", $7u^{\#}$, $asc\_height^{\#}$, $desc\_depth^{\#}$);
adjust_fit$(0, 0)$; **pickup** $crisp.nib$;
numeric $light\_hair$; $light\_hair =$ **if** $hefty$: $vair$ **else**: $hair$ **fi**;
$pos_1(curve, 90)$; $pos_2(curve, 90)$; $pos_3(curve, 90)$; $pos_4(curve, 90)$;
$lft\ x_1 = lft\ x_3 = $ hround u; $x_2 = x_4 = w - x_1$;
$top\ y_{3r} = 0$; $.5[y_3, y_4] = 0$; $y_1 - y_3 = y_2 - y_4 = x\_height$;
filldraw stroke z_{1e} -- z_{2e}; **filldraw stroke** z_{3e} -- z_{4e};   % bars
numeric $theta$, $hstem$; $theta = $ angle$(z_2 - z_1)$;
$(hstem - crisp) * $ cosd $theta = light\_hair - crisp$;
$pos_5(hstem, theta)$; $pos_6(hstem, theta)$; $pos_7(hstem, theta)$; $pos_8(hstem, theta)$;
$lft\ x_{5l} = lft\ x_{6l} = $ hround$(2u - .5light\_hair)$; $x_7 = x_8 = w - x_6$;
$top\ y_{7l} = h + o$; $bot\ y_{6r} = -d - o$; $z_7 - z_5 = z_8 - z_6 = (whatever, 0)$ rotated $theta$;
filldraw stroke z_{5e} -- z_{6e}; **filldraw stroke** z_{7e} -- z_{8e};   % stems
penlabels$(1, 2, 3, 4, 5, 6, 7, 8)$; **endchar**;

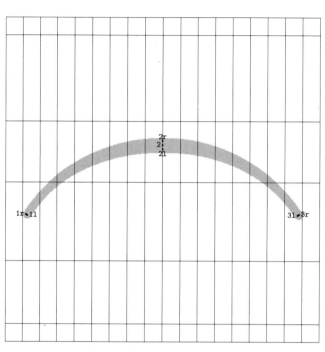

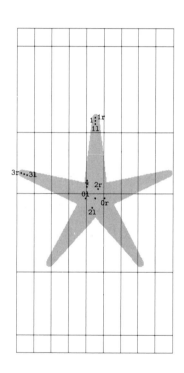

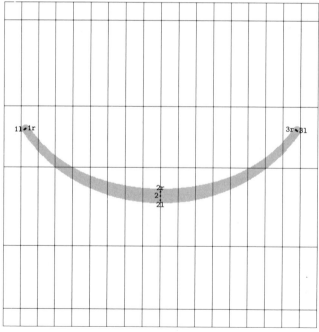

cmchar "Five-pointed star";
beginchar(oct "077", $9u^\#$, $v\_center(x\_height^\#)$);
adjust_fit(0, 0); **pickup** $tiny.nib$;
numeric $theta$; $theta = {}^{360}/_5$; % degrees between points
$pos_0(curve, 0)$; $pos_1(rule\_thickness, 90)$; $x_0 = x_1 = good.x\ .5w$;
$top\ y_{1r} = \mathrm{vround}(math\_axis + .5x\_height + .5rule\_thickness)$;
$\mathrm{ypart}(.5[z_1, z_0 + (z_1 - z_2)\ \mathrm{rotated}\ 2theta]) = math\_axis$;
$pos_2(curve, theta)$; $pos_3(rule\_thickness, 90 + theta)$;
$z_2 = z_0$; $z_3 - z_0 = (z_1 - z_0)\ \mathrm{rotated}\ theta$;
$z_4 = whatever[z_{0l}, z_{1r}] = whatever[z_{2r}, z_{3r}]$;
filldraw for $n = 0$ **upto** 4:
$\quad z_0 + (z_{1r} - z_0)\ \mathrm{rotated}\ (n * theta)$ -- $z_0 + (z_4 - z_0)\ \mathrm{rotated}\ (n * theta)$ -- **endfor**
$\quad$ cycle; % star
penlabels(0, 1, 2, 3, 4); **endchar**;

cmchar "Slur above (frown)";
beginchar(oct "137", $18u^\#$, $v\_center(.5x\_height^\#)$);
adjust_fit(0, 0); **pickup** $fine.nib$;
numeric $light\_stem$; $light\_stem = \mathrm{Vround}\ .5[vair, stem]$;
$x_1 - .5hair = \mathrm{hround}\ u$; $y_1 - .5hair = \mathrm{vround}(-d - .5hair)$; $x_3 = w - x_1$; $y_3 = y_1$;
$pos_2(light\_stem, 90)$; $x_2 = .5w$; $y_2 = good.y\ h$;
numeric $theta$; $theta = \mathrm{angle}((z_2 - z_1)\ \mathrm{yscaled}\ 3)$;
$pos_1(hair, 90 + theta)$; $pos_3(hair, 90 - theta)$;
filldraw $z_{1l}\{\mathrm{dir}\ theta\} \ldots z_{2l} \ldots \{\mathrm{dir}\ -theta\}z_{3l}$
$\quad .. z_{3r}\{- \mathrm{dir}\ -theta\} \ldots z_{2r} \ldots \{- \mathrm{dir}\ theta\}z_{1r} ..$ cycle; % arc
penlabels(1, 2, 3); **endchar**;

cmchar "Slur below (smile)";
beginchar(oct "136", $18u^\#$, $v\_center(.5x\_height^\#)$);
adjust_fit(0, 0); **pickup** $fine.nib$;
numeric $light\_stem$; $light\_stem = \mathrm{Vround}\ .5[vair, stem]$;
$x_1 - .5hair = \mathrm{hround}\ u$; $y_1 + .5hair = \mathrm{vround}(h + .5hair)$; $x_3 = w - x_1$; $y_3 = y_1$;
$pos_2(light\_stem, 90)$; $x_2 = .5w$; $y_{2l} = good.y - d$;
numeric $theta$; $theta = \mathrm{angle}((z_2 - z_1)\ \mathrm{yscaled}\ 3)$;
$pos_1(hair, 90 + theta)$; $pos_3(hair, 90 - theta)$;
filldraw $z_{1l}\{\mathrm{dir}\ theta\} \ldots z_{2l} \ldots \{\mathrm{dir}\ -theta\}z_{3l}$
$\quad .. z_{3r}\{- \mathrm{dir}\ -theta\} \ldots z_{2r} \ldots \{- \mathrm{dir}\ theta\}z_{1r} ..$ cycle; % arc
penlabels(1, 2, 3); **endchar**;

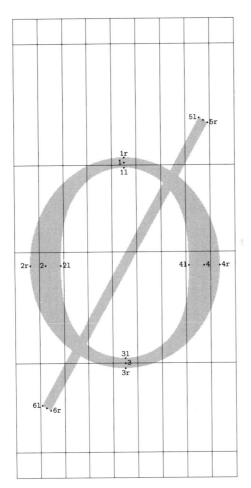

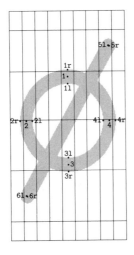

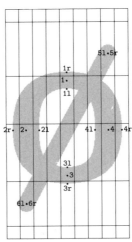

Finally we complete the lowercase alphabet, with slightly exotic letters generated by program file `romspl.mf`.

% This file contains special letters and letter combinations,
% compatible with the alphabet 'romanl'.

% Codes *'020*–*'021* and *'031*–*'034* are generated.

cmchar "Dotless letter i";
beginchar(oct "020", $5u^\#$, $x\_height^\#$, 0);
italcorr $x\_height^\# * slant - serif\_fit^\# + .5stem^\# - 2u^\#$;
adjust_fit($serif\_fit^\# + stem\_shift^\#$ **if** $monospace$: $+.25u^\#$ **fi**, $serif\_fit^\# - stem\_shift^\#$);
pickup $tiny.nib$; $pos_1(stem', 0)$; $pos_2(stem', 0)$;

$\vdots$ (a copy of part of the program for 'i' in **romanl** comes here)

$dish\_serif(2, 1, b, \frac{1}{3}, jut, c, \frac{1}{3}, .9jut)$; **fi**   % lower serif
penlabels(1, 2); **endchar**;

cmchar "Dotless letter j";
beginchar(oct "021", $5.5u^\#$, $x\_height^\#$, $desc\_depth^\#$);
italcorr $x\_height^\# * slant - serif\_fit^\# + .5stem^\# - 2u^\#$;
adjust_fit($serif\_fit^\# + 2stem\_shift^\#$ **if** $monospace$: $+.5u^\#$ **fi**,
  $serif\_fit^\# - 2stem\_shift^\#$ **if** $monospace$: $-.5u^\#$ **fi**);
pickup $tiny.nib$; $pos_1(stem', 0)$; $pos_2(stem', 0)$;

$\vdots$ (a copy of part of the program for 'j' in **romanl** comes here)

& $term.e(6, 7, left, 1, 4)$; **fi**   % arc and terminal
penlabels(1, 2, 5, 6, 7); **endchar**;

cmchar "Scandinavian letter o/slash";
beginchar(oct "034", $9u^\#$, $x\_height^\# + .5desc\_depth^\#$, $.5desc\_depth^\#$);
italcorr $h^\# * slant - u^\# - \max(.5fudge * stem^\#, .75u^\#) + .5vair^\#$;
adjust_fit($0, 0$);
$penpos_1(vair, 90)$; $penpos_3(vair, -90)$;
$penpos_2(fudged.stem, 180)$; $penpos_4(fudged.stem, 0)$;
$x_{2r} = $ hround $\max(.5u, 1.25u - .5fudged.stem)$;
$x_{4r} = w - x_{2r}$; $x_1 = x_3 = .5w$;
$y_{1r} = x_height + $ vround $1.5oo$; $y_2 = y_4 = .5x\_height - vair\_corr$; $y_{3r} = -oo$;
penstroke $pulled\_arc_e(1, 2)$ & $pulled\_arc_e(2, 3)$
  & $pulled\_arc_e(3, 4)$ & $pulled\_arc_e(4, 1)$ & cycle;   % bowl
$x_5 = x_4$; $x_6 = x_2$; $y_5 = h$; $y_6 = -d$;
numeric $theta$; $theta = $ angle$(z_5 - z_6) - 90$;
pickup $crisp.nib$; $pos_5(vair, theta)$; $pos_6(vair, theta)$;
filldraw stroke z_{5e} -- z_{6e};   % diagonal
penlabels(1, 2, 3, 4, 5, 6); **endchar**;

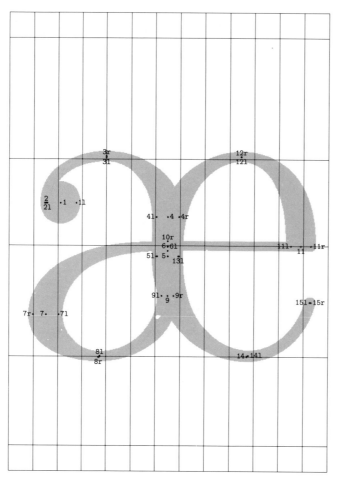

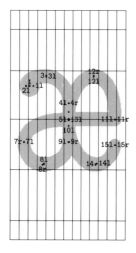

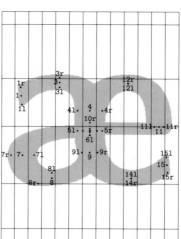

cmchar "The ligature ae";
beginchar(oct "032", $13u\#$, $x\_height\#$, 0);
italcorr $.5[bar\_height\#, x\_height\#] * slant + .5\min(curve\# - 1.5u\#, 0)$;
adjust_fit$(0, 0)$;
numeric $left\_curve$, $right\_curve$;
if $monospace$: $right\_curve = left\_curve = fudged.stem$;
else: $left\_curve = \max(tiny.breadth, \text{hround}(curve - 2stem\_corr))$;
  $right\_curve = \max(tiny.breadth, \text{hround}(curve - \textbf{if } serifs: 6 \textbf{ else}: 8 \textbf{ fi } stem\_corr))$; **fi**
pickup $tiny.nib$; $pos_{11}(right\_curve, 0)$;
$pos_{12}(vair, 90)$; $pos_{13}(mfudged.stem, 180)$;
$y_{11} = good.y\ bar\_height$; $\text{top } y_{12r} = h + \text{vround } 1.5oo$; $y_{10l} = \text{bot } y_{11}$;
$rt\ x_{11r} = \text{hround} \min(w - .5u, w - u + .5right\_curve)$;
$lft\ x_{13r} = \text{hround}(.5w - .5mfudged.stem)$; $x_{12} = .55[x_{13}, x_{11}]$;
$\{\{$ **interim** $superness := more\_super$;
  filldraw stroke $super\_arc_e(11, 12)\}\}$; % right bowl of e
$y_{13} = .5[y_{12}, y_{14}]$; $\text{bot } y_{14r} = -oo$; $x_{14} = x_{12} + .25u$;
if $serifs$: $pos_{14}(vair', 270)$; $pos_{15}(mfudged.hair, 360)$;
  $y_{15} = \max(good.y(.5bar\_height - .9), y_{14l} + vair)$; $x_{15r} = x_{11r}$;
  $(x, y_{14l}) = whatever[z_{14r}, z_{15}]$; $x_{14l} := \min(x, x_{14l} + .5u)$;
  filldraw stroke $pulled\_arc_e(12, 13)$
    $\&\ pulled\_super\_arc_e(13, 14)(.8superpull)$
    $\ldots \{x_{15} - x_{14}, 5(y_{15} - y_{14})\}z_{15e}$; % left bowl, arc, and terminal of e
else: $pos_{14}(vair, 270)$;
  filldraw stroke $super\_arc_e(12, 13)$
    $\&\ super\_arc_e(13, 14)$; % left bowl and arc of e
  pickup $fine.nib$; $pos_{14'}(vair, 270)$; $z_{14} = z_{14'}$;
  $pos_{15}(.5[vair, flare], 275)$; $rt\ x_{15r} = \text{hround}(w - .6u)$;
  $y_{15r} = good.y(y_{15r} + \frac{1}{3}bar\_height - y_{15})$; $y_{15l} := good.y\ y_{15l}$; $x_{15l} := good.x\ x_{15l}$;
  filldraw stroke $term.e(14', 15, right, 1, 4)$; **fi** % right terminal
$y_{11'r} = y_{10r} = y_{10l} + .6[thin\_join, vair]$; $y_{11'l} = y_{10l}$;
$x_{11'l} = x_{11'r} = x_{11}$; $x_{10l} = x_{10r} = x_{13}$;
fill stroke z_{10e} -- $z_{11'e}$; % crossbar
pickup $fine.nib$; $\text{top } y_{3r} = h + \text{vround } 1.5oo$;
if $serifs$: $pos_1(flare, 180)$; $pos_2(mfudged.hair, 180)$;
  $pos_3(vair, 90)$; $lft\ x_{1r} = \text{hround} \max(u, 2.1u - .5flare)$; $x_3 = 4u$;
  $y_1 = \min(bar\_height + .5flare + 2vair + 2, .9[bar\_height, h] - .5flare)$;
  $bulb(3, 2, 1)$; % bulb
else: $pos_1(\frac{5}{7}[vair, flare], 95)$; $x_{1l} = good.x\ 1.5u$; $x_{1r} := good.x\ x_{1r}$;
  $pos_3(\frac{1}{8}[vair, thin\_join], 90)$;
  $x_3 = 4.3u$; $\text{top } y_{1r} = \text{vround } .82[bar\_height, \text{top } y_{3r}]$;
  filldraw stroke $term.e(3, 1, left, .9, 4)$; **fi** % left terminal
$pos_4(mfudged.stem, 0)$; $x_4 = x_{13}$; $y_4 = \frac{1}{3}[bar\_height, h]$;
$pos_5(mfudged.stem, 0)$; $x_5 = x_4$; $y_5 = \min(y_4, y_{13})$;
filldraw stroke $super\_arc_e(3, 4)\ \&\ z_{4e}$ -- z_{5e}; % arc and stem
$pos_6(.6[thin\_join, vair], 90)$; $x_6 = x_4$; $\text{bot } y_6 = y_{10l}$;
$pos_7(left\_curve, 180)$;
$lft\ x_{7r} = \text{hround} \max(.5u, 1.5u - .5left\_curve)$; $y_7 = \frac{1}{3}[\text{top } y_{8l}, \text{top } y_{6r}]$;
$pos_8(vair, 270)$; $x_{8l} = 3.75u$; $\text{bot } y_{8r} = -oo$;

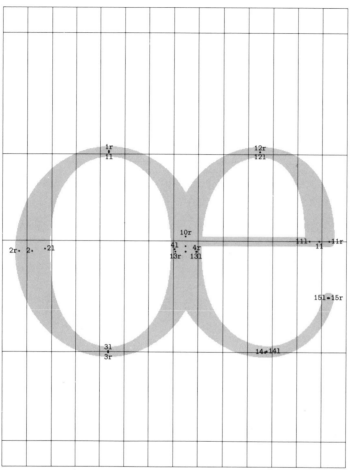

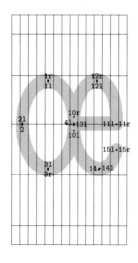

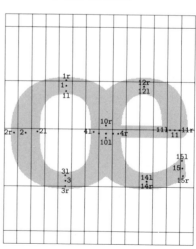

$pos_9(.5[vair, fudged.stem], 360)$; $x_9 = x_5$; $y_9 = .55bar\_height$;
$(x', y_{8r}) = whatever[z_{8l}, z_{9l}]$; $x_{8r} := \max(x', x_8 - u)$;
$\{\{$ **interim** $superness := more\_super$;
    filldraw stroke $z_{9e}\{down\} \ldots z_{8e}\{left\} \ldots \{up\}z_{7e}$ & $super\_arc_e(7, 6)\}\}$;   % bowl
if $y_9 < y_5$: **filldraw stroke** $z_{5e}\{down\} .. \{down\}z_{9e}$; **fi**   % link (usually hidden)
penlabels$(1, 2, 3, 4, 5, 6, 7, 8, 9, 10, 11, 12, 13, 14, 15)$; **endchar**;

cmchar "The ligature oe";
beginchar(oct "033", $14u^\#$, $x\_height^\#$, 0);
italcorr $.5[bar\_height^\#, x\_height^\#] * slant + .5\min(curve^\# - 1.5u^\#, 0)$;
adjust_fit$(0, 0)$;
numeric $left\_curve$, $right\_curve$;
if $monospace$: $right\_curve = left\_curve = fudged.stem$;
else: $left\_curve = \max(fine.breadth, \mathrm{hround}(curve - 2stem\_corr))$;
    $right_curve = \max(tiny.breadth, \mathrm{hround}(curve - $**if** $serifs$: 6 **else**: 8 **fi** $stem\_corr))$; **fi**
pickup $tiny.nib$; $pos_{11}(right\_curve, 0)$;
$pos_{12}(vair, 90)$; $pos_{13}(mfudged.stem, 180)$;
$y_{11} = good.y\,bar\_height$; $top\,y_{12r} = h + \mathrm{vround}\,1.5oo$; $y_{10l} = bot\,y_{11}$;
$rt\,x_{11r} = \mathrm{hround}\min(w - .5u, w - u + .5right\_curve)$;
$lft\,x_{13r} = \mathrm{hround}(.5(w + u) - .5mfudged.stem)$; $x_{12} = .55[x_{13}, x_{11}]$;
$\{\{$ **interim** $superness := more\_super$;
    filldraw stroke $super\_arc_e(11, 12)\}\}$;   % right bowl of e
$y_{13} = .5[y_{12}, y_{14}]$; $bot\,y_{14r} = -oo$; $x_{14} = x_{12} + .25u$;
if $serifs$: $pos_{14}(vair', 270)$; $pos_{15}(mfudged.hair, 360)$;
    $y_{15} = \max(good.y(.5bar\_height - .9), y_{14l} + vair)$; $x_{15r} = x_{11r}$;
    $(x, y_{14l}) = whatever[z_{14r}, z_{15}]$; $x_{14l} := \min(x, x_{14l} + .5u)$;
    filldraw stroke $pulled\_arc_e(12, 13)$
        & $pulled\_super\_arc_e(13, 14)(.8superpull)$
       $\ldots \{x_{15} - x_{14}, 5(y_{15} - y_{14})\}z_{15e}$;   % left bowl, arc, and terminal of e
else: $pos_{14}(vair, 270)$;
    filldraw stroke $super\_arc_e(12, 13)$
       & $super\_arc_e(13, 14)$;   % left bowl and arc of e
    pickup $fine.nib$; $pos_{14'}(vair, 270)$; $z_{14} = z_{14'}$;
    $pos_{15}(.5[vair, flare], 275)$; $rt\,x_{15r} = \mathrm{hround}(w - .6u)$;
    $y_{15r} = good.y(y_{15r} + {}^1\!/_3 bar\_height - y_{15})$; $y_{15l} := good.y\,y_{15l}$; $x_{15l} := good.x\,x_{15l}$;
    filldraw stroke $term.e(14', 15, right, 1, 4)$; **fi**   % terminal
$y_{11'r} = y_{10r} = y_{10l} + .6[thin\_join, vair]$; $y_{11'l} = y_{10l}$; $x_{11'l} = x_{11'r} = x_{11}$; $x_{10l} = x_{10r} = x_{13}$;
fill stroke $z_{10e} \texttt{--} z_{11'e}$;   % crossbar
pickup $fine.nib$; $pos_1(vair, 90)$; $pos_3(vair, -90)$;
$pos_2(left\_curve, 180)$; $pos_4(mfudged.stem, 0)$;
$lft\,x_{2r} = \mathrm{hround}\max(.5u, 1.25u - .5curve)$;
$z_4 = z_{13}$; $x_1 = x_3 = .5[x_2, x_4]$; $top\,y_{1r} = h + \mathrm{vround}\,1.5oo$; $bot\,y_{3r} = -oo$;
$y_2 = y_4$; $y_{2l} := y_{4l} := .52h$;
filldraw stroke $pulled\_arc_e(1, 2)$ & $pulled\_arc_e(2, 3)$;   % left half of left bowl
filldraw stroke $pulled\_arc_e(3, 4)$ & $pulled\_arc_e(4, 1)$;   % right half of left bowl
penlabels$(1, 2, 3, 4, 10, 11, 12, 13, 14, 15)$; **endchar**;

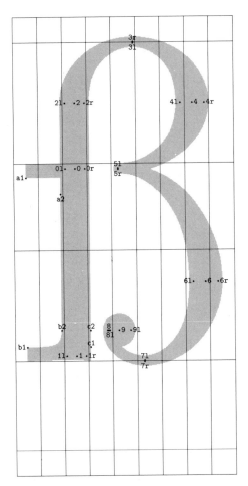

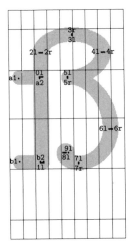

```
cmchar "German letter es-zet (sharp s)";
```
beginchar(oct "031", $4.5u^\# + \max(4.5u^\#, .5stem^\# + flare^\# + curve^\#)$, $asc\_height^\#$, 0);
italcorr $asc\_height^\# * slant - u^\#$;
adjust_fit($serif\_fit^\#$, 0);
pickup $tiny.nib$; $pos_1(stem', 0)$; $pos_2(stem', 0)$;
$lft\ x_{1l} = lft\ x_{2l} = \text{hround}(2.5u - .5stem')$; $bot\ y_1 = 0$; $y_2 = y_4 = .5[x\_height, y_3]$;
$penpos_3(vair - fine, 90)$; $fine.top\ y_{3r} = h + oo$;
filldraw stroke $z_{1e}\ \text{--}\ z_{2e}$;   % stem
numeric $stem\_edge$, $curve'$; $stem\_edge = rt\ x_{1r}$; $curve' = \text{hround}\ .5[stem', curve]$;
pickup $fine.nib$; $pos_4(curve', 0)$; $pos_5(vair, -90)$;
$pos_{2'}(stem', 180)$; $z_{2'} = z_2$; $x_3 = .5[x_2, x_4]$; $rt\ x_{4r} = \text{hround}(w - u)$;
$top\ y_{5l} = x\_height$; $lft\ x_5 = \min(lft\ x_{4l}, \text{hround}(stem\_edge + u))$;
filldraw stroke $pulled\_super\_arc_e(2', 3)(.5superpull)$
    & $pulled\_super\_arc_e(3, 4)(.5superpull)$
    & $pulled\_super\_arc_e(4, 5)(.5superpull)$;   % upper bowl
$pos_{5'}(vair, 90)$; $z_{5'} = z_5$; $pos_6(curve', 0)$; $pos_7(vair, -90)$;
$rt\ x_{6r} = \text{hround}(w - .5u) + 3eps$; $y_6 = .4x\_height$; $bot\ y_{7r} = -oo$;
if $serifs$: $pos_8(hair, -180)$ **else**: $pos_8(vair, -110)$ **fi**;
$lft\ x_{8r} = \min(\text{hround}(stem\_edge + .5u + 1), lft\ x_{8r} + x_{6r} - 2eps - x_{8l})$;
$x_7 = \max(x_{8l} + eps, .4[lft\ x_{8r}, x_6])$;
filldraw stroke $pulled\_super\_arc_e(5', 6)(.5superpull)$
    & $pulled\_super\_arc_e(6, 7)(.5superpull)$;   % lower bowl
if $serifs$: $pos_9(^5/_7[vair, flare], -180)$;
  $y_9 - (x_9 - lft\ x_{9r}) = \text{vround}\ .07x\_height$; $bulb(7, 8, 9)$;   % bulb
  $penpos_0(stem' - tiny, 0)$; $x_0 = x_1$; $tiny.top\ y_0 = x\_height$;
  $serif(0, 1, a, 0, -jut)$;   % bar
  $dish\_serif(1, 2, b, ^1/_3, jut, c, 0, epsilon)$;   % serif
else: $bot\ y_{8r} = \text{vround}\ .01h$; $x_{8l} := good.x\ x_{8l}$; $y_{8l} := good.y(y_{8l} + .5)$;
  filldraw stroke $term.e(7, 8, left, 1, 4)$; **fi**   % terminal
penlabels(0, 1, 2, 3, 4, 5, 6, 7, 8, 9); **endchar**;

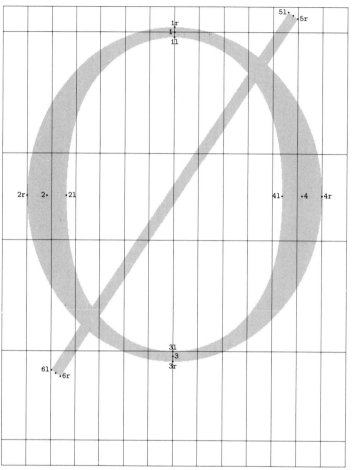

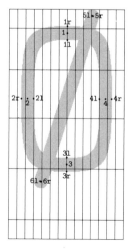

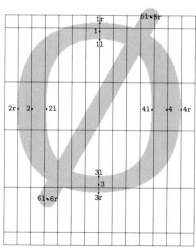

The uppercase alphabet is now completed by program file `romspu.mf`.

% This file contains special letters and letter combinations,
% compatible with the alphabet 'romanu'.

% Codes ´035 – ´037 are generated.

cmchar "Scandinavian letter O/slash";
beginchar(oct "037", $14u^\#$, $cap\_height^\# + .25desc\_depth^\#$, $.25desc\_depth^\#$);
italcorr $.7cap\_height^\# * slant - .5u^\#$;
adjust_fit$(0, 0)$;
$penpos_1(vair, 90)$; $penpos_3(vair, -90)$;
$penpos_2(fudged.cap\_stem, 180)$; $penpos_4(fudged.cap\_stem, 0)$;
if *monospace*: $x_{2r} = $ hround $1.5u$;
   interim *superness* := sqrt *superness*;   % make "Ø" not "Ø"
else: $x_{2r} = $ hround u; **fi**
$x_{4r} = w - x_{2r}$; $x_1 = x_3 = .5w$;
$y_{1r} = cap\_height + o$; $y_2 = y_4 = .5cap\_height - vair\_corr$; $y_{3r} = -o$;
penstroke $pulled\_arc_e(1, 2)$ & $pulled\_arc_e(2, 3)$
   & $pulled\_arc_e(3, 4)$ & $pulled\_arc_e(4, 1)$ & cycle;   % bowl
$x_5 = x_4 - vair$; $x_6 = x_2 + vair$; $y_5 = h$; $y_6 = -d$;
numeric *theta*; $theta = $ angle$(z_5 - z_6) - 90$;
pickup *crisp.nib*; $pos_5(vair', theta)$; $pos_6(vair', theta)$;
filldraw stroke z_{5e} -- z_{6e};   % diagonal
penlabels$(1, 2, 3, 4, 5, 6)$; **endchar**;

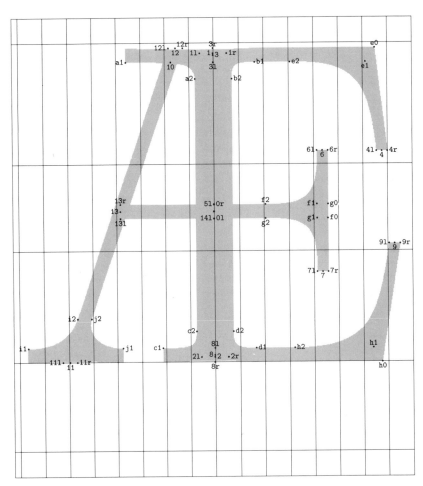

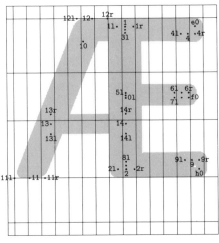

cmchar "The ligature AE";
beginchar(oct "035", $16u\#$, $cap\_height\#$, 0);
italcorr $cap\_height\# * slant - beak\_jut\# - .5u\#$;
adjust_fit($cap\_serif\_fit\#$, 0);
numeric $left\_stem$, mid_stem, $outer\_jut$, $alpha$;
$mid\_stem = \max(tiny.breadth,$ hround $.9[mfudged.hair, mfudged.cap\_stem])$;
pickup $tiny.nib$; $pos_1(mid\_stem, 0)$; $pos_2(mid\_stem, 0)$;
$lft\ x_{1l} = lft\ x_{2l} =$ hround(**if** *monospace* **or** *hefty*: .55 **else**: .5 **fi** $w - .75u$);
$top\ y_1 = h$; $bot\ y_2 = 0$;
filldraw stroke z_{1e} -- z_{2e};   % stem
pickup $crisp.nib$; $pos_3(slab, 90)$; $pos_4(mfudged.hair, 0)$;
$top\ y_{3r} = h$; $x_3 = x_1$; $rt\ x_{4r} =$ hround$(w - u)$; $y_4 = good.y(y_{3l} - beak) - eps$;
$arm(3, 4, e, beak\_darkness, beak\_jut)$;   % upper arm and beak
$pos_5(cap\_bar, -90)$; $pos_6(mfudged.hair, 0)$; $x_5 = x_1$;
$top\ y_{5l} =$ vround(**if** *hefty*: .52 **else**: .48 **fi** $[y_2, y_1] + .5cap\_bar)$;
$pos_0(cap\_bar, 90)$; $pos_7(mfudged.hair, 0)$;
$z_0 = z_5$; $x_6 = x_7$; $y_6 - y_{5l} = y_{0l} - y_7$;
if *serifs* **and not**(*monospace* **and** *hefty*): $rt\ x_{6r} =$ hround$(w - 3.65u + .5mfudged.hair)$;
    $y_6 = good.y(y_{5l} + .6beak) + eps$; $rt\ x_{9r} =$ hround$(w - .5u)$;
else: $rt\ x_{6r} =$ hround$(w - 1.5u)$; $y_6 = y_{5l} + eps$; $rt\ x_{9r} =$ hround$(w - .75u)$; **fi**
$arm(5, 6, f, beak\_darkness, 0)$; $arm(0, 7, g, beak\_darkness, 0)$; % middle arm and serif
$pos_8(slab$ **if not** *serifs*: $+ 2stem\_corr$ **fi**, $-90)$;
$pos_9(mfudged.hair, 0)$; $bot\ y_{8r} = 0$; $x_8 = x_2$; $y_9 = good.y(y_{8l} + \frac{7}{6}beak) + eps$;
$arm(8, 9, h, beak\_darkness, 1.5beak\_jut)$;   % lower arm and beak
$left\_stem =$ **if** *monospace*: $fudged.hair$ **else**: cap_hair **fi if** *hefty*: $-3stem\_corr$ **fi**;
$outer\_jut = .8cap\_jut$; $x_{11l} = l + letter\_fit + outer\_jut + .5u$; $y_{11} = 0$;
$x_{12} = x_{11l} - apex\_corr -$ **if** *monospace*: 2 **fi** u; $y_{12} = h$;
$alpha = diag\_ratio(1, .5left\_stem, y_{12} - y_{11}, x_{12} - x_{11l})$;
$penpos_{11}(alpha * left\_stem, 0)$; $penpos_{12}(alpha * left\_stem, 0)$;
fill $diag\_end(12l, 11l, 1, 1, 11r, 12r)$
    -- $diag\_end(11r, 12r, 1, 1, 12l, 11l)$ -- cycle;   % diagonal
$y_{10} = h - slab$; $z_{10} = whatever[z_{11}, z_{12}]$;
fill z_{10} -- (x_1, y_{10}) -- (x_1, h) -- z_{12} -- cycle;   % link
$penpos_{13}(whatever, angle(z_2 - z_1))$; $z_{13} = whatever[z_{11}, z_{12}]$;
$penpos_{14}(cap\_band, 90)$; $x_{14} = x_0$; $y_{13l} = y_{14l}$; $y_{13r} = y_{14r}$;
if *hefty*: $y_{14r} = .4h$; **else**: $y_{14} = y_0$; **fi**
penstroke z_{13e} -- z_{14e};   % bar line
if *serifs*: **numeric** $inner\_jut$; **pickup** $tiny.nib$;
    $prime\_points\_inside(11, 12)$;
    if $rt\ x_{11'r} + cap\_jut + .5u + 1 \le lft\ x_{2l} - .75cap\_jut$: $inner\_jut = cap\_jut$;
    else: $rt\ x_{11'r} + inner\_jut + .5u + 1 = lft\ x_{2l} - .75inner\_jut$; **fi**
    $dish\_serif(11', 12, i, \frac{1}{2}, outer\_jut, j, .6, inner\_jut)(dark)$;   % lower left serif
    $nodish\_serif(1, 2, a, \frac{1}{3}, cap\_jut + x_{1l} - x_{12}, b, \frac{1}{3}, .5cap\_jut)$;   % upper serif
    $nodish\_serif(2, 1, c, \frac{1}{3}, .75inner\_jut, d, \frac{1}{3}, .5cap\_jut)$; **fi**   % lower middle serif
penlabels(0, 1, 2, 3, 4, 5, 6, 7, 8, 9, 10, 11, 12, 13, 14); **endchar**;

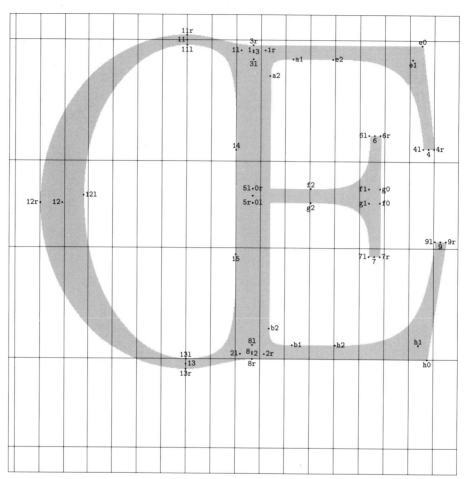

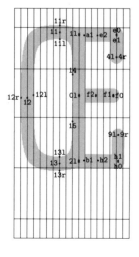

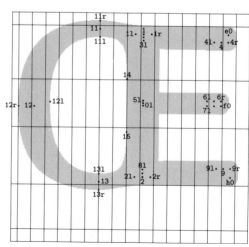

cmchar "The ligature OE";
beginchar(oct "036", $18u\#$, $cap\_height\#$, 0);
italcorr $cap\_height\# * slant - beak\_jut\# - .5u\#$;
adjust_fit($cap\_serif\_fit\#$, 0);
numeric $light\_stem$;
$light\_stem = \max(tiny.breadth, \text{hround } .8[mfudged.hair, mfudged.cap\_stem])$;
pickup $tiny.nib$; $pos_1(light\_stem, 0)$; $pos_2(light\_stem, 0)$;
$lft\ x_{1l} = lft\ x_{2l} = \text{hround } .5w$; $top\ y_1 = h$; $bot\ y_2 = 0$;
filldraw stroke $z_{1e}\ \text{-\,-}\ z_{2e}$;   % stem
pickup $crisp.nib$; $pos_3(slab, 90)$; $pos_4(mfudged.hair, 0)$;
$top\ y_{3r} = h$; $x_3 = x_1$; $rt\ x_{4r} = \text{hround}(w - u)$; $y_4 = good.y(y_{3l} - beak) - eps$;
$arm(3, 4, e, beak\_darkness, beak\_jut)$;   % upper arm and beak
$pos_5(cap\_bar, -90)$; $pos_6(mfudged.hair, 0)$;
$top\ y_{5l} = \text{vround}(.52[y_2, y_1] + .5cap\_bar)$; $x_5 = x_1$;
$pos_0(cap\_bar, 90)$; $pos_7(mfudged.hair, 0)$;
$z_0 = z_5$; $x_6 = x_7$; $y_6 - y_{5l} = y_{0l} - y_7$;
if $serifs$ and not($monospace$ and $hefty$): $rt\ x_{6r} = \text{hround}(w - 3.4u + .5mfudged.hair)$;
    $y_6 = good.y(y_{5l} + .6beak) + eps$; $rt\ x_{9r} = \text{hround}(w - .5u)$;
else: $rt\ x_{6r} = \text{hround}(w - 1.5u)$; $y_6 = y_{5l} + eps$; $rt\ x_{9r} = \text{hround}(w - .75u)$; **fi**
$arm(5, 6, f, beak\_darkness, 0)$; $arm(0, 7, g, beak\_darkness, 0)$; % middle arm and serif
$pos_8(slab$ **if** not $serifs$: $+2stem\_corr$ **fi**, $-90)$;
$pos_9(mfudged.hair, 0)$; $bot\ y_{8r} = 0$; $x_8 = x_2$; $y_9 = good.y(y_{8l} + {}^7\!/_6 beak) + eps$;
$arm(8, 9, h, beak\_darkness, 1.5beak\_jut)$;   % lower arm and beak
$penpos_{11}(vair, 90)$; $penpos_{13}(vair, -90)$;
if $monospace$: $penpos_{12}(fudged.cap\_stem, 180)$;
    interim $superness$:= sqrt $superness$;   % make "O", not "0"
else: $penpos_{12}(\text{hround}(cap\_curve - stem\_corr), 180)$; **fi**
$x_{11} = x_{13} = .5w - 2u$; $y_{11r} = h + o$; $y_{13r} = -o$; $y_{12} = .5h - vair\_corr$; $x_{12r} = \text{hround } u$;
$x_{14} = x_{15} = .5w$; $y_{14} = {}^2\!/_3 h$; $y_{15} = {}^1\!/_3 h$; $y_{12l} := .52h$;
penstroke $super\_arc_e(11, 12)$ & $super\_arc_e(12, 13)$;   % left half of bowl
fill $z_{13r}\{right\}\ \ldots\ \{right\}(x_2, 0)\ \text{-\,-}\ (x_1, h)\{left\}\ \ldots\ \{left\}z_{11r}$
    $\text{-\,-}\ z_{11l}\{right\}\ \ldots\ \{z_{14} - z_{11l}\}(.82[x_{11l}, x_{14}], .82[y_{14}, y_{11l}])$
    $\ldots\ z_{14}\ \text{-\,-\,-}\ z_{15}\ \ldots\ \{z_{13l} - z_{15}\}(.82[x_{13l}, x_{15}], .82[y_{15}, y_{13l}])$
    $\ldots\ \{left\}z_{13l}\ \text{-\,-}\ cycle$;   % right half of bowl
if $serifs$: $serif(1, 2, a, {}^1\!/_3, .5cap\_jut)$;   % upper serif
    $serif(2, 1, b, {}^1\!/_3, .5cap\_jut)$; **fi**   % lower serif
penlabels(0, 1, 2, 3, 4, 5, 6, 7, 8, 9, 11, 12, 13, 14, 15); **endchar**;

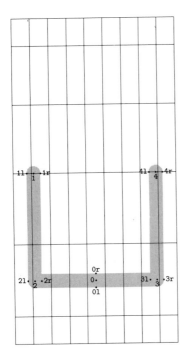

Since fonts like `cmtt10` do not include f-ligatures or dashes, they have room for other goodies. Most of the characters needed by program file `romsub.mf` are actually generated by `sym.mf` (which we shall study next); but two of the characters do not appear in any other fonts.

% This file defines characters that go into a text font when *ligs* ≤ 1.

% Character codes $'013$–$'015$, $'074$, and $'076$ are generated when *ligs* $= 1$;
% in addition, codes $'040$, $'042$, $'055$, $'134$, $'137$, and $'173$–$'175$
% are generated, if *ligs* $= 0$.

up_arrow = oct "013"; *down_arrow* = oct "014";
less = ASCII "<"; *greater* = ASCII ">";
if *ligs* = 0: *straight_quotes* = oct "042"; *minus* = ASCII "-";
  backslash = ASCII "\"; *underbar* = ASCII "_";
  left_brace = ASCII "{"; *vertical* = ASCII "|"; *right_brace* = ASCII "}"; **fi**

input *sym*;

cmchar "Straight single quote";
beginchar(oct "015", $5u^\#$, $asc\_height^\#$, 0);
italcorr $asc\_height^\# * slant + .5$ **if** *serifs*: $flare^\#$ **else**: $stem^\#$ **fi** $- 2u^\#$;
adjust_fit(0, 0);
$x_1 = x_2 = .5w$; $y_2 = \max(.5[bar\_height, x\_height] + .5vair, h - x\_height)$;
if *serifs*: **pickup** *crisp.nib*; $pos_1(flare, 0)$; $pos_2(vair, 0)$;
  $y_1 + .5stem = h$; **filldraw** circ_stroke z_{1e} -- z_{2e};   % stem and bulb
else: **pickup** *fine.nib*; $pos_1(stem, 0)$; $pos_2(vair, 0)$;
  top $y_1 = h$; **filldraw** stroke z_{1e} -- z_{2e}; **fi**   % stem
penlabels(1, 2); **endchar**;

iff *ligs* = 0: **cmchar** "Blank-space sign";
beginchar(oct "040", $9u^\#$, $bar\_height^\#$, $.5desc\_depth^\#$);
italcorr $bar\_height^\# * slant - .25u^\#$;
adjust_fit(0, 0);
numeric $thin\_vair^\#$; $thin\_vair^\# = .7vair^\#$;
define_whole_blacker_pixels($thin\_vair$);
forsuffixes \$ = 1, 2, 3, 4: $penpos_\$(thin\_vair, 0)$; **endfor**
$penpos_0(thin\_vair, 90)$; $x_0 = .5w$; $y_{0l} = \text{vround}(-d - .5thin\_vair)$;
$x_1 = x_2$; $x_3 = x_4 = w - x_1$; **lft** $x_{1l} = \text{hround } .75u$;
$y_1 = y_4 = h$; $y_2 = y_3 = y_0$;
fill z_{1l} --- z_{2l} ... (x_2, y_{0l}) --- (x_3, y_{0l}) ... z_{3r} --- z_{4r}
  .. z_{4l} --- (x_{3l}, y_{0r}) -- (x_{2r}, y_{0r}) --- z_{1r} .. cycle;   % the stroke
penlabels(0, 1, 2, 3, 4); **endchar**;

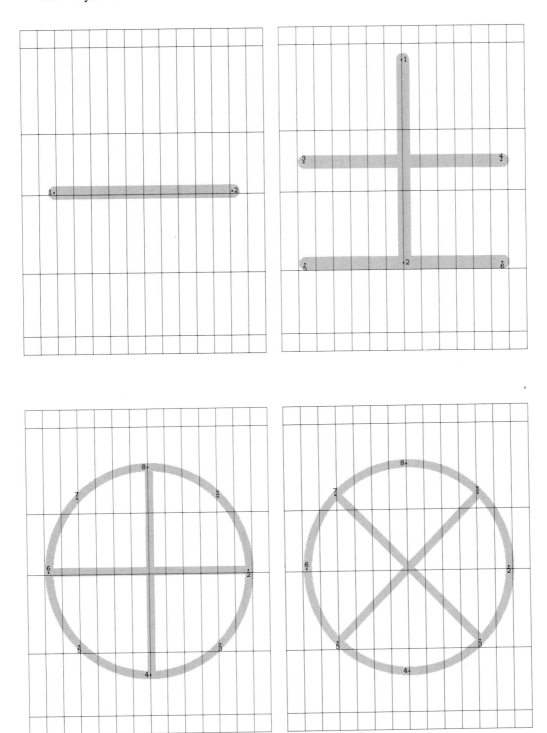

The program file `sym.mf` is used in several different ways, so it has been set up to produce characters "on demand."

% This file generates the following characters when their codes are known:
% *minus, plus_minus, o_plus, o_times,*
% *cup, cap, meet, join,*
% *down_arrow, up_arrow,*
% *left_arrow, right_arrow, double_arrow,*
% *subset, superset, elt,*
% *for_all, there_exists, false_that,*
% *less, greater, underbar,*
% *neq, leq, geq, eqv,*
% *backslash, vertical,*
% *cdot, diamond,*
% *left_brace, right_brace,*
% *straight_quotes, infty, integral.*

iff known *minus*: **cmchar** "Minus sign";
beginarithchar(*minus*); **pickup** *rule.nib*;
lft $x_1 = $ hround $1.5u - eps$; $x_2 = w - x_1$; $y_1 = y_2 = math\_axis$;
draw $z_1 \mathbin{--} z_2$;   % bar
labels$(1, 2)$; **endchar**;

iff known *plus_minus*: **cmchar** "Plus-or-minus sign";
beginarithchar(*plus_minus*); **pickup** *rule.nib*;
numeric *shiftup*; *shiftup* = vround $1.5u$;
$x_1 = x_2 = .5w$; *lft* $x_3 = $ *lft* $= x_5 = $ hround $u - eps$; $x_4 = x_6 = w - x_3$;
$.5[y_1, y_2] = y_3 = y_4 = math\_axis + shiftup$; *top* $y_1 = h + shiftup$; $y_5 = y_6 = y_2$;
draw $z_1 \mathbin{--} z_2$;   % stem
draw $z_3 \mathbin{--} z_4$;   % plus bar
draw $z_5 \mathbin{--} z_6$;   % minus bar
labels$(1, 2, 3, 4, 5, 6)$; **endchar**;

iff known *o_plus*: **cmchar** "Circle-plus operator";
beginarithchar(*o_plus*); **pickup** *light_rule.nib*; *autorounded*;
lft $x_6 = $ hround u; $x_2 = w - x_6$; $y_2 = math\_axis$; *top* $y_8 = h$;
circle_points; *draw_circle*;   % circle
draw $z_2 \mathbin{--} z_6$; **draw** $z_4 \mathbin{--} z_8$;   % bar and stem
labels$(1, 2, 3, 4, 5, 6, 7, 8)$; **endchar**;

iff known *o_times*: **cmchar** "Circle-times operator";
beginarithchar(*o_times*); **pickup** *light_rule.nib*; *autorounded*;
lft $x_6 = $ hround u; $x_2 = w - x_6$; $y_2 = math\_axis$; *top* $y_8 = h$;
circle_points; *draw_circle*;   % circle
draw $z_1 \mathbin{--} z_5$; **draw** $z_3 \mathbin{--} z_7$;   % diagonals
labels$(1, 2, 3, 4, 5, 6, 7, 8)$; **endchar**;

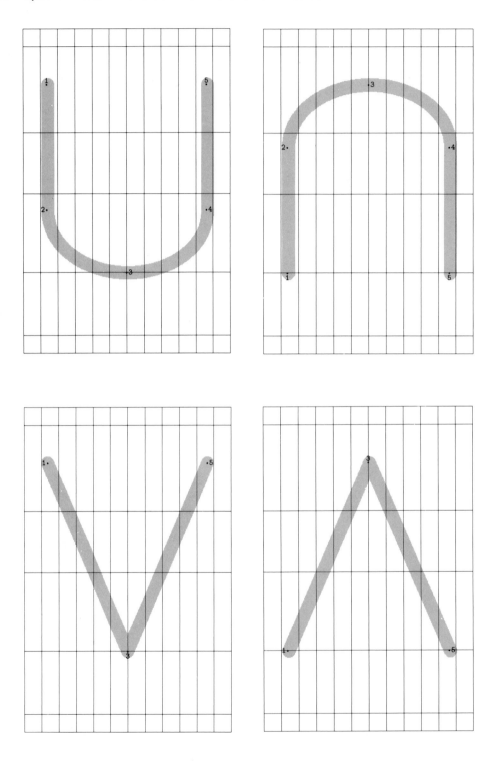

iff known *cup*: **cmchar** "Set union sign";
beginchar(cup, $12u^\#$, $.8asc\_height^\#$, 0);
italcorr $.8asc\_height^\# * slant - .5u^\#$;
adjust_fit$(0, 0)$; **pickup** $rule.nib$; *autorounded*;
lft $x_1 = $ hround u; $x_2 = x_1$; $x_3 = w - x_3$; $x_4 = x_5 = w - x_1$;
$y_1 = good.y$ $h + o$; bot $y_3 = -o$; $y_2 = y_4 = {}^2/_3[y_1, y_3]$; $y_5 = y_1$;
draw z_1 --- z_2 ... z_3 ... z_4 --- z_5;   % stems and cup
labels$(1, 2, 3, 4, 5)$; **endchar**;

iff known *cap*: **cmchar** "Set intersection sign";
beginchar(cap, $12u^\#$, $.8asc\_height^\#$, 0);
italcorr $.8asc\_height^\# * slant - .5u^\#$;
adjust_fit$(0, 0)$; **pickup** $rule.nib$; *autorounded*;
lft $x_1 = $ hround u; $x_2 = x_1$; $x_3 = w - x_3$; $x_4 = x_5 = w - x_1$;
$y_3 = good.y$ $h + o$; bot $y_1 = -o$; $y_2 = y_4 = {}^2/_3[y_1, y_3]$; $y_5 = y_1$;
draw z_1 --- z_2 ... z_3 ... z_4 --- z_5;   % stems and cap
labels$(1, 2, 3, 4, 5)$; **endchar**;

iff known *join*: **cmchar** "Lattice supremum (logical or) sign";
beginchar($join$, $12u^\#$, $.8asc\_height^\#$, 0);
italcorr $.8asc\_height^\# * slant - .5u^\#$;
adjust_fit$(0, 0)$; **pickup** $rule.nib$;
lft $x_1 = $ hround $u - eps$; $x_3 = w - x_3$; $x_5 = w - x_1$;
$y_1 = good.y$ $h + o$; bot $y_3 = -o$; $y_5 = y_1$;
draw z_1 -- z_3 -- z_5;   % diagonals
labels$(1, 3, 5)$; **endchar**;

iff known *meet*: **cmchar** "Lattice infimum (logical and) sign";
beginchar($meet$, $12u^\#$, $.8asc\_height^\#$, 0);
italcorr $.8asc\_height^\# * slant - .5u^\#$;
adjust_fit$(0, 0)$; **pickup** $rule.nib$;
lft $x_1 = $ hround $u - eps$; $x_3 = w - x_3$; $x_5 = w - x_1$;
$y_3 = good.y$ $h + o$; bot $y_1 = -o$; $y_5 = y_1$;
draw z_1 -- z_3 -- z_5;   % diagonals
labels$(1, 3, 5)$; **endchar**;

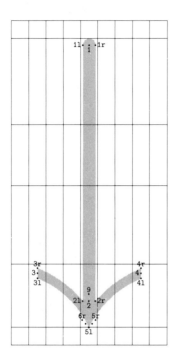

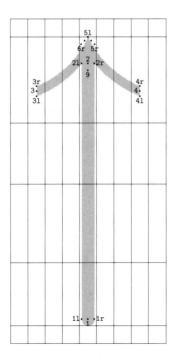

iff known *down_arrow*: **cmchar** "Downward arrow";
beginchar(*down_arrow*, $9u\#$, *asc_height*$\#$, *asc_depth*$\#$);
adjust_fit(0, 0); **pickup** *crisp.nib*;
pos_1(*rule_thickness*, 0); pos_2(*rule_thickness*, 0);
pos_3(*bar*, 90); pos_4(*bar*, 90);
lft x_{1l} = hround(.5w − .5*rule_thickness*); y_1 + .5*rule_thickness* = h;
$x_0 = x_1 = x_2$; *bot* $y_0 = -d$; $x_0 - x_3 = x_4 - x_0 = 3u + eps$;
$y_3 = y_4 = y_0 + .24$*asc_height* + *eps*;
pos_5(*bar*, angle($z_4 - z_0$)); $z_{5l} = z_0$;
pos_6(*bar*, angle($z_3 - z_0$)); $z_{6l} = z_0$;
$z_9 = .381966[.5[z_3, z_4], z_0]$;
numeric t; **path** p; $p = z_{4r}\{z_9 - z_4\} .. z_{6r}$;
t = xpart(p intersectiontimes ((x_{2r}, −d) -- (x_{2r}, h))); y_2 = ypart **point** t **of** p;
filldraw $z_0 .. \{z_4 - z_9\}z_{4l}$ -- **subpath**(0, t) **of** ($z_{4r}\{z_9 - z_4\} .. z_{6r}$)
$\quad$ -- z_{2r} --- $z_{1r} .. z_{1l}$ --- z_{2l} -- **subpath**(t, 0) **of** ($z_{3r}\{z_9 - z_3\} .. z_{5r}$)
$\quad$ -- $z_{3l}\{z_9 - z_3\} .. z_0$ & cycle; $\hspace{3cm}$ % arrowhead and stem
penlabels(0, 1, 2, 3, 4, 5, 6, 9); **endchar**;

iff known *up_arrow*: **cmchar** "Upward arrow";
beginchar(*up_arrow*, $9u\#$, *asc_height*$\#$, *asc_depth*$\#$);
italcorr .76*asc_height*$\#$ ∗ *slant* + .5*crisp*$\#$ − $u\#$;
adjust_fit(0, 0); **pickup** *crisp.nib*;
pos_1(*rule_thickness*, 0); pos_2(*rule_thickness*, 0);
pos_3(*bar*, 90); pos_4(*bar*, 90);
lft x_{1l} = hround(.5w − .5*rule_thickness*); y_1 − .5*rule_thickness* = −d;
$x_0 = x_1 = x_2$; *top* $y_0 = h$; $x_0 - x_3 = x_4 - x_0 = 3u + eps$;
$y_3 = y_4 = y_0 - .24$*asc_height* − *eps*;
pos_5(*bar*, angle($z_4 - z_0$)); $z_{5l} = z_0$;
pos_6(*bar*, angle($z_3 - z_0$)); $z_{6l} = z_0$;
$z_9 = .381966[.5[z_3, z_4], z_0]$;
numeric t; **path** p; $p = z_{4l}\{z_9 - z_4\} .. z_{6r}$;
t = xpart(p intersectiontimes ((x_{2r}, −d) -- (x_{2r}, h))); y_2 = ypart **point** t **of** p;
filldraw $z_0 .. \{z_4 - z_9\}z_{4r}$ -- **subpath**(0, t) **of** ($z_{4l}\{z_9 - z_4\} .. z_{6r}$)
$\quad$ -- z_{2r} --- $z_{1r} .. z_{1l}$ --- z_{2l} -- **subpath**(t, 0) **of** ($z_{3l}\{z_9 - z_3\} .. z_{5r}$)
$\quad$ -- $z_{3r}\{z_9 - z_3\} .. z_0$ & cycle; $\hspace{3cm}$ % arrowhead and stem
penlabels(0, 1, 2, 3, 4, 5, 6, 9); **endchar**;

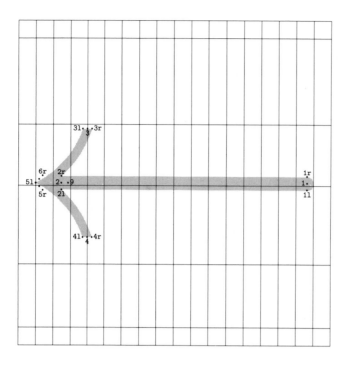

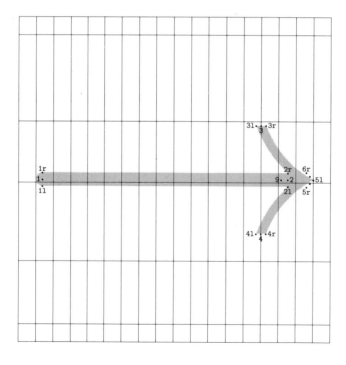

iff known *left_arrow*: **cmchar** "Leftward arrow";

compute_spread$(.45x\_height^\#, .55x\_height^\#)$;

beginchar$(left\_arrow, 18u^\#, v\_center(spread^\# + rule\_thickness^\#))$;

adjust_fit$(0, 0)$; **pickup** *crisp.nib*;

$pos_1(rule\_thickness, 90)$; $pos_2(rule\_thickness, 90)$; $pos_3(bar, 0)$; $pos_4(bar, 0)$;

$y_0 = y_1 = y_2 = math\_axis$; $x_1 + .5rule\_thickness = \mathrm{hround}(w - u)$; *lft* $x_0 = \mathrm{hround}\, u$;

$y_3 - y_0 = y_0 - y_4 = .24asc\_height + eps$; $x_3 = x_4 = x_0 + 3u + eps$;

$pos_5(bar, \mathrm{angle}(z_4 - z_0))$; $z_{5l} = z_0$; $pos_6(bar, \mathrm{angle}(z_3 - z_0))$; $z_{6l} = z_0$;

$z_9 = .381966[.5[z_3, z_4], z_0]$;

numeric t; **path** p; $p = z_{4r}\{z_9 - z_4\} \mathrel{..} z_{6r}$;

$t = \mathrm{xpart}(p\ \mathrm{intersectiontimes}\ ((0, y_{2l}) \mathrel{-\!\!-} (w, y_{2l})))$; $x_2 = \mathrm{xpart}$ **point** t **of** p;

filldraw $z_0 \mathrel{..} \{z_4 - z_9\}z_{4l} \mathrel{-\!\!-} \mathbf{subpath}(0, t)$ **of** $(z_{4r}\{z_9 - z_4\} \mathrel{..} z_{6r})$

    $\mathrel{-\!\!-} z_{2l} \mathrel{-\!-\!-} z_{1l} \mathrel{..} z_{1r} \mathrel{-\!-\!-} z_{2r} \mathrel{-\!\!-} \mathbf{subpath}(t, 0)$ **of** $(z_{3r}\{z_9 - z_3\} \mathrel{..} z_{5r})$

    $\mathrel{-\!\!-} z_{3l}\{z_9 - z_3\} \mathrel{..} z_0\ \&\ \mathrm{cycle}$;   % arrowhead and stem

penlabels$(0, 1, 2, 3, 4, 5, 6, 9)$; **endchar**;

iff known *right_arrow*: **cmchar** "Rightward arrow";

compute_spread$(.45x\_height^\#, .55x\_height^\#)$;

beginchar$(right\_arrow, 18u^\#, v\_center(spread^\# + rule\_thickness^\#))$;

adjust_fit$(0, 0)$; **pickup** *crisp.nib*;

$pos_1(rule\_thickness, 90)$; $pos_2(rule\_thickness, 90)$; $pos_3(bar, 0)$; $pos_4(bar, 0)$;

$y_0 = y_1 = y_2 = math\_axis$; $x_1 - .5rule\_thickness = \mathrm{hround}\, u$; *rt* $x_0 = \mathrm{hround}(w - u)$;

$y_3 - y_0 = y_0 - y_4 = .24asc\_height + eps$; $x_3 = x_4 = x_0 - 3u - eps$;

$pos_5(bar, \mathrm{angle}(z_4 - z_0))$; $z_{5l} = z_0$; $pos_6(bar, \mathrm{angle}(z_3 - z_0))$; $z_{6l} = z_0$;

$z_9 = .381966[.5[z_3, z_4], z_0]$;

numeric t; **path** p; $p = z_{4l}\{z_9 - z_4\} \mathrel{..} z_{6r}$;

$t = \mathrm{xpart}(p\ \mathrm{intersectiontimes}\ ((0, y_{2l}) \mathrel{-\!\!-} (w, y_{2l})))$; $x_2 = \mathrm{xpart}$ **point** t **of** p;

filldraw $z_0 \mathrel{..} \{z_4 - z_9\}z_{4r} \mathrel{-\!\!-} \mathbf{subpath}(0, t)$ **of** $(z_{4l}\{z_9 - z_4\} \mathrel{..} z_{6r})$

    $\mathrel{-\!\!-} z_{2l} \mathrel{-\!-\!-} z_{1l} \mathrel{..} z_{1r} \mathrel{-\!-\!-} z_{2r} \mathrel{-\!\!-} \mathbf{subpath}(t, 0)$ **of** $(z_{3l}\{z_9 - z_3\} \mathrel{..} z_{5r})$

    $\mathrel{-\!\!-} z_{3r}\{z_9 - z_3\} \mathrel{..} z_0\ \&\ \mathrm{cycle}$;   % arrowhead and stem

penlabels$(0, 1, 2, 3, 4, 5, 6, 9)$; **endchar**;

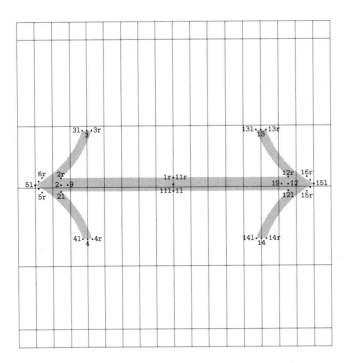

iff known *double_arrow*: **cmchar** "Left-and-right arrow";
compute_spread(.45*x_height*#, .55*x_height*#);
beginchar(*double_arrow*, 18*u*#,
$\quad$ *v_center*(**if** *monospace*: .6*asc_height*# **fi** *spread*# + *rule_thickness*#));
adjust_fit(0, 0); **pickup** *crisp.nib*;
pos_1(*rule_thickness*, 90); pos_2(*rule_thickness*, 90); pos_3(*bar*, 0); pos_4(*bar*, 0);
$y_0 = y_1 = y_2 = $ *math_axis* **if** *monospace*: + vround .3*asc_height* **fi**; *lft* $x_0 = $ hround *u*;
if *monospace*: $x_1 + .5$*rule_thickness* $=$ hround$(w - u)$ **else**: $x_1 = .5w$ **fi**;
$y_3 - y_0 = y_0 - y_4 = .24$*asc_height* $+ eps$; $x_3 = x_4 = x_0 + 3u + eps$;
pos_5(*bar*, angle$(z_4 - z_0)$); $z_{5l} = z_0$; pos_6(*bar*, angle$(z_3 - z_0)$); $z_{6l} = z_0$;
$z_9 = .381966[.5[z_3, z_4], z_0]$;
numeric t; **path** p; $p = z_{4r}\{z_9 - z_4\} .. z_{6r}$;
$t = $ xpart$(p$ intersectiontimes $((0, y_{2l})$ -- $(w, y_{2l})))$; $x_2 = $ xpart **point** t **of** p;
filldraw $z_0 .. \{z_4 - z_9\}z_{4l}$ -- **subpath**$(0, t)$ **of** $(z_{4r}\{z_9 - z_4\} .. z_{6r})$
$\quad$ -- z_{2l} --- $z_{1l} .. z_{1r}$ --- z_{2r} -- **subpath**$(t, 0)$ **of** $(z_{3r}\{z_9 - z_3\} .. z_{5r})$
$\quad$ -- $z_{3l}\{z_9 - z_3\} .. z_0$ & cycle; $\qquad\qquad$ % left arrowhead and stem
pos_{11}(*rule_thickness*, 90); pos_{12}(*rule_thickness*, 90); pos_{13}(*bar*, 0); pos_{14}(*bar*, 0);
$y_{10} = y_{11} = y_{12} = $ *math_axis* **if** *monospace*: $-$ vround .3*asc_height* **fi**;
rt $x_{10} = $ hround$(w - u)$;
if *monospace*: $x_{11} - .5$*rule_thickness* $=$ hround *u* **else**: $x_{11} = .5w$ **fi**;
$y_{13} - y_{10} = y_{10} - y_{14} = .24$*asc_height* $+ eps$; $x_{13} = x_{14} = x_{10} - 3u - eps$;
pos_{15}(*bar*, angle$(z_{14} - z_{10})$); $z_{15l} = z_{10}$; pos_{16}(*bar*, angle$(z_{13} - z_{10})$); $z_{16l} = z_{10}$;
$z_{19} = .381966[.5[z_{13}, z_{14}], z_{10}]$;
numeric t; **path** p; $p = z_{14l}\{z_{19} - z_{14}\} .. z_{16r}$;
$t = $ xpart$(p$ intersectiontimes $((0, y_{12l})$ -- $(w, y_{12l})))$; $x_{12} = $ xpart **point** t **of** p;
filldraw $z_{10} .. \{z_{14} - z_{19}\}z_{14r}$ -- **subpath**$(0, t)$ **of** $(z_{14l}\{z_{19} - z_{14}\} .. z_{16r})$
$\quad$ -- z_{12l} --- $z_{11l} .. z_{11r}$ --- z_{12r} -- **subpath**$(t, 0)$ **of** $(z_{13l}\{z_{19} - z_{13}\} .. z_{15r})$
$\quad$ -- $z_{13r}\{z_{19} - z_{13}\} .. z_{10}$ & cycle; $\qquad\qquad$ % right arrowhead and stem
penlabels(0, 1, 2, 3, 4, 5, 6, 9, 10, 11, 12, 13, 14, 15, 16, 19); **endchar**;

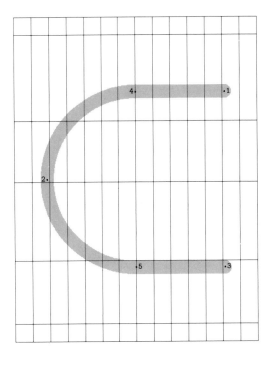

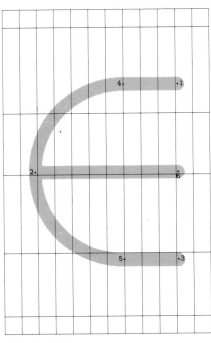

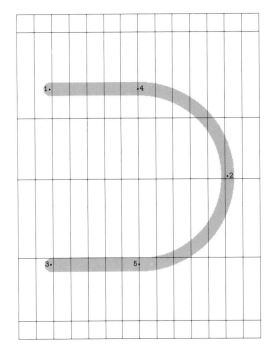

iff known *subset*: **cmchar** "Proper subset sign";
compute_spread($^5/_4 x\_height^\#$, $^3/_2 x\_height^\#$);
beginchar(*subset*, $14u^\#$, *v_center*(*spread*$^\#$ + *rule_thickness*$^\#$));
italcorr $h^\# * slant - u^\#$;
adjust_fit$(0, 0)$; **pickup** *rule.nib*; *autorounded*;
lft x_2 = hround $1.5u - eps$; $x_1 = x_3 = w - x_2$;
$y_1 - y_3 = spread$; $y_2 = .5[y_1, y_3] = math\_axis$;
$x_4 = x_5 = .5w$; $y_4 = y_1$; $y_5 = y_3$;
draw z_1 --- z_4 ... $z_2\{down\}$ ... z_5 --- z_3;   % arc and bars
labels$(1, 2, 3, 4, 5)$; **endchar**;

iff known *elt*: **cmchar** "Element sign";
compute_spread($^5/_4 x\_height^\#$, $^3/_2 x\_height^\#$);
beginchar(*elt*, $12u^\#$, *v_center*(*spread*$^\#$ + *rule_thickness*$^\#$));
italcorr $h^\# * slant - u^\#$;
adjust_fit$(0, 0)$; **pickup** *rule.nib*; *autorounded*;
lft x_2 = hround $1.5u - eps$; $x_1 = x_3 = x_6 = w - x_2$;
$y_1 - y_3 = spread$; $y_2 = y_6 = .5[y_1, y_3] = math\_axis$;
$x_4 = x_5 = .5w + u$; $y_4 = y_1$; $y_5 = y_3$;
draw z_1 --- z_4 ... $z_2\{down\}$ ... z_5 --- z_3;   % arc and bars
draw z_2 -- z_6;   % middle bar
labels$(1, 2, 3, 4, 5, 6)$; **endchar**;

iff known *superset*: **cmchar** "Proper superset sign";
compute_spread($^5/_4 x\_height^\#$, $^3/_2 x\_height^\#$);
beginchar(*superset*, $14u^\#$, *v_center*(*spread*$^\#$ + *rule_thickness*$^\#$));
italcorr $h^\# * slant - u^\#$;
adjust_fit$(0, 0)$; **pickup** *rule.nib*; *autorounded*;
lft x_1 = hround $1.5u - eps$; $x_2 = w - x_1$; $x_3 = x_1$;
$y_1 - y_3 = spread$; $y_2 = .5[y_1, y_3] = math\_axis$;
$x_4 = x_5 = .5w$; $y_4 = y_1$; $y_5 = y_3$;
draw z_1 --- z_4 ... $z_2\{down\}$ ... z_5 --- z_3;   % arc and bars
labels$(1, 2, 3, 4, 5)$; **endchar**;

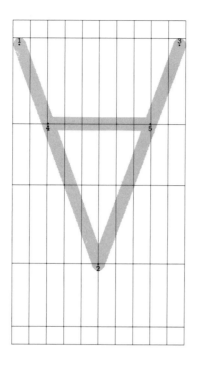

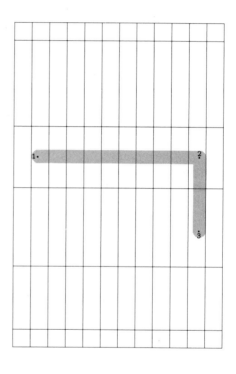

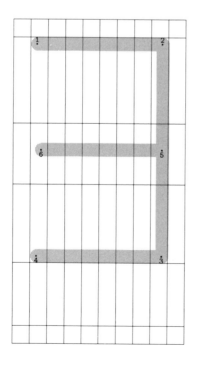

iff known *for_all*: **cmchar** "Universal quantifier";
beginchar(*for_all*, $10u^{\#}$, *asc_height*#, 0);
italcorr *asc_height*# $*$ *slant*;
adjust_fit(0, 0); **pickup** *rule.nib*;
$x_2 = good.x\ .5w;\ \ w := r := 2x_2;$
lft $x_1 = 0;\ \ x_3 = w - x_1;$
top $y_1 = h;\ \ bot\ y_2 = -o;\ \ y_3 = y_1;\ \ y_4 = y_5 = good.y\ x\_height;$
$z_4 = whatever[z_1, z_2];\ \ z_5 = whatever[z_2, z_3];$
draw z_1 -- z_2 -- z_3;   % diagonals
draw z_4 -- z_5;   % bar
labels(1, 2, 3, 4, 5); **endchar**;

iff known *false_that*: **cmchar** "Logical not sign";
beginchar(*false_that*, $12u^{\#}$, *x_height*#, 0);
italcorr *x_height*# $*$ *slant* $-\ .5u^{\#}$;
adjust_fit(0, 0); **pickup** *rule.nib*;
lft $x_1 = $ hround $u - eps;\ \ x_2 = x_3 = w - x_1;$
$y_1 = y_2 = good.y\ .5[bar\_height, h];\ \ y_2 - y_3 = 1.2(h - bar\_height);$
draw z_1 -- z_2 -- z_3;   % bar and stem
labels(1, 2, 3); **endchar**;

iff known *there_exists*: **cmchar** "Existential quantifier";
beginchar(*there_exists*, $10u^{\#}$, *asc_height*#, 0);
italcorr *asc_height*# $*$ *slant*;
adjust_fit(0, 0); **pickup** *rule.nib*;
lft $x_1 = $ hround $u - eps;\ \ x_2 = x_3 = x_5 = w - x_1;\ \ x_4 = x_6 - .25u = x_1;$
top $y_1 = h;\ \ bot\ y_4 = 0;\ \ y_2 = y_1;\ \ y_5 = y_6 = .5[y_1, y_3];\ \ y_3 = y_4;$
draw z_1 -- z_2 -- z_3 -- z_4;   % upper bar, stem, lower bar
draw z_5 -- z_6;   % middle bar
labels(1, 2, 3, 4, 5, 6); **endchar**;

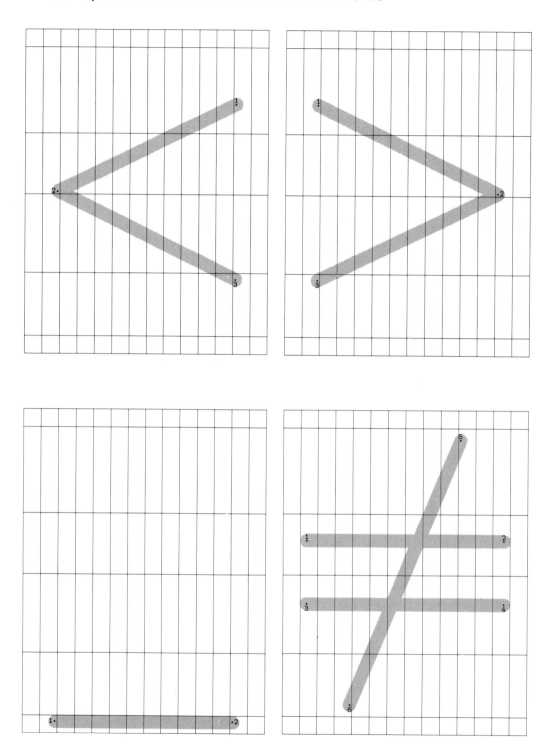

iff known *less*: **cmchar** "Less than sign";
compute_spread($5/4x\_height^\#$, $3/2x\_height^\#$);
beginchar(*less*, $14u^\#$, *v_center*($spread^\# + rule\_thickness^\#$));
italcorr $h^\# * slant - u^\#$;
adjust_fit(0, 0); **pickup** *rule.nib*;
lft $x_2 =$ hround $1.5u - eps$; $x_1 = x_3 = w - x_2$;
$y_1 - y_3 = spread$; $y_2 = .5[y_1, y_3] = math\_axis$;
draw $z_1 \mathbin{--} z_2 \mathbin{--} z_3$; % diagonals
labels(1, 2, 3); **endchar**;

iff known *greater*: **cmchar** "Greater than sign";
compute_spread($5/4x\_height^\#$, $3/2x\_height^\#$);
beginchar(*greater*, $14u^\#$, *v_center*($spread^\# + rule\_thickness^\#$));
italcorr $math\_axis^\# * slant - u^\#$;
adjust_fit(0, 0); **pickup** *rule.nib*;
rt $x_2 =$ hround($w - 1.5u$) $+ eps$; $x_1 = x_3 = w - x_2$;
$y_1 - y_3 = spread$; $y_2 = .5[y_1, y_3] = math\_axis$;
draw $z_1 \mathbin{--} z_2 \mathbin{--} z_3$; % diagonals
labels(1, 2, 3); **endchar**;

iff known *underbar*: **cmchar** "Underbar suitable for < and >";
compute_spread(($5/8 + .45$) $* x\_height^\#$, ($3/4 + .55$) $* x\_height^\#$);
beginchar(*underbar*, $14u^\#$, 0, $spread^\# - math\_axis^\# + .5rule\_thickness^\#$);
adjust_fit(0, 0); **pickup** *rule.nib*;
lft $x_1 =$ hround $1.5u - eps$; $x_2 = w - x_1$; *bot* $y_1 =$ *bot* $y_2 = -d$;
draw $z_1 \mathbin{--} z_2$; % bar
labels(1, 2); **endchar**;

iff known *neq*: **cmchar** "Unequals sign";
compute_spread($.45x\_height^\#$, $.55x\_height^\#$);
beginchar(*neq*, $14u^\#$, *v_center*($4spread^\# + rule\_thickness^\#$));
italcorr $h^\# * slant - .5u^\#$;
adjust_fit(0, 0); **pickup** *rule.nib*;
lft $x_1 =$ hround $u - eps$; $x_3 = x_1$; $x_2 = x_4 = w - x_1$;
$y_1 = y_2$; $y_3 = y_4$; $y_1 - y_3 = spread$; $.5[y_1, y_3] = math\_axis$;
draw $z_1 \mathbin{--} z_2$; **draw** $z_3 \mathbin{--} z_4$; % bars
lft $x_6 =$ hround $3.5u - eps$; $x_5 = w - x_6$; *top* $y_5 = h + o$; *bot* $y_6 = -d - o$;
draw $z_5 \mathbin{--} z_6$; % diagonal
labels(1, 2, 3, 4, 5, 6); **endchar**;

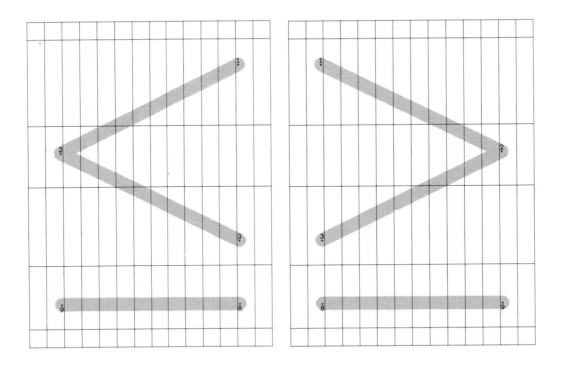

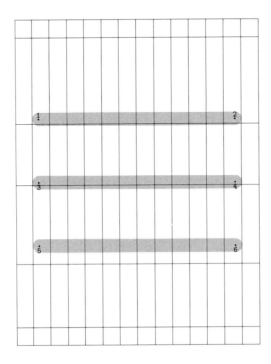

iff known *leq*: **cmchar** "Less than or equal to sign";
compute_spread$(.45x\_height^{\#}, .55x\_height^{\#})$;
spread$^{\#\prime}$:= *spread*$^{\#}$; *spread*$^{\prime}$:= *spread*;   % the spread of '='
compute_spread$(^5/_4x\_height^{\#}, ^3/_2x\_height^{\#})$;
beginchar$(leq, 14u^{\#}, v\_center(spread^{\#\prime} + spread^{\#} + rule\_thickness^{\#}))$;
italcorr $h^{\#} * slant - u^{\#}$;
adjust_fit$(0, 0)$; **pickup** *rule.nib*;
lft x_2 = hround $1.5u - eps$; $x_1 = x_3 = w - x_2$;
$y_1 - y_3 = spread$; $y_2 = .5[y_1, y_3]$; *top* $y_1 = h$;
draw $z_1 \ \text{--} \ z_2 \ \text{--} \ z_3$;   % diagonals
$x_8 = x_1$; $x_9 = x_2$; $y_8 = y_9$; $y_3 - y_9 = spread^{\prime}$; **draw** $z_8 \ \text{--} \ z_9$;   % bar
labels$(1, 2, 3, 8, 9)$; **endchar**;

iff known *geq*: **cmchar** "Greater than or equal to sign";
compute_spread$(.45x\_height^{\#}, .55x\_height^{\#})$;
spread$^{\#\prime}$:= *spread*$^{\#}$; *spread*$^{\prime}$:= *spread*;   % the spread of '='
compute_spread$(^5/_4x\_height^{\#}, ^3/_2x\_height^{\#})$;
beginchar$(geq, 14u^{\#}, v\_center(spread^{\#\prime} + spread^{\#} + rule\_thickness^{\#}))$;
italcorr $h^{\#} * slant - u^{\#}$;
adjust_fit$(0, 0)$; **pickup** *rule.nib*;
lft x_1 = hround $1.5u - eps$; $x_2 = w - x_1$; $x_3 = x_1$;
$y_1 - y_3 = spread$; $y_2 = .5[y_1, y_3]$; *top* $y_1 = h$;
draw $z_1 \ \text{--} \ z_2 \ \text{--} \ z_3$;   % diagonals
$x_8 = x_1$; $x_9 = x_2$; $y_8 = y_9$; $y_3 - y_9 = spread^{\prime}$; **draw** $z_8 \ \text{--} \ z_9$;   % bar
labels$(1, 2, 3, 8, 9)$; **endchar**;

iff known *eqv*: **cmchar** "Equivalence or congruence sign";
compute_spread$(.45x\_height^{\#}, .55x\_height^{\#})$;
beginchar$(eqv, 14u^{\#}, v\_center(2spread^{\#} + rule\_thickness^{\#}))$;
italcorr $h^{\#} * slant - .5u^{\#}$;
adjust_fit$(0, 0)$; **pickup** *rule.nib*;
lft x_1 = hround $u - eps$; $x_3 = x_5 = x_1$; $x_2 = x_4 = x_6 = w - x_1$;
$y_1 = y_2$; $y_3 = y_4 = math\_axis$; $y_5 = y_6$; $y_1 - y_3 = y_3 - y_5 = spread$;
draw $z_1 \ \text{--} \ z_2$;   % upper bar
draw $z_3 \ \text{--} \ z_4$;   % middle bar
draw $z_5 \ \text{--} \ z_6$;   % lower bar
labels$(1, 2, 3, 4, 5, 6)$; **endchar**;

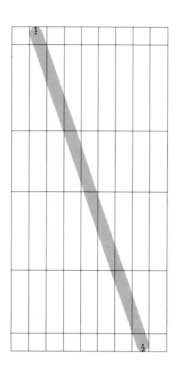

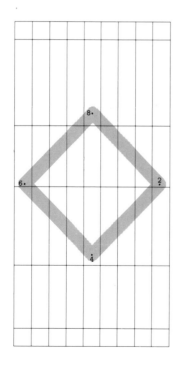

iff known *backslash*: **cmchar** "Reverse slash (backslash)";
beginchar(*backslash*, $9u^\#$, *body_height*$^\#$, *paren_depth*$^\#$);
adjust_fit(0, 0); **pickup** *rule.nib*;
lft x_1 = hround $u - eps$; *top* $y_1 = h + eps$;
rt x_2 = hround($w - u$) + *eps*; *bot* $y_2 = -d - eps$;
draw z_1 -- z_2;   % diagonal
labels(1, 2); **endchar**;

iff known *vertical*: **cmchar** "Vertical line";
beginchar(*vertical*, $5u^\#$, *body_height*$^\#$, *paren_depth*$^\#$);
italcorr *body_height*$^\#$ * *slant* + .5*rule_thickness*$^\#$ − $2u^\#$;
adjust_fit(0, 0); **pickup** *rule.nib*;
$x_1 = x_2 = good.x$ .5w; *top* $y_1 = h + eps$; *bot* $y_2 = -d - eps$;
draw z_1 -- z_2;   % stem
labels(1, 2); **endchar**;

iff known *diamond*: **cmchar** "Diamond operator";
beginchar(*diamond*, $9u^\#$, *v_center*($7u^\#$));
italcorr *math_axis*$^\#$ * *slant*;
adjust_fit(0, 0); **pickup** *rule.nib*;
numeric a; $a = (lft\ 3.5u) * $ sqrt($^{3.14159}/_2$);   % an attempt to match circle area
$x_4 = x_8 = good.x$ .5w; $w := r := 2x_4$; $x_2 = w - x_6 = good.x(x_4 + a)$;
$y_2 = y_6 = .5[y_4, y_8] = math\_axis$; $y_8 = good.y(y_2 + a)$;
draw z_2 -- z_4 -- z_6 -- z_8 -- **cycle**;   % bowl
labels(2, 4, 6, 8); **endchar**;

iff known *cdot*: **cmchar** "Period raised to axis height";
beginchar(*cdot*, $5u^\#$, *v_center*($7u^\#$));
adjust_fit(0, 0); **pickup** *fine.nib*;
numeric *dot_diam*$^\#$; *dot_diam*$^\#$ = **if** *monospace*: $^5/_4$ **fi** *dot_size*$^\#$;
define_whole_blacker_pixels(*dot_diam*);
pos_1(*dot_diam*, 0); pos_2(*dot_diam*, 90);
lft x_{1l} = hround(.5w − .5*dot_diam*);
$y_1 + .5dot\_diam$ = vround(*math_axis* + .5*dot_diam*);
$z_1 = z_2$; *dot*(1, 2);   % dot
penlabels(1, 2); **endchar**;

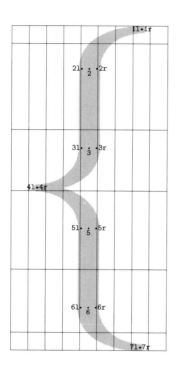

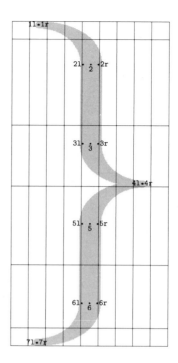

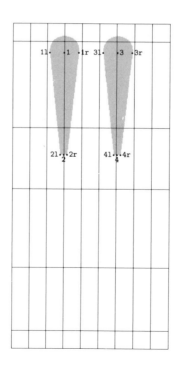

iff known *left_brace*: **cmchar** "Left curly brace";
beginchar(*left_brace*, $9u^\#$, $body\_height^\#$, $paren\_depth^\#$);
italcorr $body\_height^\# * slant + .5vair^\# - u^\#$;
adjust_fit$(0, 0)$; **pickup** *fine.nib*;
forsuffixes $\$ = 1, 1', 4, 4', 7, 7': pos_\$(vair, 0)$; **endfor**
forsuffixes $\$ = 2, 3, 5, 6: pos_\$(stem, 0)$; **endfor**
$x_2 = x_3 = x_5 = x_6; \quad x_1 = x_{1'} = x_7 = x_{7'} = w - x_4 = w - x_{4'};$
lft $x_{4l} = $ hround$(1.5u - .5vair); \quad$ *lft* $x_{2l} = $ hround$(.5w - .5stem);$
top $y_1 = h; \quad$ *bot* $y_7 = -d; \quad .5[y_4, y_{4'}] = .5[y_1, y_7] = .5[y_2, y_6] = .5[y_3, y_5];$
$y_1 - y_2 = y_3 - y_4 = (y_1 - y_4)/4; \quad y_1 - y_{1'} = y_4 - y_{4'} = y_{7'} - y_7 = vair - fine;$
filldraw $z_{1l}\{left\} \ldots z_{2l} \text{---} z_{3l} \ldots \{left\}z_{4l}$
$\text{--} z_{4'l}\{right\} \ldots z_{5l} \text{---} z_{6l} \ldots \{right\}z_{7l}$
$\text{--} z_{7r} \text{--} z_{7'r}\{left\} \ldots z_{6r} \text{---} z_{5r} \ldots \{left\}.5[z_{4r}, z_{4'r}]\{right\}$
$\ldots z_{3r} \text{---} z_{2r} \ldots \{right\}z_{1'r} \text{--} z_{1r} \text{--}$ cycle;   % stroke
penlabels$(1, 2, 3, 4, 5, 6, 7)$; **endchar**;

iff known *right_brace*: **cmchar** "Right curly brace";
beginchar(*right_brace*, $9u^\#$, $body\_height^\#$, $paren\_depth^\#$);
italcorr $math\_axis^\# * slant + .5vair^\# - u^\#$;
adjust_fit$(0, 0)$; **pickup** *fine.nib*;
forsuffixes $\$ = 1, 1', 4, 4', 7, 7': pos_\$(vair, 0)$; **endfor**
forsuffixes $\$ = 2, 3, 5, 6: pos_\$(stem, 0)$; **endfor**
$x_2 = x_3 = x_5 = x_6; \quad x_1 = x_{1'} = x_7 = x_{7'} = w - x_4 = w - x_{4'};$
rt $x_{4r} = $ hround$(w - 1.5u + .5vair); \quad$ *r* $x_{2r} = $ hround$(.5w + .5stem);$
top $y_1 = h; \quad$ *bot* $y_7 = -d; \quad .5[y_4, y_{4'}] = .5[y_1, y_7] = .5[y_2, y_6] = .5[y_3, y_5];$
$y_1 - y_2 = y_3 - y_4 = (y_1 - y_4)/4; \quad y_1 - y_{1'} = y_4 - y_{4'} = y_{7'} - y_7 = vair - fine;$
filldraw $z_{1r}\{right\} \ldots z_{2r} \text{---} z_{3r} \ldots \{right\}z_{4r}$
$\text{--} z_{4'r}\{left\} \ldots z_{5r} \text{---} z_{6r} \ldots \{left\}z_{7r}$
$\text{--} z_{7l} \text{--} z_{7'l}\{right\} \ldots z_{6l} \text{---} z_{5l} \ldots \{right\}.5[z_{4l}, z_{4'l}]\{left\}$
$\ldots z_{3l} \text{---} z_{2l} \ldots \{left\}z_{1'l} \text{--} z_{1l} \text{--}$ cycle;   % stroke
penlabels$(1, 2, 3, 4, 5, 6, 7)$; **endchar**;

iff known *straight_quotes*: **cmchar** "Straight double quotes";
beginchar(*straight_quotes*, $9u^\#$, $asc\_height^\#$, 0);
numeric $top\_width^\#$, $spread^\#$; $top_width^\# = $ **if** *serifs*: $flare^\#$ **else**: $stem^\#$ **fi**;
$spread^\# = \max(3u^\#, top\_width^\# + .5u^\#)$; **define_pixels**(*spread*);
italcorr $asc\_height^\# * slant + .5top\_width^\# + .5spread^\# - 4u^\#$;
adjust_fit$(0, 0)$;
$x_1 = x_2; \quad x_3 = x_4 = w - x_1; \quad x_3 - x_1 = spread + 2; \quad y_1 = y_3;$
$y_2 = y_4 = \max(.5[bar\_height, x\_height] + .5vair, h - x\_height);$
if *serifs*: **pickup** *crisp.nib*; $pos_1(flare, 0); \quad pos_2(vair, 0);$
$\quad pos_3(flare, 0); \quad pos_4(vair, 0);$
$\quad y_1 + .5stem = h;$ **filldraw circ_stroke** $z_{1e} \text{--} z_{2e};$ % left stem and bulb
$\quad$ **filldraw circ_stroke** $z_{3e} \text{--} z_{4e};$ % right stem and bulb
else: **pickup** *fine.nib*; $pos_1(stem, 0); \quad pos_2(vair, 0);$
$\quad pos_3(stem, 0); \quad pos_4(vair, 0);$
$\quad$ *top* $y_1 = h;$ **filldraw stroke** $z_{1e} \text{--} z_{2e};$ % left stem
$\quad$ **filldraw stroke** $z_{3e} \text{--} z_{4e};$ **fi**   % right stem
penlabels$(1, 2, 3, 4)$; **endchar**;

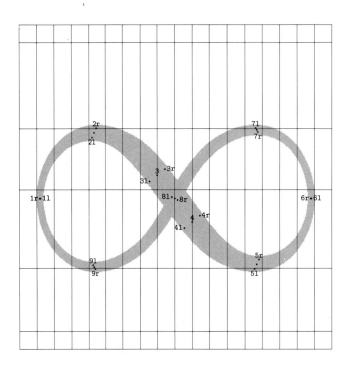

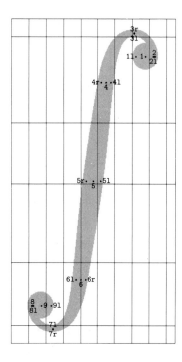

iff known *infty*: **cmchar** "Infinity";
beginchar(*infty*, $18u^\#$, $x\_height^\#$, 0);
italcorr $.7x\_height^\# * slant - .5u^\#$;
adjust_fit(0, 0); **pickup** *fine.nib*;
numeric *theta*, *phi*;
if *monospace*: $phi = -theta = 90$;
else: $phi = \mathrm{angle}(4u, h)$; $theta = \mathrm{angle}(6u, -h)$; **fi**
$pos_1(vair, 180)$; $pos_2(.5[vair, curve], 90 + .5theta)$; $pos_3(curve, 90 + theta)$;
$pos_4(curve, 90 + theta)$; $pos_5(.5[vair, curve], 90 + .5theta)$;
$pos_6(vair, 180)$; $pos_7(.2[vair, curve], 270 + .5phi)$;
$pos_8(.3[vair, curve], 270 + phi)$; $pos_9(.2[vair, curve], 270 + .5phi)$;
lft $x_{1r} = w - rt\ x_{6l} = $ hround u; $x_2 = x_9 = .4[x_1, x_8]$; $x_5 = x_7 = .6[x_8, x_6]$;
if *monospace*: $x_{2l} := x_{2r}$; $x_{5r} := x_{5l}$; $x_{7r} := x_{7l}$; $x_{9l} := x_{9r}$; **fi**
$y_1 = y_6 = .5h$; *top* $y_{2r} = $ *top* $y_{7l} = h + oo$; *bot* $y_{5l} = $ *bot* $y_{9r} = -oo$;
$x_8 = .5[x_3, x_4] = .5w$; $y_8 = .5[y_3, y_4] = .5h$;
$y_3 - y_4 = h/3$; $z_3 - z_4 = $ *whatever* $* $ dir *theta*;
filldraw stroke $z_{1e}\{up\}$ ... $z_{2e}\{right\}$ ... z_{3e} --- z_{4e} ... $z_{5e}\{right\}$
  ... $z_{6e}\{up\}$ ... $z_{7e}\{left\}$ ... $\{-$ dir $phi\}z_{8e}$ ... $\{left\}z_{9e}$ ... $z_{1e}\{up\}$;   % bowls
penlabels(1, 2, 3, 4, 5, 6, 7, 8, 9); **endchar**;

iff known *integral*: **cmchar** "Integral sign";
beginchar(*integral*, $5.25u^\# + \max(1.25u^\#, stem^\#) + 2\max(1.5u^\#, curve^\#)$,
  $asc\_height^\#$, $desc\_depth^\#$);
italcorr $asc\_height^\# * slant - .5u^\#$;
adjust_fit(0, 0); **pickup** *fine.nib*;
$pos_1(curve, 0)$; $pos_2(hair, 0)$; $pos_3(vair, 90)$; $pos_4(.6[hair, stem], 180)$;
$pos_5(stem, 180)$; $pos_{5'}(stem, 0)$; $z_{5'} = z_5$; $pos_6(.6[hair, stem], 0)$;
$pos_7(vair, -90)$; $pos_8(hair, -180)$; $pos_9(curve, -180)$;
$x_7 = w - x_3 = 2.4u$; *rt* $x_{1r} = \max(rt\ x_3 + eps, \mathrm{hround}(w - u))$; $x_9 = w - x_1$;
$x_5 = .5[x_4, x_6]$; $x_4 - x_6 = 1.5u$; *lft* $x_{5r} = \mathrm{hround}(.5w - .5stem)$;
$y_9 - .5curve = \mathrm{vround}(-.9d - o + vair)$; $y_3 - y_1 = y_9 - y_7$;
top $y_{3r} = h + o$; *bot* $y_{7r} = -d - o$; $y_5 = .5[y_3, y_7] = .5[y_4, y_6]$; $y_4 - y_6 = \frac{2}{3}(y_3 - y_7)$;
$bulb(3, 2, 1)$; $bulb(7, 8, 9)$;   % bulbs
filldraw stroke $z_{3e}\{left\}$ ... $z_{4e}\{(z_{5e} - z_{4e})$ xscaled $1.1\}$
  .. tension atleast 1 and atleast .8 .. $\{z_5 - z_4\}z_{5e}$;   % upper stem
filldraw stroke $z_{5'e}\{z_6 - z_5\}$ .. tension atleast .8 and atleast 1
  .. $\{(z_{6e} - z_{5'e})$ xscaled $1.1\}z_{6e}$ ... $\{left\}z_{7e}$;   % lower stem
math_fit(0, $-2u^\#$); **penlabels**(1, 2, 3, 4, 5, 6, 7, 8, 9); **endchar**;

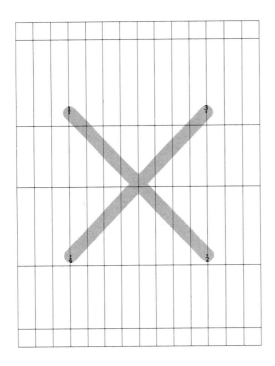

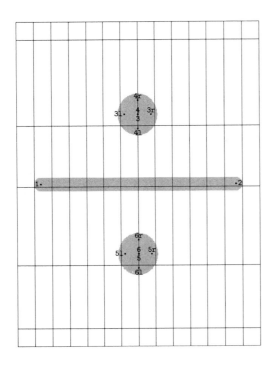

The longest program file, symbol.mf, is actually the easiest to read, because most of its characters are fairly simple (at least superficially).

% This file defines the symbols of a TeX math symbol font.
% Character codes ´000´–´0100´ and ´133´–´177´ are generated.

% (Improvements to the author's original characters were worked out in 1982
% by Ronald F. Whitney and other members of
% the American Mathematical Society.)

% Italic corrections have not been computed for most of these characters,
% since they are generally not slanted.

$minus$ = oct "000"; $cdot$ = oct "001"; $diamond$ = oct "005";
$plus\_minus$ = oct "006"; o_plus = oct "010"; o_times = oct "012";
eqv = oct "021"; leq = oct "024"; geq = oct "025";
$subset$ = oct "032"; $superset$ = oct "033";
$left\_arrow$ = oct "040"; $right\_arrow$ = oct "041";
up_arrow = oct "042"; $down\_arrow$ = oct "043"; $double\_arrow$ = oct "044";
$infty$ = oct "061"; elt = oct "062";
for_all = oct "070"; $there\_exists$ = oct "071"; $false\_that$ = oct "072";
cup = oct "133"; cap = oct "134"; $meet$ = oct "136"; $join$ = oct "137";
$left\_brace$ = oct "146"; $right\_brace$ = oct "147"; $vertical$ = oct "152";
$backslash$ = oct "156"; $integral$ = oct "163";

input sym;   % symbols common to other fonts

cmchar "Times operator";
beginarithchar(oct "002"); **pickup** $rule.nib$;
$x_1 = good.x(1/\text{ sqrt } 2)[.5w, rt\ u]$; $y_1 = good.y(1/\text{ sqrt } 2)[math\_axis, bot\ h]$;
$x_2 = x_3 = w - x_1$; $x_4 = x_1$; $.5[y_1, y_2] = .5[y_3, y_4] = math\_axis$; $y_2 = y_4$;
draw z_1 -- z_2; **draw** z_3 -- z_4;   % diagonals
labels$(1, 2, 3, 4)$; **endchar**;

cmchar "Elementary division operator";
beginarithchar(oct "004"); **pickup** $rule.nib$;
$x_3 - .5dot\_size = \text{hround}(.5w - .5dot\_size)$; $w := r := 2x_3$;
$y_3 + .5dot\_size = \text{vround}(math\_axis + math\_spread[.5x\_height, .6x\_height] + .5dot\_size)$;
$lft\ x_1 = \text{hround } u - eps$; $x_2 = w - x_1$; $y_1 = y_2 = math\_axis$;
draw z_1 -- z_2;   % bar
$pos_3(dot\_size, 0)$; $pos_4(dot\_size, 90)$; $z_3 = z_4$;
$pos_5(dot\_size, 0)$; $pos_6(dot\_size, 90)$; $z_5 = z_6$; $x_5 = x_3$; $.5[y_3, y_5] = math\_axis$;
$dot(3, 4)$; $dot(5, 6)$;   % dots
penlabels$(1, 2, 3, 4, 5, 6)$; **endchar**;

---

def $beginarithchar($**expr** $c) =$ % ensure consistent dimensions for +, −, etc.
  if $monospace$: **beginchar**$(c, 14u\#, {}^{27}/_7 u\# + math\_axis\#, {}^{27}/_7 u\# - math\_axis\#)$;
  else: **beginchar**$(c, 14u\#, 6u\# + math\_axis\#, 6u\# - math\_axis\#)$; **fi**
  italcorr $math\_axis\# * slant - .5u\#$;
  adjust_fit$(0, 0)$; **enddef**;

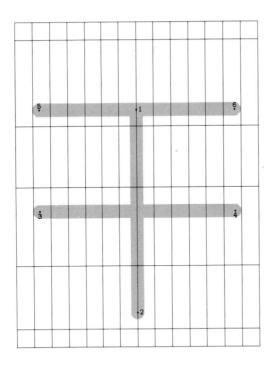

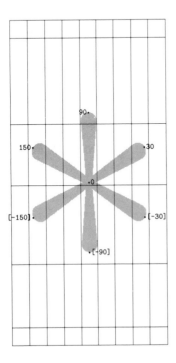

cmchar "Minus-or-plus sign";
beginarithchar(oct "007"); **pickup** *rule.nib*;
numeric *shiftup*; *shiftup* $= -$ vround $1.5u$;
$x_1 = x_2 = .5w$; *lft* $x_3 = $ *lft* $= x_5 = $ hround $u - eps$; $x_4 = x_6 = w - x_3$;
$.5[y_1, y_2] = y_3 = y_4 = math\_axis + shiftup$; *top* $y_1 = h + shiftup$; $y_5 = y_6 = y_1$;
draw z_1 -- z_2;   % stem
draw z_3 -- z_4;   % plus bar
draw z_5 -- z_6;   % minus bar
labels$(1, 2, 3, 4, 5, 6)$; **endchar**;

cmchar "Asterisk at the axis";
beginchar(oct "003", $9u^\#$, $v\_center(x\_height^\#)$);
adjust_fit$(0, 0)$;
numeric *ast_flare*; *ast_flare* $= $ hround $.7[thin\_join, stem]$;
$x_0 = .5w$; $y_0 = h - .5x\_height$;
for $d = -150$ **step** 60 **until** 150: $z[d] = z_0 + .5$ dir d xscaled $7.5u$ yscaled x_height;
  numeric *theta*; *theta* $= $ angle$(z[d] - z_0)$;
  fill $z_0 + .5(0, -thin\_join)$ rotated *theta*
    --- $z[d] + .5(-ast\_flare, -ast\_flare)$ rotated *theta*
    .. $z[d]$ .. $z[d] + .5(-ast\_flare, ast\_flare)$ rotated *theta*
    --- $z_0 + .5(0, thin\_join)$ rotated *theta* -- cycle; **endfor**   % diagonal at angle d
labels$(0, [-150], [-90], [-30], 30, 90, 150)$; **endchar**;

> The Asterism, used as a Reference,
> has a proper position for its figure;
> but for all other purposes it would be better
> to be in the middle of its Shank.
> — PHILIP LUCKOMBE, *The History and Art of Printing* (1770)

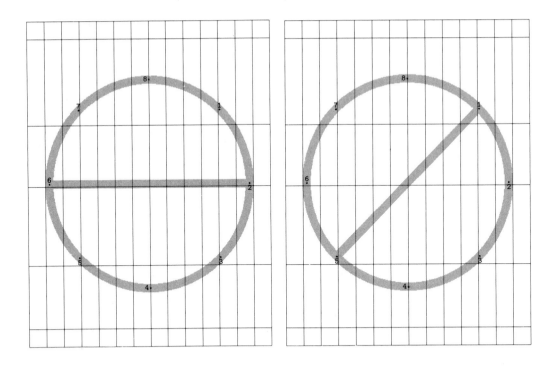

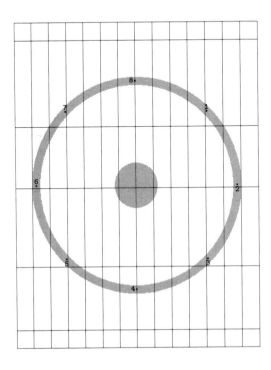

cmchar "Circle-minus operator";
beginarithchar(oct "011"); **pickup** *light_rule.nib*; *autorounded*;
lft $x_6 = $ hround u; $x_2 = w - x_6$; $y_2 = math\_axis$; *top* $y_8 = h$;
circle_points; *draw_circle*;   % circle
draw $z_2 -- z_6$;   % bar
labels(1, 2, 3, 4, 5, 6, 7, 8); **endchar**;

cmchar "Circle-divide operator";
beginarithchar(oct "013"); **pickup** *light_rule.nib*; *autorounded*;
lft $x_6 = $ hround u; $x_2 = w - x_6$; $y_2 = math\_axis$; *top* $y_8 = h$;
circle_points; *draw_circle*;   % circle
draw $z_1 -- z_5$;   % diagonal
labels(1, 2, 3, 4, 5, 6, 7, 8); **endchar**;

cmchar "Circle-dot operator";
beginarithchar(oct "014"); **pickup** *light_rule.nib*; *autorounded*;
lft $x_6 = $ hround u; $x_2 = w - x_6$; $y_2 = math\_axis$; *top* $y_8 = h$;
circle_points; *draw_circle*;   % circle
fill *fullcircle* scaled $(1.3 dot\_size + eps)$ shifted $(.5[z_4, z_8])$;   % dot
labels(1, 2, 3, 4, 5, 6, 7, 8); **endchar**;

---

def *circle_points* $=$
   $x_4 = x_8 = .5[x_2, x_6]$; $x_1 = x_3 = superness[x_4, x_2]$; $x_5 = x_7 = superness[x_4, x_6]$;
   $y_2 = y_6 = .5[y_4, y_8]$; $y_1 = y_7 = superness[y_2, y_8]$; $y_3 = y_5 = superness[y_2, y_4]$;
   enddef;

def *draw_circle* $=$
   draw $z_8\{right\} \ldots z_1\{z_2 - z_8\} \ldots z_2\{down\} \ldots z_3\{z_4 - z_2\} \ldots z_4\{left\}$
   $\ldots z_5\{z_6 - z_4\} \ldots z_6\{up\} \ldots z_7\{z_8 - z_6\} \ldots$ cycle **enddef**;

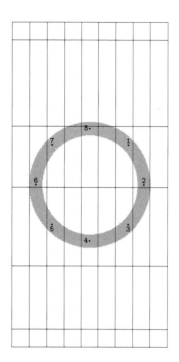

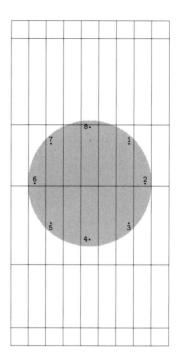

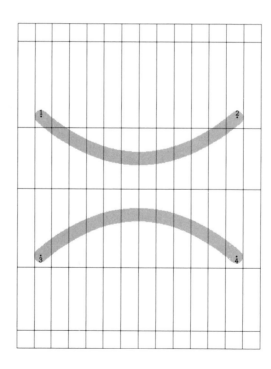

cmchar "Circle operator";
beginchar(oct "016", $9u\#$, $v\_center(7u\#)$);
adjust_fit$(0, 0)$; **pickup** *rule.nib*; *autorounded*;
lft $x_6 =$ hround u; $x_2 = w - x_6$; *top* $y_8 = h$; $y_2 = math\_axis$;
circle_points; *draw_circle*; % circle
labels$(1, 2, 3, 4, 5, 6, 7, 8)$; **endchar**;

cmchar "Bullet";
beginchar(oct "017", $9u\#$, $v\_center(7u\#)$);
adjust_fit$(0, 0)$; **pickup** *rule.nib*; *autorounded*;
lft $x_6 =$ hround u; $x_2 = w - x_6$; *top* $y_8 = h$; $y_2 = math\_axis$; *circle_points*;
filldraw $z_8\{right\} \ldots z_1\{z_2 - z_8\} \ldots z_2\{down\} \ldots z_3\{z_4 - z_2\} \ldots z_4\{left\}$
$\ldots z_5\{z_6 - z_4\} \ldots z_6\{up\} \ldots z_7\{z_8 - z_6\} \ldots$ cycle; % circle and interior
labels$(1, 2, 3, 4, 5, 6, 7, 8)$; **endchar**;

cmchar "Hardy's asymptotic equivalence sign";
compute_spread$(.45x\_height\#, .55x\_height\#)$;
beginchar(oct "020", $14u\#$, $v\_center(2spread\# + rule\_thickness\#)$);
adjust_fit$(0, 0)$; **pickup** *rule.nib*; *autorounded*;
lft $x_1 =$ hround $u - eps$; $x_3 = x_1$; $x_2 = x_4 = w - x_1$; $x_5 = x_6 = .5w$;
$y_1 = y_2 = good.y\ h$; $y_3 = y_4$; $.5[y_1, y_3] = .5[y_5, y_6] = math\_axis$;
$y_5 = good.y\ .3[y_1, y_3]$;
draw $z_1\{x_5 - x_1, 2(y_5 - y_1)\} \ldots z_5\{right\} \ldots z_2\{x_2 - x_5, 2(y_2 - y_5)\}$; % upper bar
draw $z_3\{x_6 - x_3, 2(y_6 - y_3)\} \ldots z_6\{right\} \ldots z_4\{x_4 - x_6, 2(y_4 - y_6)\}$; % lower bar
labels$(1, 2, 3, 4)$; **endchar**;

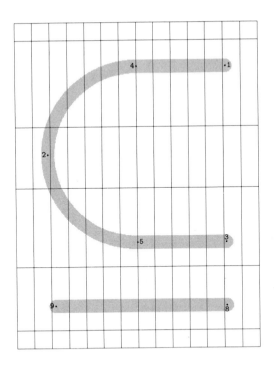

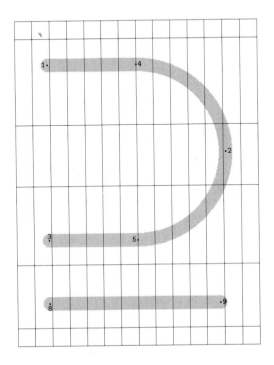

cmchar "Subset or equal to sign";
compute_spread($.45x\_height^\#$, $.55x\_height^\#$);
$spread^{\#'} := spread^\#$; $spread' := spread$;   % the spread of '='
compute_spread($^5/_4x\_height^\#$, $^3/_2x\_height^\#$);
beginchar(oct "022", $14u^\#$, $v\_center(spread^{\#'} + spread^\# + rule\_thickness^\#)$);
adjust_fit$(0, 0)$; **pickup** *rule.nib*; *autorounded*;
lft $x_2 =$ hround $1.5u - eps$; $x_1 = x_3 = w - x_2$;
$y_1 - y_3 = spread$; $y_2 = .5[y_1, y_3]$; *top* $y_1 = h$;
$x_4 = x_5 = .5w$; $y_4 = y_1$; $y_5 = y_3$;
draw z_1 --- z_4 ... $z_2\{down\}$ ... z_5 --- z_3;   % arc and bars
$x_8 = x_1$; *lft* $x_9 = x_2$; $y_8 = y_9$; $y_3 - y_9 = spread'$; **draw** z_8 -- z_9;   % lower bar
labels$(1, 2, 3, 4, 5, 8, 9)$; **endchar**;

cmchar "Superset or equal to sign";
compute_spread($.45x\_height^\#$, $.55x\_height^\#$);
$spread^{\#'} := spread^\#$; $spread' := spread$;   % the spread of '='
compute_spread($^5/_4x\_height^\#$, $^3/_2x\_height^\#$);
beginchar(oct "023", $14u^\#$, $v\_center(spread^{\#'} + spread^\# + rule\_thickness^\#)$);
adjust_fit$(0, 0)$; **pickup** *rule.nib*; *autorounded*;
lft $x_1 =$ hround $1.5u - eps$; $x_2 = w - x_1$; $x_3 = x_1$;
$y_1 - y_3 = spread$; $y_2 = .5[y_1, y_3]$; *top* $y_1 = h$;
$x_4 = x_5 = .5w$; $y_4 = y_1$; $y_5 = y_3$;
draw z_1 --- z_4 ... $z_2\{down\}$ ... z_5 --- z_3;   % arc and bars
$x_8 = x_1$; *rt* $x_9 = x_2$; $y_8 = y_9$; $y_3 - y_9 = spread'$; **draw** z_8 -- z_9;   % lower bar
labels$(1, 2, 3, 4, 5, 8, 9)$; **endchar**;

---

def *compute_spread*(**expr** *normal_spread*, *big_spread*) =
  $spread^\# := math\_spread[normal\_spread, big\_spread]$;
  $spread :=$ ceiling$(spread^\# * hppp) + eps$; **enddef**;

def *v_center*(**expr** *h_sharp*) =
  $.5h\_sharp + math\_axis^\#$, $.5h\_sharp - math\_axis^\#$ **enddef**;

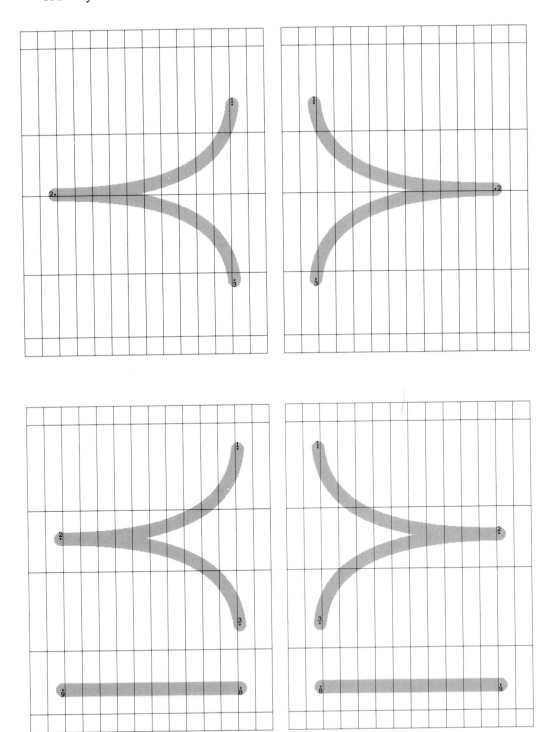

cmchar "Precedes sign";
compute_spread($5/4x\_height^\#$, $3/2x\_height^\#$);
beginchar(oct "036", $14u^\#$, *v_center*($spread^\# + rule\_thickness^\#$));
adjust_fit$(0, 0)$; **pickup** *rule.nib*; *autorounded*;
lft x_2 = hround $1.5u - epsilon$; $x_1 = x_3 = w - x_2$;
$y_1 - y_3 = spread$; $y_2 = .5[y_1, y_3]$; *top* $y_1 = h$;
draw $z_1\{-u, -spread\} \ldots \{left\}z_2$;   % upper diagonal
draw $z_3\{-u, spread\} \ldots \{left\}z_2$;   % lower diagonal
labels$(1, 2, 3)$; **endchar**;

cmchar "Follows sign";
compute_spread($5/4x\_height^\#$, $3/2x\_height^\#$);
beginchar(oct "037", $14u^\#$, *v_center*($spread^\# + rule\_thickness^\#$));
adjust_fit$(0, 0)$; **pickup** *rule.nib*; *autorounded*;
lft x_1 = hround $1.5u - epsilon$; $x_2 = w - x_1$; $x_3 = x_1$;
$y_1 - y_3 = spread$; $y_2 = .5[y_1, y_3]$; *top* $y_1 = h$;
draw $z_1\{u, -spread\} \ldots \{right\}z_2$;   % upper diagonal
draw $z_3\{u, spread\} \ldots \{right\}z_2$;   % lower diagonal
labels$(1, 2, 3)$; **endchar**;

cmchar "Precedes or equals sign";
compute_spread($.45x\_height^\#$, $.55x\_height^\#$);
$spread^{\#\prime} := spread^\#$; $spread^\prime := spread$;   % the spread of '='
compute_spread($5/4x\_height^\#$, $3/2x\_height^\#$);
beginchar(oct "026", $14u^\#$, *v_center*($spread^{\#\prime} + spread^\# + rule\_thickness^\#$));
adjust_fit$(0, 0)$; **pickup** *rule.nib*; *autorounded*;
lft x_2 = hround $1.5u - eps$; $x_1 = x_3 = w - x_2$;
$y_1 - y_3 = spread$; $y_2 = .5[y_1, y_3]$; *top* $y_1 = h$;
draw $z_1\{-u, -spread\} \ldots \{left\}z_2$;   % upper diagonal
draw $z_3\{-u, spread\} \ldots \{left\}z_2$;   % lower diagonal
$x_8 = x_1$; $x_9 = x_2$; $y_8 = y_9$; $y_3 - y_9 = spread^\prime$; **draw** $z_8 \,\text{--}\, z_9$;   % bar
labels$(1, 2, 3, 8, 9)$; **endchar**;

cmchar "Follows or equals sign";
compute_spread($.45x\_height^\#$, $.55x\_height^\#$);
$spread^{\#\prime} := spread^\#$; $spread^\prime := spread$;   % the spread of '='
compute_spread($5/4x\_height^\#$, $3/2x\_height^\#$);
beginchar(oct "027", $14u^\#$, *v_center*($spread^{\#\prime} + spread^\# + rule\_thickness^\#$));
adjust_fit$(0, 0)$; **pickup** *rule.nib*; *autorounded*;
lft x_1 = hround $1.5u - eps$; $x_2 = w - x_1$; $x_3 = x_1$;
$y_1 - y_3 = spread$; $y_2 = .5[y_1, y_3]$; *top* $y_1 = h$;
draw $z_1\{u, -spread\} \ldots \{right\}z_2$;   % upper diagonal
draw $z_3\{u, spread\} \ldots \{right\}z_2$;   % lower diagonal
$x_8 = x_1$; $x_9 = x_2$; $y_8 = y_9$; $y_3 - y_9 = spread^\prime$; **draw** $z_8 \,\text{--}\, z_9$;   % bar
labels$(1, 2, 3, 8, 9)$; **endchar**;

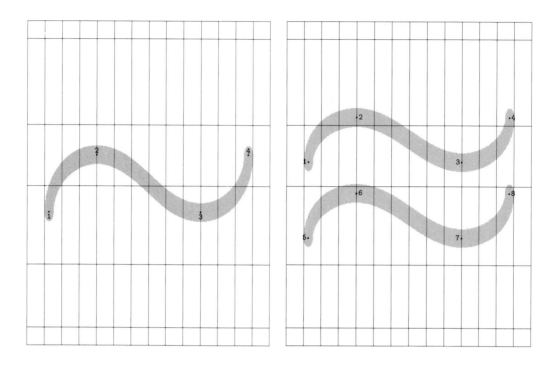

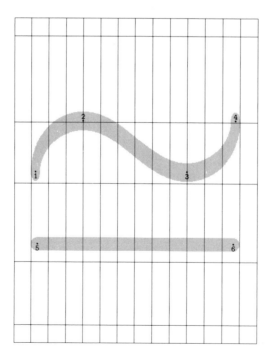

cmchar "Similarity sign";
compute_spread$(.45x\_height^\#, .55x\_height^\#)$;
beginchar(oct "030", $14u^\#$, $v\_center(spread^\# + rule\_thickness^\#)$);
adjust_fit$(0, 0)$;
pickup pencircle xscaled $.7rule\_thickness$ yscaled $1.4rule\_thickness$;
if $vair^\# > .8curve^\#$: **pickup** $rule.nib$; *autorounded*; **fi**   % monoline
lft $x_1 = $ hround u; $x_2 = 4u$; $x_3 = w - x_2$; $x_4 = w - x_1$;
bot $y_1 = bot$ $y_3 = -d$; *top* $y_2 = top$ $y_4 = h$;
draw $z_1\{up\} \ldots z_2\{right\} .. \{right\}z_3 \ldots \{up\}z_4$;   % stroke
labels$(1, 2, 3, 4)$; **endchar**;

cmchar "Approximate equality sign";
compute_spread$(.45x\_height^\#, .55x\_height^\#)$;
$spread^{\#'} := spread^\#$; $spread' := spread$;   % the spread of '='
compute_spread$(.54x\_height^\#, .66x\_height^\#)$;
beginchar(oct "031", $14u^\#$, $v\_center(spread^{\#'} + spread^\# + rule\_thickness^\#)$);
adjust_fit$(0, 0)$;
pickup pencircle xscaled $.7rule\_thickness$ yscaled $1.4rule\_thickness$;
if $vair^\# > .8curve^\#$: **pickup** $rule.nib$; *autorounded*; **fi**   % monoline
lft $x_1 = $ hround u; $x_2 = 4u$; $x_3 = w - x_2$; $x_4 = w - x_1$;
$y_1 = y_3$; *top* $y_2 = top$ $y_4 = h$; *top* $y_2 - bot$ $y_1 = spread'$;
draw $z_1\{up\} \ldots z_2\{right\} .. \{right\}z_3 \ldots \{up\}z_4$;   % upper stroke
$z_1 - z_5 = z_2 - z_6 = z_3 - z_7 = z_4 - z_8 = (0, spread)$;
draw $z_5\{up\} \ldots z_6\{right\} .. \{right\}z_7 \ldots \{up\}z_8$;   % lower stroke
labels$(1, 2, 3, 4, 5, 6, 7, 8)$; **endchar**;

cmchar "Similar or equal sign";
compute_spread$(.45x\_height^\#, .55x\_height^\#)$;
beginchar(oct "047", $14u^\#$, $v\_center(2spread^\# + rule\_thickness^\#)$);
adjust_fit$(0, 0)$;
pickup pencircle xscaled $.7rule\_thickness$ yscaled $1.4rule\_thickness$;
if $vair^\# > .8curve^\#$: **pickup** $rule.nib$; *autorounded*; **fi**   % monoline
lft $x_1 = $ hround u; $x_2 = 4u$; $x_3 = w - x_2$; $x_4 = w - x_1$;
bot $y_1 = bot$ $y_3 = $ floor $math\_axis$; *top* $y_2 = top$ $y_4 = h$;
draw $z_1\{up\} \ldots z_2\{right\} .. \{right\}z_3 \ldots \{up\}z_4$;   % stroke
pickup $rule.nib$; *lft* $x_5 = $ hround $u - eps$; $x_6 = w - x_5$; $y_5 = y_6 = math\_axis - spread$;
draw $z_5 -- z_6$;   % bar
labels$(1, 2, 3, 4, 5, 6)$; **endchar**;

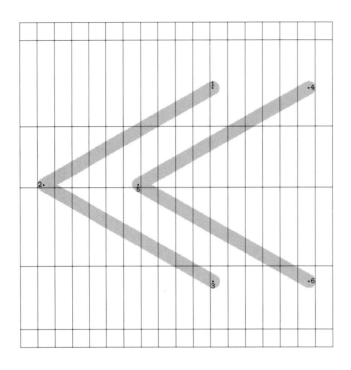

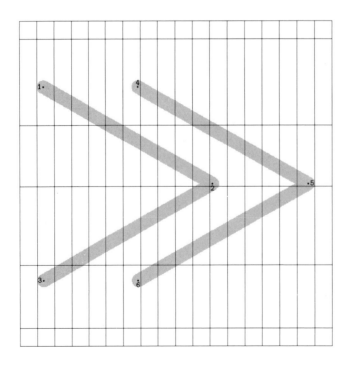

cmchar "Much less sign";
compute_spread($5/4x\_height^\#$, $3/2x\_height^\#$);
beginchar(oct "034", $18u^\#$, *v_center*(*spread*$^\#$ + *rule_thickness*$^\#$));
adjust_fit(**if** *monospace*: $-u^\#$, $-u^\#$ **else**: $0, 0$ **fi**); **pickup** *rule.nib*;
lft x_2 = hround $u - epsilon$; $x_1 = x_3$ = hround $12.5u - x_2$;
$y_1 - y_3$ = ceiling $1.1spread$; $y_2 = .5[y_1, y_3]$ = *math_axis*;
draw z_1 -- z_2 -- z_3;   % left diagonals
$z_4 - z_1 = z_5 - z_2 = z_6 - z_3$; $x_4 = w - x_2$; $y_4 = y_1$;
draw z_4 -- z_5 -- z_6;   % right diagonals
labels$(1, 2, 3, 4, 5, 6)$; **endchar**;

cmchar "Much greater sign";
compute_spread($5/4x\_height^\#$, $3/2x\_height^\#$);
beginchar(oct "035", $18u^\#$, *v_center*(*spread*$^\#$ + *rule_thickness*$^\#$));
adjust_fit(**if** *monospace*: $-u^\#$, $-u^\#$ **else**: $0, 0$ **fi**); **pickup** *rule.nib*;
lft x_1 = hround $u - epsilon$; x_2 = hround $12.5u - x_1$; $x_3 = x_1$;
$y_1 - y_3$ = ceiling $1.1spread$; $y_2 = .5[y_1, y_3]$ = *math_axis*;
draw z_1 -- z_2 -- z_3;   % left diagonals
$z_4 - z_1 = z_5 - z_2 = z_6 - z_3$; $x_4 = w - x_2$; $y_4 = y_1$;
draw z_4 -- z_5 -- z_6;   % right diagonals
labels$(1, 2, 3, 4, 5, 6)$; **endchar**;

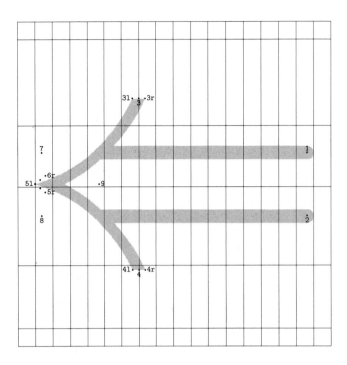

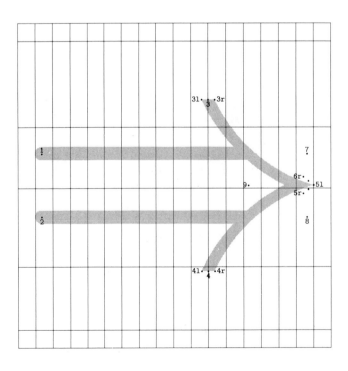

cmchar "Double leftward arrow";
compute_spread$(.45x\_height^{\#}, .55x\_height^{\#})$;
beginchar(oct "050", $18u^{\#}$, $v\_center(spread^{\#} + rule\_thickness^{\#})$);
adjust_fit$(0, 0)$; **pickup** *rule.nib*;
lft x_7 = hround $u - eps$; $x_8 = x_7$; $x_1 = x_2 = w - x_7$;
$y_1 = y_7$; $y_2 = y_8$; $y_1 - y_2 = spread$; $.5[y_1, y_2] = math\_axis$;
draw $z_1 \mathbin{--} z_7$; **draw** $z_2 \mathbin{--} z_8$; % bars
pickup *crisp.nib*; *lft* x_0 = hround $u - eps$; $y_0 = good.y\ math\_axis$;
$pos_3(rule\_thickness, 0)$; $pos_4(rule\_thickness, 0)$;
$y_3 - y_1 = y_2 - y_4 = .24asc\_height + eps$; $x_3 = x_4 = x_0 + 6u + eps$;
$pos_5(rule\_thickness, \text{angle}(z_4 - z_0))$; $z_{5l} = z_0$;
$pos_6(rule\_thickness, \text{angle}(z_3 - z_0))$; $z_{6l} = z_0$;
$z_9 = .381966[.5[z_3, z_4], z_0]$;
erase filldraw $z_0 \mathbin{..} \{z_3 - z_9\}z_3 \mathbin{--} (0, y_3)$
$\mathbin{--} (0, y_4) \mathbin{--} z_4\{z_9 - z_4\} \mathbin{..} z_0$ & cycle; % erase excess
numeric t; **path** p; $p = z_{4r}\{z_9 - z_4\} \mathbin{..} z_{6r}$;
$t = \text{xpart}(p \text{ intersectiontimes } ((0, y_0) \mathbin{--} (w, y_0)))$;
filldraw $z_0 \mathbin{..} \{z_4 - z_9\}z_{4l} \mathbin{--}$ **subpath**$(0, t)$ **of** $(z_{4r}\{z_9 - z_4\} \mathbin{..} z_{6r})$
$\mathbin{--}$ **subpath**$(t, 0)$ **of** $(z_{3r}\{z_9 - z_3\} \mathbin{..} z_{5r}) \mathbin{--} z_{3l}\{z_9 - z_3\} \mathbin{..} z_0$ & cycle; % arrowhead
penlabels$(0, 1, 2, 3, 4, 5, 6, 7, 8, 9)$; **endchar**;

cmchar "Double rightward arrow";
compute_spread$(.45x\_height^{\#}, .55x\_height^{\#})$;
beginchar(oct "051", $18u^{\#}$, $v\_center(spread^{\#} + rule\_thickness^{\#})$);
adjust_fit$(0, 0)$; **pickup** *rule.nib*;
lft x_1 = hround $u - eps$; $x_2 = x_1$; $x_7 = x_8 = w - x_1$;
$y_1 = y_7$; $y_2 = y_8$; $y_1 - y_2 = spread$; $.5[y_1, y_2] = math\_axis$;
draw $z_1 \mathbin{--} z_7$; **draw** $z_2 \mathbin{--} z_8$; % bars
pickup *crisp.nib*; *rt* x_0 = hround$(w - u) + eps$; $y_0 = good.y\ math\_axis$;
$pos_3(rule\_thickness, 0)$; $pos_4(rule\_thickness, 0)$;
$y_3 - y_1 = y_2 - y_4 = .24asc\_height + eps$; $x_3 = x_4 = x_0 - 6u - eps$;
$pos_5(rule\_thickness, \text{angle}(z_4 - z_0))$; $z_{5l} = z_0$;
$pos_6(rule\_thickness, \text{angle}(z_3 - z_0))$; $z_{6l} = z_0$;
$z_9 = .381966[.5[z_3, z_4], z_0]$;
erase filldraw $z_0 \mathbin{..} \{z_3 - z_9\}z_3 \mathbin{--} (w, y_3)$
$\mathbin{--} (w, y_4) \mathbin{--} z_4\{z_9 - z_4\} \mathbin{..} z_0$ & cycle; % erase excess
numeric t; **path** p; $p = z_{4l}\{z_9 - z_4\} \mathbin{..} z_{6r}$;
$t = \text{xpart}(p \text{ intersectiontimes } ((0, y_0) \mathbin{--} (w, y_0)))$;
filldraw $z_0 \mathbin{..} \{z_4 - z_9\}z_{4r} \mathbin{--}$ **subpath**$(0, t)$ **of** $(z_{4l}\{z_9 - z_4\} \mathbin{..} z_{6r})$
$\mathbin{--}$ **subpath**$(t, 0)$ **of** $(z_{3l}\{z_9 - z_3\} \mathbin{..} z_{5r}) \mathbin{--} z_{3r}\{z_9 - z_3\} \mathbin{..} z_0$ & cycle; % arrowhead
penlabels$(0, 1, 2, 3, 4, 5, 6, 7, 8, 9)$; **endchar**;

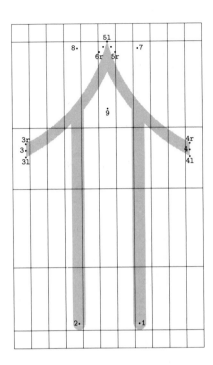

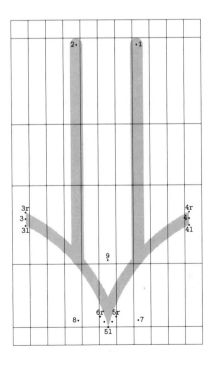

cmchar "Double upward arrow";
beginchar(oct "052", $11u^\#$, $asc\_height^\#$, $asc\_depth^\#$);
adjust_fit$(0, 0)$; **pickup** $rule.nib$;
$compute\_spread(.45x\_height^\#, .55x\_height^\#)$;
$bot\ y_1 = bot\ y_2 = -d - eps$; $top\ y_7 = h$; $y_8 = y_7$;
$x_1 = x_7$; $x_2 = x_8$; $x_1 - x_2 = spread$; $.5[x_1, x_2] = crisp.lft$ hround$(crisp.rt\ .5w)$;
draw z_1 -- z_7; **draw** z_2 -- z_8; % bars
pickup $crisp.nib$; $top\ y_0 = h + eps$; $x_0 = good.x\ .5w$;
$pos_3(rule\_thickness, 90)$; $pos_4(rule\_thickness, 90)$;
$x_2 - x_3 = x_4 - x_1 = 3u + eps$; $y_3 = y_4 = y_0 - .48asc\_height - eps$;
$pos_5(rule\_thickness, \text{angle}(z_4 - z_0))$; $z_{5l} = z_0$;
$pos_6(rule\_thickness, \text{angle}(z_3 - z_0))$; $z_{6l} = z_0$;
$z_9 = .381966[.5[z_3, z_4], z_0]$;
erase filldraw z_0 .. $\{z_3 - z_9\}z_3$ -- (x_3, h)
   -- (x_4, h) -- $z_4\{z_9 - z_4\}$ .. z_0 & cycle; % erase excess
numeric t; **path** p; $p = z_{4l}\{z_9 - z_4\}$ .. z_{6r};
$t = \text{xpart}(p\ \text{intersectiontimes}\ ((x_0, -d)$ -- $(x_0, h)))$;
filldraw z_0 .. $\{z_4 - z_9\}z_{4r}$ -- **subpath**$(0, t)$ **of** $(z_{4l}\{z_9 - z_4\}$ .. $z_{6r})$
   -- **subpath**$(t, 0)$ **of** $(z_{3l}\{z_9 - z_3\}$ .. $z_{5r})$ -- $z_{3r}\{z_9 - z_3\}$ .. z_0 & cycle; % arrowhead
penlabels$(0, 1, 2, 3, 4, 5, 6, 7, 8, 9)$; **endchar**;

cmchar "Double downward arrow";
beginchar(oct "053", $11u^\#$, $asc\_height^\#$, $asc\_depth^\#$);
adjust_fit$(0, 0)$; **pickup** $rule.nib$;
$compute\_spread(.45x\_height^\#, .55x\_height^\#)$;
$top\ y_1 = top\ y_2 = h + eps$; $bot\ y_7 = -d$; $y_8 = y_7$;
$x_1 = x_7$; $x_2 = x_8$; $x_1 - x_2 = spread$; $.5[x_1, x_2] = crisp.lft$ hround$(crisp.rt\ .5w)$;
draw z_1 -- z_7; **draw** z_2 -- z_8; % bars
pickup $crisp.nib$; $bot\ y_0 = -d - eps$; $x_0 = good.x\ .5w$;
$pos_3(rule\_thickness, 90)$; $pos_4(rule\_thickness, 90)$;
$x_2 - x_3 = x_4 - x_1 = 3u + eps$; $y_3 = y_4 = y_0 + .48asc\_height - eps$;
$pos_5(rule\_thickness, \text{angle}(z_4 - z_0))$; $z_{5l} = z_0$;
$pos_6(rule\_thickness, \text{angle}(z_3 - z_0))$; $z_{6l} = z_0$;
$z_9 = .381966[.5[z_3, z_4], z_0]$;
erase filldraw z_0 .. $\{z_3 - z_9\}z_3$ -- $(x_3, -d)$
   -- $(x_4, -d)$ -- $z_4\{z_9 - z_4\}$ .. z_0 & cycle; % erase excess
numeric t; **path** p; $p = z_{4r}\{z_9 - z_4\}$ .. z_{6r};
$t = \text{xpart}(p\ \text{intersectiontimes}\ ((x_0, -d)$ -- $(x_0, h)))$;
filldraw z_0 .. $\{z_4 - z_9\}z_{4l}$ -- **subpath**$(0, t)$ **of** $(z_{4r}\{z_9 - z_4\}$ .. $z_{6r})$
   -- **subpath**$(t, 0)$ **of** $(z_{3r}\{z_9 - z_3\}$ .. $z_{5r})$ -- $z_{3l}\{z_9 - z_3\}$ .. z_0 & cycle; % arrowhead
penlabels$(0, 1, 2, 3, 4, 5, 6, 7, 8, 9)$; **endchar**;

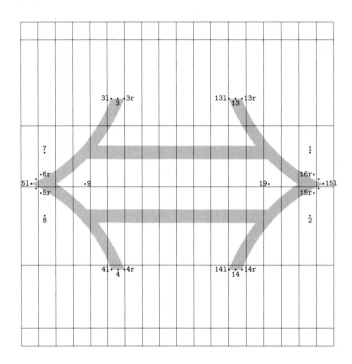

cmchar "Double left-and-right arrow";
compute_spread(.45*x_height*#, .55*x_height*#);
beginchar(oct "054", 18*u*#, *v_center*(*spread*# + *rule_thickness*#));
adjust_fit(**if** *monospace*: −*u*#, −*u*# **else**: 0, 0 **fi**); **pickup** *rule.nib*;
lft x_7 = hround $u - eps$; $x_8 = x_7$; $x_1 = x_2 = w - x_7$;
$y_1 = y_7$; $y_2 = y_8$; $y_1 - y_2 = spread$; $.5[y_1, y_2] = math\_axis$;
draw z_1 -- z_7; **draw** z_2 -- z_8;   % bars
pickup *crisp.nib*; *lft* x_0 = hround $u - o$; $y_0 = good.y\ math\_axis$;
$pos_3(rule\_thickness, 0)$; $pos_4(rule\_thickness, 0)$;
$y_3 - y_1 = y_2 - y_4 = .24asc\_height + eps$; $x_3 = x_4 = x_0 + 5u + eps$;
$pos_5(rule\_thickness, \text{angle}(z_4 - z_0))$; $z_{5l} = z_0$;
$pos_6(rule\_thickness, \text{angle}(z_3 - z_0))$; $z_{6l} = z_0$;
$z_9 = .381966[.5[z_3, z_4], z_0]$;
erase filldraw z_0 .. $\{z_3 - z_9\}z_3$ -- $(0, y_3)$
    -- $(0, y_4)$ -- $z_4\{z_9 - z_4\}$ .. z_0 & cycle;   % erase excess at left
numeric *t*; **path** *p*; $p = z_{4r}\{z_9 - z_4\}$ .. z_{6r};
$t = \text{xpart}(p \text{ intersectiontimes } ((0, y_0) \text{ -- } (w, y_0)))$;
filldraw z_0 .. $\{z_4 - z_9\}z_{4l}$ -- **subpath**$(0, t)$ **of** $(z_{4r}\{z_9 - z_4\}$ .. $z_{6r})$
    -- **subpath**$(t, 0)$ **of** $(z_{3r}\{z_9 - z_3\}$ .. $z_{5r})$
    -- $z_{3l}\{z_9 - z_3\}$ .. z_0 & cycle;   % left arrowhead
rt x_{10} = hround$(w - u) + o$; $y_{10} = good.y\ math\_axis$;
$pos_{13}(rule\_thickness, 0)$; $pos_{14}(rule\_thickness, 0)$;
$y_{13} = y_3$; $y_{14} = y_4$; $x_{13} = x_{14} = x_{10} - 5u - eps$;
$pos_{15}(rule\_thickness, \text{angle}(z_{14} - z_{10}))$; $z_{15l} = z_{10}$;
$pos_{16}(rule\_thickness, \text{angle}(z_{13} - z_{10}))$; $z_{16l} = z_{10}$;
$z_{19} = .381966[.5[z_{13}, z_{14}], z_{10}]$;
erase filldraw z_{10} .. $\{z_{13} - z_{19}\}z_{13}$ -- (w, y_{13})
    -- (w, y_{14}) -- $z_{14}\{z_{19} - z_{14}\}$ .. z_{10} & cycle;   % erase excess at right
numeric *t*; **path** *p*; $p = z_{14l}\{z_{19} - z_{14}\}$ .. z_{16r};
$t = \text{xpart}(p \text{ intersectiontimes } ((0, y_{10}) \text{ -- } (w, y_{10})))$;
filldraw z_{10} .. $\{z_{14} - z_{19}\}z_{14r}$ -- **subpath**$(0, t)$ **of** $(z_{14l}\{z_{19} - z_{14}\}$ .. $z_{16r})$
    -- **subpath**$(t, 0)$ **of** $(z_{13l}\{z_{19} - z_{13}\}$ .. $z_{15r})$
    -- $z_{13r}\{z_{19} - z_{13}\}$ .. z_{10} & cycle;   % right arrowhead
penlabels(0, 1, 2, 3, 4, 5, 6, 7, 8, 9, 10, 13, 14, 15, 16, 19); **endchar**;

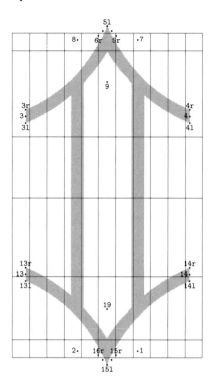

cmchar "Double up-and-down arrow";
beginchar(oct "155", $11u^\#$, $body\_height^\#$, $paren\_depth^\#$);
adjust_fit$(0, 0)$; **pickup** $rule.nib$;
$compute\_spread(.45x\_height^\#, .55x\_height^\#)$;
$bot\ y_1 = bot\ y_2 = -d - eps$; $top\ y_7 = h$; $y_8 = y_7$;
$x_1 = x_7$; $x_2 = x_8$; $x_1 - x_2 = spread$; $.5[x_1, x_2] = crisp.lft$ hround$(crisp.rt\ .5w)$;
draw z_1 -- z_7; **draw** z_2 -- z_8;   % bars
pickup $crisp.nib$; $top\ y_0 = h + o$; $x_0 = good.x\ .5w$;
$pos_3(rule\_thickness, 90)$; $pos_4(rule\_thickness, 90)$;
$x_2 - x_3 = x_4 - x_1 = 3u + eps$; $y_3 = y_4 = y_0 - .4asc\_height - eps$;
$pos_5(rule\_thickness, angle(z_4 - z_0))$; $z_{5l} = z_0$;
$pos_6(rule\_thickness, angle(z_3 - z_0))$; $z_{6l} = z_0$;
$z_9 = .381966[.5[z_3, z_4], z_0]$;
erase filldraw $z_0\ ..\ \{z_3 - z_9\}z_3$ -- (x_3, h)
  -- (x_4, h) -- $z_4\{z_9 - z_4\}\ ..\ z_0$ & cycle;   % erase excess at top
numeric t; **path** p; $p = z_{4l}\{z_9 - z_4\}\ ..\ z_{6r}$;
$t = $ xpart$(p\ $intersectiontimes$\ ((x_0, -d)$ -- $(x_0, h)))$;
filldraw $z_0\ ..\ \{z_4 - z_9\}z_{4r}$ -- **subpath**$(0, t)$ **of** $(z_{4l}\{z_9 - z_4\}\ ..\ z_{6r})$
  -- **subpath**$(t, 0)$ **of** $(z_{3l}\{z_9 - z_3\}\ ..\ z_{5r})$
  -- $z_{3r}\{z_9 - z_3\}\ ..\ z_0$ & cycle;   % top arrowhead
$bot\ y_{10} = -d - o$; $x_{10} = good.x\ .5w$;
$pos_{13}(rule\_thickness, 90)$; $pos_{14}(rule\_thickness, 90)$;
$x_{13} = x_3$; $x_{14} = x_4$; $y_{13} = y_{14} = y_{10} + .4asc\_height - eps$;
$pos_{15}(rule\_thickness, angle(z_{14} - z_{10}))$; $z_{15l} = z_{10}$;
$pos_{16}(rule\_thickness, angle(z_{13} - z_{10}))$; $z_{16l} = z_{10}$;
$z_{19} = .381966[.5[z_{13}, z_{14}], z_{10}]$;
erase filldraw $z_{10}\ ..\ \{z_{13} - z_{19}\}z_{13}$ -- $(x_{13}, -d)$
  -- $(x_{14}, -d)$ -- $z_{14}\{z_{19} - z_{14}\}\ ..\ z_{10}$ & cycle;   % erase excess at bottom
numeric t; **path** p; $p = z_{14r}\{z_{19} - z_{14}\}\ ..\ z_{16r}$;
$t = $ xpart$(p\ $intersectiontimes$\ ((x_{10}, -d)$ -- $(x_{10}, h)))$;
filldraw $z_{10}\ ..\ \{z_{14} - z_{19}\}z_{14l}$ -- **subpath**$(0, t)$ **of** $(z_{14r}\{z_{19} - z_{14}\}\ ..\ z_{16r})$
  -- **subpath**$(t, 0)$ **of** $(z_{13r}\{z_{19} - z_{13}\}\ ..\ z_{15r})$
  -- $z_{13l}\{z_{19} - z_{13}\}\ ..\ z_{10}$ & cycle;   % bottom arrowhead
penlabels$(0, 1, 2, 3, 4, 5, 6, 7, 8, 9, 13, 14, 15, 16, 19)$; **endchar**;

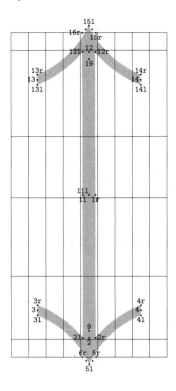

cmchar "Up-and-down arrow";
beginchar(oct "154", $9u^\#$, $body\_height^\#$, $paren\_depth^\#$);
adjust_fit$(0, 0)$; **pickup** $crisp.nib$;
$pos_1(rule\_thickness, 0)$; $pos_2(rule\_thickness, 0)$;
$pos_3(bar, 90)$; $pos_4(bar, 90)$;
lft $x_{1l} = $ hround$(.5w - .5rule\_thickness)$; $y_1 = .5[-d, h]$;
$x_0 = x_1 = x_2$; *bot* $y_0 = -d - o$; $x_0 - x_3 = x_4 - x_0 = 3u + eps$;
$y_3 = y_4 = y_0 + .24asc\_height + eps$;
$pos_5(bar, \text{angle}(z_4 - z_0))$; $z_{5l} = z_0$; $pos_6(bar, \text{angle}(z_3 - z_0))$; $z_{6l} = z_0$;
$z_9 = .381966[.5[z_3, z_4], z_0]$;
numeric t; **path** p; $p = z_{4r}\{z_9 - z_4\} .. z_{6r}$;
$t = $ xpart$(p$ intersectiontimes $((x_{2r}, -d) -\!- (x_{2r}, h)))$; $y_2 = $ ypart **point** t **of** p;
filldraw $z_0 .. \{z_4 - z_9\}z_{4l} -\!-$ **subpath**$(0, t)$ **of** $(z_{4r}\{z_9 - z_4\} .. z_{6r})$
$-\!- z_{2r} -\!-\!- z_{1r} .. z_{1l} -\!-\!- z_{2l} -\!-$ **subpath**$(t, 0)$ **of** $(z_{3r}\{z_9 - z_3\} .. z_{5r})$
$-\!- z_{3l}\{z_9 - z_3\} .. z_0$ & cycle;   % lower arrowhead and stem
$pos_{11}(rule\_thickness, 0)$; $pos_{12}(rule\_thickness, 0)$; $z_{11} = z_1$;
$pos_{13}(bar, 90)$; $pos_{14}(bar, 90)$;
$x_{10} = x_{11} = x_{12}$; *top* $y_{10} = h + o$; $x_{10} - x_{13} = x_{14} - x_{10} = 3u + eps$;
$y_{13} = y_{14} = y_{10} - .24asc\_height - eps$;
$pos_{15}(bar, \text{angle}(z_{14} - z_{10}))$; $z_{15l} = z_{10}$; $pos_{16}(bar, \text{angle}(z_{13} - z_{10}))$; $z_{16l} = z_{10}$;
$z_{19} = .381966[.5[z_{13}, z_{14}], z_{10}]$;
numeric t; **path** p; $p = z_{14l}\{z_{19} - z_{14}\} .. z_{16r}$;
$t = $ xpart$(p$ intersectiontimes $((x_{12r}, -d) -\!- (x_{12r}, h)))$; $y_{12} = $ ypart **point** t **of** p;
filldraw $z_{10} .. \{z_{14} - z_{19}\}z_{14r} -\!-$ **subpath**$(0, t)$ **of** $(z_{14l}\{z_{19} - z_{14}\} .. z_{16r})$
$-\!- z_{12r} -\!-\!- z_{11r} .. z_{11l} -\!-\!- z_{12l} -\!-$ **subpath**$(t, 0)$ **of** $(z_{13l}\{z_{19} - z_{13}\} .. z_{15r})$
$-\!- z_{13r}\{z_{19} - z_{13}\} .. z_{10}$ & cycle;   % upper arrowhead and stem
penlabels$(0, 1, 2, 3, 4, 5, 6, 9, 10, 11, 12, 13, 14, 15, 16, 19)$; **endchar**;

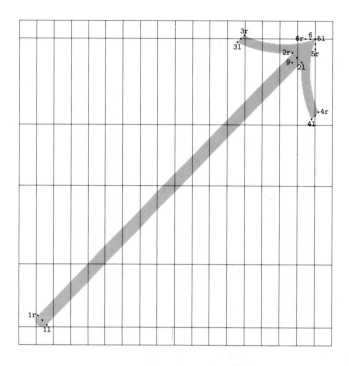

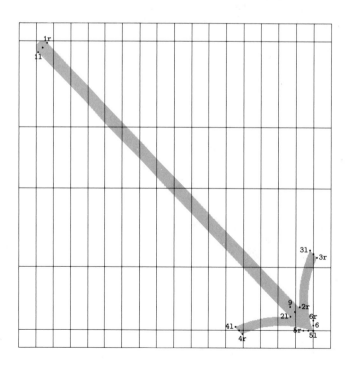

cmchar "Northeast arrow";
beginchar(oct "045", $18u^\#$, $asc\_height^\#$, $asc\_depth^\#$);
adjust_fit$(0, 0)$; **pickup** *crisp.nib*;
$x_1 - .5rule\_thickness =$ hround u; $rt\ x_0 =$ hround$(w - u)$;
$y_1 - .5rule\_thickness = -d$; *top* $y_0 = h$;
numeric *theta, delta*; $theta = \text{angle}(z_0 - z_1)$; $delta = 3u ++ .24asc\_height$;
if abs$(theta - 45) < 2.5$: $theta := 45$; $y_1 := y_0 + x_1 - x_0$; **fi**   % near-45° angle
$pos_1(rule\_thickness, 90 + theta)$; $pos_2(rule\_thickness, 90 + theta)$;
$pos_3(bar, theta)$; $pos_4(bar, theta)$;
$y_3 = y_0$; $x_4 = x_0$; $x_0 - x_3 = y_0 - y_4 = delta + eps$;
$pos_5(bar, -90)$; $z_{5l} = z_0$; $pos_6(bar, -180)$; $z_{6l} = z_0$;
$z_9 = .381966[.5[z_3, z_4], z_0]$;
numeric t; **path** p; $p = z_{4l}\{z_9 - z_4\} \mathrel{..} z_{6r}$;
$t = \text{xpart}(p \text{ intersectiontimes } (z_{1l} \mathrel{--} (z_{1l} + 2(z_0 - z_1))))$; $z_{2l} = \textbf{point } t \textbf{ of } p$;
filldraw $z_0 \mathrel{..} \{z_4 - z_9\}z_{4r} \mathrel{-\!-} \textbf{subpath}(0, t) \textbf{ of } (z_{4l}\{z_9 - z_4\} \mathrel{..} z_{6r})$
   $\mathrel{-\!-} z_{2l} \mathrel{-\!-\!-} z_{1l} \mathrel{..} z_{1r} \mathrel{-\!-\!-} z_{2r} \mathrel{-\!-} \textbf{subpath}(t, 0) \textbf{ of } (z_{3l}\{z_9 - z_3\} \mathrel{..} z_{5r})$
   $\mathrel{-\!-} z_{3r}\{z_9 - z_3\} \mathrel{..} z_0$ & cycle;   % arrowhead and stem
penlabels$(0, 1, 2, 3, 4, 5, 6, 9)$; **endchar**;

cmchar "Southeast arrow";
beginchar(oct "046", $18u^\#$, $asc\_height^\#$, $asc\_depth^\#$);
adjust_fit$(0, 0)$; **pickup** *crisp.nib*;
$x_1 - .5rule\_thickness =$ hround u; $rt\ x_0 =$ hround$(w - u)$;
$y_1 + .5rule\_thickness = h$; *bot* $y_0 = -d$;
numeric *theta, delta*; $theta = \text{angle}(z_0 - z_1)$; $delta = 3u ++ .24asc\_height$;
if abs$(theta + 45) < 2.5$: $theta := -45$; $y_1 := y_0 + x_0 - x_1$; **fi**   % near-45° angle
$pos_1(rule\_thickness, 90 + theta)$; $pos_2(rule\_thickness, 90 + theta)$;
$pos_3(bar, theta)$; $pos_4(bar, theta)$;
$x_3 = x_0$; $y_4 = y_0$; $y_3 - y_0 = x_0 - x_4 = delta + eps$;
$pos_5(bar, 180)$; $z_{5l} = z_0$; $pos_6(bar, 90)$; $z_{6l} = z_0$;
$z_9 = .381966[.5[z_3, z_4], z_0]$;
numeric t; **path** p; $p = z_{4l}\{z_9 - z_4\} \mathrel{..} z_{6r}$;
$t = \text{xpart}(p \text{ intersectiontimes } (z_{1l} \mathrel{--} (z_{1l} + 2(z_0 - z_1))))$; $z_{2l} = \textbf{point } t \textbf{ of } p$;
filldraw $z_0 \mathrel{..} \{z_4 - z_9\}z_{4r}$
   $\mathrel{-\!-} \textbf{subpath}(0, t) \textbf{ of } (z_{4l}\{z_9 - z_4\} \mathrel{..} z_{6r})$
   $\mathrel{-\!-} z_{2l} \mathrel{-\!-\!-} z_{1l} \mathrel{..} z_{1r} \mathrel{-\!-\!-} z_{2r}$
   $\mathrel{-\!-} \textbf{subpath}(t, 0) \textbf{ of } (z_{3l}\{z_9 - z_3\} \mathrel{..} z_{5r})$
   $\mathrel{-\!-} z_{3r}\{z_9 - z_3\} \mathrel{..} z_0$ & cycle;   % arrowhead and stem
penlabels$(0, 1, 2, 3, 4, 5, 6, 9)$; **endchar**;

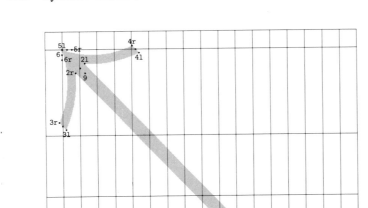

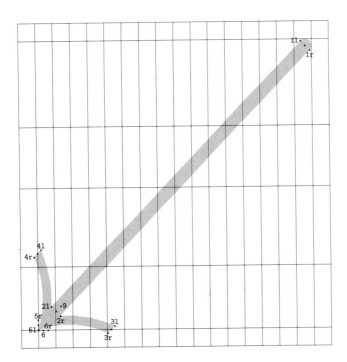

cmchar "Northwest arrow";
beginchar(oct "055", $18u^\#$, $asc\_height^\#$, $asc\_depth^\#$);
adjust_fit$(0, 0)$; **pickup** $crisp.nib$;
$x_1 + .5rule_thickness = $ hround$(w - u)$; *lft* $x_0 = $ hround u;
$y_1 - .5rule\_thickness = -d$; *top* $y_0 = h$;
numeric $theta$, $delta$; $theta = $ angle$(z_1 - z_0)$; $delta = 3u ++ .24asc\_height$;
if abs$(theta + 45) < 2.5$: $theta := -45$; $y_1 := y_0 + x_0 - x_1$; **fi** $\quad$ % near-45° angle
$pos_1(rule\_thickness, -90 + theta)$; $pos_2(rule\_thickness, -90 + theta)$;
$pos_3(bar, -180 + theta)$; $pos_4(bar, -180 + theta)$;
$x_3 = x_0$; $y_4 = y_0$; $x_4 - x_0 = y_0 - y_3 = delta + eps$;
$pos_5(bar, 0)$; $z_{5l} = z_0$; $pos_6(bar, -90)$; $z_{6l} = z_0$;
$z_9 = .381966[.5[z_3, z_4], z_0]$;
numeric t; **path** p; $p = z_{4l}\{z_9 - z_4\} .. z_{6r}$;
$t = $ xpart$(p$ intersectiontimes $(z_{1l} \text{ -- } (z_{1l} + 2(z_0 - z_1))))$; $z_{2l} = $ **point** t **of** p;
filldraw $z_0 .. \{z_4 - z_9\}z_{4r}$ -- **subpath**$(0, t)$ **of** $(z_{4l}\{z_9 - z_4\} .. z_{6r})$
$\quad$ -- z_{2l} --- $z_{1l} .. z_{1r}$ --- z_{2r} -- **subpath**$(t, 0)$ **of** $(z_{3l}\{z_9 - z_3\} .. z_{5r})$
$\quad$ -- $z_{3r}\{z_9 - z_3\} .. z_0$ & cycle; $\qquad$ % arrowhead and stem
penlabels$(0, 1, 2, 3, 4, 5, 6, 9)$; **endchar**;

cmchar "Southwest arrow";
beginchar(oct "056", $18u^\#$, $asc\_height^\#$, $asc\_depth^\#$);
adjust_fit$(0, 0)$; **pickup** $crisp.nib$;
$x_1 + .5rule_thickness = $ hround$(w - u)$; *lft* $x_0 = $ hround u;
$y_1 + .5rule\_thickness = h$; *bot* $y_0 = -d$;
numeric $theta$, $delta$; $theta = $ angle$(z_1 - z_0)$; $delta = 3u ++ .24asc\_height$;
if abs$(theta - 45) < 2.5$: $theta := 45$; $y_1 := y_0 + x_1 - x_0$; **fi** $\quad$ % near-45° angle
$pos_1(rule\_thickness, -90 + theta)$; $pos_2(rule\_thickness, -90 + theta)$;
$pos_3(bar, -180 + theta)$; $pos_4(bar, -180 + theta)$;
$y_3 = y_0$; $x_4 = x_0$; $x_3 - x_0 = y_4 - y_0 = delta + eps$;
$pos_5(bar, 90)$; $z_{5l} = z_0$; $pos_6(bar, 0)$; $z_{6l} = z_0$;
$z_9 = .381966[.5[z_3, z_4], z_0]$;
numeric t; **path** p; $p = z_{4l}\{z_9 - z_4\} .. z_{6r}$;
$t = $ xpart$(p$ intersectiontimes $(z_{1l} \text{ -- } (z_{1l} + 2(z_0 - z_1))))$; $z_{2l} = $ **point** t **of** p;
filldraw $z_0 .. \{z_4 - z_9\}z_{4r}$
$\quad$ -- **subpath**$(0, t)$ **of** $(z_{4l}\{z_9 - z_4\} .. z_{6r})$
$\quad$ -- z_{2l} --- $z_{1l} .. z_{1r}$ --- z_{2r}
$\quad$ -- **subpath**$(t, 0)$ **of** $(z_{3l}\{z_9 - z_3\} .. z_{5r})$
$\quad$ -- $z_{3r}\{z_9 - z_3\} .. z_0$ & cycle; $\qquad$ % arrowhead and stem
penlabels$(0, 1, 2, 3, 4, 5, 6, 9)$; **endchar**;

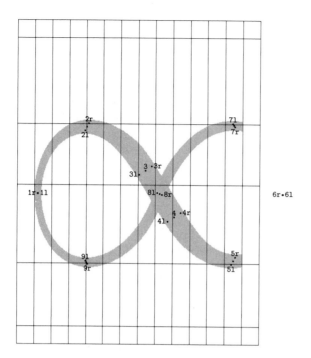

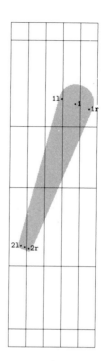

6r•61

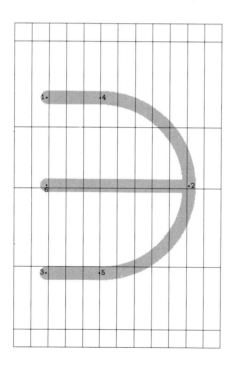

cmchar "Proportionality sign";
beginchar(oct "057", $16.5u^\#$, $x\_height^\#$, 0);
italcorr $x\_height^\# * slant - .5u^\#$;
adjust_fit$(0, -2.5u^\#)$; **pickup** *fine.nib*;
numeric *theta*, *phi*; $phi = \text{angle}(3u, h)$; $theta = \text{angle}(5u, -h)$;
$pos_1(vair, 180)$; $pos_2(.5[vair, stem], 90 + .5theta)$; $pos_3(stem, 90 + theta)$;
$pos_4(stem, 90 + theta)$; $pos_5(.5[vair, stem], 90 + .5theta)$;
$pos_6(vair, 180)$; $pos_7(.2[vair, stem], 270 + .5phi)$;
$pos_8(.3[vair, stem], 270 + phi)$; $pos_9(.2[vair, stem], 270 + .5phi)$;
lft $x_{1r} = w - $ *rt* $x_{6l} = \text{hround } u$; $x_2 = x_9 = .4[x_1, x_8]$; $x_5 = x_7 = .6[x_8, x_6]$;
if *monospace*: $x_{2l} := x_{2r}$; $x_{5r} := x_{5l}$; $x_{7r} := x_{7l}$; $x_{9l} := x_{9r}$; **fi**
$y_1 = y_6 = .5h$; *top* $y_{2r} = $ *top* $y_{7l} = h + oo$; *bot* $y_{5l} = $ *bot* $y_{9r} = -oo$;
$x_8 = .5[x_3, x_4] = .5w$; $y_8 = .5[y_3, y_4] = .5h$;
$y_3 - y_4 = h/3$; $z_3 - z_4 = $ *whatever* $* \text{dir } theta$;
filldraw stroke $z_{1e}\{up\} \ldots z_{2e}\{right\} \ldots z_{3e} \text{---} z_{4e} \ldots z_{5e}\{right\} \ldots z_{6e}\{up\}$
$\ldots z_{7e}\{left\} \ldots \{-\text{ dir } phi\}z_{8e} \ldots \{left\}z_{9e} \ldots z_{1e}\{up\}$;   % 'infinity' bowls
erase fill$(w - 3.5u, h + o) \text{ -- } (w, h + o)$
$\text{-- } (w, -o) \text{ -- } (w - 3.5u, -o) \text{ -- cycle}$;   % erase excess
penlabels$(1, 2, 3, 4, 5, 6, 7, 8, 9)$; **endchar**;

cmchar "Prime symbol (intended as superscript only)";
beginchar(oct "060", $3u^\# + \max(1.75u^\#, curve^\# + 2(curve^\# - stem^\#))$,
$.8asc\_height^\#$, 0);
adjust_fit$(0, 0)$; **pickup** *fine.nib*;
numeric *light_stem*, *heavy_stem*;
$light\_stem = \text{hround } .5[vair, stem]$; $heavy\_stem = \text{hround}(bold + 2dw)$;
$x_1 + .5heavy\_stem = \text{hround}(w - .25u)$; $y_1 + .5heavy\_stem = h$;
$x_2 - .5light\_stem = \text{hround } .5u$; $y_2 = {}^1\!/_{12}asc\_height$;
numeric *theta*; $theta = \text{angle}(z_1 - z_2) - 90$;
$pos_1(heavy\_stem, theta)$; $pos_2(light\_stem, theta)$;
filldraw circ_stroke $z_{1e} \text{ -- } z_{2e}$;   % diagonal
penlabels$(1, 2)$; **endchar**;

cmchar "Ownership sign";
compute_spread$({}^5\!/_4 x\_height^\#, {}^3\!/_2 x\_height^\#)$;
beginchar(oct "063", $12u^\#$, *v_center*$(spread^\# + rule\_thickness^\#)$);
adjust_fit$(0, 0)$; **pickup** *rule.nib*; *autorounded*;
lft $x_1 = \text{hround } 1.5u - eps$; $x_1 = x_3 = x_6 = w - x_2$;
$y_1 - y_3 = spread$; $y_2 = y_6 = .5[y_1, y_3] = math\_axis$;
$x_4 = x_5 = .5w - u$; $y_4 = y_1$; $y_5 = y_3$;
draw $z_1 \text{---} z_4 \ldots z_2\{down\} \ldots z_5 \text{---} z_3$;   % arc and bars
draw $z_2 \text{ -- } z_6$;   % middle bar
labels$(1, 2, 3, 4, 5, 6)$; **endchar**;

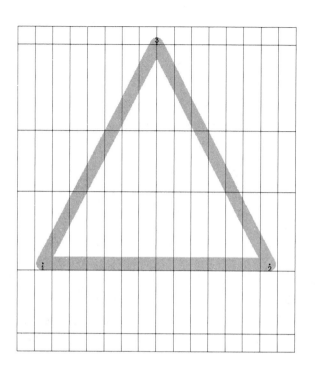

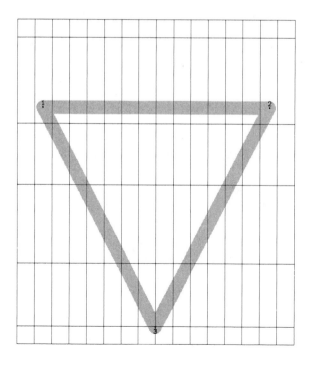

cmchar "Large triangle";
beginchar(oct "064", $16u^\#$, $asc\_height^\#$, $desc\_depth^\#$);
adjust_fit$(0, 0)$; **pickup** *rule.nib*;
bot $y_1 = 0$; $y_2 = y_1$; *top* $y_3 = h + o$;
$.5[x_1, x_2] = x_3 = good.x\ .5w$; $w := r := 2x_3$; *lft* $x_1 = \text{hround}(.5w - u * \text{sqrt } 48)$;
draw $z_1 \ \text{--}\ z_2 \ \text{--}\ z_3 \ \text{--}\ \text{cycle}$;   % stroke
labels$(1, 2, 3)$; **endchar**;

cmchar "Large inverted triangle";
beginchar(oct "065", $16u^\#$, $asc\_height^\#$, $desc\_depth^\#$);
adjust_fit$(0, 0)$; **pickup** *rule.nib*;
top $y_1 = h - d$; $y_2 = y_1$; *bot* $y_3 = -d - o$;
$.5[x_1, x_2] = x_3 = good.x\ .5w$; $w := r := 2x_3$; *lft* $x_1 = \text{hround}(.5w - u * \text{sqrt } 48)$;
draw $z_1 \ \text{--}\ z_2 \ \text{--}\ z_3 \ \text{--}\ \text{cycle}$;   % stroke
labels$(1, 2, 3)$; **endchar**;

cmchar "Zero-width slash to negate a relation";
beginchar(oct "066", $14u^\#$, $asc\_height^\#$, $asc\_depth^\#$);
adjust_fit$(0, 0)$; **pickup** *rule.nib*;
rt $x_5 = \text{hround}(w - 2.5u) - eps$; *lft* $x_6 = \text{hround } 2.5u + eps$;
top $y_5 = h + o$; $.5[y_5, y_6] = math\_axis$;
draw $z_5 \ \text{--}\ z_6$;   % diagonal
labels$(1, 2)$; *zero_width*; **endchar**;

cmchar "Maps-to relation";
compute_spread$(.45x\_height^\#, .55x\_height^\#)$;
beginchar(oct "067", $14u^\#$, $v\_center(spread^\# + rule\_thickness^\#)$);
                      % this character should be followed immediately by minus or rightarrow
adjust_fit$(0, 0)$; **pickup** *rule.nib*;
lft $x_1 = \text{hround } u$; $x_2 = x_1 + .5u$; $x_3 = x_4 = x_1$;
$y_1 = y_2 = math\_axis$; $y_1 - y_3 = y_4 - y_1 = .24asc\_height + eps$;
draw $z_3 \ \text{--}\ z_4$;   % stem
draw $z_1 \ \text{--}\ z_2$;   % bar stub
labels$(1, 2, 3, 4)$; *zero_width*; **endchar**;

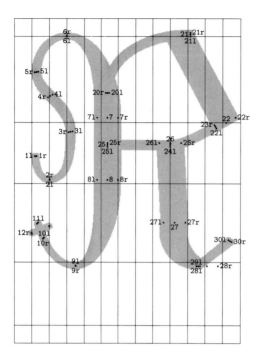

cmchar "Uppercase Fraktur R";
beginchar(oct "074", $13u^\#$, $asc\_height^\#$, 0);
adjust_fit(0, 0); **pickup** *fine.nib*;
$pos_1(hair, 0)$; $pos_2(vair, 90)$; $pos_3(\frac{1}{6}[hair, stem], 190)$;
$pos_4(\frac{1}{4}[hair, stem], 210)$; $pos_5(\frac{1}{8}[hair, stem], 190)$;
$pos_6(vair, 90)$; $pos_7(cap\_stem, 0)$; $pos_8(cap\_stem, 0)$;
$pos_9(vair, -90)$; $pos_{10}(hair, -135)$; $pos_{11}(hair, -135)$;
$pos_{12}(vair, 135)$; $pos_{13}(vair, 135)$;
$lft\ x_{1l} = lft\ x_{5r} = \text{hround } u$; $x_2 = .4[x_1, x_3]$; $rt\ x_{3l} = \text{hround } 3.5u$; $x_4 = .6[x_3, x_5]$;
$x_6 = 3u$; $lft\ x_7 = \text{hround}(6u - .5cap\_stem)$; $x_8 = x_7$;
$x_9 = 3.5u$; $x_{10} = \frac{5}{3}u$; $x_{11} = \frac{4}{3}u$; $x_{12} = u$; $x_{13} = 2u$;
$y_1 = .47h$; $bot\ y_{2l} = \text{vround } .35h$; $y_3 = \frac{1}{3}[y_2, y_6]$; $y_5 = \frac{3}{4}[y_2, y_6]$; $y_4 = .6[y_3, y_5]$;
$top\ y_{6r} = h + oo$; $y_7 = .64h$; $y_8 = .57y_7$; $bot\ y_{9r} = -o$;
$y_{10} = \frac{1}{6}y_7$; $y_{12} = \frac{1}{5}y_7$; $y_{13} = \frac{1}{4}y_7$;
$z_{11} - z_{10} = whatever * (z_{13} - z_{12})$ rotated 90;
filldraw stroke $z_{1e}\{down\}$ ... $z_{2e}\{right\}$ ... $z_{3e}\{up\}$ .. z_{4e} .. $z_{5e}\{up\}$
    ... $pulled\_arc_e(6, 7)$ .. $pulled\_arc_e(8, 9)$
    ... z_{10e} - - - z_{11e};   % flourish and left stem
filldraw stroke z_{12e} - - z_{13e};   % cross
$pos_{20}(cap\_bar, 180)$; $pos_{21}(cap\_bar, 90)$;
$x_{20} = x_7$; $y_{20} = .75h$; $rt\ x_{21} = \text{hround}(w - 3.5u + .5cap\_stem)$; $top\ y_{21r} = h + o$;
filldraw stroke $z_{20e}\{up\}$ ... $\{right\}z_{21e}$;   % top of bowl
$rt\ x_{22r} = \text{hround}(w - .1u)$; $y_{22r} = good.y\ .64h$;
numeric *theta*; $theta = \text{angle}(z_{21r} - z_{22r})$;
$pos_{22}(cap\_stem, theta - 90)$; $pos_{23}(cap\_bar, theta)$; $z_{22l} = z_{23l}$;
path p; $p = z_{20}\{up\}$ ... $(z_{21} \text{ -- } (w, y_{21}))$;
$z = p$ intersectionpoint $(z_{22l} \text{ -- } z_{22l} + (h, 0)$ rotated $theta)$;
filldraw z -- z_{21r} -- z_{22r} -- z_{22l} -- cycle;   % diagonal of bowl
$pos_{24}(cap\_bar, 90)$; $pos_{25}(cap\_bar, 90)$; $x_{24} = w - 4u$; $x_{25} = x_7$;
$y_{24} = y_{25}$; $top\ y_{24r} = \text{vround}(.52h + .5cap\_bar)$;
filldraw stroke $z_{23e}\{\text{dir}(theta + 90)\}$ ... z_{24e} - - - z_{25e};   % bottom of bowl
$pos_{26}(cap\_stem, 0)$; $pos_{27}(cap\_stem, 0)$; $pos_{28}(cap\_stem, 0)$;
$x_{26} = x_{24}$; $x_{27} = x_{26} + .25u$; $x_{28l} = w - 2.5u$; $y_{26} = y_{24r}$; $y_{27} = \frac{1}{3}y_{26}$; $bot\ y_{28} = -o$;
filldraw stroke z_{26e} -- z_{27e} ... $\{right\}z_{28e}$;   % lower diagonal
$pos_{29}(cap\_bar, 0)$; $pos_{30}(cap\_bar, -30)$; $z_{29l} = z_{28l}$;
$x_{30r} = good.x(w - .5u)$; $y_{30r} = good.y\ .09h$;
erase filldraw z_{29r} -- z_{28r} -- z_{30r} -- cycle;   % erase excess
filldraw stroke z_{29e} -- z_{30e};   % serif of lower diagonal
penlabels(1, 2, 3, 4, 5, 6, 7, 8, 9, 10, 11, 12, 13, 20, 21, 22, 23, 24, 25, 26, 27, 28, 29, 30);
endchar;

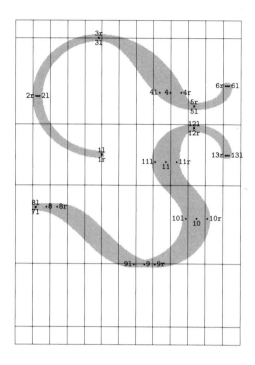

cmchar "Uppercase Fraktur I";
beginchar(oct "075", $13u^\#$, $asc\_height^\#$, 0);
adjust_fit(0, 0); **pickup** *fine.nib*;
$pos_1(vair, 270)$; $pos_2(cap\_hair, 180)$; $pos_3(vair, 90)$;
$pos_4(cap\_stem, 0)$; $pos_5(vair, 90)$; $pos_6(cap\_hair, 180)$;
$x_1 = 5u$; *lft* $x_{2r} = $ hround u; $x_3 = .5[x_2, x_{4l}]$; $x_{4r} = x_5 - .75u$;
$x_5 = .5[x_{4l}, x_{6l}]$; *rt* $x_{6l} = $ hround$(w - .5u)$;
top $y_{1l} = $ vround $.5h$; $y_2 = .5[y_1, y_3]$; *top* $y_{3r} = h + oo$;
$y_4 = .2[y_5, y_3]$; $y_6 = .3[y_5, y_3]$; *bot* $y_{5l} = $ ceiling$(\frac{1}{6}[x\_height, h])$;
filldraw stroke $z_{1e}\{left\}$ ... $z_{2e}\{up\}$ ... $z_{3e}\{right\}$
  .. z_{4e} .. $z_{5e}\{right\}$ ... $\{up\}z_{6e}$;   % upper stroke
$pos_7(vair, 90)$; $pos_8(cap\_stem, 0)$; $pos_9(cap\_stem, 0)$;
lft $x_7 = $ hround u; $z_{7r} = z_{8l}$; $x_9 = .5w + u$; $y_8 = good.y$ $.25h$; *bot* $y_9 = -oo$;
filldraw z_{8l} --- z_{8r} .. $\{right\}z_{9r} + (0, eps)$
  -- z_{9r} --- z_{9l} .. $\{left\}z_{7l}$ -- cycle;   % lower left stroke
$pos_{10}(cap\_stem, 0)$; $pos_{11}(cap\_stem, 0)$; $pos_{12}(vair, -90)$; $pos_{13}(cap\_hair, -180)$;
$x_{10} = w - 2.5u$; $x_{11r} = x_{12} - u$; $x_{12} = x_5$; $x_{13} = x_6$;
$y_{10} = \frac{1}{3}y_{12}$; $y_{11} = \frac{3}{4}y_{12}$; *top* $y_{12l} = x\_height$; $y_{13} = \frac{4}{5}y_{12}$;
filldraw $z_{9l} + (0, eps)\{right\}$ ... $\{up\}z_{10l}$
  -- $z_{10r}\{down\}$ ... z_{9r} --- z_{9l} -- cycle;   % lower link
filldraw stroke $z_{10e}\{up\}$ ... $z_{11e}\{up\}$
  ... $z_{12e}\{right\}$ ... $\{down\}z_{13e}$;   % lower right stroke
penlabels(1, 2, 3, 4, 5, 6, 7, 8, 9, 10, 11, 12, 13); **endchar**;

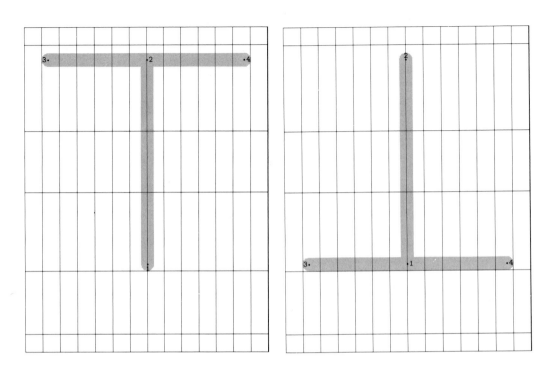

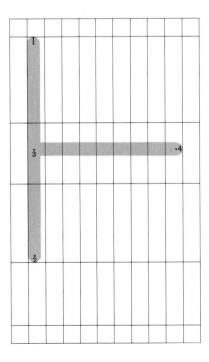

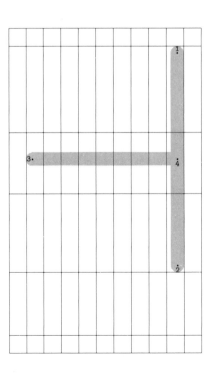

cmchar "Lattice top";
beginchar(oct "076", $14u^\#$, $asc\_height^\#$, 0);
adjust_fit(0, 0); **pickup** $rule.nib$;
$x_1 = x_2 = good.x\ .5w$; $w := r := 2x_1$; *lft* $x_3 = $ hround u; $x_4 = r - x_3$;
bot $y_1 = 0$; $y_2 - y_1 = x_4 - x_3$;
if *top* $y_2 > h$: $y_2 := bot\ h$; **fi**
$y_3 = y_4 = y_2$;
draw $z_1 \mathbin{--} z_2$;   % stem
draw $z_3 \mathbin{--} z_4$;   % bar
labels(1, 2, 3, 4); **endchar**;

cmchar "Perpendicular sign or lattice bottom";
beginchar(oct "077", $14u^\#$, $asc\_height^\#$, 0);
adjust_fit(0, 0); **pickup** $rule.nib$;
$x_1 = x_2 = good.x\ .5w$; $w := r := 2x_1$; *lft* $x_3 = $ hround u; $x_4 = r - x_3$;
bot $y_1 = 0$; $y_2 - y_1 = x_4 - x_3$;
if *top* $y_2 > h$: $y_2 := bot\ h$; **fi**
$y_3 = y_4 = y_1$;
draw $z_1 \mathbin{--} z_2$;   % stem
draw $z_3 \mathbin{--} z_4$;   % bar
labels(1, 2, 3, 4); **endchar**;

cmchar "Left turnstile";
beginchar(oct "140", $11u^\#$, $asc\_height^\#$, 0);
adjust_fit(0, 0); **pickup** $rule.nib$;
$.5[y_1, y_2] = y_3 = y_4$; $x_1 = x_2 = x_3$;
lft $x_3 = $ hround u; $x_4 = w - x_3$; *top* $y_1 = h$; *bot* $y_2 = 0$;
draw $z_1 \mathbin{--} z_2$;   % stem
draw $z_3 \mathbin{--} z_4$;   % bar
labels(1, 2, 3, 4); **endchar**;

cmchar "Right turnstile";
beginchar(oct "141", $11u^\#$, $asc\_height^\#$, 0);
adjust_fit(0, 0); **pickup** $rule.nib$;
$.5[y_1, y_2] = y_3 = y_4$; $x_1 = x_2 = x_4$;
lft $x_3 = $ hround u; $x_4 = w - x_3$; *top* $y_1 = h$; *bot* $y_2 = 0$;
draw $z_1 \mathbin{--} z_2$;   % stem
draw $z_3 \mathbin{--} z_4$;   % bar
labels(1, 2, 3, 4); **endchar**;

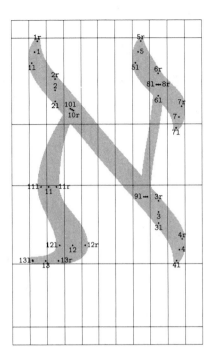

cmchar "Hebrew letter aleph";
beginchar(oct "100", $11u^\#$, $asc\_height^\#$, 0);
adjust_fit(0, 0); **pickup** *fine.nib*;
$pos_1(cap\_stem, 75)$; $pos_2(cap\_stem, 90)$; $pos_3(cap\_stem, 90)$; $pos_4(cap\_stem, 75)$;
lft x_{1l} = hround $u - eps$; $x_2 = 2.5u = w - x_3$; *rt* x_{4r} = hround$(w - u) + eps$;
top $y_{1r} = h$; *bot* $y_{4l} = 0$; $z_2 = whatever[z_{1l}, z_{4r}]$; $z_3 = whatever[z_{1l}, z_{4r}]$;
filldraw $z_{1r}\{4(x_{1l} - x_{1r}), y_{1l} - y_{1r}\} \ldots \{down\}z_{1l} \ldots z_{2l}$
   $\text{---}\, z_{3l} \ldots \{down\}z_{4l}\{4(x_{4r} - x_{4l}), y_{4r} - y_{4l}\} \ldots \{up\}z_{4r} \ldots z_{3r}$
   $\text{---}\, z_{2r} \ldots \{up\}$ cycle;   % long diagonal
$pos_5(cap\_stem, 75)$; $pos_6(cap\_stem, 90)$; $pos_7(cap\_stem, 75)$;
lft x_{5l} = hround$(w - 4u) - eps$; $x_6 = .5[x_5, x_7]$; $x_7 = x_4$;
$y_5 = y_1$; *bot* $y_{7l} = x\_height - o$; $z_6 = whatever[z_{5l}, z_{7r}]$;
filldraw $z_{5r}\{4(x_{5l} - x_{5r}), y_{5l} - y_{5r}\} \ldots \{down\}z_{5l}$
   $\ldots z_{6l}\{z_{7r} - z_{5l}\} \ldots \{down\}z_{7l}\{4(x_{7r} - x_{7l}), y_{7r} - y_{7l}\} \ldots \{up\}z_{7r}$
   $\ldots z_{6r}\{z_{5l} - z_{7l}\} \ldots \{up\}$ cycle;   % short diagonal
$pos_8(cap\_hair, 0)$; $pos_9(cap\_hair, 0)$; $z_8 = z_6$; $x_9 = x_8 - .75u$; $z_9 = whatever[z_2, z_3]$;
filldraw stroke $z_{8e}\{down\} \ldots \{down\}z_{9e}$;   % right stem
$pos_{10}(cap\_hair, -30)$; $pos_{11}(stem, 0)$;
$pos_{12}(cap\_curve, 0)$; $pos_{13}(cap\_curve, 0)$; $pos_{14}(vair, 90)$;
lft x_{11l} = hround $1.5u$; $x_{10} = x_{12} = .4[x_{11}, .5w]$; $z_{10} = whatever[z_2, z_3]$;
lft x_{13l} = hround u; $z_{13l} = z_{14l}$; $y_{11} = .5y_{10}$; $y_{12} = .2[y_{14r}, y_{11}]$; *bot* $y_{13} = 0$;
filldraw stroke $z_{10e}\{2(x_{11} - x_{10}), y_{11} - y_{10}\}$
   $\ldots z_{11e}\{down\} \ldots \{down\}z_{12e}$;   % left stem
filldraw $z_{12r}\{down\} \ldots z_{13r} \text{ ---} z_{13l} \text{ --} z_{14r}\{right\} \ldots \{up\}z_{12l} \text{ --}$ cycle; % flourish
penlabels(1, 2, 3, 4, 5, 6, 7, 8, 9, 10, 11, 12, 13, 14); **endchar**;

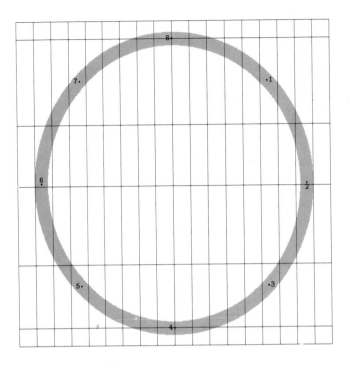

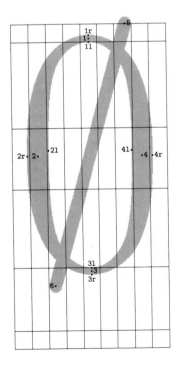

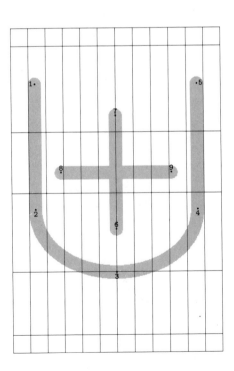

cmchar "Circle for copyright, etc.";
beginchar(oct "015", $18u^\#$, $asc\_height^\#$, $desc\_depth^\#$); *autorounded*;
adjust_fit(**if** *monospace*: $-3u^\#$, $-3u^\#$ **else**: $0, 0$ **fi**); **pickup** *rule.nib*;
lft x_6 = *hround* u; $x_2 = w - x_6$; *top* $y_8 = h + o$; *bot* $y_4 = -d - o$;
circle_points; *draw_circle*;   % circle
labels$(1, 2, 3, 4, 5, 6, 7, 8)$; **endchar**;

cmchar "Empty set symbol";
beginchar(oct "073", $9u^\#$, $body\_height^\#$, $body\_height^\# - asc\_height^\#$);
adjust_fit$(0, 0)$;
$penpos_1(vair, 90)$; $penpos_3(vair, -90)$; $penpos_2(stem, 180)$; $penpos_4(stem, 0)$;
if **not** *monospace*: **interim** *superness* := sqrt($more\_super * hein\_super$); **fi**
x_{2r} = *hround* max$(.7u, 1.45u - .5stem)$;
$x_{4r} = w - x_{2r}$; $x_1 = x_3 = .5w$; $y_{1r} = asc\_height + o$; $y_{3r} = -o$;
$y_2 = y_4 = .5asc\_height - vair\_corr$; $y_{2l} := y_{4l} := .52asc\_height$;
penstroke $pulled\_arc_e(1, 2)$ & $pulled\_arc_e(2, 3)$
    & $pulled\_arc_e(3, 4)$ & $pulled\_arc_e(4, 1)$ & cycle;   % bowl
pickup *rule.nib*; *lft* x_6 = *hround* $2u - eps$; $x_5 = w - x_6$;
top $y_5 = h + o$; *bot* $y_6 = -d - o$;
draw z_5 -- z_6;   % diagonal
penlabels$(1, 2, 3, 4, 5, 6)$; **endchar**;

cmchar "Multiset union sign";
beginchar(oct "135", $12u^\#$, $.8asc\_height^\#$, 0); *autorounded*;
adjust_fit(**if** *monospace*: $-.5u^\#$, $-.5u^\#$ **else**: $0, 0$ **fi**); **pickup** *rule.nib*;
lft x_1 = *hround* u; $x_2 = x_1$; $x_3 = w - x_3$; $x_4 = x_5 = w - x_1$;
$y_1 = good.y\ h + o$; *bot* $y_3 = -o$; $y_2 = y_4 = {}^2\!/_3[y_1, y_3]$; $y_5 = y_1$;
draw z_1 --- z_2 ... z_3 ... z_4 --- z_5;   % stems and cup
$y_8 = y_9 = .47[y_1, y_3]$; $x_8 = w - x_9 = x_1 + 2rule\_thickness + eps$;
$x_6 = x_7 = x_3$; $.5[y_6, y_7] = y_8$; $y_7 - y_6 = x_9 - x_8$;
draw z_8 -- z_9; **draw** z_6 -- z_7;   % enclosed plus sign
labels$(1, 2, 3, 4, 5, 6, 7, 8, 9)$; **endchar**;

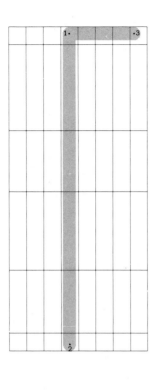

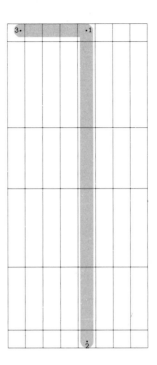

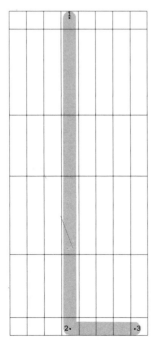

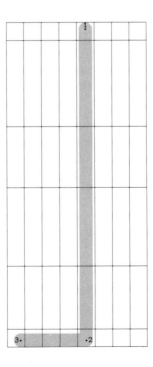

cmchar "Left ceiling bracket";
beginchar(oct "144", $8u^\#$, $body\_height^\#$, $paren\_depth^\#$);
adjust_fit$(0, 0)$; **pickup** $rule.nib$;
$x_1 = x_2 = good.x\ 3.5u$; $x_3 = x_1 + 3.75u + eps$;
$top\ y_1 = h$; $.5[y_1, y_2] = math\_axis$; $y_3 = y_1$;
draw $z_3 \text{ -- } z_1 \text{ -- } z_2$;   % stem and bar
labels$(1, 2, 3)$; **endchar**;

cmchar "Right ceiling bracket";
beginchar(oct "145", $8u^\#$, $body\_height^\#$, $paren\_depth^\#$);
adjust_fit$(0, 0)$; **pickup** $rule.nib$;
$x_1 = x_2 = good.x(w - 3.5u)$; $x_3 = x_1 - 3.75u - eps$;
$top\ y_1 = h$; $.5[y_1, y_2] = math\_axis$; $y_3 = y_1$;
draw $z_3 \text{ -- } z_1 \text{ -- } z_2$;   % stem and bar
labels$(1, 2, 3)$; **endchar**;

cmchar "Left floor bracket";
beginchar(oct "142", $8u^\#$, $body\_height^\#$, $paren\_depth^\#$);
adjust_fit$(0, 0)$; **pickup** $rule.nib$;
$x_1 = x_2 = good.x\ 3.5u$; $x_3 = x_1 + 3.75u + eps$;
$top\ y_1 = h$; $.5[y_1, y_2] = math\_axis$; $y_3 = y_2$;
draw $z_1 \text{ -- } z_2 \text{ -- } z_3$;   % stem and bar
labels$(1, 2, 3)$; **endchar**;

cmchar "Right floor bracket";
beginchar(oct "143", $8u^\#$, $body\_height^\#$, $paren\_depth^\#$);
adjust_fit$(0, 0)$; **pickup** $rule.nib$;
$x_1 = x_2 = good.x(w - 3.5u)$; $x_3 = x_1 - 3.75u - eps$;
$top\ y_1 = h$; $.5[y_1, y_2] = math\_axis$; $y_3 = y_2$;
draw $z_1 \text{ -- } z_2 \text{ -- } z_3$;   % stem and bar
labels$(1, 2, 3)$; **endchar**;

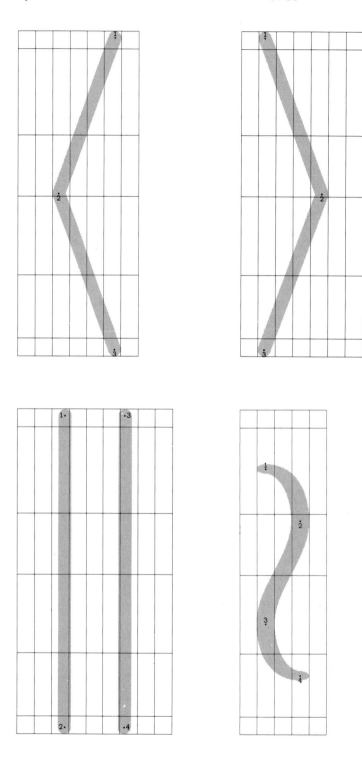

cmchar "Left angle bracket";
beginchar(oct "150", $7u^\#$, $body\_height^\#$, $paren\_depth^\#$);
adjust_fit$(0, 0)$; **pickup** $rule.nib$;
$rt\ x_1 = \text{hround}(w - u) + eps$; $\ x_1 = x_3$; $\ lft\ x_2 = \text{hround}\ 2u - 1 - eps$;
$top\ y_1 = h + eps$; $\ .5[y_1, y_3] = y_2 = math\_axis$;
draw $z_1 \mathrel{-}\mathrel{-} z_2 \mathrel{-}\mathrel{-} z_3$; % diagonals
labels$(1, 2, 3)$; **endchar**;

cmchar "Right angle bracket";
beginchar(oct "151", $7u^\#$, $body\_height^\#$, $paren\_depth^\#$);
adjust_fit$(0, 0)$; **pickup** $rule.nib$;
$rt(w - x_1) = \text{hround}(w - u) + eps$; $\ x_1 = x_3$; $\ lft(w - x_2) = \text{hround}\ 2u - 1 - eps$;
$top\ y_1 = h + eps$; $\ .5[y_1, y_3] = y_2 = math\_axis$;
draw $z_1 \mathrel{-}\mathrel{-} z_2 \mathrel{-}\mathrel{-} z_3$; % diagonals
labels$(1, 2, 3)$; **endchar**;

cmchar "Double vertical line (norm or cardinality)";
beginchar(oct "153", $9u^\#$, $body\_height^\#$, $paren\_depth^\#$);
adjust_fit$(0, 0)$; **pickup** $rule.nib$;
$x_1 = x_2$; $\ top\ y_1 = h$; $\ .5[y_1, y_2] = math\_axis$;
$x_3 = x_4 = w - x_1$; $\ y_3 = y_1$; $\ y_4 = y_2$;
$compute\_spread(.45x\_height^\#, .55x\_height^\#)$; $\ x_3 - x_1 = spread$;
draw $z_1 \mathrel{-}\mathrel{-} z_2$; **draw** $z_3 \mathrel{-}\mathrel{-} z_4$; % stems
labels$(1, 2, 3, 4)$; **endchar**;

cmchar "Wreath product";
beginchar(oct "157", $5u^\#$, $asc\_height^\#$, $asc\_depth^\#$);
adjust_fit(**if** $monospace$: $u^\#$, $u^\#$ **else**: $0, 0$ **fi**);
pickup pencircle yscaled $.7rule\_thickness$ xscaled $1.4rule\_thickness$;
if $vair^\# > .8curve^\#$: **pickup** $rule.nib$; $\ autorounded$; **fi** % monoline
$lft\ x_1 = lft\ x_3 = \text{hround}\ u$; $\ x_2 = x_4 = w - x_1$;
$top\ y_1 = \text{vround}\ .75[math\_axis, h]$;
$.5[y_1, y_4] = .5[y_2, y_3] = math\_axis$; $\ y_1 - y_2 = {}^1\!/4(y_1 - y_4)$;
draw $z_1\{right\} \ldots z_2\{down\} \mathinner{\ldotp\ldotp} \{down\}z_3 \ldots \{right\}z_4$; % stroke
labels$(1, 2, 3, 4)$; **endchar**;

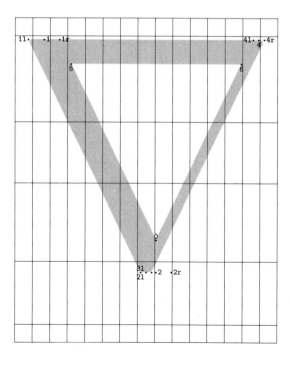

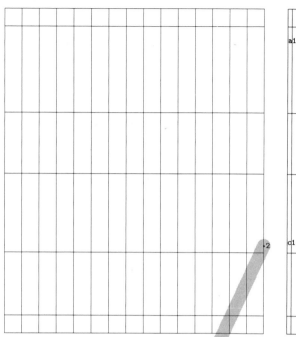

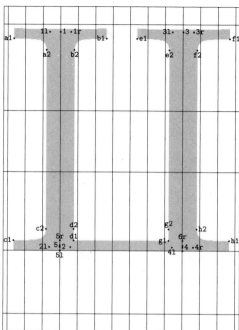

cmchar "Radical sign";
beginchar(oct "160", $15u^\#$, $rule\_thickness^\#$,
   $body\_height^\# + paren\_depth^\# - rule\_thickness^\#$);
big_sqrt; **endchar**;

cmchar "Amalgamation symbol or coproduct symbol";
beginchar(oct "161", $13u^\# + width\_adj^\#$, $cap\_height^\#$, 0);
italcorr $cap\_height^\# * slant - cap\_serif\_fit^\# + cap\_jut^\# - 2.5u^\# + \min(.5cap\_stem^\#, u^\#)$;
adjust_fit($cap\_serif\_fit^\#$, $cap\_serif\_fit^\#$);
pickup $tiny.nib$; $pos_1(cap\_stem, 0)$; $pos_2(cap\_stem, 0)$;
$pos_3(cap\_stem, 0)$; $pos_4(cap\_stem, 0)$;
$lft\ x_{1l} = lft\ x_{2l} = $ hround $\max(2u, 3u - .5cap\_stem)$; $x_3 = x_4 = w - x_1$;
$top\ y_1 = top\ y_3 = h$; $bot\ y_2 = bot\ y_4 = 0$;
filldraw stroke $z_{1e} \text{ -- } z_{2e}$;   % left stem
filldraw stroke $z_{3e} \text{ -- } z_{4e}$;   % right stem
$penpos_5(cap\_bar, 90)$; $penpos_6(cap\_bar, 90)$;
$x_5 = x_1$; $x_6 = x_3$; $y_5 = y_6$; $y_{5l} = 0$;
fill stroke $z_{5e} \text{ -- } z_{6e}$;   % bar
if $serifs$: **numeric** $inner\_jut$;
   if $rt\ x_{1r} + cap\_jut + u + 2 \leq lft\ x_{3l} - cap\_jut$: $inner\_jut = cap\_jut$;
   else: $rt\ x_{1r} + inner\_jut + u + 2 = lft\ x_{3l} - inner\_jut$; **fi**
   $dish\_serif(1, 2, a, \frac{1}{3}, cap\_jut, b, \frac{1}{3}, inner\_jut)$;   % upper left serif
   $nodish\_serif(2, 1, c, \frac{1}{3}, cap\_jut, d, \frac{1}{3}, eps)$;   % lower left serif
   $dish\_serif(3, 4, e, \frac{1}{3}, inner\_jut, f, \frac{1}{3}, cap\_jut)$;   % upper right serif
   $nodish\_serif(4, 3, g, \frac{1}{3}, eps, h, \frac{1}{3}, cap\_jut)$; **fi**   % lower right serif
math_fit(0, $.5ic^\#$); **penlabels**(1, 2, 3, 4, 5, 6); **endchar**;

cmchar "Nabla or backwards-difference operator";
beginchar(oct "162", $15u^\#$, $cap\_height^\#$, 0);
adjust_fit(0, 0);
numeric $right\_stem$, $alpha$;
$right\_stem = cap\_hair$ **if** $hefty$: $-3stem\_corr$ **fi**;
$x_{1l} = w - x_{4r} = .75u$; $y_1 = y_4 = h$;
$x_2 - x_1 = x_4 - x_3$; $x_{3l} = x_{2l} + apex\_corr$; $y_2 = y_3 = -apex\_o - apex\_oo$;
$alpha = diag\_ratio(2, right\_stem, y_1 - y_2, x_{4r} - x_{1l} - apex\_corr)$;
$penpos_1(alpha * cap\_stem, 0)$; $penpos_2(alpha * cap\_stem, 0)$;
$penpos_3(alpha * right\_stem, 0)$; $penpos_4(alpha * right\_stem, 0)$;
fill $diag\_end(2l, 1l, 1, 1, 4r, 3r) \text{ -- } diag\_end(4r, 3r, 1, 1, 2l, 1l) \text{ -- cycle}$;   % triangle
$z_0 = whatever[z_{1r}, z_{2r}] = whatever[z_{3l}, z_{4l}]$;
$y_5 = y_6 = h - cap\_vstem$; $z_5 = whatever[z_{1r}, z_{2r}]$; $z_6 = whatever[z_{3l}, z_{4l}]$;
if $y_0 > cap\_notch\_cut$: $y_0 := cap\_notch\_cut$;
   unfill $z_0 + .5right\{up\} \ldots \{z_4 - z_3\}z_6 \text{ -- } z_5\{z_2 - z_1\}$
      $\ldots \{down\}z_0 + .5left \text{ -- cycle}$;   % counter
else: **unfill** $z_0 \text{ -- } z_5 \text{ -- } z_6 \text{ -- cycle}$; **fi**   % counter
penlabels(0, 1, 2, 3, 4, 5, 6); **endchar**;

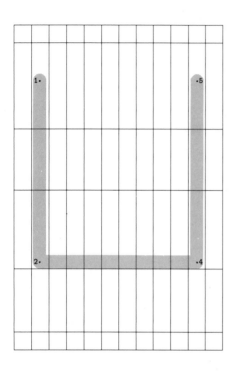

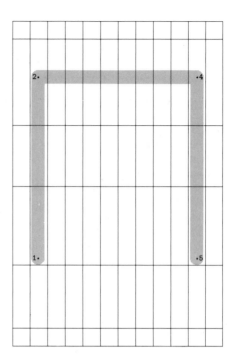

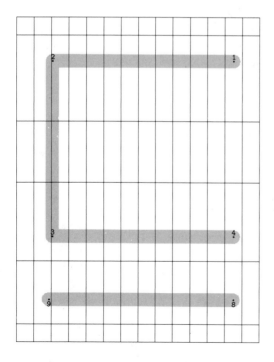

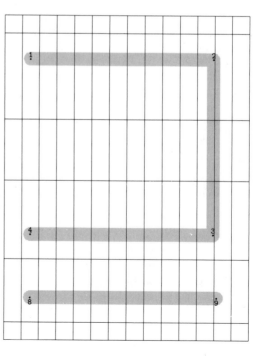

cmchar "Square set union sign (Scott lub)";
beginchar(oct "164", $12u^\#$, $.8asc\_height^\#$, 0);
adjust_fit$(0, 0)$; **pickup** $rule.nib$;
lft $x_1 =$ hround $1.1u$; $x_2 = x_1$; $x_4 = x_5 = w - x_1$;
$y_1 = good.y$ $h + o$; bot $y_2 = 0$; $y_4 = y_2$; $y_5 = y_1$;
draw z_1 --- z_2 --- z_4 --- z_5;   % stems and bar
labels$(1, 2, 4, 5)$; **endchar**;

cmchar "Square set intersection sign (Scott glb)";
beginchar(oct "165", $12u^\#$, $.8asc\_height^\#$, 0);
adjust_fit$(0, 0)$; **pickup** $rule.nib$;
lft $x_1 =$ hround $1.1u$; $x_2 = x_1$; $x_4 = x_5 = w - x_1$;
$y_2 = good.y$ $h + o$; bot $y_1 = 0$; $y_4 = y_2$; $y_5 = y_1$;
draw z_1 --- z_2 --- z_4 --- z_5;   % stems and bar
labels$(1, 2, 4, 5)$; **endchar**;

cmchar "Square subset or equal to sign";
$compute\_spread(.45x\_height^\#, .55x\_height^\#)$;
$spread^{\#\prime} := spread^\#$; $spread' := spread$;   % the spread of '='
$compute\_spread(^5\!/_4x\_height^\#, ^3\!/_2x\_height^\#)$;
beginchar(oct "166", $14u^\#$, $v\_center(spread^{\#\prime} + spread^\# + rule\_thickness^\#)$);
adjust_fit$(0, 0)$; **pickup** $rule.nib$;
lft $x_2 =$ hround$(1.5u + oo)$; $x_1 = x_4 =$ hround$(w - 1.5u) + eps$; $x_3 = x_2$;
$y_1 - y_4 = spread$; $y_2 = y_1$; $y_3 = y_4$; top $y_1 = h$;
draw z_1 -- z_2 -- z_3 -- z_4;   % bars and stem
$x_8 = x_1$; $x_9 = x_2 - oo - eps$; $y_8 = y_9$; $y_4 - y_9 = spread'$;
draw z_8 -- z_9;   % lower bar
labels$(1, 2, 3, 4, 8, 9)$; **endchar**;

cmchar "Square superset or equal to sign";
$compute\_spread(.45x\_height^\#, .55x\_height^\#)$;
$spread^{\#\prime} := spread^\#$; $spread' := spread$;   % the spread of '='
$compute\_spread(^5\!/_4x\_height^\#, ^3\!/_2x\_height^\#)$;
beginchar(oct "167", $14u^\#$, $v\_center(spread^{\#\prime} + spread^\# + rule\_thickness^\#)$);
adjust_fit$(0, 0)$; **pickup** $rule.nib$;
$x_1 = x_4 =$ hround $1.5u - eps$; rt $x_2 =$ hround$(w - 1.5u - oo)$; $x_3 = x_2$;
$y_1 - y_4 = spread$; $y_2 = y_1$; $y_3 = y_4$; top $y_1 = h$;
draw z_1 -- z_2 -- z_3 -- z_4;   % bars and stem
$x_8 = x_1$; $x_9 = x_2 + oo + eps$; $y_8 = y_9$; $y_4 - y_9 = spread'$;
draw z_8 -- z_9;   % lower bar
labels$(1, 2, 3, 4, 8, 9)$; **endchar**;

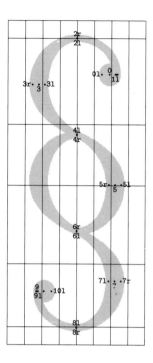

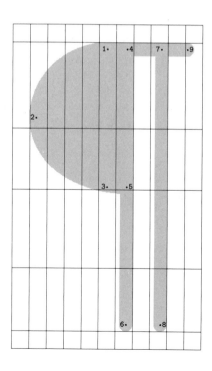

cmchar "Section sign";
beginchar(oct "170", $6.5u^\# + \max(1.5u^\#, stem^\#)$, $asc\_height^\#$, $desc\_depth^\#$);
adjust_fit$(0, 0)$; **pickup** *fine.nib*;
numeric *sstem*; $sstem = \text{hround } .75[hair, stem]$;
$pos_0(stem, 0)$; $pos_1(hair, 0)$; $pos_2(vair, 90)$; $pos_3(sstem, 180)$; $pos_4(vair, 270)$;
$pos_{5'}(sstem, 0)$; $pos_5(sstem, 180)$;
$pos_6(vair, 90)$; $pos_7(sstem, 0)$; $pos_8(vair, -90)$; $pos_9(hair, -180)$; $pos_{10}(stem, -180)$;
$top\ y_{2r} = h + oo$; $bot\ y_{8r} = -d - oo$; $y_2 - y_1 = y_9 - y_8 = (y_2 - y_8)/8$;
$y_3 = .52[y_4, y_2]$; $y_5 = .52[y_4, y_6]$; $y_7 = .52[y_6, y_8]$; $y_{5'} = .52[y_6, y_4]$;
$y_2 - y_4 = y_4 - y_6 = y_6 - y_8$;
$rt\ x_{1r} = \text{hround}(w - 1.5u)$; $lft\ x_{3r} = \text{hround } 1.25u$;
$x_2 = x_4 = x_6 = x_8 = .5w$; $x_5 = x_7 = w - x_3$; $x_{5'} = x_3$; $x_9 = w - x_1$;
$bulb(2, 1, 0)$; $bulb(8, 9, 10)$; % bulbs
filldraw stroke $z_{2e}\{left\} \ldots z_{3e}\{down\} \ldots z_{4e}\{3(x_5 - x_3), y_5 - y_3\}$
    $\ldots z_{5e}\{down\} \ldots \{left\}z_{6e}$; % upper stroke
filldraw stroke $z_{4e}\{left\} \ldots z_{5'e}\{down\} \ldots z_{6e}\{3(x_7 - x_{5'}), y_7 - y_{5'}\}$
    $\ldots z_{7e}\{down\} \ldots \{left\}z_{8e}$; % upper stroke
penlabels$(0, 1, 2, 3, 4, 5, 6, 7, 8, 9, 10)$; **endchar**;

cmchar "Paragraph mark";
beginchar(oct "173", $11u^\#$, $asc\_height^\#$, $desc\_depth^\#$);
adjust_fit$(0, 0)$; **pickup** *rule.nib*; *autorounded*;
$top\ y_1 = h$; $bot\ y_6 = -d - eps$; $y_4 = y_7 = y_9 = y_1$;
$y_8 = y_6$; $y_3 = y_5 = good.y\ .5[y_1, y_6]$;
$x_7 - x_4 = \text{ceiling}(rule\_thickness + 1.25u)$;
$lft\ x_2 = \text{hround } u$; $y_2 = .5[y_1, y_3]$; $x_4 = x_5 = x_6$; $rt\ x_9 = \text{hround}(w - .5u)$;
$x_7 = x_8 = good.x(x_9 - 1.5u)$; $x_1 = x_3 = \min(.5w, x_4)$;
filldraw $z_4 \mathbin{..} z_1\{left\} \ldots z_2\{down\} \ldots \{right\}z_5 \text{ -- cycle}$; % filled bowl
draw $z_9 \text{ -- } z_4 \text{ -- } z_6$; % left stem and upper serif
draw $z_7 \text{ -- } z_8$; % right stem
labels$(1, 2, 3, 4, 5, 6, 7, 8, 9)$; **endchar**;

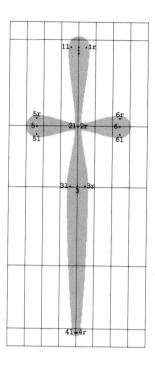

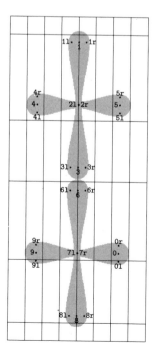

cmchar "Dagger mark";
beginchar(oct "171", $8u\#$, $asc\_height\#$, $desc\_depth\#$);
adjust_fit$(0, 0)$; **pickup** *fine.nib*;
$pos_1(stem, 0)$; $pos_2(thin\_join, 0)$; $pos_3(stem, 0)$; $pos_4(hair, 0)$;
$pos_5(stem, 90)$; $pos_{2'}(thin\_join, 90)$; $pos_6(stem, 90)$; $z_{2'} = z_2$;
$x_1 = x_2 = x_3 = x_4$; $x_1 - .5stem = $ hround$(.5w - .5stem)$; $w := r := 2x_1$;
$x_5 - .5stem = $ hround u; $x_6 = w - x_5$;
$y_1 + .5stem = h + oo$; $y_2 = y_5 = y_6$; $y_3 = .57y_2$; bot $y_4 = -d - o$;
$y_5 + .5stem = $ floor$(x\_height + .5stem)$;
filldraw circ_stroke $z_{1e}\{down\}$ .. $z_{2e}\{down\}$ .. $z_{3e}\{down\}$ .. z_{4e};   % stem
filldraw circ_stroke $z_{5e}\{right\}$ .. $\{right\}z_{2'e}$;   % left bulb
filldraw circ_stroke $z_{6e}\{left\}$ .. $\{left\}z_{2'e}$;   % right bulb
penlabels$(1, 2, 3, 4, 5, 6)$; **endchar**;

cmchar "Double dagger mark";   .
beginchar(oct "172", $8u\#$, $asc\_height\#$, $desc\_depth\#$);
adjust_fit$(0, 0)$; **pickup** *fine.nib*;
$pos_1(stem, 0)$; $pos_2(thin\_join, 0)$; $pos_3(stem, 0)$;
$pos_4(stem, 90)$; $pos_{2'}(thin\_join, 90)$; $pos_5(stem, 90)$; $z_{2'} = z_2$;
$x_1 = x_2 = x_3$; $x_1 - .5stem = $ hround$(.5w - .5stem)$; $w := r := 2x_1$;
$x_4 - .5stem = $ hround u; $x_5 = w - x_4$;
$y_1 + .5stem = h + oo$; $y_2 = y_4 = y_5 = .5[y_1, y_3]$; $y_3 - .5stem = $ ceiling$(.5[-d, h])$;
filldraw circ_stroke $z_{1e}\{down\}$ .. $\{down\}z_{2e}$;   % top stem
filldraw circ_stroke $z_{3e}\{up\}$ .. $\{up\}z_{2e}$;   % upper middle stem
filldraw circ_stroke $z_{4e}\{right\}$ .. $\{right\}z_{2'e}$;   % top left bulb
filldraw circ_stroke $z_{5e}\{left\}$ .. $\{left\}z_{2'e}$;   % top right bulb
$pos_6(stem, 0)$; $pos_7(thin\_join, 0)$; $pos_8(stem, 0)$;
$pos_9(stem, 90)$; $pos_{7'}(thin\_join, 90)$; $pos_0(stem, 90)$; $z_{7'} = z_7$;
$x_6 = x_7 = x_8 = x_1$; $x_9 = x_4$; $x_0 = x_5$;
$y_6 = y_3 - stem - 1$; $y_7 = y_9 = y_0 = .5[y_6, y_8]$; $y_8 - .5stem = -d - oo$;
filldraw circ_stroke $z_{6e}\{down\}$ .. $\{down\}z_{7e}$;   % lower middle stem
filldraw circ_stroke $z_{8e}\{up\}$ .. $\{up\}z_{7e}$;   % bottom stem
filldraw circ_stroke $z_{9e}\{right\}$ .. $\{right\}z_{7'e}$;   % bottom left bulb
filldraw circ_stroke $z_{0e}\{left\}$ .. $\{left\}z_{7'e}$;   % bottom right bulb
penlabels$(1, 2, 3, 4, 5, 6, 7, 8, 9, 0)$; **endchar**;

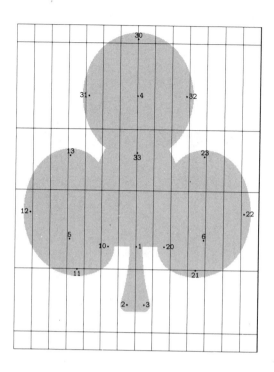

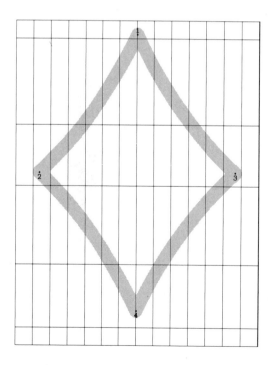

cmchar "Club suit";
beginchar(oct "174", $14u^\#$, $asc\_height^\#$, $^2/_3desc\_depth^\#$);
adjust_fit$(0, 0)$; **pickup** $rule.nib$; $autorounded$;
$x_1 = x_4 = x_{30} = x_{33} = good.x$ $.5w$; $w := r := 2x_1$;
$x_2 = good.x(x_1 - .5u) - eps$; *lft* $x_1 - rt$ $x_{10} = $ hround $.5pt$; *lft* $x_{12} = $ hround $.5u$;
$x_{11} = .6[x_{12}, x_{10}]$; $x_{13} = .5[x_{12}, x_{10}] = x_5$; $x_{32} - x_{31} = x_1 - .5u - x_{12}$;
$x_2 + x_3 = x_5 + x_6 = x_{10} + x_{20} = x_{11} + x_{21} = x_{12} + x_{22} = x_{13} + x_{23} = x_{31} + x_{32} = 2x_1$;
top $y_{30} = h + o + oo$; *bot* $y_{11} = $ *bot* $y_{21} = -o$; *top* $y_{13} = $ *top* $y_{23} = $ vround $.53h$;
$y_{30} - y_{33} = y_{13} - y_{11}$; $y_{31} = y_{32} = y_4 = .5[y_{30}, y_{33}]$; $y_{12} = y_{22} = .5[y_{11}, y_{13}]$;
$y_1 = y_{10} = y_{20} = good.y$ $.1h$; *bot* $y_5 = $ *bot* $y_6 = y_1 + .75$; *bot* $y_2 = $ *bot* $y_3 = -d$;
filldraw $z_{30}\{left\}$ ... $z_{31}\{down\}$ ... $z_{33}\{right\}$ ... $z_{32}\{up\}$ ... cycle;   % top bowl
filldraw $z_{13}\{left\}$ ... $z_{12}\{down\}$ ... $z_{11}\{right\}$ ... $z_{10}\{up\}$ ... cycle;   % left bowl
filldraw $z_{23}\{left\}$ ... $z_{20}\{down\}$ ... $z_{21}\{right\}$ ... $z_{22}\{up\}$ ... cycle;   % right bowl
filldraw $z_1\{down\}$ ... $\{2(x_2 - x_1), y_2 - y_1\}z_2$ -- $z_3\{2(x_1 - x_3), y_1 - y_3\}$
      ... $\{up\}$ cycle;   % stem
filldraw z_4 -- z_5 -- z_6 -- cycle;   % filling
labels$(1, 2, 3, 4, 5, 6, 10, 11, 12, 13, 20, 21, 22, 23, 30, 31, 32, 33)$; **endchar**;

cmchar "Diamond suit";
beginchar(oct "175", $14u^\#$, $asc\_height^\#$, $^2/_3desc\_depth^\#$);
adjust_fit$(0, 0)$; **pickup** $rule.nib$; $autorounded$;
$x_1 = x_4 = good.x$ $.5w$; $w := r := 2x_1$;
lft $x_2 = $ hround u; $x_3 = w - x_2$;
top $y_1 = h + o + oo$; *bot* $y_4 = -d - o - oo$; $y_2 = y_3 = .5[y_1, y_4]$;
draw $z_1\{x_3 - x_1, 1.5(y_3 - y_1)\}$ ... $z_3\{1.5(x_3 - x_1), y_3 - y_1\}$;   % upper right diagonal
draw $z_1\{x_2 - x_1, 1.5(y_2 - y_1)\}$ ... $z_2\{1.5(x_2 - x_1), y_2 - y_1\}$;   % upper left diagonal
draw $z_4\{x_2 - x_4, 1.5(y_2 - y_4)\}$ ... $z_2\{1.5(x_2 - x_4), y_2 - y_4\}$;   % lower left diagonal
draw $z_4\{x_3 - x_4, 1.5(y_3 - y_4)\}$ ... $z_3\{1.5(x_3 - x_4), y_3 - y_4\}$;   % lower right diagonal
labels$(1, 2, 3, 4)$; **endchar**;

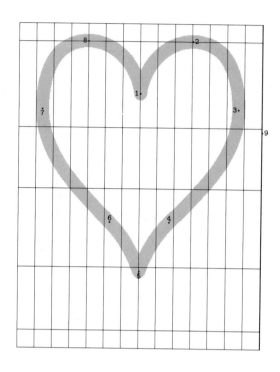

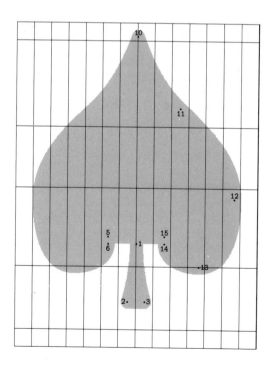

cmchar "Heart suit";
beginchar(oct "176", $14u^\#$, $asc\_height^\#$, $2/3 desc\_depth^\#$);
adjust_fit$(0, 0)$; **pickup** $rule.nib$; $autorounded$;
$x_1 = x_5 = good.x \ .5w$; $w := r := 2x_1$;
$lft \ x_7 = $ hround u; $x_8 = 4u$; $x_2 + x_8 = x_3 + x_7 = x_4 + x_6 = w$;
$y_1 = good.y \ .77h$; $top \ y_2 = h + o$; $y_3 = .7h$; $y_4 = .2h$; $bot \ y_5 = -o - oo$;
$y_2 = y_8$; $y_3 = y_7$; $y_4 = y_6$; $z_4 = whatever[z_3, z_5]$;
$x_0 = x_9 = w$; $y_0 = 1.5h$; $y_9 = .6h$;
draw $z_1\{x_2 - x_1, 8(y_2 - y_1)\} \ldots z_2\{right\} \ldots z_3\{down\} \ldots \{z_4 - z_9\}z_4$
$\ldots \{z_5 - z_0\}z_5$;   % right half bowl
draw $z_1\{x_8 - x_1, 8(y_8 - y_1)\} \ldots z_8\{left\} \ldots z_7\{down\} \ldots \{(z_4 - z_9) \text{ xscaled } -1\}z_6$
$\ldots \{(z_5 - z_0) \text{ xscaled } -1\}z_5$;   % left half bowl
labels$(0, 1, 2, 3, 4, 5, 6, 7, 8, 9)$; **endchar**;

cmchar "Spade suit";
beginchar(oct "177", $14u^\#$, $asc\_height^\#$, $2/3 desc\_depth^\#$);
adjust_fit$(0, 0)$; **pickup** $rule.nib$; $autorounded$;
$x_1 = x_{10} = good.x \ .5w$; $w := r := 2x_1$;
$x_2 = good.x(x_1 - .5u) - eps$; $lft \ x_1 - rt \ x_6 = $ hround $.5pt$; $x_5 = x_6$;
$x_7 = .5[x_8, x_6]$; $lft \ x_8 = $ hround u;
$x_2 + x_3 = x_5 + x_{15} = x_6 + x_{14} = x_7 + x_{13} = x_8 + x_{12} = x_9 + x_{11} = 2x_{10}$;
$top \ y_{10} = h + o + oo$; $y_9 = y_{11} = .7h$; $y_8 = y_{12} = .3h$;
$y_1 = y_6 = y_{14} = good.y \ .1h$; $bot \ y_5 = bot \ y_{15} = y_1 + .75$;
$bot \ y_7 = bot \ y_{13} = -o$; $bot \ y_2 = bot \ y_3 = -d$; $z_9 = whatever[z_8, z_{10}]$;
filldraw $z_{10}\{-w, -3h\} \ldots z_9\{-w, -h\} \ldots z_8\{down\} \ldots z_7\{right\} \ldots z_6 \dashrightarrow z_5$
$\text{--} z_{15} \text{ --- } z_{14} \ldots \{right\}z_{13} \ldots \{up\}z_{12} \ldots \{-w, h\}z_{11}$
$\ldots \{-w, 3h\}$ cycle;   % filled bowl
filldraw $z_1\{down\} \ldots \{2(x_2 - x_1), y_2 - y_1\}z_2 \text{ -- } z_3\{2(x_1 - x_3), y_1 - y_3\}$
$\ldots \{up\}$ cycle;   % stem
labels$(1, 2, 3, 5, 6, 10, 11, 12, 13, 14, 15)$; **endchar**;

Finally, we are ready to wrap things up, with two simple program files that are used only by the **texset** driver. The programs in **tset.mf** generate most of the non-standard ASCII symbols in TeX's extended character set.

% Special characters for "extended ASCII character set" fonts

% Two accents have been copied from **accent.mf**
% and there's also a (genuinely) blank space.

% Codes '040, '136, and '176 are generated, in addition to the following:
$cdot$ = oct "000";
$down\_arrow$ = oct "001";
$meet$ = oct "004";
$false\_that$ = oct "005";
elt = oct "006";
up_arrow = oct "013";
$plus\_minus$ = oct "014";
o_plus = oct "015";
$infty$ = oct "016";
$subset$ = oct "020";
$superset$ = oct "021";
cap = oct "022";
cup = oct "023";
for_all = oct "024";
$there\_exists$ = oct "025";
o_times = oct "026";
$double\_arrow$ = oct "027";
$left\_arrow$ = oct "030";
$right\_arrow$ = oct "031";
neq = oct "032";
$diamond$ = oct "033";
leq = oct "034";
geq = oct "035";
eqv = oct "036";
$join$ = oct "037";
$straight\_quotes$ = oct "042";
$minus$ = oct "055";
$less$ = oct "074";
$greater$ = oct "076";
$backslash$ = oct "134";
$underbar$ = oct "137";
$left\_brace$ = oct "173";
$vertical$ = oct "174";
$right\_brace$ = oct "175";
$integral$ = oct "177";

input sym;

cmchar "Blank space";
beginchar(oct "040", $6u\#$, 0, 0);
adjust_fit(0, 0); **endchar**;

cmchar "Circumflex (hat) accent";
beginchar(oct "136", $9u^\#$, $\min(asc\_height^\#, 2x\_height^\#)$, 0);

$\vdots$ (a copy of the program for '^' in **accent** comes here)

penlabels(0, 1, 2, 3, 4); **endchar**;

cmchar "Tilde (squiggle) accent";
beginchar(oct "176", $9u^\#$, $\min(asc\_height^\#, {}^{10}\!/_7 x\_height^\# + .5dot\_size^\#)$, 0);

$\vdots$ (a copy of the program for '~' in **accent** comes here)

penlabels(1, 2, 3, 4, 5); **endchar**;

The final program file, `tsetsl.mf`, is similar to `tset.mf`; the `texset` driver calls this one before setting *slant* to zero.

> % Special slanted characters for "extended ASCII character set" fonts

> % These characters were copied from `greekl.mf` and `italms.mf`
> % with character positions changed and italic corrections added to the width.

> % Codes ´002´–´003´, ´007´–´012´, and ´017´ are generated.

cmchar "Lowercase Greek alpha for extended ASCII";
beginchar(oct "002", $11u^\#$, $x\_height^\#$, 0);
italcorr $\max(^1\!/_3 x\_height^\# * slant + .5hair^\# + .5u^\#, x\_height^\# * slant - .5u^\#)$;
adjust_fit(0, $ic^\#$); **pickup** *fine.nib*;

$\vdots$ (the rest of the program for 'α' in **greekl** comes here)

penlabels(0, 1, 2, 3, 4, 5, 6, 7); **endchar**;

cmchar "Lowercase Greek beta for extended ASCII";
beginchar(oct "003", $9.5u^\#$, $asc\_height^\#$, $desc\_depth^\#$);
italcorr $.5[x\_height^\#, asc\_height^\#] * slant - u^\#$;
adjust_fit(0, $ic^\#$); **pickup** *fine.nib*;

$\vdots$ (the rest of the program for 'β' in **greekl** comes here)

penlabels(0, 1, 2, 3, 4, 5, 6, 7, 8, 9); **endchar**;

cmchar "Lowercase Greek pi for extended ASCII";
beginchar(oct "007", $10u^\#$, $x\_height^\#$, 0);
italcorr $x\_height^\# * slant + .5stem^\# - u^\#$;
adjust_fit(0, $ic^\#$);   *pi_stroke*;   % hook and bar

$\vdots$ (the rest of the program for 'π' in **greekl** comes here)

penlabels(1, 2, 3, 4, 5, 6, 7); **endchar**;

cmchar "Lowercase Greek lambda for extended ASCII";
beginchar(oct "010", $10.5u^\#$, $asc\_height^\#$, 0);

$\vdots$ (a copy of the program for 'λ' in **greekl** comes here)

penlabels(1, 2, 3, 4, 5, 6); **endchar**;

cmchar "Lowercase Greek gamma for extended ASCII";
beginchar(oct "011", $10u^\#$, $x\_height^\#$, $desc\_depth^\#$);
italcorr $x\_height^\# * slant - .5u^\#$;
adjust_fit$(0, ic^\#)$;   **pickup** *fine.nib*;

       $\vdots$ (the rest of the program for 'γ' in **greekl** comes here)

penlabels$(1, 2, 3, 4, 5, 6, 7)$; **endchar**;

cmchar "Lowercase Greek delta for extended ASCII";
beginchar(oct "012", $8u^\#$, $asc\_height^\#$, 0);
italcorr $.9asc\_height^\# * slant + .5hair^\# - 1.5u^\#$;
adjust_fit$(0, ic^\#)$;   **pickup** *fine.nib*;

       $\vdots$ (the rest of the program for 'δ' in **greekl** comes here)

penlabels$(1, 2, 3, 4, 5, 6, 7, 8)$; **endchar**;

cmchar "Partial differential sign for extended ASCII";
beginchar(oct "017", $10u^\#$, $asc\_height^\#$, 0);
italcorr $.7asc\_height^\# * slant + .5curve^\# - 1.5u^\#$;
adjust_fit$(0, ic^\#)$;

       $\vdots$ (the rest of the program for '∂' in **italms** comes here)

penlabels$(0, 1, 2, 3, 4, 5, 6, 7)$; **endchar**;

The Base File

We've now seen all of the METAFONT code that defines Computer Modern type-faces, except for the contents of the file 'cmbase.mf'. The purpose of cmbase is to provide basic routines that are needed by the programs in other files; we might say that cmbase is a "fancy" extension of the "plain" METAFONT base file de-scribed in *The METAFONTbook*. All of the standard routines of plain.mf are as-sumed to be present, although some of them are changed slightly by cmbase.mf.

The opening lines of cmbase.mf are very simple:

% The base file for Computer Modern (a supplement to plain.mf)

$cmbase := 1;$ % when *cmbase* is known, this file has been input

let cmchar $= \backslash;$ % 'cmchar' should precede each character
let generate $=$ **input**;   % 'generate' should follow the parameters

$autorounding := 0; \; smoothing := 0;$ % we do our own rounding
def $autorounded =$ **interim** $autorounding := 2$ **enddef**;

newinternal $slant, fudge, math\_spread, superness, superpull, beak\_darkness, ligs;$
boolean $square\_dots, hefty, serifs,$
$\quad monospace, variant\_g, low\_asterisk, math\_fitting;$

boolean $dark, dark_{dark}, skewed, skewed_{skewed};$ % for fast option testing
$dark = skewed =$ **false**; $\; dark_{dark} = skewed_{skewed} =$ **true**;

(The boolean variables *dark* and *skewed* provide an efficient way for subroutines like *serif* and *hook_in* to test if special variations are desired.)

The most important general routine in *cmbase* is probably the *pos* macro, which generalizes plain METAFONT's '*penpos*' by subtracting the breadth of the currently-picked-up pen:

---

newinternal $currentbreadth;$
vardef $pos_{@\#}(\textbf{expr } b, d) =$
$\quad$ **if** known b: **if** $b \leq currentbreadth$: **errmessage** "bad pos"; **fi fi**
$\quad (x_{@\#r} - x_{@\#l}, y_{@\#r} - y_{@\#l}) = (b - currentbreadth, 0)$ rotated d;
$\quad x_{@\#} = .5(x_{@\#l} + x_{@\#r}); \; y_{@\#} = .5(y_{@\#l} + y_{@\#r})$ **enddef**;

(If parameters have been set up carefully, a "bad pos" error will never occur. This error message could therefore be removed from the code for *pos*, making font generation a bit faster in a production system.)

In order to make *pos* work, it's necessary to maintain the value of *currentbreadth*, by redefining part of plain METAFONT's **pickup** macro:

---

def *numeric_pickup_* **primary** $q =$
  currentpen := *pen_*$[q]$;
  pen_lft := *pen_lft_*$[q]$; *pen_rt* := *pen_rt_*$[q]$;
  pen_top := *pen_top_*$[q]$; *pen_bot* := *pen_bot_*$[q]$;
  currentpen_path := *pen_path_*$[q]$;
  if known *breadth_*$[q]$: *currentbreadth* := *breadth_*$[q]$; **fi enddef**;

The next most important feature of `cmbase` is the **stroke** macro, which simplifies and generalizes the **penstroke** feature of plain METAFONT. When a Computer Modern program says '**stroke** $p(e)$', we get the cyclic path '$p(l)$ -- reverse $p(r)$ -- cycle', if $p(e)$ is a path whose edges are denoted by the letter e. For example, '**stroke** $z_{1e}\{left\} \mathinner{.\,.} z_{2e}$' is equivalent to

$$(z_{1l}\{left\} \mathinner{.\,.} z_{2l}) \mathbin{-\!-} (z_{2r} \mathinner{.\,.} \{right\}z_{1r}) \mathbin{-\!-} \text{cycle}.$$

Plain METAFONT's '**penstroke** $p(e)$' is exactly the same as '**fill stroke** $p(e)$', if $p(e)$ is not a cyclic path.

---

vardef *stroke* **text** $t =$
  forsuffixes $e = l, r$: *path_*$_e$:= t; **endfor**
  if cycle *path_*$_l$:
    errmessage "Beware: 'stroke' isn't intended for cycles"; **fi**
  *path_*$_l$ -- reverse *path_*$_r$ -- cycle **enddef**;

There's also '**circ_stroke** $p(e)$', which expands to '$p(l)$ -- reverse $p(r)$ $\mathinner{.\,.}$ cycle':

---

vardef *circ_stroke* **text** $t =$
  forsuffixes $e = l, r$: *path_*$_e$:= t; **endfor**
  if cycle *path_*$_l$:
    errmessage "Beware: 'stroke' isn't intended for cycles"; **fi**
  *path_*$_l$ -- reverse *path_*$_r$ $\mathinner{.\,.}$ cycle **enddef**;

Since **circ_stroke** uses '$\mathinner{.\,.}$' instead of '--', the path is roughly circular at the initial endpoint where the beginning of $p(l)$ is joined to the beginning of $p(r)$.

The next part of `cmbase.mf` contains dozens of macro definitions for specific features of the Computer Modern design. Most of these routines can be omitted here, because we've already seen them; they were sprinkled in with the program files, so that they could be studied in context. Only four of the feature-drawing routines still need to be shown, namely *diag_end* and its variants. They have been saved for this chapter because they are best considered as a unit.

The *diag_end* routine produces the outlines of diagonal strokes at the top and bottom of letters like '**X**'. These outlines are used in **fill** commands (not **filldraw**), since soft corners look better if they have different diameters of curvature in diagonal contexts. A macro call like '*diag_end*$(5r, 6r, 1, .5, 6l, 5l)$' yields the outline of a curve similar to what would be drawn by a *tiny* pen from

z_{5r} to z_{6r} to z_{6l} to z_{5l}, but it is altered so that the "sharpness" at corner z_{6r} is 1 and the sharpness at z_{6l} is .5; this means that the effective pen diameters at z_{6r} and z_{6l} are *tiny* and *.5tiny*. (Points z_{5r}, z_{6r}, z_{6l}, and z_{5l} are not actually on the path computed by *diag_end* in this example, unless *tiny* = 0.)

---

vardef *diag_end*(**suffix** *from*, $)(**expr** *sharpness_in*, *sharpness_out*)(**suffix** $$, *to*) =
  save *from_x*, *to_x*, y_-, x_-, xx_-;
  if $y_{from} > y_\$$: *tiny.bot* **else**: *tiny.top* **fi** $y_- = y_\$$;   % we assume that $y_\$ = y_{\$\$}$
  $(from\_x, y_-) = whatever[z_{from}, z_\$]$; $(to\_x, y_-) = whatever[z_{\$\$}, z_{to}]$;
  if $x_{\$\$} > x_\$$: $x_- = x_\$ + sharpness\_in * \text{length}(z_\$ - (from\_x, y_-))$;
    $xx_- = x_{\$\$} - sharpness\_out * \text{length}(z_{\$\$} - (to\_x, y_-))$;
    if $xx_- < x_-$: $xx_- := x_- := .5[xx_-, x_-]$; **fi**
  else: $x_- = x_\$ - sharpness\_in * \text{length}(z_\$ - (from\_x, y_-))$;
    $xx_- = x_{\$\$} + sharpness\_out * \text{length}(z_{\$\$} - (to\_x, y_-))$;
    if $xx_- > x_-$: $xx_- := x_- := .5[xx_-, x_-]$; **fi fi**
  $sharpness\_in[z_\$, (from\_x, y_-)]\{z_\$ - z_{from}\}$
    $\ldots \{z_{\$\$} - z_\$\}(x_-, y_\$) \mathinner{.\,.} (xx_-, y_\$)\{z_{\$\$} - z_\$\}$
    $\ldots \{z_{to} - z_{\$\$}\} sharpness\_out[z_{\$\$}, (to\_x, y_-)]$ **enddef**;

Simpler versions of *diag_end* called *diag_in* and *diag_out* are used when there is just one corner to be turned instead of two. The middle strokes of 'W' and 'w' require a third variation called *special_diag_end*:

---

vardef *diag_in*(**suffix** *from*, $)(**expr** *sharpness*)(**suffix** $$) =
  pickup *tiny.nib*; **save** *from_x*, y_-;
  if $y_{from} > y_\$$: *bot* **else**: *top* **fi** $y_- = y_\$$;
  $(from\_x, y_-) = whatever[z_{from}, z_\$]$;
  $sharpness[z_\$, (from\_x, y_-)]\{z_\$ - z_{from}\}$
    $\ldots \{z_{\$\$} - z_\$\}z_\$ + sharpness * \text{length}(z_\$ - (from\_x, y_-)) * \text{unitvector}(z_{\$\$} - z_\$)$ **enddef**;

vardef *diag_out*(**suffix** $)(**expr** *sharpness*)(**suffix** $$, *to*) =
  pickup *tiny.nib*; **save** *to_x*, y_-;
  if $y_{to} > y_\$$: *bot* **else**: *top* **fi** $y_- = y_\$$;
  $(to\_x, y_-) = whatever[z_{\$\$}, z_{to}]$;
  $z_{\$\$} - sharpness * \text{length}(z_{\$\$} - (to\_x, y_-)) * \text{unitvector}(z_{\$\$} - z_\$)\{z_{\$\$} - z_\$\}$
    $\ldots \{z_{to} - z_{\$\$}\} sharpness[z_{\$\$}, (to\_x, y_-)]$ **enddef**;

vardef *special_diag_end*(**suffix** $$, $, @, @@) =   % for top middle of w's
  if $x_{@r} \leq x_{\$r}$: *diag_end*($$r, $r, 1, 1, @l, @@l$)
  else: $z_0 = whatever[z_{\$\$l}, z_{\$l}] = whatever[z_{@l}, z_{@@l}]$;
    diag_end($$r, $r, 1, 1, $l, 0$) -- z_0 **fi enddef**;

The next part of `cmbase.mf` deals with character fitting. White space is added to or taken from the sidebearings of each character by the **adjust_fit** routine, which is either *normal_adjust_fit* or *mono_adjust_fit* depending on whether *monospace* is **false** or **true**. The width of a character as stated in its **beginchar** command is actually just a "reference width," not the true width; the subsequent command **adjust_fit**(α, β) adds $\alpha + \lambda$ extra space at the left and $\beta + \lambda$ at the right, where λ is the *letter_fit* parameter. Character programs often refer to the variable w, which is the reference width in pixels; but the final character generated by a program actually runs from $x = l$ to $x = r$, not from $x = 0$ to $x = w$. There's a *shrink_fit* variable that improves the appearance of low-resolution and medium-resolution letters. Appendix E of *The METAFONT book* discusses these adjustment routines in more detail.

---

newinternal $l, r, shrink\_fit$;   % adjustments to spacing

def *normal_adjust_fit*(**expr** *left_adjustment*, *right_adjustment*) =
$\quad l := - \operatorname{hround}(left\_adjustment * hppp) - letter\_fit$;
$\quad$**interim** $xoffset := -l$;
$\quad charwd := charwd + 2letter\_fit\# + left\_adjustment + right\_adjustment$;
$\quad r := l + \operatorname{hround}(charwd * hppp) - shrink\_fit$;
$\quad w := r - \operatorname{hround}(right\_adjustment * hppp) - letter\_fit$;
$\quad$**enddef**;

def *mono_adjust_fit*(**expr** *left_adjustment*, *right_adjustment*) =
$\quad$**numeric** *expansion_factor*;
$\quad mono\_charwd\# = 2letter\_fit\#$
$\qquad + expansion\_factor * (charwd + left\_adjustment + right\_adjustment)$;
$\quad$**forsuffixes** $\$ = u, jut, cap\_jut, beak\_jut, apex\_corr$:
$\qquad \$:= \$\# * expansion\_factor * hppp$; **endfor**
$\quad l := - \operatorname{hround}(left\_adjustment * expansion\_factor * hppp) - letter\_fit$;
$\quad$**interim** $xoffset := -l$;
$\quad r := l + mono\_charwd - shrink\_fit$;
$\quad w := r - \operatorname{hround}(right\_adjustment * expansion\_factor * hppp) - letter\_fit$;
$\quad charwd := mono\_charwd\#$; $charic := mono\_charic\#$;
$\quad$**enddef**;

extra_endchar := *extra_endchar* & `"r:=r+shrink_fit;w:=r-1;"`;

Yet another width adjustment is made when characters are being prepared for use in math formulas. This secondary adjustment occurs just before the **endchar**; in essence, **math_fit**(α, β) increases the surrounding space by α at the left and β at the right. Furthermore the italic correction is decreased by β, so that the character's effective right edge will not actually change when the italic correction is added (as it normally is within a formula). The **math_fit** routine is set either to *ignore_math_fit* or *do_math_fit*, depending on whether *math_fitting* is **false** or **true**.

---

def *ignore_math_fit*(**expr** *left_adjustment*, *right_adjustment*) = **enddef**;

def *do_math_fit*(**expr** *left_adjustment*, *right_adjustment*) =
$\quad l := l - \operatorname{hround}(left\_adjustment * hppp)$; **interim** $xoffset := -l$;
$\quad charwd := charwd + left\_adjustment + right\_adjustment$;
$\quad r := l + \operatorname{hround}(charwd * hppp) - shrink\_fit$;
$\quad charic := charic - right\_adjustment$;
$\quad$**if** $charic < 0$: $charic := 0$; **fi enddef**;

There also are a few width/height/depth adjustment routines of a miscellaneous nature: A character's width can be zeroed out by calling *zero_width*; its width in pixels can be changed from even to odd or vice-versa by calling *change_width*; and its height and depth can be increased (without changing h or d) by calling **padded**.

---

def *zero_width* = *charwd* := 0; $r := l - shrink\_fit$ **enddef**;
def *change_width* = **if** not *monospace*:   % change the width by ± 1
  if $r + shrink_fit - l = $ floor(*charwd* $*$ *hppp*): $w := w + 1$; $r := r + 1$;
  else: $w := w - 1$; $r := r - 1$; **fi fi enddef**;
def *padded* **expr** *del_sharp* =
  charht := *charht* + *del_sharp*; *chardp* := *chardp* + *del_sharp* **enddef**;

These conventions about width adjustment make it appropriate to substitute new routines for the proofsheet-ruling macros that plain METAFONT calls *makebox* and *maketicks*. The new *makebox* not only shows the adjusted edges (l, r) at the left and right of the boxes that it makes, it also puts vertical lines or slanted lines at intervals of one u; and it shows important parameters like the *asc_height*, *x_height*, and *desc_depth*.

---

def *makebox*(**text** *rule*) =
  for $y = 0$, *asc_height*, *body_height*, *x_height*, *bar_height*, $-desc\_depth$, $-body\_depth$:
    $rule((l, y)t\_, (r, y)t\_)$;   % horizontals
  endfor
  for $x = l, r$: $rule((x, -body\_depth)t\_, (x, body\_height)t\_)$;   % verticals
  endfor
  for $x = u * (1 + $ floor$(l/u))$ **step** u **until** $r - 1$:
    $rule((x, -body\_depth)t\_, (x, body\_height)t\_)$;   % more verticals
  endfor
  if $charic \neq 0$:
    $rule((r + charic * pt, h.o\_), (r + charic * pt, .5h.o\_))$;   % italic correction
  fi
  enddef;

def *maketicks*(**text** *rule*) =
  for $y = 0, h.o\_, -d.o\_$:
    $rule((l, y), (l + 10, y))$; $rule((r - 10, y), (r, y))$;   % horizontals
  endfor
  for $x = l, r$:
    $rule((x, 10 - d.o\_), (x, -d.o\_))$; $rule((x, h.o\_ - 10), (x, h.o\_))$;   % verticals
  endfor
  if $charic \neq 0$:
    $rule((r + charic * pt, h.o\_ - 10), (r + charic * pt, h.o\_))$;   % italic correction
  fi
  enddef;

rulepen := *pensquare*;

Now we come to `cmbase`'s largest routine, which is called **font_setup**. This is what gets everything off to a good start, after the parameter values have been specified but before any character programs have been performed.

The first job of **font_setup** is to establish the proper routines for fitting:

---

def *font_setup* =
  if *monospace*: **let** *adjust_fit* = *mono_adjust_fit*;
    def *mfudged* = *fudged* **enddef**;
    mono_charic$^\#$:= *body_height*$^\#$ $*$ *slant*;
    if *mono_charic*$^\#$ < 0: *mono_charic*$^\#$:= 0; **fi**
    mono_charwd$^\#$:= 9*u*$^\#$; **define_whole_pixels**(*mono_charwd*);
  else: **let** *adjust_fit* = *normal_adjust_fit*;
    def *mfudged* = **enddef**; **fi**
  if *math_fitting*: **let** *math_fit* = *do_math_fit*
  else: **let** *math_fit* = *ignore_math_fit* **fi**;

Then **font_setup** converts from resolution-independent "sharped" units to pixel-oriented units. A number of additional parameters are computed from the 62 basic ones; for example, *oo* is an overshoot correction that's essentially half of *o*, and *fudged.hair* is approximately *fudge* times *hair*. The pixel-oriented units are adjusted so that rounding does not cause aberrations at low resolutions, as explained in Chapter 24 of *The METAFONTbook*.

---

define_pixels(*u*, *width_adj*, *serif_fit*, *cap_serif_fit*, *jut*, *cap_jut*, *beak*,
  bar_height, *dish*, *bracket*, *beak_jut*, *stem_corr*, *vair_corr*, *apex_corr*);
define_blacker_pixels(*notch_cut*, *cap_notch_cut*);
define_whole_pixels(*letter_fit*, *fine*, *crisp*, *tiny*);
define_whole_vertical_pixels(*body_height*, *asc_height*,
  cap_height, *fig_height*, *x_height*, *comma_depth*, *desc_depth*, *serif_drop*);
define_whole_blacker_pixels(*thin_join*, *hair*, *stem*, *curve*, *flare*,
  dot_size, *cap_hair*, *cap_stem*, *cap_curve*);
define_whole_vertical_blacker_pixels(*vair*, *bar*, *slab*, *cap_bar*, *cap_band*);
define_corrected_pixels(*o*, *apex_o*);
forsuffixes $ = *hair*, *stem*, *cap_stem*:
  fudged.$^\#$:= *fudge* $*$ $^\#$; *fudged.*$:= hround(*fudged.*$^\#$ $*$ *hppp* + *blacker*);
  forever: **exitif** *fudged.*$ > .9*fudge* $*$ $; *fudged.*$:= *fudged.*$ + 1; **endfor endfor**
rule_thickness := ceiling(*rule_thickness*$^\#$ $*$ *hppp*);
heavy_rule_thickness := ceiling(3*rule_thickness*$^\#$ $*$ *hppp*);
oo := vround(.5*o*$^\#$ $*$ *hppp* $*$ *o_correction*) + *eps*;
apex_oo := vround(.5*apex_o*$^\#$ $*$ *hppp* $*$ *o_correction*) + *eps*;
lowres_fix(*stem*, *curve*, *flare*) 1.3;
lowres_fix(*stem*, *curve*) 1.2;
lowres_fix(*cap_stem*, *cap_curve*) 1.2;
lowres_fix(*hair*, *cap_hair*) 1.2;
lowres_fix(*cap_band*, *cap_bar*, *bar*, *slab*) 1.2;
stem′ := hround(*stem* − *stem_corr*); *cap_stem*′ := hround(*cap_stem* − *stem_corr*);
vair′ := vround(*vair* + *vair_corr*);
vstem := vround .8[*vair*, *stem*]; *cap_vstem* := vround .8[*vair*, *cap_stem*];

$ess := (ess\#/stem\#) * stem; \quad cap\_ess := (cap\_ess\#/cap\_stem\#) * cap\_stem;$
$dw := (curve\# - stem\#) * hppp; \quad bold := curve\# * hppp + blacker;$
$dh\# := .6designsize;$
$stem\_shift\# := \textbf{if } serifs: 2stem\_corr\# \textbf{ else}: 0 \textbf{ fi};$
$more\_super := \max(superness, \text{sqrt } .77superness);$
$hein\_super := \max(superness, \text{sqrt } .81225258superness); \qquad$ % that's $2^{-.3}$

Pens that will be used to draw the characters are established next. The main pens are called *fine.nib*, *crisp.nib*, and *tiny.nib*; their widths (which are integers) are called *fine.breadth*, *crisp.breadth*, and *tiny.breadth*. If the breadth is positive, a small amount *eps* is subtracted from the integer value; for example, if *fine* = 2 we set *fine.breadth* := 2, then we reset *fine* := 2 − *eps*. This slightly smaller breadth is used in calculations, so that the three points defined by *penpos* or *pos* will not coincide. Functions like *fine.lft*, *crisp.top*, and *tiny.rt* are defined so that the edges of the basic pens can easily be specified even when the pens haven't been picked up.

$clear\_pen\_memory;$
$\textbf{if } fine = 0: fine := 1; \textbf{ fi}$
$\textbf{forsuffixes } \$ = fine, crisp, tiny:$
$\quad \textbf{if } \$ > fudged.hair: \$:= fudged.hair; \textbf{ fi}$
$\quad \$.breadth := \$;$
$\quad \textbf{pickup if } \$ = 0: \textbf{nullpen else}: \textbf{pencircle} \text{ scaled } \$; \$:= \$ - eps \textbf{ fi};$
$\quad \$.nib := savepen; \quad breadth\_[\$.nib] := \$;$
$\quad \textbf{forsuffixes } \$\$ = lft, rt, top, bot: shiftdef(\$.\$\$, \$\$\ 0); \textbf{ endfor endfor}$

The next part of **font_setup** is rather technical; it's necessary only when pixels aren't square (i.e., when *aspect_ratio* $\neq$ 1). Stroke thicknesses that are vrounded to "good" vertical values must be larger than the diameters of the pens that draw the strokes, but the pen diameters have been hrounded to integer values. Nonsquare pixels make it possible to have $x < y$ yet hround $x >$ vround y; therefore the function Vround(y) = max(vround y, *min_Vround*) is used instead of vround(y) whenever it's necessary to preserve an inequality.

$min\_Vround := \max(fine.breadth, crisp.breadth, tiny.breadth);$
$\textbf{if } min\_Vround < \text{vround } min\_Vround: min\_Vround := \text{vround } min\_Vround; \textbf{ fi}$
$\textbf{if } flare < \text{vround } flare: flare := \text{vround } flare; \textbf{ fi}$
$\textbf{forsuffixes } \$ = vair, bar, slab, cap\_bar, cap\_band, vair', vstem, cap\_vstem, bold:$
$\quad \textbf{if } \$ < min\_Vround: \$:= min\_Vround; \textbf{ fi endfor}$

Now we define a few more pens for special purposes: (1) *rule.nib* is used to draw '+' and '/' and '=' and other math symbols; *light_rule.nib* is a variant that's not quite as dark. (2) *cal.nib* and *tilted.nib*, with some lighter and heavier variants, are used to draw the calligraphic capital letters of calu.mf. A few other quantities need in the calu programs are also established at this time.

$\textbf{pickup pencircle} \text{ scaled } rule\_thickness; \quad rule.nib := savepen;$
$math\_axis := good.y(math\_axis\# * hppp);$

pickup pencircle scaled **if** *hefty*: (.6[*vair*, *fudged.hair*]) **else**: *fudged.hair* **fi**;
light_rule.nib := *savepen*;
pickup pencircle xscaled *cap_curve* yscaled *cap_hair* rotated 30;
cal.nib := *savepen*;
pair *cal.extension*; *cal.extension* := (.75*cap_curve*, 0) rotated 30;
pickup pencircle xscaled *cap_curve* yscaled *cap_hair* rotated 70;
tilted.nib := *savepen*;
pickup pencircle xscaled *curve* yscaled *cap_hair* rotated 70;
med_tilted.nib := *savepen*;
pickup pencircle xscaled *cap_stem* yscaled *cap_hair* rotated 30;
med_cal.nib := *savepen*;
pickup pencircle xscaled *stem* yscaled *cap_hair* rotated 30;
light_cal.nib := *savepen*;
pickup pencircle xscaled (*cap_curve* + *dw*) yscaled *cap_hair* rotated 30;
heavy_cal.nib := *savepen*;
bot_flourish_line := −.5*u* − *o*;
pair *bend*; *bend* = (.5*u*, 0);
pair *flourish_change*; *flourish_change* = (4*u*, .2*asc_height*);
join_radius := *u*;

Finally, **font_setup** closes by defining the *currenttransform* to use when filling and drawing, and by giving values to a few more auxiliary variables.

currenttransform := *identity* slanted *slant*
    yscaled *aspect_ratio* scaled *granularity*;
if *currenttransform* = *identity*: **let** t_- = **relax**
else: **def** t_- = transformed *currenttransform* **enddef fi**;
numeric *paren_depth*#; .5[*body_height*#, −*paren_depth*#] = *math_axis*#;
numeric *asc_depth*#; .5[*asc_height*#, −*asc_depth*#] = *math_axis*#;
body_depth := *desc_depth* + *body_height* − *asc_height*;
shrink_fit := 1 + hround(2*letter_fit*# * *hppp*) − 2*letter_fit*;
if not **string** *mode*: **if** *mode* ≤ *smoke*: *shrink_fit* := 0; **fi fi**
enddef;

Two macros related to **font_setup** come next:

vardef Vround **primary** *y* = y_- := vround *y*;
    if y_- < *min_Vround*: *min_Vround* **else**: y_- **fi enddef**;
newinternal y_-, *min_Vround*;

def *shiftdef*(**suffix** $)(**expr** *delta*) =
    vardef $ **primary** *x* = *x* + *delta* **enddef enddef**;

Then there are some macros to provide "syntactic sugar":

let {{ = **begingroup**; **let** }} = **endgroup**;
def .... = .. tension atleast .9 .. **enddef**;
def *less_tense* = **save** ...; **let** ... = ... **enddef**;
def ?? = *hide*(**showvariable** *x*, *y*) **enddef**;

vardef *ic#* = *charic* **enddef**;
vardef *h#* = *charht* **enddef**;
vardef *w#* = *charwd* **enddef**;
vardef *d#* = *chardp* **enddef**;

And finally, `cmbase.mf` closes with a few macros that allow us to define conditional characters via '**iff**'. These tricky constructions are discussed in Appendix E of *The METAFONTbook*.

let *semi_* = ; ; **let** *colon_* = : ; **let** *endchar_* = *endchar*;
def *iff* **expr** *b* = **if** *b*: **let** *next_* = *use_it* **else**: **let** *next_* = *lose_it* **fi**; *next_* **enddef**;
def *use_it* = **let** : = *restore_colon*; **enddef**;
def *restore_colon* = **let** : = *colon_*; **enddef**;
def *lose_it* = **let** *endchar* = *fi*; **inner** *cmchar*; **let** ; = *fix_* *semi_* **if false enddef**;
def *fix_* = **let** ; = *semi_*; **let** *endchar* = *endchar_*; **outer** *cmchar*; **enddef**;
def *always_iff* = **let** : = *endgroup*; *killboolean* **enddef**;
def *killboolean* **text** *t* = *use_it* **enddef**;
outer *cmchar*;

Particulars, as every one knows, make for virtue and happiness;
generalities are intellectually necessary evils.
— ALDOUS HUXLEY, *Brave New World* (1932)

Font Specimens

Let us now take a look at the 75 "standard" typefaces in the Computer Modern family. The following pages list all the characters of each font, together with examples of the fonts in use.

Text types are illustrated by the complete texts of two classic works by Edgar Allan Poe: *The Raven* (1845) and *The Tell-Tale Heart* (1843). Poe's original spelling of words like 'visiter' has been retained, but a few liberties have necessarily been taken with respect to the original typography. The lines are "leaded" by 20% of their design size; for example, 10 pt type is shown with a \baselineskip of 12 pt, while 5 pt type has a \baselineskip of 6 pt.

ABCDEFGHIJKLMNOPQRSTUVWXYZ abcde
fghijklmnopqrstuvwxyz 0123456789 ÆŒØΓΔΘΛ
ΞΠΣΥΦΨΩ æœøßıȷ ` ´ ˘ ¯ ° ^ ··· ˝ ~ ¸ ﬀ ﬁ ﬂ ﬃ ﬄ
cmr17 ., ; : ¿ ? ¡ ! ' ' " " # $ % & @ - -- --- * ( ) [ ] + / =

THE RAVEN

Once upon a midnight dreary, while I pondered,
    weak and weary,
Over many a quaint and curious volume of for-
    gotten lore—
While I nodded, nearly napping, suddenly there
    came a tapping,
As of some one gently rapping, rapping at my
    chamber door.

"'Tis some visiter," I muttered, "tapping at my
chamber door—
Only this and nothing more."

ABCDEFGHIJKLMNOPQRSTUVWXYZ abcdefghijklmnopqrstu
vwxyz 0123456789 ÆŒØΓΔΘΛΞΠΣΥΦΨΩ æœøßıȷ ` ´ ˘ ˇ ¯ ˜ ° ^ ˙ ¨ " " ~
 fffiflffiffl .,;:¿?¡!'''' "" #$%&@-–—* ()[]+/=
_____ cmr12

Ah, distinctly I remember it was in the bleak December;
And each separate dying ember wrought its ghost upon the floor.
Eagerly I wished the morrow;—vainly I had sought to borrow
From my books surcease of sorrow—sorrow for the lost Lenore—
For the rare and radiant maiden whom the angels name Lenore—
Nameless *here* for evermore.

ABCDEFGHIJKLMNOPQRSTUVWXYZ abcdefghijklmnopqrstuvwxyz
0123456789 ÆŒØΓΔΘΛΞΠΣΥΦΨΩ æœøßıȷ ` ´ ˘ ˇ ¯ ˜ ° ^ ˙ ¨ " " ~   fffiflffiffl
.,;:¿?¡!'''' "" #$%&@-–—* ()[]+/=
_____ cmr10

And the silken, sad, uncertain rustling of each purple curtain
Thrilled me—filled me with fantastic terrors never felt before;
So that now, to still the beating of my heart, I stood repeating
"'Tis some visiter entreating entrance at my chamber door—
Some late visiter entreating entrance at my chamber door;—
This it is and nothing more."

ABCDEFGHIJKLMNOPQRSTUVWXYZ abcdefghijklmnopqrstuvwxyz 0123456789
ÆŒØΓΔΘΛΞΠΣΥΦΨΩ æœøßıȷ ` ´ ˘ ˇ ¯ ˜ ° ^ ˙ ¨ " " ~   fffiflffiffl .,;:¿?¡!'''' "" #$%&@-–—*
()[]+/=
_____ cmr9

Presently my soul grew stronger; hesitating then no longer,
"Sir," said I, "or Madam, truly your forgiveness I implore;
But the fact is I was napping, and so gently you came rapping,
And so faintly you came tapping, tapping at my chamber door,
That I scarce was sure I heard you"—here I opened wide the door;—
Darkness there and nothing more.

ABCDEFGHIJKLMNOPQRSTUVWXYZ abcdefghijklmnopqrstuvwxyz 0123456789
ÆŒØΓΔΘΛΞΠΣΥΦΨΩ æœøßıȷ ` ´ ˘ ˇ ¯ ˜ ° ^ ˙ ¨ " " ~   fffiflffiffl .,;:¿?¡!'''' "" #$%&@-–—*
()[]+/=
_____ cmr8

Deep into that darkness peering, long I stood there wondering, fearing,
Doubting, dreaming dreams no mortal ever dared to dream before;
But the silence was unbroken, and the stillness gave no token,

And the only word there spoken was the whispered word, "Lenore?"
This I whispered, and an echo murmured back the word, "Lenore!"

Merely this and nothing more.

---

cmr7

ABCDEFGHIJKLMNOPQRSTUVWXYZ abcdefghijklmnopqrstuvwxyz 0123456789 ÆŒØΓΔΘΛ
ΞΠΣΥΦΨΩ æœøßıȷ` ´ ˘ ¯ ˚ ˆ ˙ ˝ ˝ ¸ ﬀﬁﬂﬃﬄ .,;:¿?¡!'‘’"“” #$%&@-–—* ()[]+/=

Back into the chamber turning, all my soul within me burning,
Soon again I heard a tapping somewhat louder than before.
"Surely," said I, "surely that is something at my window lattice;
Let me see, then, what thereat is, and this mystery explore—
Let my heart be still a moment and this mystery explore;—

'Tis the wind and nothing more!"

---

cmr6

ABCDEFGHIJKLMNOPQRSTUVWXYZ abcdefghijklmnopqrstuvwxyz 0123456789 ÆŒØΓΔΘΛΞΠΣΥΦΨ
Ω æœøßıȷ` ´ ˘ ¯ ˚ ˆ ˙ ˝ ˝ ¸ ﬀﬁﬂﬃﬄ .,;:¿?¡!'‘’"“” #$%&@-–—* ()[]+/=

Open here I flung the shutter, when, with many a flirt and flutter,
In there stepped a stately Raven of the saintly days of yore;
Not the least obeisance made he; not a minute stopped or stayed he;
But, with mien of lord or lady, perched above my chamber door—
Perched upon a bust of Pallas just above my chamber door—

Perched, and sat, and nothing more.

---

cmr5

ABCDEFGHIJKLMNOPQRSTUVWXYZ abcdefghijklmnopqrstuvwxyz 0123456789 ÆŒØΓΔΘΛΞΠΣΥΦΨΩ
æœøßıȷ` ´ ˘ ¯ ˚ ˆ ˙ ˝ ˝ ¸ .,;:¿?¡!'‘’"“” #$%&@-–—* ()[]↑+/<=>

Then this ebony bird beguiling my sad fancy into smiling,
By the grave and stern decorum of the countenance it wore,
"Though thy crest be shorn and shaven, thou," I said, "art sure no craven,
Ghastly grim and ancient Raven wandering from the Nightly shore—
Tell me what thy lordly name is on the Night's Plutonian shore!"

Quoth the Raven "Nevermore."

---

cmsl12

*ABCDEFGHIJKLMNOPQRSTUVWXYZ abcdefghijklmnopqrstu
vwxyz 0123456789 ÆŒØΓΔΘΛΞΠΣΥΦΨΩ æœøßıȷ` ´ ˘ ¯ ˚ ˆ ˙ ˝ ˝ ¸
ﬀﬁﬂﬃﬄ .,;:¿?¡!'‘’"“” #$%&@-–—* ()[]+/=*

Much I marvelled this ungainly fowl to hear discourse so plainly,
Though its answer little meaning—little relevancy bore;
For we cannot help agreeing that no living human being
Ever yet was blessed with seeing bird above his chamber door—
Bird or beast upon the sculptured bust above his chamber door,

With such name as "Nevermore."

---

cmsl10

*ABCDEFGHIJKLMNOPQRSTUVWXYZ abcdefghijklmnopqrstuvwxyz
0123456789 ÆŒØΓΔΘΛΞΠΣΥΦΨΩ æœøßıȷ` ´ ˘ ¯ ˚ ˆ ˙ ˝ ˝ ¸ ﬀﬁﬂﬃﬄ
.,;:¿?¡!'‘’"“” #$%&@-–—* ()[]+/=*

But the raven, sitting lonely on the placid bust, spoke only
That one word, as if his soul in that one word he did outpour.
Nothing farther then he uttered—not a feather then he fluttered—
Till I scarcely more than muttered "Other friends have flown before—
On the morrow he will leave me, as my Hopes have flown before."

Then the bird said "Nevermore."

ABCDEFGHIJKLMNOPQRSTUVWXYZ abcdefghijklmnopqrstuvwxyz 0123456789
ÆŒØΓΔΘΛΞΠΣΥΦΨΩ æœøßıj` ´˘¯° ^˙¨˝˜ ˛‚ ﬀﬁﬂﬃﬄ .,;:¿?¡!''""#$%&@-‒—
* ()[]+/=
— cms19

Startled at the stillness broken by reply so aptly spoken,
"Doubtless," said I, "what it utters is its only stock and store
Caught from some unhappy master whom unmerciful Disaster
Followed fast and followed faster till his songs one burden bore—
Till the dirges of his Hope that melancholy burden bore,
                                    Nevermore—Ah nevermore.'"

ABCDEFGHIJKLMNOPQRSTUVWXYZ abcdefghijklmnopqrstuvwxyz 0123456789
ÆŒØΓΔΘΛΞΠΣΥΦΨΩ æœøßıj` ´˘¯° ^˙¨˝˜ ˛‚ ﬀﬁﬂﬃﬄ .,;:¿?¡!''""#$%&@-‒—*
()[]+/=
— cms18

But the Raven still beguiling my sad fancy into smiling,
Straight I wheeled a cushioned seat in front of bird, and bust and door;
Then, upon the velvet sinking, I betook myself to linking
Fancy unto fancy, thinking what this ominous bird of yore—
What this grim, ungainly, ghastly, gaunt, and ominous bird of yore
                                    Meant in croaking "Nevermore."

ABCDEFGHIJKLMNOPQRSTUVWXYZ abcdefghijklmnopqrstuvwxyz
0123456789 ÆŒØΓΔΘΛΞΠΣΥΦΨΩ æøßıj` ´˘¯˙^˙¨˜˛ .,;:¿?¡!'''
"#$%&@␣_ ()[]{}↑↓+-*/|\<=>
— cmtt12

```
This I sat engaged in guessing, but no syllable express-
        ing
To the fowl whose fiery eyes now burned into my bosom's
        core;
This and more I sat divining, with my head at ease re-
        clining
On the cushion's velvet lining that the lamp-light
        gloated o'er,
But whose velvet-violet lining with the lamp-light
        gloating o'er,
                        She shall press, ah, nevermore!
```

ABCDEFGHIJKLMNOPQRSTUVWXYZ abcdefghijklmnopqrstuvwxyz 0123456789
ÆŒØΓΔΘΛΞΠΣΥΦΨΩ æøßıj` ´˘¯˙^˙¨˜˛ .,;:¿?¡!''' "#$%&@␣_ ()[]{}↑↓+
-*/|\<=>
— cmtt10

```
Then, methought, the air grew denser, perfumed from an unseen
        censer
Swung by seraphim whose foot-falls tinkled on the tufted floor.
```

```
"Wretch," I cried, "thy God hath lent thee---by these angels he
        hath sent thee
Respite---respite and nepenthe from thy memories of Lenore;
Quaff, oh quaff this kind nepenthe and forget this lost Lenore!"
                                     Quoth the Raven "Nevermore."
```

cmtt9
```
ABCDEFGHIJKLMNOPQRSTUVWXYZ abcdefghijklmnopqrstuvwxyz 0123456789
ÆŒØΓΔΘΛΞΠΣΤΦΨΩ æœøß1ȷ`´˜¯˘˙ˆ˝˚¨¸ .,;:¡?¿!'‘'"#$%&@␣_ ()[]{}↑↓+-*/|\<
=>
```

```
"Prophet!" said I, "thing of evil!---prophet still, if bird or devil!---
Whether Tempter sent, or whether tempest tossed thee here ashore,
Desolate yet all undaunted, on this desert land enchanted---
On this home by Horror haunted---tell me truly, I implore---
Is there---is there balm in Gilead?---tell me---tell me, I implore!"
                                     Quoth the Raven "Nevermore."
```

cmtt8
```
ABCDEFGHIJKLMNOPQRSTUVWXYZ abcdefghijklmnopqrstuvwxyz 0123456789 ÆŒØΓΔΘΛΞΠΣΤΦΨΩ
æœøß1ȷ`´˜¯˘˙ˆ˝˚¨¸ .,;:¡?¿!'‘'"#$%&@␣_ ()[]{}↑↓+-*/|\<=>
```

```
"Prophet!" said I, "thing of evil!---prophet still, if bird or devil!
By that Heaven that bends above us---by that God we both adore---
Tell this soul with sorrow laden if, within the distant Aidenn,
It shall clasp a sainted maiden whom the angels name Lenore---
Clasp a rare and radiant maiden whom the angels name Lenore."
                                     Quoth the Raven "Nevermore."
```

cmsltt10
```
ABCDEFGHIJKLMNOPQRSTUVWXYZ abcdefghijklmnopqrstuvwxyz 0123456789
ÆŒØΓΔΘΛΞΠΣΤΦΨΩ æœøß1ȷ`´˜¯˘˙ˆ˝˚¨¸ .,;:¡?¿!'‘'"#$%&@␣_ ()[]{}↑↓+
-*/|\<=>
```

```
"Be that word our sign of parting, bird or fiend!" I shrieked,
        upstarting---
"Get thee back into the tempest and the Night's Plutonian shore!
Leave no black plume as a token of that lie thy soul hath spoken!
Leave my loneliness unbroken!---quit the bust above my door!
Take thy beak from out my heart, and take thy form from off my
        door!"
                                     Quoth the Raven "Nevermore."
```

cmvtt10
```
ABCDEFGHIJKLMNOPQRSTUVWXYZ abcdefghijklmnopqrstuvwxyz
0123456789 ÆŒØΓΔΘΛΞΠΣΥΦΨΩ æœøß1ȷ`´˜¯˘˙ˆ˝˚¨¸,· fffiflffiffl
.,;:¿?¡!'‘'"“” #$%&@---—* ()[]+/=
```

```
And the Raven, never flitting, still is sitting, still is sitting,
On the pallid bust of Pallas just above my chamber door;
And his eyes have all the seeming of a demon's that is dreaming,
And the lamp-light o'er him streaming throws his shadow on the floor;
And my soul from out that shadow that lies floating on the floor
                                     Shall be lifted—nevermore!
```

ABCDEFGHIJKLMNOPQRSTUVWXYZ abcdefghijklm
nopqrstuvwxyz 0123456789 ÆŒØΓΔΘΛΞΠΣΥΦΨΩ æœ
øßıȷ` ´˘ˇ¯ ˚ ^˙¨˝˜ ¸˛ fffiflffiffl .,;:¿?¡!'''"" #$%&@-–—*
()[]+/=

—————————————————————————————————— cmbx12

THE TELL-TALE HEART

True!—nervous—very, very dreadfully nervous I had been
and am; but why *will* you say that I am mad? The disease
had sharpened my senses—not destroyed—not dulled them.

ABCDEFGHIJKLMNOPQRSTUVWXYZ abcdefghijklmnopqrstuv
wxyz 0123456789 ÆŒØΓΔΘΛΞΠΣΥΦΨΩ æœøßıȷ` ´˘ˇ¯ ˚ ^˙¨˝˜ ¸˛
fffiflffiffl .,;:¿?¡!'''"" #$%&@-–—* ()[]+/=

—————————————————————————————————— cmbx10

Above all was the sense of hearing acute. I heard all things in the
heaven and in the earth. I heard many things in hell. How, then, am
I mad? Hearken! and observe how healthily—how calmly I can tell
you the whole story.

ABCDEFGHIJKLMNOPQRSTUVWXYZ abcdefghijklmnopqrstuvwxyz
0123456789 ÆŒØΓΔΘΛΞΠΣΥΦΨΩ æœøßıȷ` ´˘ˇ¯ ˚ ^˙¨˝˜ ¸˛ fffiflffiffl
.,;:¿?¡!'''"" #$%&@-–—* ()[]+/=

—————————————————————————————————— cmbx9

It is impossible to say how first the idea entered my brain; but, once con-
ceived, it haunted me day and night. Object there was none. Passion there
was none. I loved the old man. He had never wronged me. He had never
given me insult. For his gold I had no desire.

ABCDEFGHIJKLMNOPQRSTUVWXYZ abcdefghijklmnopqrstuvwxyz
0123456789 ÆŒØΓΔΘΛΞΠΣΥΦΨΩ æœøßıȷ` ´˘ˇ¯ ˚ ^˙¨˝˜ ¸˛ fffiflffiffl .,;:¿?¡!''
'"" #$%&@-–—* ()[]+/=

—————————————————————————————————— cmbx8

I think it was his eye! yes, it was this! One of his eyes resembled that of a
vulture—a pale blue eye, with a film over it. Whenever it fell upon me, my blood
ran cold; and so by degrees—very gradually—I made up my mind to take the life
of the old man, and thus rid myself of the eye forever.

ABCDEFGHIJKLMNOPQRSTUVWXYZ abcdefghijklmnopqrstuvwxyz 0123456789
ÆŒØΓΔΘΛΞΠΣΥΦΨΩ æœøßıȷ` ´˘ˇ¯ ˚ ^˙¨˝˜ ¸˛ fffiflffiffl .,;:¿?¡!'''"" #$%&@-–—*
()[]+/=

—————————————————————————————————— cmbx7

Now this is the point. You fancy me mad. Madmen know nothing. But you should have
seen *me*. You should have seen how wisely I proceeded—with what caution—with what
foresight—with what dissimulation I went to work! I was never kinder to the old man
than during the whole week before I killed him.

cmbx6

ABCDEFGHIJKLMNOPQRSTUVWXYZ abcdefghijklmnopqrstuvwxyz 0123456789 ÆŒØΓΔ
ΘΛΞΠΣΥΦΨΩ æœøßıȷ` ´˘¯˚ ^˙˝˜ ˆ˜ ˜ ‚- ﬀﬁﬂﬃﬄ .,:;¿?¡!'‘’“”#$%&@--—* ()[]+/=

And every night, about midnight, I turned the latch of his door and opened it—oh, so gently!
And then, when I had made an opening sufficient for my head, I put in a dark lantern, all closed,
closed, so that no light shone out, and then I thrust in my head. Oh, you would have laughed
to see how cunningly I thrust it in! I moved it slowly—very, very slowly, so that I might not
disturb the old man's sleep.

cmbx5

ABCDEFGHIJKLMNOPQRSTUVWXYZ abcdefghijklmnopqrstuvwxyz 0123456789 ÆŒØΓΔΘΛΞΠΣΥ
ΦΨΩ æœøßıȷ` ´˘¯˚ ^˙˝˜ ˆ˜ ˜ ‚- ﬀﬁﬂﬃﬄ .,:;¿?¡!'‘’“”#$%&@--—* ()[]+/=

It took me an hour to place my whole head within the opening so far that I could see him as he lay upon
his bed. Ha!—would a madman have been so wise as this? And then, when my head was well in the
room, I undid the lantern cautiously—oh, so cautiously—cautiously (for the hinges creaked)—I undid it
just so much that a single thin ray fell upon the vulture eye.

ABCDEFGHIJKLMNOPQRSTUVWXYZ abcdefgh ijklmnopqrstuvwxyz 0123456789 ÆŒØΓΔΘΛΞΠ ΣΥΦΨΩ æœøßıȷ` ´˘¯˚ ^˙˙˙”˜ ‚- ﬀﬁﬂﬃﬄ .,:;¿?¡ !'‘’“”#$%&@--—* ()[]+/=

cmss17

And this I did for seven long nights—every night just at midnight—but I found the eye always closed; and so it was impossible to do the work; for it was not the old man who vexed me, but his Evil Eye.

ABCDEFGHIJKLMNOPQRSTUVWXYZ abcdefghijklmnopqrstuvwxyz
0123456789 ÆŒØΓΔΘΛΞΠΣΥΦΨΩ æœøßıȷ` ´˘¯˚ ^˙˙˙”˜ ‚-
ﬀﬁﬂﬃﬄ .,:;¿?¡!'‘’“”#$%&@--—* ()[]+/=

cmss12

And every morning, when the day broke, I went boldly into the chamber, and spoke courageously to him, calling him by name in a hearty tone, and inquiring how he had passed the night. So you see he would have been a very profound old man, indeed, to suspect that every night, just at twelve, I looked in upon him while he slept.

ABCDEFGHIJKLMNOPQRSTUVWXYZ abcdefghijklmnopqrstuvwxyz 012345678
9 ÆŒØΓΔΘΛΞΠΣΥΦΨΩ æœøßıȷ` ´˘¯˚ ^˙˙˙”˜ ‚- ﬀﬁﬂﬃﬄ .,:;¿?¡!'‘’“”#$%&
@--—* ()[]+/=

cmss10

Upon the eighth night I was more than usually cautious in opening the door. A watch's minute hand moves more quickly than did mine. Never, before that night, had I *felt* the extent of my own powers—of my sagacity. I could scarcely contain my feelings of triumph. To think that there I was, opening the door, little by little, and he not even to dream of my secret deeds or thoughts.

ABCDEFGHIJKLMNOPQRSTUVWXYZ abcdefghijklmnopqrstuvwxyz 0123456789
ÆŒØΓΔΘΛΞΠΣΥΦΨΩ æœøßıȷ` ´˘¯˚^˙˝˜˝˜‚- ﬀﬁﬂﬃﬄ .,;:¿?¡!'''" ""#$%&@-‐—*
()[]+/=

— cmss9

I fairly chuckled at the idea; and perhaps he heard me; for he moved on the bed suddenly, as if startled. Now you may think that I drew back—but no. His room was as black as pitch with the thick darkness, (for the shutters were close fastened, through fear of robbers,) and so I knew that he could not see the opening of the door, and I kept pushing it on steadily, steadily.

ABCDEFGHIJKLMNOPQRSTUVWXYZ abcdefghijklmnopqrstuvwxyz 0123456789 ÆŒØΓΔΘΛ
ΞΠΣΥΦΨΩ æœøßıȷ` ´˘¯˚^˙˝˜˝˜‚- ﬀﬁﬂﬃﬄ .,;:¿?¡!'''" ""#$%&@-‐—* ()[]+/=

— cmss8

I had my head in, and was about to open the lantern, when my thumb slipped upon the tin fastening, and the old man sprang up in the bed, crying out—"Who's there?"

I kept quite still and said nothing. For a whole hour I did not move a muscle, and in the meantime I did not hear him lie down. He was still sitting up in the bed, listening;—just as I have done, night after night, hearkening to the death-watches in the wall.

ABCDEFGHIJKLMNOPQRSTUVWXYZ abcdefgh ijklmnopqrstuvwxyz 0123456789 ÆŒØΓΔΘΛΞΠ ΣΥΦΨΩ æœøßıȷ` ´˘¯˚^˙˝˜˝˜‚- ﬀﬁﬂﬃﬄ .,;:¿?¡ !'''" ""#$%&@-‐—* ()[]+/=

— cmssi17

Presently I heard a slight groan, and I knew it was the groan of mortal terror. It was not a groan of pain or of grief—oh, no!—it was the low stifled sound that arises from the bottom of the soul when over-charged with awe.

ABCDEFGHIJKLMNOPQRSTUVWXYZ abcdefghijklmnopqrstuvwxyz 0123456789 ÆŒØΓΔΘΛΞΠΣΥΦΨΩ æœøßıȷ` ´˘¯˚^˙˝˜˝˜‚- ﬀﬁﬂﬃﬄ .,;:¿?¡!'''" ""#$%&@-‐—* ()[]+/=

— cmssi12

I knew the sound well. Many a night, just at midnight, when all the world slept, it has welled up from my own bosom, deepening, with its dreadful echo, the terrors that distracted me. I say I knew it well. I knew what the old man felt, and pitied him, although I chuckled at heart.

ABCDEFGHIJKLMNOPQRSTUVWXYZ abcdefghijklmnopqrstuvwxyz 012345678 9 ÆŒØΓΔΘΛΞΠΣΥΦΨΩ æœøßıȷ` ´˘ˇ¯˚˙¨´˝˜ ,- fffiflffiffl .,:;¿?¡!'''' "" #$%& @--—* ()[]+/=

cmssi10

I knew that he had been lying awake ever since the first slight noise, when he had turned in the bed. His fears had been ever since growing upon him. He had been trying to fancy them causeless, but could not. He had been saying to himself—"It is nothing but the wind in the chimney—it is only a mouse crossing the floor," or "it is merely a cricket which has made a single chirp."

ABCDEFGHIJKLMNOPQRSTUVWXYZ abcdefghijklmnopqrstuvwxyz 0123456789 ÆŒØΓΔΘΛΞΠΣΥΦΨΩ æœøßıȷ` ´˘ˇ¯˚˙¨´˝˜ ,- fffiflffiffl .,:;¿?¡!'''' "" #$%&@--—* ()[]+/=

cmssi9

Yes, he has been trying to comfort himself with these suppositions: but he had found all in vain. All in vain; because Death, in approaching him, had stalked with his black shadow before him, and enveloped the victim. And it was the mournful influence of the unperceived shadow that caused him to feel—although he neither saw nor heard—to feel the presence of my head within the room.

ABCDEFGHIJKLMNOPQRSTUVWXYZ abcdefghijklmnopqrstuvwxyz 0123456789 ÆŒØΓΔΘΛΞΠΣΥΦΨΩ æœøßıȷ` ´˘ˇ¯˚˙¨´˝˜ ,- fffiflffiffl .,:;¿?¡!'''' "" #$%&@--—* ()[]+/=

cmssi8

When I had waited a long time, very patiently, without hearing the old man lie down, I resolved to open a little—a very. very little crevice in the lantern. So I opened it—you cannot imagine how stealthily, stealthily—until, at length, a single dim ray, like the thread of the spider, shot from out the crevice and fell upon the vulture eye.

ABCDEFGHIJKLMNOPQRSTUVWXYZ abcdefghijklmnopqrstuvwxyz 0123456789 ÆŒØΓΔΘΛΞΠΣΥΦΨΩ æœøßıȷ` ´˘ˇ¯˚˙¨´˝˜ ,- fffiflffiffl .,:;¿?¡!'''' "" #$%&@--— * ()[]+/=

cmssdc10

It was open—wide, wide open—and I grew furious as I gazed upon it. I saw it with perfect distinctness—all a dull blue, with a hideous veil over it that chilled the very marrow in my bones; but I could see nothing else of the old man's face or person: for I had directed the ray as if by instinct, precisely upon the damned spot.

ABCDEFGHIJKLMNOPQRSTUVWXYZ abcdefghijklmnopqrstuvwxyz 0123456789 ÆŒØΓΔΘΛΞΠΣΥΦΨΩ æœøßıȷ` ´˘ˇ¯˚˙¨´˝˜ ,- fffiflffiffl .,:;¿?¡!'''' "" #$%&@--—* ()[]+/=

cmssbx10

And now—have I not told you that what you mistake for madness is but over acuteness of the senses?—now, I say, there came to my ears a low, dull, quick sound, such as a watch makes when enveloped in cotton. I knew *that* sound well, too. It was the beating of the old man's heart. It increased my fury, as the beating of a drum stimulates the soldier into courage.

ABCD
EFGHI
JKLM
NOPQ
RSTU
VWXY

Z
012345
6789

BUT

cmssq8

ABCDEFGHIJKLMNOPQRSTUVWXYZ abcdefghijklmnopqrstuvwxyz 0123456789
ÆŒØΓΔΘΛΞΠΣΥΦΨΩ æœøßıȷ ˋ´ˇ˘¯˚¨´˝˜¸ fffifl ffi ffl .,;:¿?¡!'' "" #$%&@-
-—* ()[]+/=

even yet I refrained and kept still. I scarcely breathed. I held the lantern motionless.
I tried how steadily I could maintain the ray upon the eye. Meantime the hellish
tattoo of the heart increased. It grew quicker and quicker, and louder and louder
every instant. The old man's terror *must* have been extreme! It grew louder, I say,
louder every moment!—do you mark me well?

cmssqi8

ABCDEFGHIJKLMNOPQRSTUVWXYZ abcdefghijklmnopqrstuvwxyz 0123456789
ÆŒØΓΔΘΛΞΠΣΥΦΨΩ æœøßıȷ ˋ´ˇ˘¯˚¨´˝˜¸ fffifl ffi ffl .,;:¿?¡!'' "" #$%&@-
-—* ()[]+/=

*I have told you that I am nervous: so I am. And now at the dead hour of the night,
amid the dreadful silence of that old house, so strange a noise as this excited me to
uncontrollable terror. Yet, for some minutes longer I refrained and stood still. But
the beating grew louder, louder! I thought the heart must burst. And now a new
anxiety seized me—the sound would be heard by a neighbor!*

ABCDEFGHIJKLMNOPQRSTUVWXYZ abcdefghijklmnopqrstuvwxyz
0123456789 ÆŒØΓΔΘΛΞΠΣΥΦΨΩ æœøßıȷ `´˘¯°^˙¨˝˜¸ ﬀﬁﬂﬃﬄ .,;:¿?¡!'
'‘"#$%&@----—* ()[]+/=

_____ cmdunh10

The old man's hour had come! With a loud yell, I threw open the lantern and
leaped into the room. He shrieked once—once only. In an instant I dragged him
to the floor, and pulled the heavy bed over him.

ABCDEFGHIJKLMNOPQRSTUVWXYZ abcdefghijklmnopqrstuv
wxyz 0123456789 ÆŒØΓΔΘΛΞΠΣΥΦΨΩ æœøßıȷ `´˘¯°^˙¨˝˜¸
ﬀﬁﬂﬃﬄ .,;:¿?¡!'‘"#$%&@----—* ()[]+/=

_____ cmbxsl10

I then sat upon the bed and smiled gaily, to find the deed so far done.
But, for many minutes, the heart beat on with a muffled sound. This,
however, did not vex me; it would not be heard through the wall. At
length it ceased. The old man was dead.

ABCDEFGHIJKLMNOPQRSTUVWXYZ abcdefghijklmnopqrstuvwxyz
0123456789 ÆŒØΓΔΘΛΞΠΣΥΦΨΩ æœøßıȷ `´˘¯°^˙¨˝˜¸ ﬀﬁﬂﬃﬄ .,;:¿?¡!'
'‘"#$%&@----—* ()[]+/=

_____ cmb10

I removed the bed and examined the corpse. Yes, he was stone, stone dead. I
placed my hand upon the heart and held it there many minutes. There was no
pulsation. He was stone dead. His eye would trouble me no more.

ABCDEFGHIJKLMNOPQRSTUVWXYZ abcdefghijklmnopqrstuvwxyz 0123456789 ÆŒØΓΔΘΛ
ΞΠΣΥΦΨΩ æœøßıȷ `´˘¯°^˙¨˝˜¸ ﬀﬁﬂﬃﬄ .,;:¿?¡!'‘"#$%&@----—* ()[]+/=

_____ cmff10

If still you think me mad, you will think so no longer when I describe the wise precautions I took
for the concealment of the body. The night waned, and I worked hastily, but in silence. First of all
I dismembered the corpse. I cut off the head and the arms and the legs.

ABCDEFGHIJKLMNOPQRSTUVWXYZ abcdefghijklmnopqrstuvwxyz
0123456789 ÆŒØΓΔΘΛΞΠΣΥΦΨΩ æœøßıȷ `´˘¯°^˙¨˝˜¸ ﬀﬁﬂﬃﬄ
.,;:¿?¡!'‘"#$%&@----—* ()[]+/=

_____ cmfib8

I then took up three planks from the flooring of the chamber, and deposited
all between the scantlings. I then replaced the boards so cleverly, so cunningly, that no human eye—not even *his*—could have detected anything
wrong. There was nothing to wash out—no stain of any kind—no blood-
spot whatever. I had been too wary for that. A tub had caught all—ha! ha!

ABCDEFGHIJKLMNOPQRSTUVWXYZ abcdefghijklmnopqrstuv
wxyz 0123456789 ÆŒØΓΔΘΛΞΠΣΥΦΨΩ æœøßıȷ `´˘¯°^˙¨˝˜¸
ﬀﬁﬂﬃﬄ .,;:¿ ?¡!'‘"#£%&@----— ()[]+/=*

_____ cmti12

When I had made an end of these labors, it was four o'clock—still dark as midnight. As the bell sounded the hour, there came a knocking at the street door. I went down to open it with a light heart,—for what had I now to fear?

ABCDEFGHIJKLMNOPQRSTUVWXYZ abcdefghijklmnopqrstuvwxyz
0123456789 ÆŒØΓΔΘΛΞΠΣΥΦΨΩ æœøßıȷ`´˘ˇ¯°˙¨˝˜¸ fffiflffiffl .,:;¿?¡
!'''""#£%&@–--—* ()[]+/=

cmti10

There entered three men, who introduced themselves, with perfect suavity, as officers of the police. A shriek had been heard by a neighbor during the night; suspicion of foul play had been aroused; information had been lodged at the police office, and they (the officers) had been deputed to search the premises.

ABCDEFGHIJKLMNOPQRSTUVWXYZ abcdefghijklmnopqrstuvwxyz 0123456789
ÆŒØΓΔΘΛΞΠΣΥΦΨΩ æœøßıȷ`´˘ˇ¯°˙¨˝˜¸ fffiflffiffl .,:;¿?¡!'''""#£%&@––
—* ()[]+/=

cmti9

I smiled,—for what had I to fear? I bade the gentlemen welcome. The shriek, I said, was my own in a dream. The old man, I mentioned, was absent in the country. I took my visiters all over the house. I bade them search—search well.

ABCDEFGHIJKLMNOPQRSTUVWXYZ abcdefghijklmnopqrstuvwxyz 0123456789 ÆŒØΓ
ΔΘΛΞΠΣΥΦΨΩ æœøßıȷ`´˘ˇ¯°˙¨˝˜¸ fffiflffiffl .,:;¿?¡!'''""#£%&@––—* ()[]+/=

cmti8

I led them, at length, to his chamber. I showed them his treasures, secure, undisturbed. In the enthusiasm of my confidence, I brought chairs into the room, and desired them here to rest from their fatigues, while I myself, in the wild audacity of my perfect triumph, placed my own seat upon the very spot beneath which reposed the corpse of the victim.

ABCDEFGHIJKLMNOPQRSTUVWXYZ abcdefghijklmnopqrstuvwxyz 0123456789 ÆŒØΓΔΘ
ΛΞΠΣΥΦΨΩ æœøßıȷ`´˘ˇ¯°˙¨˝˜¸ fffiflffiffl .,:;¿?¡!'''""#£%&@––—* ()[]+/=

cmti7

The officers were satisfied. My manner had convinced them. I was singularly at ease. They sat, and while I answered cheerily, they chatted of familiar things. But, ere long, I felt myself getting pale and wished them gone. My head ached, and I fancied a ringing in my ears: but still they sat and still chatted. The ringing became more distinct:—it continued and became more distinct: I talked more freely to get rid of the feeling: but it continued and gained definitiveness—until, at length, I found that the noise was not within my ears.

ABCDEFGHIJKLMNOPQRSTUVWXYZ *abcdefghijklmnopqrstuvw*
xyz 0123456789 ÆŒØΓΔΘΛΞΠΣΥΦΨΩ æœøßıȷ`´˘ˇ¯°˙¨˝˜¸
fffiflffiffl .,:;¿?¡!'''""#£%&@––—* ()[]+/=

cmbxti10

No doubt I now grew very pale;—but I talked more fluently, and with a heightened voice. Yet the sound increased—and what could I do? It was a low, dull, quick sound—much such a sound as a watch makes when enveloped in cotton.

ABCDEFGHIJKLMNOPQRSTUVWXYZ abcdefghijklmnopqrstuvwxyz 0123456789
ÆŒØΓΔΘΛΞΠΣΥΦΨΩ æœøßıȷ` ´ ˘ ¯ ˚ ˆ ˙ ¨ ˝ ˜ ¸ ., ; : ¿ ? ¡ ! ' ' " " #£%&@␣_ ( ) [ ] { } ↑ ↓ +
- * / | \ < = >
_____ cmitt10

I gasped for breath---and yet the officers heard it not. I talked
more quickly---more vehemently; but the noise steadily increased.
I arose and argued about trifles, in a high key and with violent
gesticulations; but the noise steadily increased. Why would they
not be gone?

ABCDEFGHIJKLMNOPQRSTUVWXYZ abcdefghijklmnopqrstuvwxyz
0123456789 ÆŒØΓΔΘΛΞΠΣΥΦΨΩ æœøßıȷ` ´ ˘ ¯ ˚ ˆ ˙ ¨ ˝ ˜ ¸ ffififlffiffl
., ; : ¿ ? ¡ ! ' ' " " #£%&@ - – — * ( ) [ ] + / =
_____ cmu10

I paced the floor to and fro with heavy strides, as if excited to fury by the
observations of the men—but the noise steadily increased. Oh God! what
could I do? I foamed—I raved—I swore! I swung the chair upon which I
had been sitting, and grated it upon the boards, but the noise arose over
all and continually increased.

ABCDEFGHIJKLMNOPQRSTUVWXYZ abcdefghijklmnopqrstuvwxyz
0123456789 ÆŒØΓΔΘΛΞΠΣΥΦΨΩ æœøßıȷ` ´ ˘ ¯ ˚ ˆ ˙ ¨ ˝ ˜ ¸ ffififlffiffl
., ; : ¿ ? ¡ ! ' ' " " #£%&@ - – — * ( ) [ ] + / =
_____ cmfi10

It grew louder—louder—louder! And still the men chatted pleasantly, and
smiled. Was it possible they heard not? Almighty God!—no, no! They heard!—
they suspected!—they knew!—they were making a mockery of my horror!—this
I thought, and this I think.

ABCDEFGHIJKLMNOPQRSTUVWXYZ ABCDEFGHIJKLMNOPQRSTUVW
XYZ 0123456789 ÆŒØΓΔΘΛΞΠΣΥΦΨΩ ÆŒØSSIJ` ´ ˘ ¯ ˚ ˆ ˙ ¨ ˝ ˜ ¸
., ; : ¿ ? ¡ ! ' ' " " #$%&@ - – — * ( ) [ ] ↑ ↓ + / < = >
_____ cmcsc10

BUT ANYTHING WAS BETTER THAN THIS AGONY! ANYTHING WAS MORE TOL-
ERABLE THAN THIS DERISION! I COULD BEAR THOSE HYPOCRITICAL SMILES NO
LONGER! I FELT THAT I MUST SCREAM OR DIE!—AND NOW—AGAIN!—HARK!
LOUDER! LOUDER! *LOUDER!*—

ABCDEFGHIJKLMNOPQRSTUVWXYZ ABCDEFGHIJKLMNOPQRSTUVWXYZ 0123456789
ÆŒØΓΔΘΛΞΠΣΥΦΨΩ ÆŒØSSIJ` ´ ˘ ¯ ˚ ˆ ˙ ¨ ˝ ˜ ¸ ., ; : ¿ ? ¡ ! ' ' " " #$%&@␣_ ( ) [ ] { } ↑ ↓
+ - * / | \ < = >
_____ cmtcsc10

"VILLIANS!" I SHRIEKED, "DISSEMBLE NO MORE! I ADMIT THE DEED!---
TEAR UP THE PLANKS!---HERE, HERE!---IT IS THE BEATING OF HIS HID-
EOUS HEART!"

`·↓αβ⌐∈πλγδ↑±⊕ω∂C⊃∩U∀∃⊗5←→≠◇≤≥≡∨ !"#$%&'()*+,-./0123456789:;<=>?`
`@ABCDEFGHIJKLMNOPQRSTUVWXYZ[\]^_'abcdefghijklmnopqrstuvwxyz{|}~∫`

cmtex10

\TeX's internal code is based on the American Standard Code for
Information Interchange, known popularly as ''ASCII.'' There
are 128 codes, numbered 0~to~127; we conventionally express the
numbers in octal notation, from \oct{000} to \oct{177}, or in
hexadecimal notation, from \hex{00} to \hex{7F}. In the ASCII
scheme, codes \oct{000} through \oct{040} and code \oct{177}
are~assigned to special functions; for example, code \oct{007}
is called |BEL|, and it means ''Ring the bell.'' The other 94
codes are assigned to visible symbols.

`·↓αβ⌐∈πλγδ↑±⊕ω∂C⊃∩U∀∃⊗5←→≠◇≤≥≡∨ !"#$%&'()*+,-./0123456789:;<=>?`
`@ABCDEFGHIJKLMNOPQRSTUVWXYZ[\]^_'abcdefghijklmnopqrstuvwxyz{|}~∫`

cmtex9

Ever since ASCII was established in the early 1960s, pecple have had
different ideas about what to do with positions \oct{000}--\oct{037}
and \oct{177}, because most of the functions assigned to those codes are
appropriate only for special purposes like file transmission, not for
applications to printing or to interactive computing. It turned out that
manufacturers soon started producing line printers that were capable of
generating 128 characters, 33~of~which were tailored to the special needs
of particular customers; part of the advantage of a standard code was
therefore lost.

`·↓αβ⌐∈πλγδ↑±⊕ω∂C⊃∩U∀∃⊗5←→≠◇≤≥≡∨ !"#$%&'()*+,-./0123456789:;<=>?`
`@ABCDEFGHIJKLMNOPQRSTUVWXYZ[\]^_'abcdefghijklmnopqrstuvwxyz{|}~∫`

cmtex8

An extended ASCII code intended for text editing and interactive computing was
developed at several universities about 1965, and for many years there have been
terminals in use at Stanford, MIT, Carnegie-Mellon, and elsewhere that have 120
or~121 symbols, not just~95. Aficionados of these keyboards (like the author of
this book) are loath to give up their extra characters; it seems that such people
make heavy use of about 5~of the extra~25, and occasional use of the other~20,
although different people have different groups of five. For example, the au-
thor developed \TeX\ on a keyboard that includes the symbols |←|,~|↓|, |≠|, |≤|,
and~|≥|, and he finds that this makes it much more pleasant to type class notes,
technical papers, and computer programs of the kind he likes to write; his logi-
cian friends make heavy use of the |∀| and~|∃| keys; and so on.

$\Gamma\Delta\Theta\Lambda\Xi\Pi\Sigma\Upsilon\Phi\Psi\Omega\alpha\beta\gamma\delta\epsilon\zeta\eta\theta\iota\kappa\lambda\mu\nu\xi\pi\rho\sigma\tau\upsilon\phi\chi$
$\psi\omega\vartheta\varpi\varrho\varphi\leftarrow\longleftarrow\rightarrow\longrightarrow\,◦▷◁0123456789.,</>\star$
$\partial ABCDEFGHIJKLMNOPQRSTUVWXYZ\flat\natural\smile\frown$
$\ell abcdefghijklmnopqrstuvwxyz\imath\jmath\wp\vec{}\,\hat{}$

cmmi12

$$\wp(z - p) + (\partial^2/\partial z^2)\ln\theta(z - p) = 2\pi\zeta_\varpi(z).$$

$\Gamma\Delta\Theta\Lambda\Xi\Pi\Sigma\Upsilon\Phi\Psi\Omega\alpha\beta\gamma\delta\epsilon\zeta\eta\theta\iota\kappa\lambda\mu\nu\xi\pi\rho\sigma\tau\upsilon\phi\chi$
$\psi\omega\varepsilon\vartheta\varpi\varrho\varsigma\varphi\leftharpoonup\leftharpoondown\rightharpoonup\triangleright\triangleleft 0123456789.,</>\star$
$\partial ABCDEFGHIJKLMNOPQRSTUVWXYZ\flat\natural\sharp\smile\frown$
$\ell abcdefghijklmnopqr\,stuvwxyz\imath\jmath\wp\vec{}\,\hat{}$
— cmmi10

$-\cdot\times*\div\diamond\pm\mp\oplus\ominus\otimes\oslash\odot\bigcirc\circ\bullet\asymp\equiv\subseteq\supseteq\leq\geq\preceq\succeq\sim\approx\subset\supset\ll\gg\prec\succ$
$\leftarrow\rightarrow\uparrow\downarrow\leftrightarrow\nearrow\searrow\simeq\Leftarrow\Rightarrow\Uparrow\Downarrow\Leftrightarrow\nwarrow\swarrow\propto\prime\infty\in\ni\bigtriangleup\bigtriangledown/\not\forall\exists\neg\emptyset\Re\Im\top\bot$
$\aleph\mathcal{ABCDEFGHIJKLMNOPQRSTUVWXYZ}\cup\uplus\sqcap\wedge\vee$
$\vdash\dashv\lfloor\rfloor\lceil\rceil\{\}\langle\rangle\|\updownarrow\Updownarrow\backslash\wr\sqrt{}\amalg\nabla\int\sqcup\sqcap\sqsubseteq\sqsupseteq\S\dagger\ddagger\P\clubsuit\diamondsuit\heartsuit\spadesuit$
— cmsy10

Here's some 10-point math: $\hat{a}_0^a + \breve{b}_1^b - \tilde{c}_2^c \times \dot{d}_3^d / \grave{e}_4^e \oplus \acute{f}_5^f \ominus \ddot{g}_6^g \otimes \check{h}_7^h \oslash \bar{\imath}_8^i \odot \vec{\jmath}_9^j$.

$\Gamma\Delta\Theta\Lambda\Xi\Pi\Sigma\Upsilon\Phi\Psi\Omega\alpha\beta\gamma\delta\epsilon\zeta\eta\theta\iota\kappa\lambda\mu\nu\xi\pi\rho\sigma\tau\upsilon\phi\chi$
$\psi\omega\varepsilon\vartheta\varpi\varrho\varsigma\varphi\leftharpoonup\leftharpoondown\rightharpoonup\triangleright\triangleleft 0123456789.,</>\star$
$\partial ABCDEFGHIJKLMNOPQRSTUVWXYZ\flat\natural\sharp\smile\frown$
$\ell abcdefghijklmnopqr\,stuvwxyz\imath\jmath\wp\vec{}\,\hat{}$
— cmmi9

$-\cdot\times*\div\diamond\pm\mp\oplus\ominus\otimes\oslash\odot\bigcirc\circ\bullet\asymp\equiv\subseteq\supseteq\leq\geq\preceq\succeq\sim\approx\subset\supset\ll\gg\prec\succ$
$\leftarrow\rightarrow\uparrow\downarrow\leftrightarrow\nearrow\searrow\simeq\Leftarrow\Rightarrow\Uparrow\Downarrow\Leftrightarrow\nwarrow\swarrow\propto\prime\infty\in\ni\bigtriangleup\bigtriangledown/\not\forall\exists\neg\emptyset\Re\Im\top\bot$
$\aleph\mathcal{ABCDEFGHIJKLMNOPQRSTUVWXYZ}\cup\uplus\sqcap\wedge\vee$
$\vdash\dashv\lfloor\rfloor\lceil\rceil\{\}\langle\rangle\|\updownarrow\Updownarrow\backslash\wr\sqrt{}\amalg\nabla\int\sqcup\sqcap\sqsubseteq\sqsupseteq\S\dagger\ddagger\P\clubsuit\diamondsuit\heartsuit\spadesuit$
— cmsy9

Here's some 9-point math: $\hat{k}_0^k * \breve{l}_1^l \star \tilde{\ell}_2^\ell \diamond \dot{m}_3^m \circ \dot{n}_4^n \bullet \acute{o}_5^o \div \ddot{p}_6^p \cup \check{q}_7^q \cap \bar{r}_8^r \uplus \vec{s}_9^s$.

$\Gamma\Delta\Theta\Lambda\Xi\Pi\Sigma\Upsilon\Phi\Psi\Omega\alpha\beta\gamma\delta\epsilon\zeta\eta\theta\iota\kappa\lambda\mu\nu\xi\pi\rho\sigma\tau\upsilon\phi\chi$
$\psi\omega\varepsilon\vartheta\varpi\varrho\varsigma\varphi\leftharpoonup\leftharpoondown\rightharpoonup\triangleright\triangleleft 0123456789.,</>\star$
$\partial ABCDEFGHIJKLMNOPQRSTUVWXYZ\flat\natural\sharp\smile\frown$
$\ell abcdefghijklmnopqr\,stuvwxyz\imath\jmath\wp\vec{}\,\hat{}$
— cmmi8

$-\cdot\times*\div\diamond\pm\mp\oplus\ominus\otimes\oslash\odot\bigcirc\circ\bullet\asymp\equiv\subseteq\supseteq\leq\geq\preceq\succeq\sim\approx\subset\supset\ll\gg\prec\succ$
$\leftarrow\rightarrow\uparrow\downarrow\leftrightarrow\nearrow\searrow\simeq\Leftarrow\Rightarrow\Uparrow\Downarrow\Leftrightarrow\nwarrow\swarrow\propto\prime\infty\in\ni\bigtriangleup\bigtriangledown/\not\forall\exists\neg\emptyset\Re\Im\top\bot$
$\aleph\mathcal{ABCDEFGHIJKLMNOPQRSTUVWXYZ}\cup\uplus\sqcap\wedge\vee$
$\vdash\dashv\lfloor\rfloor\lceil\rceil\{\}\langle\rangle\|\updownarrow\Updownarrow\backslash\wr\sqrt{}\amalg\nabla\int\sqcup\sqcap\sqsubseteq\sqsupseteq\S\dagger\ddagger\P\clubsuit\diamondsuit\heartsuit\spadesuit$
— cmsy8

Here's some 8-point math: $\hat{t}_0^t \triangleleft \breve{u}_1^u \triangleright \tilde{v}_2^v \wr \dot{w}_3^w \vee \dot{x}_4^x \wedge \acute{y}_5^y \dagger \ddot{z}_6^z \ddagger \breve{\aleph}_7^\aleph \amalg \bar{\Delta}_8^\Delta \backslash \vec{\mathcal{A}}_9^\mathcal{A}$.

$\Gamma\Delta\Theta\Lambda\Xi\Pi\Sigma\Upsilon\Phi\Psi\Omega\alpha\beta\gamma\delta\epsilon\zeta\eta\theta\iota\kappa\lambda\mu\nu\xi\pi\rho\sigma\tau\upsilon\phi\chi$
$\psi\omega\varepsilon\vartheta\varpi\varrho\varsigma\varphi\leftharpoonup\leftharpoondown\rightharpoonup\triangleright\triangleleft 0123456789.,</>\star$
$\partial ABCDEFGHIJKLMNOPQRSTUVWXYZ\flat\natural\sharp\smile\frown$
$\ell abcdefghijklmnopqr\,stuvwxyz\imath\jmath\wp\vec{}\,\hat{}$
— cmmi7

$-\cdot\times*\div\diamond\pm\mp\oplus\ominus\otimes\oslash\odot\bigcirc\circ\bullet\asymp\equiv\subseteq\supseteq\leq\geq\preceq\succeq\sim\approx\subset\supset\ll\gg\prec\succ$
$\leftarrow\rightarrow\uparrow\downarrow\leftrightarrow\nearrow\searrow\simeq\Leftarrow\Rightarrow\Uparrow\Downarrow\Leftrightarrow\nwarrow\swarrow\propto\prime\infty\in\ni\bigtriangleup\bigtriangledown/\not\forall\exists\neg\emptyset\Re\Im\top\bot$
$\aleph\mathcal{ABCDEFGHIJKLMNOPQRSTUVWXYZ}\cup\uplus\sqcap\wedge\vee$
$\vdash\dashv\lfloor\rfloor\lceil\rceil\{\}\langle\rangle\|\updownarrow\Updownarrow\backslash\wr\sqrt{}\amalg\nabla\int\sqcup\sqcap\sqsubseteq\sqsupseteq\S\dagger\ddagger\P\clubsuit\diamondsuit\heartsuit\spadesuit$
— cmsy7

Here's some 7-point math: $\hat{\mathcal{B}}_0^\mathcal{B} \sqcup \check{\mathcal{C}}_1^\mathcal{C} \sqcap \tilde{\mathcal{D}}_2^\mathcal{D} \pm \acute{\mathcal{E}}_3^\mathcal{E} \mp \dot{\mathcal{F}}_4^\mathcal{F} \cdot \dot{\mathcal{G}}_5^\mathcal{G} \equiv \ddot{\mathcal{H}}_6^\mathcal{H} \in \breve{\mathcal{I}}_7^\mathcal{I} \asymp \bar{\mathcal{J}}_8^\mathcal{J} \ni \vec{\mathcal{K}}_9^\mathcal{K}$.

cmmi6

ΓΔΘΛΞΠΣΥΦΨΩαβγδεζηθικλμνξπρστυφχ
ψωεϑϖϱςφ←−→→◦◦◁▷◁0123456789.,;</>⋆
∂ABCDEFGHIJKLMNOPQRSTUVWXYZ♭♮♯⌣⌢
ℓabcdefghijklmnopqrstuvwxyzıȷ℘⃗ ̂

cmsy6

−·×∗÷⋄±∓⊕⊖⊗⊘⊙○∘∙⊂≍⊑⊒≤≥≶≷∼≈⊂⊃≪≫⊲⊳
←→↑↓↔↗↘≃⇐⇒⇑⇓⇔↖↙∝∞∈∋△▽/∀∃¬∅ℜℑ⊤⊥
ℵABCDEFGHIJKLMNOPQRSTUVWXYZ∪∩⊎∧∨
⊢⊣⊔⊓{}⟨⟩‖↕↨\≀√∐∇∫⊔∩□⊐⊒§†‡¶♣♢♡♠

Here's some 6-point math: $\hat{\mathcal{L}}_0^{\mathcal{L}} \leq \check{\mathcal{M}}_1^{\mathcal{M}} \prec \tilde{\mathcal{N}}_2^{\mathcal{N}} \preceq \acute{\mathcal{O}}_3^{\mathcal{O}} \ll \grave{\mathcal{P}}_4^{\mathcal{P}} \subset \dot{\mathcal{Q}}_5^{\mathcal{Q}} \subseteq \ddot{\mathcal{R}}_6^{\mathcal{R}} \sqsubseteq \breve{\mathcal{S}}_7^{\mathcal{S}} \vdash \bar{\mathcal{T}}_8^{\mathcal{T}} \approx \vec{\mathcal{U}}_9^{\mathcal{U}}.$

cmmi5

ΓΔΘΛΞΠΣΥΦΨΩαβγδεζηθικλμνξπρστυφχ
ψωεϑϖϱςφ←−→→◦◦◁▷◁0123456789.,;</>⋆
∂ABCDEFGHIJKLMNOPQRSTUVWXYZ♭♮♯⌣⌢
ℓabcdefghijklmnopqrstuvwxyzıȷ℘⃗ ̂

cmsy5

−·×∗÷⋄±∓⊕⊖⊗⊘⊙○∘∙⊂≍⊑⊒≤≥≶≷∼≈⊂⊃≪≫⊲⊳
←→↑↓↔↗↘≃⇐⇒⇑⇓⇔↖↙∝∞∈∋△▽/∀∃¬∅ℜℑ⊤⊥
ℵABCDEFGHIJKLMNOPQRSTUVWXYZ∪∩⊎∧∨
⊢⊣⊔⊓{}⟨⟩‖↕↨\≀√∐∇∫⊔∩□⊐⊒§†‡¶♣♢♡♠

Here's some 5-point math: $\dot{\mathcal{V}}_0^{\mathcal{V}} \geq \grave{\mathcal{W}}_1^{\mathcal{W}} \succ \tilde{\mathcal{X}}_2^{\mathcal{X}} \succeq \acute{\mathcal{Y}}_3^{\mathcal{Y}} \gg \dot{\mathcal{Z}}_4^{\mathcal{Z}} \supset \dot{\Sigma}_5^{\sigma} \sqsupseteq \breve{\Upsilon}_6^{\upsilon} \sqsupseteq \Phi_7^{\phi} \dashv \Psi_8^{\psi} \sim \vec{\Omega}_9^{\omega}.$

cmmib10

ΓΔΘΛΞΠΣΥΦΨΩαβγδεζηθικλμνξπρστυφχ
ψωεϑϖϱςφ←−→→◦◦◁▷◁0123456789.,;</>⋆
∂ABCDEFGHIJKLMNOPQRSTUVWXYZ♭♮♯⌣⌢
ℓabcdefghijklmnopqrstuvwxyzıȷ℘⃗ ̂

cmbsy10

−·×∗÷⋄±∓⊕⊖⊗⊘⊙○∘∙⊂≍⊑⊒≤≥≶≷∼≈⊂⊃≪≫⊲⊳
←→↑↓↔↗↘≃⇐⇒⇑⇓⇔↖↙∝∞∈∋△▽/∀∃¬∅ℜℑ⊤⊥
ℵABCDEFGHIJKLMNOPQRSTUVWXYZ∪∩⊎∧∨
⊢⊣⊔⊓{}⟨⟩‖↕↨\≀√∐∇∫⊔∩□⊐⊒§†‡¶♣♢♡♠

Here's some bold 10-point math: $\hat{A}_0^{\Gamma} + \breve{B}_1^{\Delta} - \tilde{C}_2^{\Theta} \times \acute{D}_3^{\Lambda} / \grave{E}_4^{\Xi} \oplus \dot{F}_5^{\Pi} \ominus \ddot{G}_6^{\Sigma} \otimes \breve{H}_7^{\Phi} \oslash \bar{I}_8^{\Psi} \odot \vec{J}_9^{\Omega}.$

cmex10

$$\int_{-\infty}^{\infty} \left(\frac{\text{RAVEN}}{\Pi\acute{\alpha}\lambda\lambda\alpha\varsigma} + \heartsuit_{\tau\breve{\epsilon}\lambda-\tau\bar{\alpha}\lambda} \right) d\varphi \longrightarrow \left\{ \overset{\cdot\cdot}{\frown} \begin{array}{c} \text{THE} \\ \text{END} \end{array} \overset{\smile}{} \right\}.$$

General Index

The following pages list all appearances of the principal constituents of the programs in this book. An <u>underlined</u> entry is a page number where the relevant quantity is defined; for example, the parameter '*apex_corr*' is defined on page 5, the macro/subroutine '*arm*' is defined on page 377, and the standard font 'cmr10' is defined on pages 10–11.

The names of people, organizations, concepts, and fonts can also be found here, mixed in with the program parts.

At the end of this general index, which is "algebraic," there's another kind of index that is more "pictorial": You can use the charts in the second index to go from a character shape to the page on which that shape is defined.

*Generally speaking, if an entry has more than a dozen page references,
it may be too broad,
and possibly should be divided into two or more primary entries.*
— ADDISON-WESLEY, *Guide for Authors* (1982)

	´0	´1	´2	´3	´4	´5	´6	´7
´00x	Γ 171	Δ 173	Θ 175	Λ 177	Ξ 179	Π 181	Σ 183	Υ 185
´01x	Φ 187	Ψ 189	Ω 191	ff 421	fi 423	fl 425	ffi 427	ffl 429
´02x	ı 443	J 443	` 49	´ 49	ˇ 51	˘ 53	¯ 53	° 55
´03x	¸ 57	ß 449	æ 445	œ 447	ø 443	Æ 453	Œ 455	Ø 451
´04x	˝ 57	! 265	ʺ 141	# 267	$ 361	% 269	& 363	' 281
´05x	(271	) 271	* 275	+ 275	, 277	- 143	. 277	/ 277
´06x	0 285	1 287	2 289	3 291	4 293	5 295	6 297	7 299
´07x	8 301	9 303	: 279	; 279	¡ 265	= 279	¿ 367	? 365
´10x	@ 283	A 369	B 371	C 373	D 375	E 377	F 379	G 381
´11x	H 383	I 385	J 387	K 389	L 391	M 393	N 395	O 397
´12x	P 399	Q 401	R 403	S 405	T 407	U 409	V 411	W 413
´13x	X 415	Y 417	Z 419	[273	" 141	] 273	^ 51	˙ 59
´14x	ʻ 281	a 307	b 309	c 311	d 313	e 315	f 317	g 319
´15x	h 323	i 325	j 327	k 329	l 331	m 333	n 335	o 337
´16x	p 339	q 341	r 343	s 345	t 347	u 349	v 351	w 353
´17x	x 355	y 357	z 359	– 143	— 145	ʺ 61	~ 61	¨ 59

For example, the program for 'Γ' appears on page 171. This is the font coding scheme produced by the **roman** driver file when *ligs* = 2. (In roman fonts with *variant_g* set **true**, the program for 'g' appears on page 321.)

	´0	´1	´2	´3	´4	´5	´6	´7
´00x	Γ 171	Δ 173	Θ 175	Λ 177	Ξ 179	Π 181	Σ 183	Υ 185
´01x	Φ 187	Ψ 189	Ω 191	↑ 463	↓ 463	' 456	ı 265	¿ 367
´02x	ı 443	J 443	` 49	´ 49	ˇ 51	˘ 53	¯ 53	° 55
´03x	¸ 57	ß 449	æ 445	œ 447	ø 443	Æ 453	Œ 455	Ø 451
´04x	␣ 456	! 265	" 479	# 267	$ 361	% 269	& 363	' 281
´05x	(271	) 271	* 275	+ 275	, 277	- 459	. 277	/ 277
´06x	0 285	1 287	2 289	3 291	4 293	5 295	6 297	7 299
´07x	8 301	9 303	: 279	; 279	< 473	= 279	> 473	? 365
´10x	@ 283	A 369	B 371	C 373	D 375	E 377	F 379	G 381
´11x	H 383	I 385	J 387	K 389	L 391	M 393	N 395	O 397
´12x	P 399	Q 401	R 403	S 405	T 407	U 409	V 411	W 413
´13x	X 415	Y 417	Z 419	[273	\ 477	] 273	^ 51	_ 473
´14x	' 281	a 307	b 309	c 311	d 313	e 315	f 317	g 319
´15x	h 323	i 325	j 327	k 329	l 331	m 333	n 335	o 337
´16x	p 339	q 341	r 343	s 345	t 347	u 349	v 351	w 353
´17x	x 355	y 357	z 359	{ 479		477	} 479	~ 61	¨ 59

This is the font coding scheme produced by the **roman** driver file when *ligs* = 0.

	´0	´1	´2	´3	´4	´5	´6	´7
´00x	· 477	↓ 463	α 543	β 543	∧ 461	¬ 471	∈ 469	π 543
´01x	λ 543	γ 544	δ 544	↑ 463	± 459	⊕ 459	∞ 481	∂ 544
´02x	⊂ 469	⊃ 469	∩ 461	∪ 461	∀ 471	∃ 471	⊗ 459	⇄ 467
´03x	← 465	→ 465	≠ 473	◇ 477	≤ 475	≥ 475	≡ 475	∨ 461
´04x	542	! 265	" 479	# 267	$ 361	% 269	& 363	' 281
´05x	(271	) 271	* 275	+ 275	, 277	− 459	. 277	/ 277
´06x	0 285	1 287	2 289	3 291	4 293	5 295	6 297	7 299
´07x	8 301	9 303	: 279	; 279	< 473	= 279	> 473	? 365
´10x	@ 283	A 369	B 371	C 373	D 375	E 377	F 379	G 381
´11x	H 383	I 385	J 387	K 389	L 391	M 393	N 395	O 397
´12x	P 399	Q 401	R 403	S 405	T 407	U 409	V 411	W 413
´13x	X 415	Y 417	Z 419	[273	\ 477	] 273	^ 543	− 473
´14x	' 281	a 307	b 309	c 311	d 313	e 315	f 317	g 319
´15x	h 323	i 325	j 327	k 329	l 331	m 333	n 335	o 337
´16x	p 339	q 341	r 343	s 345	t 347	u 349	v 351	w 353
´17x	x 355	y 357	z 359	{ 479		477	} 479	~ 543	∫ 481

This is the font coding scheme produced by the `texset` driver file.

	´0	´1	´2	´3	´4	´5	´6	´7
´00x	Γ 171	Δ 173	Θ 175	Λ 177	Ξ 179	Π 181	Σ 183	Υ 185
´01x	Φ 187	Ψ 189	Ω 191	↑ 463	↓ 463	' 456	¡ 265	¿ 367
´02x	I 145	J 145	` 49	´ 49	ˇ 51	˘ 53	¯ 53	˚ 55
´03x	¸ 57	SS 145	Æ 453	Œ 455	Ø 451	Æ 453	Œ 455	Ø 451
´04x	‐ 57	! 265	” 141	# 267	$ 361	% 269	& 363	’ 281
´05x	(271	) 271	* 275	+ 275	, 277	- 143	. 277	/ 277
´06x	0 285	1 287	2 289	3 291	4 293	5 295	6 297	7 299
´07x	8 301	9 303	: 279	; 279	< 473	= 279	> 473	? 365
´10x	@ 283	A 369	B 371	C 373	D 375	E 377	F 379	G 381
´11x	H 383	I 385	J 387	K 389	L 391	M 393	N 395	O 397
´12x	P 399	Q 401	R 403	S 405	T 407	U 409	V 411	W 413
´13x	X 415	Y 417	Z 419	[273	“ 141	] 273	ˆ 51	˙ 59
´14x	‘ 281	A 369	B 371	C 373	D 375	E 377	F 379	G 381
´15x	H 383	I 385	J 387	K 389	L 391	M 393	N 395	O 397
´16x	P 399	Q 401	R 403	S 405	T 407	U 409	V 411	W 413
´17x	X 415	Y 417	Z 419	– 143	— 145	˝ 61	˜ 61	¨ 59

This is the font coding scheme produced by the `csc` driver file.

	´0		´1		´2		´3		´4		´5		´6		´7	
´00x	Γ	171	Δ	173	Θ	175	Λ	177	Ξ	179	Π	181	Σ	183	Υ	185
´01x	Φ	187	Ψ	189	Ω	191	ff	199	fi	201	fl	203	ffi	205	ffl	207
´02x	$\imath$	245	$\jmath$	245	\`	49	´	49	˘	51	˘	53	¯	53	˚	55
´03x	¸	57	β	249	æ	247	œ	247	ø	245	Æ	453	Œ	455	Ø	451
´04x	˝	57	!	265	”	141	#	267	£	239	%	269	&	241	’	281
´05x	(	271	)	271	*	275	+	275	,	277	-	143	.	277	/	277
´06x	0	193	1	193	2	193	3	195	4	195	5	195	6	197	7	197
´07x	8	197	9	197	:	279	;	279	i	265	=	279	¿	243	?	243
´10x	@	283	A	369	B	371	C	373	D	375	E	377	F	379	G	381
´11x	H	383	I	385	J	387	K	389	L	391	M	393	N	395	O	397
´12x	P	399	Q	401	R	403	S	405	T	407	U	409	V	411	W	413
´13x	X	415	Y	417	Z	419	[	273	“	141	]	273	ˆ	51	˙	59
´14x	‘	281	a	209	b	209	c	211	d	211	e	213	f	213	g	215
´15x	h	215	i	217	j	217	k	219	l	219	m	221	n	221	o	223
´16x	p	223	q	223	r	225	s	225	t	227	u	227	v	227	w	229
´17x	x	229	y	231	z	231	–	143	—	145	˝	61	~	61	¨	59

This is the font coding scheme produced by the `textit` driver file when *ligs* = 2.

	´0	´1	´2	´3	´4	´5	´6	´7
´00x	Γ 171	Δ 173	Θ 175	Λ 177	Ξ 179	Π 181	Σ 183	Υ 185
´01x	Φ 187	Ψ 189	Ω 191	α 147	β 147	γ 149	δ 149	ϵ 151
´02x	ζ 151	η 153	θ 153	ι 153	κ 155	λ 155	μ 155	ν 157
´03x	ξ 157	π 159	ρ 159	σ 159	τ 161	υ 161	ϕ 161	χ 163
´04x	ψ 163	ω 165	ε 165	ϑ 167	ϖ 167	ϱ 169	ς 169	φ 169
´05x	← 431	← 431	→ 433	→ 433	` 435	' 435	▷ 435	◁ 435
´06x	0 251	1 251	2 253	3 255	4 257	5 259	6 261	7 261
´07x	8 263	9 263	. 437	, 437	< 437	/ 437	> 437	⋆ 441
´10x	∂ 233	A 369	B 371	C 373	D 375	E 377	F 379	G 381
´11x	H 383	I 385	J 387	K 389	L 391	M 393	N 395	O 397
´12x	P 399	Q 401	R 403	S 405	T 407	U 409	V 411	W 413
´13x	X 415	Y 417	Z 419	♭ 439	♮ 439	♯ 439	⌣ 441	⌢ 441
´14x	ℓ 233	a 209	b 209	c 211	d 211	e 213	f 213	g 215
´15x	h 215	i 217	j 217	k 219	l 219	m 221	n 221	o 223
´16x	p 223	q 223	r 225	s 225	t 227	u 227	v 227	w 229
´17x	x 229	y 231	z 231	$\imath$ 235	$\jmath$ 235	$\wp$ 235	→ 237	⌢ 237

This is the font coding scheme produced by the `mathit` driver file.

	´0	´1	´2	´3	´4	´5	´6	´7
´00x	− 459	· 477	× 483	∗ 485	÷ 483	◇ 477	± 459	∓ 485
´01x	⊕ 459	⊖ 487	⊗ 459	⊘ 487	⊙ 487	◯ 525	∘ 489	• 489
´02x	≍ 489	≡ 475	⊆ 491	⊇ 491	≤ 475	≥ 475	⪯ 493	⪰ 493
´03x	∼ 495	≈ 495	⊂ 469	⊃ 469	≪ 497	≫ 497	≺ 493	≻ 493
´04x	← 465	→ 465	↑ 463	↓ 463	↔ 467	↗ 509	↘ 509	≃ 495
´05x	⇐ 499	⇒ 499	⇑ 501	⇓ 501	⇔ 503	↖ 511	↙ 511	∝ 513
´06x	′ 513	∞ 481	∈ 469	∋ 513	△ 515	▽ 515	/ 515	ʼ 515
´07x	∀ 471	∃ 471	¬ 471	∅ 525	ℜ 517	ℑ 519	⊤ 521	⊥ 521
´10x	ℵ 523	𝒜 123	ℬ 123	𝒞 123	𝒟 125	ℰ 125	ℱ 125	𝒢 127
´11x	ℋ 127	ℐ 127	𝒥 129	𝒦 129	ℒ 129	ℳ 131	𝒩 131	𝒪 133
´12x	𝒫 133	𝒬 133	ℛ 135	𝒮 135	𝒯 135	𝒰 137	𝒱 137	𝒲 137
´13x	𝒳 139	𝒴 139	𝒵 139	∪ 461	∩ 461	⊎ 525	∧ 461	∨ 461
´14x	⊢ 521	⊣ 521	⌊ 527	⌋ 527	⌈ 527	⌉ 527	{ 479	} 479
´15x	⟨ 529	⟩ 529	∣ 477	∥ 529	↕ 507	⇕ 505	\ 477	≀ 529
´16x	√ 531	Ⅱ 531	∇ 531	∫ 481	⊔ 533	⊓ 533	⊑ 533	⊒ 533
´17x	§ 535	† 537	‡ 537	¶ 535	♣ 539	◇ 539	♡ 541	♠ 541

This is the font coding scheme produced by the `mathsy` driver file.

	´0	´1	´2	´3	´4	´5	´6	´7
´00x	(69	) 71	[73	] 77	⌊ 75	⌋ 79	⌈ 75	⌉ 79
´01x	{ 81	} 85	⟨ 91	⟩ 91	| 101	‖ 101	/ 93	\ 93
´02x	(69	) 71	(69	) 71	[73	] 77	⌊ 75	⌋ 79
´03x	⌈ 75	⌉ 79	{ 81	} 85	⟨ 91	⟩ 91	/ 93	\ 93
´04x	(69	) 71	[73	] 77	⌊ 75	⌋ 79	⌈ 75	⌉ 79
´05x	{ 81	} 85	⟨ 91	⟩ 91	/ 93	\ 93	/ 93	\ 93
´06x	(69	) 71	⌈ 73	⌉ 77	⌊ 73	⌋ 77	| 73	| 77
´07x	⎧ 83	⎫ 87	⎩ 83	⎭ 87	{ 83	} 87	' 83	| 95
´10x	\ 69	/ 71	| 69	| 71	⟨ 91	⟩ 91	⊔ 103	⊔ 103
´11x	∮ 115	∯ 115	⊙ 119	⊙ 119	⊕ 105	⊕ 105	⊗ 105	⊗ 105
´12x	Σ 107	Π 109	∫ 113	∪ 117	∩ 117	⊎ 119	∧ 121	∨ 121
´13x	Σ 107	Π 109	∫ 113	∪ 117	∩ 117	⊎ 119	∧ 121	∨ 121
´14x	⊔ 111	⊔ 111	⌢ 63	⌢ 63	⌢ 63	~ 65	~ 65	~ 65
´15x	[73	] 77	⌊ 75	⌋ 79	⌈ 75	⌉ 79	{ 81	} 85
´16x	√ 99	√ 99	√ 99	√ 99	√ 101	| 101	⌈ 101	‖ 97
´17x	↑ 95	↓ 95	╱ 89	╲ 89	╲ 89	╱ 89	⇑ 97	⇓ 97

This is the font coding scheme produced by the `mathex` driver file.